www.wadsworth.com

wadsworth.com is the World Wide Web site for Wadsworth Publishing Company and is your direct source to dozens of online resources.

At wadsworth.com you can find out about supplements, demonstration software, and student resources. You can also send e-mail to many of our authors and preview new publications and exciting new technologies.

wadsworth.com
Changing the way the world learns®

Current Systems in Psychology

History, Theory, Research, and Applications

Noel W. Smith

State University of New York at Plattsburgh

Wadsworth
Thomson Learning™

Australia • Canada • Mexico • Singapore • Spain •
United Kingdom • United States

Executive Editor: Vicki Knight
Acquisitions Editor: Marianne Taflinger
Editorial Assistant: Suzanne Wood
Marketing Manager: Jenna Opp
Marketing Assistant: Jessica McFadden
Project Editor: Pam Suwinsky
Print Buyer: Karen Hunt

Production Editor: Carol O'Connell, Graphic World Publishing
  Services
Compositor: Graphic World, Inc.
Cover Designer: Roger Knox
Cover Image: Roger Knox
Cover Printer: Phoenix Color
Printer/Binder: RR Donnelley & Sons/Crawfordsville

For permission to use material from this text,
contact us by
  Web: www.thomsonrights.com
  Fax: 1-800-730-2215
  Phone: 1-800-730-2214

Library of Congress Cataloging-in-Publication Data
Smith, Noel W.
    Current systems in psychology : history, theory, research,
and applications / Noel W. Smith.
        p.   cm.
    Includes bibliographical references and index.
    ISBN 0-8304-1484-8
      1. Psychology. 1. Title.

  BF121 .S574   1999
  150—dc21
                                    99-052275

For more information, contact
Wadsworth/Thomson Learning
10 Davis Drive
Belmont, CA 94002-3098
USA
http://www.wadsworth.com

International Headquarters
Thomson Learning
290 Harbor Drive, 2nd Floor
Stamford, CT 06902-7477
USA

UK/Europe/Middle East/South Africa
Thomson Learning
Berkshire House
168-173 High Holborn
London WC1V 7AA
United Kingdom

Asia
Thomson Learning
60 Albert Street #15-01
Albert Complex
Singapore 189969

Canada
Nelson/Thomson Learning
1120 Birchmount Road
Scarborough, Ontario M1K 5G4
Canada

Dedicated to those students who strive to know

Contents in Brief

Contents

Major tenets: The environment is only a source of inputs for an internal processor that converts the inputs into such outputs as perceptions, memories, images, decisions, and other cognitive events. Causality is linear: inputs are processes in a sequence of coding, storage, and reconstruction. Hypotheses are deduced from theories and tested empirically in laboratory settings. **Locus of control:** Because the person contains and produces the cognitive events, the system is organocentric.

Major tenets: Laboratory methods, animal studies, statistics, and mechanistic S-R formulations miss meanings and self-determination that should be central to psychology. Borrowing of methodologies and mechanisms from the physical sciences must be replaced with the study of human goal striving, free choices, self-fulfillment, inner reality, and individual uniqueness. **Locus of causality:** Because the person contains and produces his or her own causality, the system is organocentric.

Major tenets: According to object relations theory, human attachment to such objects as the therapist or the parent is a relational bond and it is innate. The bond with the therapist is central in therapeutic change. The theory replaces Freud's psychosexual development with development of the self. Another prominent theory, one of action language, describes concrete actions of the individual rather than attributing these actions to instincts, drives, energies, and other biophysical forces. **Locus of causality:** Because causality comes largely from the individual—though less so than with orthodox theory—the system is organocentric.

Major tenets: Behavior is selected in accordance with its consequences—the principle of reinforcement. Because of the high consistency of reinforced responses, single organisms provide reliable data out of which predictability and control can be realized. Statistics and group comparisons are unnecessary. In contrast with contingency-governed (reinforced) behavior, rule-governed behavior is shaped by the speaker's verbal descriptions of contingencies rather than actual contingencies of reinforcement. **Locus of causality:** Because responses are largely shaped by the environment, the system is envirocentric.

Major tenets: Contrary to the assumptions in psychology that behavior is chaotic and has only statistical regularity, the co-relationships of social settings and physical objects result in predictable patterns of behavior called behavior settings. These are independent of individual personalities. The behavior setting has control mechanisms for both objects and people that keep the patterns stable. These principles are discovered from observation of natural events. **Locus of causality:** Behavior is a function of the environment; hence, the system is envirocentric.

Major tenets: Modern claims to objective knowledge about the world have no warrant. Knowledge is totally relative to the social group in which it is constructed. It is no more than social agreement as formed by language. All we can ever know are these cultural meanings. Truth is no more than coherency, and error is disagreement. **Locus of causality:** Because the system is centered on social constructions, it is sociocentric.

Major tenets: The individual and the world are in never ending developmental process. Each exchange brings further changes to both the person and the world. This dialectic process precludes static states and implies opposites or bipolarities in interaction. Resolution of opposites leads to new conflicts and further change. **Locus of causality:** Because of the interdependence of the individual and the world in which causality is the relationship between them, the system is often noncentric; but prominent versions are reductionistic to biology and are thereby organocentric.

Major tenets: By beginning with observable events rather than with abstractions (constructs) such as mind, processing, and brain powers, a complex of interdependent events called the interbehavioral field can be identified. An active person in interaction with an active world is the locus of psychological events. Biology, chemistry, physics, and culture participate in all psychological events, but psychology as a field of person-object interactions has its own level of functioning and its own principles and is not reducible to any of the participating conditions that comprise it. All psychological events ranging from imagining to talking consist of interdependent field relationships. **Locus of causality:** Because causation itself consists of the interbehavioral field rather than some component of it, the system is totally noncentric.

Major tenets: Subjectivity is not a mental or private event but behavior that can be communicated objectively by means of sorting statements (Q sorting) and factor analysis of the sorts. Whereas group means—R methodology—masks all subjectivity as well as forcing subjects into the experimenter's mold rather than allowing them to express their own viewpoint, Q methodology reveals what viewpoints people share and don't share in various combinations. **Locus of causality:** The system adopts a basis in interbehavioral psychology and is therefore noncentric.

Major tenets: People live in more than a mechanical and physical world. They live in a world of meanings that most of psychology has ignored but which should form the core of psychology. Meanings are relationships. Objects act on persons just as persons act on them. People relate to objects by intentionality, a reaching forth to embrace the object. This is consciousness. Consciousness is not in us but in the intentional relationship. Consciousness as a relationship replaces mind-body dualism and reduction of psychology to brain physiology. **Locus of causality:** Causality is primarily a relationship, and therefore the system is noncentric.

Preface

While teaching an upper division undergraduate course "history and modern systems of psychology" over a period of several years, I kept looking for a textbook that would tell the students what today's systems of psychology are saying. The numerous textbooks that go by titles such as "History and Systems of Psychology" include limited coverage of systems beyond about 1950. These books are oriented primarily toward what I would call classical systems such as Titchener's structuralism, the Chicago school of functionalism, Gestalt psychology, associationism, and behaviorism from Watson to Hull. They cover the classical figures in psychoanalysis but never the current ones. That brings the coverage up to mid-twentieth century. Usually parts of chapters will be devoted to Skinner's behavior analysis, some developments in cognitive psychology, a few paragraphs on such humanistic psychologists as Maslow and Rogers, and there may be a brief mention of one or two other systems. Nowhere can one find an extended treatment of the numerous current systems in psychology.

In order to get beyond the first half-century of the twentieth century, I put together readings on some of the current systems, but I still needed a systematic treatment. Finally, I decided that the only way to get one was to write it myself. It seemed to me that such a treatment should include theory, research, and applications together with cross-comparisons and a critique. It should set the systems in a historical perspective to indicate what traditions they draw from, and it should provide some principles of logic of science against which these systems could be compared. It should be aimed at upper-division undergraduate courses but should also be useful to graduate students, perhaps as a handbook. I began writing chapters and distributing them to students for use in class. That went well, so I persisted. Because the project turned out to occupy more than four years and consume all of my available time, I now understand why no one else had produced such a text.

A major disadvantage in writing about a large number of current systems is that no one can be an expert in all of them. Many people devote their careers to just one system, or even to a subdomain of one system. Therefore, errors both of omission and commission are inevitable. In many cases I used secondary sources to find primary sources, and secondary sources necessarily never reflect the latest work. I also used current databases, which somewhat mitigate that shortcoming, but databases are never complete, and my searching technique is not always totally successful or totally effective. Consequently, I have undoubtedly missed some important sources, quite apart from the question of properly interpreting and integrating all the information. Often the problem was one of too much information: some systems are a bottomless pit of sources that perhaps not even a specialist could master in its entirety. In such cases I had to determine which were the most important sources, a never fully successful effort: even rather obscure publications can hold valuable insights, and these are easy to overlook or pass by.

Although the problem of covering an enormous body of literature is a common one, the problem of preferences and biases is unavoidable. This includes selection of component topics—that is, what to put in or leave out; how to organize the topics; how much space to give to each topic; and what distinctions to make (orientation bias). Authors rarely tell the reader what their biases are. For example, textbooks in psychology today are replete with references to "processing information," yet the authors seldom indicate that this is a theoretical construction and not an observed event. They offer no alternatives to this construction. Similarly, one finds references to sense data, biological basis of behavior, brain storage, language production centers, neural messages or neural signals, cues, mental processes, inputs, and sundry other theoretical constructions that authors refer to as if they were observed events. (Chapter 2, pp. 48–49 examines the distinction between constructions and events.) Psychology may be the sorriest of all disciplines from the point of view of hidden biases.

Having said that, I am obliged to relate my own orientation bias. It is what I broadly refer to as "contextual interactionism" (Smith, 1973). That is, I regard a psychological event as an interaction between an organism and an object in a given context. These interactions include reasoning, imagining, perceiving, learning, knowing, and so forth. Because of the context, the psychological event cannot be reduced to biology, chemistry, or physics, although these fully participate in the event. The various participating components provide some of the potential or enabling factors for the larger organization of events that comprise the psychological event. Change any participating event—a broken leg, a brain lesion, a different context—and the interaction changes. Mind-body, cognition-behavior, brain-behavior, and other dualisms are obviated, as is an empty organism (the assumption that biology is irrelevant). Causality of interactions are not internal factors—mind, brain, cognition—nor external factors (environ-

ment). Causality is not *inside* or *outside* but *comprised of the entire interaction in context*. This approach applies in varying degrees to the systems of division V (chapters 9–12). In addition to contextual interactionism, I also find admirable characteristics in some of the other systems, along with characteristics that seem not-so-admirable.

I have tried to keep my biases in check, but I have not hesitated to present contextual interactionist approaches as alternatives to traditional formulations, especially in chapter 2, section 2. The traditionalists, however, have seldom given coverage to the contextual interactionists and have thereby precluded the possibility of an informed choice.

I have given each system coverage in accordance with what I understand about it and have drawn it mostly from the proponents of that system. In the critique of each chapter, I have generally let others speak, but have sometimes added my own evaluations. The concluding section of each chapter consists mostly of my own point of view in assessment of what the system has accomplished and/or where it seems to be headed.

I am grateful to the colleagues and students who read parts of the manuscript and offered suggestions for improvement: Charles Baxter, Stephen Brown, Dennis Delprato, Katy Dunham, James Herrick, Parker Lichtenstein, Paul Mountjoy, Gretchen Sando, Marilyn Smith, and William Tooke.

I would be pleased to receive specific suggestions for improvement from students, instructors, or other readers in the event that a revised edition should ever be warranted.

N. W. Smith
Department of Psychology
State University of New York
Plattsburgh, NY 12901
e-mail: nwsmith@plattsburgh.edu

PART

I

Introduction to
the Systems

Introduction

Chapter Outline

WHAT IS A SYSTEM?

This book is about systems in psychology, but what constitutes a system? Nearly forty years ago Melvin Marx (1963) advanced two definitions that are still useful: a system "broadly refers within psychology to a cluster of theoretical propositions and methodological biases (e.g., behaviorism, psychoanalysis)" (p. 9) or consists of "an organization and interpretation of the data and theories of a subject matter with emphasis upon a particular methodology (metatheory) and working assumptions (postulates)" (p. 43). Both definitions indicate the centrality of theory and methodology. To this I would add, after an even earlier writer (McGeoch, 1933), that systems should have coherency and unity. All of the systems selected for inclusion here have a theoretical orientation, and most but not all—cognitive psychology is the major exception, and even it has some common themes—have coherence and unity. As for methodology, some, such as dialectic and interbehavioral psychology, are eclectic; but most use one or a restricted group of methodologies (see chapter 14). Marx's reference in his second definition to postulates is also important and is treated later in this chapter. Lichtenstein (1967), in defining a scientific system as "a framework or scaffolding which permits the scientist to arrange his data in an orderly and meaningful way" (p. 323), follows Marx and McGeoch in emphasizing organization—but he stresses particularly that which a system gives to observations.

For the purposes of this book, a system in psychology is an orderly and logical construction for dealing with data and theories of the subject in a unified and coherent manner; it uses a set of postulates (even if implicitly) and usually a single methodology.

TEN SYSTEMS PLUS SIX

I have selected ten current systems for full chapter treatment and another six for shorter treatment in chapter 13. Psychoanalysis followed by interbehavioral psychology is the oldest, and social constructionism the most recent of the ten. Dialectical psychology, as a philosophy, has the oldest roots, going back 3000 years to the Chou Dynasty in China and 2500 years to the Hellenic or Golden Age of Greece in Europe. Of the sixteen, direct realism, which comes out of Australia, may be the most recent, although evolutionary psychology is also rather recent. Cognitive psychology is clearly the dominant system today. The most coherent and truly systematic is interbehavioral psychology, and the least is either humanistic psychology or the piecemeal cognitive psychology—although individual branches are sometimes more systematic than the whole.

Cognitive psychology has the longest chapter and dialectic psychology the shortest. If dialectic psychologists feel shortchanged, I hope they will let me know what important matter should be added. If cognitivists feel that that chapter is too long and unwieldy, I'm open to their suggestions on what to remove.

The selections bring together in one place the theoretical diversity of psychology so that students can more readily comprehend it. One cannot make an informed choice without knowing what the alternatives are. In undergraduate courses students may be exposed to cognitive psychology and behavior analysis, with a touch of psychoanalysis and humanistic psychology. Seldom do they learn about phenomenological psychology, operant subjectivity, interbehavioral psychology, or eco-behavioral science. This volume is intended to provide them with that information and thereby expand their ability to (a) compare the strengths and weaknesses of each system and (b) make an informed judgment about each. Only through broad exposure can the student become adequately informed.

The consequences of not having such information are well illustrated by the case of a psychologist who claimed that the world we see about us is a deception. He argued that the information coming through our sense organs gets transformed and converted into nothing but an illusion of the outer world. Further, he declared that there is no way this interpretation of what we see can be wrong (Attneave, 1974). Unfortunately, he knew too little about the alternatives to make an informed choice and could only render the dogmatic assertion that no other possibility exists. In another example, a social constructivist (chapter 8) writes, "It is not that constructivists deny the existence of external reality, it is just that there is no way of knowing whether what is perceived and understood is an accurate reflection of that reality" (Marshall, 1996, p. 30). Similarly, Stam (1990) asserts that one cannot bypass the mental. Whether these assertions are right or wrong, I hope that this book will help students broaden their horizons and recognize that alternatives are possible.

ORGANIZATION OF THE BOOK

Chapters 1 and 2: The Beginning

Following this introductory chapter, chapter 2 provides a sketch of the major concepts of psychology from hunter-gatherers to the present time as a background to the current systems. It traces the evolution of concepts that the current systems draw from. (For more detail see Hergenhahn [1997], Kantor [1963, 1969], and Leahy [1997].) Chapter 2 also surveys issues in the logic of science as they apply to the systems.

Chapters 3 to 13: Four Categories of Systems

A glance at the table of contents will show that these chapters are grouped into four divisions, according to whether they center causation on (a) the organism (organocentric), (b) the environment (envirocentric), (c) the social group (sociocentric), or (d) no single source of causation (noncentric: contextual interactional). The systems are alphabetized in each division, and the six covered in chapter 13 are also alphabetized.

No grouping is perfect, and one could make a case for another arrangement of the systems. Post modernism and social constructionism (chapter 8) are actually forms of envirocentrism—the social group is the only recognized component of the environment. But because this one component is the sole determiner of what we can know about anything, the category of sociocentric seems appropriate. Dialectical psychology (chapter 9) in the noncentric category could be classified as organocentric, especially by the Chinese and Russian dialectical psychologists. They often give preeminence to the brain as a causal condition of behavior. Phenomenological psychology (chapter 12), also in the noncentric category, edges in the direction of organocentrism. Proponents who introduce variations into a system or who combine parts of systems into hybrids can, of course, change the picture radically. Some cognitivists, for example, advocate reorientations that would move cognitive psychology distinctly in the direction of envirocentrism or noncentrism. Schafer has moved psychoanalysis strongly in the direction of noncentrism, but most others in the system remain well within organocentrism.

Chapter 14: Retrospective

The final chapter looks back over the systems, summarizes their central assumptions about causality, reviews their applied and research features, and returns to principles of logic of science (introduced in chapter 2) as criteria for use of constructs. It also briefly considers some problems of methodologies.

CHAPTER ORGANIZATION

Chapters 3 to 12 have nine to twelve major sections. All chapters begin with a table of contents and an introduction, followed by one or two sections on historical development and some major issues the system addresses. Fundamental principles of the system may be set forth in the development and issues section or in a separate section. The postulate system (see below) is presented, and then subsequent sections deal with research, applications, and psychotherapy or clinical psychology, in that order. Of course, not all chapters include all three of these subtopics. For instance because of its significance, psychotherapy is generally separated from the other applications. In the case of research, in cognitive psychology and behavior analysis it is too intimately linked with theory to be relegated to a separate section.

The last four sections are the same for all chapters: *First,* "Relations to Other Systems"; *second,* a critique offering evaluative commentary on the system; *third,* an overview of what system has contributed to psychology and/or of where it might be going; and *fourth,* references.

POSTULATE SYSTEMS

Every chapter has a section on postulates. Postulates are simply assumptions or propositions that serve as fundamental principles for further analysis and are often written out as a set. In order to understand the fundamental assumptions of theoretical systems, a written postulate system is essential. In most cases the proponents of systems are not very explicit about their assumptions. To fill that void, I have provided a postulate system for a major proponent of each of the ten systems to which I have given a full chapter. These postulate systems are often necessarily inferential and consequently may be unacceptable to the system's proponents. Those proponents, however, should have been more explicit about their postulates— explicit at all levels of generality. Pronko (1988) points out that everyone uses postulates, even if unwittingly, and that often these "silent assumptions [are] mistaken for hard facts" (p. 155). If a reader is going to judge whether a proponent of a system has anything worth saying, the proponent needs to tell the reader exactly what a system's postulates are or at least cite a source where the reader can find them.

A few proponents of particular systems have recognized the importance of clarifying their assumptions. Here is an example:

"Making our philosophical assumptions explicit will facilitate the understanding of multifaceted phenomena in Community Psychology. Without explicit assumptions, researchers run the risk of tacitly endorsing assumptions that they themselves may not consider to be valid, authentic, apt, or robust for conducting research in Community Psychology." (Kingry-Westergaard & Kelly, 1990, p. 23) These authors set forth ten "theoretical propositions" that comprise a limited postulate system. In establishing five criteria for a systematic psychology, McGeoch (1933), specifies explicit postulates as one of the five.

That every body of knowledge is grounded on postulational operations is almost trite, but that these operations need to be recognized and made explicit is a principle less commonly observed. Such explicit recognition not only makes clear one's premises to begin with, which is necessary if a consistent structure is to be erected upon them, but it clears the ground for understanding and intelligent criticism. In systematic controversies one can find much discussion which would have been impossible had the 'schools' represented laid bare their postulates at the outset. (p. 6)

In social constructionism (chapter 8) Gergen (1994) provides a set of assumptions, as does Maslow in humanistic psychology (chapter 4), and a few others have been semi-explicit about their assumptions. The most thoroughgoing postulates are those that Kantor (1959) has provided for interbehavioral psychology. He has written an entire book about these postulates and the relation of the interbehavioral system to them.

I have used his hierarchical model of a postulate system for organizing the postulates for each of the ten systems. At the base of the hierarchy and the most general of the levels are the *protopostulates,* the assumptions of a science that guide and control the details of investigation and influence the conduct of scientific workers. For example, does science deal only with events that may be observed or closely inferred from observation? Or does it also include the assumption of events that transcend nature? Does it assume ultimates or final truths, or is it always evolutional and corrigible?

Next are the *metapostulates,* which provide the supportive assumptions for the particular science.

In biology, these would include the principle of evolution as opposed to fixed species; in geology, gradual tectonic uplift, erosion, deposition, and so on over billions of years rather than a biblical catastrophic flood; in physics, the inclusion of relativistic principles rather than exclusively absolutistic events; in psychology, the question of whether a psychological event is centered in the organism, the environment, the social group—or not centered at all. (The chapter organization of ten systems in this book is based on these four causal propositions at the metapostulate level.) At the top of the hierarchy the *system postulates* provide the system that is structured on the subject matter and its rules of operation. The following alternative postulates, for example, follow directly from the metapostulate about centering or causation: the activity of organisms is (a) purely biological; (b) biological plus mental; (c) produced by the environment; (d) some combination of a, b, and c; or (e) interactions of organisms and objects as part of a field or context. In practice, the appropriate level for a particular postulate is often ambiguous, but the hierarchy nevertheless provides a useful starting point for examining assumptions. To enable the student to more readily make comparisons of these assumptions, the appendix brings together the ten postulate systems in one place.

REFERENCES

Attneave, Fred. 1974. How do you know? *American Psychologist* 29: 493–511.

Gergen, Kenneth J. 1994. *Relations and Relationships: Soundings in Social Construction.* Cambridge, MA: Harvard University Press.

Hergenhahn, B. R. 1997. *An Introduction to the History of Psychology,* 3rd ed. Belmont, CA: Wadsworth.

Kantor, J.R. 1959. *Interbehavioral Psychology: A Sample of Scientific Science Construction.* Bloomington, IN: Principia.

—. 1963. *The Scientific Evolution of Psychology,* vol. 1. Chicago: Principia Press.

—. 1969. *The Scientific Evolution of Psychology,* vol. 2. Chicago: Principia Press.

Kingry-Westergaard, Cynthia, & James G. Kelly 1990. A contextualist epistemology for ecological research. In *Researching Community Psychology: Issues of Theory and Methods.* Edited by P. Tolan, C. Keys, F. Chertok, & L. Jason. Washington, DC: American Psychological Association.

Leahey, Thomas H. 1997. *A History of Psychology: Main Currents in Psychological Thought,* 4th ed. Upper Saddle River, NJ: Prentice-Hall.

Lichtenstein, Parker. 1967. Psychological systems: Their nature and function. *Psychological Record* 17:321–40.

Marshall, Hermine H. 1996. Clarifying and implementing contemporary psychological perspectives. *Educational Psychologist* 31:29–34.

Marx, Melvin. 1963. The general nature of theory construction. In *Theories in Contemporary Psychology.* Edited by Melvin Marx. New York: Macmillan.

McGeoch, John A. 1933. The formal criteria of a systematic psychology. *Psychological Review* 40:1–12.

Pronko, N. H. 1988. *From AI to Zeitgeist: A Philosophical Guide for the Skeptical Psychologist.* Westport, CT: Greenwood Press.

Smith, N. W. 1973. Contextual interactionists: A symposium. *Psychological Record* 23:281–82 (full symposium, 283–342).

Stam, Henderikus J. 1990. Rebuilding the ship at sea: The historical and theoretical problems of constructionist epistemologies in psychology. *Canadian Journal of Psychology* 31:239–53.

CHAPTER 2

Historical Background and Logic of Science

Chapter Outline

HISTORICAL BACKGROUND

He who observes the development of things from the beginning will have the most advantageous view of them.—Aristotle, *Politikon*

Those who cannot remember the past are condemned to repeat it.—George Santayana, *Life of Reason I*

From Hunter-Gatherers to Hellenic Greeks and Naturalistic Psychology

When and Where Did Mind-Body Dualism Begin? Have humans always assumed a mind and a body? Did such a dualism come down to us from the pre-Socratic Greeks? Has this dualism always been a part of psychology? A careful examination of the historical records shows that the answer to all three questions is "no." Yet the common assumption in psychology is that belief in a supernatural mind is a heritage from our primitive ancestors (for example, Denmark, 1980; Skinner, 1963; Wile, 1977). However, the earliest records of psychological concepts found among hunter-gatherers, Indo-Europeans, Egyptians, Mesopotamians, Hebrews, and Chinese, clearly show that this dualism was not always a given.

What difference does this make? If this were just a matter of antiquarian interest, only antiquarians would need to consider it. But the question of whether a science of the mind is possible, or whether psychology is about a mind at all, is the central question around which modern psychology developed. It remains central, in one form or another, to the character of several current systems in psychology. Psychology has gone in cycles—first declaring itself a study of mind, then a study of behavior, then some systems declaring again in favor of mind. History cannot directly answer the question of whether psychology is about mind or behavior or both, but it can serve as a tool of analysis. If it can tell us when and where psychophysical dualism arose,[1] such a disclosure will indicate that dualism did not always exist and is not an inevitable way of thinking. It also indicates the alternative that existed prior to the concept of dualism. Finally, history informs us about the conditions or sources from which dualism arose, and that knowledge may allow us to judge whether those sources are compatible with a science of psychology.

---

1. There are any number of dualisms, and dialectics (chapter 9) places major emphasis on such opposites in conflict. The *mind-body* dualism is specifically a *psychophysical* dualism in which "psych-" refers to something outside of time and space; having no physical properties; transcending the physical. *Physical,* in turn, refers to that which is solely in time and space. Such terms as "nonphysical," "incorporeal," "transcendental," "transpatial," "transnatural," "supernatural," and "unextended" all refer to something beyond the physical. "Unextended" means not having spatial extension; having no dimensions. "Metaphysical" could also be added to the list. Aristotle used the term to mean "after the physics," but it has come to mean "beyond physics"; having no referent in the physical world.

Hunter-Gatherers and Herders. Among groups whose way of life was hunting and gathering or herding livestock, the concept of life-force or life-power was widespread. It took such forms as breath, smoke, liveliness, cloud, shadow, image, etc. (Smith, 1985). One of the most common was breath, and lines from nose and mouth depicted in cave art in France and Spain (Smith, 1992) suggest that it may go back to the ice age of 15,000 or even 30,000 years ago (Clottes, 1996). The last breath of the fallen warrior in the *Iliad* was the *psuché*,[2] a term that became the root of the word "psychology" (Smith, 1989). To expire is to breathe out and also to die. It is to lose one's life-force. Similarly, "spirit" in its Latin origins referred to breath.

Two versions of this life-force were widespread among hunter-gatherers and early farmers and herders (Hultkrantz, 1953; Bremmer, 1983). One, essentially free of the body, occurred in sleep, fainting, and ecstasy. It might be called the "free power." It was immortal, and in the afterlife it could take another form such as that of an animal. The second version was active while the individual was awake and was often identified with breath. It could be called the "body power." It played a role in such psychological activities as thinking, feeling, and perceiving. However, the particulars of the two types vary from group to group. Usually both the free power and the body power are called "soul," but in our time this word has a meaning infused with Christian supernaturalism that would have been unknown to these groups.

Hunter-gatherers typically attributed events in nature—sickness, good fortune, the availability of food, weather conditions, the changing seasons, the fate of enemies, the creation of landscape features, springs of water, and so on—to these life-forces. These animistic forces were greater than human power and therefore super*human*. But they were not beyond nature, not super*natural*—that is, not beyond the time-space dimensions of the natural world (Saliba, 1976; Spiro, 1966). For lack of a better term we can refer to this orientation as "naturalistic animism." The common references to a spirit or soul usually refer to breath or blood or life itself (Smith, 1985, 1989). The Native Americans found it difficult to reconcile the Christian nonphysical soul with their own belief systems (Hultkrantz, 1953) because the cleft between soul and nature was contrary to their own rootedness in nature. Consistent with this naturalistic view of the life-force, ethnologists have found no evidence for a mind concept, inner-outer distinction, or other evidence of a psychophysical dualism (for example, Fortes, 1949, 1965; Lienhardt, 1961).

Early and Non-Western Civilizations. The first urban centers for which a deciphered written record exists show an orientation toward the world and toward humans similar to that of the hunter-gatherers. In the earliest Mesopotamian state, Sumer, the major gods were personifications of nature (Smith, 1993b). The chief sky god was An, the earth goddess Ki, and the universe *an-ki* ("earth-sky"). Enlil was "Lord Wind," where *en* meant "lord" and *lil* "wind." Appropriately, Enlil was also life breath and animation. There is no mind-body or physical-nonphysical dualism in these concepts, nor in the Mesopotamians' four modes of being: luck, fate, vitality, and individual corporeality (Oppenheim, 1964; Smith, 1974, 1993b).

The heart was the locus of many psychological events for the Mesopotamians, Egyptians, Chinese, Greeks, Mayans, and many others. (The heart's change of rate in affective situations and its relation to change in breathing is easy to observe.) In Egypt's New Kingdom period (2000–1780 BCE[3]) the god of feeling and touch (Sia) is in the heart. Vignettes illustrate the heart as weighed against justice, a feather, at the time of death. This weighing was a prelude to the fate of the individual. Among the modes of being of the Egyptians, the *ba* was closely associated with breath and was

---

2. In Greek the word is ψυχή, approximately "psuché" in transliteration.

3. BCE, meaning Before the Common Era, is a substitute for B.C.; and CE, meaning Common Era, substitutes for A.D. Historians are increasingly using these designations to replace the Christocentric ones.

the life-energy in the afterlife (Smith, 1990b). New Kingdom period depictions show it as a bird with a human head, sometimes breathing into the nostrils of a mummy. Zabkar (1968) points out that because no dualism existed in Egyptian culture, the *ba* was neither an internal nor an external entity, nor was it a spiritual force opposed to a material force. "The dualistic view that man is constituted of two distinct elements . . . is alien to the Egyptian. . . ." (p. 113). Further, "So foreign was the idea of immateriality or spirituality to the concept of the Ba that the Christianized Egyptians found the word *ba* inadequate to express the Christian idea of a soul . . ." (p. 56). For the Egyptians, animals, gods, and humans were all in continuity with one another.

In China, too, the gods are quite materialistic. They are like human beings but more powerful and totally unlike the Western supernatural god (Kuo & Lam, 1968; Maspero, 1978; Granet; 1975/1922). Many educated Chinese, especially Confucian scholars, were atheistic. The indigenous Chinese belief system is concrete. The mystical is absent, and abstractions are of little interest. Ritual is performed for its effectiveness. Two groups of life-forces are accepted, *yin*—primarily the body, particularly blood—and *yang*—based on breath. In Daoism the *chi* is the breath or vitality of the *Dao*. Many psychological functions are seated in the heart, and psychology in Chinese is *xinli xue,* "study of the rule of the heart" (Petzold, 1987). Mind-body dualism was absent from indigenous Chinese beliefs but has entered from abroad. Many Chinese have studied in the West and brought dualism into Chinese psychology (Yue, 1994; Petzold, 1994). Buddhism, imported from India, has also brought with it the mind-body duality (Kuo, 1976).

The Japanese view everything in interdependence and consequently have no mind-body dualism. Humans are in continuity with other forms of nature (Maruyama, 1974; Watanabe, 1974), and they are in continuity with the nature gods of the indigenous religion, Shintoism. The Japanese do not separate self and environment, for neither can be defined as independent of the other (Kojima, 1984).

Indo-Europeans. A single language family that probably originated somewhere around the Black Sea about six thousand years ago stretched from India to Europe and west to Iceland (and beyond, due to European colonization). It includes such languages in the East as Bengali, Urdu, Farsi, and Hindi, and in the West as Russian, Albanian, Greek, French, Icelandic, Keltic, and English. This language family provides additional information about early psychological concepts (Smith, 1989).

The earliest Indo-European text is the *Rig Veda.* Although its date is unknown, one archaeological artifact connected with its authors dates to roughly 5700 years ago (Hicks & Anderson, 1991). The *Rig Veda* is primarily a ceremonial work containing numerous tributes to the beauty and character of nature. Its gods are nature gods and some, such as the Mesopotamian gods, have the same name as the corresponding part of nature.

A few relevant terms from the *Rig Veda* are instructive. *Manas,* usually translated as "mind" or "spirit," is located in the heart, but it is a function of the entire body and means only "thinking" or "thought," not mind *as opposed to* body (Bhawe, 1960). (A major psychology journal in India is called *Manas.*) Behavior is associated with breathing and other organic processes and is a life-function. *Atman* means breath or wind. In the *Rig Veda* there is no psychophysical dualism.

The Prehellenic Greeks left us the great epics of Homer, the *Iliad* and the *Odyssey.* In these works we again find gods with the same names as the natural entities to which they refer (such as Gaea [Earth] and Eros [Love]), indicating a continuity between nature itself and the life-forces that are assumed to be a causative part of it (Smith, 1989). These life-forces are in continuity with humans as well as other aspects of nature and play a causative role there as well.

In her presidential address to the American Psychological Association, Florence Denmark (1980) claimed that the original meaning of *psyche* was "soul" and "spirit" and that modern psychology can unite the intangible and the physical. But, as noted above, *psuché* ("psyche") did *not* mean something intangible or nonphysical in

Homer. It was the last breath of life, a free power that continued into the afterlife as a shadow and without senses. The loss of *psuché* was the loss of life in this world. The term at that time had no distinctive psychological meaning.

The psychological terms that Homer did use were functions of the body. Five are worth considering here (Smith, 1989):

- Feeling, a function of the heart, *kardia*.
- *Menos*, associated with impulsive acts and rage, situated in the chest. *Menos* comes from the same Proto-Indo-European root as English "mind" and Vedic "manas."
- *Frenes*, located in the chest or midriff or in the lungs around the beating heart has two different characteristics. One is a contemplative or intellectual function of an affective type, involving such feelings as awe, contentment, joy, and appreciation of beauty. The second characteristic is also affective, but it gave rise to such terms as "frenetic," "frantic," "frenzy," and "schizophrenia." The intellectual character of *frenes* took on the meaning of "mind" many centuries later and gave us the word *phrenology,* the belief that contours of the skull reflect personality characteristics. *Fren* or *frenes* occurs 350 times in the Homeric works, mostly as a psychological event.
- *Nóos* (later *nous*) resides in the chest and is a rational function and life energy. *Nóos* is an appreciation or immediate understanding of something, such as recognition of a solution to a problem. Centuries later Aristotle made *nous* the highest function of *psuché,* which in turn was the primary life-function of the entire organism—"the first grade of actuality of a natural body" (Aristotle, *De Anima*, 412a, 30).[4]
- Impulsive and irrational affective functions such as joy, anger, fear, grief, and desire for revenge belong to *thumos*. Unlike *psuché's* free power, *thumos* is active when one is awake. It is etymologically related to breath and vapor and resides in the chest or in *frenes*.

---

4. For a history of the transition from Homer's nonpsychological meaning of *psuché* to Aristotle's use of it in a systematic psychology, see Smith (1974).

Because *kardia, menos, frenes, nóos,* and *thumos* center around the chest, heart, lungs, and breathing, it appears that Homeric peoples considered these body components and functions to be the source of affective and intellectual behavior.

The Old English epic *Beowulf* written around the eighth century CE has much in common with other Indo-European epics such as the *Iliad* and *Odyssey, Táin Bó Cuange* of the Kelts, *Poetic Edda* and *Prose Edda* of the Norse, the Icelandic sagas, and some quasi-narrative features of the *Rig Veda,* in that psychological acts are typically associated with regions or organs of the body. *Sawol* that became our word "soul" has several meanings, all closely related to life-functions (Smith, 1989). For one, it refers to thoughts which are from the breast (l. 2818), and these depart at the time of death. It also refers to afterlife (ll. 184, 2422, and 2820) and to intellect or reason (l. 1742). When the soul is pierced in battle (l. 801), life is destroyed; and one who is soulless is dead (ll. 1406, 3303). When the dragon bites Beowulf, he is bloodied with life's gore (*sawuldriore,* l. 2693). These usages point to (a) life itself, loss of life, or afterlife, (b) blood as life, and (c) life actions of thinking and reasoning. They clearly do not point to any nonphysical or spiritual entity as we now use the word. Similarly, the Hebrew term *nefesh* (note: a Semitic language, not Indo-European), translated as "soul," meant a person's "living being" or "acting being" (Murtonen, 1958).

Hellenic Psychology: Naturalism Without Animism

Presocratic Greeks. The Greeks usually called themselves Hellenes, although Aristotle and later the Romans referred to them as Graikoi, hence Greek. The Hellenic period extends from the time of Greek intellectual and cultural attainment of about 600 BCE to the death of Alexander in 323 BCE. The earliest of these Hellenic peoples were the first we know of to reject animistic and mythological explanations and attempt to understand nature on its own terms. For example, they tried to understand the behavior of matter by reasoning about its fundamental constituents which they believed to be air, earth, fire, and water. As crude as this was, in principle it is the same as the 96+ elements that we now know compose matter. They asked why the sun moves across the sky, and determined that it was self-moved, thereby rejecting the myth that Apollo and his horses pulled it across the sky. In the fifth to fourth centuries BCE, Leucippos (fl. 440) and Democritos (460–370) set forth the theory that the behavior of matter could be explained by the character of invisible particles they named "atoms." These philosophers were replacing animistic naturalism with philosophical naturalism, the prelude to scientific naturalism.

Socrates (469–399). In the fifth century Socrates used naturalistic philosophy to explain why one cannot accurately understand human behavior by consulting body parts. The setting for this explanation is a scene in the *Phaedon* of Plato in which Socrates is awaiting his execution after an Athenian court convicted him. He has chosen death rather than exile (*Criton*), and his friends want to remove him from the prison and take him to another city. Socrates refuses. He explains that one cannot, by referring to his bones and muscles and other body parts, explain his decision to remain in Athens and accept his execution, nor can one explain his talking to his friends by referring to sound and air and hearing. If it were up to his body parts, rather than remaining in a seated position, they would get up and run off to another city to avoid death. They would act "by their own idea of what was best" (*Phaedon,* 99b).[5] One can only explain his actions by taking account of the fact that, as an Athenian citizen, he believed it was "right and honourable" (99a) to obey the state and accept its penalties. To attribute his actions to his body parts, he insists, would be a "confusion of causes and conditions" (99a). That is, without his

body parts he could not carry out his intentions, but to claim that he acts *because* of them is erroneous. Those who do not think through the matter "cannot distinguish the cause from the condition without which the cause would never be the cause" (99b).

Here in the fourth century BCE we have a forthright statement that warns us not to confuse causes with conditions. In terms often used today, we should not confuse *necessary* conditions with *sufficient* conditions. That is, the body parts are necessary for Socrates to carry out his actions, but they are not sufficient by themselves. His decision requires not only the necessary biological conditions but also his lifetime history as an Athenian citizen, with the meaning of honor and rightness that that personal history includes. Were Socrates to be transported to the twenty-first century and hear that his behavior was due to his brain, he would have found this equally unacceptable, insisting that the brain might be necessary for his decision but could not sufficiently explain it. If the decision were up to his brain, it would have caused his body to run off to save itself.

Plato (427–347). Plato's interest in psychological events is rather incidental to other interests and is scattered through his works. Reasoning is connected with mathematical analysis and the achievement of ideas and imagination with art production. Recollection is a response to something that substitutes for what is now absent. Seeing color is the joint action of the eye and the appropriate movement of the object. Affect, too, is related to motion and influenced by conditions of health, deprivation or restoration, and intellectual achievement.[6] Contrary to the views of his Homeric predecessors, he places neither affect nor any other psychological event in the heart or in any other body part.

Because we know Plato as a thinker rather than a doer, we do not expect to find him engaging in an empirical demonstration. But he does just that:

---

5. The numbers and letters in Plato's works refer to a 1578 Paris edition by Henri Estienne of the Greek text in which numbers are pages and letters are sections. These designations became the standard that continues in use today.

6. See Kantor, 1963, for an extensive review and analysis of Plato's psychological concepts. For a briefer analysis, see Smith, 1993b.

Place the right hand in a vessel of cold water and the left in a vessel of hot water. Then place both hands in a vessel of water of intermediate temperature. The right hand will feel hot and the left hand cold. Plato used this demonstration to show the relativity of the senses. Such relativity, he argues, forces us to go beyond the unreliable senses and consider the idea of a true temperature that is real and permanent and lies beyond the sensed temperature. Plato considered the inaccurate senses mere indicators of a more perfect or ideal form of things.

Some authors have attributed psychophysical dualism and mysticism to Plato (for example, Leahey, 1987). It is true that he gave both reality and supreme status to Ideas, the eternal archetype of things that are ideal patterns of existence and more real than objects we sense. His intense interest in geometry influenced this process of turning abstractions into real things, for he viewed geometric figures as only representations of reality. Plato was looking for the ultimate character of the world that was beyond the senses. The senses could be in error, but rationality could get beyond appearances to the ultimate reality, the most perfect instance, the Ideal in a world beyond the heavens.

Plato used myths, allegories, parables, and other imaginative devices to dramatize his points; but he tells us that one "ought not to assert that the descriptions which I have given of the soul and her mansions is exactly true" (*Phaedon*, 114). To take these stories literally is to miss much of what he is trying to say. His "fanciful notions of immortality, persistence, and transmigration are typical Platonic myths designed to reinforce his moral exhortation" (Kantor, 1963, p. 106), and are based on stories from the cult of Orphism (Green, 1990). He used transmigration, for example, to illustrate reminiscence—which he believed was an act of recollection. Plato did not assume anything outside the time and space dimensions of the world, the assumption intrinsic to psychophysical dualism. "It is traditional to think of Plato as the classical dualist, but actually his dualism is not the culpable dualism of matter and spirit. What he was differentiating was construction mainly in the form of mathematical formulae from the objects that were being described or discussed" (Kantor, 1981a, p. 17).

As for the charge of mysticism, the close partner of dualism, an editor of translations of Plato addressed this question (Cairns, 1961). He concluded that Plato uses logic and rationality to arrive at intelligibility, not faith based on intuition and feelings which is the stock in trade of the mystic.

Aristotle (384–322). The first Western systematic psychology came out of the biological studies of Aristotle. Accordingly, one might expect it to be organocentric but instead it had a continuity with Socrates and Plato, presenting psychological events as more than a mere function of body parts. However, he does recognize the participation of biological structures and functions, and ascribes to the heart and the connecting blood vessels a regulating role (Everson, 1997). From his biological studies he came to recognize that many activities of organisms were not just functions of biological structures but were inextricably related to the objects with which the organism was engaged. Psychological events occurred as joint actions of object and organism (Kantor, 1963; Randall, 1960; Shute, 1944; Smith, 1971, 1974, 1977, 1993b; Tolman, 1994).[7] His *psuché*[8] as the actualization of

---

7. Aristotle's translated works have been given Latin titles. Most of his psychology is in *De Anima*, but important parts are also found in some shorter works: *De Sensu* and others are collected in a book known as *Parva Naturalia*, and in Books VIII and IX of *Historia Animalium*. The numbering system is based on the Bekker edition of the Greek text, published in Berlin in five volumes, 1831–1870. A designation such as *De Anima* 412b, 31, means page 412, column b, line 31 of the Bekker edition. The system does not correspond to pagination, to single rather than double columns, or to line breaks of other editions or translations. Even so, because the system is numerically sequential, locating a passage with it is not difficult.

For the student who would like further sources on Aristotle's psychology in addition to those of Aristotle himself, or could use some help with his difficult writing, three relatively old works are outstanding as an introduction: a very short book by Shute (1944), chapter five of Randall (1960), and chapter nine of Kantor (1963).

8. Most translators translate *psuché* as "soul"—an acceptable rendering if the original meaning in *Beowulf* were intended but grossly misleading by the present understanding of the word in accordance with religious meaning.

Figure 2.1. Contrast between *Psuché* as an Agent or Thing and *Psuché* as a Relationship.

the body's potential (*De Anima*, 412a, 28–29)[9] was somewhat organocentric, but he described the actual activity as an interaction or joint action of organism and object. Figure 2.1 suggests the distinction between later views of *psuché* as a causal agent (usually a supernatural one) and Aristotle's meaning.

In the first approach, the object causes the *psuché* to produce, for example, a sensation or motive or mental act which causes a response. In Aristotle's approach, *psuché* consists of an interaction as indicated by the double-headed arrow. It is not a thing nor an agent, has no independent existence, and cannot cause anything. It exists only as a relationship. All the action is between the responding organism and the object.

For instance, sensing requires both a potential of the organism to sense and an object with the potential to be sensed, a sensible object (*De Anima*, 418–25; *De Sensu* 436–40). The sense organ must be able to change in such a way as to accommodate the form of the thing sensed (Everson, 1997). Sensing also requires a medium of contact, such as light or sound. For visual sensing, if (a) light has actualized the transparent, such as air or water; (b) an object with the potential to be sensed is present; and (c) an organism with the potential to sense the object is also present, the joint action of the sensible object and the sensible organism comprises the sensing act (Smith, 1971, 1983). The object and organism are interdependent but not fused. "The activity of the sensible object and that of their percipient sense is one and the same

activity, and yet the distinction between their being remains" (*De Anima*, 425b, 26–27), just as sound is in both the striking object and the struck, each in its own way (*De Anima*, 420a, 19–20). Thus, sensing is the joint actualization of two potentials and is localized not in the object or in the organ but in their relationship. Nor is it a conversion of light rays into a representation of the object as some prominent theories of perception today assume. For Aristotle, light rays are one necessary condition for seeing an object, but we don't see light rays. The interaction of an organism that can see and a seeable object in air that is lighted is the seeing. When Aristotle considers not just sensory qualities but identification of objects such as "the son of Diares" (*De Anima*, 418a, 20–24) he accepts that the entire organism rather than a specific sense organ is involved.

In imagining (*De Anima*, 428–434), one reacts to an absent object by means of another object. Even animals such as ants, bees, and grubs engage in sensing; but he avers that they do not imagine. Further, sensing is usually accurate (contrary to Plato) whereas imagining is usually false. Nevertheless, imagining functions in close connection with sensing and can occur with the same sense organ when the original object is no longer present. Imagining, together with sensing, allows us to recognize such characteristics of things as unity, movement, rest, magnitude, figure, and number, and the indirect qualities of things—such as the white object as "the son of Diares." The image represents the absent object as a residual movement. Thinking, reasoning, and calculating are possible because of detachment from the original object (Kantor, 1963; Randall, 1960).

Just as sensing is not located in the organism, neither is thinking. Thinking requires previous

---

9. "The *psuché* is the form of the living body. To give the form of a body is to specify what kind of thing it is. To be a living body is to possess some capacity for activity, and so the *psuché* will be the capacity for the activity whose possession defines the body in question" (Everson, 1997, p. 290).

sensing but then becomes independent of it, and this relative detachment from objects allows for the complex act of thinking. Both judging and imagining are involved in thinking and provide room for errors, whereas sensing, because it involves contact with objects, is, with few exceptions, without error. Thinking involves comparison and reason, and these allow us to apprehend universals—that is, generalities rather than particular things—such as straightness or unity. As for the object side, those things that are thought about have only form and no matter. Hence the thing thought about and the thought itself are the same. Thoughts reside in *nous,* the highest function of *psuché*.[10] But *nous* is nowhere. It has existence only as the thinking act itself, and that act is a joint product of the form of the thing thought about and the thinking organism (*De Anima,* 429b, 33). "In every case *nous* which is actively thinking is the object which it thinks" (*De Anima,* 431b, ff.). A syllogism or a mathematical formula, for example, exists only as the act of "*nousing.*"

Aristotle also considered remembering and recollecting, reasoning, appetite or motivation, dreaming, knowing, affect, intellectual activity, and a number of topics that we would consider closer to biology than to psychology—such as sleep and waking, youth and old age, life and death, respiration, and lengthiness and brevity of life, as well as nutrition and locomotion—to be a part of *psuché*. These topics all had a unity that derived from his biopsychological orientation. Out of that orientation came the analysis that not all activities could be understood as the functioning of biological structures but involved another level of organization involving organism-object relationships. Thus, in the fourth century BCE Aristotle provided an alternative to reduction of psychological events to biological structures such as the sense organs or the brain. Despite his biopsychological perspective he was the first to develop a systematic psychology that was not

organocentric and does not contain any psychophysical dualism.

Translator and commentator Richard Sorabji gives a slightly mentalistic interpretation of Aristotle's work on memory by relating him to the British empiricists, but he recognizes that Aristotle "has no word, not even any concept, corresponding to our 'mental'" (Sorabji, 1972, p. 15). Deborah Modrak (1987) imposes a mind-body dualism on Aristotle and then purports to show how well he deals with what she has imposed. For Aristotle, the psychological event is not *in a mind* or in any organ but comprises a different level of organization than organ functions, one of organism-object interdependence. Just as organism-object interdependence obviates reducing the event to biology, it also obviates the internal-external distinction of mentalism. Aristotle's psychology "manifests a better sense of what is required in that science, and its contemporary successors, than many who are still engaged in it" (Everson, 1997, p. 288).

Conclusions. So far this brief review has found no evidence for any psychophysical dualism among hunter-gatherers, Indo-Europeans, Hellenic Greeks, Chinese, and Japanese. It has shown, instead, that organocentric psychology prevailed until Socrates repudiated it, Plato gave no room for it, and Aristotle, in developing the first naturalistic and systematic psychology, provided a distinct alternative. These historical developments teach us that psychophysical dualism, contrary to statements by some psychologists (see p. 10), has not always been present and is not an inevitable way of thinking. An alternative to both organocentric and dualistic psychology was present by the fourth century BCE. The next section will address the remainder of the projected historical information: when and where dualism arose and under what conditions.

Hellenistic Greeks and Psychophysical Dualism

Coping Philosophies. The Hellenistic period extends from the end of the Hellenic era in 323 to 30

---

10. *Nous* gets translated as "mind," but this is clearly misleading. It is best to leave it untranslated and examine how Aristotle is using it. See Homer's usage in Section 1.1.

BCE when Rome gained dominance. The first century and a half (323–146) was characterized by dictators, military empires, scientific and technological achievements, and philosophies oriented not toward knowledge of the world (like Plato's and Aristotle's schools) but toward dealing with growing insecurities. Sparta totally vanquished Athens in 404 BCE and the succeeding century was beset by strife that facilitated the conquest of Greece by Philip and his son Alexander (356–323). During this period of warfare, Socrates was executed (399 BCE). With Alexander's conquest of Greece and the huge region extending south to Egypt and east to India, peace briefly followed. Then the death of Alexander and the breakup of his empire created further strife, and Aristotle fled Athens to avoid the same fate as Socrates. As the political organization and various institutions of the Greek city-state that had provided so much sense of stability, pride, and accomplishment waned and disappeared, Greek self-assuredness diminished. The *polis* or city-state of the Greeks disintegrated, and authoritarian government took its place. The loss of the cherished polis and personal identification with it left "a void at the heart of things, a rootlessness that was one of the Hellenistic age's most enduring and characteristic features" (Green, 1990, p. 388). An eminent Hellenistic historian describes the tumult of the time:

One war followed another, wars between the leading monarchies, regional wars, domestic wars within the monarchies and city-states, revolutions of the natives against the Greeks. And all the wars became more and more destructive, more and more cruel, more and more demoralizing. Not satisfied with destroying by their own hands what had just been created, the Hellenistic powers invited a new partner into their destructive game. The shadow of Rome appeared on the Western horizon, and Rome soon took an active part in the political life of the Hellenistic world, first as protector of Greek liberty against the monarchies, next as benevolent adviser in the internal affairs of the Hel-

lenistic states, and finally as an exacting and ruthless master of the Greek cities and Hellenistic monarchies alike. (Rostovtseff, 1938–1939, p. 16)

Interest in the natural world, including psychological events, gave way to social concerns and to philosophies oriented toward coping with the growing insecurities of life. At the outset these philosophies were naturalistic, consistent with the Hellenic orientation toward the world but soon began abandoning any interest in nature. Five of these philosophies were especially prominent, and four of them gave us terms that we use today: skeptic, cynic, stoic, and epicurean. While they do not relate directly to psychological principles, they are themselves psychological products of social conditions.

■ The *skeptics* challenged humankind's ability to know truth. One must suspend judgment, become non-attached, and thereby find tranquility in a dangerous world. The skeptics contributed both to a negative attitude and to a healthy suspicion about assertions.

■ The most negativistic were the *cynics*[11] ("dog-like"), who desired to live like dogs by rejecting all that is normally valued by humans. They held that the only good is virtue. It alone leads to happiness, and it can be attained by curtailing all desires and loyalties. (Note the similarity to Buddhism, which also arose under conditions of insecurity and taught that those who have no desires will not be troubled by whatever happens.) Riches, honor, freedom, health, even life are not merely matters of indifference but are actually contemptible. One should despise civilization, its laws, and its morals. One should deny allegiance to everything including family, friends, and country. The cynics paraded their poverty, their antagonism to pleasure, and

---

11. "Cynic" transliterates as *kunikos* from *kuvikós*. "Kunikos" looks so different from cynic because (a) the "k" sound of the Latin "c" became an "s" sound in French in some words and was passed on to us in the Norman conquest of England, and (b) the upper case of the Greek letter upsilon is Y.

their indifference to others as the essence of their virtue. In their rejection of the world and their indifference to it, they were shielded from suffering: they had nothing to lose.

- *Stoics,* named for the *stoa* or porch where the philosophy was taught, sought to teach virtue or the art of right living. To achieve this one must be able to use logic and physics to understand the universe. According to their physics, *theos* (divinity), *psuché,* matter, force, relationships, and virtue and vices are all made of matter. Humans differ in their physics from the rest of the universe only in having reason, through which they can govern action. By reason, they know virtue to be harmonious with the true nature of humanity. Reason tells them that power, glory, riches, health, and even life are not virtues; nor are desire, pain, poverty, misery, or death evils. Therefore they are indifferent to them. Through reason humans can become free of desires and masters of themselves. The wise welcome whatever befalls them. They can roll with the punches (our meaning of "stoical") because their strength lies in rational insight. When life is unendurable a stoic can triumph by committing suicide. Stoics give up life as they give up desire, and in doing so maintain their independence. Another aspect of the stoic philosophy is that a life of reason is not possible without social duties, justice, mercy, and friendship. Reason is the basis of society and unites humans. Citizenship is of little importance, but the social unity of all rational humans of all societies is of great importance. This concept provided the basis of Christian universal human brotherhood. Stoicism took a more mystical turn in Rome, contributing further to Christian doctrine.

- The Greek city of Cyrene, south of Athens on the north African coast, was prosperous and rich. The *Cyrenaics* initially sought immediate pleasure as the highest good, though what is pleasurable differs from person to person. But Hegesias, known as the Death-Persuader, held that happiness is an illusion and that the only goal worth pursuing is death as relief from pain. It was clearly an escapist philosophy.

- According to the *Epicureans* (named for Epicuros [340–270]) one's primary goal in life is pleasure, and the supreme pleasure is tranquillity. Both the path of indulgence or that of deprivation or rigor are counterproductive. One should strive for maximum enjoyment with the minimum of distress. Virtue is not an end in itself but a means to happiness, and to the extent it leads to happiness, one should seek it. Epicureans viewed all of the universe and all events as composed of atoms. This left no room for the paranormal or superstitious beliefs that the tumultuous conditions of the fourth and third centuries were fostering. Even death, Epicuros wrote, "is nothing to us, because when we are, death is not; and when death is, we are not." Epicureans examined atoms and the void—the entirety of existence—to find the certainty, calmness, and confidence needed to cope with the political and social conditions that faced them. One who is learned and wise is freed from fear.

Hellenistic Science. Much of the intellectual development now shifted from Athens to Alexandria, a city that Alexander founded on the delta of the Nile after his conquest of Egypt. It was a crossroads of commerce and brought in diverse groups of people with equally diverse intellectual traditions, ranging from mystical concepts of the Orient to the objective naturalism of the Greeks. Its great library and museum functioned much as a university does, even offering living quarters and dining rooms. The library contained many books by Hellenic writers, most of which are now lost. In this setting flourished such studies as astronomy, mathematics, medicine, physics, and, to a lesser extent, biology; but psychology received only limited attention after Aristotle. Verbalistic intellectual practices (e.g., allegories, puzzles, compilations, verbal formulae) that were a major element in the advent of psychophysical dualism replaced naturalistic psychology. It is somewhat ironic that psychology as a discipline did not participate in this scientific flowering, yet *the orientation away from nature and toward trans-nature or the nonphysical was itself a psychological response to social conditions.*

Aristarchos (310–230), whose teacher was from Aristotle's Lyceum, recognized that the earth and other planets circled the sun. The earth's revolution on its axis brought night and day. Because of lack of parallax effects—the stars were not displaced with respect to one another from different viewing positions on the earth—he correctly inferred that the stars were an enormous distance away. A point at the center of earth's orbit is to the size of that orbit as the orbit is to the distance from the stars (Sarton, 1959). Aristarchos triangulated the moon and sun to measure their distance from the earth (Singer, 1959). While his measurements were inaccurate, his method was sound. Eratosthenes (275–195) of Cyrene was versed in many disciplines and was the chief librarian at Alexandria. By measuring the angle of a shadow cast by sunlight at the time of the summer solstice at two cities of different latitudes and known distance apart, he calculated the size of the earth to an accuracy of less than one percent. Other luminaries of the time included Euclid (fl. 300 BCE) with his work in geometry; Archimedes (287–212) with his achievements in physics and technology; Diaphontos (3rd c. BCE) with the development of algebra; and Hipparchos who produced an accurate star chart with coordinates. However, most study of a psychological nature went toward developing philosophies of coping rather than toward understanding such events as perceiving, thinking, imagining, and the like.

Greco-Roman Turmoil. Despite these Alexandrian achievements, darkness was already on the horizon. Heavy taxes under the rulers of Alexander's former empire, such as the Ptolemies of Egypt and the Seleucids of Syria, and confiscation of property for debts brought the peasants to their knees. Rural peasant farmers were exploited by traders in the cities as well as by the government. Those in manufacturing and cottage industries also suffered. A tiny minority, primarily rulers and their courtiers, high-level bureaucrats, merchants, and loan sharks became very rich. Most of the rest were near starvation, and the overall standard of living declined. In such Greek cities as Athens and Corinth and along the coast of what is now Turkey

in cities like Ephesos and Miletos, wealthy individuals provided food to the starving. They also built public works—temples and gymnasiums—to avert unrest and resentment against the elite (Green, 1990). Widespread warfare drained the Greek economy and provided large numbers of slaves. "Rising prices, low wages, and the competition of slave labor meant a perennially bleak outlook for the unskilled or semiskilled free worker" (Green, 1990, p. 390). Slavery prevented the redistribution of wealth through wages and precluded new markets for goods and services as well. Yet hoarded wealth was huge. "There were riches galore for the taking, and generals from Sulla to Antony were not slow to skim the cream. What they left, the tax collectors (*publicani*) and provincial governors soon absorbed" (Green, 1990, p. 390). The following describes the lot of the common people of these centuries:

> Their life was hard and gloomy, and became ever gloomier, their material hardships were great, the prices high, the incomes small and ever diminishing, the insecurity of their daily lives tremendous. For example, no one was safe even for one day from being made a prisoner of war, or from being kidnapped by pirates and thus from becoming a slave perhaps to the end of his days. Their city, their beloved *polis*, was no longer able to give its people protection. Even the most glorious cities like Athens and Rhodes were deeply humiliated and demoralized. Nor did the proud kings prove to be more efficient: in truth they were broken reeds. No wonder that in such an atmosphere the despicable Graeculus of the Roman writers was born: demoralized, dishonest, a professional liar and flatterer, a selfish profiteer and exploiter, each man hoping to attain at least a minimum amount of well-being for himself and his one or two children. . . . (Rostovtseff, 1938–39, p. 18–19)

In Italy conditions were no better. Roman enslavement of populations greatly increased after 223 BCE when a Roman army destroyed Mantinea in Greece (Walbank, 1993). Between 200 and 150 the Romans took *a quarter million slaves or more* (by way of comparison, Athens had a population of about 100,000), but they began the practice as early as 296 (Green, 1990). Many slaves went to the wheat fields and cattle farms of Sicily and southern Italy where they worked in chain gangs. In Rome itself the slave population at one time was 75 percent of the total. The slaves in Sicily rebelled in the years from 136 to 131 BCE and again from 104 to 101. They were subjected to horrible retribution and massacred. Concerned that a few wealthy persons were eliminating the middle class and the peasantry by concentrating land and wealth, Tiberius, one of the two Gracchus brothers, was elected tribune in 133 BCE with a pledge to support the dispossessed. After obtaining passage of a law to redistribute public lands, he was assassinated. His brother Gaius was elected in 121 and carried out a number of reforms to help the poor. He too was murdered, his reforms were annulled, and the social and political wars resumed. "The two centuries preceding the Christian era had been a period of uninterrupted misery. For a time the Roman peace gave the world rest, but after the Antonine days happiness departed from the ancient world" (Angus, 1975, p. 306).

Hellenistic Verbal Obsessions and the Prelude to Psychophysical Dualism. In such a setting it is understandable that even privileged intellectuals began to turn away from a miserable world and to look for more personal satisfactions. The amalgamation of Greek and Eastern ideas that came together in Alexandria facilitated this development. Greek objectivity and interest in nature met Indian interest in the ineffable, illusion, and *nirvana*. Monotheism came in from the Zoroastrian religion in Persia and from Hebrew texts from Palestine. People and their viewpoints from Mesopotamia, Carthage, and even China intermixed. Textual analysis and interpretation replaced observation and the give and take of argument. Scholars deemphasized Greek science and valued the *word* that revealed underlying reality. The Greek interest in rhetoric as the art of disputation and persuasion was transformed into textual analysis. The

Alexandrians undertook the study of grammar, an objective project which gave increasing power to words and decreasing attention to the referents of the words.

In the second century BCE, Dionysius Thrax refined the *allegorical method* of obtaining underlying meanings from grammatical structures. This allowed scholars to read into texts meanings other than what the texts appeared to say—that is, allegorical rather than literal meanings. Philon, a Jewish scholar at Alexandria, became the foremost allegorist. He attempted to show that Greek writers such as Plato and Aristotle drew their inspiration from the Hebrew scriptures. Thus, he fused Hebrew religion and Greek science. With some prior models from Poseidonios the Stoic, he also transformed the Hebrew god from one of anger, jealousy, vengeance, favoritism, vanity (requiring worship and sacrifice), and other human characteristics to a perfect personal creator. Philon's god was utterly above the physical world, beyond comprehension, eternal, unchanging, the One. We cannot speak of what he is but only of what he is not, and yet he fills the heart with ecstasy and prophesy (Randall, 1970a). Philon had gone beyond the merely superhuman and had verbally constructed the supernatural. This transformation set the stage for the emergence of a nonphysical and spiritualistic psychology juxtaposed with the physical body—psychophysical dualism (Kantor, 1963).

Greco-Roman Sects. The period from 146 to 30 BCE was one of further decline. It began with Rome's final conquest of the East and ended at the battle of Actium which brought Ptolemy's Egypt under Roman rule. This period saw class conflict, civil wars, and economic imperialism. Piracy flourished; the ruling class was corrupted by new wealth; the working classes were servile. Civil war, international war, and class conflict were rampant. The danger of enslavement or death was great. In this climate rose despair, pessimism, and asceticism (Murray, 1955; Rostovtseff, 1957). Roman soldiers and sailors brought in cults from the East that promised a blissful afterlife. These flourished and began to replace the indigenous Roman beliefs that had promised little in the hereafter. In response to these conditions, the intellectual community created the supernatural as a domain to which the debased world did not apply.

In addition to this verbal obsession of the intellectuals, a more characteristic response to the social conditions of the general public (which, however, included many intellectuals) was an interest in cults or sects, magic, and divining the future. This trend gained intensity as early as the fifth century BCE and continued through the Roman period. These practices offered certainty in a time of uncertainty and fear. They empowered the practitioner to control destiny and suffering. While observances of the old Olympic gods continued, these were more customary than meaningful. Meanwhile an increasing preoccupation with Fate ("Tyche"), usually meaning inevitable death, was developing. Predestined fate could be predicted; and, therefore, one could divine the future. A great many methods, such as reading the pattern of smoke or of birds in flight or the content of dreams, were devised. But astrology, which originated in Babylon and then passed to Egypt and on to Greece and Rome, gradually became the dominant method. Ironically, great advances in mathematics and astronomy occurred parallel with this obsession with astrology.

Many sects were rooted in seasonal festivals celebrating and assuring the rebirth of the seasons. By extension, these sects came to mean the rebirth of oneself in a better world beyond the tribulations of this one. The most prominent such sects involved Isis and Osiris, gods of Egypt; Attis and the Great Mother or Cybele from Phrygia (now central Turkey); Mithra from Persia (now Iran); and Jesus Christ from Palestine. Among others were Baal from Syria; the Jewish god Yahweh (ineffable JHWH, meaning "to be" and "to breathe" constructed as Yahweh or Jehovah) from Palestine; Dionysos and Orpheus from Thrace (northern Greece, southern Bulgaria, and northwestern Turkey); Herakles (Roman Hercules) from Greece; and Adonis from Mesopotamia. All but Baal, Yahweh, and Cybele died and were said to have

been resurrected, but even these three were tied to resurrection through association with another deity (Baal and Cybele with Attis, and Yahweh with Christ). Herakles, Orpheus, and Jesus were all born in human form, suffered cruel deaths, and were then raised to Heaven by their divine fathers, from whence they would provide benefits to their devotees. These gods were all given the title "Lord." The devotees all sought to live a pure life and worship a pure god and to develop a sense of brotherhood (Brandon, 1963, 1969; Eliade, 1954, Haydon, 1967; James, 1960, 1961, Turcan, 1996).

Among these beliefs and rituals are some of the many themes that found their way into Christianity, whose theologians (for example, Origin) were incensed over the similarities between "pagan" sects and their own, not realizing that Christians were the borrowers rather than vice-versa. These various sects, including Christianity, all served a similar psychological function—offering hope for a better life hereafter and a feeling of certitude and tranquillity in the present. Over a period of four centuries the pursuit of truth had changed to a pursuit of salvation, the investigation of events of nature to the building of verbalizations, and a relishing of the pleasures of life to a focusing on preparations for death.

Greco-Roman Spiritualism: Supernatural Psyche. Rome brought peace (*pax Romana*) to the regions it ruled, but it ruled with a cruel and oppressive hand. Roman taxes were no less crushing than those of Hellenistic rulers, and eventually they destroyed the middle class while wealth-controlling landlords refused to pay taxes. In addition, it took the Romans four hundred years to learn to administer their enormous territories of highly diverse peoples. By the time they became proficient in the reign of Diocletian (284–305), the empire was already disintegrating (Barnes, 1965). Even so, the Roman's militant peace brought trade—mostly by Greeks, Syrians, and Jews—and spread both Middle Eastern culture and the Greek culture that eventually prevailed and passed down to us.

For Skeptics, Cynics, Stoics, Cyrenaics, and Epicureans "deliverance was sought *in* the world.

Then, as this longing grew, salvation was looked for *from* the world" (Randall, 1970a, p. 9). During the Hellenistic age a *personalism* had developed in which taking care of one's self superseded civic duties (Kantor, 1963). The worth of the individual and the equality of all—especially as Stoic doctrine later combined with Hebrew doctrine in Christianity—became what many now regard as the most valuable heritage of that period (Randall, 1970a). As time and conditions wore on, personalism gave way to *spiritism,* the separation of humans from other animals by attributing to them a supernatural *psuché,* which we will now call "psyche" or "mind" to reflect this meaning.

The beginnings of psyche as a supernatural agent are not as clear as the beginnings of a supernatural deity, but by the first century BCE the Roman poet Horace (65–8), writing in the Epicurean tradition, denied the existence of gods and an afterlife. Lucretius (95–55), also a Roman Epicurean, in his *On the Nature of Things,* railed against the superstitions of his time, including both supernaturalism and superhumanism. True to the tenets of his philosophy he presented a psychology based on atoms, as proposed by Democritos. This was the last naturalistic psychology for centuries to come. Lucretius argued for the materiality of mind:

> When the nerve-racking impact of spear gashes bones and sinews, even if it does not penetrate to the seat of life, there ensues faintness and a tempting inclination earthwards and on the ground a turmoil in the mind and an intermittent faltering impulse to stand up again. The substance of the mind must therefore be material, since it is affected by the impact of material weapons." (Lucretius, 1951, III, 178–80)

The fact that he was arguing the point suggests that someone was saying just the opposite. In another passage, he argued that only two things make up all existence: bodies and space. The fact that everybody senses things means that bodies exist, and unless we accept this no rational conclusions are possible. Further, space must exist for the bodies to be situated and to move about. There

is no third thing additional to bodies and space. Apparently, Lucretius's denial of a "third thing" referred to a claim for a supernatural agent that does not occupy space. Lucretius also propounded a remarkable theory of evolution through natural selection that is close to today's understanding.

Christian Continuation of Hellenistic Spiritism. When the Christian Church Fathers, the Patristics, began to develop their theology, they drew from the Hellenistic scholars the practice of building allegorical constructions of which the biblical book of Revelation is an example. They also attempted to allegorize away the failure of the predicted second coming (called "the failure of the parousia" by theologians). Apropos of psychology, they continued the Hellenistic construction of supernaturalism by further expounding on the psyche as the supernatural component of humans, analogous or parallel to the supernatural character of God and sharing His/Her spiritual character. Generally, psyche was unitary, noncorporeal, the source of thinking and choosing, and was linked with God and immortality. Because perceiving involved corporeal sense organs, the Patristics relegated it to the body. Still, arguments about the nature of psyche spanned several centuries of Patristic formulations (Kantor, 1963). By the third century, Hippolytus, a Patristic of Greek background, excoriated the notable Greek and Roman writers. He declared that he could make no sense of Aristotle's *De Anima.* The enormous gulf between the thinking of the Greek Aristotle and the Greek Hippolytus could not be more clear. Hippolytus was dismissing all non-Christian writing on natural and moral topics so that he could replace them with Christian theology.

The adherence to Greek rationality and the construction of a theology inevitably led to difficulties. In the fourth century, Gregory of Nyssa (d. 394) recognized that the union of the body and the psyche is inconceivable. The psyche cannot be within the body, for that would put it in physical space, nor can it be outside the body, for that too would give it a spatial location. It is inexplicable and incomprehensible how one can contact the other. We cannot think or speak of what the relationship can be, only recognize that what one does the other does in a corresponding manner. Thirteen centuries later a German philosopher, Gottfried Leibnitz, used this same explanation of correspondence together with an analogy of clocks (see p. 36) in an attempt to explain how psychophysical dualism works.

> The whole set of Christian doctrines and dogmas with their problems concerning the relation of the man-God to God and the triune God to man, formed a basis for the dual character of man so that, on the one hand, he is a natural being, a biological organism, and, on the other, a creative soul, a psychic substance, and a set of mental functions. (Kantor, 1963, p. 236)

The theological treatment of psychological events still influences psychology today. Questions of mind-body relations, consciousness, ego, self, psychic or mental processes, mental powers produced by the brain, sensations, diseases of the mind, and many other abstract entities in psychology have descended from Christian theology. Even the question about the very subject matter of psychology remains in dispute because of this influence. Is psychology about a mind? behavior? mind and behavior? experience? cognition and behavior? social constructions?

Conclusions. We can now more fully address the questions set forth at the outset of the chapter. A review of the evidence shows that mind-body dualism has not always existed. Nor has it always been a part of systematic psychology, for it does not appear in Aristotle. It is not an inevitable way of thinking. In the Western world we find it first appearing in the first or second century BCE among the intellectuals at Alexandria as they began to abandon the study of nature and to become preoccupied with words. This occurred in a turmoil of endless warfare and hardships in which the creation of a caring god who transcended the physical world and could somehow relate to the needs of humans was of greater interest than the

study of the world that posed such a threat. The importation of mystical concepts from the East no doubt facilitated the process. The larger public found solace in the salvation sects, one of which—Christianity—combined salvation beliefs with the intellectual traditions of the Alexandrian scholars and created the supernatural psyche as the personal agent that corresponded with the supernatural god constructed by Philon and others. The Patristic theologians divided psychological events between the psyche and the body. Mind-body dualism descends to psychology today from this heritage. Thus, according to some psychologists, the sense organs of the body receive stimulation and the mind perceives or interprets it; similarly, when the mind is under prolonged stress, the body develops disorders.

Knowing the conditions under which dualism arose and was elaborated allows us to decide, in accordance with any particular value system or orientation, whether its source is one upon which we choose to build a system of psychology or whether we prefer an alternative, such as that which Aristotle pioneered. The modern systems offer such choices, some with similarities to Aristotle, some dualistic, and some mechanistic.

A Comparison with India

A similar trend occurred earlier in India. There, too, were long periods of insecurity and suffering and an intelligentsia able to develop abstractions (Smith, 1990a). The evidence begins with the *Rig Veda* which describes the veneration of nature and the worship of nature gods of an Indo-European tribe called Aryas (Aryans). These people settled in a delimited area of north central India around what is now Delhi, where they apparently filled all the suitable land but kept growing in population. This led to hardship, tribal conflict, and starvation (*Rig Veda* 10.33.2–3). At this point in the story, the verses become increasingly mystical, involving search for abstract or allegorical explanations of existence (10.129.4). With a growing population and no fertile space into which they could expand, the Aryas fighting increased, their sacrifices became more lavish and more frequent, the rituals became more involved, and a hierarchy of priests developed to administer these complex rituals. In a succeeding work, the *Yajur Veda,* sacrifices become the preoccupation, and these begin to include humans. The nature gods recede into the background while an abstract god, Prajapati, becomes the highest power. The *Yajur Veda* tells of a quest for the non-world where the troubles of the real world do not hold and where attempts to control the environment by proper sacrifice prevail. Warfare is rampant, and probably starvation as well. In still later books, the *Brahmanas,* the most important power is still Prajapati—the Who? the undefined. Asceticism and expiation of error are growing in importance. The nondefined, the ineffable, becomes prominent, as does a gloomy, pessimistic expectation of death and rebirth. In these works an "unlimited" mind is present and identified with the Ultimate. The real becomes the unseen, the unimaginable, the ineffable, the inscrutable, the all of being and not being. The world of pain and sorrow become mere illusion.

In the early parts of the *Rig Veda,* breath (atman) is a life-function and its departure is the end of life. In the later parts of the work *atman* is an abstract creative force. In a succeeding text, the *Atharva Veda,* the *atman* reunites with the body in the afterlife and becomes identified with Prajapati and the All. By the time of the *Brahmanas, atman* means "self" with a spiritistic slant, and embraces the individual's total powers. There is a pursuit of the unobservable "essence" of things. Essence is the reality. Essence is atman. In a lesson about the essence of things, a teacher asks a pupil to divide a fig. The pupil does so and sees tiny seeds. Then the teacher asks him to divide a seed. He does so and then sees nothing. That, his teacher says, is the essence. The essence of nothing is what is real. It is atman, and "you are that" (*Chhandogya Up.* 6.8.6, 6.9.4, 6.10.13, et al.). Atman and the universal spirit, Brahman, are in essence the same. They are incorporeal, beyond space, and un-

demonstrable. Here is the first fully developed supernaturalism—beyond space and time, totally beyond nature, supernatural. But once this pinnacle is reached it is not very satisfactory. There is nowhere to go. Nothing can be done with it. Therefore, mere physical acts, whether of meditation or prayer, cannot affect it or be affected by it, for they are acts of a physical body with dimensions, movements, substance, and so on. In contrast, Brahman transcends such physical limitations and is infinite. The transcendent does not occupy time or space in which such acts occur. Accordingly, some passages say that Brahman is unknowable by the senses or by teaching. Others that he is beyond understanding (*Mundaki Up.* 2.2.1) or even "above the unknown" (*Kena Up.,* 3) and beyond conception (*Kena Up.,* 11).

Some of the *Upanishads* describe the *atman* in mostly psychological terms. It is the means of seeing, hearing, smelling, speaking, remembering, desiring, and willing. Atman is also Prajapati and Brahman as well as earth, wind, space, water, light, and numerous other things. Although *manas* (deriving from the same Indo-European root as "mind") is sometimes equated with *atman,* more often *manas* retains the physical characteristics of the body while *atman* is the transcendental element that makes for a mind-body dualism.

After the *Upanishads* came the *Sutras,* written between 600 and 200 BCE. In the later ones even the tangible physical qualities of the world, those known to the senses, are illusions. All but Brahman is internal and mental. Thus, the physical world of *manas* with its thoughts, feelings, and perception is only illusion, and one can know one's true self only through *atman,* pure spirit. Only Brahman is real and external, and he produces the world of appearances in a series of emanations. The next step, *Vedanta* philosophy, incorporated everything into supernaturalism, leaving no physical world at all. Because Vedanta philosophy allows for only the nonphysical, it is commonly claimed that this philosophy does not comprise a psychophysical dualism. But Vedanta continues to imply a physical-nonphysical dualism by contrasting supernaturalism with an illusory physical world. Vedanta philosophy is the end point of the evolution from naturalism to supernaturalism.

When the Indian writers began developing a systematic psychology, they did so in accordance with their culture. The psychology that resulted was a psychophysical dualism and was organocentric. For example, when they attempted to explain sensing, they recognized that an eye cannot see its own seeing. Consequently, they proposed that *manas* must be looking at what the eye sees. But they also recognized that *manas* could not see its own seeing either. Therefore *buddhi* (intellect) must see what *manas* sees. But what sees what *buddhi* sees? It must be the supernatural personal spirit *atman*. One text stops at that point, but in another text the great universal spirit *Brahman* looks at what *atman* sees. This infinite regress was a consequence of a physical-nonphysical/inner-outer dualism that evolved over a period of many centuries and became an integral part of this early systematic psychology. Aristotle did not face such a problem with his non-dualistic and non-centrist approach. For him, sensing was an organism-object interaction.

In sum, in the face of grievous social conditions over long periods of time, an intelligentsia consisting of the Brahman priesthood constructed a supernatural and psychophysical world whose evolution can be traced from the later books of the *Rig Veda* to a fully developed form in the *Upanishads*. Asceticism and meditation, intertwined with supernaturalism and with procedures for avoiding desire and for considering the world as illusion, provided an escape from those life conditions. The systems of philosophy that followed this dealt with a number of distinct psychological events. These tend to have inner and often mystical characteristics consistent with an evolution away from the embeddedness in nature of the *Rig Veda* and toward a transcendental conceptualization. The evolution of atman from breath or wind to the nonphysical half of a mind-body dualism illustrates this development. Figure 2.2 suggests the evolution from animistic naturalism to supernaturalism and mind-body dualism in both Indian and European cultures.

The Fall of the Roman Empire to the Rebirth of Science

Roman Science, Technology, and Encyclopedias. The Romans brought Greek craftsmen, astronomers, bankers, musicians, boat builders, and other skilled workers to Rome. The Romans did not continue Greek science but turned this knowledge and skills to such projects as building roads and aqueducts, improving health and hygiene, refining cartography, and developing architecture. Educated Romans accepted with Eratosthenes that the earth was spherical, and some accepted the heliocentric principle of Aristarchos. Most Roman works were compilations of previous knowledge, but Vitruvius (31 BCE-14 CE) wrote ten volumes of relatively original material on architecture, including an analysis of acoustics. The rediscovery of his works in the Middle Ages led to a return to Roman architecture. Also original was Marcus Agrippa's (63–12) work on engineering, geography, and map-making. Among the Roman encyclopedists, Aulus Celsus (fl. early 1st c.) wrote on numerous topics, but only his medical works, a summary of Alexandrian medicine, have survived. Galen (131–200), a Greek physician living in Rome, combined his own medical discoveries with other medical lore and emphasized purpose in the creation of the human body. Because purposiveness suited Christian theology, his work became doctrine in the Middle Ages and an impediment to new investigations. The most famous of the encyclopedias was Pliny's (23–79) thirty-seven-volume *Natural History,* a mixture of fact and myth. Varro (116–27) also compiled encyclopedias on a variety of topics, little of which involved his direct observation. His best work was on agriculture. This great trust in written words rather than in observation followed the later Hellenistic scholars and continued to predominate down through the Middle Ages. The Romans made gains in structural engineering but "did little or nothing to advance natural science. On the other hand, they did much to degrade science and to block strictly scientific impulses by compiling vast pseudoscientific works like Pliny's *Natural*

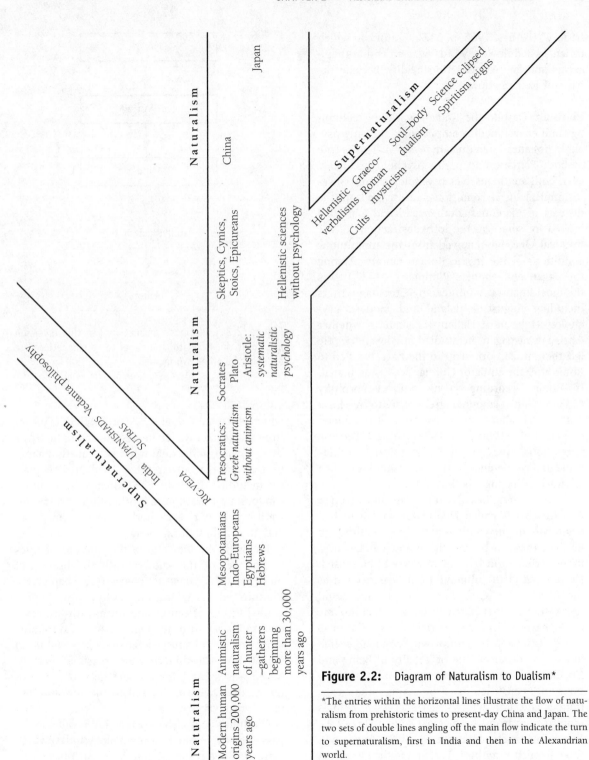

Figure 2.2: Diagram of Naturalism to Dualism*

*The entries within the horizontal lines illustrate the flow of naturalism from prehistoric times to present-day China and Japan. The two sets of double lines angling off the main flow indicate the turn to supernaturalism, first in India and then in the Alexandrian world.

History" (Barnes, 1965, p. 262). Oratory, in which cadences and flowery words were an end in themselves and far removed from reality, became the basis of Roman education.

Plotinus. Despite the Roman works of technology and encyclopedic compilations, the only psychologies after Lucretius are mystical. This is true of both Patristic and pagan psychologies. However, both are themselves psychological responses to inimical social conditions, an escape from the distress of the times. Both pagan and Christian looked for solace in the lofty abstractions of the mystical One, far removed from the tumultuous conditions of life in the Roman empire. Among the pagan philosophers Plotinus (204–270) was the most important, influencing Christian writers including Augustine, Islam, and modern psychology. Like most Hellenistic scholars, whether Christian or pagan, he studied at Alexandria. He left there in 243 on a trip to the East, but fled to Rome after the emperor Gordian was assassinated. In Rome, according to his student Porphyry (233–304), he "laboured strenuously to free himself and rise above the bitter waves of this blood drenched life" (Porphyry, 1934, par. 23). Because parenthood was so clearly physical, Plotinus avoided any reference to his parents and was even ashamed of having a body.

Plotinus drew heavily from Plato but inverted him in what is called Neo-Platonism. Plato had begun his inquiry with sensory events, although he held these to be unreliable and looked for a more perfect form beyond what could be sensed. He referred to the ultimate form of perfection as the Idea or the One. For example, one could never draw a perfect circle on a wax tablet but one could have an *idea* of a perfect circle. Plotinus's (1954) inversion began not with concrete events but with a mystical One or Totality of Being and Not-Being from which emanated other abstractions or constructions—something like drips from a faucet in which each successive drip is more distant from the original source (Fig. 2.3). These emanations comprise reality. Plotinus gives three explicit examples. The first is the One from

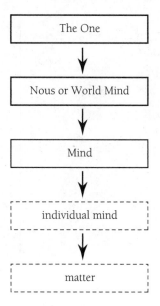

Figure 2.3. Plotinus's Emanations. In this inversion and spiritizing of Plato, the upper three emanations are explicit, the other two implicit.

which emanates Nous or World Mind (*psuché*) from which, in turn, emanates Mind. Implicitly or by extension, individual mind is a fourth emanation, and at the outer reaches (or depths) is matter, including the body. The human spirit or mind can look up toward pure World Mind or down toward evil matter. The mind engages in knowing, and the highest form of knowing is a mystical union with the One. From this tradition comes the merger of the knower with the known of modern social constructionism (see chapter 8). Plotinus advocated turning away from the degraded things of senses and inward toward one's own mind, a part of the One. There is no immortality, and so one must merge one's personal mind with the World Mind and lose personal identity. As he was dying, Plotinus said he was trying to return the Divine in himself to the Absolute Divine (Porphyry, par. 2).

Plotinus's approach to perception is one that he passed down to much of psychology today, which maintains the same assumptions. An object acts on a sense organ, and the organ acts on the mind; the mind then creates the qualities of the object—the object's texture, color, hardness, odor, flavor, and so on. It is not the object that is perceived but a psychic representation. This view is held by organocentric systems, especially orthodox cognitive psychology (chapter 3), but is opposed by envirocentric and noncentric systems. Plotinus's emphasis on an inner agent or process is also common to organocentric systems. Memory, he believes, has no relation to the body but belongs entirely to the mind where recording of past events occurs. Mind and body cannot affect one another. Thinking and reasoning, like remembering, transcend the physical although they produce such feelings as anger. Inevitably, his mind-body separation landed him in some contradictions, but it was he who refined and perfected the mystical approach that combined with Greek rationalism to become a platform for intellectual development for succeeding centuries. Its appeal was its program for escape from the turmoil of the Roman world. Plotinus's work opened the way for the development of Christian theology. It "influenced Christian thought very directly for over a thousand years . . . and the most influential of the church fathers, [was] Augustine" (Barnes, 1965, p. 264). Augustine (see below) himself further influenced psychology.

After about 235 the Roman army took on the major role of government in the face of disintegrating social and political conditions. The army established emperors who served as puppets until it executed them. The emperors could not successfully govern the widespread provinces or contain the graft that permeated the government. Instability grew, poverty increased, and interest in public affairs died.

In order to have a single religion in support of his administration, in 313 Constantine made Christianity the official Roman religion. Under Theodosius (375–395, Emperor of the East and 392–395, Emperor of the West), all other religions were banned and Christians, once the persecuted, became the persecutors. The growing power of Christianity accompanied a growing rejection of everything pagan including Greek science.

Augustine (354–430). In Plotinus's day there was still some respect for Greek scholarship, but by the fifth century little but spirit was of interest. The fourth to fifth centuries were the age of another prominent intellectual figure, Augustine. For Plotinus, spirit was superior to nature; for Augustine, nature was transformed into spirit. For Plotinus, the Absolute was distant; for Augustine the Absolute was close and personally real. This was a time of rampant corruption, disregard for law and order, decay of public buildings, abandonment of frontier military posts, wholesale desertions from the army, widespread looting by the disinherited, and the selling of children into slavery. Finally the mighty city of Rome itself, unable to protect its citizens from invasion by Goths from the north, fell in 476. Tolerance for Greek scholarship ended in 529 when the emperor Justinian closed Plato's academy—along with Aristotle's Lyceum and other Greek schools—and ended a nine-century continuity.

Augustine admonished people to despise the world and turn fully to the spiritual life. He denounced all science of pagan origin as well as their religious beliefs. Only internal truth had any validity. In *The City of God Against the Pagans,* he insisted that Rome's fall was due to its worldly character, for no state can long endure based on human values and human relationships rather than on spiritual ones. In his *Confessions* he interiorized Plotinus's doctrines. The human mind can contain the entire world and the image of god (Fig. 2.4). Mind and memory are so expansive that one need only examine oneself and avoid study of the world. This is the basis of the introspective tradition in psychology. It is also the basis of the widespread belief in modern psychology—a belief to which orthodox cognitive psychology gives central status—that the world is represented internally. What Barnes (1965) calls Augustine's "personal sex neuroses" (p. 304) have also descended to us. In a reaction against his own libertine youth, Augustine blamed human problems on the

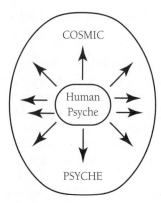

COSMIC

Human
Psyche

PSYCHE

Figure 2.4. Augustine's Interiorization of the Cosmos*

*Derived from interiorizing Plotinus.

original sexual intercourse of Adam and Eve for which Eve was to blame. His indictment of women and denunciation of sex have plagued the Western world down to the present.

In the period of Augustine any lingering science faded out of European culture, and that loss heralded the Dark Ages. However, in the eastern Roman empire at Byzantium, knowledge of pagan Greek science continued and contributed to the Arab transmission of knowledge to Europe in the thirteenth century.

The Dark Ages and Returning Security. A few glimmers of light remained during the Dark Ages, mostly in the monasteries. Few but monks learned to read and write. Boëthius (480–524), a competent scholar, planned to translate all of Plato and Aristotle into Latin. He completed only a part of Aristotle's logic before Theodoric, the Gothic emperor, executed him. Had he succeeded with his plans, the intellectual history of Europe might have been radically different. Plato's *Timaeus* was known during the Dark Ages, as were a few other remnants of Greek scholarship. About 430 Capella, in an allegorical story, described the seven liberal arts as the maidservants of a bride. They were grammar, rhetoric, logic, geometry, arithmetic, astronomy, and music. Although these originated in pagan Greek and Roman scholarship

(the geometry, arithmetic, and music compiled and translated by Boëthius), they became the basis for medieval education and eventually a requirement for the Master of Arts degree in all of Europe. Priscians' (6th c.) grammar was read, and so was a history by Orosius (5th c.), one of Augustine's followers, which claimed to depict the dire conditions of the pagan world. Cassiodorus (490–580) urged monks to learn about medicinal plants for use in their infirmaries. The English monk, Bede the Venerable (673–735), studied time reckoning and popularized the BC/AD dating system that Dionysius Exiguus (d. ca. 545) had developed. Isidore (560–636) compiled what was known of pagan and Christian literature. But by the eighth and ninth centuries not much of even the theologically contaminated Greek and Roman science remained. Even the grammar studies of Priscian and the earlier Donatus (4th c.) disappeared. One notable writer of the Dark Ages who knew Greek was John Scotus Erigena (810–880) whose work was mostly mystical theology, heavily influenced by Plotinus. His theories of angels strongly influenced medieval art.

The Dark Ages are distinguished not only by loss of classical scholarship but also by the replacement of logic with faith, appeal to the authority of the Patristics, neoplatonic mysticism, and myth. In the ninth century Erigena revived an emphasis on logic, but only upon the return of Aristotle's complete logical works in the twelfth century did scholars begin once again to employ rigorous logical tools. And this led to the extreme of seeking final truth in logic rather than in examining nature.

The early part of the Dark Ages was marked by raids and devastation all over Europe by Goths, Vikings, Vandals, Danes, Angles, Saxons, and others. Some large areas became devoid of people as populations fled the attackers. In the ninth and tenth centuries Viking, Saracen (Muslim), and Hungarian attacks devastated Europe (Bautier, 1971). The situation was little better on the political side, for the feudal system brought a very low standard of living for the peasants.

The Dark Ages, from about 500–1000, descended only on the West, for this was a period of commercial progress in the Byzantine and Muslim realms. Trade and industry prospered. In the intellectual area, Byzantine scholars studied and commented on Greek works and transmitted these to surrounding areas, including the Muslim world where scholars of diverse nationalities and backgrounds translated and studied them and in some cases made advancements.

Partial stability returned to Europe by the ninth century, but social order had to wait until the twelfth (Barnes, 1965). The eighth and ninth centuries experienced a beginning of cultural recovery in some parts of Europe, and in the eleventh century a reawakening of science began. The crusades brought back to Europe a recognition that a world of knowledge, technology, advanced commercial development, and splendor existed in the Byzantine and Muslim worlds. Meanwhile, European society was becoming more secular with the development of towns and commerce. *The returning stability and security was probably an important if not essential psychological factor in rendering that society more receptive to further secular developments such as the reentry of science and technology.* Prosperity, comfort, and well-being seem to correlate well with reduced interest in militarism and religious zeal, just as poverty and insecurity tend to correlate with the opposite. It is usually the underprivileged who support revolutions and conquest and advocate extreme religious beliefs, whereas the comfortable seek peace and increased commerce. (This correlation is imperfect—as correlations always are in complex situations.)

The construction of castles and cathedrals led to development of skilled building trades and technological know-how. Warfare also brought technological innovation and an interest in basic scientific principles. The University of Salerno in Italy was established as early as the ninth century for medical studies, and the University of Bologna in 1088 for law studies. The University of Paris began about 1200, and Oxford and Cambridge in

England were of similar vintage. They were followed in succeeding centuries by others in Italy, Germany, Scotland, Portugal, Czechoslovakia, and Poland. Although these universities were more doctrinaire than free thinking, more sectarian than secular, they served to organize studies and stimulate further understanding.

Transformation of the English Words Mind and Soul. During the early and middle Middle Ages, the English terms that refer to psychophysical dualism changed from their earlier naturalistic meanings to those of dualism. Figure 2.5 indicates this development in relation to psuché/psyche. In their earliest recorded usage, the three terms all have naturalistic meanings. The nonphysical or immaterial meaning of "psyche," beginning about the second century BCE, gives rise to that meaning of "soul" in the ninth century CE and of "mind" in the twelfth century CE (these words, due to the Christian influence, substitute for "psyche").

"Mind" initially had the naturalistic meaning of intention, as in "I have a mind to take a walk," or memory, as in "keep in mind"—meanings it has retained to the present. It was also used for thinking in "have a mind of," but we no longer hear this usage. These meanings have not changed much from the Proto-Indo-European root *men-* of more than 6000 years ago, which referred to thinking and remembering. Similar naturalistic meanings descending from Proto-Indo-European continued as *mens* in Latin and as *manas* in Vedic and Sanskrit of ancient India. In the twelfth century, under the influence of Christianity, the word mind came to mean a nonphysical counterpart to the body. Soul, and more especially mind, became institutionalized in Western culture as a determining agent for human activity. In keeping with the beliefs of the Christian theologians, the assumption is that nature has divided us into two parts in which mind—and in later centuries *brain*—serves as an agent to direct and control the body. "Mind" and "soul" are interchangeable when the reference is to immaterial entity.

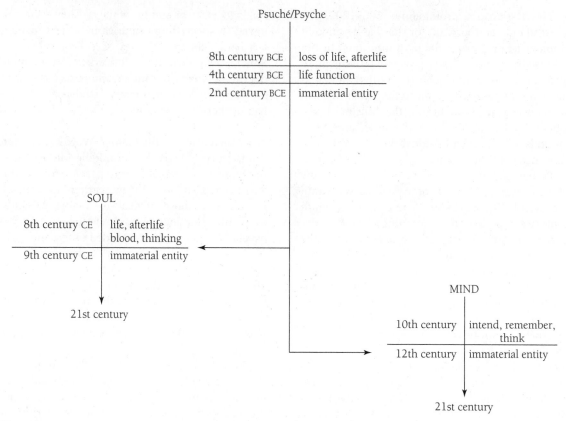

Figure 2.5. The Evolution of Greek *Psuché*/Psyche and Its Influence on English "Soul" and "Mind"

Arab Transmission. Perhaps the most important single development in the return of science was the bizarre twist of history in which the Arabs transmitted back to Europe the Europeans' own fund of Greek and Roman accomplishments, of whose existence Europeans had barely been aware. The Arabs' new religion, Islam, had spread by the sword but it tolerated the diversity of peoples it conquered.[12] It swept west across northern Africa and up into Spain and pushed east to India into what is now Pakistan, reaching its zenith by 750.

Unlike Europe, the Arab world never faced a long period of insecurities and miseries. Perhaps for this reason they never tried to retreat from the physical world but instead developed commerce and took considerable interest in science and technology. These varied peoples and nations established universities at Baghdad, Bukhara, Cairo, Cordoba, Damascus, and Seville. Like the Romans,

---

12. Actually, little of what we refer to as "Arab" was ethnically Arab. The accomplishments in trade, commerce, industrial production, architecture, and science are attributed to those under the Muslim empire who used Arabic as a common language, just as Europe used Latin. These included Syrians, Indians, Persians, Egyptians, Palestinians, Spaniards, and so on. Neither were all of these people Muslim, even though they lived under Muslim control. For example, a number of important "Arab" contributors to philosophy, science, mathematics, and technology were Jews and some were Hindus. Since the Arabic language was the single point in common, we can do no better than to continue referring to them as "Arabs," while recognizing their varied ethnicity.

they mostly collected and wrote commentaries—usually spiritistic and Neoplatonic—on earlier works, but they also made new advancements. These advancements occurred in such areas as mathematics (al-Khwarizmi, d. c 850; Abu-l-wafa, d. 998; Ibn Yunus, d. 1009; Omar Khayyám, d. 1124; Nazir al-Din, d. 1274), astronomy (al-Battani; astrology was more prevalent however), chemistry (Rhazes, d. 924), mechanics (Omar Khayyám), optics (al-Hazen, 965–1039; Kamal ad-Din, d. 1320), geography (al-Khwarizmi; al-Balkhi, d. 934; al-Musudi, d. 957; al-Maqdisi, 10th c.), medicine (Rhazes, Ali ibn Abbas, d. 994; Ibn Sina/Avicenna, 980–1037; Ibn Zuhr/Avenzoar, 1113–1162; Ibn Khatima, d. 1369; Masawaih al-Mardini, d. 1015), and surgery (Abu-l-Qasim/Abulcasis, d. 1013). From India they passed on the number system that we use today, and al-Khwarizmi may have invented the all-important zero. From China or Egypt, they brought alchemy, the forerunner of chemistry.

Much of this transmission occurred in Spain. Moorish Spain was peaceful and productive with Spanish, Moorish, and Jewish cultures living together in mutual tolerance. High levels of craftsmanship and industry flourished. The Moors developed extensive irrigation projects that made agriculture more productive than ever. But with all this prosperity, the Moors lost their religious zeal and their military potency and could not successfully defend against the zealous Europeans who were unwilling to tolerate Muslims on European land. As a consequence of their Spanish conquests, the Europeans discovered a great number of classical pagan books in Arabic and immediately began translation, much of it accomplished by Jews at Toledo after its capture in 1085. Jews knew the requisite languages. The Catholics then expelled the Jews in 1492, and many of them dispersed to the Netherlands and the eastern Mediterranean where they used their skills, commercial contacts, and monetary assets to the advantage of their new homelands. Some rediscovery of pagan classical scholarship came from monasteries in Ireland and England where monks continued to keep Greek alive, and from southern Italy where the Greek-speaking population remained in contact with Byzantine Greece.

Among the translations were the works of Aristotle, including his biology and psychology. Albertus Magnus/Albert the Great (1193 or 1206–1280) at the university of Paris introduced Aristotle to Europe and attempted to reconcile him with Christian belief. However, an Arab commentator Averroës (1126–1198) had given Aristotle a Neoplatonic interpretation that centered around denial of the immortality of the soul. In 1209 the Council of Paris declared Aristotle's *De Anima* forbidden and in 1212 did the same with his *Metaphysics* and *Physics* along with the Arab commentaries. Thomas Aquinas (1225–1274), a student of Albert, defended Aristotle against the Augustinians and the Averroists by providing a Christian interpretation of his works and giving reason an equal place with faith. With this distorted interpretation, Aristotle's psychology and other works entered the mainstream of European thinking.

The Reestablishment of Science. From the time of the Patristics, psychology had been the handmaiden of theology. It was institutionalized in this form during the Middle Ages, especially with the work of Aquinas. Consequently, it was a topic not for scientific treatment but for metaphysical speculation concerning characteristics of the soul. Even physics, medicine, and astronomy were tied to Aristotle, Galen, and Ptolemy, respectively, as doctrinal truth. Recommendations for a scientific approach based on inductive evidence and experimentation—instead of solely on deductive reasoning as laid out by Aristotle (who also advocated inductive procedures)—began to emerge from the work of Albert and his observations and experiments connected with Aristotle's biology; from that of Roger Bacon (1214–1294) and his experimentation with optics; and from that of Witelo/Vittelo (c. 1270) who greatly advanced optics. Most of these efforts were intended to support theology. These thirteenth-century rudiments of science were not total innovations. They were already laid down by the Greeks and by the additional work of the Arabs. Gradual advancement in science continued, and in the sixteenth century an important landmark was the publication by Copernicus (1473–1543) of his treatise on the heliocentric theory that rejected the geocentrism of Ptolemy. This harks back to Aristarchos seventeen centuries earlier and to late medieval writers who also suggested the concept. About 1600 Galileo (1564–1642) began systematic experiments in physics that resulted in a repudiation of Aristotle's physics—important because the doctrinaire use of a non-Hellenic Aristotle had to die before science could proceed unhampered. Galileo also made important observations of the moon, planets, stars, and sun with a telescope, which led him to support Copernicus. The Church in 1616 forced him, under threat of torture, to renounce the movement of the earth around the sun. As regressive as this coerced renouncement was, it was trivial compared with the Church's punishment of Giordano Bruno whom it burned alive in 1601 for his theological and scientific heresies.

As revolutionary as Galileo was in physics, he adhered to traditional beliefs in psychology: sensory qualities such as tastes, odors, sounds, heat, tickling, and colors are only in the person and have no real existence as do shape, quantity, size, and motion (*Il Saggiatore,* 1624). This viewpoint was quite different from Aristotle's, in which sensory qualities are a joint product of sensible object and sense organ. Galileo's distinction between the qualities that he believed were only products of a mind and had no physical existence came to be called *secondary qualities,* whereas those that had physical qualities of shape, quantity, size, and motion were called *primary qualities*—one type occupying a nonphysical and the other a physical realm consistent with theology and comprising a psychophysical dualism. This dualism of secondary and primary qualities became an important part of such philosophies as positivism and British empiricism (see below) and eventually of the organocentric psychologies including cognitive psychology (see chapter 3). The noncentric psychologies, especially phenomenological psychology (see chapter 12), interbehavioral psychol-

ogy (see chapter 10), ecological realism (see chapter 13), and probabilistic epigenetic psychology (see chapter 13) have rejected psychophysical dualism and have been closer to Aristotle on this issue.

In the sixteenth century Andreas Vesalius (1514–1564) made major advancements in anatomy, and William Gilbert (1540–1603) discovered magnetic fields, including that of the earth. A book by Ludovicus Vives (1494–1549) called *On the Soul and Life* connected supernatural concepts of the soul with physiology, a pattern that, in various forms, extends from the time of the Patristics to the present. It (a) invokes a spiritistic psychology and (b) reduces psychology to biology.

In the seventeenth century, scientific development gained momentum—all of it building on earlier advances. Johannas Kepler (1571–1630) calculated the orbits of the planets, William Harvey (1578–1657) demonstrated that—contrary to Galen—blood circulated through the body, and Robert Boyle (1627–1691) began scientific chemistry. Christiaan Huygens (1629–1695) contributed to scientific advancement in numerous areas including the wave theory of light. Isaac Newton's (1642–1727) work in physics united separate measurements into laws of gravity and motion that govern the planets in their orbits as well as the movement of objects on earth. His work in optics had a bearing on psychology. He took a position consistent with that of Galileo that colors do not physically exist but are created in the brain. According to this doctrine, we look at a colorless world and by an unexplained process manufacture the colors in our brain cells, then project them onto the objects. The yellow and orange of the tulip is not in the tulip but in the viewer. Psychology books typically present this as fact, but interbehavioral psychology (chapter 10) and ecological perception (chapter 13) challenge it.

In the eighteenth century Benjamin Franklin (1706–1790) made systematic advances in the understanding of electricity. He invented the lightening rod, which after much resistance replaced the ringing of church bells to ward off storms (with a marked drop in death rate of bell ringers whose bell steeples often drew lightening). Antoine Lavoisier (1743–1794) made far-reaching advances in chemistry before the French Revolutionists guillotined him. In psychology, Anton Mesmer (1734–1815) demonstrated that he could use imagining through suggestion to achieve the same effects as religious exorcism by a priest, though he erroneously believed his results were due to "animal magnetism," an analogy to magnetism of iron. An eminent historian and social scientist (Barnes, 1965) regards these centuries as one of the most outstanding periods of intellectual achievement in Western civilization since the time of Hellenic Greece:

> The Hellenic thinkers brought free inquiry into the world, questioned the supernaturalism of Oriental antiquity, raised reason to a position of supremacy, directed philosophy towards a solution of human problems, and created a scientific habit of thought. The scientists, philosophers, and critical thinkers of the period from 1600 to 1800, carrying on the work of progressive medieval scholars, performed much the same function in freeing western Europe from the protective blanket of orthodox medievalism. They, too, challenged the older supernaturalism, elevated reason, defended free thinking, brought philosophy down to earth, and achieved important scientific discoveries. (p. 668)

Most scientific work occurred outside the universities, for they were still under the control of the Church, and the Church was not receptive to investigations that cast doubt on its doctrines. Scientific academies, such as the Royal Society of England and the French Academy of Sciences, organized much of the research. The projects were made possible in part by the mercantile trade that produced many wealthy persons who had the leisure and means to undertake scientific investigations ("gentlemen scholars"). The work was also consistent with the interests of a large middle class, more focused on improving life in this world than in preparing for the next. Philosophy began to emerge from theology as a focus on rationality rather than faith and on understanding rather than

salvation. An essential enabling ingredient in the rise of philosophy and science was political and economic stability.

The eighteenth century is often called the Age of Enlightenment. The power of nobles and clergy was reduced and that of the peasants increased. The French and the American revolutions helped bring recognition of human rights and a demand for political equality. These revolutions also highlighted the role of social factors in psychological events and the value of studying human activities as important in their own right, while reducing deference to theology. Heretofore only cognitive acts such as thinking, sensing, and imagining had received attention. In this period feelings began to receive their due, requiring observation of behaviors. This trend began to look toward a psychology based on such observations (Kantor, 1969). People with psychotic problems began to receive humane treatment, rather than being viewed as possessed by demons. In France, Philippe Pinel (1745–1826) removed the chains from psychotic people and initiated the development of modern psychiatry.

In the nineteenth century, Julius Meyer (1830–1895) in Germany and Dimitri Mendeleev (1834–1907) in Russia, by building on the work of others, devised the periodic table of the elements. This showed the systematic relationship of elements that comprise all matter and became fundamental to both chemistry and physics. Another important scientific milestone was Charles Darwin's (1809–1892) massive evidence for biological evolution, repudiating the theological belief in special creation. Still another was Friedrich Wöhler's (1800–1882) demonstration that organic urea could be obtained from inorganic ammonium cyanate. Thus, not only are life forms continuous with one another through evolution, but the organic and inorganic are also continuous, and one cannot maintain a divine power ("vitalism") in the organic that separates it absolutely from the inorganic. The periodic table suggests that even the elements are in continuity.

Despite these revolutionary advancements in the physical and biological sciences, psychology did not participate as a systematic science. In fact there was no identifiable discipline called "psychology," but rather an assumption derived from theology and now taken up by seventeenth century philosophy that soul or mind produced such activities as thinking and willing. How this nonphysical agent could act on the body became a great philosophical debate. Only toward the end of the nineteenth century did psychology begin to emerge as an independent discipline, still carrying much of the baggage of its past.

Attempts to Reconcile the Soul/Mind to Nature. A soul outside the bounds of nature proved as difficult for philosophers of the seventeenth and succeeding centuries to deal with as it had been for Gregory of Nyssa in the fourth century (see p. 23). No one tackled the question directly by questioning the validity of the construct as Lucretius had in the first century. In fact the father of modern philosophy, René Descartes (1596–1650), just assumed an interaction with the body without examining the logic of such an interaction. He held that mind/soul is *unextended* (has no physical dimensions) and resides in the pineal gland in the head. From that central location it regulates spirits contained in brain cavities and directs them through the nerves to cause muscles to move. Mind can even act independently of the body and produce pure thought, whereas the brain can produce only imagining and perceiving. When body and mind act together in sensing and imagining, the interaction takes place in the pineal gland. Descartes's contemporaries vigorously attacked him for his theory of interactionism. How, they asked, could a mind, which has no physical properties, interact with something nonphysical? It would have to become physical itself in order to have an impact on something physical. And how could it reside in the pineal gland or anywhere in physical space if it had no physical dimensions— that is, did not *extend* into space? This question still plagues all attempts to relate mind and body and is often called the "Cartesian dualism." We will see further attempted solutions, all of them futile and most of them by means of analogy.

(Descartes also used analogies, those of mechanical and hydraulic body functions, but did not apply them to mind-body.) The pitfall was the starting point, a supernatural construct inherited from 2000 years earlier rather than events of the world.

Baruch Spinoza (1632–1677), one of Descartes's critics, attempted to solve the Cartesian dualism by proposing that both mind and body are attributes of a single ultimate God who acts on both, rather than mind acting on body or vice-versa. He drew from his trade of lens grinding the analogy of a convex-concave lens. If one looks at the lens from the inside it is concave but from the outside it is convex, yet it is one lens. Similarly, from the inside we find the unextended attribute of thought and from the outside the extended attribute of body or motion. These correspond to each other because they are attributes or aspects of a single God. This *double aspect* theory still assumes two disparate things but has been used by any number of theorists as a presumed solution to mind-body dualism.

Attempting to get around the problem of how mind and body could interact, Gottfried Leibnitz (1646–1716) in close accord with Gregory of Nyssa, proposed a clock analogy. God created mind and body in perfect harmony, each following its own independent laws, just as a clock maker might make two clocks that are always in agreement although neither has any influence on the other. This means that when one's mind decides it is time to leave the classroom, the body gets up and walks out, not because mind acts on body but because the two are perfectly synchronized by a divine act of the creator. This doctrine is called "preestablished harmony." It is a product of Leibnitz's proposal that God has arranged irreducible spiritual forces called "monads", having no extension. These monads, none of which has any influence on any other, exist in a hierarchy—based on Plotinus's emanations—with God as the supreme monad. A unified mind, as a monad, reflects different degrees of clarity; sensation is haziest; perception is intermediate; and apperception is complete clarity. Ideas, such as mathematical truths, are innate and contained in the unified mind.

Less interested in solving the mind-body problem or in elaborating the characteristics of a theological soul than in the function of a mind in human knowledge, John Locke (1632–1704) rejected the views of Descartes and Leibnitz that argued for innate ideas and proposed that all knowledge comes from experience, a view called "empiricism" (or British empiricism because of other British writers who held similar positions). His famous analogy was the infant's mind as a blank slate on which experience writes. We gain knowledge through sensation of the outer world and reflection of the inner. He followed the Plotinus-Galileo-Newton model of two worlds by declaring that "secondary qualities" such as odor, taste, touch, sound, pleasure, pain, and color are produced by the organism and are unextended, unlike "primary qualities" such as shape, solidity, number, and movement that are independent of mind and are extended.

Taking his cue from Locke, George Berkeley (1685–1753) reasoned that if secondary qualities are in the mind there is no reason why primary qualities are not also in the mind. Therefore, everything is in the mind. Because sensations exist only in someone's mind, objects are just packages of sensations. The physical world has no existence independent of minds. Even so, he emphasizes the importance of experience in associating one sensation with another. Insisting that extended matter could not act on unextended experience, Berkeley abolished one half of the mind-body dualism and proposed a *monism* in which all existence is spirit. This has much in common with the Vedanta philosophy of India (p. 25) and is the logical extreme of Augustine. An anonymous jokester captured Berkeley's position in a limerick:

There was a faith-healer of Deal,
Who said, "Although pain isn't real,
If I sit on a pin,
And it punctures my skin,
I dislike what I fancy I feel."

David Hume (1711–1776), a Scotsman, rejected both mind and spirit as unverifiable and thereby went a step beyond Berkeley. Our experience, he argued, consists of a collection of sensations or "impressions" and these, by habit of association (experience of seeing things occur together), results in attributing causality to the impressions. The impression of causality and other associations consists of mental gravity that brings these mental particles together. Like Locke and Berkeley, he reduced qualities of the world to mental sensations. Despite his dismissal of mind, mind serves as a kind of theater where successive sensations appear and mingle with others and with various situations and associate by psychic gravity. Mind is nothing but a collection of sensations. This position, building on the work of other British empiricists, brings to a climax the atomistic mind as against the unified mind of those on the European continent (philosophy continental). The atoms of the mind arise from the world, whereas the continental mind's unity assumes innate ideas or innate organization of sensations from the world. The atomistic mind promoted by Hume is a radical departure from the unified soul/mind of the Patristics, Augustine, Plotinus, Thomas Aquinas, Descartes, Leibnitz, and others.

Following in the tradition of Leibnitz, Christian Wolff (1679–1754) in Germany supported the unified mind. The mind, he held, does not associate mental atoms but is an apperceptive unity with numerous innate powers or faculties. Wolff was the first to use the term "psychology" in book titles. In two books he provided systematic though spiritistic treatments that replaced such terms as "psychosophy" and "pneumatology" and gave psychology the status of a discipline distinct from philosophy. Despite recommending psychology's inclusion among the other sciences, he insisted that it is a natural theology that deals with a natural God, not a science of observation and quantification. Although he tried to maintain the mind-body parallelism of Leibnitz while rejecting the notion of preestablished harmony, he allowed that sensory organs could affect the mind.

Up to this point we have found two major theories of knowledge ("epistemology"), neither of which shows any recognition of the need to observe what humans actually do. The first is a philosophy of *rationalism* from continental Europe. It received impetus from Descartes and Spinoza and was further expressed by Leibnitz and Wolff. It takes its name from the belief that all truth can be found by human reason. With variations from one writer to another, it assumes (a) an internal and an external world (psychophysical dualism); (b) that humans have innate, internal organizing systems for the information from the external world and/or that knowledge itself is innate or instinctive; and (c) that the mind is a unified whole. Rationalism's theater today is in varying degrees the organocentric systems of psychology. It also shows up in the phenomenology of Husserl and the existentialism of Sartre (chapter 12). The second theory is the British *empiricism* of Locke and Berkeley and especially of Hume, contending that knowledge comes from experience, inner as well as sense experience. It assumes—again, with variations among writers—(a) an internal and external world (like rationalism); (b) that knowledge comes from experience; and (c) that the mind is atomistic—composed of mental atoms, ideas, or particles of some sort. Aspects of this show up in some current systems of psychology, especially in the form of environmental influences.

In addition to rationalism and empiricism, a third theory of knowledge that gets attention in psychology today—much of it critical—is *positivism*. It began with Auguste Comte (1798–1857) who advocated (a) leaving behind the immature stages of mind that look for causality and explanation; and (b) advancing to the stage of positivism that rejects religion and supernaturalism, and replaces them with science. Everything not based on observation he would discard. One cannot objectively investigate the mind but one can objectively investigate behavior as the mind's product, he insisted. A version of positivism by the physicist Ernst Mach (1838–1916) held in common with the British empiricists that all we can know with any certainty are our sensations and that science is therefore dependent on these sensations and their correlations. In fact, the external world of science is constructed by the organization of internal sensations.

Rationalism, empiricism, and positivism all regard sensations as the doorway to the mind and therefore gave major emphasis to them. Both Comte and Mach were empiricists in that they believed that knowledge comes from experience, by which they meant psychic sensations. It is noteworthy that all three theories of knowledge accept the knower's sensations but question the knowability of the thing sensed—a direct legacy of medieval theology in which the soul stood supreme and the debased body and world were only necessary evils, adjuncts to its immortality. These one-sided theories of knowledge continue into some of the current systems, especially the organocentric, such as cognitive (chapter 3) and humanistic psychology (chapter 4). One current system (chapter 8) absorbs the known into the knower, somewhat akin to Berkeley's theory.

A later version of positivism called "logical positivism" also insisted that valid knowledge depends on sensory experience. It advocated that theoretical terms must be defined by the operations used to determine the character of the thing or event, and hypotheses must be logically (hence, *logical* positivism) deduced from theory and then empirically[13] tested. Logical positivism has come under heavy criticism.

The advent of materialism in the eighteenth century brought no direct challenge to the validity of the mind-body duality but rather a variation on it: mind is dependent on material. That variation, however, presented the belief that mind requires physical properties, a view developed by the French materialists. Drawing on a new analogy, Julien de La Mettrie (1709–1751) declared that a human is "an assemblage of springs" and "the soul is but a principle of motion, or a sensible material part of the brain . . . a principal spring of the whole machine . . . such that all the others are only an emanation from it (La Mettrie, 1912/1748, p. 135). Just as we found Plotinus's emanations in Leibnitz's monads, here we find his influence also,

---

13. Here the word "empirical" refers to observation or factual evidence, a related meaning to its use as "experiential," referring to "mental."

reinterpreted as springs. The great mystic's impact continued to help confine psychology to spiritistic assumptions. For La Mettrie, brain as a mainspring produces mind or soul. Mind is an *epiphenomenon,* an appearance that accompanies matter, a byproduct. Using another analogy consistent with epiphenomenalism, Pierre Cabanis (1757–1805), a physician, declared that just as the stomach digests food the brain digests impressions and secretes thought. This proposal was an attempt to convert psychology to biology and thus remove it from the grasp of theology. Mind as brain product was a significant departure from mind as spirit, although spirit still played a role. This epiphenomenalism finds a number of supporters today and is also called "emergentism," meaning that mind emerges out of brain.

Drawing heavily from Locke and combining the atomistic mind of the British and the unified mind of the continent, one of the most influential philosophers of all, Immanuel Kant (1742–1804) proposed that the physical world gives rise to nonphysical sensations. Like Descartes, Kant raises a question about a mechanism for such a connection. The mind runs these atomistic units through innate categories and synthesizes them into an appearance ("phenomenal thing") of the world. This appearance is all we can ever know about the world although, contrary to Berkeley, the world does exist as a physical "thing in itself." The mind he called "the transcendental unity of apperception." That is, it transcends the physical world and is unified. Apperception supplies the unification of sensations into meanings ("unity of apperception," from Leibnitz). What we experience as objects are only phantoms in us. The phenomenal thing that appears to be the world we know is just an internal representation. Consequently, we live in a double world—a real physical world that we can never know and a mentally constructed nonphysical one that we do know. Kant was following the tradition of the Alexandrians and others down through the centuries, allowing verbalizations that do not refer to observations to get in the way of genuine observations of human actions and the circumstances of those actions. In fact, Kant repudiated observation. He insisted that because psychological events are transcendental they could never be experimented on or quantified. If one accepts that they are indeed transcendental, Kant is absolutely right. One cannot quantify or experiment on spirits. Nor can one reconcile a transcendental mind with a physical body. Looking back we can see that Kant's internal world theory systematizes the beliefs of Augustine, and Kant's thesis that sensory qualities are created by the organism now gives us the Plotinus-Galileo-Newton-Locke-Berkeley-Hume-Kant theory of perception. Kant's double world is the strictest form of a one-sided theory of knowledge and is central to cognitive psychology (chapter 3), but that system, consistent with Cabanis, often assumes that the brain produces the representations.

Table 2.1 illustrates seven points of view on the physical body and the nonphysical mind.

Table 2.1			
Attempts to Reconcile Mind with Body			
Theorist	**Attempted Solution**	**Analogy**	**"Solution" Symbolized**
Descartes	interaction		M⟵⟶B
Spinoza	double aspect	lens	Ⓜ🅱
Leibnitz	preestablished harmony: parallelism	clocks	M ‖ B
Berkeley	no body or world; all is spirit		Ⓜ 🅱̶
Hume	no body or mind, only impressions	gravity	Ⓜ̶ 🅱̶
La Mettrie	epiphenomenalism	springs	Ⓜ
Cabanis		digestion	🅱

Descartes made no effort to resolve the dilemma, and it is not clear whether Hume intended to offer a solution. The other five clearly sought an answer.

Despite efforts to resolve the dilemma by analogy, a very weak form of argument, these mutually contradictory entities—the physical and nonphysical or extended and unextended—could not be brought together any more readily than one can have a circle be squared. They are contradictions in terms. One can go on *talking* about their relationships, as theologians have done for 2000 years, just as one can *talk* about a square circle, but neither has any referent in observable events. Because science is based on observation, psychophysical dualism can never be part of science, even though it remains a part of theology and of philosophies that overlook the contradiction. None of these seven men nor anyone else of the period questioned whether it was necessary to assume a dualism or what an alternative might be. That was simply not conceivable at the time. The next step was to convert mind into biology as the locus of mind, a step that Vives and Newton had already taken and in which Cabanis and a number of others followed. That effort continues in psychology to the present day, despite mysteries it presents that are as great as those of psychophysical dualism. An alternative to both dualism and biologizing was as old as Aristotle but was not recognized because of the medieval version of his philosophy. That alternative, however, was redeveloped in the twentieth century and is represented in some current systems. Awareness of it is an essential ingredient in making an informed choice.

Biologizing the Mind. Nineteenth-century advances in physiology provided a biological model by means of which psychology might be separated from its mentalistic philosophy and given the status of a natural science. Charles Bell (1774–1842) in England and Francois Magendie (1783–1855) in France independently discovered the distinction between sensory and motor nerves. Bell suggested that each sensory nerve conducted one kind of experience. Visual nerves convey only visual experiences, and auditory nerves convey only auditory experiences. An eminent pioneer, German physiologist Johannes Müller (1801–1858), extended this to mean that each quality of experience comes only through the specific quality or energy of a particular nerve. This is the doctrine of "specific nerve energies." Each particular nerve has a specific energy and provides a specific sensation regardless of the type of stimulus. With one stroke he had assimilated Kant to biology. In effect, he said that we don't respond to the real world, only to our nerve endings, just as Kant said we respond only to our apperceptive phenomena. Müller was quite specific that the nerves and the brain, not the external world, support the soul and give it content. Kant's double world gained a biological component.

Hermann von Helmholtz (1821–1894), an even more eminent physiologist, also accepted the model of Kant and elaborated on Müller's doctrine: sensory organs are analyzers, and the kind of impulses they send determines the nature of the sensations received. It was only a small step for others to move the analyzers to the brain, thus naturalizing the soul by biologizing it. The concrete nervous system became the underpinning for the ethereal soul. Helmholtz's continuity with Kant and Müller gives us the Plotinus-Galileo-Newton-Locke-Berkeley-Hume-Kant-Müller-Helmholtz double-world model of perception.

Experimental Psychology and the Classical Schools: The Struggle with Dualism

Psychophysics. Experimental psychology has no single beginning, but the work of Ernst Weber (1795–1878) was seminal. A physiologist and anatomist, as well as a collaborator with his physicist brother in studies of electricity, he measured magnitude of stimulation to determine the minimal amount necessary in order for subjects to discriminate between stimuli. He found that ratios rather than absolute amounts governed the discriminations. For example, when a weight is 40 ounces, a subject will detect a difference at about 39 ounces, and when it is 20 ounces the subject will detect a difference at 19.5 ounces. Therefore, the ratio for weights is about 1 to 40. For light it is about 1 to 300. An inch added to your height would be barely noticeable, but an inch added to your nose would be conspicuous because the ratio is different. This became known as Weber's Law. It was a remarkable achievement for a discipline that was still not an autonomous subject but a part of philosophy, a discipline claimed by Kant to be unquantifiable and not subject to experimentation. The achievement was possible because Weber, at least in his operations, ignored the venerable abstractions of theology and philosophy and did exactly what other scientists were doing. He made systematic observations, in this case of the responses of humans. No doubt he was influenced by his work in physics as well as by his training in physiology.

Weber's successor in this work was Gustav Fechner (1801–1887), a religious mystic trained in medicine, who had some experience in physics. Fechner called this type of study "psychophysics," meaning the relation of the psyche to the physical. He explicitly conceived of psychophysics as a form of mind-body dualism. By mathematical conversion he established a more refined version of Weber's Law in which the response, to which he gave the mentalistic designation "sensation," varied in a linear fashion as the stimulus varied logarithmically. His formula is called "Fechner's Law." His intention was to establish a scientific relationship between matter and spirit, the body and the soul. What his formula actually described was the relation between the magnitude or sensitivity of the response and the magnitude of the stimulus. By referring to "sensation," he confused measurements of the concrete response with the ancient doctrine of mind and soul. Although he was actually measuring responses, he believed he was measuring a mental unit. What he was doing and what he thought he was doing were entirely different. But that was characteristic of early psychology and, some would argue, continues in some systems to the present day.

Voluntarism: The First Classical System. The pivotal figure in the establishment of experimental psychology was Wilhelm Wundt (1832–1920). Although he obtained a position in philosophy at the University of Leipzig, he was trained in medicine and physiology. Thus, like Weber and Fechner, he was a part of the movement within physiology that separated psychology from philosophy and took it into the realm of experimental studies. His inspiration came from the work of Weber, Fechner, and Donders (1818–1889)—who subtracted simple reaction systems from complex reaction systems to obtain the speed of the mind ("mental chronometry")—and other experimentalists. Wundt's study with Müller and his experience in Helmholtz's physiology laboratory influenced him to apply the methods of physiology to the study of mind, and he referred to his work as "physiological psychology." This designation referred only to his methods and did not imply that psychology could be reduced to physiology. In fact, Wundt denied the possibility of such a reduction, for he believed he was studying irreducible "consciousness," a term that was beginning to replace "mind" and "soul."[14] But because mental phenomena were not directly accessible to the physical methods of experimentation, Wundt insisted that he was studying only the outward manifestations, the "outworks" of mind or consciousness. Thus, he continued the mind-body dualism and to some extent the dictum of Kant that one could not experiment on mental phenomena. Both the mental and the physical, Wundt claimed, have laws of causality, that of the mind

---

14. "Consciousness" is from Latin *cum/con*—"with"—and *scio*—"I know". "Conscio" means "knowing together" or "I share with someone the knowledge that. . . " The state of knowing with oneself is *conscienta*, whence "conscience." In other words, "consciousness" means sharing knowledge with someone and "conscience" means knowing by oneself. "Consciousness" took on the meaning of "conscience," an internal process or entity. These words entered the English language in the seventeenth century, and within about a century their original naturalistic meanings gave way to transcendental ones (see Lewis, 1960; *Oxford Universal Dictionary on Historical Principles*, 1955).

being psychic rather than physical. Experimental procedures would disclose its principles.

In one of his experiments he found that when subjects viewed letters or words for a brief duration, they recalled more of the content when they had seen words than when they'd seen only random letters. Consciousness, he concluded, contains more content as a synthesis than as unsynthesized elements. It consists of a domain of elements or ideas, some of which are central and readily perceived. Others are more peripheral, such as the letters presented but not identified, are outside the center of attention and not apprehended. Drawing from Leibnitz and Kant, he proposed that those idea-elements in the center of consciousness are synthesized into wholes by the mechanism of apperception. Apperception also provides for thinking and language. Wundt's system receives the name "voluntarism" because of his belief that the will voluntarily apperceives and synthesizes mental elements. Wundt's experiments were mostly on perception, attention, and reaction time; but he wrote ten volumes on *Völkerpsychologie* that covered myth, language, art, and religion. These subjects, he claimed, were beyond the pale of experimentation. Only history could reveal the evolution of mind through various stages of culture and higher mental processes.

Students came from Europe and from North America to study with Wundt and then returned to their homes, some to establish laboratories and some to work in other areas of psychology. Wundt's inspiration for an independent and experimental psychology was pervasive but no one closely adhered to his system.

Memorization. Hermann Ebbinghaus (1850–1909) was inspired by Fechner to engage in experimental psychology but had not heard of Wundt's dictum that it was not possible to experiment on "higher mental processes." He chose memorization, invented nonsense syllables to minimize the effects of prior learning (though he also used words), and used himself as a subject. Among his important findings was that forgetting is rapid at first and then slows, and that *relearn-*ing requires fewer trials than original learning. Ebbinghaus has been praised for (a) carrying psychology into the experimental study of "higher mental processes," (b) the precision of his work, and (c) his introduction of statistical analysis to psychology. He has been criticized for using meaningless rather than meaningful material and for fostering the application of a mechanistic methodology that is derived from the physical sciences and is inappropriate for psychology. Ebbinghaus's work with learning was a forerunner of interest in that subject by functionalists, behaviorists, and cognitivists.

The Würzburg School. One of Wundt's close students, Oswald Külpe (1862–1915), established an experimental laboratory at the University of Würzburg in which he purported to experiment with thinking which Wundt claimed was not subject to experimentation but only to historical analysis. Despite major controversies that arose over the issue and some of the findings, the school broadened the scope of experimental psychology beyond discrimination ("sensation") and reaction time. For example, Bühler (1879–1964) claimed to find a thought element that corresponded to a sensation element, and Ach (1871–1964) identified an unconscious act called a "determining tendency."

Structuralism. Another of Wundt's students, Edward Titchener (1867–1927) had studied at Oxford and was thoroughly imbued with British empiricism, especially the proposals of James Mill (1773–1836), a Scottish clergyman. Mill held that the mind consists of complex ideas composed of simple ideas and sensations, all held together by a kind of gravitational attraction. Ideas of bricks and mortar combine into the more complex idea of a wall and, together with other hierarchies of ideas, produce the more complex idea of a house. (His son, John Stuart Mill, 1806–1873, took this a step further, using another analogy to say that some ideas combined like a chemical compound to become totally different from any of their constituent parts.) Titchener accepted the British empiricists's position that laws of the mind are those of the association of sensations. His program used experimental procedures to discover elementary sensations (along the lines of Mill) that compose the mind. Because he was looking for the structure of the mind, he called his system "structuralism." He denied a Wundtian mechanism of apperception, which he regarded as mystical, and replaced it with empiricist associations by contiguity. His method was to train subjects to introspect their minds and observe raw sensations uncontaminated with meaning. Initially, he assumed consciousness to be an epiphenomenon of the brain but eventually favored the positivist approach of pure description.

Functionalism and behaviorism vigorously attacked the assumptions of structuralism. This together with the fact that structuralism could not produce consistent experimental results led to its demise. Kantor (1969) raises the rhetorical question, "Did the experimentalists of this period work with transcendental sensations or did they study the reactions of certain persons, called subjects, to certain things, called stimulus objects?" (p. 301).

Those whose influences stemmed from the atomistic mind, such as Titchener, for the most part attempted to reduce psychology to sensations and a physiology of nerves and brain, which they believed produced the sensations. Those of the unified mind persuasion studied thinking, willing, memorizing, forgetting, and other varied behaviors, and were reluctant to reduce these to brain functions.

Functionalism. This American school of psychology was influenced by William James (1842–1910), who in turn was influenced by Darwin. James emphasized that psychology must deal with the function of consciousness rather than with structure or content. The function of consciousness is to enable the individual to adapt to the environment. Instead of existing as pieces or elements, consciousness flows as a stream and actively shapes its environment. This was not much like the "mental atoms" of British empiricists, but James did cling to *ideas* in consciousness as the ba-

sis of will and the cause of behavior. His support of instincts was more consistent with innate faculties proposed by Scottish philosophy—and by such continental rationalists as Leibnitz and Wolff—than with the British empiricists. However, he allowed that instincts could change with the individual's experience, and that repetition of behavior creates habits by forming fixed pathways in the brain through which energy can more readily flow. (Evolutionary psychology, discussed in chapter 13, takes some of its inspiration from James's instincts.) Because habits improve our accuracy and efficiency, they are functional—in fact they serve as enormous fly-wheels that keep society on its course. Habits allow the individual little change after age thirty, and therefore should be developed very carefully. James's psychology included emotions, habits, cognitions, will, and religious experiences.

John Dewey (1859–1952) added a stream of behavior to the stream of consciousness, thereby reinforcing mind-body dualism. He also insisted that stimulus and response are functionally related to each other and are not separate entities: A child who is burned by a candle flame develops a new functional response to the flame as its meaning changes the stimulus function from attractive to painful. The response and the meaning of the stimulus are interdependent. Behavior is an adaptive act, and its stimulus-response components form an interrelated sequence: 'the seeing-of-a-light-that-means-pain-when-contact-occurs" (Dewey, 1896, p. 360).

Much of the development of functionalism took place at the University of Chicago, first with Dewey and then with James Angell (1869–1949), who had been a student of James and Dewey. Angell set forth three principles of functional psychology: (a) a mental stream is a part of a larger biological stream and mediates between the organism and the environment; (b) consciousness enables the organism to survive by mediating with the environment and takes over from habit when new adjustments are needed; and (c) mind and body act as a unit to enable the organism to survive. In short, the mind is a function of the organism that serves to promote its adaptation to surroundings.

Harvey Carr (1873–1954), also at Chicago, emphasized that behavior that enables survival in one situation is most likely to be repeated when the same situation arises again. He called this the "adaptive act." This placed an emphasis on learning, and learning became an important focus of functionalism, which facilitated its later absorption by behaviorism. Carr held that mental activities are both experiences *and* reactions of biological organs. Had he gone the next step and said that mental activities *are* the reactions of organs, he would have stated a behavioristic position.

At Columbia University Robert Woodworth (1869–1962) developed "dynamic psychology," sometimes included as a version of functionalism. He is best known for his formula S—O—R, in which O for "organism" has a function similar to Carr's adaptive act. The O mechanism mediates between the environment (S) and the response (R). It is a need or drive that produces different behaviors in the same environment depending on which drive is present. The O was another representation of mind, psyche, consciousness, sensations, ideas, and so forth, and became central to *methodological behaviorism* within which it went by such names as "drive" or "cognitive map" (see below).

Edward Thorndike (1874–1949), an American engaged in studies of animal learning, concluded that animals' minds do not reason, nor do they associate things. They learn by trial and error as a consequence of reward or punishment. His Laws of Effect involving reward and punishment were forerunners of Skinner's reinforcement principles. His Law of Exercise states that responses are strengthened in direct proportion to the number of times a connection has occurred and to the duration and vigor of the connection. The S $\rightarrow$ R bonds weaken with disuse. He called his psychology "connectionism". It was a protobehaviorism.

Behaviorism. This school has its roots in a number of predecessors. Positivism and empiricism give rise to the belief that all knowledge is based

on "sense data," but the observation component of positivism—not sense data—is connected with behaviorism. Empiricism's emphasis on experience became its concentration on learning. In Russia Ivan Sechenov (1829–1905) conducted experiments on animals that led him to conclude that thought does not produce action. Instead, external stimulation produces *both* internal thought and external action, and both depend on brain reflexes. Vladimir Bekhterev (1887–1927) engaged in human conditioning studies by applying electric shock to a finger preceded by a sound. He retained physiological explanations but advocated that psychology should deal only with behaviors. Ivan Pavlov's (1857–1927) conditioning experiments with dogs was going on at about the same time and came to the attention of John Watson (1878–1958). Watson had a particular interest in animal behavior and was exposed to the work of other animal researchers who also influenced him. One cannot get introspection from a nonhuman animal, thus the necessary emphasis on behavior. Watson's degree work at Chicago and his faculty position there exposed him to the functionalists who were moving increasingly away from introspection and toward learning studies. His move to Johns Hopkins University brought him into further contact with people whose viewpoints reinforced his behavioristic direction.

In his initial declaration of behaviorism Watson (1913) maintained only that it was unnecessary to make "consciousness a special object of observation" (p. 174). This is "methodological behaviorism" in which one does not deny consciousness but skirts it methodologically. Six years later he announced that he could find no evidence for William James's stream of consciousness, but he did find evidence for a stream of behavior (Watson, 1919). This is "strict" or "radical behaviorism," the first total break with mind-body dualism in 2000 years.

Watson believed that humans are infinitely malleable through learning. He adopted Pavlovian conditioning as the basis of this learning and lopped off one side of the mind-body dualism by converting the body into a learning machine. The brain is not the seat of a soul or even the seat of behavior. It is only a relay organ between stimulation and response. He included thinking and language in behavior by regarding them as subtle actions of the body. His main thrust was fourfold: he gave impetus to (a) objective methods of investigation over introspection; (b) behavior as a replacement for mental contents (sensations, ideas, apperception); (c) a goal of prediction and control rather than explanation; and (d) the view that animals and humans do not differ qualitatively from each other and that the same observational methods can be used on humans as on animals. Watson took the terms "stimulus" and "response" from biology, and behaviorism became S → R psychology. The world of stimulation is an antecedent condition, or an input, and the response a consequence of it, or an output. This is based on an analogy with biophysics in which the direct stimulation of a prepared muscle results in a reflexive contraction. A more refined behaviorism, according to Natalicio (1985), was that of Smith and Guthrie (1921) who "introduced into psychology an interpretive focus of ordinary experience, in behavioral language, a work considerably more consistent and sophisticated than Watson's early speculations" (p. 3).

Behaviorism divided into camps of methodological behaviorists and radical behaviorists, both conducting learning studies with rats. The former carried more influence than the latter. Especially prominent among methodological behaviorists was Clark Hull (1884–1952) at Yale. He followed the logical positivists by operationally defining an unobservable drive state, formulating a theory of learning based on these drives, and then deducing hypotheses to be tested on rats. At the University of California at Berkeley Edward Tolman (1886–1959) attempted to explain the learning behavior of rats by positing a rat's "cognitive map" of the maze. Drives and cognitive maps were much like Woodworth's O, and because they intervene between stimulus and response are called "intervening variables." Critics charged that they were a return to the old mind/sensation/apperception/ consciousness dressed up in a new guise to sound

scientific. Among the radical behaviorists, Guthrie (1886–1959) developed a learning theory strictly in S → R terms and avoided all semblance of mentalism, including intervening variables. Radical behaviorism continues today as B. F. Skinner's (1904–1990) behavior analysis (see chapter 6).

Although behaviorism dominated American psychology from about the 1930s to the 1950s, both strict and methodological behaviorism eventually lost their following. They had promised to start with simple learning of animals. As these principles became clear through experimentation, they moved on gradually and systematically to the more complex human behaviors. Unfortunately, animal learning turned out to be (a) very complex, (b) possibly irrelevant to both human and nonhuman animals because of the artificiality of laboratory studies, and (c) not necessarily applicable to humans. In the background of behaviorism's focus on animal learning was (a) biological evolution, indicating a continuity among species; and (b) British empiricism's emphasis on experience, which inspired the statement in the Declaration of Independence that "All men are created equal." The latter was a characteristic American credo to which behaviorism implicitly subscribed and to which it would presumably contribute the evidence. Behaviorism's major shortcoming may have been that it "made psychology a renunciatory discipline definitively retreating in the face of such complex and important types of behavior as imagining, perceiving, attending, feeling, and other basic human activities" (Kantor, 1969, p. 367). In addition, mentalism, with its long and pervasive cultural entrenchment, was always just below the surface and could not remain permanently suppressed.

The failure of the promise of behaviorism together with a continued covert clinging to mentalism were important factors leading to behaviorism's replacement—except for behavior analysis— by cognitive psychology (see chapter 3) which continues behaviorism's methodology and retains its emphasis on learning. Cognitivism regards remembering, perceiving, and other cognitions not as behaviors but as mental processes akin to a computer program. It considers these mental processes to be internal representations of the external world (in some versions, the representations are not so much pictures as hypothetical structures that code for memories, perceptions, etc.). Thus behaviorism's replacement reverted to (a) the mind-body dualism, (b) the double world of Kant and his innate determiners of the mind, and (c) the Plotinus-Galileo-Newton-Locke-Berkeley-Hume-Kant-Müller-Helmholtz model of perception.

Mind-body dualism never really disappeared from psychology. Although somewhat suppressed from the 1930s to the 1950s, it was present all along in methodological behaviorism. Eventually, it came roaring back through much of psychology. Stimulus-response learning was so mechanistic and constraining that investigators found it unsatisfactory. In looking for an alternative they saw only mentalism. The fascination with computers provided an irresistible new analogy for the mind, and the proverbial pendulum swung back to the mentalistic side. Mentalistic constructions are now used freely in psychology with little critical regard (Jenkins, 1993).

Beyond Behaviorism. One of the first to delineate a psychological event not as mere behavior of an organism and not as a mental process but as an interaction between object and organism was Frederick Woodbridge (1867–1940), a member of the school of natural philosophy at Columbia University. He argued, for example, that seeing is not exclusively in the organism but is "an interaction or relation between the organism and its surroundings effected by means of the eye" (1909, p. 368), a position much like that of Aristotle. The nervous system cannot see or hear, he noted, but it provides unity by coordinating the discriminations of the sense organs, and this unity is consciousness.

Also emphasizing organism-environment interactions (not mind-body interactions) rather than mechanistic inputs and outputs was the Chinese investigator of animal behavior, Zing-Yang Kuo (1898–1940). He had been a student of Tolman but was more influenced by Watson, even though he was also critical of him. He gave full attention to bi-

ology but as an enabling or limiting condition, rather than a determining condition, of animal behavior. His psychology is now called "probabilistic epigenetic psychology" (chapter 13). A little earlier J. R. Kantor (1888–1984) took account of a context ("field") of interdependent interactions and developed a thoroughgoing systematic psychology (chapter 10) complete with formal postulates and extension into such complex "interbehaviors" as knowing, orienting, choosing, thinking, and others. Because in his system the psychological event is a complex of relationships of concrete events, it has no need for mentalistic constructions or reduction of psychology to brain. However, the brain and other components of the organism's biology receive full recognition as participating conditions in the field, as they do in Kuo's system.

James Gibson's (1904–1979) ecological perception and the development of it into ecological realism arrived at broadly similar characteristics after shedding its more traditional constructions (chapter 13, §3). William Stephenson's operant subjectivity (chapter 11) adopts interbehaviorism as its theoretical basis and provides a rigorous methodology for studying subjectivity—that is, the subject's point of view—objectively. This methodology opens up for systematic study the so-called mental or cognitive events that behaviorism was never able to adequately deal with. It offers an alternative to the mechanistic computer constructs of cognitivism and to statistical procedures that discard uniqueness. Community psychology (chapter 13) also takes a person-environment orientation with an applied orientation. Dialectical psychology (chapter 9) is interactional or bipolar and takes into account the developmental history and context of the interaction. Russian and Chinese dialecticians are usually reductionistic to biology, most others less so.

These noncentric approaches have stepped outside the long tradition we have traced from Hellenistic Greece[15] although, as always, predecessors

---

15. Kuo's Chinese background may have placed him outside the tradition from the start and made it easier for him to formulate an alternative to the Western mechanism and mentalism.

paved the way. Despite the fact that they offer an alternative to both mentalism and mechanism, they have received little attention, for the weight of tradition—or the great flywheel of habit, to use William James's metaphor—continues to invoke the venerable mind and its incarnation in the brain.

Gestalt Psychology. The rationalists and empiricists clashed when Gestalt psychology (not to be confused with Fritz Perls's gestalt therapy, chapter 4) came on the scene. The Gestalt psychologists argued that mind is not divisible into elements, not even elements that can be combined as chemical compounds (as J. S. Mill proposed) or consolidated by apperception (as Leibnitz and Wundt held). The Gestaltists insisted that the mind has innate powers that give a Gestalt—a whole or pattern—to things, and this applies to perceiving and to thinking alike. For example, when we look at things we do not see separate spots that must be combined into an object such as a tree. Instead we innately relate the components by such principles as proximity, similarity, and set (what we anticipate seeing) into a unit "tree." And learning to solve a problem consists not of trial and error as Thorndike held but of discovering the critical component to the solution that contributes to the whole. Learning is gaining *insight*. Wolfgang Köhler (1887–1967) attempted to provide a physiological basis for Gestalt organization by an analogy he drew from electrical fields. He proposed that sensory stimulation enters electrochemical fields in the brain and is restructured into wholes. Further, the configuration of fields of force in the brain and the configuration of the object in the world correspond to each other point by point; they are "isomorphic" with one another. The individual perceives the configurations in the brain as perceptions. Here too, as with Müller and Helmholtz, we find the biologizing of Kant's unity of apperception. His double world is restated as isomorphism and his innate categorization as Gestalt organization.

The social psychologist Kurt Lewin (1890–1947) applied Gestalt psychology to groups. In his "group dynamics," the behavior of each individual is determined by the pattern of the energy of the entire group—just as the brain, in gestalt theory, determines sensory elements. This theory influenced humanistic psychology (chapter 4) and its involvement in such human potential movements as T-groups and encounter groups. Lewin also influenced ecological psychology (chapter 7), community psychology (chapter 13), and environmental psychology (chapter 13) through his emphasis on behavior as a function of environment.

Summary and Conclusions

Primitive psychological concepts posited life-forces in everything. In humans the life-forces that determined behavior were often biological organs, especially the heart. Aristotle put psychology on a fully naturalistic course when he described the interaction of organism and environment rather than constructing a determining force within the organism. In the following centuries deleterious social conditions turned intellectuals inward, away from the world, and converted *psuché* from a life-function to a supernatural inner determiner. India had earlier made a similar transformation under similar circumstances. Christian theologians developed *psuché* into an inner psychology, and this approach dominated thinking throughout the Middle Ages and beyond. As other sciences freed themselves from theology, psychology remained bound to it; but it gained the attention of philosophy as that discipline began to pull away from theology. Philosophies such as rationalism, empiricism, and positivism gave psychology greater scope but retained psychophysical dualism and disagreed primarily on whether the soul was unified or atomistic. Rather than turning to observations of nature, philosophers attempted to naturalize the soul by means of analogies and biologizing. Even when experimental psychology arrived, investigators continued to believe that they were studying something intangible that could be accessed only indirectly.

The classical systems in psychology from the late nineteenth century to about the 1950s or 60s were primarily reactions to these age-old problems and for the most part continued to interpret their observations in terms of sensations/mind/consciousness/intervening variables—no matter how sophisticated those observations became as they adapted laboratory methodologies. Only slowly and to a limited degree did they turn to descriptive accounts of their data as other sciences were doing. Radical behaviorism alone discarded the mentalistic constructs, but in doing so it turned to mechanistic accounts. Some noncentric systems avoided mind-body dualism, mechanism, and biological reductionism by focusing on interdependent object and organism operating in a context. Other current systems have remained close to the tradition coming down to us from the Church Fathers or have turned heavily to the environment (for example, eco-behavioral science). Psychoanalysis (chapter 5), both a classical and a current system, built its original theory on the innate mental structures of the rationalists and on energies and forces of physics, thus clinging to mind-body dualism of the theologians while striving for the scientific status of an established science. Humanistic psychology (chapter 4) substitutes "self" for mind. The postmodernists and social constructionists (chapter 8) deny the validity of rationality and of science, yet turn to logic and scientific cross-cultural studies to justify their own position. In some versions they accept a merging of the knower and the known of Plotinus and in other versions embrace the unknowable world of Kant.

History shows us that it is primarily mind-body dualism and the various reactions to it that have created in psychology such wide disagreements about what comprises its basic subject matter. These disagreements began to emerge after the Middle Ages when the soul became an increasingly puzzling topic, both logically and empirically (observationally). And yet history also shows us that mind-body dualism is a creation of only the last 2000 years. Alternatives to it and to biological reductionism were available in the fourth century BCE but went unrecognized by later thinkers. They are available again today but are still seldom noticed. Whether these alternatives

are valid or invalid is a different issue, but unless we recognize and consider them we do not provide ourselves with the basis for an informed choice. Generally, mainstream psychology has not considered them, but has allowed only cultural assumptions from the past to determine the character of various systems of psychology.

Psychology today is not only in disagreement about its subject matter but is highly fragmented in its theoretical and methodological approaches. This is due in part to increasing specializations but also to age-old disagreements about mind construction. Once again it is appropriate to raise questions similar to those raised early in this chapter. Is psychology a study of mind and its representations of a separate real world? Is it a study of behaviors influenced by a cognitive mind? Or is it just behaviors? Is it the action of the environment on the organism? Is it the action of the brain on the organism? Or is it interrelations of organism and environment in a context?

LOGIC OF SCIENCE

Many topics could be included under the heading "logic of science" (also called "philosophy of science"). Those presented here are the ones that seem most central to the sixteen systems described in this book. These topics in most cases are not mutually exclusive but overlap to one degree or another. In fact, in some respects they are all subsets of the distinction between constructs and events and the way these are applied.

Constructs vs. Events

The Distinction. A construction or "construct" is, as the name indicates, something that is constructed rather than observed. It is an invention, an abstraction, a contrivance. In fact anything that is not the original event is a construct: a theory, a hypothesis, a principle, a mathematical formula, a diagram, a measurement. Even a description is a construct, for it is not the thing that it describes. Descartes's soul, Leibnitz's monads, Hume's impressions, Locke's ideas and sensations, La Mettrie's springs, Kant's transcendental unity of apperception, Müller's specific nerve energies, J. S. Mill's mental chemistry, Woodworth's O, and Köhler's isomorphism, to name but a few, are all constructs. What is critical, however, is whether the construct is derived from the event or imposed on it (Ebel, 1974; Kantor, 1957, 1962; Lichtenstein, 1984; Observer, 1983). In all these instances the construct was drawn from traditional cultural sources and imposed on the events. The events are seeing, believing, remembering, thinking, imagining, and other concrete human actions, not nerve energies, sensations, and the like. An event is anything that happens, whether we know about it or not.

The authors of a recent book on psychology's theoretical issues describe the volume as a "comprehensive guide" (Bem & Looren de Jong, 1997) yet do not mention the critical issue of constructs. The debates over many centuries about the nature of mind also failed to recognize the nature of constructs and their confusion with events. The authors are in venerable company.

The distinction between constructs and events is critical. It determines theory, research designs, applications, and even knowability. Wundt held that we cannot know consciousness, only its effects. And he was right that we cannot know an ephemeral construct. But did he need to invoke it or could he simply have referred to the responses he was actually measuring? Were Titchener's subjects introspecting their elementary sensations, or were they making sensory discriminations of objects and events? Posner and Raichel (1994, p. 24) well illustrate the confusion between constructs and events. They show a graph in which they claim to plot the brain on a horizontal axis and mind on the vertical. They do plot the imaging techniques of the brain at varying levels of detail, but the "mind" turns out to be time.

As another example of confusing constructs and events, in an effort to justify unobservables in psychology, Bornstein (1988) claims that "psychologists investigate feelings, motivations, and other internal processes." Here he lumps together an event and a construct under another construct: internal processes. Let's examine each of these in order to see what the alternatives are.

■ If you receive an A on a paper, you probably agree that your joy is a real event. A feeling, then, is an event consisting of a person in interaction with the thing felt about, such as joy upon seeing an A on a paper.

■ Why did you work hard for the A? You must have been motivated. But what is a motive? It isn't anything in itself, but it should have a specific referent in identifiable events. Perhaps you bet a friend a bagel that you could get an A. Motivation is a construct of causality, not an event, but it can be a useful summarizing term if it has identifiable referents. However, contrary to Bornstein, we don't investigate the motive as such, for it is only an abstraction, a construct. What we investigate are the specific conditions that lead to a particular behavior.

■ Bornstein's final example, internal processes (which he intends as an all-embracing category) is also a construct rather than an event. It assumes that nature has divided us into two parts. If referents for inner processes can be specified, the inner-outer distinction no longer holds. For identifiable events of nature—the joy of the A, the bet that was one influencing factor on the hard work to earn the A— become the focus rather than a constructed duality. But the construct of internal processes is usually one of mind-body dualism that has no such referents.

Bornstein goes on to justify unobservables in psychology by way of claiming that gravity is an unobservable that physicists study indirectly. On the contrary, gravity is not an unobservable. It is an event involving the relationship of bodies in space, and this relationship may be observed, measured, and described mathematically. We may similarly observe events of humans in relationship with their surroundings and describe these relationships rather than starting with cultural constructs and imposing them on the investigations. The alternatives are available for the choosing.

A possible reason for adopting unobservables, Kantor (1979) suggests, is that we interact with our surroundings in two different ways. One involves observation and manipulation whereas the other is more subtle and includes hunches, assumptions, and knowing. Because the latter type of reaction is more remote from the original event, the scientist may suppose that he or she is dealing with one thing when it is actually something else (see also p. 67 on analogies). Cultural is perhaps an even greater influence, but we are not locked into culture; we change our culture through our actions, and consequently change in orientation about cultural constructs is not impossible (Kantor, 1938, 1973).

Despite some claims that "theoretical terms" (constructs) and observational terms are equally inferential and unreliable, several empirical studies of these terms support the greater reliability and validity of the latter and the clear distinguishability of the two (Clark & Paivio, 1989). Investigators found that "observational terms refer more directly to observable phenomena than do theoretical terms and are relatively more stable and definite in their meanings" (p. 510). Further, "the data suggest that scientists do and ought to maintain distinct attitudes toward observational and theoretical terms when thinking about or communicating scientific ideas. Observational terms have more stable and universal meanings, and participate in statements that can be empirically validated by virtue of their concrete referents" (p. 510).[16]

Should a system be construct-based or event-based? That is, do the proponents begin with constructs with which they interpret events, or do they begin with events and develop their constructs from those events? Kantor (1981b) argues that "In general a valid logic of science must be founded on a full appreciation of the relations between events and constructs" (p. 6) including the clear distinction between them. Lichtenstein (1984) echoes a similar point:

---

16. Ironically, the authors couched their studies in constructs whose referential base has been questioned by a number of others (see chapter 3).

When one follows carefully what is entailed in scientific work we have a basis for distinguishing among data, investigative operations, and constructions. The construction phase becomes particularly important when it is realized that it is here that most disagreement in science arises. Constructs are more likely to be sound when they are derived from direct contact with events whether involving manipulations and measurement or not. Unfortunately scientists when they are in the grip of tradition are usually unaware of the fact. Thus astronomers found circular orbits for the planets reasonable and biologists described in detail the homunculi [little men] in sperm cells. (p. 471)

Constructs with Time-Space Coordinates. Constructs are necessary in science, and when properly used always have concrete referents: they refer to things or events. Inferences are constructs which play an important role in science. In the fifth to fourth century BCE, Democritos observed the behavior of matter and inferred that it was composed of tiny particles that he called "atoms." Although he could not verify their existence, their space-time coordinates gave them the potential to be observed if they existed. In the twentieth century the development of adequate instrumentation finally permitted the verification of these inferred particles. In contrast, the historical constructs imposed on human actions had no time-space coordinates but transcended space and time. For that reason analogies were invented—constructs about constructs—and the brain as a concrete organ became the substitute for these immaterial agents. But as a psychological organ, the brain too is a construct (see pp. 60–64).

Estes (1989) favorably cites Bohr, Einstein, and Hull as using abstract inferred "representations" (constructs). Bohr proposed that the atom had electrons spinning around a nucleus. This arrangement has space-time coordinates that provide for potential verification. The construct has been an extremely useful one in physics and chemistry and continues to be useful even though it is now considered of doubtful validity. Einstein proposed that gravity consisted of space curved from the mass of bodies in it, and this construct successfully predicted the path of the light of a star as it passed near the sun. In contrast to these scientific constructs, Hull's drives had no time-space coordinates despite his efforts to hold to the views of the logical positivists and define them by operations. His highly influential learning theory based on these drives and the predictions about behavior deduced from the theory crumbled for both conceptual and empirical (observational) reasons.

Types of Constructs. Sometimes the confusion between constructs and events results from using the term "variable" for things and events as well as for constructs. When the word refers to a stimulus condition, a response, a context, a body condition, or other concrete thing, a variable is a thing or event. When it refers to "intervening variables" such as Woolworth's O, Hull's drive, and Tolman's cognitive map, it is a construct. Consciousness, cognition, experience, and mind are also used as intervening variables.[17] As Kantor (1957) points out, intervening variables originated with Tolman (1936) for the explicit purpose of finding a place for mental processes in his formulation, and Tolman took them from James who described mental life as intervening between impressions on the body and responses of the body to the outer world. The intervening constructs became unobservable events and took on causal powers: a drive, instinct, or mind was said to cause behavior.

Anyone not influenced by the presuppositions of traditional philosophy can easily see that what are called intervening variables are actually supervening "variables." When intervening variables are identified with such factors as fatigue, previous training, or abnormality of the organisms they are extravening or setting fac-

tors [context]. If we persist in keeping before us the events with which we actually work we will not confuse authentic hypotheses, namely, constructs regulated and controlled by the events that set the investigative problems, with the licentious products of autistic creation. (Kantor, 1957, p. 59)

Marr (1983) points out that

Newton suggested the possibility . . . that an all-pervading "aether" served as the medium for such phenomena as gravitation and light. Psychology has been replete with mental aethers that mediate between stimuli and responses. Indeed, cognitive psychology seems to be paralleling classical physics in the search for an understanding of the structure and mechanics of the mental aether . . . Such models can always be expanded or elaborated to accommodate whatever data might be obtained. . . . (p. 13)

And they are accommodating because they have a base in no more than verbal constructions. One argument advanced for intervening variables, however, is that they combine a number of factors into a single term thereby making it easier to work with them (Wasserman, 1983, p. 8). Critics would hold that such combining can all too easily obscure the multiple interactions that are occurring and can replace those events with a hypothetical causal entity. Nevertheless, it is a common practice to combine a number of related behaviors into a construct such as motivation or personality by way of descriptive summary, but the motivation or personality does not then intervene. As descriptions these constructs do not cause the behaviors that they describe.

Lewin (1951) influenced eco-behavioral science (chapter 7), environmental psychology (chapter 13), and community psychology (chapter 13) with his construct of B = f(P,E), where B = behavior, P = person, and E =environment. P is the person's mind, or what Lewin called life space; and the formula shows the behavior *separated* from the person who is behaving with the life space. Behavior is the function of a construct (P) and a thing or

---

17. Sometimes a distinction is made between an intervening variable and a hypothetical construct. The latter is then applied to something that is supposed to have actual existence, such as the atoms of Democritos, but has "surplus meaning" beyond the observations from which it is inferred. "Surplus meaning" is another troublesome construct, and it seems to be another word for "mind."

event of the environment (E). He doesn't explain how this is possible. Similarly, Mahoney (1977) proposed that cognition (read *mind*), environment, and behavior all influence each other. Consequently, he has two events interacting with a construct. In close accord with this, Bandura (1989) presented his "triadic reciprocal causation" in which environment, behavior, and person (read *mind*) interact. Again, two events are interacting with a construct, the logic of which is not clear. So far as we know, only things and events can interact with each other, not things and constructs. Mahoney's and Bandura's triads differ from Woodworth's S—O—R only in that they are in reciprocal relations rather than in linear (straight line) cause and effect. Clarifying exactly what the events are as opposed to imposing constructs (such as a person's mind) would lead to better identification of all the relevant events and a better scientific understanding on which to build applications. Lewin also gave impetus to cognitivism by his premise that "human action is critically dependent on the cognitive processing of information—that is, on the world as cognized rather than the world as it is" (Gergen, 1985, p. 269). This, of course, is a version of Kant's double world.

These formulations make clear that any intervening variable—whether triadic or linear—presumes a causal relationship between that construct and an event, in other words a presumed mind-body causal relation. Because a construct is not a thing but an abstraction and can therefore never be observed (although its referent, if it has one, could be observed), such an arrangement lies forever outside observation and verification. (Observation can be traditional laboratory studies, interviews, Q sorts, case studies, biography, field observations, etc.) What happens in practice, however, is that the investigator observes events but reports them as the operation of constructs, such as mind or processing, and imposes them on the events he or she observes. The confusion between events and constructs goes back to the Hellenistic scholars who became obsessed with verbalizations. Yet things and events are all that anyone anywhere has ever observed or ever can observe.

Although scientific work is mostly a matter of constructions, it does not follow, Kantor (1957) notes, "that hypothetical entities may be arbitrarily created" (p. 59). *Descriptive constructs,* he holds, are most valid and useful when they derive directly from contacts with events. They are of decreasing validity and usefulness when they are (a) analogies, (b) borrowed from other fields (such as biology), and (c) total inventions such as intervening variables. *Explanatory constructs* (causality) may relate psychology to biology, chemistry, and social events but may not be reduced to them. They are more analytical than simple description in relating things and events (Kantor, 1983), but they may still be regarded as forms of description. Explanation builds a body of knowledge when one functional description is integrated with another which has already been functionally related to still others. *Manipulative constructs* involving problems, theories, and hypotheses can be validated only if "securely connected with events" (1957, p. 59).

Criteria for Constructs. Are there any explicit standards for regulating scientific constructs? The following list from Kantor (1957, 1978, 1981b) consists of standards consistent with scientific advancement. Others could be added. Proponents of social constructionism (chapter 8) would reject most of these criteria and hold that all claims to knowledge or truth are invalid constructs—except within the social group that constructs them—and have no warrant beyond that group. Such a social group could be scientific researchers whose claims are no better than those of myth-makers, they insist.

- Distinguish carefully between constructs of all types and the original events.
- Avoid all constructs derived from traditional cultural and philosophical sources.
- When means for obtaining critical information is lacking, keep constructs extremely tentative— and *never* base them on unobservables.
- Note that only constructs derived directly from observed events have the potential of validity.
- Take an adequate sample of events so that the interrelationships of events may be observed.

- Begin all investigations with observations from which constructs may be derived; avoid starting with constructs and interpreting results in terms of those constructs.
- Keep interpretive constructs consistent with the events observed; do not base them on other constructs.
- Anchor all constructs—such as intelligence, motivation, and attitudes—in observed referents and avoid giving them independent existence as things or causes.
- Use only constructs which are corrigible.
- Avoid turning participating conditions, or those that may be necessary for the event, into determining conditions (see pp. 61–64).
- Recognize the different levels of organization of things and events and keep explanatory constructs consistent with this recognition.
- Distinguish between the knower and the thing known and avoid merging them (see p. 67).
- Derive postulates from observation.
- Avoid adopting unobservable constructs or analogies for what is unknown and regard admission of ignorance as a scientific virtue (see p. 67).
- Use only those constructs that are observable at least in principle, for it is only through observation that science is possible.

Does the observability criterion rule out "private" and "subjective" events? Not according to some proponents.

All too often constructs become circular. Barber (1981), a prolific researcher in hypnosis, points out that hypnosis has typically been defined by a trance state: we know that someone is hypnotized because he or she is in a trance. Then we explain the person's hypnotic behavior by the trance. In other words, the definition of hypnosis as a trance state is not independent of what the trance is supposed to explain. Barber discarded the trance construct completely and described hypnosis as directed imagining that is continuous with other behaviors with which we are familiar. An understanding of hypnosis, he argues, does not require a hypothetical construct of trance. By distinguishing the construct from the event he was able to develop an entirely different understanding of hypnosis. Circularity also enters into a fundamental construct in psychoanalysis: Freud originally *defined* libido as sexual needs and then began to use it to *explain* sexual behaviors (MacCorquodale & Meehl, 1951). Another instance of circularity occurs when psychometrists create a scale to measure a construct such as alienation or intelligence and then define the construct with the scale.

As other examples of circular constructs, Ebel (1974) points to intelligence, motivation, and creativity. We hear that an individual works hard because he is motivated, and we judge that he's motivated because he works hard. Ebel compares these explanatory constructs to tree nymphs ("dryads") and other animistic powers of hunter-gatherers. The title of his paper, "And Still the Dryads Linger," indicates his thesis that we have not yet expunged these animistic explanations from psychology. They linger on as intelligence, personality traits, libido, etc. We even refer to various amounts of intelligence, motivation, and creativity as if they were *things* with quantity. Constructs such as intelligence are important but should, he contends, be limited to an indication of functional relationships, for these relationships are all that explanation can be. Nor should we allow complexity of our subject matter to

> keep us from recognizing our dryads for what they are—partial descriptions that masquerade as causal explanations. This need not keep us from understanding how useless they are in our search for understanding of behavioral phenomena. Let us be on guard against their deceptive pretentions. Let us make behavioral science, limited and imperfect as it is, inhospitable to them. They can only weaken it. (p. 491)

To summarize the position of Barber and Ebel, we need to be aware of circularity in constructs and keep our definitions and explanations independent of each other. For instance, if we define motivation as working hard, we must look elsewhere for explanations of *why* people work hard.

Those explanations, according to Ebel, would be confined to descriptions of functional relationships of variables, not of invented dryads. Such constructs as intelligence, motive, and personality are useful descriptions of specified behaviors, but they do not cause the behaviors they describe. Clarence doesn't have a high grade point average *because* he is intelligent. His high grade point average is a measure or description of intelligent behavior. A person doesn't behave in some typical way because of his or her personality. That typical behavior *is* personality. "Personality" is a shorthand term for those particular behaviors. A child isn't distractable *because* of an attention-deficit hyperactivity (ADHD) disorder. The term only *refers* to distractibility and other behaviors that sometimes cluster with it.

If we consider causality the same as explanation, the search for explanation then becomes a search for functional relationships. Along these lines British philosopher Bertrand Russell attempts to avoid dryads in physics. He points out that "Electricity is not a thing, like Saint Paul's cathedral; it is a way in which things behave. When we have told how things behave when they are electrified, and under what circumstances they are electrified, we have told all there is to tell" (quoted by Cole, 1983). Whether dryads appear in some of the systems covered in this book, the reader will be able to decide.

Another viewpoint, however, one calling itself "realist" and linked in some degree with social constructionism (chapter 8), argues that we should be looking for causal mechanisms rather than functional relationships (Manicus & Secord, 1983). The causal mechanism, in this view, are not events but are multilayered acts of people, which range over the disciplines of biology, physics, and sociology as well as psychology and include biography, context, motives, interests, and purposes. These mechanisms enter into life as it is lived—a viewpoint that shares some common ground with humanistic (chapter 4) and phenomenological (chapter 12) psychology. Some social constructionists (chapter 8) and some humanistic psychologists deny altogether that ob-servation can be objective or that it has any useful role in psychology.

The Mind Construct. Mind in its various incarnations is *the* major construct in psychology. We have seen that in English usage it historically referred to concrete events and still retains some of those meanings but that under the influence of theology it also developed nonphysical meanings. If we use mind to refer directly to such events as thinking, knowing, discriminating, and imagining—as a shorthand summary for those specific events—it is a useful construct as long as we recognize that it is *not* those events and *does not* cause them. If it is considered a separate and unobservable causal force intervening between the world and the body, it does not meet criteria for a scientific construct, such as those advanced by Kantor. Instead it is a restatement of the old theological psyche or soul—a thing, process, agent, or power. This is *reification,* the act of attributing real existence to an abstraction as, for example, in the statement "the phenomena of consciousness are real" (Manicus & Secord, 1983, p. 406) and "mental processes exist" (Kukla, 1989, p. 793). The following also illustrates reification: "The human mind is an adaptive system. It chooses behaviors in the light of its goals, and as appropriate to the particular context in which it is working" (Simon, 1992, p. 156). The author has turned a construct into a thing and given it self-acting powers. However, Jenkins (1993) is quite uncritical. His earlier research showed the interdependence of recalling (remembering) and context and thereby supported a contextualist interpretation as against an associationist position derived from British empiricism (Jenkins, 1974). He believes that we can decide as "a matter of taste" whether to use "inferred constructs of the mentalistic sort" (Jenkins, 1993, p. 360).

Mind is a cultural construct, not a scientific one. It does not derive from observation but from cultural tradition as our historical survey showed. We might choose to use it but should be clear about it origins and its character. What we observe either by direct or indirect means are such events as perceiving, learning, speaking, and believing. If we use mind as a summary term for one or more of these, we must not fall into the circularity of giving it power to cause those same events; and we must not lose track of the fact that such events are referents and that mind does not exist independent of them.

These statements about the mind construct apply equally well to the consciousness construct except that consciousness is a recent invention and is used with greater vagueness. ". . . It has been in vogue to agree that the set [of necessary and sufficient conditions for consciousness] is impossible to define; to disagree on what the set consists in; to talk of consciousness as an emergent property of *the* brain . . . and to discuss the brain as if it controlled, but was not controlled by, the body" (Shapiro, 1997, p. 840). Sometimes consciousness seems to be the same as mind, and at other times an author uses it as something different. One can find lists of different meanings that could apply equally well to mind, but the lists offer no distinctions between the two (English & English, 1958). Searle (1998) tells us that "the essence of the mental is conscious states" (p. 39). Given that "essence," "mental," and "conscious states" are all constructs, we are left in even thicker fog.

Often consciousness seems to be used in the context of attending and perceiving an object. If so, what is consciousness apart from the perceived color, odor, shape, usage, meaning, and so on? What else is its referent? The word has recently become the topic of a series of conferences and of a great outpouring of books (Shapiro, 1997). Rarely do any of these recognize it as a construct (Smith, 1997). Instead the brain receives a "resident ghost called consciousness" (Grossberg, 1972, p. 249).

In some contexts "self" has become a term for "mind," just as "mind" substituted for "soul." *The self* is especially prominent in humanistic psychology (chapter 4). In that context self functions as a causative agent that exercises will power and directs the body. For example, "His alcoholic self won't allow him to stop drinking." However, when "self" is used as a term for behavior patterns—an alcoholic self, a fun-loving self, a nice-guy self, a vengeful self—it is merely a descriptive construct and is unlikely to be problematical as long as the referents to the events are clear.

Modes of Expression. Some scholars recommend always referring to psychological events as participles or verbals: sensing rather than sensation, knowing rather than knowledge, thinking rather than thought, imagining rather than imagination. This recommendation seeks to keep us alert to the fact that we are dealing with human events rather than with things. This is helpful, but one cannot easily apply it to intelligence or personality, even though they too refer to some pattern of actions for which the label is a convenient form of reference. The contextual interactionists such as community psychologists (chapter 13), interbehaviorists (chapter 10) and phenomenologists (chapter 12) point out that even the participle/verbal form fails to indicate that the *action* is actually an *interaction*; that is, when we think, we think about *something*; when we sense, we sense *something*; when we speak, we speak about *something*. Nevertheless, using participles/verbals wherever possible may help avoid reification.

Along the same lines, consider the following: do "people experience visual mental images" (Kosslyn, 1995, p. 6), or do people imagine? The first refers to constructs and the second to events. The assumptions are quite different in the two. Other modes of expression either invoke a mind-body dualism or refer to a whole person or a person's behavior. For example, does it take a keen mind to solve complex problems, or a does it take a bright person? Does Tom's personality cause problems, or is his behavior inappropriate? Does Ann use her imagination, or does she imagine (or behave imaginatively)? In short, do we give the person credit or do we invoke an impersonal construct to carry out the action? Note the impersonal and autonomous character of mind in the following passage: "It [mind] chooses behaviors in the light of its goals, and as appropriate to the particular context in which it is working . . . It can learn" (Simon, 1992, p. 156).

Mentalists and nonmentalists operate from vastly different postulate systems. That is why, as indicated in chapter 1, it is so important for the advocates of each system to set forth their postulates, and to do so at all levels of generality in order to provide full disclosure. Ten postulate systems, some of them necessarily inferred, are presented in the Appendix for direct comparisons.

Mind-Body Dualism

According to one writer, "the scientific mind-body problem concerns the relation between two sets of theories" (Mandler, 1985, p. 29). It might be contended, in contrast, that the mind-body problem is not a scientific problem but a culturally assumptive one; and that it is not about two sets of theories, but is a single assumption about a construct (mind) and a thing (body). Following is a survey of some of the major viewpoints on the mind-body question.

Epiphenomenalism. Among the classical approaches to the mind-body assumption, is the one called Cartesian dualism after René Descartes. This proposed clear-cut interaction of nonphysical mind and physical body still has a few supporters (Eccles & Robinson, 1984; Popper & Eccles, 1977; Vendler, 1984). An approach much more commonly invoked today is *epiphenomenalism,* the belief that body produces mind much as a steam engine produces a whistle, or that "mind has evolved from other bodily functions" (Tolman, 1987, p. 221). This also goes by the name of emergentism: the mind emerges from the brain. For example, "self-conscious mind is conceived best as an emergent property of a specifiable brain organization" (Pribram, 1986, p. 514). The philosopher John Searle (1992) subscribes to this view and to the analogy of Cabanis that compares the brain with digestion. The pioneer in split brain studies, Sperry (1988, 1993), also subscribes to it but also posits a kind of Cartesian interaction of mind and body. In its most common form today it suggests that the brain produces information processing. *Identity theory,* in contrast, holds that mind does

not emerge as some ghostly thing without substance, but that it is nothing but substance— substance in the form of brain cells. Brain is identical with mind. A version of this is called "eliminativism," meaning that any account of human action that does not eliminate all but neural action as the explanatory construct for the action is unscientific and dualistic (for example, Mahner & Bunge, 1998). Some versions of this dismiss mind altogether. One problem with the constructs of identity and eliminativism is that no one has ever found a thought or a perception or an emotion in neurons. How an electrochemical impulse of a neuron could be the color green or love or a memory of visiting grandparents is unclear. Epiphenomenalism, identity theory, and eliminativism face the question of what it is that observes the epiphenomenon or the electrochemical impulse. What sees the green excreted by the neuron or feels its passion of love? Or what sees or feels its byproduct? Can it see itself or feel itself?

This is the same problem that the early psychologists of India faced when they put seeing in the eye, but then recognized that an eye could not see its own seeing and so named a series of prior seeings. Because the search for a beginning point goes back infinitely, this is called an "infinite regress." One attempt to avoid having a little man (homunculus) sitting inside the head interpreting whatever comes in and another interpreting for that one and so on infinitely is to treat images as computer simulations (Kosslyn, 1983). This is another example of the use of an analogy to attempt to solve the problem of the mind construct.

Whereas the eliminativists have argued that only a reduction of psychology to neurology can eliminate dualism, one analyst has argued to the contrary that giving causality to neurons ("material events") is itself a dualistic position.

Dualism does not require that there be no brain! Indeed, dualism does not even necessarily require that mental events not be the effects of neural causes. A modest dualism only asserts that there *are* mental events. To show, then, that such events are somehow caused by material events, far from establishing the validity of a monist position, virtually guarantees the validity of a dualist position. (Robinson, 1986, pp. 435–36)

Another writer goes much further:

Probably the most confusing and futile procedure for ameliorating the deficiencies of the mentalistic tradition is to assert that the brain is the seat of consciousness or mind. One of the many attempts to rationalize a belief in soul or mind is to make consciousness an epiphenomenon hovering over the brain. But this clearly emphasizes the presence of spirits and is no solution of any mind-body problem. Accordingly the next suggestion is to substitute the brain for the mind altogether. Thus the faculties of the soul have been made into centers in the brain. Cognitivists believe that psychology can be scientific by equating pure phantasms of the soul with functions of a tangible organ. Of course the entire identification is purely verbal and involves spurious interpretations of an important organ, the functions of which are quite other than the identity theory attempts to make out. (Kantor, 1978, p. 336)

The following are further examples of epiphenomenalism and are usually connected with cognitive psychology. (See chapter 3 for more details on the first three.)

■ *Computations and mental representations:* Cognitions operate on representations, that is, on an internal world represented symbolically. This is the classical viewpoint that goes back to Kant. The world we experience is only an illusory representation of a real world and follows computational rules—that is, symbol manipulation.

■ *Connectionist networks:* In one version inputs from the world are weighted for categorizing and the responses to the weighted categories are the representations. In another version the representations are images that arise from spreading neural activations that carry meaning structures from a central network to peripheral structures.

■ *Dynamic representations:* Mental states, such as memories and perceptions, are meanings that emerge from brain-environment relationships through coordination by dynamic change over time. The brain permits but does not create or represent the relationship. The mental states are "dynamic representations" specific to the environmental event.

■ *Functionalism:* Mental processes are real events with causative power that adapt the individual to the environment and interpret the world. Functionalism emphasizes mental actions rather than mental things. Among the departures from classical functionalism the most important gives biology the role of enabling the actions rather than of containing them. In that characteristic it resembles dynamic representations. Some functionalists have used the analogy that function is to the body as a computer program is to a computer. Just as a program can run on different computers, the same mental process can operate with different individuals or even with different species.

■ *Holographic representation:* Pribram (1986) turns to brain and analogical analysis to resolve the mind-body issue: "either an input from the senses or from some central sources . . . will activate the spectrally encoded memory trace to produce an image" (p. 514). Although he doesn't tell us what sees this image, he proposes that the brain is a "spectral analyzer" that functions analogously to a hologram which operates in a manner similar to Leibnitz's monads in that each bit of information is distributed in such a way that it represents the whole. Thus, Plotinus's emanations (fig. 2.3) reach us as hypothetical neural holograms through Leibnitz and Pribram. Dualism is resolved, Pribram argues, through the proposal that "image (and object) and holographic record are transforms of each other, and the transformations involved are highly reversible" (p. 517). Skinner (chapter 6), Kantor (chapter 10), and Sartre and Merleau-Ponty (chapter 12) would argue that imagining is a form of action, not a form of reproduction as the representation construct assumes; and therefore, no computer or hologram analogy and no infinity of interpreters is required.

Mechanical Analogy: Watt Steam Engine Governors. This analogy draws from James Watt's invention for controlling the speed of steam engines (which is now used on other types of engines as well). As engine speed increases and the weights whirl more rapidly, centrifugal force moves them further out from the center where they activate controls that govern speed. The action can be described mathematically as a dynamic system (Van Gelder, 1995). This contrasts with a computational-representation system that would compute the position of the weights with procedures that use symbol representations such as numbers and would employ self-causing hypothetical agents (homunculi) to act upon them. The governor analogy dispenses with symbols in the head that purport to represent the world and with the way the symbols are handled. The approach turns to the operation of states in space just as the flyweights of the governor adjust the speed of the engine when they change spatial position. In this scenario, cognition is a reaction to the environment involving a servo-mechanism. The individual's movement through space—while reacting to push and pull, to approach and avoidance of a governor—is reminiscent of Lewin's valences in life space, a kind of tension-system in which objects attract or repel. Both draw from physics the action of forces upon the individual. This approach, if it avoids mind-body dualism, does so by adopting a more mechanistic system than Watson's S → R.

Vibration Analogy: Wooden Door. This analogy attempts to avoid the brain theories of dualism, epiphenomenalism, and identity theory by arguing that the brain is a substratum inseparable from consciousness, as a wooden door vibrates in response to a sound wave (Ellis, 1995).

Intentionality. This construct is best known from Husserl's (see chapter 12) usage, in which the mind relates to something beyond itself. From the Latin meaning of "intentionality," it *stretches forth* to the object. That is, the mind ("consciousness" is the term often used) is always *about* something external to itself. To Merleau-Ponty and Sartre (chapter 12) this means that there is nothing in consciousness, for consciousness is always a relationship between the person and the object. That you are conscious of the clock as the class period nears an end is to say that you and the clock are in a relationship to each other, and this relationship is one of meaning. The clock is not in your consciousness, it is up there on the wall. Nor is it a representation in your neurons. Nor is it a mere physical contrivance to which you respond mechanically. It is something that means an imminent end of the class activities, and this meaning is comprised by the intentional relationship. The meaning is irreducible to any of its components. Physical objects cannot react with intentionality, and that is why psychology cannot be properly studied mechanistically as a physical science and why methodologies borrowed from the physical sciences are inappropriate. This version of intentionality moves further away from the traditional mind-body assumption than others summarized to this point, especially because of the bidirectional dialectic of person-world interchange (though retaining some unidirectionality) between person and object. But other versions, especially those more influenced by Husserl, are unidirectional and organocentric: consciousness goes from the person to the object. Other than close followers of Merleau-Ponty, intentionality is usually used as another form of mind-body dualism.

With the occasional exception of intentionality, all these approaches to the mind-body question fail to recognize that mind is a construct, not an existing thing. The proponents then impose it on the events they observe. By beginning with this cultural construct rather than with events in nature, observers have to resort to reductionism, analogies, representations, and other verbal devices to deal with it. For example, "all actions and thoughts require some underlying representation, some theoretical structure that constructs and produces the observable aspects of human thought and action" (Mandler, 1985, p. 31). The next section describes an approach that does not begin with this construct but instead begins with the observed events.

The Mind Construct Replaced with Events: Contextual Interactionism. S—R psychology was the first to eliminate the mind construct altogether. Two objections to it will indicate its perceived shortcomings and why it has diminished as a contender in approaches to the mind-body problem. First, if we give someone a problem to solve and the stimulus, and wait for a solution, our likely response will be, "It is blatantly obvious here that an exclusive focus on observable stimuli and responses is uninformative about what is really of interest—the thought processes and strategies involved in problem solution" (Eysenck & Keane, 1990, p. 3). Second, quoting Watson on predicting the response from the stimulus or identifying the stimulus from the nature of the response, Jenkins (1993) notes that "It is hard to appreciate fully what a severe constraint this is! It demands that stimuli and responses be in a one-to-one mapping; it admits no possibility of different sets of stimuli having the same effect on responses or of different responses occurring to the same stimulus complex depending on the state or disposition of the organism" (p. 356).

Despite these identifications of some of the shortcomings of S—R psychology, the types of available alternatives seem to be seldom noticed, as the following will illustrate: "It does not seem to be generally known among psychologists that all manifest behavior depends on underlying psychological mechanisms—information-processing devices, decision rules, and so on—in conjunction with contextual input into those mechanisms. No behavior can be produced without them" (Buss, 1995, p. 1). Behavior the author regards as only a surface or "manifest" event for which something hidden or "underlying" (recall Wundt's "outworks," as opposed to the inner phenomena) must be responsible. Perhaps the author is right and perhaps he is wrong, but the statement implies that no alternatives exist. He continues, "All psychological

theories—be they cognitive, social, developmental, or clinical—imply the existence of internal psychological mechanisms . . . It is clear that no behavior can be produced in the absence of psychological mechanism" (p. 2). What is clear is that the author is not making an informed choice. He does not know what alternatives are available and takes the only position he knows, the orthodox mind-body stance. Similarly, the philosopher Searle (1998) declares, "If we know anything about how the world works, we know that the brain does produce consciousness" (p. 39).

Because the contextual interactionists receive extended treatment in other chapters as did intentionality above, a sketch here will suffice. Both Merleau-Ponty's phenomenological psychology (chapter 11) and J. R. Kantor's interbehavioral psychology (chapter 10) deal with Jenkins's objection to the behavioristic assumption of a 1-to-1 relation between stimulus and response by noting that stimulus objects have functional meanings that differ from the physical characteristics of the object; and responses have response functions that differ from the mere configuration of the response. These functional relations comprise meanings. They also emphasize that the setting and response are interdependent, and thus interaction in context is an indispensable part of the total event; and they note the importance of the medium of contact, such as light or sound. Consequently, they avoid the "exclusive focus on observable stimuli and responses" that Eysenck and Keane object to while adhering to actual events rather than to constructs. They also reject causality as linear inputs and outputs (or as inputs, mental processing, and outputs). They replace linearity with a complex of interdependent events.

Kantor puts the stimulus object and its stimulus function, along with the response and its response function, together with setting factors, medium of contact, and interactional history as a set of interrelations in a system that he calls the "interbehavioral field." The total field comprises the psychological event. The field is a construct that *derives* from the observed component events. As a part of this complex field of interactions he examines "the thought processes and strategies involved in problem solution" that Eysenck and Keane call for. Yet constructs such as mind, drive, will, motive, processing, or other determiners are never needed. Such hypothetical constructs between the individual and the world would be superfluous. The field of interactions itself comprises events from the most subtle and covert, such as imagining, to those easily observed, such as conversation. Thus, imagining is not mental and conversing bodily, nor is one cognition and the other behavior. All are interbehaviors that may be observed in some manner. For Kantor the psychological event consists of (a) the individual (b) with a personal history (c) engaged in imagining something or perceiving something (d) in some setting. This approach differs radically from the assumption of a hypothetical agent causing behavior, or that nature has divided people into inner and an outer. The emphasis in "psychological event" is on "event," and "psych-" is closer to Aristotle's *psuché* than to most meanings of psyche. We will see in the next section how contextual interactionism deals with biology.

The Chinese investigator Z.-Y. Kuo (chapter 13) developed a quite similar system confined to nonhuman animals. Probably because of his cultural background, even though he was trained in the United States, he was less inclined than native Westerners to invoke Western cultural constructs. He emphasized the interdependent stimulus object, total environment context, status of anatomical structures and their functional capacities, physiological conditions of the organism, and developmental history of the organism—all as interdependent, interacting events that comprise the animal's behavior. He imposed no hypothetical forces.

Contextual interactionists emphasize the individual in context who perceives, chooses, reasons, socializes, and learns, not an impersonal mind (or neural network, cognition, self, intervening variable, etc.) that operates his or her body. It is a person with a history of meanings, meanings comprised of interactions with things, that makes up the psychological event. Moreover, the person-object interaction is the heart of the event. Ed (in conjunction with what is to be learned), not Ed's mind, learns developmental psychology. Roberta (in conjunction with what she thinks about), not Roberta's neural network, works out a research design. Socrates (together with relevant objects and events), not Socrates' bones and muscles, decided to accept his death sentence. When John studies comparative psychology, his mind is not processing information. Instead, John as a whole person (jointly with the subject matter) is learning about animal behavior. Pat (together with substitute objects and events) is homesick for her parents; it is not her brain that is homesick. The emphasis is on events as relationships, as interactions, as interdependencies. In this approach constructs are the functional descriptions, not the causes, of those events.

Reductionism

A professor of psychology relates how an insightful student brought to his attention an inconsistency in his own assumption that some disorders were psychogenic (caused by a mind) and some somatogenic (caused by the body), while relegating them all to brain functions:

> One time a student asked: "I don't understand. Just now you said there's a difference between psychogenic and somatogenic disorders, but earlier you said that everything ultimately depends on the brain. But if that is so, why is there a difference?" Then she just looked at me. At that point, after a moment's embarrassment, I was forced to think about what reductionism is really about. (Gleitman, 1984, p. 426)

We have seen that some of the attempts to deal with mind-body dualism have involved converting mind into brain. The result is that this organ must play a biological and psychological role. The proponents of mind as brain (identity theory) or brain as the producer of mind (epiphenomenalism) or brain as the explanatory construct that must eliminate all others to be scientific (eliminativism) point to the vast literature on brain imaging, brain damage, brain ablation, and other studies that show the action of one portion or another of the brain in a great array of actions. This, they hold is evidence of the brain's containment and production of behavior (or "mental processes"). For example, "Inferences from reaction time data, recordings of event-related brain potentials, and other results of experimental observations have led to the acceptance of the idea that cognitive operations are taking place in the brains of sensing and behaving organisms" (Pribram, 1986, p. 507). Others are skeptical and observe that much brain postulation, especially in cognitive psychology, is even less direct than the imaging and extirpation studies. "Psychologists continually observe people behaving in some patterned way, only to present their observations in terms of theories postulating all manner of unobserved electrical circuitry" (Rychlak, 1993, p. 933).

Kendler (1988) tells us that for psychology to become a natural science on a par with the "hard sciences" it must be treated as a biological science. The belief that the brain produces psychological events is so endemic in psychology that it hardly needs further elaboration. It is a belief that comes out of an organocentric assumption, that the organism's actions are essentially self-caused (also called "self-acting"). The remainder of this section will treat an alternative viewpoint about the role of biology in psychology. (See chapter 3 for various views on the role of the brain in cognition and for discussion of cognitive neuroscience.) The alternative is characteristic of noncentric systems and envirocentric systems but has received the most attention from Skinner's behavior analysis (chapter 6) and from two contextual interactionists: Kuo—probabilistic epigenetic psychology (chapter 13)—and Kantor—interbehavioral psychology (chapter 10). Among the arguments against the brain doctrine are (a) the assumption of self-causation and (b) the failure to distinguish between the brain as a *necessary* condition for psychological action and the brain as a *sufficient* condition for such action.

■ *Self-causation.* If the brain causes human actions, what causes brain actions? Is the brain a patriarch, itself uncaused, issuing commands? We either have to assume that the brain is self-caused—and we have no evidence that anything in the universe is self-caused—or accept an infinite regress with no starting point and consequently no action. Various efforts to get around this have employed feedback loops and other contrivances, but are ultimately no more satisfactory. The following passage from Dewey and Bentley (1949) describes what they see as the shortcomings of both imposed constructs and self-causation.

> The "mind" as "actor," still in use in present-day psychologies and sociologies, is the old self-acting "soul" with its immortality stripped off, grown dessicated and crotchety. "Mind" or "mental," as a preliminary work in casual phrasing, is a sound word to indicate a region or at least a general locality in need of investigation; as such it is unobjectionable. "Mind," "faculty," "I.Q.," or what-not as an actor in charge of behavior is a charlatan, and "brain" as a substitute for such a "mind" is worse. Such words insert a name in place of a problem, and let it go at that; they pull out no plums, and only say, "What a big boy am I!" The old "immortal soul" in its time and in its cultural background roused dispute as to its "immortality" not as to its status as "soul." Its modern derivative, the "mind," is wholly redundant. The living, behaving, knowing organism is present. To add a "mind" to him is to try to double him up. It is double-talk; and double-talk doubles no facts. (pp. 131–132)

■ *Brain as a Necessary but Not a Sufficient Condition.* Much of the attribution of behavior to brain is a confusion of necessary and sufficient conditions. That is, the brain is *necessary* for all organismic events but it does not carry out the action alone. It is not *sufficient*. To put it another way, it *participates* in all actions but does not *determine* them. It is only one part of a complex of events that together make up causation. Consider the following examples of the role of chemistry and of biology in psychology. A disease known as phenylketonuria (PKU), an inability to metabolize phenylalanine, is a metabolic disorder that if untreated leads to intellectual retardation. Although the proper metabolism of phenylalanine is necessary for normal intellectual development, one cannot thereby conclude that intellectual development is produced by such metabolism or that intelligence is located in that metabolism.

Similarly, one cannot conclude that a deficit in speech following a brain lesion means that that part of the brain produces speech, or even that speech has a locus there. The deficit only demonstrates that the impaired part of the brain is necessary for normal speech. Many other factors are also necessary for speech, such as speech organs, a history of learning a language, and a setting where speech is appropriate. Intellectual development and all other psychological events require the entire complex of events and are not reducible to any one of them. It is important to study metabolism in PKU. Likewise, it is important to study the role of cone cells in color perception in order to understand color blindness, for without the necessary equipment color perception is impaired. But, as Socrates recognized, these participating or enabling conditions must not be lifted out of their biological relationships and given autonomous power. To turn neurons into a sufficient condition for a complex group of interacting events is to fly in the face of observation. They do not contain or produce the event. Psychological action occurs as a result of the entire complex that comprises it: the biology, the object reacted to and its evolved meaning, the context, and the individual's personal history. Together these provide sufficiency. We cannot legitimately give the brain as a necessary condition the load of the entire complex.

The brain is better understood not as an autonomous and self-caused Boss but as a complex coordinating organ, one condition that enables and participates in the occurrence of such psychological events as attending, perceiving, generalizing, and so on. The brain as a Boss is another form

of psychophysical dualism, for it explains the observed (for example, speech behavior as a physical event) with the unobserved and unobservable (mind, soul, or fictitious neurology as the psychic event). But what of the hundreds of experiments that show the action of neurons in problem solving, recalling, and other events? Do they not demonstrate that the locus of these events is in those neurons? In response to such questions or assumptions, it is important to note that no one has ever observed a color, a face, a memory, an emotion, an image, or symbol manipulation in neurons. Nor has anyone observed a neuron sending a *message* or even a *signal;* messages and signals require formulators and interpreters. What the investigators actually observe are electrochemical *impulses* or, in imaging techniques, indications of blood flow. Physiological events of chemistry, electricity, physics, and cellular interactions are the activities of the brain, and they are important to understand.

The morphological and physiological development of the C.N.S. [central nervous system] is intricately related to the ontogeny of other organs or other parts of the body and to external stimulation and other stimulative factors of the environmental context during the developmental history of the individual. Nevertheless, the behavioral epigeneticist will have no part in conventional conceptualization making the brain the seat of mind, intelligence, innate behavior, memory, learning, motivation, emotion, etc. . . . And unlike the operant behaviorist who regards the activities of the C.N.S. as irrelevant to his behavior studies, the epigeneticist believes that laboratory investigations of every part of the nervous system are a major part of his scientific responsibilities. There should be no mystery about the brain; the only mystery is that of the Western tradition of thought, which, since the ancient Greeks, has made a real myth out of the brain. To the Chinese whose thinking is still not tainted by Western culture, man's soul resides in his heart. Perhaps both are wrong . . . The C.N.S. acts merely as the excitatory, inhibitory, and coordinating center for the activities of other parts of the body in the whole gradient system of behavior. (Kuo, 1967, pp. 194–95)

Even if we assume coding rather than a picture or an emotion in the brain, we must then assume a decoder whether called feed-back loops or a homunculus. And if the decoded image of, say, a face is in the brain rather than part of person one is looking at or imagining, we have to ask what looks at the decoding. What the imaging experiments demonstrate is an increased activity of blood flow in certain brain areas when perceiving or imagining a face is occurring. It is a reasonable inference (meets the criteria for scientific constructs) that neurons in that region are sending more impulses. It is not a reasonable inference that the neurons, in turn, are recalling something. Neurons are not anthropomorphic beings. What the investigators do observe, by any number of methods in common use, is that the *individual* is perceiving something (or recalling or problem solving, etc.). It is a reasonable inference that the neurons *participate* in these events in which blood flow increases and that they may be *necessary* for the recalling to occur, but the experiments do not demonstrate *sufficiency* and they do not demonstrate images, representations, or coding.

The proponents of this contextual interactionist view of the brain give full accord to the participation of biology just as they give full accord to a personal history, social influences, the situation and other observed participants, but they do not attribute cause of the entire event to any one of them. In such a view, a psychological event is not something in the head, in the mind, in neurons, in hormones, or in DNA molecules but is comprised of the total interactional complex. Only that total complex is causality = sufficient conditions = the psychological event. But aren't psychosomatic disorders and placebos a clear indication of brain or mind-body acting on the body? In this view, biological components are part of the total interactional pattern whether they injure the body, as in so-called psychosomatic disorders, or have a healthy effect,

as in many applications of placebos—just as social and developmental factors may be injurious or healthy.

In short, this alternative to orthodoxy argues that mind-body dualism is irrelevant to psychology whether as a mysterious agent or cause or incarnated as brain. Mind in a body or body without a mind is not an observed event. What counts is the individual interacting with surrounding things and events in a context and accumulating a history of such interactions that bear on each new interaction.

We hear a similar point of view from an endocrinologist about the role of testosterone in aggression (Sapolsky, 1997). This male hormone has been blamed for male aggression, but extensive studies have shown that an elevated level of testosterone is an *effect* of the aggressive behavior, not the cause, although it can increase the level of aggression once aggression has started. Genes are involved in the regulation of testosterone, but genes operate in interrelationship with other conditions. Even if we work out the full human genome, it will not explain why any given individual behaves as he or she does, for environment and social context are interdependent with biology. Oyama (1985), a developmentalist, also rejects the "gene-environment dualism" in which genes act on the organism but are themselves self-caused. Genes are only one of many interactants, she argues. Keller (1983, 1995) and Spanier (1995) also find interactional effects, but note that the literature fails to recognize the findings and continues to report linear cause and effect (see chapter 8). A theoretical biologist points out that genes produce proteins but do little else. How these proteins play out is interdependent on numerous conditions (Goodwin, 1995).

Genes, however, may preclude normal behavior when they are defective, as in PKU, or may result in neural malfunctions that contribute to maladaptive behavioral interactions such as may be the case with attention-deficit hyperactivity disorder (Barkley, 1998); but even so, interactions with other conditions of biology and environment are no less important. The interaction may involve genes, cells, organism, context, and culture (Gottlieb, 1997). The following from an introduction to an issue of a science magazine *Discover,* is apropos. "We are more than our genes. We are our genes in a particular place and time, whole people interacting with others in an infinitely variable world. Only through that experience do we become who we are" (Zabludoff, 1998, p. 6).

Social and Environmental Reductionism. While most reductionistic attempts in psychology are biological, in recent years social constructionism (chapter 8) has led a movement to reduce psychology to social processes. For example, Stam (1990) assumes that the only alternative to mentalism or biological reductionism is social constructionism: that is, that no truth or reality exists beyond what a particular social group believes (constructs) it to be. "At the outset, psychology took itself to be the science of the mental" (p. 240); "there is still no simple way to bypass the problems of the mental, and psychology remains true, in this respect, to its intellectual heritage" (p. 241). Like Bornstein, Stam lumps together constructs and events. Consciousness, perception, and attention, he says, have received "a systematic and rigorous theoretical and empirical analysis" (p. 240). He believes that the behaviorism of Watson, Hull, and Skinner "all failed to satisfy the criteria, for a science that would take mental events seriously" (p. 241). A counter argument is that they failed in part because of a culture that believed in mental events and wanted to restore them and in part because the mechanistic character of the approaches of Watson (and to some extent Hull, who did have a mental construct as an intervening variable that he called "drives") did not take into account the complex human activities that the culture believed were mental. Stam believes that psychology must deal with the mental in terms of intentionality: "Mental phenomena include an object intentionally within themselves" and this is "exclusive to mental phenomena" (p. 240). For eco-behavioral science (chapter 7), the reduction is to the behavior setting—such as an airport terminal, chess game, workplace, class-room, and so on where we follow predictable patterns of behavior.

Conclusion. The contextual interactionists point out that all reductionistic efforts assume that what is on the surface, the behavior actually performed, is only superficial and that something more fundamental is the cause—whether it be cognitive mechanisms, neural networks, unconscious urges, motives, instincts, libido, ego, id, drives, experience, self, or social processes. Further, they note that reductionism also tends to assume the operation of single causes—such as brain or behavior setting—to assume linear cause and effect while neglecting interdependent actions. They conclude that biological reductionism is always mentalistic despite proponents' claims to avoid mentalism. It is mentalistic because it assumes that a hypothetical power causes behavior; whether we call that power mind or brain or something else hardly matters. It remains an explanatory construct not *derived from* observation but *imposed on* observation.

If we choose to follow the criterion listed on pp. 52–53 and take an adequate sample of events, the contexual interactionists say, we are less likely to reduce the multiple events of human organisms functioning in their environments to a single cause, whether that proposed cause be such *things and events* as classical conditioning, reinforcement, genes, testosterone, and social processes or whether it be such *constructs* as minds, brain powers, information processing, and Oedipus complexes. If instead we choose to follow more traditional implicit criteria of founding investigations on traditional constructs, we will continue to have a traditional psychology of mentalism and reductionism. Thus, by being informed we can base our choice both on what we know to be available and on the consequences of those choices.

Privacy and Subjectivity

An implicit and sometimes explicit tenet of cognitivism is that cognition is a private event and must be dealt with by inference. No one can know another person's mind; experience is subjective and private; and people often don't reveal their true feelings. This viewpoint arose in the seventeenth century with Descartes's treatment of the nonphysical mind as an inner private realm. It has come under attack by a number of psychologists. Kantor (1922, 1982) argued that such events as thinking, believing, and feeling are just as objective as the events of geology or chemistry. Each event in the universe is unique, whether a falling leaf or a thought, and each is equally objective. Each observation of any event has its own standpoint. I am in a position to observe a falling leaf; you are not. I am in a position to observe my own toothache; you are not. You are in a position to take a reading from a dial; I am not. Ratliff (1962) noted that a toothache is no more private to him than a light that he turns on, and Zuriff (1972) contended that loudness is private in the same way that a hiccup is. We do not attribute privacy to magma formations beneath the earth or to digestion, and we have no more reason to do so with psychological events, for these are equally concrete: "The only privacy of 'my toothache' is that the event is bounded by a framework of conditions that at this time and place it is this particular organism that is a factor in the situation" (Observer, 1973, p. 564). "Everything is public in the sense of being directly or inferentially available for observation" (Observer, 1981, p. 104). That is, one or another component of the interactions is almost always available for observation (Smith, 1993a). Kantor (1982) argues for the objectivity of subjectivity, and this is the position of Stephenson (1953) in devising his Q methodology (chapter 11) to provide objective and quantitative measures of subjectivity. In Stephenson's system the only difference between subjectivity and objectivity is that from my standpoint my response is subjective and from your standpoint that same response is objective.

According to these arguments, then, we could conclude that the criterion that all scientific constructs must be observable—at least in principle— does not rule out subjective events, those attributed to a mind. So-called privacy is not a limitation in psychology any more than in any other science, for it has no special meaning beyond the fact that all events in nature have various degrees of accessibility to observation, and all are observed from one or another viewpoint and by one or another method. Magma plumes beneath the earth, tube worms on the ocean floor, stellar explosions, DNA replication, and human imagining are all events of nature. All require special technology or methodologies to study. To divide them into private and nonprivate confers no advantage but only makes for confusion. In fact psychology may be in a better position than such sciences as physics, geology, archaeology, and astronomy which cannot obtain verbal reports from their objects of investigation. Rather than being unique in having the problem of privacy, psychology may be advantaged in having a lesser problem.

Knowability

Psychology would be of little interest if it did not attempt to advance knowledge. The empiricist tradition, in its general meaning in the sciences, holds that systematic observation and analysis of events of nature allow us to discover principles of nature, some of which are universal (e.g., gravity) and some of which are relative to a particular situation (e.g., whether we perceive a fire as warming or destructive). This has been a prominent guiding assumption of scientific and philosophical inquiry for several centuries in Western culture. British empiricism, with its specific meaning of all knowledge derived from experience, was influential in some envirocentric systems of psychology—such as behaviorism—even though behaviorists have not usually subscribed to its doctrine that experience consists of sense data. Ironically, many organocentrists, such as cognitivists, have.

Another point of view is the rationalism of continental Europe. This organocentric approach emphasizes innate organizing capacities for knowledge and has played a major role in cognitive psychology. In the tradition of Kant it contends that "there is no outside, impartial viewpoint capable of analyzing individual knowledge independent of the individual exhibiting this knowledge . . .

knowing, consciousness, and all other aspects of human experience are seen from the point of view of the experiencing subject . . . we can perceive the reality in which we live only from within our perceiving order" (Guidano, 1995, p. 94). Gergen (1994b) has attacked this position for implying that if we respond to our perceptions of the world instead of to the world itself, we have no way to begin hypothesis testing or other methods of inquiry. Similarly, the cognitivist's "cognitive mapping" or determination of mental templates of the world is problematic. Finally, because a real world is unknowable, science and knowledge cannot exist. Gergen has also attacked the empiricist tradition in science with the argument that what is taken to be empirical data is not absolute but subject to the interpretations of the particular social group that collects the data.

Gergen's (1994a) own approach to knowing, a sociocentric one, argues that knowing is totally relative to social discourse. Knowing is only what a particular social group holds to be true at a given time, and "socially constructed" knowledge has no claim to truth beyond that group. From this point of view, the law of gravity has no universality. It is only what a group of scientists have agreed upon and have given a mathematical form; its truth is confined to them. Even the statement that context is important in whether a fire means warmth or destruction carries no truth beyond the group that declares it to be true. This sociocentric system of psychology is called "social constructionism." It draws from postmodernism (chapter 8), and its proponents claim that biological organization, language conventions, and cultural processes produce our reality.

Somewhere in the middle of these views is one that attempts to avoid the definitive character of the empiricist tradition, the unknowable world of the rationalists, and the total relativism of the social constructionists. It suggests that empirical research provides limited evidence of possible causal or functional relationships, not conclusive demonstrations of such relationships. Psychological research becomes more a support to theory than a test of theory (Martin & Thompson, 1997).

Similarly, an approach called "neorealism" recognizes the social, historical, and linguistic conventions that influence decisions, interpretations, methodologies, theories, values, and other constructions used in psychology. It also holds that cultural relativism can be bridged to some extent, as evidenced by the fact that people learn to communicate across cultures, but that, because most questions in psychology are within, not across cultures, the cross-cultural question does not usually arise (Martin & Thompson, 1997).

Much of the disagreement about knowability stems from traditional philosophy's division of knowing and the known into "epistemology" and "ontology" as well as its establishment of empiricism, rationalism, and positivism, and more recently postmodernism (chapter 8)—and postmodernism's psychological offshoot, social constructionism. Beginning in Alexandrian times, thinkers set themselves apart from their surroundings and eventually called knowledge of themselves "epistemology" and their assumptions about separated reality "ontology" (Kantor, 1981a). These two major branches of modern philosophy are restatements of mind-body dualism. Epistemology asks such questions as whether other minds exist and whether knowledge of anything but one's own mind is possible (solipsism). It often assumes that the senses convey knowledge, but overlooks the organism's interactions with its surroundings (Kantor, 1981a). Ontology asks if an external world exists and if so how we can know what it is like and whether scientific findings of regularity and laws in nature are creations of humans rather than reflections of nature. These questions address cultural constructs rather than observable events. Kantor (1962) takes a no-nonsense approach to such questions:

> Such problems however, can never arise from the study of the scientist's work which plainly reveals that knowledge depends upon things, not things upon knowledge. To achieve knowledge and attain exact descriptions and explanation we must improve our contact with events . . . The spurious problems of "reality" and the existence

of an external world arise from the simple confusion of things with reactions to them. When observations are difficult, when observers are deficient (color blind), when relations between things observed and observers vary, those who are dominated by philosophic tradition conclude that observations contribute to the existence of observed things. (pp. 17–18)

Wolpert (1993) notes that the philosophers' assumption of unknowability in science would also apply to ordinary knowledge that the sun rises in the east. He warns us "not to mix up the philosophers' problems in dealing with truth, rationality and reality with the success or otherwise of science" (p. 106).

Most philosophers have looked for the basis of knowledge in such philosophical theories as empiricism, rationalism, positivism, and pragmatism, but German philosopher Martin Heidegger (1962) contends that knowing begins not in philosophy but in the social community and everyday activities. Philosophy derives from this communal knowledge, he contends, not vice-versa: philosophy is not itself a beginning point of knowledge. Similarly, John Dewey (Dewey & Bentley, 1949), an American educator, psychologist, and philosopher, maintained that knowledge has no theoretical basis at all but consists of humans in interaction with their environments, a mutual relationship of acting and being acted upon. Philosopher of science and psychologist J. R. Kantor (1962, 1981a) would also place knowing in the relationships of people with their world and reject such constructs as innate determiners, sense data, and such absolutes as total relativity.

What, then, is knowledge? Is it what springs from philosophical theories? Is it an innately structured internal representation of an external world? Is it sensations from the environment? Is it creations of a mind? Is it only whatever a social group agrees upon? Or is it the product of the interaction of people and their surroundings? Probably the only approach from which science can actually operate is to take the beginning point of knowledge as that which develops from daily contact between people and things and to take scientific knowledge as a more refined and systematized contact with things.

Analogies

Because psychology has long confused constructs with events and started its inquiry with constructs borrowed from the general culture such as inner and outer, mind and body, it has tried to deal with the resulting dilemmas not by turning to the events themselves, but by turning to even more constructs in the form of analogies. Such analogies have included parallel clocks (Leibnitz), optics (Spinoza), gravity (J. Mill), chemistry (J. S. Mill), blank tablet (Locke), vibrations (Hartley), digestion (Cabanis), chronometers (Donders), evolution (James), electrical fields (Köhler), biomechanics (Watson), and vectors (Lewin). Then came telephone switchboards, computers, holograms (Pribram), and even engine governors (Van Gelder) and vibrating doors (Ellis). Of these, computers have received, by far, the most attention.

Analogies are useful devices for clarifying an issue or for adding color or drama to an account of some event, but they are very weak as arguments. When we treat humans as if they are computers or computer programs, we treat them as what they are not (Blewitt, 1983). "Analogical inferences can only reasonably be used in cases where there are sufficient relevant similarities and no relevant differences between the cases where the projected property is known to hold and the cases where that property is being inferred to hold" (Stemmer, 1987). Seldom if ever have the analogizers applied such rigorous criteria to psychological events. Another writer notes that despite the usefulness of metaphors, they eventually break down as we draw increasingly exact parallels with the things they represent (Barton, 1994). Why do we slip into troublesome metaphors and analogies?

> When speaking and writing about ideas that cannot be proved by logical thinking or physical experience, it is inevitable that analogies and metaphors are used; and, in all discussions

of a philosophical, metaphysical or religious nature, it is necessary to remember the part played by language in the formation of concepts and beliefs. (O'Grady, 1989, p. 146).

Is this passage about the mind-body construct or brain powers? It could very well be, but it is actually about beliefs in the Devil. The principles are the same: a culturally constructed belief with concrete referent which gets developed by such verbal devices as analogy and metaphor. The author goes on to show how people react to their own construction of the Devil and build upon it. She could just as well have referred to some of psychology's dryads.

What is an alternative to psychology by analogy? Simply founding our investigations on concrete events, rather than on constructs, and thereby obviating analogies. This procedure would also provide an alternative to the mind-body construct and to biological and social reductionism. Such a remedy, however, requires that we learn to distinguish between constructs and events. Then we can use descriptions (verbal, mathematical, diagrammatic, etc.) of observed functional relationships as scientific constructs that may be validated, invalidated, or modified by further observations. Or we can continue with analogies, reductionism, imposed constructs, and the dilemmas of the past. Knowing the alternatives at least gives us a choice.

REFERENCES

Angus, S. 1975. *The Mystery-Religions: A Study in the Religious Background of Early Christianity,* 2nd ed. New York: Dover.

Bandura, Albert. 1989. Human agency in social cognitive theory. *American Psychologist* 44: 1175–84.

Barber, Theodore X. 1981. *Hypnosis: A Scientific Approach.* South Orange, NJ: Power Publishers.

Barkley, Russell A. 1998. Attention-deficit hyperactivity disorder. *Scientific American* 279 (September): 66–71.

Barnes, Harry E. 1965. *An Intellectual and Cultural History of the Western World,* 3rd rev., 3 vols. New York: Dover.

Barton, Scott. 1994. Chaos, self-organization, and psychology. *American Psychologist* 49: 5–14.

Bautier, Robert-Henri. 1971. *The Economic Development of Medieval Europe.* London: Thames and Hudson.

Bem, Sacha, & Huib Looren de Jong. 1997. *Theoretical Issues in Psychology: An Introduction.* London: Sage.

Bhawe, S. S. 1960. *The Soma-Hymns of the Rig-Veda: A Fresh Interpretation, Part II.* Baroda, India: Oriental Institute.

Blewitt, Edward. 1983. The computer analogy in psychology: Memory as interbehaviour or information processing? In *Reassessment in Psychology: The Interbehavioral Alternative.* Edited by N. W. Smith, P. T. Mountjoy, & D. H. Ruben. Lanham, MD: University Press of America.

Bornstein, Robert F. 1988. Radical behaviorism, internal states, and the science of psychology: A reply to Skinner. *American Psychologist* 43: 819–21.

Brandon, S. G. F., ed. 1963. *The Saviour God.* Manchester, England: Manchester University Press.

———. 1969. *Religions in Ancient History.* New York: Scribner's.

Bremmer, Jan. 1983. *The Early Greek Concept of the Soul.* Princeton, NJ: Princeton University Press.

Buss, David M. 1995. Evolutionary psychology: A new paradigm for psychological science. *Psychological Inquiry* 6: 1–30.

Cairns, Huntington. 1961. Introduction. In *The Collected Dialogues of Plato Including the Letters.* Translated and edited by Edith Hamilton & Huntington Cairns. New York: Pantheon Books.

Clark, James M., & Allan Paivio. 1989. Observational and theoretical terms in psychology. *American Psychologist* 44: 500–512.

Clottes, Jean. 1996. Thematic changes in upper palaeolithic art: A view from the Grotte Chauvet. *Antiquity* 70: 276–88.

Cole, K. C. 1983. The forces of nature. *Discover* (August): 32–33.

Denmark, Florence L. 1980. Psyche: From rocking the cradle to rocking the boat. *American Psychologist* 35: 1057–65.

Dewey, John. 1896. The reflex arc concept in psychology. *Psychological Review* 31: 357–70.

Dewey, John, & Arthur F. Bentley. 1949. *Knowing and the Known.* Boston: Beacon Press.

Ebel, Robert L. 1974. And still the dryads linger. *American Psychologist* 29: 485–92.

Eccles, John, & Daniel. N. Robinson. 1984. The wonder of being human: Our brain and our mind. New York: Free Press.

Eliade, Mircea. 1954. *The Myth of the Eternal Return: Cosmos and History.* Princeton, NJ: Princeton University Press.

Ellis, R. D. 1995. *Questioning Consciousness: The Interplay of Imagery, Cognition, and Emotion in the Human Brain.* Philadelphia: John Benjamins.

English, Horace B., & Ava C. English. 1958. *A Comprehensive Dictionary of Psychological and Psychoanalytic Terms: A Guide to Usage.* New York: Longmans, Green.

Estes, William K. 1989. William K. Estes. In *History of Psychology in Autobiography,* vol. 3. Edited by G. Lindzey. Stanford, CA: Stanford University Press.

Everson, Stephen. 1997. *Aristotle on Perception.* Oxford, England: Clarendon Press.

Eysenck, Michael W., & Mark T. Keane. 1990. *Cognitive Psychology: A Student's Handbook.* Hove and London: Erlbaum Associates.

Fortes, Meyer. 1949. *The Web of Kinship among the Tallensi: Second Part of an Analysis of the Social Structure of a Trans-Volta Tribe.* London: Oxford University Press, International African Institute.

———. 1965. Some reflections on ancestor worship in Africa. In *African Systems of Thought: Studies Presented and Discussed at the Third International African Seminar in Salisbury.* Edited by Meyer Fortes & Germain Dieterlen. London: Oxford University Press.

Gergen, Kenneth J. 1985. The social constructionist movement in modern psychology. *American Psychologist* 40: 266–75.

———. 1994a. The limits of pure critique. In *After Postmodernism: Reconstructing Ideology Critique.* Edited by Herbert W. Simons & Michael Billig. London: Sage.

———. 1994b. *Relations and Relationships: Soundings in Social Construction.* Cambridge, MA: Harvard University Press.

Gleitman, Henry. 1984. Introducing psychology. *American Psychologist* 39: 421–27.

Goodwin, Brian C. 1995. *How the Leopard Changed Its Spots: The Evolution of Complexity.* London: Phoenix Giants.

Gottlieb, Gilbert. 1997. Synthesizing Nature-Nurture: Prenatal Roots of Instinctive Behavior. Mahwah, NJ: Erlbaum.

Granet, Marcel. 1975/1922. *The Religion of the Chinese People.* Edited and translated by Maurice Freedman. New York: Harper & Row.

Green, Peter. 1990. *Alexander to Actium: The Historical Evolution of the Hellenistic Age.* Berkeley: University of California.

Grossberg, John M. 1972. Brain wave feedback experiments and the concept of mental mechanism. *Journal of Behavioral Therapy and Experimental Psychiatry* 3: 245–51.

Guidano, Vittorio F. 1995. Constructivist psychotherapy: A theoretical framework. In *Constructivism in Psychotherapy.* Edited by Robert A. Neimeyer & Michael J. Mahoney. Washington, DC: American Psychological Association.

Haydon, A. Eustace. 1967. *Biography of the Gods.* New York: Ungar.

Heidegger, Martin. 1962. *Being and Time.* New York: Harper & Row.

Hicks, Harry H., & Robert N. Anderson. 1991. Analysis of Indo-European Vedic Aryan head—4th millennium B. C. *Journal of Indo-European Studies* 18: 425–46.

Hultkrantz, Åke. 1953. *Conceptions of the Soul among North American Indians: A Study in Religious Ethnology.* Stockholm: The Ethnological Museum of Sweden.

James, E. O. 1960. *The Ancient Gods: The History and Diffusion of Religion in the Ancient Near East and the Mediterranean.* New York: Putnam.

———. 1961. *Seasonal Feasts and Festivals.* New York: Barnes & Noble.

Jenkins, James J. 1974. Remember that old theory of memory? Well, forget it! *American Psychologist* 29: 785–95.

———. 1993. What counts as behavior? *Journal of Mind and Behavior* 14: 353–64.

Kantor, J. R. 1922. Can the psychophysical experiment reconcile introspectionists and objectivists? *American Journal of Psychology* 32: 481–510.

———. 1938. The operational principle in the physical and psychological sciences. *Psychological Record* 2: 3–32.

———. 1957. Events and constructs in the science of psychology; Philosophy: Banished and recalled. *Psychological Record* 7: 55–60.

———. 1962. *The Logic of Modern Science.* Chicago: Principia Press.

———. 1963. *The Scientific Evolution of Psychology,* vol. 1. Chicago: Principia Press.

———. 1969. *The Scientific Evolution of Psychology,* vol. 2 Chicago: Principia Press.

———. 1973. Segregation in science: An historico-cultural analysis. *Psychological Record* 23: 335–42.

———. 1978. Cognition as events and as psychic constructions. *Psychological Record* 28: 329–42.

———. 1979. Wundt, experimental psychology and natural science. *Revista Mexican de Análisis de la Conducta* 5: 117–29.

———. 1981a. *Interbehavioral Philosophy.* Chicago: Principia Press.

———. 1981b. Interbehavioral psychology and the logic of science. *Psychological Record* 31: 3–11.

———. 1982. Objectivity and subjectivity in science and psychology. *Revista Mexicana de Análisis de la Conducta* 8: 3–10.

———. 1983. Explanation: Psychological nature, role in scientific investigation. *Revista Mexicana de Análisis de la Conducta* 9: 29–38.

Kantor, J. R., & N. W. Smith. 1975. *The Science of Psychology: An Interbehavioral Survey*. Chicago: Principia.

Keller, Evelyn F. 1983. *A Feeling for the Organism: The Life and Work of Barbara McClintock*. San Francisco: Freeman.

———. 1995. *Reflections on Gender and Science*. New Haven, CT: Yale University Press.

Kendler, Howard H. 1988. Behavioral determinism: A strategic assumption? *American Psychologist* 43: 822–23.

Kojima, Hideo, 1984. A significant stride toward the comparative study of control. *American Psychologist* 49: 972–73.

Kosslyn, Stephen M. 1983. *Ghosts in the Mind's Machine: Creating and Using Images in the Brain*. New York: Norton.

———. 1995. *Image and Brain: The Resolution of the Imagery Debate*. Cambridge, MA: MIT Press.

Kukla, Andre. 1989. Nonempirical issues in psychology. *American Psychologist* 44: 785–94.

Kuo, You-yuh. 1976. Chinese dialectical thought and character. In *Contributions to Human Development*. Edited by J. F. Rychlak. Basel, Switzerland: Karger.

Kuo, Zing-yang. 1967. *The Dynamics of Behavior Development: An Epigenetic View*. New York: Random House.

Kuo, Zing-yang, & Yut-hang Lam. 1968. Chinese religious behavior and the deification of Mao Tse-Tung. *Psychological Record* 18: 455–68.

La Mettrie, Julien O. de. 1912/1748. *Man a Machine*. Translated by G. C. Bussey & M. W. Calkins. Chicago: Open Court.

Leahey, Thomas H. 1987. *A History of Psychology: Main Currents in Psychological Thought,* 2nd ed. Englewood Cliffs, NJ: Prentice-Hall.

Lewin, Kurt. 1951. *Field Theory in Social Science: Selected Theoretical Papers*. Edited by Dorwin Cartwright. New York: Harper.

Lewis, C. S. 1960. *Studies in Words*. Cambridge, England: Cambridge University Press.

Lichtenstein, Parker E. (1984). Interbehaviorism in psychology and in the philosophy of science. *Psychological Record* 34: 455–75.

Lienhardt, Godfrey. 1961. *Divinity and Experience*. London: Oxford University Press.

Lucretius. 1951. *On the Nature of the Universe = De Rerum Natura*. Translated by R. E. Latham. Harmondsworth, England: Penguin Books.

MacCorquodale, Kenneth, & Paul E. Meehl. 1951. Operational validity of intervening constructs. In *Psychological Theory*. Edited by Melvin H. Marx. New York: Macmillan.

Mahner, Martin, & Mario A. Bunge. 1998. *Foundations of Biopsychology*. Berlin, Germany: Springer.

Mahoney, Michael J. 1977. Reflections on the cognitive learning trend in psychotherapy. *American Psychologist* 32: 5–13.

Mandler, George. 1985. *Cognitive Psychology: An Essay in Cognitive Science*. Hillsdale, NJ: Erlbaum.

Manicus, Peter T., & Paul F. Secord. 1983. Implications for psychology of the new philosophy of science. *American Psychologist* 38: 399–413.

Marr, Jack. 1983. Memory: Models and metaphors. *Psychological Record* 33: 12–19.

Martin, Jack, & Janice Thompson. 1997. Between scientism and relativism: Phenomenology, hermeneutics and the new realism in psychology. *Theory and Psychology* 7: 629–52.

Maruyama, M. 1974. Paradigmatology and its applications to cross disciplinary, cross professional, and cross cultural communication. *Cybernetica* 171: 135–56, 237–81.

Maspero, Henri. 1978. *China in Antiquity*. Translated by Frank A. Kierman. Amherst: University of Massachusetts.

Modrak, Deborah K. W. 1987. *Aristotle: The Power of Perception*. Chicago: University of Chicago Press.

Murray, Gilbert. 1955. *Five Stages of Greek Religion*. Garden City, NJ: Doubleday.

Murtonen, A. The living soul: A study of the meaning of the word *naefaes* in the Old Testament Hebrew language. *Studia Orientalia* 23: 3–105.

Natalicio, Luiz. 1985. Behaviorism at seventy: Implications for a philosophy of science of psychology. *Revista Interamericana de Psicologia* 19: 1–18.

Observer. 1973. Private data, raw feels, inner experience, and all that. *Psychological Record* 23: 563–65.

———. 1981. Concerning the principle of psychological privacy. *Psychological Record* 311: 101–106.

———. 1983. Meanings as events and as constructions in psychology and linguistics. *Psychological Record* 33: 433–40.

O'Grady, Joan. 1989. *The Prince of Darkness: The Devil in History, Religion and the Human Psyche*. New York: Barnes & Noble.

Oppenheim, A. Leo. 1964. *Ancient Mesopotamia: Portrait of a Dead Civilization*. Chicago: University of Chicago Press.

Oyama, Susan. 1985. *The Ontology of Information: Developmental Systems and Evolution*. Cambridge, England: Cambridge University Press.

Petzold, Matthias. 1987. The social history of Chinese psychology. In *Psychology in Twentieth-Century Thought and Society*. Edited by Mitchell G. Ash & William R. Woodward. Cambridge, England: Cambridge University.

———. 1994. Chinese psychology under political pressure: A comment on Guoan Yue. *Theory and Psychology* 4: 277–79.

Plato. *The Dialogues of Plato, 4th ed., 4 vols. Translated by* B. Jowett. Oxford: Clarendon Press.

Plotinus. *1954.* First to Fifth Enneads. Translated by Stephen MacKenna. Boston: Branford.

Popper, Karl R., & John C. Eccles. 1977. The self and its brain. Berlin, Germany: Springer-Verlag.

Porphyry. 1934. On the life of Plotinus and the arrangement of his work. In *The Essence of Plotinus, Extracts from the Six Enneads and Porphyry's Life of Plotinus.* Translated by Stephen McKenna. New York: Oxford University Press.

Posner, Michael I., & Marcus E. Raichle. 1994. Images in Mind. New York: Scientific American Library.

Pribram, Karl H. 1986. The cognitive revolution and mind/brain issues. *American Psychologist* 41: 507–520.

Randall, John H. 1960. *Aristotle.* New York: Columbia University Press.

———. 1970a. *Hellenistic Ways of Deliverance and the Making of the Christian Synthesis.* New York: Columbia University Press.

———. 1970b. *Plato: Dramatist of the Life of Reason.* New York: Columbia University Press.

Ratliff, Floyd. 1962. Some interrelations among physics, physiology, and psychology in the study of vision. In *Psychology: A Study of a Science,* vol. 4. Edited by Sigmund Koch. New York: McGraw-Hill.

Robinson, Daniel N. (1986). *An Intellectual History of Psychology.* Madison: University of Wisconsin Press.

Rostovtseff, M. I. 1938–1939. The Mentality of the Greek world and the afterlife. *Harvard University Divinity School Bulletin: 5–25.*

———. *1957.* The Social and Economic History of the Roman Empire, 2nd rev. ed., 2 vols. Oxford: Clarendon Press.

Rychlak, Joseph F. 1993. A suggested principle of complementarity for psychology. *American Psychologist* 48: 933–42.

Saliba, J. A. 1976. Religion and the anthropologist, part 1. *Anthropologia* 18: 179–208.

Sapolsky, Robert M. 1997. *The Trouble with Testosterone and Other Essays on the Human Predicament.* New York: Scribner.

Sarton, George. 1959. *A History of Science: Hellenistic Science and Culture in the Last Three Centuries B. C.* New York: Wiley.

Searle, John. 1992. *The Rediscovery of Mind.* Cambridge, MA: MIT Press.

———. 1998. God, mind, and artificial intelligence. *Free Inquiry* 18 (4): 39–41.

Shapiro, Yanina. 1997. The consciousness hype: What do we want explained? *Theory and Psychology* 7: 837–56.

Shute, Clarence. 1944. *The Psychology of Aristotle.* New York: Columbia University Press.

Simon, Herbert. 1992. What is an "explanation" of behavior? *Psychological Science* 3: 150–61.

Singer, Charles. 1959. *A Short History of Scientific Ideas to 1900.* London: Oxford University Press.

Skinner, B. F. 1963. Behaviorism at fifty. *Science* 149: 951–58.

Smith, Noel W. 1971. Aristotle's dynamic approach to sensing. *Journal of the History of the Behavioral Sciences* 7: 375–77.

———. 1974. The ancient background to Greek psychology. *Psychological Record* 24: 309–324.

———. 1977). Aristotle. *International Encyclopedia of Psychiatry, Psychology, and Neurology,* vol. 6. New York: Van Nostrand.

———. 1983. Sensing is perceiving: An alternative to the doctrine of the double world. In *Greek and Interbehavioral Psychology: Selected and Revised Papers,* 2nd ed. Edited by N. W. Smith. Lanham, MD: University Press of America.

———. 1985. Belief systems—A psychological analysis. *Mankind Quarterly* 25: 195–225.

———. 1989. Indo-European psychological concepts and the shift to psychophysical dualism. *Mankind Quarterly* 30: 119–27.

———. 1990a. The evolution of psychophysical dualism in ancient India: From the Rig Veda to the Sutras. *Mankind Quarterly* 31: 1–15.

———. 1990b. Psychological concepts under changing social conditions in ancient Egypt. *Mankind Quarterly* 30: 317–27.

———. 1992. *Ice Age Art: Its Psychology and Belief System.* New York and Berne: Peter Lang.

———. 1993a. Alternatives to recurring problems in psychology. In *Greek and Interbehavioral Psychology: Selected and Revised Papers,* 2nd ed. Edited by N. W. Smith. Lanham, MD: University Press of America.

———. 1993b. Introduction. In *Greek and Interbehavioral Psychology: Selected and Revised Papers,* 2nd ed. Edited by N. W. Smith. Lanham, MD: University Press of America.

———. 1997. Consciousness: Event or construct? In *Investigations in Behavioral Epistemology.* Edited by Linda J. Hayes & Patrick M. Ghezzi. Reno, NV: Context Press.

Smith, Stevenson, & Edwin R. Guthrie. 1921. *General Psychology in Terms of Behavior.* New York: Appleton-Century-Crofts.

Sorabji, Richard. 1972. *Aristotle on Memory.* Providence, RI: Brown University Press.

Spanier, Bonnie. 1995. *Im/Partial Science: Gender Ideology in Molecular Biology.* Bloomington: Indiana University Press.

Sperry, R. W. 1988. Psychology's mentalist paradigm and the religion/science tension. *American Psychologist* 43:607–613.

———. 1993. The impact and promise of the cognitive revolution. *American Psychologist* 48: 878–85.

Spiro, M. E. 1976. Religion: Problems of definition and explanation. In *Anthropological Approaches to the Study of Religion.* Edited by Michael Banton. London: Tavistock.

Stam, Henderikus J. 1990. Rebuilding the ship at sea: The historical and theoretical problems of constructionist epistemologies in psychology. *Canadian Journal of Psychology* 31: 239–53.

Stemmer, Nathan. 1987. The hypothesis of other minds: Is it the best explanation? *Philosophical Studies* 51: 109–151.

Stephenson, William. 1953. *The Study of Behavior: Q-Technique and Its Methodology.* Chicago: University of Chicago Press.

Tolman, Charles. 1987. Dialectical materialism as psychological metatheory. *The Analysis of Psychological Theory: Metapsychological Perspectives.* Edited by S. Hendrikus, T. B. Rogers, & K. J. Gergen. New York: Hemisphere.

———. 1994. What is living and what is dead in Aristotle's psychology. *Theory and Psychology* 4: 433–36.

Tolman, Edward C. 1936. Operational behaviorism and current trends in psychology. *Proceedings of the 25th Anniversary Celebration of the Inauguration of Graduate Studies.* Los Angeles: University of Southern California Press.

Turcan, Robert. 1996. *The Cults of the Roman Empire.* Oxford: Blackwell.

Van Gelder, T. 1995. What might cognition be, if not computation? *Journal of Philosophy* 91: 345–81.

Vendler, Zeno. 1984. *The Matter of Minds.* Oxford: Clarendon.

Wade, N. 1982. The Editorial Notebook: Smart apes, or dumb? *New York Times,* April 30.

Walbank, F. W. 1993. *The Hellenistic World,* rev. ed. Cambridge, MA: Harvard University Press.

Wasserman, Edward A. 1983. Is cognitive psychology behavioral? *Psychological Record* 33: 6–30.

Watanabe, M. 1974. The conception of nature in Japanese culture. *Nature* 183: 279–82.

Watson, John B. 1913. Psychology as the behaviorist views it. *Psychological Review* 20: 158–77.

———. 1919. *Psychology from the Standpoint of a Behaviorist.* Philadelphia: Lippincott.

Wile, D. B. 1977. Questioning Sperry's bridge from brain to mind to value. *American Psychologist* 32: 987–89.

Wolpert, Lewis. 1993. *The Unnatural Nature of Science.* Cambridge, MA: Harvard University Press.

Woodbridge, Frederick J. E. 1901. Consciousness, the sense organs, and the nervous system. *Journal of Philosophy, Psychology, and Scientific Method* 10: 5–15.

Yue, Guoan. 1994. More on Chinese theoretical psychology: A rejoinder to Matthias Petzold. *Theory and Psychology* 4: 281–83.

Zabkar, L. V. 1968. *A Study of the Ba Concept in Ancient Egyptian Texts,* vol. 34 in *Studies in Ancient Oriental Civilization.* Chicago: The Oriental Institute of the University of Chicago.

Zabludoff, Marc. 1998. Fear and longing. *Discover* (May): 6.

Zuriff, G. E. 1972. A behavioral interpretation of psychophysical scaling. *Behaviorism* 1: 118–33.

Organocentric Systems

CHAPTER 3

Cognitive Psychology: Mentalism, Computer Analogies, and a Double World

INTRODUCTION

The student who begins reading psychology textbooks will soon encounter statements about human information processing. The texts state that information from the outside world comes into the organism through the senses and is processed by the nervous system or the cognitive system. If the texts subscribe fully to the cognitive position, they will say that internal encoders, decoders, retrieval mechanisms, attenuators, feedback loops, storage systems, and so on are the mechanisms of the nervous system. In effect, according to this system, the human organism, especially the nervous system, is much like a computer program. The student will recognize terminology that draws heavily from these devices. In addition to computer similarities, the texts also tell the student that the neural computer-like mechanisms provide a representation of the outer world.

This approach returns psychology to an earlier focus on the constructs (see chapter 2, p. 54) "mind" and "higher mental processes," and these constructs are what the term "cognition" embraces. Usually it ties mind into brain under one or another theory and seeks to find structures of mind that can be represented as computer-like flow diagrams, although a number of recent theories have departed from this and moved to connectionist networks (see p. 83) and other constructions. Cognitivism deals with perception, learning, memory, language, thinking, and imagining but gives less attention to other activities—such as emotion, abnormality, personality, or individual differences. Learning and memory, especially, have been mainstays of its research and theory; but attention, perception, problem solving, thinking, and imagining are also considered. Sometimes two forms of cognitivism are recognized: One form maintains that *all* psychological events have a cognitive component; the other confines the subject to symbolic thought and therefore excludes memory, perception, thinking, and so on. Both forms assume that our perception of the world is not just a function of a stimulus but also of mental structures that determine the perception and give it its characteristics.

A few other systems such as operant subjectivity (chapter 11), interbehaviorism (chapter 10), and ecological perception (chapter 13) have given attention to cognitive behavior but have not used such constructs as processing, mind, consciousness, brain causation, and inner representation. These constructs are typical of cognitive psychology and differentiate it from other approaches to cognition.

The cognitive system has become dominant in psychology during the last half of the twentieth century. Its viewpoint (actually a diversity of viewpoints) fills the pages of technical journals and books, both experimental and theoretical, as well as the textbooks. It has so permeated American psychology with the construct of information processing as analogous to a computer that one might expect the public to associate the word psychology with the study of humans as computers. Yet the popular association seems to remain Freud and psychoanalysis.

Because cognitive psychology looms so large, it necessarily generates criticism and diversity of viewpoints both within and outside its ranks. In fact, it is hardly a single system but many that are loosely related. In addition, *cognitive science* has come on the scene with its multidisciplinary approach, of which cognitive psychology is but one component, although the boundary between the two is not distinct. Such topics as psycholinguistics, philosophy, anthropology, neuropsychology, and computer science, are a part of cognitive science (Hunt, 1989), and all receive varying degrees of attention in cognitive psychology as well; but cognitive science gives much more attention to seeking human-like characteristics in computers (AI or artificial intelligence) as well as computer-like characteristics in humans. Garfield (1990b) finds fundamental disputes an ongoing part of cognitive science. But he also sees a methodological unity in (a) the interest in discovering the characteristics of intelligent behaviors, (b) "the notion" that the manipulation of symbolic representations makes intelligent behavior possible, (c) the descriptions of these operations as computations, and (d) the search for the transaction of these processes in brains. No special distinction will be made here between cognitive psychology and cognitive science. Both will be referred to as "cognitivism." Wallace (1996) sees just two unifying features—the assumptions that (a) mental representations are involved in all cognition, and (b) the computer analogy is the best approach to understanding these representations.

EARLY DEVELOPMENT AND SOME ISSUES

Behaviorism and Cognitivism

When John Watson (1913) set forth his behaviorism in 1913 it was a "methodological behaviorism." He did not deny mind, he simply advocated that psychology could safely ignore it. That is, its *methodology* would not include mind. In 1919 he denied the existence of mind, espousing "radical behaviorism." (Skinner gave the term a somewhat different meaning, see chapter 6.) Methodological behaviorism retained mind in a number of substitute forms, such as drives (Hull), cognitive maps (Tolman), and other "intervening variables," unobserved causal agents intervening between stimulus and response. But both methodological and radical behaviorism studied mostly learning and gave little attention to thinking, imagining, and other cognitive behaviors. And much of the study of learning was mechanistic, employing constructs of conditioning and reinforcement. As the decades wore on and journals filled with these studies, the promise that behaviorism would begin with simple animal conditioning and progress to the most complex human behaviors remained stalled at the animal starting box. (Skinner's behaviorism, called behavior analysis, has extended much further than methodological behaviorism.)

Despite this failure to achieve stated goals, these classical forms of behaviorism amassed a great deal of information about learning, some of which still makes its way into introductory psychology textbooks as part of a rather standard body of knowledge of psychology. They also de-

veloped a highly sophisticated methodology and application of statistics. When cognitive psychology came on the scene, it introduced both continuities and a discontinuity.

Continuities:

■ It adopted the statistics and methodology of behaviorism, rejected its mechanistic classical conditioning approach, and substituted another, more high-tech mechanism—the computer.

■ It continued behaviorism's stimulus and response mechanisms as input and output mechanisms.

■ The information processing brain that cognitivism posited offered continuity with methodological behaviorism's emphasis on variables such as drives, mental maps, brain powers that intervene between the stimulus and response, the S—O—R construct, as it is sometimes written.

■ It continued behaviorism's procedures of deducing hypotheses from theory (the hypothetico-deductive method) and of emphasizing learning and memory.

■ It continued methodological behaviorism's practice of using operational definitions for its constructs—that is, a response (an operation) defines a mental construct.

■ It continued the behavioristic belief in hierarchies but changed the hierarchy from simple conditional responses whose hierarchies produce complex behaviors to one in which complex mental processes are "compounded from the more elementary ones" (Simon & Newell, 1964, p. 290). Leahy (1992) sees no essential difference between methodological behaviorism and cognitive psychology.

Discontinuity:

■ It discarded non-human animals[1] as subjects and made brain/mind central to *programs* of information processing. In giving centrality to brain as a psychological organ and ignoring the stimulus (except as inputs) and the response

---

1. Animal studies are beginning to become a factor in cognitivism (for example, Roitblat & Meyer, 1995).

(except as outputs) it emphasized *internal causality* as opposed to S → R behaviorism's *external causality*. This important discontinuity is due to the fact that cognitivism and behaviorism each draw from a different philosophical tradition. Cognitivism draws from German rationalism, in which innate organizing capacities determine mental events, and from the mind-body dualism of the seventeenth-century French philosopher René Descartes (Wallace, 1996). In contrast, behaviorism draws from British empiricism, in which the environment determines behavior. But when cognitivism borrowed behaviorism's methodological assumptions, it stepped partly into the empiricist camp as well.

An interest in cognitive events was not new to psychology. Meyering (1989) attributes to Helmholtz, a pioneering nineteenth-century German physiologist, the origin of the assumption that a mind makes order out of sensory material. As a cultural concept, the belief in an ordering mind or soul comes down to us from theologians of the Hellenistic and Roman periods and thus has less than scientific beginnings (Kantor, 1963). In addition to Helmholtz, others in the nineteenth century attempted to connect cognition with mentalism: Fechner's psychophysics (mind and physical stimulus), Wundt's concern with psychic causality, Donder's mental chronometry, etc. In the late nineteenth and earlier twentieth century came the rise of structuralism, functionalism, Gestalt psychology, associationism, humanistic psychology (chapter 4), and Tolman's brand of methodological behaviorism (i.e., the theory that rats used hypothetical mental maps to find the way through mazes)—all emphasizing mentalistic cognitivism. Besides Tolman's maps, other methodological behaviorists had their own intervening variables such as drives and brain powers. Also in the twentieth century there arose the nonmentalistic approaches to cognitive events mentioned above.

Many cognitivists have continued the behavioristic tradition of conducting research in the laboratory by experimenting with groups of subjects and using traditional statistical analyses of group means (R methodology; see chapter 11) while others have turned their laboratories into facilities for physiological studies connected with "mental processes." Still others have turned to computer modeling and mathematics for theory development, and a few have combined two or more procedures. They also continue some of the earlier assumptions of the introspectionists but without attempting to introspect on the mind (Neisser, 1976). That is, they assume a mostly internal mechanism and largely ignore interactions with the world.

Some Major Early Contributors

Cognitive psychology draws from a number of sources. One of these is communications engineering, especially the work of Shannon (1948). He referred to information as the electrical changes that occurred in telephone transmission and described the changes mathematically. When a system has one of two possible states and the state of one depends on the other, an observer can discover something about the non-present state from the one that is present. In other words, "information" meant the structural characteristic of the message. Although Shannon's work was important in designing communication systems and computers, it had little utility for understanding human knowledge. Weaver (1949) was explicit that "information" as used by engineers had no connection with human knowledge. Even so, the engineering usage reinforced interest in the construct of information as a fundamental process in humans alone and in the structures that accommodate information processing. In this formulation psychology was simply following in the long tradition that began with its philosophical predecessors, trying to understand its subject matter by analogy (see chapter 2, p. 67).

It was Herbert Simon who pioneered the idea that computers could be programmed to imitate human cognition. Through his background in political science and administration, he had developed an interest in decision making in organizations, and he extended this to humans. Together with colleagues he provided computer simulations of problem solving (Newell, Shaw, & Simon, 1958; Newell & Simon, 1961); expanded this to perception, verbal learning, and concept formation; and drew strong parallels between humans and computers (Simon & Newell, 1964). Another important landmark was Chomsky's (1959) review of Skinner's book *Verbal Behavior* and his argument that language was not just a matter of learning but required internal constructs.

Piaget (Furth, 1981) also contributed to the search for mental structures. Drawing from his background in biology, he proposed the analogy that mind goes through progressive qualitative stages just as an embryo's structures change qualitatively. Another seminal figure was Ulrich Neisser (1967) who promoted the information processing construct and was influential in establishing cognitive psychology as a dominant system. He held that experience is produced by the person. A page of print is a remote stimulus, while the pattern of light rays striking the retina comprise a more direct ("proximal") stimulus. But even the more direct stimulus is unlike the real object that produced it and unlike the constructed experience, all of which is information processed by the brain. In other words, we don't interact with the page of print. Instead, our brains reconstruct the page as inputs, pass them from one processing system to the next, and provide a representation of the page as a sort of internal image that only *appears to be* the page of print "out there." Neisser's book presented the earliest general coverage of cognitive psychology. He later modified his position and gave a greater role to the environment as influenced by the ecological approach of Gibson (Neisser, 1976; see chapter 13, p. 374).

CONCEPTS, ISSUES, AND RESEARCH

"Cognition" refers to knowledge, and cognitive psychology directs its efforts toward understanding the mechanisms involved in human knowing.

In general, the system advances the following propositions:

(a) The environment comes to the organism by way of energies. These energies serve as signals that are detected by the sense organs. This is the beginning of knowledge.

(b) Learning is also a method of acquiring knowledge, and this is an encoding process.

(c) The encoded knowledge is stored in brain circuitry.

(d) When the knowledge is retrieved from storage, it is decoded. This knowledge, according to one major theory, is an *internal representation* of the outer world and occurs in two forms:

　(1) a perception-based form consisting of representations or images of sights, sounds, smells, tastes, and tactual qualities

　(2) a memory of episodes abstractly representing principles or meanings of things, such as scientific concepts or grammatical rules of a language.

(e) The knowledge may be further processed by converting to language that follows the grammatical rules.

From these characteristics we can identify four main constructs in representational cognitivism:

(a) The human organism is an information processor that converts the world into symbols.

(b) The symbols, after further processing, are representations of that world.

(c) The processing and representations are produced by neurons in the brain.

(d) The locus of cognition is in the systems of internal states or processing mechanisms, while its relations with the environment are limited to inputs for processing.

Although not all cognitivists would fully accept all these assumptive constructs, and some might entirely reject one or more, they reflect the tenor of much of cognitive psychology.

In contrast with Skinner (who assumed that the principle of reinforcement and its particulars could embrace much of psychological behavior) or with Hull (who assumed that learning could be understood entirely in terms of drive reduction) the cognitivists assume that a great many principles from many research areas are involved in psychological theory. As part of the behavioristic legacy, cognitivism theory is often tested with research. For that reason, this chapter does not list research in a separate section but describes it in connection with theory.

Three Theoretical Approaches about Representations

Computations and Mental Representations.
Cognitivists often use such terms as information processing, mental computations, symbol manipulating, and rule-following interchangeably. Usually these are said to involve or result in mental representations. Deciding, remembering, thinking, and other cognitions are processes that operate on representations. The world is represented internally in symbolic form. This construct of representation can be quite thoroughgoing:

> We have no direct *immediate* access to the world, nor to any of its properties . . . Whatever we know about reality has been *mediated,* not only by the organs of sense but by complex systems which interpret and reinterpret sensory information. (Neisser, 1967, p. 3)

> Naively, it seems to us that the outside world, the world around us, is a given; it is just there . . . We all feel as if our experiencing of the world around us were quite direct. However, the apparent immediacy of this experience *has* to be more or less illusory because we know that every bit of our information about external things is coming in through our sense organs, or has come in through our sense organs at some time in the past. All of it, to the best of our knowledge, is mediated by receptor activity and is relayed to the brain in the form of Morse code signals, as it were, so that what we experience as the "real world" and locate outside ourselves cannot possibly be anything better than a

> *representation* of the external world. (Attneave, 1974, p. 493)

In other words, according to these cognitivists, the world that seems so real to us is no more than an illusion. We live in a double world, an internal illusory world that we know and an external real world that we don't know. Attneave asserts, following the passage quoted above, that there is no possibility that this view can be wrong. More recently Buss (1995) has claimed that psychologists don't usually know that behavior is only a manifestation, a surface event, that requires a variety of cognitive mechanisms in order to be produced and that cannot occur without them.

The symbolic representations of the world are mental events between the two physical events of "sensing energy and using nerve impulses to release the energy for muscle contractions" (Johnson-Laird, 1993, p. xiii). Two major ways (and some variations) have been proposed in which the world is internally represented by our computer brains. One of these consists of images from a particular sense modality. The modality that gets the lion's share of attention is vision, but proponents hold that the representation could be from any sense modality: odor (for example, lilacs in bloom) or sound ("The Star Spangled Banner"). These images are analogs of the actual object or occurrence and are called "analogical representations." The second kind of representation is called "propositional representation." These are not restricted to any sense modality but are language-like. They consist of ideas and follow rules for combining together. It should be noted that cognitivists who are "eliminativists" insist that no representations exist, only brain functions. They *eliminate* representations. One version of this position is called "identity" theory because it holds that brain function and mind are identical. The "non-eliminativists" argue for the reality of representations that brain functions produce. This is also called "epiphenomenalism" or "emergentism": representations arise or emerge out of biological operations of the brain and are not identical with brain operations. Variations occur on these themes, and Garfield (1990a, 1990b), as a "naturalist," argues that representations are not an internal state of organism (or computer) but a relationship of organism (or computer) to the environment, just as being a parent is not an internal state but a relationship with offspring. The role of biology from this viewpoint, is to provide the capabilities—whether computational or some other mechanism for the organism—"to enter into particular kinds of relations to its environment" (1990b, p. xxiv).

Studies of the imaginative manipulation of various objects have become part of the standard body of cognitive literature that appears in most cognitive textbooks. To determine whether objects as imagined are parallel to objects in the real world, investigators (Cooper & Shepard, 1984; Shepard, 1971; Shepard & Cooper, 1982) presented subjects with pairs of three-dimensional shapes formed with cubes. The subjects saw each member of the pair in a degree of rotation different from that of the other member. The subjects' task was to decide whether the two members of the pair were the same or a different shape. The time it took to decide was proportional to the angular differences (the amount that the viewing angle of one shape was rotated further around than the other). The same was true of two-dimensional objects that rotated in one plane, like clock hands. This suggested to the authors that (a) the subjects imaginatively rotated one shape until it matched the viewing angle of the other, and (b) the imagery corresponded to actual three-dimensional objects the drawings represented in perspective and not to the flat two-dimensional drawings that were actually present. In further experiments subjects imagined a rotating shape. When a test shape (either the imagined one or a mirror image) was presented at any point of rotation that matched the shape of the imagined shape at that same point of rotation (individualized for each subject), the response time for determining whether the shape was the same or different from the imagined shape was uniform—about half a second.

Therefore, the subjects engaged in a complete imaginary rotation including intermediate angles. With these two findings, further supported by a variety of experiments, the experimenters concluded that the subjects imaginatively rotated objects in direct correspondence with real objects. They suggest that spatial imagination has evolved to correspond to structures in the physical world and become a part of innate processes, perhaps in line with the innate, uniform, grammatical structure that Chomsky believes all humans have before it gets altered into the language of the community.

Along similar lines, in a series of experiments to study imaging, the experimenters (Kosslyn, Ball, & Reiser, 1978) gave subjects a fictitious map with important objects marked by Xs and asked them to memorize the map and then draw it from memory. After they accomplished this the experimenters asked them to imagine the map and concentrate on one of the objects. Next they instructed the subjects to scan the map and find a second object. The time it took the subjects to scan from one object to another corresponded directly to the actual distance between the objects, closer objects taking less scanning time than more distant objects.

Paivio (1971, 1986) proposed one coding system for representations of images and another for verbally based symbols. Each of the two systems has subdivisions which send references from one system to the other—such as between an object and the word for the object. In one of Paivio's (Paivio & Csapo, 1973) experimental tests, he presented subjects with words referring to objects and asked the subjects to either imagine them or pronounce the words. Later they had to recall them. During recall, subjects were successful twice as often for imagined objects to which the words referred than for pronounced words—thereby indicating the superiority of nonverbal encoding over verbal encoding and suggesting a dual system. The imagining was as successful as when pictures are recalled. Paivio interpreted the results to support his theory.

Criticisms of some fundamental assumptions of mental representations came from Pylyshyn (1973). He noted that if images are like pictures, one needs a seer to see the picture and another seer to see the seeing of the first seer and so on infinitely. Skinner (1963) had earlier pointed out the same problem: the notion of an internal world that is a copy of the outer world raises the question of who/what sees the picture in the head. Pylyshyn further argued that if processing has both a verbal and a nonverbal basis, the encodings must be somehow connected, and this requires a third coding system to intercede between them or direct them. Kosslyn (1980, 1981, 1983) countered that Pylyshyn's interceding propositional processing agent needed another coding system to direct it and so on infinitely, just as Pylyshyn himself had argued about the image needing a seer or homunculus. Kosslyn (1983, 1994; Kosslyn & Koenig, 1992) gave attention to an attempt to get around the logical requirement of a homunculus. Relying in part on studies with PET scans, Kosslyn (1994) argued that imagery and perception utilize the same mechanisms in the brain and do not imply the need for a seer.

Kosslyn proposed what he felt was a more adequate theory than Pylyshyn's. He argued that images are not pictures but processes in which the spatial relations of components are maintained in a special medium of space. This involves (a) two kinds of storage files in long term memory and (b) a medium of space or *spatial medium*. In one of these files, *propositional files,* is information about parts of objects and how the parts are related. In the second kind, *image files,* is information about images and how the spatial medium represents them. The spatial medium is where the image occurs. The medium is sharpest or in best focus in the center and less so toward the edges. The medium has a grain, and its coarseness further limits the viewing of details, and it has a limited size. The representation is no sooner formed in the medium than it begins to fade. The image files provide coordinates for points on the object represented, while the propositional files provide properties of the object and their relationships.

For example, the image file would contain the co-ordinates of a basic face or of parts of the face of a friend. The propositional file would have a list of characteristics—nose, eyes, mouth—and of how these components are related to the basic face: one mouth at lower center, nose centered above mouth, and two eyes spaced evenly above the nose. When someone imagines the face, the image files and the propositional files feed into the medium of space. But forming an image involves still further processes. The image process seeks the basic face in the propositional file and upon finding it, a *picture* process reads the coordinates and forms the basic image in the highest resolution part of the spatial medium and fills that area. A *find* process obtains the parts and then the *put* process puts them on the image. Thus the processing of images adds parts to a basic structure, according to Kosslyn's theory.

Kosslyn (1978) tested the limited size of the spatial medium as proposed by the theory. He asked subjects to imagine an animal at a distance, moving increasingly closer until the image filled their imaginary visual space. Their estimates of the distance of the animal at its closest corresponded directly with the relative size of the animal. A rabbit was imagined very close when it filled the area; a dog was further away, and a horse the furthest. The results supported that component of his theory, as did a test of granularity. In a task in which subjects imagined a clock, the time required to respond was proportional to the imaginary distance and increased as the imaginary distance increased, in accordance with Kosslyn's framework (Amorim & Stucchi, 1997).

Pylyshyn (1981, 1984) set forth criticisms about theories of imagery that supplemented his previous criticisms. He argued that images that function in a special medium must be part of the organism's structure and therefore cannot be modified by propositional conditions such as *beliefs and goals*. But if images can be so modified, then they must also be propositional. Pylyshyn (1984) confirmed the finding of Kosslyn, Ball, and Reiser (1978) that when subjects imaginatively scan an imaginary map, the time it takes to get from one point to another directly corresponds to the measured distance. But if they were instructed to shift quickly from one point to the other, the relationship no longer held. If they were instructed to imaginatively run between points, they crossed the distance more quickly than when imaginatively walking. Because of these changes in imagery with instruction, images could not be part of the organism's structure. They must be propositional and not a separate entity or process. He concludes that images are representations that reflect reality but that no special representational system is involved. Using a variety of evidence including PET studies of the brain, Kosslyn (1994) argues that (a) the mechanisms of object recognition are in large part those of imagery but that imagery assists with object recognition, and (b) imagery is depictive (pictorial) as well as propositional.

Garfield (1988) argues that the beliefs and goals in Pylyshyn's theory are indeed important but that they and other attitudes are not entities located in the head that should produce theories about cognitive events. Rather, such cognitive theories should explain how human interactions with the environment develop beliefs and desires. Also questioning the computational/representational theories, Putnam (1975, 1988) provided demonstrations that meanings are not mental creations in the head but are partly a product of the physical and cultural environment. Because computational theories posit strings of symbols in the mind, these theories must explain how the symbols are connected with the world but cannot adequately do so, argues Looren de Jong (1995). "A computer has no access to the real-world things referred to by its representations" (p. 240). Drawing from Putnam's work and carrying the analysis into a comparison of computational theories and connectionist theories (below), Looren de Jong comes down on the side of the connectionists. He also argues for a relational concept of mind along the lines of the ecological psychology of Gibson (chapter 13, p. 374) to replace both internal and external causality (Looren de Jong, 1997).

Connectionist Networks. Connectionism departs from a rule-following computational system in which the internally represented world has no close relations with the actual world. Connectionism adheres to representations but proposes that these representations are responses to inputs from the world—which are weighted to categorize them (Bechtel, 1990)—or that they are images resulting from neural activations spreading from a central network of meaning structures to peripheral structures (Lundh, 1995).

The proponents of this construction emphasize patterns of activation in networks as an analogy with neural networks, rather than built-in symbols and rules. The theory proposes that a complex of nodes stimulate or inhibit each other and are interconnected to form a unit. The nodes have a hierarchical structure of inputs and outputs, with some receiving external inputs, some having intermediary functions, and others outputting to other units. The patterns of these activations or inputs from one node to another follow a set of rules (algorithms, as in computer programming) that affect the strength of inputs and outputs among nodes. The network stores representations, such as a view of a tree or the odor of baking bread, in the distribution of activated nodes. Because of the great number of patterns possible, the odor and the tree, or even two different odors, will not conflict with one another unless they are quite similar.

Just as the nodes can stimulate or inhibit one another, so too do *units* of nodes—groupings of nodes—stimulate and inhibit one another, and each produces a single output by taking the total weight of the inputs from all nodes. Units also have a hierarchy that parallels that of nodes. The units learn an algorithm to produce an output pattern to an input pattern from the world without following any built-in rules. In this theory, because numerous nodes are operating simultaneously and in multilayers, the processing is parallel rather than serial, contrary to most flow diagrams of processing (Balard, 1986; Hinton & Anderson, 1981; Holyoak & Thagard, 1990; McClelland et al., 1986; Rumelhart & McClelland, 1986; Smolensky, 1988). Smolensky (1995) proposes that mental representations are vectors that occur not in a unit but as an activity pattern whose properties explain the composition of the representation without requiring causal relations. Fodor (1997) argues that Smolensky's theory implicitly uses the structure of "Classical mental representation theory" without acknowledging it and then claims the efficacy of the theory without the classical structure.

One proposed vision of how the network learns is that when the initial output pattern is incorrect, a comparison with the correct response occurs. The system works back through the network and adjusts the units toward a correct pattern on the next occasion. For example, if you were trying to learn the German word *Naturwissenschaft* (science) but kept thinking *Naturwunderkeit* or couldn't think of the word at all, you would check the form in a word list. Then the network would begin the adjustments. After a number of trials and corrections the network would have all the correct algorithms in place. Consequently, the network that was not preprogrammed with rules for the German word would develop its own program within the nodes and units of nodes. Tienson (1990) notes that something in the back propagation must change weightings in an appropriate manner, but no such mechanism is proposed nor is it clear how it could work.

Another approach to connectionist networks is a form of "constructivism." It argues that the neural structures from which cognitions operate are not innate but develop from interaction with the environment (Quartz, 1993). Learning algorithms incorporate the addition of structure as well as modifying weighted inputs. This constructivism theory "allows for the structure of the learning system's environment to play a central role in the construction of the representations that underlie the system's ability to learn in that environment" (p. 239).[2] The author argues that this constructivist approach, with its allowance for learning to add new connections and structures,

has important advantages over the innate and fixed neural structures of PDP (parallel distributed processing). As neural structure becomes more complex through learning, the power of representation becomes greater and novel representations can occur. In support of this position, the author cites thirty years of neurobiological research showing increasing complexity of postnatal neural development and its adaptability that directly influences brain structure.

Because it is not clear how the brain can represent and process symbols, the theory has tried to provide a model of how representation might occur. It holds, for example, that the representation of the word *Naturwissenschaft* is distributed in a pattern within a unit or across units, and the storage lies in the strengths of connections. These patterns of connections allow the reproduction of *Naturwissenschaft*. In experiments in which the form of words influenced identification of similar forms of words ("morphological priming"), the investigators reported that the results supported a connectionist interpretation in which the effects occur because of the activation characteristics of a connectionist network despite the lack of any explicit representation of word forms in the network (Rueckl et al., 1997).

This connectionist theory, it should be noted, is in conflict with cognitive neuropsychology that argues for localization of brain functions, and connectionism does little with biological explanations of cognition (Kosslyn & Koenig, 1992). It is also in conflict with the viewpoint of cognition as rule-based representations or as symbolic. The opponents of connectionism hold it to be a return to associationism in computer guise (Pinker & Mehler, 1988).

Dynamic Representations. This approach (Port & van Gelder, 1995) accepts mental states but rejects symbolic manipulation and connectionist processing. It holds that mental states are brain-environment relationships as well as brain functions. The representational properties of biological behavior, the proponents argue, require time to gain stability; consequently, time is an intrinsic

---

2. Note the emphasis on the nervous system's environment and the nervous system's—rather than the person's—ability to learn.

property of such behavior. Both symbolic and connectionist representations are static, discrete things, inconsistent with the continuous temporal character of events of biology. It is dynamic temporal change that coordinates body and environment for meanings to emerge, and meanings define mental states. Rather than involving an internal set of symbols for an object in the world, a mental state such as memory or perception is a "dynamic representation" specific to an environmental event of the world. The nervous system supports the organism-environment relationship but does not create it or represent it. This is borne out, proponents contend, by the fact that species with quite different neural structures behave in functionally equivalent ways. A source of inspiration for this position is Gibson's (chapter 13, p. 374) work in ecological perception, which indicates that the environment provides information for meaningful events as such events occur in the organism-environment relationship.

Memory

Storage and Processing Approaches. An important experiment not only for memory but for cognitive psychology in general was that of Sternberg (1966, 1969), who studied mental scanning of items in memory. His subjects memorized a list of syllables or digits and then were presented with another syllable or digit. Their task was to determine as quickly as possible whether or not the test item was already in the list they had memorized and to say "yes" or "no" accordingly. He found that the more items in memory, the longer the response time, whether or not the test item was already in the memorized list. He concluded that a search of memory involves a serial sequence of comparisons between the new item and each one in memory and continues to the end of the list even when a match occurs. But why would a subject continue scanning after finding a match? A possible answer is found in further data: each item added to the memory set required an additional 38 milliseconds of response time, giving a scanning

rate of 25 to 30 items per second. This suggests that because the scanning is so rapid, it is more efficient to go the full course before deciding "yes" or "no" than to do it after every comparison. The findings are contrary to expectation and unlikely to be found by any means other than experimentation. Sternberg provided a chart showing the flow of information between memory set and test item and coordinated this with a linear equation describing the relationships. His theory became one of the most influential in cognitive psychology and influenced a large number of experimenters to test the theory.

Many cognitivists consider memory to consist of two types of stores. One store contains short-term memories and the other long-term memories. When we hear the name of a person we have just met, the name goes into a sensory store and moves into the short-term store as we rehearse it in order to use it again. If we do not continue the rehearsal or use of the name, it quickly decays or is replaced by new information in the short term store. If we associate the name with someone or something we know, it may move into long-term storage. Continued rehearsal or usage can also accomplish the transfer. Short-term storage is encoded in sounds and long-term in meaning. Retrieval of information from the long-term store is often slower because of the great amount of information it contains that must be searched. An additional short-term store is also frequently assumed to hold sensory information.

The classical experiment that purported to demonstrate a permanent memory store was that conducted by Penfield (1958a, 1958b), a neurosurgeon at Montreal's Neurological Institute. He used an electric probe to stimulate various parts of the cortex surface of the brain of epileptic patients whose skulls were opened for surgery. He used only a local anesthetic on the scalp, the skull and brain being insensitive to touch and even to cutting. The patients were awake and able to report on the electrical stimulation. Some of the reports were essentially biological, such as a tingling or numbness in some parts of the body. Others were psychological, such as visual scenes or memories of previous experiences. Still others were limited to sounds, colors, or tactile sensations. Skinner (1963) suggests that it is

> simpler to assume that it is the behavior of seeing, hearing, and so on which is aroused than that it is some copy of earlier environmental events which the subject then looks at or listens to. Behavior similar to the response to the original events must be assumed in both cases—the subject sees or hears—but the reproduction of the events seen or heard is a needless complication. (p. 955)

Fewer than 8 percent of the patients responded, and a number of those who did respond were probably relating reconstructions rather than memories. Most reports were vague. A serious deficiency in the procedure was that no independent observers were present as a check on the accuracy of Penfield's observations and descriptions. Valenstein (1973) remarked that "The impression exists that if electrodes are placed in a specific part of the brain, a particular behavior can inevitably be evoked. Those that have participated in this research know that this is definitely not the case" (p. 87).

A proposed alternative to the duplex (triplex if a sensory store is included) theory of memory holds that memory functions according to a series of stages of information processing (Craik & Lockhart, 1972). In the first stage such information as the name we hear upon meeting a person is processed according to the acoustical (sound) characteristics perceived. In a later stage the meaning is processed according to some meaning we have given it. As the processing continues to deeper levels, it coordinates with an organized complex of knowledge. For example, the name of the new acquaintance comes to mean someone who is a member of a bowling team and whose superior skills are important for the success of the team. Whereas the duplex theory assumes that rote learning will move information from short-term to long-term memory, the stages of processing theory argue that meaningful and organized rehearsal in the processing operation is essential for retention.

Another memory theory proposes that memory consists of (a) procedural memory, which provides connections between stimuli and responses, including complex stimulus relationships; (b) semantic memory, which permits internal representations and manipulative constructions of the world; and (c) episodic memory, which enables the individual to retain a memory of personal experiences and to go back in time to review the memory. The theory further proposes three relationships: (a) procedural memory is independent of the other two, whereas semantic memory is to some extent tied to procedural memory and episodic memory to both; (b) each type of memory is connected with a form of awareness—procedural with non-awareness, semantic with awareness, and episodic with self-awareness; and (c) each memory system is a part of a different neural system, which has had a distinctive evolution (Tulving, 1985).[3] Because PET scans showed higher blood flow in the right expanded limbic system of the brain for novel than for familiar stimuli and in certain other areas for complex pictures, Tulving et al. (1994) conclude that these regions are the sites of an encoding network for visual/spatial novelty stimulation. Reviewing the literature on the manner in which four memory systems deal with four types of dissociation, Tulving (1996) finds evidence for multiple long-term memory systems and their neural basis.

The construct of mind is often considered to be spatial, with various items of memory residing at single points within that space. Because of the diversity of memory that is presumed to be in the long-term store—roller-skating skills, knowledge of the streets of one's home town, recipe for baking brownies, commands for running a computer program, language skills, and so on—it is unlikely

---

3. Quite a number of memories have been proposed by one or another cognitivist. Neiworth (1995) lists long-term, short-term, working, reference, procedural, declarative, episodic, semantic, implicit, and explicit. This is reminiscent of the way in which Clark Hull kept multiplying hypothetical drives to meet experimental findings and an earlier generation of psychologists proliferated instincts.

that they are all stored in a uniform manner. And the assumption that information gets into long-term storage by rehearsal ignores the fact that without rehearsal one remembers long after the event one's own wedding or the major events of a motion picture.

In an attempt to handle some of these problems, some memory researchers have turned to theories of PDP. This still implies a space but one in which components are stored at different locations. The PDP theory assumes that humans routinely engage in parallel processing rather than processing in serial or linear chains of events in sequence. According to McClelland's (1981, 1986) theory of PDP, learning is a process of reinforcing the connections between stored units that collectively represent the total thing remembered. In remembering, one accesses one or more of the units, each of which represents several related things which in turn activate other units for a full retrieval. This kind of memory storage and retrieval would enable a single cue or a few incomplete or even erroneous cues to activate the memory. In serial processing the erroneous cue would make retrieval impossible. Parallel processing, the theory holds, also allows one to fill in missing information, not from knowledge about the particular things remembered but from stored information of the same type about other things. It also has the flexibility to handle the storage and retrieval of the diverse knowledge each person has and to account for long-term storage without rehearsal. Because the adaptive networks are free of traditional mediators and representations, they are merely adaptive according to the historical conditions of selection.

Estes (1980) reviewed the research that speaks to the comparison of computer memory and short-term human memory. He covered six points of comparison between human and computer memory and found important differences in all of them. In general, the difference is that computers display rapid access and high precision whereas human memory is "robust" and general purpose. Humans don't have to be as rapid and precise as computers, but what they do remember provides rapid adaptation to the environment. Further,

the more we learn about the human memory, the less it seems to fit the stereotyped idea of a simple repository. It seems to be not at all like a storeroom, a library, or a computer core memory, a place where items of information are stored and kept until wanted, but rather presents a picture of a complex, dynamic system that at any given time can be made to deliver information concerning discrete events or items it has had experience with in the past. In fact, human memory does not, in a literal sense, store anything; it simply changes as a function of experience. The storehouse analogy . . . can be pernicious in a consideration of where research efforts should be concentrated, or of how intellectual function can be improved in some general way. (p. 68)

Alternative Directions. In order to predict a subject's behavior it is necessary to know the subject's goals, the character of the task and its environment, and most important of all the operational or personality characteristics ("control structures") of the subject, contends Jenkins (1981). But cognitive theorists typically use flow diagrams instead of attempting to discover the operational characteristics, which are almost never modeled. Without the operational characteristics, Jenkins argues, the sequence of alternative possibilities is almost infinite for a given task, leaving theoretical issues unsettled. Cognitive theories of the mind are actually models of the subject's specific modes of performance of the task. With new materials or a new task the mental model has to be patched with "new memories, new functions, and the like until it becomes so cumbersome that it is finally abandoned" (p. 216–17), and this goes on without end. "We are wasting our time trying to get a general model by building little special models of particular (and arbitrary) laboratory exercises" (p. 217).

Jenkins provides an experiment to show that when we present stupid or meaningless tasks to subjects they behave in kind. ". . . If we run stupid experiments, we can have stupid theories. The stupid theories will appear correct because the subjects can become as stupid as we require them to be" (p. 219). He notes that some classical experiments also illustrate this principle. Thorndike's cats in the puzzle box could only engage in trial and error because that was all that was available to them in the experiment. Köhler's apes solved problems by insight because that was all the experimental situation permitted. Similarly, Hull's rats learned reinforced responses that resulted in drive reduction and Toman's rats learned by cognitive maps because of the restrictions in each case. To further make his case, Jenkins cites studies that demonstrate how little we can generalize from one experimental situation to another. At most, the experiments generalize to slightly different classes of events.

A bit of history suggests some further problems. In an attempt to understand the fundamentals of learning and memory, Ebbinghaus invented the nonsense syllable as the most elementary unit he could conceive of. The nonsense syllable represented the British empiricists-associationists belief in elements or atoms of the mind. The syllables removed context and the subject's operational characteristics and prior knowledge from the experimental situation. Similarly, Watsonian and methodological behaviorists believed that, if they thoroughly studied conditional responses, they would eventually arrive at the most complex human behaviors. Yet systems psychologists and human-factors psychologists have shown that in order to succeed in improving complex systems, one must first deal with the condition that contains the greatest variance. The smaller sources have little effect until the major one is controlled. The contrary assumption, that we must first study the simplest analyzable units and build to more complex behaviors, runs from British empiricism to behaviorism to cognitivism and has usually been the operational mode of psychology. Consequently, psychology has made little progress. Jenkins insists that we must abandon it, for "to study complex relations one must be dealing with enough elements to form the relations" (Jenkins, 1981, p. 225).

In an extensive program of research Jenkins (Jenkins, 1974, 1981; Jenkins, Wald, & Pittenger, 1978; Pittenger & Jenkins, 1979) demonstrated

that remembering is interdependent with its context, including situations in which the remembering occurs, the nature of the remembering task, the skills and knowledge of the rememberer, and what the rememberer believes and knows. The sources of the rememberer's beliefs and his or her ways of structuring the experience are also important. Further "we cannot deal with memory without dealing with instructions, perception, comprehension, inference, problem solving, and all the other processes that contribute to the construction of events" (Jenkins, 1974, p. 794). *"Memory is not a box in a flow diagram"* (p. 794, author's italics). To answer questions about memory we must designate what kinds of analyses of it will be useful for a particular purpose or understanding and what particular events are of interest.

Watkins (1990) argues that the search for hypothetical mediators for memory is unproductive. Mediators are either stores or traces left behind in the brain after the original event. Mediationism produces a plethora of theories that are of interest primarily only to those who advance them and are unlikely to be abandoned until the author leaves the scene. These theories, he believes, establish a level of complexity that experimental techniques cannot adequately deal with. He recommends a procedure that his own memory research has followed, that of treating memory as a function of (a) the environment and the "state of mind" of the rememberer and (b) the rememberer's history. This approach, he believes, would lead to "straightforward" research questions and to findings that would become accumulative. It would contrast with the present situation of diverse theories with no connection among the findings. Along these lines a number of memory researchers have turned to natural conditions in which memory occurs (see Neisser, 1982, for a volume of these).

Semantic Networks

This model (Anderson, 1983; Collins & Loftus, 1975; Meyer & Schvaneveldt, 1971) rests on the assumption that knowledge consists of associations. These associations reside in nodes linked to each other in various degrees of strength. The word "pillow" might be more strongly linked to "bed" than to "door," while "head" and "blanket" would be somewhere in between. "Bed," "pillow," and "blanket" could form part of a linked network with "pillow" at the center and could have various degrees of activation strength. Other semantic associations could be "where is" (a good restaurant) and "sand-beach-sun." Learning about similarities can increase association strength or form a new link. For example, if a child learns that one pronounces the *w* in "between," "twig," "twin," "twice," "twenty," and "twelve" and that all refer to "two," it may be easier for the child to learn a new link: that "two" is spelled with a *w* even though it is not pronounced. Likewise, the different sounds of *o* in "one" and "only."

Alzheimer subjects, who were part of a study in the Baltimore Longitudinal Study of Aging, were tested on tasks of generating as many words as possible in sixty seconds—either words naming fruits or vegetables (closed categories) or words beginning with F, A, or S (open categories). At 2.5 years prior to the presumed onset of the disease, they produced fewer examples of closed categories (especially of uncommon fruits and vegetables) than did matched normal subjects, but they produced as many associations to open categories as did normals. This suggests that the ability to provide uncommon associations in semantic networks changes early in the development of the disease and might be used for early diagnosis (Weingartner et al., 1993). Schwartz et al. (1996) presented Alzheimer subjects rated as mildly to moderately demented with successive single words on a computer screen. The words referred to objects that the subjects could imagine (as opposed to abstract words). Normal elderly and college students served as controls. The words were preceded by the experimenter's oral statement of a category. The subject's task was to decide whether the word fit the category or not and to indicate the answer by pressing a right or left button. Measures of reaction time and electrical activity of the brain (event-related brain potential, or ERP) showed that the Alzheimer subjects with at least a mild degree of dementia were not substantially different from the control subjects and therefore demonstrated no clear breakdown of the semantic network, as has usually been assumed.

Production Systems

These systems are based on "if . . . then" rules such as "if tuition goes up again, (then) I may not be able to enroll next semester" . . . These rules have long been in use in systems of logic and have been brought into cognitive psychology on the assumption that a long-term *memory store* holds many "if . . . then" rules while a *working memory store* holds information that is being processed. The working memory (a) receives the information that tuition may go up, (b) searches long-term memory for the appropriate "if" rule, and (c) evokes the corresponding conclusion—"then"—that enrollment may not be affordable. When more than one pairing is possible, the working memory picks the best one. Production systems are useful in analyzing such activities as games—chess is a cognitivist's favorite—and trouble-shooting a defect in machinery or in electronics. Such systems have also been applied to problem solving (Newell & Simon, 1972) and to other cognitive and noncognitive behaviors, such as learning and operant conditioning of animals, respectively (Holland et al., 1986). Thompson and Mann (1995) showed that the extent to which subjects perceived necessity depended on whether they confronted "p only if q" or "if p, then q." This perception rather than the strictly logical relationship was an important variable. The authors conclude that it seems unlikely that different reasoning tasks are mediated by a single mechanism.

Psycholinguistics

An influential landmark in this topic was the work of Chomsky (1957, 1965), a linguist at Massachusetts Institute of Technology. Chomsky argued that a universal form of grammar is genetic in every human being. As the child matures the grammatical form unfolds and is modified by the language community of which the child is a part. This accounts for certain structural similarities in all languages. Chomsky's work stimulated considerable research in language development. This research found that the construct of innately generated grammar did not handle performance models (Smith, 1982) and showed no distinctive sequence of grammatical development and no universal principles of any kind (Schlesinger, 1984, cited in Eysenck & Keane, 1990). It did show that language development is far more complicated than Chomsky had assumed and is highly individualized. The rate of development and the sequence of grammatical structures varies from child to child. The development of syntax is interdependent with context, memory, and other factors (Lachman, Lachman, & Butterfield, 1979). These findings are along the lines of the psycholinguistics advanced by Kantor (1928, 1977), who argued that living language is not static structures such as words and phonemes that the linguist constructs, nor is it transmission of symbols from one mind to another. It is an interactive process between speaker and listener involving referents (the thing referred to), gestures, intonation, context, prior statements, and what the speaker knows about the listener's comprehension—all constantly changing as the discourse continues and as listener and speaker switch roles. Similarly, Garfield (1990a) suggests that language consists not only of information contained in utterances but also what is

> implied by the social context and relevant conventions that define the framework within which the discourse occurs, and which contribute the information conveyed and received by its recipients . . . It involves attention to implicature, presumed motives, stereotyped interactions, etiquette, and an unending web of similar nonlinguistic facts that nonetheless determine the significance of the linguistic events to be understood. (p. 13)

Although Chomsky's theory now has little standing in psychology, it served to stimulate considerable research in psycholinguistics.

Seidenberg (1997) proposes that innate capacities for language may be in "the form of biases or sensitivities toward particular types of information inherent in environmental events such as language" (p. 1603), not in a preformed knowledge of grammar. He holds that a variety of sources of information indicate that the way in which the brain is organized may limit how we learn language, but does not determine the principles of acquiring language or its use.

Artificial Intelligence

Some of the roots of this approach lie in the work of Turing (1950), a British mathematician who proposed a test to determine whether a computer has human intelligence. An interrogator with prepared questions poses questions to a computer and to a human; both of them concealed from her. The human, like the computer, answers the questions on a screen and does so truthfully while trying to convince her that he really is human. The computer responds through a program designed to enable it to answer in a human-like manner. If the interrogator cannot consistently and accurately differentiate the two in a series of tests, the computer has passed the "Turing test" and is said to have human intelligence. Critics say that success in such a test indicates only a simulation of human intelligence, not identity with it. Proponents claim that the two are actually identical: machine intelligence is human intelligence and human intelligence is machine intelligence. Searle (1990, 1992), a philosopher, argues that both humans and machines manipulate symbols but that only humans add meaning to the symbols. He assumes that the biological brain produces psychological events and uses several analogies to demonstrate that brain events are different from computer events. For example, "you could not run your car by doing a computer simulation of the oxidation of gasoline . . . It seems obvious that a simulation of cognition will similarly not produce the effects of the neurobiology of cognition" (1990, p. 29).

The first empirical studies, those of Newell and Simon (1961), examined humans who were thinking aloud as they solved problems in symbolic logic. Using those studies, they designed computer programs that followed similar procedures. Because one could simulate the other, they concluded that the same principles governed both the computer and the humans. Simulations in other tasks such as concept formation (Gregg & Simon, 1967) and verbal learning (Feigenbaum, 1970) followed. The computer programs, however, used specific programming for each task rather than using a few basic principles to solve a variety of problems in the manner of humans. To meet that shortcoming, Simon and Newell (1964, 1971) developed the General Problem Solver Program to find logical proofs, work cryptogram problems, and play chess. In line with human performance, the program was not specific to a particular task but could attack a variety of tasks. In playing chess the program worked from a decision tree in which alternatives and the consequences of each were assessed. Each decision or subgoal led to a new decision process.

Simon and Newell, unlike some AI proponents, do not assume that humans are like computers, but rather that computers can be programmed to operate like humans. They use flow charts to represent the hypothetical mental structures. The extent of match between the operation of the computer program and a human indicates the extent of artificial intelligence obtained. According to Weizenbaum (1976), a computer scientist at MIT, the General Problem Solver is a programming language for writing programs to conduct very specific tasks, not a general theory. If it is intelligence, the intelligence is very different from that of humans which can take context into account. Kurzweil (1985), another computer scientist, denies that Simon and Newell's artificial intelligence simulates human intelligence. An algorithm in a program, he avers, does not mean that the same algorithm occurs in a brain, only that it *could* be the same. We should, he believes, continue to develop machine intelligence for its own utility. When computers can parallel process rather than serial process, that innovation will bring us closer to complex systems like brain functions.

Campbell (1989), a science writer, observes that AI systems fail with rule-based approaches, particularly in pattern recognition. It seems clear to him that humans do not operate according to rules as computers do, even when they are attempting to apply logic. Instead, they seem to use their accumulation of knowledge and experience to find a satisfactory solution. He finds connectionism a better approach than AI. A review of the AI literature led Dreyfus and Dreyfus (1986) to conclude that AI had not lived up to its promise and showed no evidence that it ever would. Today, few AI advocates claim that computer programs simulate human thinking. Most simply try to write programs that can succeed at human intellectual tasks, such as translation of languages and playing chess. But even efforts to program computers to translate languages—such as Systran, used by the European Commission—can provide only a rough conversion which allows an interested party to decide whether a more accurate human translation might be worthwhile (Browning, 1996).

Cognitive Neuroscience

One of the earliest devices for studying subtle biological components of psychological responses was the electromyogram (EMG). It measures electrical potential (voltage) produced in muscles and is useful for indicating level of activation of a muscle or muscle group when a person is imagining an activity that involves that muscle. For example, voltage generated in arm muscles when one imagines lifting a weight, in the tongue during silent speech, in the eye muscles during visual imagining, and in the forearms of deaf mutes (Jacobson, 1932; Max, 1937). When subjects were completely relaxed and not generating voltage in the muscles, they had difficulty imagining (Jacobson, 1930, 1932). Shaw (1938) was unable to obtain such localization, but he did report increased action potential of all muscle groups during imagining. Some of the researchers used these results to suggest that such subtle action as imagining is a *behavior* in the form of minute muscle action, not something presumed mental. For example, "Since the arm muscles are a focal mechanism for speech in the deaf, our results thus lend some support to the behavioristic form of the motor theory of consciousness" (Max, p. 337). Shaw (1938) considered the muscle action in imagining to be a vestigial remnant of the original response: "during the revival of vestigial responses one can expect to be present any muscular activity that accompanied the original response" (p. 215). The cognitivists, on the other hand, assume that EMG does indicate a mind. Cacioppo and Petty (1981) have been using EMG to attempt to show how muscle action accompanies mental information processing and supplements verbal and overt behavioral measures of mind. In addition to assuming a duality of body-mind or body and brain, they regard skeletomuscular responses "as the doorways to the neuromuscular paths that interface the brain to the external environment" (p. 454).

Cacioppo and Petty (1981) conducted a series of experiments to attempt to show such a relationship. In one of these, the subjects' task was to decide whether a word was printed in all capitals or an adjective was descriptive of themselves (self-descriptive). For the self-descriptive task, subjects had to compare the meaning of the word with themselves, but for the capitalization task they had only to notice the appearance of the letters. They pressed a button to respond yes or no after the stimulus was removed. It was anticipated that the self-description task required more silent language associations than the recognition task and should show greater EMG activity of muscles used in speech processing. Similarly, judging a mismatch between adjective and self should also evoke more covert linguistic processing than a match. Electrodes were placed adjacent to the lips—above muscles used in forming sounds with the lips—and on the nonpreferred arm. The results showed that the expectations were confirmed: speech muscles showed greater EMG activity than arm muscles. In a second experiment, subjects attended to a particular characteristic of a spoken stimulus, such as whether a word that would follow rhymed or was similar in meaning to

a word given earlier. Muscle responses were in accord with those in the first experiment. When covert language processing events were occurring, only the muscles of the lips, not the arm muscles, showed involvement. Additional experiments also found that speech muscles of the lips, chin, and throat showed "active processing" rather than passivity when the subjects heard something advocated that they might or might not agree with.

These results would not, of course, differentiate between a behavioristic account of EMG and a cognitive account. The behaviorist would substitute behavioristic terms for computer processing terms just as the cognitivist has replaced behavioral terms with those from computer processing.

The goal of cognitive neuroscience is to find how neurophysiology produces cognitive events or how a psychological event is a function of neurophysiology, specifically a 1:1 relationship (Sarter, Berntson, & Cacioppo, 1996). Brain imaging devices have greatly facilitated the study of brain functions in relation to such behaviors as thinking, imagining, and so on. These devices include functional magnetic resonance imaging (fMRI), positron emission tomography (PET), computed tomography (CT), and magnetoencephalography (MEG) (Beardsley, 1997; Posner & Raichle, 1994; Raichle, 1994). PET is the most advanced of these. PET and fMRI measure not neural activity but blood flow. Electroencephalography (EEG) remains valuable, especially when used at the brain surface. Blood flow and volume, metabolism, balance of acids and bases, chemical factors involving receptors, and transmitter metabolism are additional measures. Ablation studies with animals and observation of brain damage in humans are still useful, as is stimulation of brain cells. These are often used in conjunction with brain imaging (Gabrieli, 1998).

The procedures of cognitive neuroscience involve manipulating cognitive events and examining the neural events or manipulating neural events and examining the effect on cognitive events. PET and MRI show functional anatomy, and electrical recordings show the sequence of neural events. Using these together, one can view (a) the regions of activity and their sequences as the individual speaks, problem solves, imagines, and so on; or (b) the characteristic of brain activity in abnormal behaviors (Andreasen, 1997). A recent finding of the latter: PET and MRI studies show decrements in the activity of the subgenual prefrontal cortex of some individuals with bipolar disorders; the implications of the decrement are unknown (Drevits et al., 1997).

When brain imaging shows an area to be active, such as when an individual is happy, this does not demonstrate that happiness is localized in that area, for other "levels of analysis" may be involved, note Sarter, Berntson, and Cooper (1996). (By "levels of analysis" the authors apparently mean different levels of neurological organization rather than the organism's organized relationship with conditions of the environment and its own history of such relationships as some other systems—such as dialectical, interbehavioral, and phenomenological psychology—would hold.) The authors point out that with brain imaging one can conclude only that the area is a *necessary* condition. It would be a *sufficient* condition if electrical or chemical stimulation produced the cognitive event. That is, if stimulation of a brain area cause speech or problem solving, one could conclude that that area is the locus of the speech or problem solving, and the 1:1 relationship would obtain. The authors believe that such evidence may be on the horizon for the activity of attending to stimuli.

In a series of experiments in which experimenters presented words to subjects in a variety of ways or subjects generated words under prescribed arrangements, brain imaging procedures showed two pathways for use of verbs: areas called the *anterior cigulate* of both the left frontal cortex and the left temporal cortex plus the left cerebellum as one pathway and the *bilateral Sylvan-insular cortex and the left medial extrastriate cortex* as the second pathway. Further studies show a role for the dorsal area of the left posterior cortex when subjects hear the words and a more ventral area when they see the words. The reviewer (Raichle,

1994) refers to the "processing" of words by these brain areas, but processing, of course, is a construct. The observed event consists of increased blood flow as one of the biological components of the response to words as stimuli. Blood flow does not demonstrate that these regions store or produce or remember words, only that they are involved—necessary conditions, perhaps, but not sufficient conditions.

In memory experiments, MRI imaging of the prefrontal cortex during memory tasks shows a middle section to be the most active part when the subjects are remembering a face (Courtney et al., 1997). When subjects try to remember letters that they saw in a sequence, the active region partly overlaps the one found by Courtney et al. (Cohen et al., 1997). The authors assume storage regions of working memory and consider various issues such as whether or not the results reveal an executive function. A review of neuroimaging memory studies shows that knowledge of any type involves several lobes of the brain (Gabrieli, 1998).

In "blind sight" and related studies (Milner, 1971; Weiskrantz et al., 1974; Weiskrantz, 1986), even though the occipital cortex is destroyed, the individual accurately points to objects but reports being unable to see them. Similarly, with the corpus-callosum cut such patients can correctly match or point to objects on the blinded side but declare that they are not visible. (However, the effects are very slight, and some of the responses suggest that the patients were on the edge of recognizing something there.) Blind sight has been called "divided consciousness" or described as perceptual processing without awareness. A situation that may be related to this is the blind spot that everyone has. This is the area of the retina occupied by the optic nerve, where photoreceptors are necessarily absent. The brain is said to "fill in" the section of our visual field where we are blind so that we never notice it. Dennett (1991) argues that the brain is ignoring the gap rather than filling in. He also proposes that the brain ignores the jerky movements our eyes make called "saccadic movements." But if one assumes that the brain is what sets the limits or provides the opportunities rather than acting as a causal agent, we might reach a different conclusion. We could conclude that, simply because we don't have the biological equipment to do so (Smith, 1997), we don't see the empty section of the visual field or a jerky world of eye movements.

Cognitive neuroscience needs to consider brain deficits, some of them massive, that do not produce cognitive deficits. British neurologist John Lorber (Berker et al., 1992; Lewin, 1980; Priestly & Lorber, 1981) reports that brain scans show that half of the most severe hydrocephalic patients, those with 95 percent of the cranium filled with cerebrospinal fluid, have no intellectual impairments. In one case a student had virtually no brain but scored 126 on an I.Q. test, obtained a first-class honors degree in mathematics, and was socially normal. Thompson (1959) found that even after he had removed 99 percent of rats' cortexes they retained learned responses to position of food in a T-maze—even with delayed reinforcement. Further, they were able to learn new positions as well as the control animals who had no cortical destruction. What do these cases mean for such constructs as an information processing brain and localized functions? These cases cut to the very core of cognitive neuroscience: because it assumes that the brain is the container and producer of psychological events, its credibility may be in jeopardy if it ignores these findings.

Recent Trends

Some different directions in memory theory and research have been presented under the heading of "Memory" above. Here a few other trends will be mentioned.

Not only was Neisser (1967) one of the early systematic cognitivists; he was also one of the first of them to turn at least partly in another direction (1976). His work anticipated some recent trends. Rather than continuing to assume that "knowing subjects are closed systems, not situated in a world" (Bem & Keijer, 1996, p. 465), Neisser

(1976, 1982, 1985) gives equal emphasis to (a) the information that the world provides (after Gibson, chapter 13, p. 374) and (b) the "schema" or "schemata" of the organism that accepts the information. Schema are organizations of past responses into ways of dealing with new situations (Bartlett, 1932). Schema influence and are influenced by each such situation. Neisser suggests that they are part of the nervous system including receptors, afferent fibers, efferent fibers, and probably many other structures and processes that serve to select some portions of information and not others. Directing much of his attention toward perception, he asks: How is it that, if organisms construct perceptions of the world, these perceptions can be so accurate? And—if information is simply picked up from the world, why do perceptual errors occur? Neisser insists that we see objects, not representations: no inner creature is looking at pictures in the brain. At the same time, the world provides the information that organisms utilize. "By constructing an anticipatory schema, the perceiver engages in an act that involves information from the environment as well as his own cognitive mechanisms. He is changed by the information he picks up." This changes "the perceptual schema so that the next act will run a different course" (1976, p. 57).

Drawing from ecological psychology and other environmentally oriented concepts, some cognitivists have used this broadened approach in such areas as aging and cognition, psychobiology, social cognition, personality, affect, sex differences in a number of different cognitive skills, and others (Schlechter & Toglia, 1985).

Bem and Keijer (1996) find that cognitivism is changing its concept of mind from "a disembodied rational entity, immersed in its own thoughts" (p. 450) to one that is adaptable to the environment. Mind is not an agent that causes itself "but a way of constructing meanings in the world" (p. 450). Bem and Keijer see teleological (goal orientation) or functional constructs as the new direction. Function, they hold, is more than internal structure or brain structure. It is the adaptiveness of the organism to its surroundings. In this scenario mind becomes a group of functions that relate to the goal of the person using the functions. Activities, which cognitivism has heretofore ignored, rather than entities become central. That is, beliefs, desires, and memories give way to the activities of believing, desiring, and remembering. Further, these functions do not occur in body parts, but the parts provide the conditions that permit the functions to occur. Mind also provides interpretations of objects, giving meaning to them. Bem and Keijer cite a special issue of *Cognitive Science* (1993) entitled "Situated Action" as an important presentation of this changing direction. They note that much of this trend arises not from traditional cognitivism but from "socially and culturally oriented psychologists" (p. 464) and from social constructionism, robotics, and neuroethology. We may also note that these developments find similarities in dialectical psychology (chapter 9), interbehavioral psychology (chapter 10), phenomenological psychology (chapter 12), and some others (chapter 13).

In a realistic task in which teachers devise a method of teaching algebra, the investigator (Hall, 1996) refers to the task as one of "situated cognition." He argues that representations in such realistic situations are shared activities rather than mental structures. They are activities of joint engagement rather than things that individuals have. These ongoing interactions are omitted from cognition studies and yet are critical in effective teaching, he maintains.

IMPLICIT POSTULATES

No cognitive psychologist has made explicit exactly what system of assumptions (postulate system) he or she is using. What cognitivists do provide the reader are only general statements about information processing, mental structures, and other constructs and assumptions about the role of biology. Consequently, only these statements are available from which to infer the postulates. Because there is no single leader or formulator in

cognitive psychology, any number of persons might be appropriate as examples of this system. Herbert Simon's formulation is selected here for its seminal character which played a major role in the rise of cognitivism in psychology:

■ *Protopostulates* (general guiding assumptions about science)
1. Science involves both observation of events and employment of cultural constructs such as mind and body.
2. Knowledge comes from interpreting observation of events in terms of these constructs.
■ *Metapostulates* (supportive assumptions for a particular science)
1. Psychology is based in biology.
■ *Corollary:* Psychology is not an autonomous science but is dependent on biology.
2. Biology includes the dual role of biological functions and psychological functions.
3. Psychological events are produced by specialized biological tissue and do not involve the entire organism.
■ *Postulates* (subject matter assumptions)
1. Humans are part body and part mind, and mind is different from behavior.
2. The construct of existential mind includes storage and transformational properties.
3. Experience is produced by the person's mind.
■ *Corollary:* Mind is self-causative.
4. Mind construction acts to transform information.
■ *Corollary:* Humans live in a double world—an outside physical world and an inside world that experiences the outside world as it is transformed and reconstructed by the mind.
5. Causation is linear: inputs are processed in a sequence of coding, storage, and reconstruction.
6. Human cognition is sufficiently similar to computer programs that it can be effectively studied as analogous to them.
7. The only role the environment plays in cognition is to provide sensory inputs from which the brain creates its own world.

8. Psychology gives preeminence to constructs; whereas events are merely indicators of these constructs.

PSYCHOTHERAPY

Cognitive therapy attempts to deal with the ways in which people structure their situations and they try to cope with their perceptions of those situations. It sets its sights on how people can improve their perceptions and their coping through various cognitive exercises. Its most controversial assumption is that all psychopathologies involve cognitive distortions, although the particulars differ from case to case (Haaga & Davison, 1991).

One of the pioneers in cognitive therapy was Beck (1963, 1964, 1967), who observed in depressed clients not the reflections in their dreams of anger turned inward as psychoanalysis holds, but dreams in which they were victims. He developed a theory of depression based on negative thought processes and established a therapy that would enable clients to deal with this negativism cognitively. Beck gives his clients exercises to help them identify and replace their feelings of worthlessness, gloom, enormous burdens, lack of hope for the future, and so on. The clients survey and list their own automatic negative thoughts, identify relations between thoughts and feelings, and replace negative thoughts with more objective or positive ones.

If the depression is severe, the starting point may involve working out a schedule of simple activities for each day, activities that are easy to monitor such as getting out of bed, brushing teeth, and so on. Simple but specific objectives that the client agrees to can be gradually added. This may include modes of thinking. As activity increases, more and more cognitive procedures can be introduced, such as recording negative thoughts and feelings and finding alternatives. At a more advanced stage of treatment, the client may examine assumptions underlying the negativism and compare them with evidence or logic.

Beck (1989) has applied similar procedures to marriage counseling. He presents nine stages in the counseling process, some of which overlap.

(1) Identify negative emotional reactions, determine what situations elicit them, and begin to recognize what automatic thoughts link the emotions with the situations.

(2) Imagine a relevant scene, identify the automatic thoughts, and list them.

(3) Practice identifying automatic thoughts. For example, "He doesn't care about me," "I can't do anything right," and "She's always so demanding."

(4) Imaginatively relive an upsetting event and identify the automatic thought.

(5) Ask whether the automatic thought was warranted, what the evidence is for it, what contrary indications exist, and what alternative explanations are possible.

(6) Seek a rational explanation for the behavior to replace the automatic one. For example, "He doesn't care about me" could become "He gives me little attention when he wants to relax, but he shows his caring at other times."

(7) Test the explanation. For example, a husband believes his wife is indifferent because she doesn't love him anymore. Rationally, however, he wonders (stage 6) if her responses are due to his being inadequately attentive to her, perhaps not showing enough interest. He could test this by inquiring about something she is concerned about and offering suggestions.

(8) Reframe: reinterpret as positive a characteristic that has been perceived as negative. For example, what the wife perceives as criticism from her husband could be reinterpreted as constructive suggestions.

(9) Practice labeling the distortions as polarized (all-or-nothing), overgeneralization (drawing conclusions from few observations), tunnel vision (selecting a small detail from a larger event), personalization (assuming oneself to be the cause of negative behavior when other factors are responsible), negative (global) la-

beling (applying a negative label to a *person* rather than to the person's *action*). Labeling helps the individual recognize misinterpretations and exaggerations of a spouse's behavior.

Needless to say, progressing through these stages requires carefully constructed exercises and considerable practice to be effective.

An emphasis on interpersonal process of therapist and client is one of many adaptations and variations that have developed in cognitive therapy (Safran & Segal, 1990). This therapy is not about interpretations—the authors reject interpretations—but about modifying cognitive schema that are closely connected to emotions. The therapist uses his or her own feelings to explore hypotheses about the client's interpersonal patterns. The client is urged to become an active partner with the therapist in examining thoughts and beliefs in order to disconfirm those that are inaccurate.

The practitioners of cognitive therapy have extended it to a great variety of conditions of which the following—from the compendium by Dattilio and Freeman (1992a)—is a partial list: generalized anxiety, performance anxiety, social phobia, posttraumatic stress disorder, panic, stress, dysthymia, suicidal tendencies, child sexual abuse, bulimia, obesity, cocaine addiction, schizophrenia, borderline personality, homosexuality, poststroke depression, multiple personality, and chronic pain.

Dattilio and Freeman (1992b) list (a) twelve cognitive treatment strategies, (b) seven behavioral techniques, and (c) homework utilized by cognitive therapists. A few of these cognitive techniques are described briefly below:

■ *Downward arrow.* The therapist responds to a client's statements with "If so, then what?" in order to stimulate thoughts and beliefs which help reveal the client's assumptions. It helps him or her understand what thoughts lead to other thoughts and the (lack of) logic involved.
■ *Labeling of distortions.* This enables the client to identify thoughts and see the patterns of the thoughts.

■ *Questioning the evidence.* This helps the client to practice determining the validity of a belief until such questioning becomes an automatic procedure.
■ *Examining options and alternatives.* The client reviews all options and alternatives to see that he or she is not trapped but has a way out and can generate new options.
■ *Reattribution.* The client recognizes that he or she cannot be blamed for all problems and finds sources of causation in a number of persons or conditions.
■ *Cognitive rehearsal.* The client imaginatively rehearses being assertive, getting acquainted with people, and so on.

Other cognitive techniques include idiosyncratic meaning, decatastrophizing, advantages and disadvantages, paradox or exaggeration, turning adversity to advantage, and replacement imagery.

The behavioral techniques differ from the cognitive in that they are overt rather than covert responses and include assertiveness training, behavioral rehearsal (engaging in an act rather than imagining it as in cognitive rehearsal), graded task assignment, bibliotherapy (reading as a supportive measure), relaxation and meditation, social skills training, and shame-attacking exercises. Homework assignments provide additional practice beyond what can occur in the therapy sessions and is a collaborative effort between therapist and client.

Homework may be of a variety of types (and is used in other therapies as well). Sometimes printed forms are used for practice in cognitive restructuring. In one example (Sank & Shaffer, 1984), at the top of a form called "Homework for Cognitive Restructuring" is the label Activating Event followed by a blank line. Below it are spaces for Irrational Beliefs (automatic thoughts), Disputes (questions), and Rational Beliefs (replies). Following these spaces are lines marked Consequences (emotions, physical discomfort) and Effects (affective, behavioral, cognitive). Also available is an Advanced Homework Sheet for Cognitive Restructuring that adds to the previous form Consequences of Irrational Belief and Effects of Rational Beliefs.

A psychiatrist known to the author includes in his treatment of DWI (Driving While Intoxicated) cases a homework requirement of searching newspapers daily for accounts of DWI and accidents involving alcohol. The clients bring the clippings to the therapy sessions and discuss some of the contents. Between sessions the task helps keep clients thinking about drinking and driving so that they will be less likely to have a drink and then drive away.

Cognitive therapy, unlike classical cognitivism, takes account of the situation. In fact, most cognitive therapies combine procedures with behavior therapy. This merging began in part with Beck in his pioneering work, and a large literature has now developed on cognitive-behavioral therapy. The authors in the volume edited by Dryden and Golden (1987) describe several varieties of this hybrid, including rational-emotive therapy (see chapter 4), rational behavior therapy, cognitive-behavioral hypnotherapy, multi-modal therapy, and cognitive behavior modification. Some of the merging has gone the other way as behavior therapists began including cognitive methods in their practices. A growing cooperation between cognitive behaviorism and community psychology is also occurring (see chapter 13, p. 370) (Kirschenbaum & Ordman, 1984), and much of this is aimed at intervention.

RELATION TO SOME OTHER APPROACHES

Behavior Analysis

Cognitivism assumes hypothetical internal forces as the cause of behavior. Behavior analysis turns to observed environmental conditions for causal conditions. Cognitivism constructs theories from which it deduces hypotheses, runs experimental tests on these hypotheses using groups, and applies statistics to compare group differences. In contrast, while employing no theories, deductions, or group comparisons, behavior analysis explores with single subjects the functional relationships between environment and behavior. It is empirical and inductive, while cognitivism is hypothetical and deductive.

Humanistic Psychology

Humanists and cognitivists see eye to eye only on making mind central and believing it to be internal and largely autonomous or self-caused. The humanist version of mind is the self and its potential for self-fulfillment, while the cognitivist version is that of an information processing brain. The humanist's mind construct with its actualizing tendencies and self-fulfillment is based on an analogy with biology presented by Kurt Goldstein in which organisms reorganize and reactualize themselves. The cognitivist's mind is based on an analogy with computer programs. Both systems emphasize humans and deemphasize animals.

The humanists consider cognitivism little more than behaviorism in masquerade. In their view, it continues the artificiality of laboratory experiments and merely substitutes computer mechanisms for conditioning mechanisms. Humanists note that cognitivism ignores what they consider important: purposiveness in human conduct, the whole person, self-actualization, the joyful characteristics of life rather than the pessimistic or sorrowful, the person throughout his or her life-span, and freedom of choice rather than determinism.

Interbehavioral Psychology

Cognitivists and interbehavioralists are just about at opposite poles. Cognitivists start with constructs about internal mechanisms of information processing, mental representation, and encoding, and interpret their data accordingly. That is, the constructs precede the observations rather than following them. Observations are then interpreted in terms of the constructs. Interbehaviorism starts with observed events of organisms in interaction with their surroundings and notes the changes that occur as a history of the interactions taking place. The more recent cognitivist trend that treats mind as activity in an environment (Bem & Keijzer,

1996) brings the two closer together, but this trend's continuing treatment of mind as a separate agent that gives meaning to objects comprises a mind-body dualism that interbehaviorism rejects. For interbehaviorism, the interaction *is* the meaning; meaning is not provided by a hypothetical separate agent. For example, one does not see a face and then process the face or have a mental product so that the face means Alice Collins. Instead, seeing the face *is* perceiving Alice Collins. Cognitivism reduces psychological events to biology—actions of the brain. Interbehaviorism considers the brain to be only one of many factors—such as other biological functions, setting conditions, and interactional history—that constitute psychological action.

Operant Subjectivity

This system is directed toward the objective measurement of subjective responses. Consequently, it would appear to be of interest to cognitivists, but they have ignored it. Cognitive psychology uses R methodology (see chapter 11), which compares group means and discards individual characteristics as an "error term." Operant subjectivity, also known as Q methodology, centers on uniqueness: persons are variables rather than test items, and individuals are sorted into similar factors. R measures from the investigator's point of view; Q measures from the participant's point of view.

Q methodology rejects hypothetico-deductive models (deducing hypotheses from theory as opposed to the empirico-inductive process of drawing inferences from observed events), brain reductionism, linear cause and effect of computer processing models, and mind-body dualism. Where cognitivism assumes that behavior is only the surface appearance of hidden processes, Q takes behavior as the fundamental datum. Consequently, cognitivism starts with constructs of hidden operations in the brain whereas Q starts with the observed events of human tasks that, through Q sorts, determine shared meanings. Despite these differences, the rigorous measurements of subjectivity that Q provides could be of service to cognitivism and to cognitive therapy—but only if those

measurements are not converted to R, in which case the subjectivity would be obscured.

Phenomenological and Existential Psychology

The cognitivists' assumption of causation of memory, perception, and other psychological events by internal hypothetical structures is quite different from the phenomenologist's focus on meanings and their dependence on the person-world relationship. To the cognitivist, the chair is an input of sensory stimulation that must be converted into a representation of the object and appear to be out there in the room instead of in the head. To the phenomenologist, the chair is not in consciousness but in the world, and its meaning as a chair is that of the human-world relationship that comprises consciousness. For consciousness is directedness toward an object. The world is not what we think but what we live.

> For the cognitivist theorist this directedness flows one way, towards the object which, then, cannot help but become an abstraction: it is created by my mental acts and the condition for its formation is a divorce between the acts and the object; knowing is standing back from something, freeing it from the self's idiosyncrasies. What we know is at once created by and distant from us. But adopt the view [phenomenological] that the object is the ground of our acts, not their outcome, and we must admit the knower is constituted in the act of knowing by the objects as much as the object by the act. To talk of the world as constructed is as true (and as false) as talking of the person as constructed by the world, for self and world are jointly revealed to one another. I am defined by the world as I define the world. (Bolton, 1987, p. 239)

For the phenomenologist, the subject's role in an experiment is truly subjective. For the cognitivist, the subject is an object whose responses are measured objectively in highly constrained—artificial, the phenomenologist would say—situations.

Psychoanalysis

The assumption of classical psychoanalysis that internal forces of id, ego, and superego are the causes of behavior has its parallels in cognitivism's assumptions of internal mental structures that produce cognition. Some cognitivists have even developed theory and research about unconscious forces that also have an echo in psychoanalysis. But where Freudian psychoanalysis finds the libido (pleasure/sex) power to be a fundamental source of energy, cognitivists seem to be completely uninterested in sex. The nearest cognitivism can come to the all-pervasive libido is in its construct of information processing. Some of the current versions of psychoanalysis have rejected these traditional constructs of sexual and aggressive forces, and the comparisons would not hold in those cases.

Psychoanalytic theory emphasizes the individual's history that shapes the id and ego and creates the superego; or, in some recent versions, the history with a caregiver that shapes the self. For the purpose of explaining observed behaviors such as learning or imagining, cognitivism proposes individual theories about each hypothetical structure but gives little attention to the history of reactions or any condition of the environment.

CRITIQUE

Despite cognitivism's dominance, it seems to have almost as many opponents as partisans. Some varied criticisms follow. Few are closely related to any other and they therefore are in no particular order. The final subsection relates some counter-criticisms.

Context versus Unnatural Experimental Tasks

Neisser (1976), who abandoned some of his own former cognitivist assumptions, levels the same criticism at the cognitivists that were once aimed at the behaviorists: "A satisfactory theory of human cognition can hardly be established by exper-iments that provide inexperienced subjects with brief opportunities to perform novel and meaning-less tasks" (p. 8). Psychology, he suggests, should not assume fixed mechanisms that perform processing tasks but should "come to terms with the sophistication and complexity of the cognitive skills that people are really capable of acquiring, and with the fact that these skills undergo systematic development" (p. 8). Although he finds that cognitivism claims such achievements as discovering various types of memory and describing strategies that occur in problem solving, he also holds that it does not do justice to human nature. It operates out of context, uses experimental designs that ignore the environment, and tests subjects on unnatural tasks (Neisser, 1985). Jenkins (1981) has advanced similar arguments. Reed (1987), like Neisser, draws inspiration from Gibson and rejects both the cognitivists' internal causation by cognition and the behaviorists' external causation by stimulation. He turns to what he regards as the "correct question" of "how people come to know the meaningful environment" (p. 166).

Developmental and Social Factors

Examining the growing interest in childhood cognition, Valsiner (1991) charges that cognitivism has engaged in "a systematic de-emphasis on affect, context, culture, and history [of the organism]" (p. 483). It has turned to mental representations that have limited utility for developmental processes. Representations are static concepts that do not relate to development. Despite research that indicates that models of computational processes do not handle the data well, the fascination with technological devices keeps these assumptions alive. The assumptions of cognitivism have led investigators away from developmental processes to those that are already established. Developmental cognitive psychology asks what specific cognitive functions of children can be activated at specific ages in different situations rather than what events bring them to given levels of functioning. A survey of developmental cognitive publications shows that they seldom address what it is that develops or how. Their investigations go no further than to record the presence or absence of particular functions at particular age levels. Valsiner argues that development is a social process interdependent with the growth of cognitive skills. Cognitive theory has made no theoretical progress in "the assumption of the stability of the explanatory mechanisms themselves" and is "not a 'revolution' but merely a 'restoration' of the mentalistic argumentation of the 1890s, now refreshed by computer models" (p. 490).

From China also comes a complaint about the failure to recognize social influences. Zhu (1985, cited by Yue, 1994) argues that cognitivists neglect psychological activity as social practice and as object-subject interactions, as well as the way in which cognition and emotion are united in interactional interchange. Therefore they fail to reveal creativity, initiative, and sociality. Gergen (1994) also charges that cognitivism has neglected the problems of the real world in which people operate. Why does it not address such problems as conflict, aggression, cooperation, alienation, power, exploitation, and political and religious belief? Sarbin and Kitsuse (1994) agree with the cognitivists that humans process information, but they insist that the processing consists of social practices.

Computer Brain

A critical evaluation of the analogy of the computer brain comes from Kantor (1978), who concludes that such analogizing is a procedure of "coining or converting of terms without regard to the things and events involved" (p. 581). He argues that brain action is one of the interacting *biological* functions of the organism and that to convert it into a *psychological* organ that thinks and perceives "wrenches a major organ from its proper place in the biological economy." He finds "no place in scientific psychology for any imaginary brain operations or invented psychic processes" (Kantor, 1979, p. 19). Skinner (1989) finds a gap in knowledge between the stimulus and the organism's response and between consequences and

the changes in behavior that occur as a result. He believes that only brain science can fill the gap, but he sees it as only a matter of filling in information, not providing a different explanation of the same thing. The brain cannot explain behavior, for what it does is part of what must be explained (Skinner, 1990). Swartz (1958), one of the early critics, in addition to criticizing the brain-computer analogy asks why psychology is so eager to forfeit its birthright, why it attributes to biology or chemistry or physics its own domain of events. Why does it not expand its own expertise in dealing with interactions of organisms and objects instead of turning them over to a different science? And, Marr (1988) asks, why should a computer be used to explain the behavior of the organism that designed, built, and programmed it?

Psychologists "cast their gaze backward to the ancient faculty psychology and dragged forth the dogma of cognition from the bipartite division of soul, mind, or consciousness" (p. 158), according to Observer (1978). Unlike the recycling of industrial materials that can be used for valuable products, the recycling of spiritistic constructs is an impediment to scientific progress. However, the *constructed* psychic structures and functions of cognitivism must be distinguished from *observed* cognitive events such as remembering and thinking, Observer contends.

Similarly, Blewitt (1983) questions the appropriateness of borrowing analogical models from non-psychological events such as computing machines and insists that all psychological descriptions must come from the actual events that comprise them. He notes that when computers are treated "as if" they function like humans (for example, Simon, 1990) the result is to treat psychological events as what they are not. When computers are treated the same as humans (for example, Johnson-Laird, 1993), such treatment overlooks vast differences. Cognitive events, he argues, occur as a relation between the person and the thing cognized, not in an autonomous, self-commanding computer brain. The environment does not enter the organism to be processed. It remains where it is. What goes on in the organism are physiological processes involving chemistry, electricity, and physics, not psychological events. Psychological events are organism-environment interactions.

> The organism does not consume the environment, process it, and regurgitate it as a response; there is no "input" or "output." Organism and environment come into contact with each other, and it is the various forms of contact that constitute the subject matter of psychological events. In terms of psychological events nothing goes on between "input" and "output" because nothing goes in or comes out. The subject matter of psychology is not the "stuffing" in between the stimulus and response. Rather, the interaction between the stimulus and response is the psychological event. (Blewitt, 1983, p. 397)

The following passage from the authors of a cognitive book, one on thinking, argue that presumed brain mechanisms are really behaviors:

> While it is clear that a person does accumulate and remember ways of behaving and normally does behave in a way that is consistent with his present circumstances, there is no clear evidence in logic or in data that these behaviors are really internal psychical units that get stored, processed, searched for, selected, and invoked by some set of internal storage or processing devices. That argument only leads to regressive questions about the mechanisms underlying the mechanisms. It is not an accident that the description of symbolic processes (the functions of some alleged symbolic device) is given in behavioral terms, such as storing, sorting, and selecting. That in itself is a strong clue that rather than being functions of a device at all, they are functions of a person, i.e. part and parcel of or, better, parameters of his behavior. (Bourne, Eckstrand, & Dominowski, 1971, p. 13)

Marr (1983) also observes that physiological explanations are based on behavior rather than on physiology and are created by psychologists rather than physiologists. He suggests that if we want to know how the brain works we should study the brain itself. Studies of patterns of brain responses to seeing show complex physiological processes, but they do not tell us how we see a human face. And the proposals for presumed retrieval, he finds, are "bizarre":

> Mechanisms suggested for this putative process are so bizarre that it is difficult to understand how anyone ever took them seriously. Consider again the process of recognition. In one case, I am said to recognize your face by matching it with a representation in memory. How do I know which representation to bring forth in order to match it with your face: That process itself must be a form of recognition—so we have not solved any problems, only deferred their resolution. Extend this reasoning to the recognition of an *image* of your face. Presumably I have a representation of an image of your face which I must now match with the image, etc., etc. (p. 18)

Pronko (1988) notes that evidence that the brain processes, controls, stores, remembers, and executes functions is totally lacking. Even if we assumed that it did these things we would have to explain how that might be possible before we could use it to explain human activity. He concludes that these computer attributes of the brain are nothing less than pure myth: what we know as fact is that the brain participates in such events as thinking and remembering, but so do a lot of other conditions both biological and non biological, and it is these acting together that comprise cognitive and other interactions.

Cognition as Director

According to Mixon (1987), the cognitive assumption that humans are organized in a hierarchy is an illusion. There is no mind or cognitive processor at the top running everything down through the ranks. Instead, complex relationships are at work—ways of thinking, moving, feeling, and speaking as well as environmental contingencies. "People simply are not (even by analogy) machines impervious to environment and controlled by cognitive processes" (p. 40). We do what we do not by cognitive direction but by gaining skills through time and practice. We can't, for example, just decide to think like a Zen master. We have to practice the skill. That cognitions are not initiating causes of behavior is also argued by Flora and Kestner (1995).

Heuristics

A prominent claim of cognitivists, especially Simon (Newell & Simon, 1972; Simon, 1990) is that the information-processing model provides an effective means of searching for scientific principles about cognition. Morris, Higgins, and Bickel (1982), on the other hand, argue that there is no guarantee that the questions heuristics asks will be useful or even scientific, and in fact asking one type of question may preclude asking another that is equally or more important. Further, the kind of questions and answers that come from cognitivism are so far removed from the actual events of the person in the environment that it is difficult to integrate them with anything concrete.

Representationism

Skinner (1977) questions the logic of the assumption that we respond to a representation of the world rather than to the world itself. If knowing is a matter of constructing mental copies of actual things, how do we know the copies? he asks. Do we make copies of the copies and copies of the copies of the copies, and so on? When we move about in an area do we construct maps that we look at and follow or do we follow the area itself? If it is a map, do we then have a map of the map? On the contrary, he declares, "the body responds to the world, at the point of contact; making copies would be a waste of time" (p. 6). Similarly, he questions the "copy theory" for remembering (Skinner, 1989). We can copy things we see, but how can we copy what we do? Even if we model the behavior, we can't store it. When we remember

what something looks like, we do what we did when we first saw it. Seeing it required no copy then nor does remembering it now. Recognizing is re-cognizing, responding once again as we did in the first place. Memorizing is acting so as to respond in the future as we are acting now.

A theory of direct realism (see chapter 13, p. 371) also takes up the arguments against representationism. And Gergen (1994) argues that the construct of mental representations would mean that scientists, too, must be in contact with only their own representation, not with a real world; ultimately a science of psychology cannot exist, and the world has no known reality. We would know only the world as represented. Yet cognitivists, by seeking objective truth about such constructs as schemas and mental nodes disparage the importance of the very constructs they attempt to understand (Gergen, 1985). Gergen (1994) further argues that if cognitive schemas are the means by which we know the world and they are innate, we would require an almost unlimited number of them. And of the many that are clearly environmental, such as countless new words acquired in a lifetime, it is unclear how a child who does not yet have those schemas can understand the parents in order to acquire them. He also outlines the conundrums and contradictions of cognitive mapping and cognitive production of overt behavior, and he concludes that the problems all derive from cognitivism's mind-body dualism.

In defense of the theories of representation, it is important to note that some cognitivists have moved far from the copy theory that Skinner criticizes. Some have eliminated mediators, and some treat the brain as a participant rather than as a determiner.

Mind versus Behavior

Of the several traditional meanings of mind, Skinner (1989) finds that cognitivism has adopted the one referring to a doer or executor. It is the autonomous agent that takes command. It is the mind, not the person but a double of the person, that organizes what comes in through the senses and perceives the world. Yet if one substitutes "person" for the mind in that description the meaning does not change: "The mind is limited in rate of computation" versus "the person is limited in rate of computation." Skinner concludes that "cognitive processes are behavioral processes; they are things people do" (p. 17). Even the attempt to describe mind as what the brain does is a misleading construct, he observes (Skinner, 1987). For the brain is the body, and therefore mind is what the body does, what the *person* does. It is behavior.

Jaremko (1979) finds two shortcomings with mentalistic explanations: (a) The use of internal events as explanation requires another behavior to explain that one. Assuming that internal events cause behavior avoids analyzing the complex events that can be observed. The causes of behavior lie in the history of relations with the environment, and mentalistic explanations overlook this. Cognitions are behaviors and are no more causes than any other behaviors. (b) Mental events as hypothetical constructs have been proposed as explanations of what intervenes between stimulus inputs and response outputs. An anticipation may be postulated as such an intervening event. We are stimulated, then anticipate something, and then respond. But what is an anticipation? It can't be a cause, it can only be one component in a chain of events comprised of interactions with the environment. At some point we must discontinue arguing that intervening constructs cause one another and revert back to observed behaviors. If anticipation is a genuine event, then it is a behavior and can be described as a behavior. "Cognition has never been observed but a cognitive behavior is always observable to at least one person" (p. 551).

Lichtenstein (1995) observes that behaviors are the fundamental data used to test the mentalistic theories, and Jenkins (1981) argues similarly that what the cognitivists assume to be models of mind are models of the ways in which subjects perform particular tasks. With new models come new patchworks of memories, stages, and functions that are finally abandoned as they become too cumbersome, he notes. Neisser (1976) suggests that an emphasis on "what actually hap-

pens" (p. xi) needs to replace abstractions and presuppositions.

Cognitivists assume an independent process that thinks for the person rather than acknowledging the person who is actually doing the thinking, charges Rychlak (1995). Making a point similar to that of Jaremko about ignoring *behavior*, he notes that to the cognitivist the *person* is a group of mechanisms influenced by some source other than the person. He argues that treating humans as computing machines is unproductive, for computers cannot produce meanings and purpose that are central to humans. He cites the original usage of "information" in conjunction with engineering to indicate that the usage was unrelated to any meanings in the message being transmitted.

Disunity

Holley & Stack (1992) observe a lack of coherence among the various topics. As a result of a lot of proposed separate domains of cognition, the cognitivists have developed little theory that connects other domains of research, they observe. Flora and Kestner (1995) make a similar charge: cognitivism has no unity that would bring together its research or even its topics or references. They contend that it has not advanced our understanding of human activity despite the fact that over the past thirty years it has produced huge volumes of material about information processing. In their opinion, cognitivism is not only wrong but "impedes scientific progress" (p. 587).

Operational Definitions and Hypothetico-Deductive Method

To claim that experimental procedures or methods of observation define unobserved hypothetical entities and powers is a misuse of operational definitions (proposed in physics) according to Kantor (1938), Leahy (1980), and Verplanck (1996). This procedure was employed by the methodological behaviorists to define such constructs as drives. Hull, for example, defined a drive state by hours of deprivation of food or water. This procedure came under fire beginning in the 1930s and is now drawing the same criticism when cognitivists employ it to indicate such unobserved powers as mind, processing, representations, connectionist networks, and other constructs. For example, to define short-term and long-term memory by experimental procedures and then use the responses from the experiment as evidence of corresponding memory systems gives an appearance of reality to such constructs but is specious, claim the critics.

In the hypothetico-deductive method, theorists use models or theories to deduce hypotheses and then see how well the data fit the hypothesis. They assume that if the fit is close the functional relationships are those specified by their theory. Verplanck (1996) describes this procedure as resulting in

postulated (guessed at, dreamed up) theoretical entities to which are assigned properties that, rather than being produced by data, produce the ingeniously-designed experiments that then produce the very data that led to the postulation. These "bootstrapped" data generate statements purporting to explain or describe behavior in terms of agents and processes of mind or of brain (or some parts thereof) which determine the subject's actions. Environmental objects and events become "information," which the "brain," the "mind" or "consciousness" then "processes," thus "causing" the behavior measured, which (surprise!) had, in fact, been determined by the apparatus and the instructions to the subject.

The experimental results (and generalizations) so produced are then evaluated on the criteria set by the currently fashionable methodology for "truth-evaluation." . . . [This] relies on the application of deductive, rather than inductive logic. It neglects the categorization of behavior in terms other than those imposed by the vocabulary [the cognitivists] begin with.

Inferences in Science

Simon (1990) claims that both humans and computers use symbols for intelligent behavior and that this has been demonstrated by programming computers to perform the tasks that humans perform and then showing that humans use the same processes. "The physical symbol system hypothesis has been tested so extensively over the past 30 years that it can now be regarded as fully established" (p. 3). The flaw in this type of argument, addressed by Blewitt and by Pronko above, is that the argument does not establish that *only* symbolic behavior or computer processing can account for the observed behaviors. This point is further examined by Morris, Higgins, and Bickel (1982) who note that such a claim violates the law of equifinality. This means that any number of different conditions may produce the same result. Logically, it is known as the error of "affirming the consequent." That is, in inductive logic (as opposed to deductive logic, such as syllogisms and mathematics) one can never conclude with absolute certainty that A alone causes B, only that the probability is strengthened as other conditions or possibilities are eliminated. One can describe the changes in a person's behavior and infer that the person had the capability to make such a change without violating equifinality, but this is not an explanation or an indication of causality. As soon as one infers that cognitive event A must produce the observation of B, equifinality is compromised and the consequences unjustifiably affirmed. This is because no evidence exists that A *must* produce B. After observing the behavior and inferring the capabilities for that behavior, we cannot then also infer cognitive processing, mental powers, or other controlling power. All sciences use objective inference, but this is limited to

functional relationships between behavior and the environment, whereas in cognitive science objective inferences are made about processes supposedly occurring at another level of analysis . . . Within properly conducted [science], inaccurate inferences are easily dispelled because they are about behavior-environment relationships that can be objectively analyzed. Errors in inferences about theoretical cognitive processes, however, are almost impossible to dispel because of the ephemeral and unobservable nature of those processes. . . . (Morris, Higgins, & Bickel, p. 114–15)

Theory and Methodology

According to Gergen (1994), the fact that cognitive psychology has its basis in the philosophy of German rationalism (innate mental structures that organize external signals from the world) demands a rationalist theory, but it has no overall metatheory (theory of theory) at all. A rationalist theory would characterize people as "information searching and concept sustaining" (p. 26), but cognitivism has only computer analogies. Further, contends Gergen, it should—but does not—have a rationalist methodology. So it borrows its methodology from behaviorism (experiments on subjects, control groups, dependent and independent variables, tests of hypotheses, quantification) that draws from British empiricism. This puts cognitivism squarely into contradictions. The conception of the person using inherent cognitive mechanisms to structure information from the world means that a person cannot claim accurate knowledge of the external world, for the representations are determined by the character of the cognitive system. Therefore, the scientist cannot be an authority about any part of the world including the cognitive system. Further, any attempts to correct cognitive bias would be subverted by the proclivities of the cognitive schemas required for the information processing. Experimental subjects are also captives of their mental schemas, which preclude them from meeting the requirements of the methodology. In short, according to Gergen, cognitive psychology has no philosophy of science to justify cognitive metatheory; and, because the empiricist methodology that it uses is inconsistent with its theoretical claims, the methodology cannot support those claims.[4]

---

4. Although Gergen is equally critical of behaviorism, he finds that it has a coherent metatheory and a consistent methodology, both derived from empiricism.

Criticism and Counter-Criticism

Vera and Simon (1993) have contended that the call for environmental context (especially as found in Gibson's work) is unnecessary, for the environment and the functional meaning of objects are represented in the head. Wells (1996) counters by noting that the cognitivists' own admission that "the external real-world situations are too rich and complex to be captured fully and accurately by a robot's internal models of them" (Vera & Simon, 1993, p. 46) contradicts their claims elsewhere that symbolic representation systems are universal and can account for any situation in the real-world. He argues that, contrary to Vera and Simon's claim, "situativity theory" cannot be subsumed under cognitivism; the two stand as competing approaches. One pair of critics (Baars & McGovern, 1994) of the critics has complained that critics of cognitivism (in a book they reviewed) have not provided alternative evidence to cognitivism. However, Marr (1988) contends that research will not establish one system or another: this can only occur through the logical examination of issues.

Krantz's (1969) study of earlier systems speaks to this issue of the basis of disagreement. He found that a comparison of experimental evidence between structuralists (Titchener) and functionalists (Baldwin) in the late nineteenth century was ineffective because of the totally different context from which each faction was arguing. Perhaps statements of postulates would have at least made the reason for disagreement clearer.

CONCLUSIONS

Cognitivism has clearly put cognitive behaviors back into psychology after they had been ignored by some schools of behaviorists (though receiving attention under other less well known systems). Henceforth, they will almost inevitably remain an important part of psychology. It has also had the effect of making the constructs of computer processing and mental representations highly institutionalized in psychology and other sciences. One possibility for the future, largely because of this institutionalization, is that this framework will remain the dominant viewpoint and provide limited room for others, as is now the case. With cognitivists training graduate students to continue in the cognitivist tradition, with both specialized and more general journals supporting the cognitive "paradigm" (to use Kuhn's [1970] term), with cognitivist referees reviewing grant applications for granting agencies, with promotion committees often favoring the system, and with careers spent in the system, changes do not readily occur; and other systems find it difficult to compete. Nor does cognitivism lend itself to the kind of accumulative knowledge that brings about the eventual shifts in paradigms that Kuhn claims in physics.

Still, methodological behaviorism was once dominant in the United States, but it was edged out or absorbed as cognitivism took over many of its features (while behavior analysis retains the status it has held for several decades). A second possibility, then, is that the many critics from outside this framework, and a few within it, will form a seriously competing counter-force that emphasizes cognition as interactional events consisting of an interdependent organism and environment, history of the organism, and the person as an adapting organism rather than as a computing brain. Such an approach would also attempt research with complex interdependencies rather than testing the simplest elements. Some combination of orientation toward these events and continued constructs of a processing brain, perhaps as a connectionist system, could become dominant.

So far, traditional cognitivism with its multiple parts seems well entrenched in the institutionalized networks that feed and nourish it. The critics' impact has been minimal. It will be interesting to watch the play-out between Goliath and the many little Davids in future years, but Goliath is more a multiple personality than a single entity. He is made up of diverse components and many contending viewpoints. The major battleground may be between these contending personalities, some of which remain well entrenched in orthodox computer analogies while others are evolving away from traditional constructs and toward organism-environment interactions. Perhaps the latter is only an aberration, and the traditionalists will prevail. The battle is joined.

REFERENCES

Amorim, Michel-Ange, & Natale Stucchi. 1997. Viewer- and object-centered mental explorations of an imagined environment are not equivalent. *Cognitive Brain Research* 5: 229–39.

Anderson, John R. 1983. *The Architecture of Cognition.* Cambridge, MA: Harvard University Press.

Andreasen, Nancy C. 1997. Linking mind and brain in the study of mental illness: A project for a scientific psychopathology. *Science* 275: 1586–93.

Attneave, Fred. 1974. How do you know? *American Psychologist* 29: 493–511.

Baars, Bernard J., & Katharine McGovern. 1994. How not to start a revolution. Review of *Against Cognitivism: Alternative Foundations for Cognitive Psychology.* London: Harvester Wheatsheaf, 1991. *Contemporary Psychology* 39: 370–71.

Balard, D. H. 1986. Cortical connections and parallel processing. *Behavioral and Brain Sciences* 9(1): 67–120.

Bartlett, Frederick C. (1932). *Remembering: A Study in Experimental and Social Psychology.* New York: Macmillan.

Beardsley, Tim. 1997. The machinery of thought. *Scientific American* 277, no. 2 (November): 78–83.

Bechtel, W. 1990. Connectionism and the philosophy of mind: An overview. In *Mind and Cognition: A Reader.* Edited by William G. Lycan. Oxford: Blackwell.

Beck, Aaron. 1963. Thinking and depression: 1. Idiosyncratic content and cognitive distortions. *Archives of General Psychiatry* 9: 324–33.

———. 1964. Thinking and depression: 2. Theory and therapy. *Archives of General Psychiatry* 10: 561–71.

———. 1967. *Depression: Clinical, Experimental, and Theoretical Aspects.* New York: Hoeber.

———. 1989. *Love Is Never Enough.* New York: Harper-Perennial.

Bem, Sacha, & Fred Keijzer. 1996. Recent changes in the concept of cognition. *Theory and Psychology* 6: 449–69.

Blewitt, Edward. 1983. The computer analogy in psychology: Memory as interbehaviour or information processing? In *Reassessment in Psychology: The Interbehavioral Alternative.* Edited by N. W. Smith, P. T. Mountjoy, & D. H. Ruben. Lanham, MD: University Press of America.

Bolton, Neil. 1987. The programme of phenomenology. In *Cognitive Psychology in Question.* Edited by Alan Costall & Arthur Still. Brighton, Sussex, UK: Harvester.

Bourne, L. E.; B. R. Ekstrand; & R. L. Dominowski. 1971. *The Psychology of Thinking.* Englewood Cliffs, NJ: Prentice-Hall.

Browning, John. 1996. The Rosetta hack. *Scientifc American* 275 (5): 38.

Buss, David M. 1995. Evolutionary psychology: A new paradigm for psychological science. *Psychological Inquiry* 6: 1–30.

Cacioppo, John T., & Richard E. Petty. 1981. Electromyograms as measures of extent and affectivity of information processing. *American Psychologist* 36: 441–56.

Campbell, Jeremy. 1989. *The Improbable Machine: What the Upheavals in Artificial Intelligence Research Reveal about How the Mind Really Works.* New York: Simon & Schuster.

Chomsky, Noam. 1957. *Syntactic Structures.* The Hague: Mouton.

———. 1959. Review of B. F. Skinner's *Verbal Behavior. Language* 35: 26–58.

———. 1965. *Aspects of the Theory of Syntax.* Cambridge, MA: MIT Press.

Collins, Allan M., & Elizabeth F. Loftus. 1975. A spreading-activation theory of semantic processing. *Psychological Review* 82: 407–428.

Cooper, Lynn A., & Roger N. Shepard. 1984. Turning something over in the mind. *Scientific American* 251, no. 6 (December): 106–114.

Craik, F. I. M., & R. S. Lockhart. 1972. Levels of processing: A framework for memory research. *Journal of Verbal Learning and Verbal Behavior* 11: 671–84.

Dennett, Daniel C. 1991. *Consciousness Explained, Elbow Room, and Brainstorms.* Boston: Little, Brown.

Drevits, W. C.; J. L. Price; J. R. Simpson;, R. D. Todd; T. Reich; M. Vannier; & M. E. Raichle. 1997. Subgenual prefrontal cortex abnormalities in mood disorders. *Nature* 386: 824–27.

Dreyfus, Hubert L., & Stuart E. Dreyfus. 1986. *Mind over Machine: The Power of Human Intuition and Expertise in the Era of the Computer.* New York: Free Press.

Dryden, Windy, & William L. Golden, eds. 1987. *Cognitive-Behavioral Approaches to Psychotherapy.* Cambridge, MA: Hemisphere Publishing.

Estes, William. 1980. Is human memory obsolete? *American Scientist* 68: 62–69.

Eysenck, Michael W., & Mark T. Keane. 1990. *Cognitive Psychology: A Student's Handbook.* Hove & London: Erlbaum Associates.

Feigenbaum, E. A. 1970. Information processing and memory. In *Models of Human Learning.* Edited by D. A. Norman. New York: Academic Press.

Flora, Stephen A., & Jane Kestner. 1995. Cognitions, thoughts, private events, etc. are never initiating causes of behavior: Reply to Overskeid. *Psychological Record* 45: 577–89.

Fodor, Jerry. 1997. Connectionism and the problem of systematicity (continued): Why Smolensky's solution still doesn't work. *Cognition* 62: 109–119.

Freeman, Arthur, & Frank M. Dattilio, eds. 1992a. *Comprehensive Casebook of Cognitive Therapy.* New York: Plenum Press.

———. 1992b. Introduction to cognitive therapy. In *Comprehensive Casebook of Cognitive Therapy.* Edited by A. Freeman & F. M. Dattilio. New York: Plenum Press.

Furth, Hans G. 1981. *Piaget and Knowledge: Theoretical Foundations,* 2nd ed. Chicago: University of Chicago Press.

Gabrieli, J. D. E. 1998. Cognitive neuroscience of human memory. *Annual Review of Psychology* 49: 87–115.

Garfield, Jay L. 1988. *Belief in Psychology: A Study in the Ontology of Mind.* Cambridge, MA: MIT Press.

———. 1990a. Convention, context, and meaning: Conditions on natural language understanding. In *Foundations of Cognitive Science: The Essential Readings.* Edited by Jay L. Garfield. New York: Paragon House.

———. 1990b. Introduction. In *Foundations of Cognitive Science: The Essential Readings.* Edited by Jay L. Garfield. New York: Paragon House.

Gergen, Kenneth J. 1994. *Realities and Relationships: Soundings in Social Construction.* Cambridge, MA: Harvard University Press.

Gregg, L., & H. A. Simon. 1967. Process models and stochastic theories of simple concept formation. *Journal of Mathematical Psychology* 41: 246–76.

Haaga, David A., & Gerald C. Davison. 1991. Cognitive change methods. In *Helping People Change: A Textbook of Methods,* 4th ed. Edited by Frederick H. Kanfer & Arnold P. Goldstein. New York: Pergamon Press.

Hall, Rogers. 1996. Representation as shared activity: Situated cognition and Dewey's cartography of experience. *Journal of the Learning Sciences* 5: 209–238.

Hinton, Goeffrey E., & James A. Anderson. 1981. *Parallel Models of Associative Memory.* Hillsdale, NJ: Erlbaum Associates.

Holland, J. H.; K. J. Holyoak; R. E. Nisbett; & P. Thagard. 1986. *Induction: Processes in Inference, Learning, and Discovery.* Cambridge, MA: MIT Press.

Holly, Patricia, & Janet Stack. 1992. Do cognitive psychologists share a paradigm? A second look. *Bulletin of the Psychonomic Society* 30: 65–66.

Holyoak, K. L., & P. Thagard. 1990. A constraint satisfaction approach to analogical mapping and retrieval. In: *Lines of Thinking: Reflections on the Psychology of Thought,* vol. 1. Edited by K. J. Gilhooly, M. T. Keane, R. Logie, & G. Erdos. Chichester, UK: Wiley.

Hunt, Earl. 1989. Cognitive science: definition, status, and questions. *Annual Review of Psychology* 40: 603–629.

Jacobson, Edmund. 1930. Electrical measurements of neuromuscular states during mental activities. *American Journal of Physiology* 95: 694–702.

———. 1932. Electrophysiology of mental activities. *American Journal of Psychology* 44: 677–95.

Jaremko, Matt E. 1979. Cognitive behavior modification: Real science or more mentalism? *Psychological Record* 29: 547–52.

Jenkins, James J. 1974. Remember that old theory of memory? Well, forget it! *American Psychologist* 29: 785–95.

———. 1981. Can we have a fruitful cognitive psychology? In *Nebraska Symposium on Motivation, 1980.* Edited by J. H. Flowers. Lincoln: University of Nebraska Press.

Jenkins, J. J.; J. Wald; & M. B. Pittenger. 1978. Apprehending pictorial events: An instance of psychological cohesion. In *Minnesota Studies in the Philosophy of Science,* vol. 9. Minneapolis: University of Minnesota Press.

Johnson-Laird, Philip N. 1993. *Human and Machine Thinking.* Hillsdale, NJ: Erlbaum Associates.

Kantor, J. R. 1928. Can psychology contribute to the study of linguistics? *Monist* 38: 630–48.

———. 1938. The operational principle in the physical and psychological sciences. *Psychological Record* 2: 3–32.

———. 1963. *The Scientific Evolution of Psychology,* vol. 1. Chicago: Principia Press.

———. 1977. *Psychological Linguistics.* Chicago: Principia Press.

———. 1978. Man and machines in psychology: Cybernetics and artificial intelligence. *Psychological Record* 281: 575–83.

———. 1979. The role of cognitive institutions in psychology and other sciences. *Revista Mexicana de Análisis de la Conducta* 5: 7–20.

Kirschenbaum, Daniel S., & Arnold M. Ordman. 1984. Preventive interventions for children: Cognitive behavioral perspectives. In *Cognitive Behavior Therapy for Children.* Edited by Andrew W. Meyers & E. Edward Craighead. New York: Plenum Press.

Kosslyn, Stephen M. 1980. *Image and Mind.* Cambridge, MA: Harvard University Press.

———. 1981. The medium and the message in mental imagery: A theory. *Psychological Review* 88: 44–66.

———. 1983. *Ghosts in the Mind's Machine: Creating and Using Images in the Brain.* New York: Norton.

———. 1994. *Image and Brain: The Resolution of the Imagery Debate.* Cambridge, MA: MIT Press.

Kosslyn, S. M.; T. M. Ball; & B. J. Reiser. 1978. Visual images preserve metric spatial information: Evidence from studies in image scanning. *Journal of Experimental Psychology: Human Perception and Performance* 4: 47–60.

Kosslyn, Stephen M., & Olivier Koenig. 1992. *Wet Mind: The New Cognitive Neuroscience.* New York: Free Press.

Krantz, David L. 1969. The Baldwin-Titchener controversy. In *Schools of Psychology.* Edited by David L. Krantz. New York: Appleton-Century-Crofts.

Kuhn, Thomas S. 1970. *The Structure of Scientific Revolutions,* 2nd ed. Chicago: University of Chicago Press.

Kurzweil, Raymond. 1985. What is artificial intelligence anyway? *American Scientist* 73: 258–64.

Lachman, Roy; Janet L. Lachman; & Earl C. Butterfield. 1979. *Cognitive Psychology and Information Processing: An Introduction.* Hillsdale, NJ: Erlbaum.

Leahy, Thomas H. 1980. The myth of operationism. *Journal of Mind and Behavior* 1: 127–43.

———. 1992. The mythical revolutions of American psychology. *American Psychologist* 47: 308–318.

Lewin, R. 1980. Is your brain really necessary? *Science* 210: 1232–34.

Lichtenstein, Parker E. 1995. Review of *Cognitive Approaches to Human Perception,* by Soledad Ballesteros. *Psychological Record* 45: 327–28.

Looren de Jong, Huib. 1995. Representations: Naturalist versus computationalist. In *Trends and Issues in Theoretical Psychology.* Edited by I. Lubek, R. Van Hezewijk, G. Pheterson, & C. W. Tolman, New York: Springer.

———. 1997. Some remarks on a relational concept of mind. *Theory and Psychology* 7: 147–72.

Lundh, Lars-Gunnar. 1995. Meaning structures and mental representations. *Scandinavian Journal of Psychology* 36: 363–85.

Mani, Kannan, & P. N. Johnson-Laird. 1982. The mental representation of spatial descriptions. *Memory and Cognition* 10: 181–87.

Marr, Jack. 1983. Memory: Models and metaphors. *Psychological Record* 33: 12–19.

Max, Louis William. 1937. Experimental study of the motor theory of consciousness–IV: Action-current responses in the deaf during awakening, kinaesthetic imagery and abstract thinking. *Journal of Comparative Psychology* 24: 301–344.

McClelland, James L. 1981. Retrieving general and specific information from stored knowledge of specifics. *Proceedings of the Third Annual Meeting of the Cognitive Society,* 170–72.

McClelland, James L.; David E. Rumelhart; & the PDP Research Group, eds. 1986. *Parallel Distributed Processing,* vols. 1–2. Cambridge, MA: MIT Press.

Meyer, D. E., & Roger W. Schvaneveldt. 1971. Facilitation in recognizing pairs of words: Evidence of a dependence between retrieval operations. *Journal of Experimental Psychology* 90: 227–34.

Meyering, Theo C. 1989. *Historical Roots of Cognitive Science: The Rise of Cognitive Theory of Perception from Antiquity to the Nineteenth Century.* Dordrecht, The Netherlands: Kluwer Academic.

Milner, B. 1971. Interhemispheric difference in the localization of psychological processes in man. *British Medical Bulletin* 27: 272–77.

Mixon, Don. 1987. On not-doing and on trying and failing. In *Cognitive Psychology in Question.* Edited by Alan Costall & Arthur Still. Brighton, Sussex, UK: Harvester.

Morris, Edward K.; Stephen T. Higgins; & Warren K. Bickel. 1982. Comments on cognitive science in the experimental analysis of behavior. *Behavior Analysis* 5: 109–125.

Neisser, Ulrich. 1967. *Cognitive Psychology.* New York: Appleton-Century-Crofts.

———. 1976. *Cognition and Reality.* San Francisco: Freeman.

———, ed. 1982. *Memory Observed.* San Francisco: Freeman.

———. 1985. Toward an ecologically oriented cognitive science. In *New Directions in Cognitive Science.* Edited by Theodore M. Schlechter & Michael P. Toglia. Norwood, NJ: Ablex Publishing.

Neiworth, Julie. 1995. The integration of content with context: Spatiotemporal encoding and episodic memories in people and animals. In *Comparative Approaches to Cognitive Science.* Edited by Herbert Roitblat & Jean-Arcady Meyer. Cambridge, MA: MIT Press.

Newell, Allen; J. C. Shaw; & Herbert A. Simon (1958). Elements of a theory of human problem solving. *Psychological Review* 65: 151–66.

Newell, Allen, & Herbert A. Simon. 1961. Computer simulation of human thinking. *Science* 134: 2011–2117.

———. 1972. *Human Problem Solving.* Englewood Cliffs, NJ: Prentice-Hall.

Observer. 1978. The recycling of cognition in psychology. *Psychological Record* 28: 157–60.

Paivio, Allan. 1971. *Imagery and Verbal Processes.* New York: Holt, Rinehart & Winston.

———. 1986. *Mental Representations: A Dual Coding Approach.* Oxford: Oxford University Press.

Paivio, Allan, & Kalman Csapo. 1973. Picture superiority in free recall: Imagery or dual coding? *Cognitive Psychology* 5: 176–206.

Penfield, Wilder. 1958a. *The Excitable Cortex in Conscious Man.* Springfield, IL: Thomas.

———. 1958b. Some mechanisms of consciousness discovered during electrical stimulation of the brain. *Proceedings of the National Academy of Sciences* 44 (2): 51–66.

Pinker, Steven, & Jacques Mehler, eds. 1988. *Connections and Symbols.* Cambridge, MA: MIT Press.

Pittenger, John B., & James J. Jenkins. 1979. Apprehension of pictorial events: The case of a moving observer in a static environment. *Bulletin of the Psychonomic Society* 13: 117–120.

Port, Robert F., & Timothy van Gelder, eds. 1995. *Mind as Motion: Explorations in the Dynamics of Cognition.* Cambridge, MA: MIT Press.

Posner, Michael I., & Marcus E. Raichle. 1994. *Images of Mind.* New York: Scientific American Library.

Pronko, Henry. 1988. *From AI to Zeitgeist: A Philosophical Guide for the Skeptical Psychologist.* New York: Greenwood Press.

Putnam, Hilary. 1975. The meaning of "meaning." In *Language, Mind and Knowledge,* vol. 7 of *Minnesota Studies in the Philosophy of Science.* Edited by K. Gunderson. Minneapolis: University of Minnesota Press.

———. 1988. Reductionism and the nature of psychology. In *Mind Design: Philosophy, Psychology, Artificial Intelligence.* Edited by John Haugeland. Cambridge, MA: MIT Press.

Pylyshyn, Zenon. 1973. What the mind's eye tells the mind's brain. *Psychological Bulletin* 80: 1–24.

———. 1979. Imagery theory: Not mysterious—just wrong. *Behavioural and Brain Sciences* 2: 561–63.

Quartz, Steven R. 1993. Neural networks, nativism, and the plausibility of constructivism. *Cognition* 48: 223–42.

Raichle, Marcus E. 1994. Images of the mind: Studies with modern imaging techniques. *Annual Review of Psychology* 45: 333–56.

Reed, Edward S. 1987. James Gibson's ecological approach to cognition. In *Cognitive Psychology in Question.* Edited by Alan Costall & Arthur Still. Brighton, Sussex, UK: Harvester.

Roitblat, Herbert L., & Jean-Arcady Meyer, eds. 1995. *Comparative Approaches to Cognitive Science.* Cambridge, MA: MIT Press.

Rueckl, Jay G.; Michelle Mikolinski; Michal Raveh; Caroline S. Miner; & Frank Mars. 1997. Morphological priming, fragment completion, and connectionist networks. *Journal of Memory and Languages* 36: 382–405.

Rumelhart, David G., & James L. McClelland. 1986. *Parallel Distributed Processing: Explorations in the Microstructure of Cognition,* vol. 1. Cambridge, MA: MIT Press.

Rychlak, Joseph F. 1995. A teleological critique of modern cognitivism. *Theory and Psychology* 5: 511–31.

Safran, Jeremy D., & Zindel V. Segal (1990). *Interpersonal Process in Cognitive Therapy.* New York: Basic Books.

Sank, Lawrence I., & Carolyn S. Shaffer. 1984. *A Therapist's Manual for Cognitive Behavior Therapy in Groups.* New York: Plenum Press.

Sarbin, Theodore R., & John I. Kitsuse. 1994. A prologue to constructing the social. In *Constructing the Social.* Edited by Theodore R. Sarbin & John I. Kitsuse. London: Sage.

Sarter, Martin; Gary G. Berntson; & John T. Cacioppo. 1996. Brain imaging and cognitive neuroscience. *American Psychologist* 51: 13–21.

Schlechter, Theodore M., & Michael P. Toglia, eds. 1985. *New Directions in Cognitive Science.* Norwood, NJ: Ablex Publishing.

Schlesinger, I. 1984. What is a theory of language development a theory of? Unpublished paper.

Schwartz, Tanya; Marta Kutas; Nelson Butters; Jane S. Paulsen; & David P. Salmon. 1996. Electrophysiological insights into the nature of the semantic deficit in Alzheimer's disease. *Neuropsychologia* 34: 827–41.

Searle, John R. 1990. Is the brain's mind a computer program? *Scientific American* 262, no. 1 (January): 26–31.

———. 1992. *The Rediscovery of the Mind.* Cambridge, MA: MIT Press.

Seidenberg, Mark S. 1997. Language acquisition and use: Learning and applying probabilistic constraints. *Science* 275: 1599–1603.

Shannon, Claude E. 1948. A mathematical theory of communication. *Bell Systems Technical Journal* 27: 379–423, 623–56.

Shaw, William A. 1938. The distribution of muscular action potentials during imaging. *Psychological Record* 2: 195–216.

Shepard, Roger N., & Lynn A. Cooper. 1982. *Mental Images and Their Transformations.* Cambridge, MA: MIT Press.

Shepard, R. N., & J. Metzler. 1971. Mental rotation of three-dimensional objects. *Science* 171: 701–703.

Simon, Herbert A. 1990. Invariants of human behavior. In *Annual Review of Psychology.* Palo Alto, CA: Annual Reviews.

Simon, Herbert A., & Allen Newell. 1964. Information processing in computer and man. *American Scientist* 52: 281–300.

———. 1971. Human problem solving: The state of the theory in 1970. *American Psychologist* 26: 145–59.

Situated action. 1993. *Cognitive Science* 17 (1): special issue.

Skinner, B. F. 1963. Behaviorism at fifty. *Science* 140: 951–58.

———. 1977. Why I am not a cognitive psychologist. *Behaviorism* 5: 1–10.

———. 1987. Whatever happened to psychology as the science of behavior? *American Psychologist* 42: 780–86.

———. 1989. The origins of cognitive thought. *American Psychologist* 44: 13–18.

———. 1990. Can psychology be a science of mind? *American Psychologist* 45: 1206–1210.

Smith, N. W. 1997. Consciousness: Event or construct? In *Investigations in Behavioral Epistemology.* Edited by L. J. Hayes & P. M. Ghezzi. Reno, NV: Context Press.

Smith, Terry L. 1982. Chomsky's cognitivism at twenty-five from the perspective of Skinner's "Behaviorism at Fifty." *Papers in the Social Sciences* 2: 23–32.

Smolensky, Paul. 1988. On the proper treatment of connectionism. *Behaviorism and Brain Sciences* 11: 1–74.

———. 1955. Connectionism, constituency and the language of thought. In *Connectionism.* Edited by Cynthia Macdonald & Graham Macdonald. Cambridge, MA: Blackwell.

Sternberg, Saul. 1966. High speed scanning in human memory. *Science* 153:652–54.

Sternberg, Saul. 1969. Memory scanning: Mental processes revealed by reaction time experiments. *American Scientist* 57: 421–57.

Swartz, Paul. 1958. A note on the computing machine analogy in psychology. *Psychological Record* 8: 53–56.

Thompson, R. 1959. Learning in rats with extensive neocortical damage. *Science* 129: 1223–24.

Thompson, Valerie A., & Jacqueline M. Mann. 1995. Perceived necessity explains the dissociation between logic and meaning: The case of "Only If." *Journal of Experimental Psychology: Learning, Memory, and Cognition* 21: 1554–67.

Tienson, John L. 1990. An introduction to connectionism. *Southern Journal of Philosophy* 26: 57–84.

Tulving, Endel. 1985. How many memory systems are there? *American Psychologist* 40: 385–98.

———. 1996. Classifying human long-term memory: Evidence from converging dissociations. *European Journal of Cognitive Psychology* 8: 163–83.

Tulving, Endel; Hans J. Markowitsch; Shitij Kapur; Reza Habib. 1994. Novelty encoding networks in the human brain: Positron emission tomography. *Neuroreport* 5: 2525–28.

Turing, Alan M. 1950. Computing machinery and intelligence. *Mind* 59: 433–60.

Valenstein, E. S. 1973. *Brain Control: A Critical Examination of Brain Stimulation and Psychosurgery.* New York: Wiley.

Valsiner, Jaan. 1991. Construction of the mental: From the "cognitive revolution" to the study of development. *Theory and Psychology* 4: 477–94.

Vera, A. H., & H. A. Simon. 1993. Situated action: A symbolic interpretation. *Cognitive Science* 17: 33–46.

Verplanck, William S. 1996. Cognitivism, as an operation-analytic behaviorist views it. Paper read at the Third International Congress on Behaviorism and the Sciences of Behavior, October 7–10, Yokohama, Japan. Available: <http://funnelweb.utcc.utk.edu/~wverplan/cognitivism.html>

Wallace, William A. 1996. *The Modeling of Nature: Philosophy of Science and Philosophy of Nature in Synthesis*. Washington, DC: Catholic University of America Press.

Watkins, Michael J. 1990. Mediationism and the obfuscation of memory. *American Psychologist* 45: 328–35.

Watson, John B. 1913. Psychology as the behaviorist views it. *Psychological Review* 20: 158–77.

———. 1919. *Psychology from the Standpoint of a Behaviorist*. Philadelphia: Lippincott.

Weaver, W. 1949. Recent contributions to the mathematical theory of communication. In *Mathematical Theory of Communication*. Edited by C. E. Shannon & W. Weaver. Urbana: University of Illinois.

Weingartener, Herbert J.; Claudia Kawas; Robert Rawlings; & Martha Shapiro. 1993. Changes in semantic memory in early stage Alzheimer's disease patients. *Gerontologist* 33: 637–43.

Weiskrantz, L. 1986. *Blindsight: A Case Study and Its Implications*. Oxford: Oxford University Press.

Weiskrantz, L.; E. K. Warrington, M. D. Sanders, & J. Marshall. 1974. Visual capacity in the hemianopic field following a restricted occipital ablation. *Brain* 97: 709–728.

Weizenbaum, Joseph. 1976. *Computer Power and Human Reasons*. San Francisco: Freeman.

Wells, Andrew. 1996. Situated action, symbol systems and universal computation. *Minds and Machines* 6: 33–46.

Yue, Guoan. 1994. Theoretical psychology in China today. *Theory and Psychology* 4: 261–75.

Zhu, Zhixiang. 1985. On modern cognitive psychology. *Beijing Normal University Journal* 1: 9–14.

CHAPTER 4

Humanistic Psychology: Meaning, Inner Reality, and Self-Causation

INTRODUCTION

If we hear that psychology is about self-actualization, creativity, love, autonomy, self, existence, joy, grief, meaning, need-gratification, purpose, and choice, we might wonder what some of the terms mean, but we would probably conclude that these are important sounding topics that we would like to understand better. These topics might also sound more relevant to real life than a psychology that emphasizes conditioning of rats and pigeons and more intriguing than such topics as learning, perceiving, motivation, the "neural basis" of behavior, "mental" measurement, research methodology, and "information processing" that survey courses in psychology are typically devoted to. They might even sound like what many people, before they begin to study psychology, assume that psychology is about. They are some of the topics that are centerpieces of humanistic psychology.

DEVELOPMENT AND ISSUES

Early History and Principles

Humanistic thinking emerged during the Renaissance in Europe, beginning in the fourteenth century. It held that laws, art, government, and even traditions must be measured in terms of their effects on people rather than in terms of their contribution to a future heavenly paradise. People should be free to determine their lives, and neither church nor state should dictate.

Later, in the United States a version of humanism called *transcendental humanism* developed from a literary movement in the nineteenth century exemplified by Ralph Waldo Emerson and Henry David Thoreau. This movement held that important truths develop from intuitions rather than from objective evidence. Transcendentalists opposed slavery and all types of doctrine. Both the opposition to established theological doctrine and the social protests of transcendentalism were connected with the formation of the Unitarian (later, Unitarian-Universalist) Church that set forth no

creed[1] but encouraged all people to decide for themselves what to believe. Components of this organization later sponsored "human potential" groups associated with humanistic psychology (Back, 1973).

Humanistic psychology began in the 1950s and formally came into being in the 1960s as a protest against (a) the presumed environmental forces that determine behavior according to behaviorism and (b) the presumed unconscious forces that determine behavior according to psychoanalysis. Accordingly, it called itself the "Third Force." Its proponents wanted to move away both from the mechanistic conditioning of the behaviorists (in which, as they saw it, the individual is a passive automaton at the mercy of the environment) and from the deterministic instincts of psychoanalysis (in which the dark forces of the id involving murder, incest, and destruction engage in combat with the superego). They also wanted to move away from the research methodologies and statistics that psychology had borrowed from the physical sciences. They felt that laboratory experiments with rigorous controls and quantification of results missed what was most important in human activity.

Experience and meaning rather than behavior should be the primary data of psychology, they argued. External observation that neglects thinking and feeling is inadequate. Internal data can be gathered from artistic creations, literary products, biographies, and interviews. Humans are unique. The study of rats and pigeons or other "lower" animals will not lead to an understanding of humans, nor will the study of conditional responses or statistics of personality traits. Humans make free choices and are not governed by reinforcements or unconscious forces, they claim. In making choices each individual has the responsibility to develop a set of values that will serve as a guide to finding a meaningful and fulfilling life. Such

---

1. Originally "unitarian" referred to belief in a single god rather than in the three gods of trinitarianism. This small denomination is often found in college communities where it appeals to students and academic staff.

an achievement they call self-realization or self-actualization. Whereas conventional psychology has been obsessed with rigorous experimental design rather than with problems, humanistic psychology is problem-centered. It complains that conventional psychology loses the individual in a mass of statistics. The emphasis must shift to the uniqueness of the individual, who has the potential to come to know him or herself and can thereby know others. Through art and the humanities we can increase this knowledge and share it with others for mutual self-fulfillment.

The prime mover in this protest was Abraham Maslow. His dissatisfaction with conventional psychology and the resistance of mainstream psychology journals to publishing his works led him to instigate a new movement. He was joined by Anthony Sutich, a California psychotherapist. They attracted others who were also disaffected, and together they organized the American Association for Humanistic Psychology (later dropping "American"), which eventually became the Saybrook Institute, named for the Connecticut location of their first meeting in 1964. The first issue of their newsletter called for those who objected to (a) the view of humans as "a composite of part functions," (b) a psychology derived from the methods of physics, and (c) clinical practice derived from medicine to join the movement. The association's newsletter grew into the *Journal of Humanistic Psychology*.

The views of some of those who were important in the founding of the organization is instructive. Gordon Allport (1960, 1961) was a personality psychologist who began to doubt the appropriateness of applying methods of the natural sciences to psychology although he formulated the concept of personality traits and developed tests to measure them objectively. In the mid 1940s he led a separation of clinical and social psychologists, cultural anthropologists, and sociologists at Harvard into a new department of social relations. Allport emphasized the importance of growth, or *becoming*, as directed toward goals—the topic of goals being largely ignored by conventional psychology. He held that psychology had stressed group norms and other statistics ("nomothetic") and had largely overlooked individual experiences ("idiographic").

Carl Rogers' (1942, 1951, 1961) nondirective or client-centered therapy was influential in that it made a radical break from the theory and practices of psychoanalysis and allowed the individual to direct his or her own way to recovery and fulfillment. The counselor, rather than exercising authority, would offer acceptance, honesty, and understanding that would allow the client to remove the social impediments to growth. It was the client who had the acumen for his or her own growth, not the counselor. Rogers' personality theory assumed a "phenomenal field" consisting of the person's entire life experiences. One region of this, the "self," includes the way we relate to and value both ourselves and others. The self is constantly evaluating regions of the phenomenal field and is healthiest when it is in congruence with the "ideal self"—that is, when the self as it would like to be is much like the self as it is.

The personality theories of Henry Murray, Gardner Murphy, George Kelly, and Abraham Maslow were also important (Smith, 1990).[2] Maslow (1954) was not as opposed to psychoanalytic theory as was Rogers, but he wanted to add a brighter and healthier side to it. He proposed a theory of motivation that became well known, appearing in most introductory psychology texts as well as in books on motivation and personality. It posited a hierarchy of innate human needs: Physiological needs such as hunger, thirst, and sex must first be satisfied. Then the person's need for safety and security; next, the need for love and a sense of belonging; and then self-esteem—acceptance and respect for one's self. Once these "deficiency needs" are met, the highest potential can be realized. This is self-actualization. It might lie in the fine arts for one person, in scholarship for another, and in climbing a mountain for a third. Maslow believed that self-actualized people are

---

2. Taylor (1995) has shown that personality theory played a major role in the establishment of humanistic psychology.

the healthiest and that a study of their values can lead to a scientifically confirmed universal ethical system. These would include such values as truth, goodness, beauty, gaiety, justice, and joy. Those who are self-actualized reach "peak experiences" in which they transcend their usual mode of being, obtain their greatest power, and become one with the cosmos, living fully in the here and now in a euphoric high. Those who fail to become self-actualized become neurotic, sick, and nonauthentic (Maslow, 1961).

Rogers (1961) held that achieving authenticity should be the goal of each individual, and this means to follow one's own directives rather than those of others. Each person has a "true self" that is his or her "inner core," and this is authenticity; it is already fully developed and available. No self-development is required. To gain authenticity or self-actualization one must actualize one's person by living in accordance with that authentic core. It is more a matter of discovering the true self than of creating it. Neher (1992) points out that "where behaviorists have traditionally said 'you can become whatever you want, and we'll show you how,' Maslow, and other nativist theorists, have said, 'You can become whatever your native potential allows you to become, and nothing else'" (p. 96).

Rogers (1985) believed that humanistic psychology had considerable impact on American culture but little impact on academic psychology. He found that no doctoral program or internship program with that orientation and with the approval of the American Psychological Association exists anywhere in the country. Its research methods have also had little influence because most humanistically trained psychologists go into clinical psychology and do not take academic positions in major universities.

Actualizing tendency, self-actualization, and growth tendency are biological analogies based on Kurt Goldstein's argument that an organism reorganizes and self-actualizes itself after injury (De-Carvalho, 1990b; 1991). Gestalt psychology supplied the concept of wholeness of experience and its role in determining behavior. (Gestalt psychol-

ogy should not be confused with *gestalt therapy,* which is completely unrelated; gestalt therapy later contributed to the techniques used in group encounters.) Existential psychology (see chapter 12) also had considerable influence, especially on Maslow and Rollo May (1961, 1967, 1983). As set forth by existentialism, these two men affirmed an emphasis on the centrality of immediate experience in what it means to be human. But they were unenthusiastic about existentialism's pessimism, its tenet that dread accompanies the recognition of the freedom to be responsible for oneself in the universe—a universe without meaning. They were also critical of Sartre's (1943/1957) arguments that humans and their freedom are "nothingness of being" (p. 441). According to May, we have succumbed to materialism and abandoned the meaningfulness of the humanities. Much of this, he believes, is due to our universities having extensively replaced the study of the humanities and arts with the impersonal sciences and technologies (e.g., accounting, computers, and physical sciences). The latter direct us toward a passive existence that has no meaning. Only when we recognize how devoid we are of meaning and experience the despair that goes with that recognition will we have genuine choice and self-fulfillment, he insists.

Although humanistic psychologists were quite specific about what they opposed, they were less so about what they favored. The following are some of the latter as stated by Henry Murray in his keynote address at the Saybrook conference in 1964.[3] The object of study will be (a) humans rather than animals, (b) the whole person both in all its essential characteristics and as an integrity, (c) the person throughout the life span, (d) the internal person as a complement to the external, (e) the person in the natural world rather than in a laboratory, (f) the positive and joyful characteristics of the person, (g) volitional activity, (h) a philosophy of life involving a system of values through time. The list-

---

3. Although the address is unpublished, Taylor (1995) has given an account of it from the archived manuscript.

ing goes on without any clear consistency or over-all framework. Simpson's (1977) list includes "use of energy flows and the natural ability of the body to balance itself" and, borrowing from transpersonalism (see p. 118), "the spiritual dimension" (p. 76). Charlotte Buhler (1971), a psychiatrist and early president of the Association for Humanistic Psychology, set forth the principal interests as (a) the person as a whole, (b) the core of the life span (may be unconscious but usually "traceable"), (c) intentionality (conscious and unconscious "orientation to the world"), and (d) motivation and goal setting. To her, "The common denominator of these concepts is that all humanistic psychologists see the goal of life as using your life to accomplish something you believe in, be it self-development or other values. From this they expect a fulfillment toward which people determine themselves" (p. 381). More recently, DeCarvalho (1990b) published this list: (a) The person is a holistic unit that selects and organizes stimuli and also responds indirectly to stimuli by emitting responses to them; (b) humans act with purpose and self-motivation; (c) humans have the capacity to direct their own existence. Maslow called this last item "self-actualization"; Gordon Allport called it "functional autonomy"; and Rollo May and Carl Rogers—borrowing from the existentialists—called it "authenticity."

Underlying the diverse declaration of principles, Sass (1989) believes four concepts comprise its "centrality": (a) freedom of choice as against cause-and-effect determinism; (b) uniqueness of every individual; (c) privacy or subjectivity or inner reality; and (d) self-transparency, the "wellspring of freedom and locus of uniqueness and privacy" and the "source of certitude and clarity about human existence" (p. 442).

In a thoroughgoing attack on conventional psychology, Rychlak (1976, 1988) holds that psychology has gone the route of the physical sciences and has expunged both dialectical thinking that deals with opposites and bipolar relationships (replacing it with unipolar or linear cause and effect) and teleology (final cause or purpose) toward which things are directed. He charges that the for-

mulators of theories of nature made them conform to research methods and that this confounding of theory and method brought a mechanistic view of humans that became information processing and cybernetic models. In contrast, humanistic psychology turns to introspective reports and the resulting teleological accounts: humans not only respond to stimuli but also direct themselves toward goals and alternative goals that they conceptualize. It is toward these goals (teleological responses) that they logically act. Teleology "is the tie binding all humanists" (p. 217). It is because we recognize alternatives that our behavior tends to be bipolar or dialectic, he insists. Rychlak, unlike some other humanistic psychologists, insists that humanistic psychology cannot rely on philosophy and the arts for its science but must engage in rigorous research to validate its theories.

Rychlak assumes a mind in a body, a mind that thinks dialectically. A stimulus leads the mind to think about petting a golden retriever and also about its opposite, *not* petting a golden retriever. The mind can freely choose to act or not act on its thoughts. Thinking and other cognitive events are not limited by the stimulus: the mind actively contributes to the content beyond what the stimulus provides; it structures and gives meaning to the world. He sets forth a "logical learning theory" involving goal direction ("telosponse"). Behavior, he tells us, is not S—R bonds but is aimed toward completing goals that have meaning. People learn in order to improve their meaningful understanding of experience. Learning is a two-step process involving bipolarity of the thing observed and the referent to it. This enables teleological reasoning in which one pole points to the other and removes the person's understanding from contact with one of the poles. That allows for arbitrariness in choosing. Only in this way is meaningful understanding possible.

According to humanistic psychology, all individuals are continuously becoming what their capacities allow. They choose their course of life and accept their own responsibility for their selfhood and their attainment of their existence. To achieve the highest level of which they are capable, they must be functionally autonomous (according to Allport) or self-aware and centered (according to May). According to Maslow, the self must have a spontaneous integration and then engage in actualizing its potential through its "instinctoid," which presses it forward. The instinctoid is a biological potential that one discovers and brings to actualization by a creative process (Maslow, 1968). In contrast to such a biological determiner, May argued that the process of becoming occurs not through biology but by means of confronting anxieties that arise in the contingencies of existence and the self-awareness this produces. Rogers held that human nature is fundamentally good and with adequate opportunities will fulfill its inherent growth potential. Maslow, too, believed in goodness and that self-actualization will occur under favorable conditions. May, on the other hand (May, 1961, 1967), with some of his roots in existentialism, argued for evil and anxiety along with goodness as important determiners of being, authenticity, choice, and meaning.

Davidson (1992) notes two approaches to the system's emphasis on distinctiveness of humans. One of these comes from secular humanism, which uses evolutionary development to place humans at a position qualitatively different from that of other animals. Secular humanism is closely allied with philosophy of science and other nonreligious sources. It holds that humans create God in their own image rather than vice-versa, and that all improvements in human conditions must come from human efforts, not from a god or gods. People have the capability to develop their own ethics, values, and philosophy of life and will do so if they are not impeded by dogmatism and authorities. The second approach, transpersonal psychology, finds the distinctiveness in spirituality: "human beings are an incarnation of the Divine, created in the image of the Creator, and therefore set apart from the rest of the creation by virtue of their potential for enlightenment" (p. 146). This approach derives from mysticism, Neoplatonism, and Eastern religions. Maslow (1968) anticipated "transpersonal, transhuman" psychology "centered in the cosmos rather than in human needs and interests" (p. iv) as a "Fourth Psychology" that would be higher than Third Force humanistic psychology.

Transpersonal Psychology, the Counterculture, and the New Age

Transpersonal psychology has been closely allied with humanistic psychology, sharing some of the same founders and some of the same journal editors. As humanistic psychology became more established and focused on self-development, encounter groups, and psychotherapy for individual growth, Maslow and his close colleague Anthony Sutich departed from it in order to foster spirituality, altered states of consciousness, and the nurturing of inner experience. They founded transpersonal psychology and established the *Journal of Transpersonal Psychology,* just as they had done with humanistic psychology. Transpersonal psychology was "dedicated to the study of ultimate human capacities, unitive consciousness, peak experiences, ecstasy, mystical experiences, and self-transcendence" (Taylor, 1992, p. 289–90). It relates to Hinduism, Judaism, Christianity, Sufiism (Persian/Iranian sect of Islam), shamanistic vision quests, Emerson's transcendentalism, Neoplatonism, parapsychology, Islam, Buddhism, and other sources of mysticism; and it utilizes various methods of meditation as a means of controlling "states of consciousness." Tart (1975) particularly fostered the connection with Sufi and other forms of mysticism and continues to promote the occult in humanistic psychology (Tart, 1992).[4] Transpersonal psychology draws its economic base from its appeal to the New Age (occult) whose devotees buy its books and establish its channels of communication from public lectures, conferences, alternative medicine practiced at a network of health care clinics, advertising in alternative publications, and mass marketing of books (Taylor, 1992). More recently it has utilized the Internet.

---

4. See Randi (1982) for an exposé of some of Tart's parapsychology work.

According to Vitz & Modesti (1993), proponents of New Age hold that traditional religion and philosophy together with science have not only failed us but constitute part of the problem. They seek to revolutionize society around mysticism or spiritualism by establishing networks around the globe for the purpose of achieving a new world society. They have succeeded to some extent by spreading alternative or holistic medicine and by playing a central role in the human potential movement "where the discovery of one's inner potential is the source of positive personal transformation" (p. 47). The boundaries of the movement keep shifting as new beliefs and rituals develop; but some tenets can be identified, such as, (a) all existence is one whether god, human, or inanimate object; (b) all existence is god; (c) people are god; (d) one can recognize these truths through inner transformation to cosmic consciousness, self-realization, enlightenment, etc., through techniques taught by New Agers; (d) a cosmic oneness is fundamental to all religions; and (e) a consciousness of all this will bring about peace and bliss. Upper middle-class Americans who come from crumbling mainline Protestant groups or who were former Catholics comprise most of the New Age proponents. They are often linked with the drug culture and its connection with religious experiences such as those of shamanism. Some contributing social factors to the New Age movement are (a) the growing rootlessness and decline of cultural traditions across the country; (b) the human potential movement in California with its Esalen Institute, as well as varied occult practices especially in the southern part of that state, where several religions intermingle; (c) the humanistic psychology of Maslow and his "peak experience" concept as well as his support of the Esalen Institute and transpersonal psychology; (d) Carl Rogers' contribution to humanistic psychology with his self-centered therapy; (e) the advent of the *Journal of Transpersonal Psychology* in which academics and other intellectuals legitimized the concept of transcendent or spiritual highs by which, as some held, one could find one's internal divine self and unite it

with the cosmic divine; and (f) Carl Jung's advancement of religion and mythology as a part of an unconscious.

Transpersonal psychology was a component of the counterculture that arose in connection with psychedelic drugs and protest over the Vietnam War. Those who used drugs as a religious sacrament were known as "hippies." During a short period when they opposed the war, supported love and peace, turned away from traditional society, and advocated living by simple ideals, they were called "flower children." Humanistic psychology and the counterculture were born at about the same time—in the 1960s. By 1969 the counterculture had taken over humanistic psychology (Taylor, 1995); this was facilitated by a number of points of "resonance" (Smith, 1990):

- Fulfillment of the individual quite apart from any commitment to other people
- Belief in the perfectibility of humans, while neglecting social and political conditions
- Emphasis on self-disclosure or "letting it all hang out," together with casual intimacy and disregard for long-term relationships
- Self-indulgence in the present while ignoring the future and long-term goals
- Seeking whatever is immediately pleasurable, including drugs and sex
- Denigration of science and rationality and embrace of the occult.

"Sensitivity training" and "personal growth"—sometimes involving such techniques as nude psychotherapy, physical constraints while being "stimulated" (known variously as Z process therapy, attachment therapy, and rage reduction), and "touchy-feely" procedures—were common. At conferences the transpersonal emphasis on the part of the leadership of humanistic psychology was so pervasive that Smith (1982) complained that "the humanistic psychology movement was running away from the human in search of the supernatural and the divine" (p. 4).

As the counterculture movement infiltrated and took over humanistic psychology, many of its early members fled from it. The encounter group movement, especially as represented by the Esalen Institute in California, was an especially influential part of the counterculture. Encounter groups were intense group exercises, often marathon sessions, that sought holistic emotional experiences here and now through free-wheeling group interactions that put intense pressure on individual participants to provide full disclosure about themselves and to experience intense feelings. Friction between academics and practitioners arose at Esalen; and when Maslow insisted on maintaining intellectual responsibility, Fritz Perls called him "a sugar-coated fascist" (Russell, 1992). Yoga, meditation, and massage were prominent at Esalen. In Smith's (1990) appraisal, these groups "seemed to compensate for culturally engendered lack of meaning (faith), hope, and community" (p. 13) but were, he notes, also sleazy and shallow. He (1978) indicates that with the influence of transpersonalism, humanism "loses sight of the finite humanness of everyday life in the pursuit of the ineffable" (p. 29). Some critics have referred to humanistic psychology as "human-mystic psychology."

The Future

Smith (1990) seems to see the end of humanistic psychology as an academic discipline but suggests two current movements that might possibly continue its principles: (a) the recurrence of holistic personality approaches that could replace situationism, and (b) life-span human development involving a dialectic between individuals and their social setting in its historical change. In examining the attacks on psychology from many quarters and the predictions of its breakup into several separate disciplines, Smith (1994) suggests that cognitive psychology may go its own way to deal with "human reflexivity" but that developmental, personality, and social psychology will remain as a core of "human science" to work with community development, human development, psychotherapy, and education. Research and theory will continue with "the usual conception of science as aiming at progressive approximation of truth in regard to causal analysis of conditions and consequences, but make intrinsic reference to human meanings and values" (p. 114). Thus, he sees humanistic psychology's future role not as making fundamental reforms, but as adding a new dimension that this orientation deems crucial.

Giorgi (1992b) argues that since the meaning of being human is central to the approach, it should focus its efforts on rigorously analyzing these meanings. Sass (1989) suggests that it may gradually move away from humanistic concepts and incorporate more transpersonal psychology.

Chaos theory questions whether linear and predictable events are universal, and on the other hand it shows that complex and seemingly random events have an underlying order. Krippner, therefore, (1994) suggests that it provides a possible basis for a psychology that emphasizes creativity and health, and uses qualitative research methods that would be compatible with humanistic psychology.

SEMI-EXPLICIT POSTULATES

The founder of humanistic psychology, Maslow, seems to be the most appropriate person to provide a postulate system for the system. He has set forth a set of "assumptions" and a set of "propositions" from which a number of postulates can be fairly directly derived (Maslow, 1968), and other portions of his writings provide additional information for inferring postulates.

■ *Metapostulates* (supportive assumptions for a particular science)
   1. Psychological events are "biologically based."
      Corollary 1: Psychology is dependent on biology.
      Corollary 2: Psychological events are caused by biology or biology's mind.
   2. Psychological events are partly unique and partly universal—the universal component being the biological influence.
   3. Psychological events are not mechanisms but meanings.
   4. Psychological events are both natural and mystical.

■ *Postulates* (subject matter assumptions)

1. Humans are part body and part mind or self, and self is different from behavior and from body.
   Corollary: Psychology gives preeminence to constructs.
2. The self has biologically determined values that are socially neutral or good rather than destructive or evil.
3. The biological determinants are weak and easily changed by the environment.
4. Biology presents a hierarchy of needs from tissue needs to social and personal needs.
5. Humans are self-causative.

RESEARCH

It is not always clear what comprises humanistic research and what does not. The criterion used here is that the researchers themselves identify it as humanistic or that other humanistic psychologists refer to it as such. Some of the research also carries an existential or phenomenological label.

Because humanistic psychologists believe that controlled laboratory research or quantification totally miss what is uniquely human about human beings, they have typically opposed this type of research. Those few who do quantitative research often use rating scales (Ebersole & Quiring, 1991; Prasinos & Tittler, 1984); but these too involve a mechanistic or technological approach and are therefore objectionable, according to Giorgi (1992b). The phenomenological-existentialist approach that Giorgi prefers, advocates ignoring reliability and validity as well as numbers and starting with the subject matter, adapting the methodology to it. Believing that meaning reveals itself in language, Reason and Rowan (1981) recommend the use of language methods. Aanstoos (1987; cited in Polkinghorne, 1992) finds five major qualitative methods in use and twelve or more auxiliary ones. There are also those who would accept all methodologies (for example, Lindauer, 1974; Rychlak, 1988; Tageson, 1982) as long as

they maintain a balance and focus on what is central to humanistic psychology. In contrast to the others, Rychlak (1988) argues that because quantitative methods of the behavioral sciences are independent of theory, they are suitable; and he uses them in his own research.

According to Davidson (1992), the "major weakness [of humanistic psychology] is that it is perceived as having yet to produce much of lasting impact" (p. 148). It cannot, he holds, rest on philosophical statements but must overcome its resistance to systematic research and go forward with empirical studies that deal with the concrete lives of people by using such methodologies as those of phenomenology, ethnology, and narrative research.

Controlled Studies

As a test of his "logical learning theory," Rychlak (1976, 1988) has conducted an extensive program of research on affective responding or reinforcement *value*—that is, the conceptual value of something as opposed to reinforcement of a behavior pattern. The conceptual values we attribute to something make it possible to choose a course of action to the pay-off or to its opposite (petting a golden retriever, not petting a golden retriever)—thus a dialectical process. He ran a series of experiments with nonsense syllables rated for their reinforcement value of like or dislike and followed these with recognition of words, faces, and pictures. His results supported the theory. For example, oppositionality in learning (dialectical responding) is supported by the fact that people learn the opposite meaning of disliked words at a higher rate than the opposite of liked words. Students perform better on liked than on disliked tasks and remember liked faces better than disliked ones. Rychlak has extended his work to personality characteristics and found that those characteristics correlate with degree to which the person likes a task. In other words, Rychlak is trying to show that learning is not a mechanical coupling of stimulus and response as classical and operant conditioning would suggest; rather, he contends that people learn best when they can direct their choices to those things they value.

Prasinos and Tittler (1984) correlated college students' scores from a questionnaire on lovestyles with those on five other scales. Because the "agapic" lovestyle (altruistic, gentle, and caring) correlated significantly with (a) life regard (setting goals and moving toward fulfillment); (b) spirituality; (c) self-esteem; (d) ego strength (translating intentions into action and maintaining tension control); and (e) lovingness, it was the most "successful." The high self-esteem suggested that loving others requires first loving oneself. In descending order after agapic was "ludic" (promiscuous), "erotic" (seeking an ideal body type), "storgic" (gradually developing affection and anticipation of long term commitment), "pragmatic" (fitting age, education, and other demographic requirements), and "manic" (obsessive, jealous, requiring repeated reassurance). The manic lovestyle correlates with anxiety about death and has minimal—or even negative—relations with self-esteem. All lovestyles showed some correlation with the manic scale. Each lovestyle, the researchers hold, has a distinctive "psychological structure." It is "a major component of the self" and indicates the "larger existential matrix of the individual": "How one loves is part of the picture of how one relates to life and to the fact of one's existence" (p. 108).

Ebersole and Quiring (1991) developed the Meaning in Life Depth (MILD) scale to complement one called Purpose in Life Test (PIL). The PIL measures strength of meanings as shown by feelings and enthusiasm. The MILD is more intellectual than affective, measuring the constituents of meanings. The examinee writes paragraphs that are scored on degree of meaning according to five criteria. It has shown that those with high scores on meaning are "generally hard-working, successful, mature, socially adjusted, relatively conventional older people" (p. 122).

In an effort to see if volitional behavior is self-determined, Howard (1992) gave subjects instructions to try engaging in some action during a block of time and, during alternate periods, to try not to so engage (try or try not to eat junk food, try or try not to procrastinate, try or try not to exercise, etc.). Because they could comply when the behavior was ethically neutral (not harmful to anyone) but had increasing difficulty as the ethical consequences became greater, he interprets the results to demonstrate self-causing will power.

Jourard (1978) used a self-disclosure questionnaire (forty items of personal information) to determine whether astrological signs of college students related to their self-disclosure patterns. He found no statistically significant relationships.

Most humanistic psychotherapists have resisted any efforts to evaluate their work. They have felt that subjective testimony is all that is needed and all that is appropriate. But Rogers (Rogers & Diamond, 1954) felt the need for evaluation and conducted the first controlled study of psychotherapy. Q-sorts, TAT or Thematic Apperception Test (invented by Murray, the keynote speaker at the Saybrook conference), rating scales, and recorded interviews were used to compare a therapy group with control groups. The results from the various devices were complex, but among the findings, as shown by Q-sorts comparing self with ideal self, the therapy group was significantly different from control groups in showing the self gradually becoming more like the ideal self. The authors suggested that this indicated a rise in self-esteem and improved adjustment. In general, the results showed that client-centered therapy provided marked improvement in the clients' adjustment. Despite Rogers' recognition of the need for evaluation of therapy and the exemplary model he set, he later endorsed encounter groups without any objective evidence of their benefits.

Another study that used TAT, Rorschach ink blots, and Q-sorts for self and ideal self selected for detailed analysis a person who was described as extremely happy (Ricks & Wessman, 1966). The authors noted that psychology showed little interest in happiness. In a section of the journal about the contributors, the editors questioned the congruity between humanistic psychology and Q methodology's factor analysis.

Qualitative Studies

Using survey questions, "active interviews," and participant observation, Bellah et al. (1985) studied more than two hundred white, middle-class Americans over a five-year period. They investigated "what resources Americans have for making sense of their lives, how they think about themselves and their society, and how their ideas related to their actions" (p. x). They included (a) love and marriage and how it shaped people's lives, (b) therapists and clients on self-understanding and their view of relationships and commitments, (c) people in voluntary organizations on their reasons for involvement and its contributions to their meaning in life, (d) people in political organizations for their perspectives on society in general and how political work meshed with their private lives. They found that many people were devoted to improving themselves by practices or training and often in so doing found "something that transcends them" (p. 290). As traditional ways of life that gave meaning to life have declined, improvised ways have taken their place, such as sports, arts, and exercise regimens. Some people are torn between a competitive public world and private attempts to make competition tolerable. Some have tried to reconcile the two. All are attempting to adapt traditions to present situations. Although there is widespread dissatisfaction with current social conditions, most do not seek any major change in national life and hold out hope for the good life. Many find temporary ways of dealing with "our damaged social ecology" (p. 294), but some feel we will sink into despotism unless we reform.

Using a broad population, Fishir and Wertz (1979) taped and transcribed fifty interviews with victims of crimes. They sought information about what it is like to be a crime victim that statistics cannot provide. The procedure consisted of first writing a synopsis of each case, focusing on the essentials of each person's experience and using a close approximation to each individual's words. Then they looked for sequences of events and personal meanings that were present across cases and wrote the results as a narrative. This

they condensed to the existential meanings of victimization—that is, the personal meanings that would make sense of the experience. Then going back to individual synopses, they looked for experiences that would exemplify all victims of crimes and the essential constituents of the psychological organization of such an experience. The last produced a lengthy account.

Another study, this one of women, also involved taped and transcribed interviews (Belenky et al., 1986). The authors describe the study as "five different perspectives from which women view reality and draw conclusions about truth, knowledge, and authority" (p. 3) and, with an unclear connection to the first characterization, also as their wish to "explore with women their experience and problems as learners and knowers as well as to review their past histories for changing concepts of self and relationships with others" (p. 11). The informants were drawn from a broad population of 135 women including 90 from educational institutions of various types and 45 from agencies for those needing assistance with mothering. The interviews, each lasting two to five hours, asked each to tell about life *from her point of view* [author's emphasis]" (p. 11). They designed some sections of the interview to provide specific scores, and these were scored blindly by independent scorers. They grouped perspectives on knowing into five categories and developed additional coding categories for experiences of developing beings and of the learning environment. From their findings they concluded that education could help women more if it used more "connection over separation," more acceptance than assessment, more cooperation than debate, more respect for firsthand experience, and more encouragement of students to pursue their own ways of working.

In order to determine "personal constructs," the individual's perspectives or "construing" of an experience, Botterill (1989) used five conversations with one person before and after his tour of Japan. Using computer analyses of a Repertory Grid he extracted the personal constructs as they changed at various points. The findings in each case were used in the subsequent conversation. Photographs he had taken in Japan were also used. In the last conversation, "Sam was struck by the extent of what he saw as an advancement in his thinking over the period of the research" (p. 291).

A highly unusual topic and methodology is Reed's dream incubation (1976).[5] The participant goes through preparation procedures including contemplating the dream's purposes, choosing personal symbols and a revered benefactor, and spending a day in symbolic purification. This is followed by the incubation ceremony, discussion and role playing, and sleep in the sacred place. Reed finds that the dreamers report "a subtle yet quite encouraging change in their relationship to their dreams" (p. 66). The intention is "to help the incubant become more self-sufficient in growth" (p. 67).

Unpublished Dissertations

Rogers (1985) summarizes a number of unpublished doctoral dissertations that he feels deserve publication in some form, both because of their quality and because of the range of methods and topics they demonstrate. The following is a summary of his summary: Colleen McNally studied her own experiences of "really feeling sensitive" and found that it involved (a) being open and (b) being touched. As a test of Maslow's hierarchy of needs, Marcine Johnson used a Q-sort with thirty female psychotherapy clients. As predicted, it showed greater feelings of discontent after brief therapy that was judged effective than at the beginning of therapy. Using written descriptions, Debora Brink found similarities as well as statistical differences between physics graduate students and psychology graduate students in terms of intellectually meaningful experiences. The physicists found some of their meaningful experiences in playful approaches and esthetic qualities whereas the psychologists did not mention these. By employing

eight observers, Sara Walinksy made intense observation of a single case, a fourteen-year-old boy with learning difficulties. She found quite different characteristics in different situations, varying from normal to intellectually precocious to affectively disordered. Kathleen Lisowski used sign language to interview deaf older adults to reveal their coping mechanisms and personalities. Using observation in the natural setting, Sally Wood studied a couple for one month prior to the birth of their first child and for two months afterward. The period of disruption following the birth, she found, was especially important in the transformation from a couple to a family. Suzanne Shaw interviewed those from a medical school who had participated two years earlier in a week of encounter group experiences and those who hadn't. Sixty percent of the participants reported beneficial interpersonal changes but only twenty percent of the nonparticipants so reported. Rogers lists still others by title and author involving such topics as heroin experiences, meaning of illness, adult-child relations, character of mystery, discovery of solitude, and experiences of siblings of schizophrenics.

APPLICATIONS

Other than psychotherapy and group experiences, the two main applied areas to which humanistic psychology has contributed are industrial/organizational psychology and educational psychology. However, some of the concepts and practices were pioneered, as humanistic psychology acknowledges, before it was born (Massarik, 1992; Richards & Combs, 1992).

Education

In education the system advances the position that the educational process should address the interests, desires, and goals of the pupil rather than those of the educator. Education should help pupils clarify such values as beauty, justice, freedom, truth, and responsibility, and it should promote the growth of self-concept and self-actualization so that the child may reach his or her

---

5. Reed left a professorship at Princeton University to pursue experimental dream research. The article reported here marked the departure point.

potential. It must foster the child's (a) creativity, (b) emotional health, and (c) being a person (Buhler, 1971). The teachers should use their experiential worlds to relate to that of the pupil. Curricula should include subjective experience as well as facts and skills; and rote memory and teacher presentations should make room for cooperative experiences, dialogue, and group discussion. A humanistic textbook for students in an educational curriculum states that "the way pupils feel in school is more important than anything else" (Bassett, 1978, p. ix) and that learning is "a by-product of the choosing process rather than . . . a product of the teacher's instructions" (p. 253). It calls for learners to become self-actualized through choosing their own activities and regulating their own participation.

What have been broadly called humanistic or progressive approaches to education began before humanistic psychology came on the scene in the elementary schools of the 1930s through the influence of Teachers College of Columbia University (Butts, 1955). Emphasis was on (a) the *experiences* of the learner rather than the subject matter to be learned; (b) the *wholeness* of the learner, requiring purposeful activities interesting to the learner; and (c) the *creativity* of the learner that engaged his or her participation in establishing, planning, conducting, and evaluating his or her own activities. The teacher became not a source of knowledge but a facilitator. What should be learned were not facts for an examination of mastery but the meanings the learning has to the individual in further experiences. The approach then added the social importance of the learning to the child's life and subsequently included attention to emotional needs. Educators extended this philosophy to secondary schools where courses in social living—and sometimes also the "experience curriculum" of elementary schools—became a part of the curriculum. When humanistic psychology developed, it was quite compatible with this orientation and contributed to it.

For the future, Richards and Combs (1992) call for (a) more school counseling, (b) the fostering of healthy self concepts, (c) training of teachers to become less managers and more facilitators, (d) the inclusion of pupils in all decision making, (e) more personal relationships between teachers and pupils, and (f) more individualized instruction and multicultural education. "In the main, our present schools are the products of objective-behaviorist thinking no longer adequate for today's students or for society's pressing demands" (p. 383).

The non-directive and self-actualizing educational views of Maslow and Rogers together with William Coulsen were tried out in the California schools. Van Kaam (1993), the person who established existential-phenomenological psychology at Duquesne University and who voiced his objection to the educational plan, describes the results:

> The unfortunate consequences, the resulting complaints by parents and children, the scientific appraisal by experts of the outcomes of this experiment were not encouraging. To the dismay of Maslow and Coulson other schools, educational institutes, and programs began blindly to imitate the absolutely non-directive education process. They did not consult the outcomes of the scientific evaluations. Coulson and Maslow traveled far and wide to warn educators and parents that he himself, Maslow, and Rogers had been too optimistic in their expectations of an education for children that was totally non-directive. (p. 265)

The experiment clearly demonstrated that "decision-making beyond the region of one's knowledge, expertise, and life experience would be counter-productive" (van Kaam, 1993, p. 265). It is important to recognize that Richards and Combs' call for pupil participation in decision making is not the same as non-directive education. In a broad-based study Aspy and Roebuck (1988) found that when teachers manifested Rogers' advocacy of "empathy, congruence, and unconditional positive regard," the pupils performed better than without these conditions. They note that good treatment does not preclude the teaching of content but "that it is essential to be humanly decent *in order* to teach students something" (p. 17). Hamachek, while advocating a humanistic educational psychology (1987), makes a similar point and goes so far as to say "humanistic principles translated to the level of classroom practices sometimes offer too little by way of structure and organization and sometimes expect too little in terms of student output and achievement" (p. 179).

A version of humanistic education called "critical humanism" begins with "individual feelings, which are brought into contact with external forces that then contribute to the form those feelings take" (Nemiroff, 1992, p. 89). The teacher uses a dialectic analysis of individuals and groups to reach "a locus of authentic discourse" (p. 89) so that members of the group can find their internal resources to contribute to their own and the group's understanding. This, claims the author, is empowering and makes possible meaningful discussions about how social institutions mediate and control people's lives. "When these explanations are attached to personal experiences and feelings, the ensuing insights become catalysts for change in people's attitudes, self-esteem, and courage to engage in projects for change" (p. 90).

Industry and Organization

According to Massarik (1992), Maslow's hierarchical motivation theory has been employed in industrial/organizational work in the management of employees at various levels in the hierarchy and in helping workers to self-actualize their work. Rogers' client-centered approach has also been influential in interviewing techniques, employee counseling, and assessment procedures. His approach to potential for growth has affected personnel policies, training, and organizational development. Maslow and Rogers have also been involved in small-group training with a humanistic orientation. At UCLA such training has been offered to managers for a period of more than forty years, Massarik notes.

PSYCHOTHERAPY

A variety of humanistic psychotherapies has developed. What these have in common is an effort to work from the client's point of view, to be accepting and nonjudgmental, and to place the source of therapeutic change with the client.

Bohart and Tallman (1996) review the research on the effectiveness of psychotherapies and find that self-help is about as effective as professional therapy of whatever type. And humanistic therapy primarily encourages self-help. The authors conclude that what makes any therapy work is the active client, and any procedure or technique should be in the service of helping the client take charge of his or her life. "The gifts the therapist gives are, first of all, a safe working space in which clients can dialogue and creatively think, experience, and explore. Second, therapists give procedures that clients can use to create new experiences for themselves and through such creation develop new perspectives and new solutions. Third, therapists give their own interactive experience and feedback" (p. 26).

Therapies of Actualizing Potential

These therapies are heavily influenced by Maslow and Rogers. They assume a biological potential that only needs encouragement and opportunities to unfold and grow. The outlook is optimistic; it sees humans as positive and joyous with an overwhelming tendency toward goodness. The forms these therapies take is diverse and continuing to grow as originators refine their own methods and as new people take them up and try out their own ideas. The following is a sample.

Client-Centered Therapy. Rogers' non-directive or client-centered therapy is the first of the humanistic therapies and, though used in its classic form by no one today, continues to be a source of inspiration for its philosophy. With it Rogers led a radical change in psychotherapy. He referred to "clients" rather than using the passive term "patients." The clients were not treated for a sickness but allowed to use their own values and life-direction to realize their potentials—no history taking, no diagnosis, no record keeping, no couch, no interpretations, no suggestions or directions of any kind. Not even any questions or requests such as "tell me more about . . .". As a means of enabling clients to develop their own self-understanding and growth, the therapist would only rephrase and reflect back the clients' statements, often as a feeling. For example:

> *Client:* My father would get angry with me whenever I wanted to do something my own way.
>
> *Therapist:* You feel that your father was often angry with you.
>
> *Client:* Not really often, but whenever I wanted to be my own self.
>
> *Therapist:* You wanted to do what was satisfying to you without your father's anger.
>
> *Client:* Yeah, that's what I wanted.
>
> *Therapist*: Uh-huh.

When the client runs out of something to say, the therapist remains silent until the client once again resumes with another step of discovery. The silences are part of the therapeutic process.

Heuristic Therapy. Moustakas (1990) developed a heuristic (discovery) research method and a procedure for the therapeutic application of it: In the *initial engagement* the therapist creates a climate of openness, trust, and a kind of mutual bonding. The core theme or problem to deal with also emerges. In *immersion* the therapist enters into the client's world, appreciating and communing without prejudice, comprehending the whole and all of its facets. During *incubation* insights come without laboring for them. In *indwelling* the therapist "mingles freely" with the critical components, "dwelling inside them" to become aware of the core themes so that deeper understanding develops. Next comes *illumination.* The therapist finds the major structures and themes and dwells inside each one to understand its deeper meanings. Dur-

ing the interactions the therapist presents his or her perspective ("internal frame of reference") to the client to see how it might match that of the client.

> This process of coming to be known through the internal frame of reference and through dialogues between the therapist and the person in therapy facilitates a breakthrough in therapeutic relations. It often represents the first time in a person's life that being understood is complete, and is consistent with one's own understanding . . . As a therapist I verbalize the knowledge I have obtained through immersion and indwelling, and the person verifies, elaborates, and corrects it. The respective frames of reference of the person in therapy and the therapist are in harmony. (p. 111)

The therapist also uses his or her *intuition* based on past experiences. It can be corrected if wrong, and when it is correct it allows moving on to richer meanings. According to Moustakas, heuristic psychotherapy "brings one into touch with creative resources, enables one to develop a new view of self and life, and makes possible movement toward authenticity, self-efficacy, and well-being" (p. 124).

Most of the humanistic therapies are heuristic approaches in that clients are helped to discover their own potentials and to self-actualize them. The Center for Humanistic Psychology in Detroit, Michigan, is an independent graduate school that offers degrees and training in humanistic clinical and educational psychology and emphasizes heuristics (Kostere, 1987).

Strategic Therapy. In describing a strategic humanistic therapy, Mandanes (1993) insists that people are not determined by a Creator, genes, social context, parental treatment, privation, instincts, or chemistry. The wealthy merely have more choices than do the poor. She admits that changing the social context is the most expeditious way to change people in therapy, but she insists that all individuals can change themselves.

The goal of strategic therapy is to increase choices. She provides the following example of the procedure in family therapy. A wife was resentful that her husband regularly neglected her and favored his mother. He had told his mother that they had had to get married due to pregnancy, but in reality they had planned both the marriage and the pregnancy. The strategic therapist—holding no brief for an Oedipus complex or the necessity of working through it, prescribing no medicine for chemical changes, and exploring no hypothetical childhood causes—saw that the husband had never communicated to all parties that it was his wife whom he had chosen as first in his life. She instructed the husband to phone his mother during a therapy session and clarify his priorities to his mother. Several calls were necessary before the wife was satisfied and a new beginning was possible. "This is a therapy of action, where each person takes responsibility for his or her own life, and where the therapist takes responsibility for the work of the therapy" (p. 75).

Experiential Therapy. In this procedure the therapist experiences whatever the client is experiencing. Mahrer (1993) gives four steps:

1. A strong, full feeling is the first goal, and this activates "some inner experiencing." Gendlin (1977) describes the attempt to get a "felt sense" or a "felt edge" of a problem. This is something felt that doesn't yet make sense. The therapist slows the client down to dwell on it. Whatever feeling comes is welcomed, and it should feel right and give a sense of relief.
2. The client and therapist welcome and savor the inner experience and their bond to each other.
3. The client becomes the inner experience and uncouples from the previous personality. The client and therapist find an incident in the client's life and then live this scene together with joy.
4. The client lives this new person in scenes of the future.

Mahrer (1993) has taken experiential therapy a stage further to what he calls *transformational therapy.* The therapist doesn't stop at just experiencing the client's feelings but is transformed into "really and fully living and being in these immediate, vivid, alive, real scenes and situations . . . Instead of being empathic with the person, you are fully being the person. Instead of knowing the person's world, you are living it" (p. 34). He considers transformational therapy more powerful than experiential therapy.

The Power Within. A device for therapy called the "Power Within" uses twelve steps (Chapin, 1989):

(1) Establish that the purpose of the technique "is to create a subjective reality from which the client can therapeutically benefit" (p. 449).
(2) Apprise the client of literature about the procedure.
(3) Indicate what steps in the procedure could be helpful to the client.
(4) Review with the client what he or she can expect.
(5) Elicit guided imagery.
(6) Through imagery help the client find the "Power Within."
(7) Help the client address his or her concern to the "Power."
(8) Promote a dialogue between the client and the "Power."
(9) Review the themes of the dialogue or ask the "Power" to do so and thank the "Power" for its guidance.
(10) Conclude the imagery by suggesting to the client that he or she can remember or forget whatever he or she wishes.
(11) Explore with the client how the experience can be utilized.
(12) Integrate the themes into therapy.

Example: a twenty-year-old college student suffering from anorexia nervosa had a serious conflict with her mother from which she was unable to withdraw. The "Power Within" that she imagined "suggested that she felt guilty and therefore deserving of the abuse. The truth, it said, was that she was a child doing what children do and that her mother was acting irrationally and abusively. The advice given to the client was to care about herself, stand up for herself, and realize that she could walk away from her mother's irrational demands" (p. 453).

Therapies of Becoming

The humanistic-existentialist therapies have a somewhat distinctive characteristic. They deal more with nonrational behavior and take a more pessimistic view of humans than do those that assume a process of actualizing a biological potential. They see society as dehumanizing people through its regimens and hierarchical bureaucratic structures and thereby impeding self-actualization. Alienation and emptiness, they claim, are widespread in our culture as we lose a sense of community and tradition and attempt to compensate with "food, drug-induced experiments, status-laden consumer items, sexual experiments, or pop spiritualism" (Bugental & Bracke, 1992, p. 29). Their approach is to emphasize the client's ability to understand and deal with the problems. This method works best with those clients who are intelligent and verbal and who can face painful issues and grapple with them and less well—obviously—with those who do not have these characteristics (Lowenstein, 1993). It is a long-term procedure.

DeCarvalho (1990a) describes the approach this way: Ordinary awareness of things is the process of becoming. But self-awareness is becoming that results in self-actualization and authenticity. Becoming is not the result of actualizing a biological core á la Rogers and Maslow but is a product of the intentionality of the self—its relatedness to things. The process of self-awareness can occur at either a personal or a cultural level. The *personal level* involves reflecting on the process of becoming in which the reflecting process itself changes that very process, and this continues in endless cycles of change and becoming. In the case of anxiety,

One is anxious when one is no longer able to reflect upon one's own state of anxiety. In that case, one is totally submerged in the process of becoming anxious. One is, in other words, totally anxious. Self-reflection or contemplation upon one's anxiety, however, changes that state of anxiety. Self-actualization is possible only on the second instance. (p. 255)

Any awareness of becoming changes the static process of becoming to the dynamic process of self-actualization. The *cultural level* of self-actualization involves the self's reflecting on the characteristics of the culture and choosing among the possibilities the culture offers. This may be compared with non-reflection and non-actualization in which the self merely becomes a component of the culture or identifies with it without ever examining the choices or recognizing that choices are available. Mere becoming as in the Rogers-Maslow conception is the static process of becoming, but self-reflection is the dynamic process that leads to self-actualization, or authentic becoming.

Psychotherapy is directed toward the client's becoming self-aware and thereby finding direction and leaving behind the sense of hopelessness of life. "The patients ought to understand that their life is a process of becoming, that they are condemned to become, and that if they do not choose (or, choose not to choose) then either their culture, sub-culture or someone in their lives will chose for them" (p. 256–57). Frequently a crisis will "awaken the patient to his or her own inevitable and some times dreadful need to become an authentic individual" (p. 257), for a painful experience brings the individual into confrontation with the inauthentic self, an encounter that otherwise would not occur. The most effective crisis is anxiety about death, the recognition of one's own impending annihilation, for this makes living personal and meaningful. Humanistic-existential psychotherapies train the individual to transform him or herself from casual, oblivious becoming to authentic, aware becoming in which personal choices are clarified. Self-actualization occurs because "the self is a product of its own intentionality" (p. 257).

In reference to Rogers' empirical studies of his own client-centered therapy, Severin (1973)

insists that Rogers "is engaging in a form of abstraction which is clearly a violation of existential philosophy" (p. 297). Apparently, humanistic-existentialists would consider inappropriate any attempt to evaluate the effectiveness of the psychotherapy.

Legitimate Humanistic Psychology Therapies?

Two prominent psychotherapies, gestalt and rational-emotive (RET), are accepted or partly accepted by some humanistic psychologists but rejected by others as being within the framework of humanistic psychology. RET is also often considered a cognitive—or cognitive-behavioral—therapy.

Rational-Emotive Therapy. RET attempts to deal directly with maladjustment. It holds that people train themselves in neurotic conflict by unknowingly engaging in irrational thoughts and that they can reverse this process by replacing irrational thoughts with rational ones. The role of the therapist is to take an authoritative position as an expert, confront the client with the irrational thoughts, render the thoughts explicit, and force him or her to reject the thoughts. Because the thought patterns are long-standing, the therapist cannot bring about a permanent change. The client him or herself must learn to actively combat the irrational thoughts on a continuing basis for life. Therapy also consists of helping people find or create new meanings. RET insists that people can best find fulfillment and self-actualization after they have overcome the impediments of their dysfunctions and that an understanding and attack on the core philosophies from which the dysfunctions arise will lead to a more rational pattern.

Because many irrational beliefs are quite tenacious, RET also deals with emotions (hence "rational-emotive") with a variety of conditioning and cognitive techniques.[6] RET assumes that be-

lief in conditions that *must* or *must not* be leads to emotional disturbance: "I *must* do it right." "I *must* be normal." "I *have to* do my best." "I *must not* appear unintelligent." In RET these "musts" and "must nots" *must* be countered with rationality.

The therapists unconditionally accept their clients and teach them to accept themselves as well. RET proponents claim that most other therapies foster clients' increasing dependence on the therapist's approval whereas RET avoids this by helping clients accept themselves quite independently of what the therapist thinks about them. Besides being supportive and instructive, it is active-directive (as opposed to non-directive), and, in fact, it can be quite aggressive in attacking irrational beliefs. It attempts to enable clients to replace irrational thinking with a rational and realistic understanding of their own qualities and capabilities with which they and they alone can solve their own problems. While some of its tenets and procedures square with humanistic psychology and some do not, its founder Albert Ellis considers it to "stem from a secular humanist outlook" (Ellis, 1992, p. 357). The emphasis on *secular* humanism as a philosophy sets RET apart from the mysticism, religion, or spiritualism that have pervaded humanistic psychology, he points out. He sees RET's greatest future application in education (Ellis, 1993).

Gestalt Therapy. Developed by Perls (1969), this therapy attempts to clarify a core self-concept that is self-denigrating, a product of past pain and defenses against the pain (Korb, Gorrell, and Van de Riet, 1989). Gestalt therapy does not require the client to give an account of his or her problem nor does it take a history. Rather, it turns to life as it is rather than as it was or should be. The therapist tries to heighten whatever the client is experiencing: If the client is tense, dramatize tension; if anxious, increase the anxiety. The therapist might ask the client to imaginatively place the anxiety in an empty chair and speak to it. Then the client could take the place of the anxiety and speak back. If a wife feels resentment at her husband's treatment of her and is reluctant to confront him, she will be

---

6. This point is very similar to Quinn's (1993). Because of the "phenomenon of holding stubbornly to dysfunctional patterns of behavior" (p. 14), he finds it necessary to add an intervention to Rogers' empathy and unconditional acceptance.

encouraged to have an imaginary dialogue. The effort is to move from talking about problems in life to immediately living that life. If a client tries to avoid crying, the therapist invites him or her to deliberately cry; if she is nervously rubbing one hand with the other, to do so deliberately and exaggeratedly. Other devices that gestalt therapists use where appropriate include art, body language, dreams, exaggeration of speech or motion, reversal of a statement, and verbally rehearsing fears and expectations. The therapist might invite the client to stand up and shout at herself/himself, to think out new patterns, to imagine differently, to deliberately practice a symptom or an awareness, to try out any number of new behavior patterns. The therapist may function either as a participant or as an observer. In the observer mode the therapist leaves behind his or her experiences and enters a direct relation with the client, challenging or reflecting the client's statements and feelings. In the participatory mode the therapist shares viewpoints, feelings, and experiences.

Perls tried to direct attention to body feelings and to various awarenesses. These become concrete here and now. The client may role-play two opposing characteristics of his or her personality, the "me" and any of the diverse "not-mes"—some of which, he maintained, come from other people who have become incorporated into the person. The dialogue may be with a critical part and a criticized part, each speaking from an empty chair. The client and therapist are active partners in the therapeutic process.

Perls insisted that no one self is the real self, that there are many selves which keep changing as life changes. We are what we are here and now, not some static thing. The many selves or people we are can be integrated and accepted whether we like them or not.

With progress on clarifying the core concept, the client begins to make decisions and to develop a more fulfilling life. Family, school, or workplace may need attention, but the focus is the client's own vitality and process of living. The client must decide to change self-defeating self-concepts and become self-supportive. The old painful and unfulfill-

ing defenses and self-concepts make way for true potentials to be actualized. Over time the client begins to trust the new self-supportive beliefs.

RELATION TO SOME OTHER APPROACHES

Behavior Analysis

A number of comparisons and debates have centered around these two approaches (for example, Matson, 1973; Rogers & Skinner, 1956; Wandersman, 1976; Wann [humanism misnamed phenomenology], 1964). As the humanists see it, the major difference is that behavior analysts seek external control and deny free will while humanists try to work from the inside by enabling the self to make free choices that will lead to personal fulfillment. Not surprisingly, the behavior analysts have a different interpretation.

Smith (1978) wishes to use both behaviorism's "external" understanding and humanism's "internal" understanding. E. Geller (1995) analyzes how the two might be brought together for a more effective approach on "actively caring for the environment" than either of them alone. Newman (1992) does this for psychotherapy, education, and public policy after carefully correcting the misinterpretations of behavior analysis and presenting the views of major figures in humanistic psychology. He shows that they both have their roots in a broader philosophy of naturalistic humanism and are complementary to each other: humanism provides a goal of human fulfillment without a method whereas behavior analysis provides a method without a guiding philosophy. He notes that they both hold that "persons must be treated as ends unto themselves" (p. 69) with "maximum benefit" for each individual and concludes that science and reason should be used "to achieve the goal of human fulfillment in this world" (p. 117).

Behavior analysis's development of self-management might not be far from some of the humanistic concerns about self-control as opposed to external control, even though, according to the behavior analysts, "the locus of control is not within the individual but rather within the environment designed by the individual" (Newman, 1992, p. 83). It can be used for maintaining exercise regimens, smoking cessation, weight control, and other long-term programs. The two might have different conceptualizations of the dynamics while possibly agreeing on the values.

Probably less agreement would occur in educational philosophy. Would humanist authors, (Richards & Combs, 1992) who claim that objective behavioral thinking fails to meet society's needs, reject the use of approval, reassurance, encouragement, and acceptance—the reinforcers that behavior analysts would find indispensable? The answer is probably "yes," unless the reinforcers are without condition—given regardless of what the pupil does.

Cognitive Psychology

Humanistic psychologists applaud the fact that cognitivists brought mind back into psychology. The fact that they both favor mind-body dualism and organocentrism (organism the cause of its own action) and deemphasize animal studies may be the only points the two have in common. For the cognitivists mind has become processing, cognition, and mental (or brain) representation. For the humanistic psychologists it is self and terms related to self.

The humanists point out that cognitivism took over from behaviorism the orientation toward a mechanistic theory and a laboratory methodology. They see cognitivism as little more than disguised behaviorism. That cognitivists regard mind as a passive processor of information that contributes nothing additional to environmental inputs to the knowing relationship is anathema to them, as is its non-teleological approach.

Phenomenological and Existential Psychology

Both phenomenological and humanistic psychologies share an emphasis on giving priority to what is meaningful to people rather than regarding the world as comprised of impersonal and physicalistic things to which people respond as in operant or classical conditioning. But they differ in that phenomenological psychologists such as Sartre and Merleau-Ponty look more to meanings in the relationships between people and their meaningful world. Meaning is always person-in-the world or person-in-context, though Bucklew (1955) and Ratner (1971) charge that phenomenological psychology actually falls short in its treatment of the role of the world in the person-world relationship. Friedman (1976) is close to phenomenological psychology when he says "the word 'self' has no meaning, I submit, apart from the way we respond to life situations. . . . Only when I forget myself and respond with all myself to something not myself, only then do I even have a self; for only then does my true uniqueness emerge" (p. 12). But most humanistic psychologists, in contrast, seek meanings inside the individual—in the "relations of the individual's person with his own inner, authentic self" (Orlov, 1992, p. 41). This inward entity they refer to as "self," "ego," "consciousness," "mind," or "experience." Even "person" they often use as the inner agent as, for example, "Stimulus—*Person*—Response" (Hamachek, 1987, p. 166). As such, they advocate dualism both implicitly and explicitly whereas phenomenological psychologists to some extent replace such dualism with person-world relationships.

American humanistic psychology has adapted some of European existentialism with the result, Yalom (1980) notes, that the former is more optimistic than the latter, perhaps due to experiences in the Western hemisphere that differ from conditions in Europe. This difference is revealed in humanistic psychology's reference to development of potential rather than recognition of limits, of peak experiences rather than anxiety, of personal encounters rather than isolation, and of awareness rather than acceptance.

Operant Subjectivity or Q Methodology

The criticisms of standard experimental psychology and its methodology have some echoes in Q methodology's objections to "R" methodology, which neglects the subject's point of view (chapter 11). Rogers used Q sorting to measure the efficacy of client-centered therapy but employed R methods that converted subjectivity into a predetermined objectivity, thereby obscuring the subjectivity that humanistic psychology seeks. In its intended form as Stephenson designed it, Q could be invaluable to humanistic psychology's major theme of understanding and promoting human subjectivity. Rogers (1985), in fact, calls for more use of Q. Nevertheless, a major division exists between the humanistic psychology's use of "self" and that of Stephenson. For Stephenson, "self" is the communicable subjectivity of the individual, not a separate agent or mind as it is in humanistic psychology. A similar difference exists in the terms "subjective" and "objective." For Stephenson, subjectivity is self-reference; objectivity is reference from someone else's point of view. One person can do a Q-sort that reflects his or her own subjectivity while another person can do an objective sort of that person. There is no inside or outside, no mind-body distinction, no subjective-objective dichotomy as in humanistic psychology.

Psychoanalysis

Although humanistic psychology originally set itself against the assumptions of the biological determinism of psychoanalysis and its view of the human as sinister, more recent developments in that system, such as those of Kohut (chapter 5), have emphasized the self while Gill has brought in purpose and meaning. It is somewhat ironic that humanistic psychology had its beginnings in a reaction against behaviorism and psychoanalysis as a "third force" but now has some elements in common with current schools of psychoanalysis. In a comparison of similarities and differences between Kohut and Carl Rogers, Kahn (1985) concludes that Kohut integrated many of Rogers' concepts into psychoanalysis and in so doing bridged the gap between humanistic psychology and psychoanalysis.

CRITIQUE

The criticisms of this system have been rather diverse. The following categories have few common elements and are given in no particular order, but the final category attempts to summarize the system's strengths.

Social and Environmental Conditions

A Chinese critique holds that the inner potential that humanistic psychology assumes to determine human nature is similar to an instinct. This exaggerates internal factors and overlooks sociohistorical development, as does the restriction to the individual and the environment (Lin, 1985, cited by Yue, 1994). Pan (1988, cited by Yue, 1994) argues that personal actualization should replace Maslow's self-actualization because self-actualization puts undue emphasis on personal effort and overlooks the role of social influences. Mao Tse-Tung would be in agreement with humanistic psychology about the importance of people's taking an active role in determining their own future; but the individual is in a dialectical, not autonomous, relationship with the group. And because the limits of human potential change as the group changes, self-actualization to any significant degree is impossible (Ho, 1988). Self-actualization must be a part of group change.

Prilletensky (1992) reviews a number of critiques of humanistic psychology on self-centering versus social context and finds considerable accord on views similar to those of Lin and of Yue. He notes that an underlying assumption of humanistic psychology is that if everyone becomes self-actualized, social reforms will occur automatically and the world will become a good place for everyone. Racism, homelessness, crime, poverty, and injustices will vanish. Realistically, he feels, the attempt to place all the burden on the individual means that social conditions that need addressing get neglected.

When helping individuals living in materially depriving and emotionally injurious environments, much more than psychological help is needed . . . Improved social conditions will derive neither from retreatism nor from a magic extension of the effects of self-actualization on a number of fortunate individuals. Social betterment is more likely to occur as a result of social action. (p. 322)

To the extent that they have been successful in replacing social action with self-action, the proponents may have actually supported the status quo. In the workplace, Prilletensky notes, where they have introduced T-groups and other measures believed to be humanizing, a number of studies (that they ignore) show that worker participation and control is an illusion. The workers are only talking, not actually participating or contributing to management decisions. The form has changed, he argues, not the structure.

It should be noted that humanists deny that they exclude social factors and other environmental conditions; but if they include them, few have communicated that fact nor is it found in statements of principles. Even group events are intended to actualize the individual. This self-serving orientation has brought a continuing stream of criticism. Nevertheless, a few proponents have addressed environmental conditions. For example, Nevill (1977) points out the need for efforts on all fronts to remove social barriers to the opportunity for women to live fulfilling lives and to eliminate sexual stereotypes for the benefit of all. Others have called for support for preserving the bio-ecosystem as essential environmental conditions to the quest for fulfilling lives. Polkinghorne (1983) and Rychlak (1984) also make room for the contextualized individual.

Communicating What Is Private

Sass (1989) compares humanistic psychology with hermeneutics (interpretations), a related concept to which the former sometimes refers, and concludes that the former is far more extreme in its emphasis on "inner" experiences than the latter. He finds puzzling how any form of communication about the "inner" could be possible with the privacy and uniqueness humanists posit for it. Yet empathic knowing and understanding is highly important to them.

Education

Engelmann and Carnine (1982) charge that, in education, "perhaps the greatest impediment to intelligent instruction comes from investigators who purport to be humanistic" (p. 376). Engelmann and Carnine regard such humanism as a "guaranteed formula for disaster." Feelings of empathy and understanding of the child's culture, they claim, cannot replace the need for instructional techniques and programs that will facilitate learning. Learning should be reinforcing and, if not fun, at least "challenging and engaging." If the educator fails, "the children will be seriously preempted from doing things with their lives, such as having important career options and achieving some potential values for society . . . We know that the intellectual crippling of children is caused overwhelmingly by faulty instruction—not by faulty children" (p. 376). That contention is consistent with the following:

A massive research project, called Project Follow-Through (Stebbins et al, 1977; Watkins, 1988) used fifty-one school districts with experimental groups called "Basic Skills," "Cognitive-Conceptual," and "Affective-Cognitive." The pupils made gains only in the Basic Skills group, and this consisted of "direct instruction" and "behavior analysis," the two having much similarity. They included carefully designed and tested instructional material following sequential steps, immediate feedback to pupil responses, material from previously learned lessons, and practice to mastery. The other groups made no gains (scored even lower than they would have without the procedures). As a result of their achievements, the "Basic Skills" group even had the highest scores on self-esteem. Without a sense of solid achievement, efforts to nurture positive self-concepts were not very successful. The data, largely ignored (Carnine, 1984; Morrell, 1998), show that "self concept [is] a consequence of acquisition of basic skills" and not "a necessary antecedent condition for learning" (Watkins, 1988, p. 9). A meta-analysis of thirty-seven additional studies fully confirm the earlier results of the superiority of direct instruction (Adams & Engelmann, 1996). Further research on self-esteem shows that it does not affect either personal goals or performance (Bandura, 1997). A review of research on humanistic teaching did not find any benefits from it but did find positive outcomes as a result of a teacher's clarity, enthusiasm, businesslike and task oriented procedures, good questioning skills, etc. (Selakovich, 1984).

A book called *Dumbing Down Our Kids: Why America's Children Feel Good about Themselves But Can't Read, Write, or Add* presents a plethora of data on the poor performance of American primary and secondary pupils compared with those in other countries (Sykes, 1995). American high school students, for example, spend 1,460 hours on such subjects as history, science, and mathematics whereas those in Japan spend 3,170 hours, in France 3,280 hours, and in Germany 3,528 hours. According to Sykes, educators totally refuse to consider alternatives to present policies and at a major conference on the state of American education "declared with insouciant arrogance" that the job of schools "was teaching health and physical fitness, social and civic responsibility, creativity, use of leisure, humaneness, and positive self-concept" (p. 238). Apropos of this, a father is said to have observed that in the past parents took their children to the circus and the school taught them to read, but now the school takes them to the circus and the parents teach them to read (Clifford, 1975). A strong case can be made for the need for a national assessment system against which all school performances could be compared and standards toward which they could all work (Cromer, 1997; Ravitch, 1995). A rejoinder to these criticisms presents counter-statistics and argues that parents want their children to engage in sports, watch considerable television, own their own cars, and so on. The authors claim that parents "do *not* favor an education that assigns vast amounts of homework or that encourage students to become high-achieving drudges" (Berliner & Biddle, 1995, p. 52).

Table 4.1 offers a summary of the characteristic policies of American education and some of the consequences, according to critics. Humanistic psychology did not produce the "experience

Table 4.1

Educational Policies and the Effects According to Critics

Policies	Effects of Policies
Assume (a) all meaningful learning must come from within, (b) no one can teach anyone anything but can only facilitate, (c) the facilitator can only provide the opportunity for the pupil to take responsibility for his or her own learning, (d) no one teaching approach is more effective than any other, (e) all learning styles are individual and no one is more effective than any other, and (f) learning problems are due to individual weaknesses.	Grade inflation, weak educational standards, erosion of standards in such examinations as the New York State Regents examination, low achievement score tests in mathematics, physics, and geography compared with pupils of other countries, and poor pupil performance that results in increasing numbers of students taking remedial courses at the college level.
Assume purpose and motivation come from within, and motivation must be present before learning can be effective.	Education establishment blames parent and pupil for failure to establish internal motivation and thereby failure to learn.

continued

Table 4.1

Educational Policies and the Effects According to Critics continued

Policies	Effects of Policies
Avoid anything that might thwart the pupil.	Low standards, lack of challenges.
Provide freedom of choice of learning patterns.	Finding how many different ways a problem can be solved rather than selecting the most efficient way. Emphasis on divergent over convergent problem solving.
Provide life-fulfilling experiences via "meaningful" experiences and immersion.	Superficial learning. Exposure to many extraneous general-wholistic concepts with a primary emphasis on love of learning and building of self-esteem.
Assume that quantitative research misses what is uniquely human, and only individual experience is important.	Reliance on anecdotal evidence rather than systematic comparisons.

curriculum" but together with postmodernism and social constructionism (see chapter 8, pp. 232 and 235), it has helped to reinforce and extend those policies. In addition, through their influence in teacher training colleges these two psychologies/philosophies have, in some school systems, directly modified policies toward their own viewpoint. The influences of social constructivism (chapter 8) currently appear to be more pervasive than those of humanistic psychology.

Self-Actualization Theory

L. Geller's criticism (1982) of the self-actualization theory is that because the theory places total responsibility for values and attitudes on the individual and allows no place for environmental conditions, evil must spring from the individual. Yet since the theory holds that self-actualization is a biological capacity, what determines which direction it takes if not external conditions? If predetermined nature is in harmony with itself, Maslow cannot account for the evil and pathology in the world. If it is not in harmony, his theory collapses because there is no mechanism for determining healthy or unhealthy directions. To resolve the dilemma,

Geller notes, he needs to allow for environmental influence; but that "would undercut the range and application of his theory by making human needs and the self social" and then a hierarchy of needs could "no longer function as a ground for a universal theory of self-actualization" (p. 66). In the theory, the environment does play a role in enabling or impeding the satisfaction of the lower level needs but has nothing to do with the way in which predetermined nature unfolds. Geller also takes Maslow to tasks on his usage of "needs." They are not, he insists, blind impulses but are in concrete relation to something. They are "dependent upon and unintelligible apart from a particular sociohistorical context" (p. 68). He refers to Maslow's theory as "genetic reductionism" and therefore as not psychological. The theory, he argues, "is unable to capture what is truly distinctive and unique about human needs and selfhood" (p. 67).

Neher (1991) also observes a number of problems and inconsistencies with the Maslowian theory.

(a) Maslow expressed concern that the culture was undermining human potentials; yet this is an impossibility according to his theory.

(b) The biological process of natural selection by which needs could become autonomous is unclear.

(c) The requirement of satisfying lower needs in order to reach self-actualization and the avoidance of anything that might thwart them, indicates that children should always find gratification and never experience any deprivation. Yet a number of research studies show the inimical effects of pampering on the child and even the need for some deprivation in order to avoid boredom.

(d) When deprivation of a lower need level does occur, the theory provides no way to move on up the hierarchy, yet self-actualization can occur only when deprivation is absent.

(e) Examples of behavior that contradict points of the theory are plentiful. For example, Abraham Lincoln and Eleanor Roosevelt whom Maslow cites as self-actualized both experienced considerable deprivation and should never have reached this apex according to the theory. Others, Maslow himself found, had achieved gratification of needs but were neurotic or had not found meaning in life.

Buss (1976) points out still another contradiction in the Maslowian theory. Those who struggle to meet lower level needs, particularly the underclass, cannot get past the lower level, for the social change they require is not a part of the theory. The theory demands that all change come from the individual. Buss considers this a class psychology oriented toward the privileged and irrelevant to the non-privileged.

Vitz and Modesti (1993) claim that the emphasis on "self-worship" and self-actualization has often led to divorce and other interpersonal breakdowns, and to a gradual realization for many that they can never achieve the requirements for self-actualization. Career failures, impaired health, and other inimical events result, they say. Richards and Combs (1992) claim that "such representations focus on particular aspects of humanistic writings to the exclusion of others and fail to acknowledge the significance of quality human interrelation-

ships" (p. 381). Perhaps so, especially in the educational realm that they refer to; but the theme of "self" is pervasive in the literature and that of "interrelationships" is scant. Buhler (1971) tells us that humanistic psychology wishes to reform education and psychotherapy by emphasizing interrelationships rather than technique: Psychotherapy should replace transference with a therapist-client dialogue and make satisfaction of the client's values a major goal. Education should stress creativity, being a person, and emotional health. Although some interrelationships might be involved in these goals, they remain primarily about self.

Mind-Body Dualism

The proponents call for holism as a major tenet yet carve the human into mind, body, consciousness, spirit, self, and similar constructs. Consequently they keep a firm position in mind-body dualism. In that assumption they have not departed from psychoanalysis or the successor to methodological behaviorism, cognitive psychology, despite their rejection of those psychologies. They not only carve up the individual but also carve the individual out of the world of which that person is a part. In ignoring that larger context, they treat the person as self-causative, and many proponents argue explicitly for this assumption.

To assume that experience is a determinant of behavior rather than considering that experience *is* behavior, is a statement of mind-body dualism: it presumes that experiences, feelings, thoughts, etc. are something separate from behavior. Four examples: Landsman (1977) calls for this dualism in his insistence on "behavior *and* experience"; Rosini (1977) declares that "behavior is a function of experience" (p. 162); Hamachek (1987) claims that "both the inner person and the outer world" influence behavior *and* feelings (p. 169); and Krippner (1994) offers a triad of "behavior, experience, and intentionality" (p. 53). Similarly, the emphasis on self as causative of behavior is a substitute for the word "mind" and plays the same role. Despite the emphasis on person or human, it is with some proponents (Rychlak, for example) a separate mind, not the person, that thinks. An impersonal hypothetical construct rather than the human being—or human being and thing thought about relationship—gets the credit. The construct of an internal mind, self, consciousness, or spirit is fraught with problems that have plagued both philosophy and psychology for centuries, but humanistic psychology implicitly assumes its validity and ignores these problems.

Question of Locus of Causality

The approach assumes self-causation in positing that organisms select stimuli and are self-motivated. This also shows up in the assumption of self-actualization. The assumption that the environment causes the individual's actions or that the individual is self-caused are not the only possibilities for the locus of causality, despite the fact that humanistic psychologists indicate recognition of only those two. One alternative is that causality lies in part in the relationship between the individual and the thing reacted to. Giorgi (1992a) indicates the need for "human science" to consider the interrelationship between the person and the object:

> Thus when daydreaming, the boundary of the phenomenon may be the heavens; when remembering it could be the beginning of the twentieth century; when anticipating, it could be even within the skin of a heavy body; when caring, it could be with unfortunate sufferers; and so on. The philosophers have already expressed this notion: humans are becoming embodied selves in the world with others. A human is always being meaningfully in a situation. (p. 216)

In addition to the person and the thing reacted to, causation also involves the context in which the individual is relating to the object and the life-time of personal history that he or she brings to it. Causality as a complex of interrelated events is an important alternative to the assumption of single causality, whether environmental or self.

Unconditional versus Conditional Reinforcement

Rogers' belief in using unconditional approval to facilitate personal growth runs counter to empirical evidence (Newman, 1992). For example, if reinforcement is not contingent upon cooperative behavior, cooperation does not develop (Hart et al., 1968). The behavior analysts have abundant evidence that behavior is selected by its consequences and not by non-consequences. However, Rogers' client-centered therapy may not have been totally unconditional. In an experiment in which subjects said as many words as they could think of during a period of time and the experimenter (Greenspoon, 1955) said "mmm-hmm" whenever subjects uttered a plural noun, the number of plural nouns became significantly greater than in a control group. Similarly, the plural nouns dropped to control group levels when the experimenter discontinued "mmm-hmm." These results suggest that the client-centered therapist is subtly and unknowing shaping the client's responses, despite efforts to avoid doing so. Nevertheless, the therapy is about as close to being non-directive as it is possible to get. It is also necessary to make a distinction between unconditional acceptance of the *person* and unconditional acceptance of any particular *acts* of that person. A parent can love his or her child while approving or disapproving of any particular act of that child. It is presumably the former that Rogers advocates.

Negative Behaviors and Other Criticisms

Rychlak (1979) suggests that the emphasis on freedom should include such negative choices as selfishness, manipulativeness, and misanthropy. Such positives as joy, love, and authenticity are only one part of being human. But those who wish to admit negative behaviors as genuine become outcasts among proponents of this psychology, he notes.

Campbell (1984), a former executive officer of the Association for Humanistic Psychology, lists a number of criticisms that been leveled against humanistic psychology that she feels must be addressed. Those not already discussed include: (a) a focus on bizarre treatments and ineffective therapies; (b) dogmatic attitudes that claim only experiencing is necessary, as opposed to explaining; (c) a viewpoint restricted to the elite—the white, middle-class population; and (d) vague tenets with inadequate research support.

Strengths

Humanistic psychology has spawned a number of lively journals that publish theory, reviews, techniques, debates, biographies, histories, research, and quite often criticisms of the approach—many of the criticisms by people who are proponents. This indicates a healthy willingness to examine the problems and attempt to come to grips with them. The steady flow of articles into the journals indicates continuing interest and support of the position and its advancement by proponents. That it receives attention in most textbooks on the history of psychology (Wertz, 1992) suggests a recognition of its significance by others. There is little doubt that humanistic psychologists have been among those casting light on the importance of giving subjectivity and meanings their due and persuading many others to do likewise, even some who maintain their allegiance to another approach. It has given attention to such subjects as joy, play, dying and death, love, loneliness, and creativity (though it has not been alone in doing so). Despite the damage the counterculture has done to this approach, it seems to continue to maintain a steady voice through publications and to make contributions to applied areas. It offered one of the early alternative psychotherapies to psychoanalysis and continues to point out the problems with current mechanistic concepts in psychology.

CONCLUSIONS

The criticisms are numerous and varied, but the majority center around what the critics consider an extreme position on the autonomous self.

These criticisms contend that the belief that individuals cause their own actions overlooks the multiplicity of conditions that comprise causality, including those that are environmental and social, many of which need as much or more remedy—when remedy is needed—than the individual. Trying to enable the individual to find fulfillment while ignoring inimical surrounding conditions strikes many as irrational. (Most forms of psychotherapy try to change only the person, and are therefore subject to the same charge.)

One frequently finds the question raised in the humanistic literature about why the approach has garnered so little growth and influence. Certainly, the embracing of the counterculture is one reason that is acknowledged. But another is very likely its centering on the autonomous self. While it has drawn attention to the problems with mechanistic approaches of both behaviorism and cognitivism, it has looked for a self-causing power in the organism for an alternative. In so doing it has created its own form of extremism—where behaviorism and cognitivism ignore meanings and the individual, humanistic psychology ignores the environment.

There are two forms that humanistic psychology could take if it elected to incorporate the environment. One is to maintain psychophysical dualism and refer to environmental causes and self causes as separate. For example, Smith (1978) recommends that behaviorism's "external" understanding needs to be used along with humanism's "internal" understanding for an adequate account of selfhood. But he is "deeply puzzled about how to fit them together" (p. 33). Internal "interpretation" and external "causes" are complementary, though a "mystery" to him.

The other is to use a model such as Merleau-Ponty's phenomenological psychology or Sartre's existential psychology (from which it draws some of its inspiration) in which meanings consist of person-world relationships (intentionality[7]).

---

7. Husserl's usage of "intentionality" is somewhat more mentalistic. It comes from the organism and reaches out ("intends") to the object.

"Internal" and "external" become meaningless constructs, and thereby the locus of causes or content becomes meaningless. All action takes place as a relationship, and that is the locus of meaning. (Q methodology [chapter 8], interbehavioral psychology [chapter 7], and some forms of dialectical psychology [chapter 4], as well as phenomenological psychology [chapter 9] have adopted this position.) That would solve Smith's puzzle, although the existentialist-phenomenologists address somewhat different activities (especially the phenomenologists, who are more interested in perception than the existentialists) and use different methodologies (no interviews, questionnaires, or statistical analyses) and to that extent could never be fully integrated with humanistic psychology—but could be complementary.

Either form—separate causes from self and environment or causality as contextualized person-environment interactions—would probably attract many more supporters, and one might predict that it would provide more effective applied programs as well. Of the first type, Tyler (1992) describes an ecosystem for humanistic educational psychology that consists of systems programs (interactions of components) drawn from technology, phenomenology, and ecological psychology.

Those humanistic psychologists who accept quantitative as well as qualitative research are in harmony with supporters of other approaches who maintain that no one form of research is going to answer all questions, that each methodology offers useful information that the other does not, and that all are needed. The proponents have accorded a little recognition to Q methodology, which is rigorously quantitative yet provides information strictly from the point of view of the subject. Perhaps further efforts toward a balance of methodologies would advance both its program and its acceptance by the rest of psychology.

As a number of writers have noted, humanistic psychology's major influence has been in psychotherapy, and most of its students enter that vocation or others in human services. Probably few if any therapists conduct therapy strictly along the lines of non-direction that Rogers pioneered, but

his emphasis on getting major participation by the client has had a great impact on many forms of psychotherapy and counseling. Humanistic psychotherapy has even joined hands with behavior therapy and cognitive therapy in some instances, suggesting a recognition of both the strengths and weaknesses of each as well as the way they can complement each other in those instances.

Humanistic psychology has no interrelated body of concepts that would make it a system. It has no consistent content and no agreed upon methodology. It is more of an orientation (Shaffer, 1978) with a number of roughly agreed-upon principles, some of them rather vague and only loosely related; but that seems to be no great disadvantage. What do seem to be disadvantages are (a) its inconsistency in claiming to value wholeness while rendering the person into many pieces; (b) its severing of the individual from that individual's context; and (c) as a consequence of b, its attributing self-causation to the individual, largely ignoring environmental conditions including those that are social. All three of these stem from the implicit and explicit acceptance of psychophysical dualism. As a practical matter, its tie-in with the occult has also been detrimental; and much of that, too, is based on psychophysical dualism. Yet dualism is an issue that proponents seem to ignore. The French phenomenological-existentialist psychologists, Merleau-Ponty and Sartre, though not thoroughly clear of it themselves, could serve as useful models on that score as well as on getting the individual back into context, especially because proponents often refer to these systems for inspiration or as part of their heritage.

Let's consider the two "forces" that humanistic psychology was rebelling against in the 1960s: behaviorism and psychoanalysis. Behaviorism is alive today primarily in the form of behavior analysis, and that system has broadened considerably and is continuing to broaden from its earlier narrow focus on animal conditioning. Cognitive psychology took over from methodological behaviorism its procedure and some of its assumptions and has become the dominant "force" today, but it is not monolithic. That psychology with its various pieces, together with behavior analysis, are now the two major "forces." It is questionable whether psychoanalysis is even a distant third. Psychoanalysis as a theory has never had much influence in academic psychology, and today in the clinical field it is only one of a great many psychotherapies. In addition to behavior analysis, cognitivism, and humanistic psychology, additional systems such as those covered in this book are also on the scene. The term "third force" is now an anachronism.

Finally, the term "humanistic psychology" is somewhat confusing. It is fully compatible with few if any of the humanistic philosophies, even though it shares their ancestry. Perhaps "self psychology" would be clearer and more appropriate.

REFERENCES

Aanstoos, C. M. 1987. A comparative survey of human science psychologies. *Methods* 1 (2): 1–36.

Adams, Gary L., & Siegfried Engelmann. 1996. *Research on Direct Instruction: 25 Years Beyond Distar.* Seattle, WA: Educational Achievement Systems.

Allport, Gordon W. 1955. *Becoming: Basic Considerations for a Psychology of Personality.* New Haven, CT: Yale.

———. 1960s. *Personality and Social Encounter.* Boston: Beacon.

———. 1961. *Pattern and Growth in Personality.* New York: Holt, Rinehart & Winston.

Aspy, David N., & Flor E. Roebuck. 1988. Carl Rogers's contributions to education. *Person-Centered Review* 3: 10–18.

Back, Kurt W. 1973. *Beyond Words: The Story of Sensitivity Training and the Encounter Movement.* Baltimore, MD: Penguin.

Bandura, Albert. 1997. *Self Efficacy: The Exercise of Self-Control.* New York: Freeman Press.

Bassett, T. Robert. 1978. *Education for the Individual: A Humanistic Introduction.* New York: Harper & Row.

Belenky, Mary F.; Blythe M. Clinchy; Nancy R. Goldberger; & Jill M. Farule. 1986. *Women's Ways of Knowing: The Development of Self, Voice, and Mind.* New York: Basic Books.

Bellah, Robert N.; Richard Madsen; William M. Sullivan; Ann Swidler; & Steven M. Tipton. 1985. *Habits of the Heart: Individualism and Commitment in American Life.* Berkeley: University of California.

Berliner, David, & Bruce J. Biddle. 1995. *The Manufactured Crisis: Myths, Fraud, and the Attack on America's Public Schools.* Reading, MA: Addison-Wesley.

Bohart, Arthur C., & Karen Tallman. 1996. The active client: Therapy as self-help. *Journal of Humanistic Psychology* 36: 996.

Botterill, T. David. 1989. Humanistic tourism: Personal constructions of a tourist: Sam visits Japan. *Leisure Studies* 8: 281–93.

Bucklew, John. 1955. The subjective tradition in phenomenological psychology. *Philosophy of Science* 22: 289–99.

Bugental, James F. T., & Paul E. Bracke. 1992. The future of existential-humanistic psychotherapy. *Psychotherapy* 29: 28–33.

Buhler, Charlotte. 1971. Basic theoretical concepts of humanistic psychology. *American Psychologist* 26: 378–86.

Buss, Allan R. 1976. Development of dialectics and development of humanistic psychology. *Human Development* 19: 248–60.

Butts, R. Freeman. 1955. *A Cultural History of Western Education: Its Social and Intellectual Foundations,* 2nd ed. New York: McGraw-Hill.

Campbell, Elizabeth. 1984. Humanistic psychology: The end of innocence. *Journal of Humanistic Psychology* 24: 6–29.

Carnine, Douglas. 1984. The federal commitment to excellence. Do as I say, not as I do. *Educational Leadership* 4: 87–88.

Chapin, Theodore J. 1989. The power within: A humanistic-transpersonal imagery technique. *Journal of Humanistic Psychology* 29: 444–56.

Clifford, Geraldine J. 1975. *The Shape of American Education.* Englewood Cliffs, NJ: Prentice-Hall.

Cromer, Alan. 1997. *Connected Knowledge: Science, Philosophy, and Education.* New York: Oxford University Press.

Davidson, Larry. 1992. Philosophical foundations of humanistic psychology. *Humanistic Psychologist* 20: 136–57.

DeCarvalho, Roy José. 1990a. The growth hypothesis and self-actualization: An existential alternative. *Humanistic Psychologist* 18: 252–58.

———. 1990b. A history of the "third force" in psychology. *Journal of Humanistic Psychology* 30: 22–44.

———. 1991. The humanistic paradigm in education. *Humanistic Psychologist* 19: 88–104.

Ebersole, Peter, & Gogi Quiring. 1991. Meaning of life depth. *Journal of Humanistic Psychology* 31: 113–35.

Ellis, Albert. 1992. Secular humanism and rational-emotive therapy. *Humanistic Psychologist* 20: 349–58.

———. 1993. Reflections on rational-emotive therapy. *Journal of Consulting and Clinical Psychology* 61: 199–201.

Engelmann, Siegfried, & Douglas Carnine. 1982. *Theory of Instruction: Principles and Applications.* Irvington.

Fishir, Constance T., & Frederick J. Wertz. 1979. Empirical phenomenological analysis of being criminally victimized. In *Duquesne Studies in Phenomenological Psychology,* vol. 3. Edited by Amedeo Giorgi, Richard Knowles, & David L. Smith. Pittsburgh: Duquesne University.

Friedman, Maurice. 1976. Aiming at the self: The paradox of encounter and the human potential movement. *Journal of Humanistic Psychology* 16 (2): 5–34.

Geller, E. Scott. 1995. Actively caring for the environment: An integration of behaviorism and humanism. *Environment and Humanism* 27: 184–205.

Geller, Leonard. 1982. The failure of self-actualization theory: A critique of Carl Rogers and Abraham Maslow. *Journal of Humanistic Psychology* 22: 56–73.

Gendlin, Eugene T. 1977. Experiential focusing and the problem of getting movement in psychotherapy. In *Humanistic Psychology: New Frontiers.* Edited by Dorothy D. Nevill. New York: Gardner Press.

Giorgi, Amedeo. 1992a. The idea of human science. *Humanistic Psychologist* 20: 202–217.

———. 1992b. Whither humanistic psychology? *Humanistic Psychologist* 20: 422–38.

Greenspoon, Joel. 1955. The reinforcing effect of two spoken sounds on the frequency of two responses. *American Journal of Psychology* 68: 409–416.

Hamachek, Don E. 1987. Humanistic psychology: Theory, postulates, and implications for educational processes. In *Historical Foundations of Educational Psychology.* Edited by John A. Glover & Royce R. Ronning. New York: Plenum.

Hart, B. M.; N. J. Reynolds; D. M. Baer; E. R. Brawley, & F. R. Harris. 1968. Effects of contingent and noncontingent social reinforcement on the cooperative play of a preschool child. *Journal of Applied Behavior Analysis* 1: 73–76.

Ho, David Y. F. 1988. The conception of human nature in Mao Tse-Tung thought. In *Asian Contributions to Psychology.* Edited by A. C. Paranjpe, D. Y. F. Hoe, & R. W. Rieber. New York: Praeger.

Howard, George S. 1992. Projecting humanistic values into the future: Freedom and social activism. *Humanistic Psychologist* 20: 260–72.

Jourard, Sidney M. 1978. Astrological sun signs and self-disclosure. *Journal of Humanistic Psychology* 18: 53–56.

Kahn, Edwin. 1985. Heinz Kohut and Carl Rogers: A timely comparison. *American Psychologist* 40: 893–904.

Korb, Margaret P.; Jeffrey Gorrell; & Vernon Van De Riet. 1989. *Gestalt Therapy: Practice and Theory,* 2nd ed. New York: Pergamon.

Kostere, Kim J. 1987. A brief account of the center for humanistic studies. *Humanistic Psychologist* 15: 56–58.

Krippner, Stanley. 1994. Humanistic psychology and chaos theory: The third revolution and the third force. *Journal of Humanistic Psychology* 34 (3): 48–61.

Landsman, Ted. 1977. Psychology as the science of behavior and experience. In *Humanistic Psychology: New Frontiers.* Edited by Dorothy D. Nevill. New York: Gardner Press.

Lin, Fang. 1985. On western humanistic psychology. *Social Sciences in China* 5: 69–88.

Lindauer, Martin S. 1974. *Psychological Study of Literature: Limitations, Possibilities, and Accomplishments.* Chicago: Nelson-Hall.

Lowenstein, L. F. 1993. Humanism-existentialism as a basis of psychotherapy. *International Journal of Mental Health* 22: 93–102.

Madanes, Cloe. 1993. Strategic humanism. *Journal of Systemic Therapies* 12: 69–75.

Mahrer, Alvin R. 1993. Transformational psychotherapy sessions. *Journal of Humanistic Psychology* 33: 30–37.

Maslow, Abraham H. 1954. *Motivation and Personality.* New York: Harper.

———. 1961. "Eupsychia-the-good-society." *Journal of Humanistic Psychology* 1 (1): 1–11.

———. 1968. *Toward a Psychology of Being,* 2nd ed. New York: Van Nostrand.

Massarik, Fred. 1992. The humanistic core of industrial/organizational psychology. *Humanistic Psychologist* 20: 389–96.

Matson, Floyd W. 1973. *Without/Within: Behaviorism and Humanism.* Monterey, CA: Brooks/Cole.

May, Rollo. 1961. *Existential Psychology.* New York: Random House.

———. 1967. *Psychology of the Human Dilemma.* Princeton, NJ: Van Nostrand.

———. 1983. *The Discovery of Being: Writings in Existential Psychology.* New York: Norton.

Morrell, Robert F. 1998. Project follow through: Still ignored. *American Psychologist* 53: 318–26.

Moustakas, Clark. 1990. *Heuristic Research: Design, Methodology, and Applications.* Newbury Park, CA: Sage Publications.

Neher, Andrew. (1991). Maslow's theory of motivation: A critique. *Journal of Humanistic Psychology,* 31, 98–112.

Nemiroff, Greta H. (1992). *Reconstructing Education: Toward a Pedagogy of Critical Humanism.* New York: Bergin & Garvey.

Nevill, Dorothy D. (1977). Feminism and humanism. *Humanistic Psychology: New Frontiers,* ed. By Dorothy Nevill. Gardner Press.

Newman, Bobby. (1992). *The Reluctant Alliance: Behaviorism and Humanism.* Buffalo, NY: Prometheus.

Orlov, A. B. (1992). Carl Rogers and contemporary humanism. *Journal of Russian and East European Psychology*, 30, 36–41.

Pan, Shu. (1988). The psychological problems of personal actualization and social actualization. *Social Sciences in China*, 5, 52–67.

Perls, Frederick S. (1969). *Ego, Hunger, and Aggression: The Beginning of Gestalt Therapy*. Random House.

Polkinghorne, Donald E. (1983). *Methodology for the Human Sciences: Systems of Inquiry*. Albany, NY: State University of New York.

Polkinghorne, Donald E. (1992). Research methodology in humanistic psychology. *Humanistic Psychologist*, 20, 218–242.

Prasinos, S., & B. I. Tittler. (1984). The existential context of love styles: An empirical study. *Journal of Humanistic Psychology*, 24, 95–112.

Prilletensky, Isaac. (1992). Humanistic psychology, human welfare and the social order. *Journal of Mind and Behavior*, 13, 315–328.

Quinn, Ralph H. (1993). *Journal of Humanistic Psychology*, 33, 6–23.

Randi, James. (1982). *Flim-Flam! Psychics, ESP, Unicorns, and Other Delusions*. Buffalo, NY: Prometheus.

Ratner, Carl. (1971). Principles of dialectic psychology. *Telos*, 9, 83–109.

Ravitch, Diane (ed.) (1995). *Debating the Future of American Education: Do We Need National Standards and Assessments?* Washington, DC: Brookings Institute.

Reason, Peter, & John Rowan (eds.). (1981). *Human Inquiry: A Sourcebook of New Paradigm Research*. Wiley.

Reed, Henry. (1976). Dream incubation: A reconstruction of a ritual in contemporary form. *Journal of Humanistic Psychology*, 16, 53–70.

Richards, Anne C., & Arthur W. Combs. (1992). Education and the humanistic challenge. *Humanistic Psychologist*, 20, 372–88.

Ricks, David. F., & Alden E. Wessman. (1966). Winn: A case study of a happy man. *Journal of Humanistic Psychology*, 6 (1), 2–16.

Rogers, Carl R. (1942). *Counseling and Psychotherapy*. Houghton Mifflin.

Rogers, Carl R. (1951). *Client-Centered Therapy, Its Current Practice, Implications, and Theory*. Boston: Houghton Mifflin.

Rogers, Carl R. (1961). *On Becoming a Person*. Houghton Mifflin.

Rogers, Carl R. (1985). Toward a more human science of the person. *Journal of Humanistic Psychology*, 25, 7–24.

Rogers, Carl R., & Rosalind F. Diamond. (1954). *Psychotherapy and Personality Change: Co-ordinated Research Studies in the Client-Centered Approach*. University of Chicago.

Rogers, Carl R., & B. F. Skinner. (1956). Some issues concerning the control of human behavior. *Science*, 128, 1057–66.

Rosini, Lawrence A. (1977). Research perspectives in the psychological study of experience. In *Humanistic Psychology: New Frontiers*, ed. by Dorothy D. Nevill. Garden Press.

Russell, David. (1992). Humanistic psychological centers for scholarship and personal growth. *Humanistic Psychologist*, 32, 397–406.

Rychlak, Joseph F. (1976). Psychological Science as a Humanist Views It. In *Nebraska Symposium on Motivation*, 1975, Vol. 73, ed. by Arnold J. William. Lincoln, NB: University of Nebraska.

Rychlak, Joseph F. (1979). A primer of the primrose-path psychology [Review of the book Humanistic Psychology by John B. P. Shaffer]. *Contemporary Psychology*, 24, 471–72.

Rychlak, Joseph F. (1984). Newtonianism and the professional responsibility of psychologists: Who speaks for humanity? *Professional Psychology: Research and Practice*, 15, 82–95.

Rychlak, Joseph F. (1988). *The Psychology of Rigorous Humanism*, sec. ed. New York Universities.

Sartre, Jean-Paul. (1943/1957). *Being and Nothingness*, trans. by Hazel E. Barnes, Methuan. (Original: *L'Etre et le Néant*. Gallimard)

Sass, Louis A. (1989). Humanism, hermeneutics, and humanistic psychoanalysis: Differing conceptions of subjectivity. *Psychoanalysis and Contemporary Thought*, 12, 432–504.

Selakovich, Daniel. (1984). *Schooling in America: Social Foundations of Education*. Longman.

Severin, Frank T. (1973). *Discovering Man in Psychology: A Humanistic Approach*. McGraw-Hill.

Shaffer, John B. (1978). *Humanistic Psychology*. Englewood Cliffs, NJ: Prentice-Hall.

Simpson, Elizabeth L. (1977). Humanistic psychology: An attempt to define human nature. In *Humanistic Psychology: New Frontiers*, ed. by Dorothy D. Nevill. Garden Press.

Smith, Brewster. (1978). Humanism and behaviorism: Theory and practice. *Journal of Humanistic Psychology*, 18, 27–36.

Smith, M. Brewster. (1982). Psychology and humanism. *Psi Chi Newsletter*, 8 (1), 1–7.

Smith, M. Brewster. (1990). Humanistic psychology. *Journal of Humanistic Psychology*, 30, 6–21.

Smith, M. Brewster. (1994). "Human science"—REALLY! *Journal of Humanistic Psychology*, 34, 111–116.

Stebbins, S. L.; R. G. St. Pierre; E. C. Proper; R. B. Anderson; & T. R. Cerva. (1977). Education as Experimentation: A Planned Variation Model. Vol. IV-A-D. An Evaluation of Follow Through. Cambridge, MA: ABT Associates.

Sykes, Charles J. (1995). *Dumbing Down Our Kids: Why America's Children Feel Good about Themselves but Can't Read, Write, or Add.* St. Martin's Press.

Tageson, C. William. (1982). *Humanistic Psychology: A Synthesis.* Homewood, IL: Dorsey.

Tart, Charles T. (ed.) (1975). *Transpersonal Psychology.* Harper & Row.

Tart, Charles T. (1992). Perspectives on scientism, religion, and philosophy provided by parapsychology. *Journal of Humanistic Psychology, 32,* 70–100.

Taylor, Eugene. (1992). Transpersonal psychology: Its several virtues. *Humanistic Psychologist, 20,* 285–300.

Taylor, Eugene. (1995). "What is man, psychologist, that thou art so unmindful of him?": A note on the historical relation between classical personality theory and humanistic psychology. Twenty-Seventh Annual Meeting of the Cheiron Society, Bowdoin College, Brunswick, Maine, June 22–25, 1995.

Tyler, Ken. (1992). The development of the ecosystemic approach as a humanistic educational psychology. *Educational Psychology, 12,* 15–24.

van Kaam, Adrian. (1993). Psychology as a human science and the human science of transcendent formation. *Studies in Formative Spirituality, 14,* 247–270.

Vitz, Paul C., & Deirdre Modesti. (1993). Social and psychological origins of new age spirituality. *Journal of Psychology and Christianity, 12,* 47–57.

Wandersman, A.; P. Poppen; & D. Ricks (eds.) (1976). *Humanism and Behaviorism: Dialogue and Growth.* New York: Pergamon.

Wann, T. W. (ed.) (1964). *Behaviorism and Phenomenology: Contrasting Bases for Modern Psychology.* University of Chicago.

Watkins, Cathy L. (1988). Project Follow-Through: A story of the identification and neglect of effective instruction. *Youth Policy, 10* (7), 7–11.

Wertz, Frederick J. (1992). Representations of the "third force" in history of psychology textbooks. *Humanistic Psychologist, 20,* 461–476.

Yalom, Irvin D. (1980). *Existential Psychotherapy.* Basic Books.

Yue, Guoan. (1994). Theoretical psychology in China today. *Theory and Psychology, 4,* 261–275.

CHAPTER 5

Psychoanalysis: Departures from Most of Freud

Chapter Outline

INTRODUCTION

Most students of psychology have probably been asked by friends whether they can psychoanalyze people. This erroneous identification of psychology with psychoanalysis on the part of those who have not studied psychology indicates the extent to which a familiarity with at the least the stereotypes of psychoanalysis has permeated our culture. And yet psychoanalysis has had only a minimal impact on academic psychology, and no more than a moderate one on clinical psychology. Even so, it is included in all introductory psychology books and all personality texts. The major influence of psychoanalysis in the United States has been in the medical field, specifically in psychiatry where it ruled supreme in the American Psychiatric Association until the 1980s. At that time drugs that could quickly treat maladaptive symptoms began to overshadow the slow and questionable process of psychoanalytic therapy.

Such terms as "libido" for sexual responses and "psychoanalysis" for psychodiagnosis have entered popular parlance, and novelists and playwrights have publicized psychoanalysis by using its themes. In fact, it was writers who publicized psychoanalysis and contributed to its influence in the early part of the twentieth century.

Although we associate psychoanalysis with Freud, it has splintered off into many categories, some of which have moved a considerable distance from Freud's system. This chapter will treat Freud's original system only briefly, then deal equally briefly with some of the well known people he inspired. It will devote greater space to more current developments, such as those of Roy Schafer and of object relations theory culminating with Heinz Kohut and others.

THEORETICAL DEVELOPMENT

Founding Orthodoxy and Deviations from Orthodoxy of the First Generation

Sigmund Freud. As is well known, Freud (1935, 1938, 1969) was the originator of this system that is both a personality theory and a method of psychotherapy. Freud assumed a special form of energy in the organism called the "libido," a kind of sexual tension. It manifests itself primarily in the "id" which directs much of the libido's energy. The id follows solely the pleasure principle, seeking gratification of sexual tension. A second component of psychic structure is called the "ego." It grows out of the id and seeks to minimize pain and maximize pleasure through realistic selection of behaviors, but it is still driven by the pleasure principle. A third component of psychic structure, the "superego," derives from the ego. It takes on the parent's moral values and suppresses the id's pleasure seeking tendencies. Warfare develops among these three psychic forces, with the ego mediating between the pleasure driven id and the pleasure suppressing superego. In early childhood the id has the upper hand, but as the child matures the ego gains increasing control. The ego suppresses unacceptable impulses of the id as required by the superego. Energy from the libido not only drives this psychic conflict but also gives rise to a death instinct and an opposing life instinct. One of the goals of psychoanalytic therapy is to bring all these forces into harmony through a kind of dialectic process. But many of Freud's followers did not accept the death instinct construct and consequently did not apply it.

The libido's energy is also directed toward erogenous zones of the body, giving rise to the psychosexual stages that unfold over the first five years of life. These are successively the oral, anal, and genital stages. Development can become fixated at any of these stages with resulting neurotic symptoms characteristic of that stage. Overeating, smoking, drinking, or garrulousness results from fixation ("cathexis") at the oral stage. The compulsive person is fixated at the anal stage. The teenager's obsession with sex is fixation at the genital stage. The ego increasingly wrests control of the libidinous energy from the id and attaches the energy to objects. In the earliest development the attachment is to the infant's own body, leading to "narcissism" or self-love. Later, when the attachment is to the parent of the opposite sex, the "oedipal" conflict (sometimes called the "electra" conflict for the girl, but usually "oedipal" for both sexes) is born. This occurs in the genital stage. All but a small part of these developments lie in the unconscious mind. The preconscious between the unconscious and the conscious mind also contains some memories, which are more readily available to the ego than are those in the unconscious.

Because of their libidinous energy, people have fundamental sexual and aggressive needs that function independently of their environment—but if the environment blocks them, neurotic symptoms develop. Everything people do, without exception, is for the purpose of discharging sexual or aggressive energy. If the discharge is blocked by the superego's feeling of guilt, the conflict between the need for discharge and the superego's repression of traumatic wishes or memories produces such neurotic symptoms as depression, phobias, anxiety, and sexual dysfunctions. Because the anxieties that give rise to the symptoms are unconscious, they do not respond to reason and are not available for examination. Efforts to expose them meet with resistance. These resistances take the form of defense mechanisms such as projection (attributing to someone else one's own shortcomings), reaction formation (claiming to oppose what one actually desires), introjection (assimilating an object such as the parent into the ego or superego), and repression (forcing unacceptable thoughts into the unconscious). Through free association these traumatic memories can be recovered and explored. When they are fully understood—and *only* when they are understood—the neurotic symptoms will disappear.

Freud distinguished between what he called "transference neurosis" and "narcissistic neurosis." The transference neuroses consist of such disorders as obsessions and hysteria. He held that they show up in disguised form in the transference processes—when the patient transfers feelings from the parents to the analyst. The narcissistic neuroses include such disorders as paranoia, depression, and schizophrenia, do not show up as transference, and thus cannot be observed. In the past, psychoanalysts usually did not try to treat narcissistic disorders, but Kohut's work of recent years has focused on this (see p. 153).

Alfred Adler. Among Freud's early followers the most prominent were Adler and Jung, both of whom broke with Freud and forged new schools of psychoanalysis. Adler (1917, 1927a, 1927b, 1939) saw the infant not as a sexual creature but as one that is helpless and needs total care from the more powerful adults. This dependence on adults produces feelings of inferiority and creates a striving to gain power and independence. The will to power is the driving force for Adler (although a person can, he proposed, also engage in a flight into sickness), and male sexuality is a symptom of striving to overcome female domination. Women, on the other hand, feel inferior because of their underprivileged status in society. He also maintained that sexual problems are not causes of neurotic behavior but are forms in which neurosis appears.

Adler rejected the biological instincts of Freud and substituted the social relationships within the family, especially the child's position in the birth order of siblings. It is the individual and the social environment that come into conflict, not instinctive forces inside the individual. Adler also largely deemphasized the unconscious and emphasized the belief in future possibilities, often unrealistic, toward which individuals strive. Thus, he accentuated the future in contrast to Freud's accent on the past. Adler called his approach *individual psychology*. As a therapy it was a kind of re-education. It dealt aggressively with overt problems and did so in a short period of time, in contrast with the multi-year duration of Freud's psychoanalytic therapy. Adler's terms "inferiority complex" and "sibling rivalry" gained wide usage.

Adler was a forerunner of more socially oriented psychoanalysts. His rejection of the instincts and deemphasis on the unconscious also find echoes in current trends. His stress on the future and on re-education foreshadowed some characteristics of many current psychotherapies, and his recognition of women's cultural disadvantages and consequent adjustment problems is the theme of a number of movements today.

Carl Jung. Contrary to Freud, Jung (1926, 1927, 1928, 1933, 1963) maintained that it is not just the past that is responsible for neurotic conditions but also the present—and one's goals and intentions for the future as well. For Jung the ego is fully conscious. It represses memories into the personal unconscious. Buried more deeply is a collective unconscious that contains "archetypes." These are instincts inherited by all members of our species or race. They result from the experiences of our ancestors and predispose us to perceive and to think in particular ways. These archetypes also contain symbols, and Jung claimed to have discovered the archetypes by examining the symbols of art and myth across cultures and periods of time. The archetypes include (a) the "persona," the mask that we present to other people, which is masculine for men and feminine for women; (b) the "anima," the feminine side of men, and the "animus," the masculine side of women; (c) the "shadow," an animal instinct that goes back to our prehuman form and involves immoral impulses; it may surge out of the shadow into the unconscious and even into the personal conscious; and (d) the "self," which integrates all the others into a unified being. The self appears only in middle age and often uses religion or mystical experiences for its integrating role.

Jung divided people into "introverts" and "extroverts," and these terms became as widely used as Adler's "inferiority complex" and "sibling rivalry." Introverts and extroverts could be paired in any combination with the four—and only four—functions of intuiting, sensing, feeling, and thinking. Any two of these may predominate and suppress the other two and be paired with introversion or extroversion. This results in typologies such as a thinking-intuiting introvert, perhaps a creative scientist who likes to work alone. Jung held that these primordial urges could be directed toward the divine or toward self-actualization, but if not adequately handled by the ego they could produce a neurosis or even a psychosis. He largely rejected scientific evidence and turned to mythology and art for his inspiration. Neurosis is the suffering of the soul that has not found the meaning embedded in it. He urged his patients to use their willpower and to seek the divine. It is not surprising that he has greatly influenced New Agers and others seeking the mystical.

Deviations from Orthodoxy of the Second Generation

Karen Horney. Horney (1937, 1939, 1945, 1950) trained at the Berlin Psychoanalytic Institute. After working at the Institute for a few years she emigrated to the United States where she arrived during the economic depression of 1929–1942. She found that money rather than sex was usually the major source of neurotic behavior in the United States. She concluded that the driving force of neurosis was "basic anxiety" stemming from the child's feeling of isolation and helplessness in a hostile world. The problem began with neurotic parents whose failure to provide security and love for the child led to anxiety and deviant behavior. She held that *any* deviation from normality, not just pathological conditions, was rooted in this condition. The child attempts to cope with anxiety by developing a neurotic symptom that prevents the anxiety from occurring, but the symptom itself is crippling.

Contrary to Freud, she held that sexual problems are one *type* of neurotic symptom, not a *cause* of neurosis. The child internalizes the expectations and goals of others and develops an idealized self-concept that is often unrealistic in terms of both personal and cultural limitations. The failure to reach his or her ideals produces conflicts and anxiety. The pursuit of security produces compliant individuals who are affectionate and outgoing; self-reliant and perfectionistic people who relate poorly to others; and manipulative persons who are cynical and exploitive of others. Most people can fit one of these descriptions, depending on the situation. Where Freud saw humans as biological beings who are difficult to change, Horney saw the bright prospect of eliminating neuroses by improving society and families. She directed her psychotherapy toward helping people resolve conflicts by letting the real-self take control of the ideal-self and overcome self-hatred. People develop such hatred along with the drive to perfection because of unrealistic beliefs about what they should accomplish. Through "self-realization" they can achieve harmony with others and reduce conflict and anxiety.

Horney wrote a series of papers attacking Freud's theory of female sexual development and asserted the role of culture—as opposed to male or female anatomy—in producing differences in the psychology of men and women. She found Freud's psychoanalysis male-centered, disparaging to women, and based on stereotypes. She delineated the history and culture of patriarchal discrimination against women and called for a more enlightened understanding (Horney, 1967). Her work had an important influence on women's studies.

Erich Fromm. Fromm (1941, 1947, 1955) trained at the Berlin Psychoanalytic Institute and migrated to the United States as did Horney. Like Horney, he also emphasized social conditions, but unlike her he focused primarily on historical and political conditions. He was heavily influenced by Karl Marx. Fromm contended that problems begin in the dependency of infants on their parents, and the infant's lack of animal instincts to cope with the world. As infants are weaned and begin to mature, they are insufficiently capable of coping with their surroundings. This is because (a) human reasoning ability has replaced the animal's instinctive ability to cope; and (b) humans are no longer united with other humans as they once were by myth and religion. Where the clan once gave individuals security and helped them cope with the world, they are now alone.

This alienation increased in the late Middle Ages, he claims, when merchants began a capitalistic system that required individual initiative and self-reliance. During the Reformation, even the human being's identity with God began to fade. Freedom and independence followed, but at the cost of security. In the industrial capitalist world, social belonging is missing. Fromm advocated a humanistic socialism in which individuals regain their security by achieving a loving brotherhood with others, based on cooperation and mutual support. The unsatisfactory alternative to humanistic socialism is an authoritarian system, either political or religious, which fosters frustration and hostility.

Harry S. Sullivan. Sullivan (1947, 1953), an American born psychiatrist, thought that Freud's system was essentially valid but that it needed to consider cultural factors. He conceived of personality as involving a psychic tension or "dynamism" that somewhat parallels the libido of Freud. This overt or covert energy transfer involves some part of the body. One source of this tension arises from biological requirements such as hunger, thirst, and sex. Relieving these tensions gives satisfaction, and fulfilling them completely produces exaltation. This seems to be Freud's pleasure principle. The second source of tension is threats, either actual or imagined, that create anxiety or—in extreme cases—terror. Anxiety interferes with interpersonal relations, confounds thinking, and upsets the sequence of satisfying needs. Reduction of anxiety creates feelings of security. Anxiety usually arises from insecurities created when the child was nursing.

Sullivan converted Freud's psychosexual stages of development to seven social stages, but he is best known for his viewpoints on schizophrenia. He insisted that psychiatry must deal with "disordered living . . . not an impossible study of an *individual* suffering mental disorder" (1962, p. 258), for personal individuality is only an illusion. We do not stand alone, autonomous and individual; we are inseparable from our interpersonal situations. Therefore, *situations*, not sick *individuals* must be the focus of the research on—and therapy for—schizophrenia. As a consequence of this conviction, Sullivan centered his treatment on entire families. These viewpoints are close to those of the social constructionists (chapter 8) and, in its clinical phase, of family therapy.

Erik Erikson. Of the theorists reviewed here, Erikson (1963, 1968) remained closest to Freud's original system. Even so, he gave much greater emphasis to social factors. He held that one's ego and one's self or sense of identity develop over an entire life span and that adult experiences can help heal childhood wounds. To Freud's psychosexual stages he added additional ones and modified the others, identifying a total of eight stages comprising the life cycle. Each one includes a conflict or crisis, a psychological struggle that enters into the development of personality. The dialectical outcome (see chapter 9 on dialectics) can be either negative or positive, but the person must resolve the crisis in order to remain healthy and avoid neurotic symptoms. For example, in the first, or "oral-sensory," stage, if the nursing procedure is satisfactory the infant responds with trust; and the first social situation is off to a good start. If the mother frequently ignores the infant's hunger, the infant feels threatened and develops mistrust.

Especially from adolescence onward, the exterior economic, political, and social environments are important in shaping interior emotional development and thereby entering into changes in ego modification. Erikson is well known for his formulation of the adolescent "identity crisis." In this crisis the individual becomes confused, is truant or leaves school, and resorts to drugs, alcohol, dereliction, vandalism, and sometimes crime. Erikson regards this identity crisis as the most important crisis in one's life. Its satisfactory resolution requires the support of parents and others and is essential for successful marital and sexual relations. In young adulthood the conflict is intimacy versus isolation, and in adulthood it is despair versus integrity. Erikson retained many of the fundamentals of Freud's stages of psychosexual development but gave them a more social orientation.

Heinz Hartmann. Working from the viewpoint of biological adaptation, Hartmann (1939, 1960, 1964) reformulated a good deal of traditional psychoanalysis. He eliminated many inconsistencies and made it more systematic and integrated. He also removed the dialectical polarities of id demands versus ego defense, fixation versus anti-

fixation, life instinct versus death instinct, pleasure principle versus reality principle, and others. Perhaps his most celebrated accomplishment was giving the ego more autonomy and more complex functions than it received in Freud's conceptualization (in which it was an outgrowth of the id). Thus, the analysand (patient) could use his or her autonomous ego functions to take a more active role in assessment and interpretation of thoughts, memories, dreams, and transference. Prior to Hartmann's work, analysts assumed that any disagreement with the analyst's interpretation was due to resistance and negative transfer.

Hartmann also attributed to the ego an aggressive role as important as that of the libido, and removed its instinct of self-preservation. Hartmann's work led a movement within psychoanalysis that conceived of the ego as more prominent than orthodox theory had held it to be. This development is sometimes called "ego psychology."

Under his reformulations, the superego too gained independence; and id, ego, and superego became equally important in their respective roles in a newly defined tripartite psychic structure. According to Schafer (1970), "Hartmann was the guiding genius of modern Freudian theory" (p. 445). He opened up alternative approaches to psychoanalysis without necessitating the rejection of Freud's clinical insights and methods. This modification was an important step in the evolution of psychoanalytic theory along with the social and cultural emphasis that theorists from Adler to Sullivan provided.

More Deviations: Object Relations Theory

In object relations theory, people are usually the objects—especially parents or other caretakers and the therapist. The theory proposes that the patient's object-relationship with the therapist is a major factor in therapeutic change. It holds that the human attachment to objects does not derive from libidinal functions but has its own innate basis. In object relations, instinctual drive gives way to "the actual relational bond between the self and its objects" (Liff, 1992, p. 578). Object relations is a more radical break with orthodoxy than Hartmann's ego psychology (Eagle & Wolitzky, 1992) and, in fact, replaces ego with self. Self appears "closer to actual experience" than ego, the ego being "a remote construct" (Liff, p. 579) that did not serve well the more severe conditions that psychoanalysis was addressing.

Melanie Klein. Kleinian theory (1935, 1964) deals with both instincts and object relations. Life and death instincts drive the child's mental activity, but these instincts are attached to objects— usually the parents. The infant is able to relate immediately to both external objects and those of internal fantasy because a primitive ego is present at birth.

According to Klein, by six to twelve months the child's world is fraught with intense conflict in which its innate aggressiveness, hate, envy, death wish, and desire vie with its love for its mother. The infant develops a "schizoid position": it perceives the breast as good and bad, good because it provides nourishment and comfort and bad because it is not always available. The mother's body is the fountain of profound love, satisfaction, and sexual gratification yet can invoke envy and despair that the helpless infant can only endure. Consequently, the infant feels hostility and a desire to injure or defile the mother by biting, clawing, or excreting on her yet has intense feelings of guilt over the evil thoughts. The ego splits into good and bad parts and takes with it the death instinct that was present at birth. This it projects to the breast which threatens the infant and causes the infant to feel persecuted. The other part of the ego makes the breast an ideal object, a life object. Thus, finding gratification at the breast leads to persecution and the threat of annihilation on the one hand, and comfort, love, and nourishment on the other. The fear that the death instinct will prevail over the ideal object creates the "paranoid-schizoid position." The splitting of the ego is schizoid, and the anxiety is paranoid. "Position" indicates that the condition is not a temporary stage of development but continues throughout life (Segal, 1988). The split of

both object and ego into good and bad parts allows the infant to project destructive impulses out to the bad objects.

When the infant begins to distinguish people as a whole, it recognizes a connection between father and mother, and this produces the oedipal complex. It fantasizes its parents in intercourse, wants those same gratifications for itself, and feels deprived. In fantasy the infant attacks and incorporates the parents as part of its inner world. By incorporating breasts as part-objects and persons as whole-objects, the infant projects its destructive impulses and then faces the threats of both internal guilt and projected external deprivation of what it has destroyed. The infant despairs over loss of the good object that it has destroyed, and this gives rise to the "depressive position."

The Melanie Klein-Anna Freud Dispute. Klein was a pioneer in child analysis, working with children as young as two-and-one-half years of age. She engaged children in psychoanalytic sessions in which play overcame the child's limited language skills and became the equivalent of adult free association. She interpreted what she saw in play as the unconscious manifestation of innate conflicts and used this material to construct her theory. To her, all play indicated transference (Donaldson, 1996); and, as with adults, she reported that transference neurosis occurred between the analyst and the child. The procedures of adult analysis were applicable to the child, including interpretation of the sexual meaning of play, oedipal conflicts, desires to kill the parents, and other assertions from the theory.

In flight from Nazi persecution, Anna Freud, daughter of Sigmund Freud, settled in London and, like Klein, became a member of the British Psychoanalytic Society. She had been developing her own procedure for analysis of children and had been critical of Klein's methods. She insisted that the child's superego was weak and that its dependence on its parents precluded an adult type of analysis and transference. For her, the goal of child analysis was to strengthen the ego against id impulses through education. By understanding the reasons for its behavior and the consequences, the child learns to abandon bad behavior. This it achieves through dream analysis that brings the unconscious into consciousness. In contrast to Klein, Anna Freud rejected any sexual interpretation of play and brought in the parents to support the child and to learn to improve their relationships with him or her. Klein allowed no role for the parents and sought to reduce anxiety caused by a powerful superego that produced guilt over the child's hostile fantasies about the parents (Donaldson, 1996).

Klein claimed that her position was a direct counterpart to Sigmund Freud's adult procedure, while Anna Freud's was a revision. Anna defended her approach as a necessary adaptation to the unique character of children and charged that Klein's procedure was inappropriate for children. While the British Psychoanalytic Society rallied around Klein, psychoanalysts in Europe—especially Vienna—and in the United States favored Anna Freud (Viner, 1996). These different national reactions might have been influenced by the British stress on hereditary development and the European emphasis on social and environmental influences and educational programs (Donaldson, 1996). Klein's theory continues to have a major influence in British psychoanalytic circles. Some of Klein's followers abandoned instincts, turned to the environment, and further developed the theory of object relations that became central to British psychoanalysis (Donaldson, 1996; Kavaler-Adler, 1993). Two figures were particularly important in this development.

Wilfred Bion. Bion held that by adding the paranoid-schizoid and depressive positions to Freud's oedipus complex, Klein had refined and extended psychoanalysis; but he defined the schizoid-paranoid position as feelings of disintegration and meaninglessness. He advanced the concept that learning or knowing truth (called K for knowing) and evading knowing (called minus K) (Spillius, 1994) were as instrumental in this integration or disintegration. He gave the mother the role of knowing the emotions of her child, thereby

contributing to its thoughts about its own emotions and being able to tolerate those thoughts.

Bion's contribution to psychoanalytic theory is five-fold: recognition of (a) the role of the mother in personality development; (b) the environment and the relation of internal and external factors; (c) the need for the self to have empathy with itself and with an object that empathically contains the self (Grotstein, 1981); (d) the containing function as well as an interpretive function of the analyst for facilitating analysis; and (e) the cognitive element in emotional development.

Donald Winnicott. Winnicott began his career as a pediatrician but became concerned with the psychological behaviors of his patients and their mothers. He underwent a ten-year analysis, became a supporter of Klein, and analyzed her twenty-two-year-old son (Padel, 1991).

Borrowing from Klein and his own work with children, he began setting forth his own version of object relation theory. He proposed that the mother's protection of the infant allows the infant to put together the concept of "mother" and to feel itself a person through the mother's caring for its body. Object relations begin through receiving the mother's breast precisely when the infant desires it and without signaling its desire, thereby giving the infant the illusion that it has created the breast. Most mothers, according to Winnicott, not only know the infant's needs before it signals but also know when it can wait and that it will signal its needs when they arise. In this manner the infant learns that it is not a unity with the mother but separate from her (Winnicott, 1951; Phillips, 1988).

When the developing child feels threatened, it splits into a true self that goes into hiding to avoid its demise and a false self that complies with the parents' demands to divert attention away from the true self and thereby protect it. Winnicott believed the individual could relive these events of his or her infancy and with the help of the analyst correct the errors of the relations with the mother, especially the transition period in which he or she discovered separateness from the mother. The analyst can best provide healing by compensating for shortcomings of the parental treatment. Treatment consists of a new "holding environment" in which the client can feel safe while reliving the conflicts of the object relations in which transference with the analyst plays a major role.

Heinz Kohut: Self Theory. *Self and Selfobject.* Kohut (1971, 1977) developed his directions for theory and practice out of his experience with persons with severe personality disorders consisting of the closely related constellation called "borderline states" and "narcissism" and his inability to successfully treat them using traditional psychoanalysis. Narcissistic individuals show very unstable self-esteem and are highly sensitive to disappointments and failures to which they respond with intense shame, rage, and depression (Mann, 1996). Borderlines are underachievers, have unstable relationships (although they cannot stand to be alone), have low self-esteem, and may use drugs or alcohol and engage in sexual promiscuity. As Kohut tried to listen from their viewpoints, he believed that they were not engaging in sexual or aggressive fantasies or struggling with wishes or drives but were simply attempting to improve the sense of self.

Traditional psychoanalysts had widely regarded narcissistic disorders as (a) developing from intrapsychic conflict between imperious drives and the defenses against them, and (b) remaining untreatable by psychoanalysis. Kohut, in contrast, saw the problems as (a) emanating from unsatisfactory relationships with the caregiver, usually the mother, which produced a deficient sense of self, and (b) treatable as disorders of self.

Kohut's construct of self is closely connected to what he called the "selfobject," the caregiver, usually the mother. A "selfobject" is an object because, in the form of a person, it is actually separate from the individual; but a selfobject is subjectively a part of the individual's functioning of self. Three types of relationships provide selfobjects as an outcome of the person's attempt to satisfy narcissistic needs. They occur as the child (a) idealizes the strengths and values of the parents; (b) seeks self-esteem

from acceptance, approval, and admiration by the parents; and (c) develops a sense of community with others through peers. These all represent instances of selfobject transference as the individual strives to meet his or her needs. When the therapist is fulfilling the self's needs, the therapist becomes the selfobject. Kohut's selfobject replaced Freud's instinctual drives.

Initially the child experiences the caregiver as an extension of his or her own system of self as the caregiver interacts with the child by gazing, vocalizing, and engaging in body movements. It is in the first two months of life that the caregiver becomes a part of the child's self. Symbolic play that occurs between ages 1.5 and 4 years ushers in another stage of selfobject development. The child regards the selfobject as part of the play even when the selfobject is not immediately present. As the child engages in self-talk, the selfobject is the recipient even though it appears to be the child itself. Play produces a nuclear self around stories and other forms of pretending that help form it. As the parent responds favorably to the child, the parent and others become a part or a single self system of the child.

When the parent's responses to the child are incongruous with child's experiences, the parent becomes a separate entity in an outer world, not a part of the self and its inner world. A different pattern emerges for this outer world, involving language forms and clear goals. When interacting with the outer world, the child keeps the self world separate and in the background.

Self is the experience of one's own self. It is the way in which individuals permanently structure their feelings, beliefs, memories, etc., as their sense of "me." The nascent self provides guidelines for the goals that individuals strive to achieve during their lifetime. The psychologically healthy person attempts to follow the course of this blueprint. Throughout life, the self requires selfobjects, but these are more functions than persons. Such functions might be social, interpersonal, and religious, furnished by spouse, employer, mentor, and/or therapist. But selfobject is always an internal process, not just interpersonal relations.

Treatment of Narcissism. Kohut and Wolf (1978) tell us that the unfulfilled narcissistic needs of childhood cry out for gratification, for long-delayed fulfillment. But the needs lie hidden behind "clamorous assertiveness" and "a wall of shame and vulnerability" (p. 423). The analyst must show patients that they constantly seek praise because of unrealized needs of their childhood and that their rage arises from feelings of hopelessness and helplessness, and from their inability to effectively demand the fulfillment of their needs. As the patient gradually comes to recognize these conditions, he or she will begin to examine the needs openly and with self-understanding. And as repression of the childhood narcissistic needs ceases, he or she may again repress them at the slightest feeling of any rebuff. When the analyst can keep the recognition of these needs in the open, they will gradually change from a hunger for power into normal self-assertiveness and from grandiosity into normal ideals.

Kohut (1979) offers the case of "Mr Z" in which he used orthodox analysis five times a week for four years, then five and a half years later used his procedure for analysis of the self which he had developed in the interim. Analysis of the self, like orthodox analysis, occurred five times a week for four years. In his summary comparison of the two series of sessions, the differences are striking. In the orthodox analysis of Mr Z, Kohut describes the symptoms as showing "overt grandiosity and arrogance due to imaginary oedipal victory" while below the "repression barrier" was "castration anxiety and depression due to actual oedipal defeat." The orthodox treatment resulted in superficial success, but the patient came back because of continuing problems.

The second series presents a more complex situation. The patient showed "overt arrogance, 'superior' isolation" due to continuing efforts to unite with the idealized mother. As long as the patient remained a subsidiary of the mother, she was willing to authenticate his superiority over the father. At the conscious level the patient had "low self-esteem, depression, masochism, (defensive) idealization of mother" and below the repression bar-

rier "(non-defensive) idealization of his father; rage against the mother; self-assertive male sexuality and exhibitionism." The therapy occurred in two stages. In the first, Mr Z faced his fear of disuniting from his mother and thereby losing the self with which he was familiar. The second stage made conscious "the rage, assertiveness, sexuality, and exhibitionism of his independent self" that had been repressed. This brought him face to face with "traumatic overstimulation and disintegration fear." Kohut reports a successful conclusion to Mr Z's analysis of self.

Kohut Compared with Freud. In a comparison of Freud and Kohut, Ornstein (1996) finds that Freud regarded the infant as engaging in an ongoing conflict with the world, whereas Kohut assumed an infant preadapted to live harmoniously in the world. Disorders of the self Kohut saw as deficiencies in development rather than Freudian conflicts.

Although Kohut replaced Freud's psychosexual development with the development of self, he did not reject the construct of an oedipal conflict. He held that a child enters the oedipal phase of development with guilt and anxiety. A feeble and fragmented self does not handle the conflict successfully. In contrast, the child with a strong, cohesive self—and with strong selfobjects who accept his or her oedipal longings with empathic understanding and acceptance—will meet the challenge successfully. Indeed, the experience produces even greater consolidation of the self. In general, the child whose selfobjects support the child's innate potential rather than imposing their own expectations will facilitate the flowering of the child's talents. When the self has not had the opportunity to develop to its potential, the role of the analyst is to understand the analysand's experiences and to provide interpretations that "set up a working-through process that re-creates in the analysis a situation that provides protracted, development-enhancing exposure to optimal frustrations. It is this opportunity, insufficiently provided to the analysand in childhood, that is offered once more by analysis" (Kohut, 1984, p. 210). On the strength of Kohut's theoretical formulation and success in treatment, his followers have formed the International Council for Self Psychology.

Applications to Students. Kohut's theory has been extended to students' relationships with their mentors (Mehlman & Glickauf-Hughes, 1994). The student's mentor becomes a selfobject. In a healthy relationship, the selfobject transference is temporary as the student internalizes the mentor's functions as an idealized figure and a source of self-esteem. In a less healthy relationship the professor does not meet all the student's needs, and the student feels a deficiency. When the student is excessively narcissistic, his or her need for approval is impossible to fulfill, so the student feels great disappointment, reduced self-esteem, and even depression. The authors suggest that therapists working with college students must recognize the primitive needs involved in selfobject transferences in order to help resolve problems with mentors and to increase the students' self-esteem.

Revisions. Among new directions is a growing recognition that a selfobject is neither an object nor a self but the subjectivity of a relationship (Bacal, 1995). The concept of intersubjectivity facilitates self psychology's advancement into a more complete relational system (Stolorow, 1995). From this perspective, instead of seeing self-experiences, therapists increasingly see selfobject relationships with the analyst as the means of promoting development and improvement of the self. At the same time, the concept of selfobject transference frees the analyst from instinct theory and its impediments to treatment (Basch, 1995). Psychoanalysis becomes an empathic-introspective approach involving intersubjectivity. Kernberg (1992) puts a heavy emphasis on feelings. He proposes that they are the building blocks of drives. The feeling of sexual excitement gives rise to the libido drive as rage does to the aggression drive. Object relations infused with feelings also produce drives, thereby broadening the focus from body functions to social functions.

Radical Revision: Replacement of Freud's Psychodynamics and Metapsychology. The term "dynamics" comes from Greek via physics, referring to "power" or "force." "Psyche" in Hellenistic Greek refers to "mind" or "soul."[1] Hence, "psychodynamics" is "mental forces." "Psychodynamics" specifically refers to a psychology based on principles of physics in which forces, energies, and entities are invoked as causes or resultants. Drawing on such mechanistic physics, as well as on a mechanistic biology of instincts and drives, Freud described internal forces acting on the person, rather than considering such alternatives as (a) actions of the environment on the person or (b) interactions of the person and the environment. The system that psychodynamics produces is "metapsychology" which, according to Gill (1983), simply means psychoanalytic theory as opposed to its clinical procedures. Among those calling for a complete rejection of metapsychology are Gill (1973, 1976), Holt (1974, 1989), G. Klein (1973), and Schafer (1976). Meissner (1979) points out that this group has a background in psychology that facilitates their movement away from the biological thinking of those trained solely in medicine. Schafer's critique of metapsychology and his proposed replacement for it follow.

Roy Schafer: Action Language

Anthropomorphizing via Physics and Biology. Psychoanalysis, Schafer (1976) argues, has taken the language of physical science (such as structures, discharges, energies, and forces) while dispensing with reasons, choices, and intentions—which are really fundamental to psychoanalysis. Activity became a function (of an id or ego), reasoning became a force, thinking became representations, feeling became discharges, and struggling with intentions and feelings became structures and adaptations. In addition, psychoanalysis adopted a deterministic position, and, as a consequence, never referred to choosing. This language borrowed from physics and evolutionary biology

---

1. In the period of Greek history preceding the Hellenistic—which historians call the Hellenic period—Aristotle treated *psyche* as life-function. Although traditionally translated as "soul," psyche had no internal-external reference or transcendental character. Such meanings developed in the Hellenistic period. See chapter 2.

(functions, adaptations, etc.) precludes the emphasis on subjectivity which should be central. Because of this language, Freud had to anthropomorphize his constructs in order to change physical mechanisms and structures into meanings. He spoke of the ego, for example, as an independent entity that made choices and created meanings. It was a mind within a mind.

Schafer finds the same shortcomings in Kohut's theory: self is an independent thing that makes demands, an ego-thing. (He also finds self used in so many different ways that it offers no clarity.) *The self of the neo-Freudians also has the same reified status and anthropomorphic function in its reference to experiential acts. "Moreover, in some of its usages, such as 'self-actualization,' 'the self' is set up not only as the existential referent of behavior but as, all at once, the motor, the fuel, the drive, and the end point of the journey of existence. It is ironic that self as 'the' self has become an It"* (Schafer, 1976, p. 117). This anthropomorphizing, he holds, has the major disadvantage of taking meaningful action and responsibility away from the actions of the human being. Psychoanalysis must remove psychodynamics from its theory and give the action back to people, he insists.

Action Language. Because such Freudian terms as id, energy, fixation, sublimation, and the unconscious, are mechanistic and anthropomorphic, Schafer finds it necessary to set forth a new language system for psychoanalysis that speaks always of concrete *actions* of the individual. In so doing, he attempts to preserve what he believes are Freud's important insights while at the same time redirecting the system in such a way as to better accommodate present understandings of the role of development and culture and to meet the requirements of an adequate philosophy of science. He approaches this goal by describing all events with verbs or adverbs and avoiding nouns and adjectives. Accordingly, he not only expurgates such nouns as ego and libido but such adjectival modifiers as "rigid defense" and "an intense emotion." He will not speak of "internalization" except as an imaginary act, for there is no other meaning for "inside." He avoids the verb

"has" in reference to possession, as in "*has* an impulse" or "*has* a habit." Rather, the person *acts* impulsively or *acts* habitually. Consistent with these rules, he substitutes active voice for passive voice. For example, it is more direct and informative to use active voice and say "the analysand gradually came to understand why she was resisting" than to use passive voice and say "an understanding of resistance was gradually achieved."

Such terms as "psychodynamics"—along with forces, impulses, drives, psychic energy, resultant, and the other physicalistic terms to which it refers—need to be expunged, Schafer insists. But he wishes to retain id as "a way of acting erotically or aggressively that is more or less infantile in its being irrational, unmodulated, unrestrained, heedless of consequences and contradiction, thoroughly egocentric, and more than likely associated with those vivid and diffuse [and mostly unconscious] physiological processes that fall under the common heading of excitement or arousal" (p. 195–196). While modifying Freud with action language, Schafer attempts to retain such "fundamental discoveries" of Freud as infantile and unconscious modes of acting, the role of wishing, and the history of responding to body stimuli. "Motive" is another psychodynamic term. It refers to an entity that provides a moving force—as electricity or steam are moving forces for motors and engines. "A motive," "the motive," "underlying motive," "having a motive," and "weak motives" or "strong motives" imply a force that produces an end product qualitatively different from the force itself. This usage obscures meaningful actions, the reasons a person engages in a particular action. What is important to Schafer's version of psychoanalysis is how reasons for actions appear to the individual, consciously, unconsciously, or preconsciously. To look for causes beyond such reasons requires seeking a cause of the cause and so on infinitely (an "infinite regress").

Schafer emphasizes that action itself is the subject of psychoanalysis, not something additional that makes action occur. And it is *people* who engage in these actions. Schafer avoids speculation and theorizing about unverifiable assumptions concerning early infancy, including such hypothetical forces as an instinctual drive that causes action. The upshot of this approach, although Schafer does not explicitly say so, is to change the attribution of causality from presumed entities to actions of people. Descriptions of actions become the descriptions of causality that replace the anthropomorphized forces of physics and biology as causality. This action does not have to be visible. Thinking, remembering, hoping, fantasizing, and even inhibiting or remaining silent are all actions. Human activity is meaningful and has some intention or goal. "There is nothing the psychoanalytic interpretation can deal with that is not action as here defined" (p. 139). Only neurological and other biological processes are not actions in Schafer's definition of action. He distinguishes actions from behavior in that actions refer to the individual's point of view whereas behavior "is what the independent observer or experimenter says it is" (p. 370).

The emphasis on actions provides the analysand with a far wider array of implications, interrelationships, choices, and consequences of actions than does psychodynamics, Schafer maintains. In the therapeutic process, analyst and analysand work together to examine the influences of the past on the present, especially those from infancy, always from the perspective that the influences are actions. The analyst and analysand regard the influences as products of both person and circumstance. The analysand as always engaged in creating meanings, fantasizing, and being responsible. Theories of infantile sexuality illustrate these interrelationships of person and situation. As analysis proceeds with action words, the analysand increasingly accepts life as action and decreasingly disclaims depersonalized actions—"the impulse overwhelmed me," "my mind is filled with doubt," "the future will not be kind to me." "I will" and "I won't" replace "I must" and "I can't." "I choose," "I know," and "I prefer" occur more frequently as insight improves. Insight itself is what the analysand *does* rather than what he or she *possesses*. It is growing subjective action rather than the ego's strengthening and diminishing of

control over the id and superego. "The person *is* his or her own impulse, defense, insights, and so forth; for they are his or her own actions" (p. 147).

The following passage illustrates how Schafer replaces metapsychology with action language while retaining some traditional Freudian constructs:

> In the resolution of the oedipus complex, the child's incestuous wish must be renounced. First, we must reject the isolation of the idea of the oedipus complex or the idea of incestuous wishes from the idea of the child's actions. Also we must change the passive voice to the active in order not to leave the agent of renunciation indefinite; for it is only by using the active voice that we unquestionably require there to be a specific author of the action in question. This translation might then read, "In ceasing to act oedipally, the child no longer regards its parent in an intensely sexual and rivalrous way." We might then go on to detail how the child accomplishes this remarkable feat, for example, by repressing, identifying, reversing, and displacing, and by consistently condemning any overt act or conditional act through which he or she might regard the parents in this now frightening and objectionable light. (p. 208)

In general, reasons for one's actions replace explanation by metapsychology and motives, and this makes the actions more comprehensible. As language replaces psychic determinism and physical explanation, the usual distinction between explanation and description no longer holds; for, in Schafer's system, description by action words *is* the explanation. As one psychoanalyst expresses it, "by limiting psychological reference to the actions themselves, the new language allows for explanation only in terms of the meanings or 'reasons' according to which actions are characterized" (Fourcher, 1977, p. 137).

Wishes and Slips. These words provide additional examples of Schafer's modifications of psychoanalytic terminology and the way in which words can attribute causality. Wishes are not blocked or frustrated and do not initiate action, he insists. People act to block their own wishes. People initiate action. Similarly, there is no slip of the tongue, and words do not slip out. Neither tongues or words have any independent action. Rather, these are instances in which the analysand engages in two actions simultaneously, one intended and the other unintended.

Conflict. Analysts typically treat conflict in the language of physics or biology, a resultant of forces or opposed impulses. It is then an intrapsychic struggle between these forces or impulses. But in actuality, according to Schafer, a reference to conflict is based on the analysand's simultaneous engagement in two contradictory actions such as defying and complying or attacking and protecting. People, not psychic energies, create the symptoms.

Mind? The presumed entity "mind" is used variously, according to Schafer, as (a) a place ("the thought stuck in my mind"), (b) an autonomous agent ("my mind tells me") and (c) a separate existence from "me" ("my mind was wandering"). Because the language of mind allows us to observe or comment on it as something apart, the individual can disclaim ownership of the action. Yet mind is not a possession or a causal force. It is what we do. Instructions to "say whatever comes into your mind" or "whatever occurs to you" are counterproductive, for they allow the analysand to disclaim responsibility: it is the mind that is responsible. But the mind is not a place where ideas enter or where an agent acts independently of the person. It can only be the person acting—thinking, wishing, feeling, etc.—who must take responsibility for his or her own actions. And so the phrasing should be on the order of "What does this lead you to think next?" or "What do you relate to that situation?"

Experience. Experience is not something in a mind, available to introspection. It is the giving of meaning to entities, the "construction of personal or subjective situations" (p. 368). Thus, it too is an action.

Internalization. We often say that someone has internalized some values or inhibitions or other attributes or processes. But "Inside what?" Schafer asks. We do not mean inside the brain or inside the body, although biological structures are necessary for "mental processes." We may mean inside the mind or inside the ego. Yet we do not define mind or ego in such a way as to give it location and thereby an inside. Inside the self is equally unsatisfactory, for in Freudian theory self is descriptive only and has no structure or function that could provide an interior. More generally, self points to the person, as does "I" or "me"; it is a way of representing the individual. Schafer argues that adolescents in their struggle for independence from their parents think about self and identity in an infantile and concrete way, and psychoanalysis has adopted "these archaic experiential reports" (p. 193) into its own theoretical framework. "Intrapsychic," "inner world," and "introjection" are all variations on "internalization" and have the same shortcomings.

If we ask where a thought or a dream resides, we must conclude that it can't be in a mind, for mind itself has no location. Nor does a person keep ideas or feelings pent up inside. It is more accurate to say that a person thinks, dreams, ideates, and feels. In action terms, "introjection," traditionally regarded as an incorporated object, means something fantasized which is retained with some characteristic form of activity. Schafer contends, however, that "privacy" is a legitimate term, referring to "what is not communicated." Apropos, "intrapsychic" is "the person's private and to a large extent unconscious remembering, imagining, planning, etc., and doing so more or less emotionally" (p. 160). Here is one example of Schafer's translation of "inner": "Your chronic deep sense of worthlessness comes from the condemning inner voice of your mother" becomes "You regularly imagine your mother's voice condemning you, and, agreeing with it, regard yourself as being essentially worthless." He concludes that internalization refers to an act of fantasy rather than to a process.

Can a person hold anger inside? Can it spill out? Psychoanalysts speak of anger as displacing, discharging, and turning upon itself. These references assume that anger has substance, quantity, extension, and location. But if it discharges or expresses itself, where does it go? Schafer asks. And is the space it formerly occupied now empty or filled with something else? To say instead that a person behaves angrily directs attention to what the person is actually doing and avoids the discrepancy between observation and theory. Another of Schafer's translations: "It was an old anger you finally got out" becomes "You finally acted angrily after all" (p. 174).

Externalization. Schafer finds "externalization" as unsatisfactory as "internalization," for it implies the two locations, internal and external. A reference to "external reality" or "external world" can only mean subjective action. "Projection" is traditionally used to refer to expelling something from the inside to the outside, such as a wish that one attributes to someone else rather than to oneself. But in action language it converts to a fantasized relocating of the wish.

Consequences of Exclusive Action Language. Fourcher (1977) finds considerable strength in Schafer's action language—including a demystification of much of psychoanalysis—but also a major shortcoming when it is used exclusively. It does not allow for understanding *why* one class of actions differs from another—only a description of *how* the actions differ. If, for example, "the unconscious is only a mode of action and there is no way of differentiating why one mode of action occurs rather than another, such as unconscious rather than conscious, the basis of meaning and understanding is absent.

The Narrative Approach. More recently Schafer (1983, 1985) has turned to viewing psychoanalysis as dealing less with the past and more with the present. It becomes a narrative procedure that replaces the traditional interpretation about hidden motives. As the analysand tells and retells stories around such psychoanalytic themes as erogenous body zones (with their related swallowing, retaining, expelling, etc.) and the conceptualizations of feelings and ideas (such as food, urine, babies, etc.), the neurotic characteristics are transformed in the revised narratives. These revisions are more adaptive and coherent, which Schafer claims, is therapeutic.

Schafer considers language to be a means of constructing events, and this construction is what the analyst needs to understand. Language as narration constitutes experience. Reality exists in the telling. Leary (1989) points out that this implies that an experience such as oedipal attraction does not exist apart from the present-time act of telling. Because even "facts" to Schafer are only what the analyst's theory construes them to be, psychoanalysis has to deal with *constructing the present* instead of *reconstructing the past.* Nevertheless, the past remains important in clarifying the present narration.

Donald Spence. Spence (1982) takes a position similar to Schafer's. For him, all narrations are fables about the past in which fact and fantasy are so intertwined that it is impossible to discriminate one from the other. Memories of childhood incest may be nothing more than unverifiable tales. This he calls "narrative truth" rather than "historical truth." Since there is no knowable truth, the only guidelines are those of aesthetics and pragmatics. What is important is whether the clinician has made the story an artistically coherent one from which the client can benefit. Improvement in the client's condition occurs by helping him or her find new truths rather than by dealing with historical facts. Wallace (1988) critically describes this view as one in which "no one can call us to account, that we can believe what we please as long as it is pretty and helps somebody" and one that is "convenient for witch doctors, astrologers, chiropractors, and politicians" (p. 142).

Spence (1994) charges that almost all of psychoanalytic theory arises from rhetorical argument rather than from multiple observations and inductive generalizations. The title of his book sums up his position rather well: *The Rhetorical Voice of Psychoanalysis: Displacement of Evidence by Theory.* He reviews such shortcomings as (a) selective reporting of cases to illustrate a contention, (b) deference to authority rather than utilization of independent objective evidence, (c) dependence on the analyst's memory of just what was said instead of the use of transcripts or recordings, and (d) unquestioning acceptance of the author's statement of events and his or her interpretation of them. Spence has no quarrel with case materials as data, only with their unsystematic and biased usage. Omission of detail, he indicates, is the main source of uncritical acceptance of a conclusion. As a remedy he advocates making verbatim recordings of complete series of sessions and using computers to analyze them. By this means it should be possible to find coherences and causal relationships that the analyst would overlook, test hypotheses, avoid biases, and provide a data base open to public inspection.

Merton Gill. Gill (1983, 1992) discards Freud's metapsychology and replaces it with hermeneutical (interpretive) science and social constructionism, a science of human meanings constructed by participants. This is a turn to interpretations in which no single interpretation is correct or true; the best is the one that is most coherent at the time. Gill espouses transference and countertransference as co-constructed by analyst and analysand. Both analyst and patient bring to the therapeutic procedure their own socio-historial and conscious and unconscious experiences, which interact in a unique way for each dyad (analyst-analysand). Each shapes and is shaped by the other. The communicative process between them produces an intersubjective field. This is a two-person psychology (interpersonal regression and transference) complemented with a one-person psychology (intrapsychic) consisting of the private experiences of each individual involving internalization of external conditions that the individual brings to the intersubjective field. The analyst should not determine what is distorted or symbolic but attempt to understand how the analysand's perspective is a reasonable reaction to the analyst's behavior.

Gill believes that innate drives function earlier in the infant than do social interactions; but they too, as part of one-person psychology, interact with the environment (Silverman, 1996). Sexual and aggressive motives as well as self and relations are hermeneutically bodily—not mechanistically

bodily, as Freud assumed. The analyst must include in his analysis the bodily feelings of castration anxiety, bisexuality, etc., as part of the process in which analyst and analysand construct each other's psychic reality.

Gill rejects Kohut's self psychology and its use of empathy because it assumes some absolute knowledge about the patient to which the empathy is directed. Gill thinks Sullivan's (p. 149) major shortcoming was to neglect internal object relations while covertly emphasizing personality as "*ongoing* social relationships" (p. 539). Another shortcoming, he avers, was Sullivan's neglect of the role of the body. Sullivan rejected biophysical explanations and replaced them with subjective experience, making psychiatry a study of interpersonal relations.

Joseph Weiss and Harold Sampson: Unconscious Plan. As the public has become less fascinated with psychoanalysis, the profession has turned increasingly inward, "appealing more and more exclusively to mental health professionals and consumed with internal rivalries and turf battles" (Rosbrow, 1993, p. 530). With the advent of large numbers of self-help movements to fill a huge void, Rosbrow suggests that a variety of psychoanalysis pioneered at the San Francisco Psychotherapy Research Group might provide a bridge to these movements. This approach, largely developed by Weiss (1986, 1990) and Sampson (1992a, 1992b), has discarded the libido as a determining force and accepted patients' abilities to be agents in their own therapeutic processes. The procedure has four components: (a) the patient's unconscious goals, (b) the "pathogenic beliefs" that are impediments to achieving the goals, (c) the tests the patient uses to accept or reject beliefs in connection with the analyst, and (d) the insights available to the patient for rejecting the beliefs. The patient, not the analyst, is always regarded as the agent to bring about change. The analyst's task is to help the patient disconfirm painful beliefs and feel secure.

The approach emphasizes exploring the origin of the patient's "pathogenic beliefs" and inferring from them the life history so the patient can understand the past and how he or she has interpreted it. It holds that unconscious shame, guilt, and fear derive from real experiences rather than from biological drives and libidinous energies. While much of current psychoanalysis focuses on the present and on interpersonal relations, this approach re-emphasizes remembering. Neurosis arises not so much from unfulfilled wishes as from unconscious beliefs and memories. The patient tests the analyst by relating to him or her some traumatic relationship and hopes for a favorable interpretation. In "transference testing," the analyst plays the role of the parent and the patient the role of the child. The analyst's acceptance of the childhood behavior helps the patient relinquish pathogenic beliefs. The roles may also be reversed with similar benefit. As the analyst passes the patient's tests, the patient gains a sense of safety and can release memories from repression, integrating the past with the present. This approach is notable for discarding almost all Freudian metapsychology and retaining only repression of childhood trauma. It is also notable for attempting to empirically test its theories with carefully controlled studies using raters and judges (for example, Norville, Sampson, & Weiss, 1996; Silberschatz, Sampson, & Weiss, 1986).

A THEORY IN CRISIS?

Major revisions in Freud's system began with his first followers and continue to the present. Hartmann's revisions in the 1960s were the only attempt to rework the entire system to bring it order and consistency while retaining its fundamental metapsychology. Since then the diversity of viewpoints has become ever greater, with present trends toward (a) dialogue and (b) intersubjectivity (Schafer, 1995). "Dialogue" refers to the approach in which verbal and nonverbal interchanges between analyst and analysand bring about new understandings and changes. "Intersubjectivity" refers to relationships with others, real or imagined, that comprise the context of each individual's thinking and feeling. Sandler

(1996) finds a discrepancy between what analysts indicate publicly and what they do privately. Publicly they are often orthodox in their theory, but privately they stray from doctrine in order to conduct effective therapy. Meares (1996) holds that playing this double game impedes the development of more adequate theory.

Edelson (1988, 1989) fears that the system is "a theory in crisis." He notes (a) the serious challenge by Grünbaum (1984) (see p. 169) to its empirical basis and the few cogent rejoinders; (b) the indiscriminate incorporation of developmental, cognitive, and other psychologies into the system; and (c) the failure to develop an adequate research program. He notes that theories abound; but few offer findings to substantiate what he believes to be the strong foundation that Freud put in place, especially concerning the unconscious and sexuality. Further, many methods of psychotherapy compete, each claiming to be more effective, efficient, and versatile than psychoanalytic therapy. In addition to establishing research programs, he believes that psychoanalysis needs to clarify its "core theory," and he attempts do this.

What he sees as the core is based on a distinctly mind-body dualism. Here are a few of his tenets:

■ Psychoanalysis is theory of the mind, not of interpersonal relations.

■ Mental states are entities that represent objects or events in the world.

■ These representations are symbolic, and by means of dream work and defense mechanisms the mind operates on them to produce a different mental state.

■ Through imagination, sexual wishes play a vital role in constructing unconscious fantasies about internal and external objects, the internal ones located inside the mind.

The theory asks about the contents of mental events and attempts to explain why people remember, believe, and dream what they do. Psychoanalysis holds that the mind does not just correlate with these effects but actively causes them. Unconscious sexual fantasies produce, by means of causal mechanisms, events that can be observed—what is remembered or dreamed.

Common today, in contrast with Edelson's careful and systematic view, is an eclecticism in which the analyst chooses pieces of theory and practice from various sources, often provisionally, with no coherent overall viewpoint about psychoanalysis. Even the eclectics and most revisionists, however, continue to assume the sexuality of the infant and the conflicts that sexuality produces. As a major pillar of psychoanalytic theory, the removal of this sexuality assumption would put the entire theory in jeopardy, perhaps bring it tumbling down. Some revisionists are close to that point and are under criticism by those who worry about the system (for example, Barratt, 1978; Ellman & Moskowitz, 1980; Leary, 1989; Meissner, 1979). The "unconscious plan" of Weiss and Sampson leaves little of Freudianism but repression. Can that single pillar balance the entire edifice? Whether it would need to would depend on how many analysts subscribe to it or to a similar view. In any case, a trend among a number of analysts away from metapsychology is clear. The number of pillars seems at least to be diminishing.

SEMI-EXPLICIT POSTULATES

Perhaps, among currently prominent psychoanalysts, Schafer's postulates are the most important to understand. They are far from classical psychoanalysis and possibly far from the center point of psychoanalytic thinking today. Nevertheless, they have been influential in bringing a number of psychoanalysts to critically reappraise some assumptions of the system. The following postulates seem implicit in Schafer's writings:

■ *Protopostulates* (general guiding assumptions about science)
  1. Reality consists not only of events of physics, chemistry, and biology but also of the meanings of things to people ("psychic reality").
  2. Only through use of language rules do we come to systematically understand anything.

Such rules provide coherency, establish, facts, and determine criteria of consistency.
■ *Metapostulates* (supporting assumptions for a particular science)
  1. Psychological events have meanings and cannot be accurately described by the terminology of physics or biology. These meanings are those of the person whose actions comprise them, and in that sense they are subjective.
  2. Individuals consciously control their own choices and determine their own destinies.
  3. Description is explanation. A description of reasons as actions replaces physicalistic ("dynamic") constructs.
  4. Actions of people are paramount, and explanation by entities must be abjured along with the distinction between internality and externality (or mind and body).
■ *Postulates* (subject matter assumptions)
  1. Psychological events consist of actions and must be referred to in action language.
  2. Actions of humans involve choosing, setting goals, striving for goals, and finding meanings.
  3. Actions need not necessarily be visible. Thinking, knowing, feeling, fearing, ideating, and fantasizing are as fully action events as are audible verbalizations.
  4. Erotic and aggressive actions and conflicts are endemic to childhood and are influential in later behavior.
  5. Many actions are unconscious, preconscious, and/or conscious.
  6. Actions are products of both person and circumstance.
  7. Language as narration comprises experiences, and present reality is constructed from such narration. No one narration is more true than another, but each is a different way of representing reality.

RESEARCH

Psychoanalysis has generally lacked a connection with university research tradition and expertise.

Much of the training of psychoanalysts is done in private institutes, usually with physicians as trainees. Most practicing physicians have little training in research. Nevertheless, psychoanalysts have been increasingly calling for research, in part to provide support for claims that have come under considerable criticism for lack of empirical validation.

The earliest survey of experiments and observations designed to test psychoanalytic principles examined 166 such studies and found no support for the contentions the system makes (Sears, 1943). Eysenck and Wilson (1973) reviewed studies of patterns of toilet training and breast weaning that failed to correspond to neurotic traits as demanded by Freud's theory.

Case Studies

Qualitative. Discovery by clinical observation has always been the primary methodology of psychoanalysis. Kohut (1995) argues that psychoanalytic theory comes from inner experiences observed through introspection and empathy, and that implies the case study. Edelson (1984, 1988, 1989) recommends that a methodology of case studies, both single cases and series of cases, should be the major research approach. The cases should be able to establish that unobservable entities such as unconscious fantasies exist and that they have causal powers for the behaviors they produce. For example, the theory finds support by showing how each element in a latent content corresponds with each element in a manifest content; or how a theoretical entity, such as unconscious fantasy and its contents, offers a better explanation than a rival explanation; or how the unconscious fantasy typically leads to a neurotic symptom. Case studies, he suggests, will provide little predictive power but should be explanatory of what has already occurred. They can be used to test conjectures and provide evidence for the soundness of causal inferences and explanations and can also provide generalizations with cases— and between cases—about minds.

In an example of research using case studies, Glymour (1974, 1980) applied a strategy of "bootstrapping" to a case called the Rat Man that Freud reported. In bootstrapping, at least one fact and one hypothesis form a conjunction with at least one additional fact and with the same or a different hypothesis. To support a conjunction of hypotheses and of the theory that gives rise to the hypotheses, the hypotheses must meet certain criteria. In the Rat Man case, a man felt guilt over his father's death. Two psychoanalytic hypotheses ensue: (a) He felt guilty unconsciously as well as consciously; and (b) he had an unconscious wish for his father's death. According to psychoanalytic theory, these two hypotheses entail each other and still another hypothesis—that before the age of six his father punished him for masturbating. This last prediction was disconfirmed, and Freud revised the set of hypotheses. This showed that the case method can be used to disconfirm as well as to confirm hypotheses, a crucial requirement for any scientific method and the theory it tests. Edelson and Glymour argue for the validity of this strategy whereas Grünbaum (1980) rejects it.

Quantitative. A case study that illustrated rigorous research (Luborsky & Mintz, 1974) concerned momentary forgetting that is regarded as a neurotic symptom due to the analysands' emotional involvement in transference to the analyst. Momentary forgetting, then, should be most frequent in the context of greatest emotional involvement. In the case of a thirty-one-year-old woman whose symptom was "a difficulty with men," she selected younger men with whom to have relationships, felt that they treated her unfairly, and rejected them. In the analysis, she rather often momentarily forgot what she was about to say. From a tape recording of the sessions investigators selected segments just before and after such forgetting, selected corresponding segments from a control subject who did *not* momentarily forget, and asked judges to rate the remarks on a five-point scale of thirteen categories. The category of High Involvement with Therapist reached a peak just before the forgetting episode, while Shame rose immediately after the forgetting. On these and other measures she rated significantly differently from the control subject. Her dysfunction usually appeared after feelings of rejection, helplessness, and high involvement with the therapist. In the course of the treatment, the expectation of rejection was the most important of several problems. The analytic sessions did not resolve her fear of rejection.

A review of three generations of attempts to assess outcomes of psychoanalytic therapy show major methodological shortcomings that usually render conclusions uncertain, but gradual refinements in the methodologies have produced some clarity (Wallerstein, 1996). Continuing improvements, Wallerstein suggests, may provide "truly accelerating breakthroughs" (p. 570).

Q Method

Edelson also allows that psychoanalytic methodology can use other methods. He feels that such quantitative methods as placing a person on a scale to indicate some degree of whatever the scale purports to measure is unsatisfactory. However, he finds that a quantitative method that allows the person to measure him- or herself with respect to others is useful, and the method that does this is Q methodology (chapter 11), which he believes allows for examination of "mental representations."[2]

Edelson (1989) describes a Q-sort study in which he participated. Participants sorted sixty items toward which they felt both ownership—such as my mother, my body, my self—and also affective conditions such as pain and loss. The results showed that, for one person, one factor (cluster of correlations) was centered on mother and self; another on father, self, and body; and a third on pain and loss. This allowed the analysts to discover the viewpoint ("representation") of a dual identification with both parents and the char-

acteristics of each identification. For a second participant, only two factors ("representations") emerged, one showing the relationship between pain and loss and the other of self, father, mother, and body.

Using Q method with both analyst and client—in order to provide a firm measurement of a client's actual feelings rather than the analyst's interpretation of them—Stephenson (1985) found factors confirming that the transference was real. The transference from client to analyst was quite marked and possibly also occurred from analyst to client. Another Q study examined a theory of narcissism that holds that the mass media play a central role in the social development of our narcissistic personalities (Goldman, 1991). The single subject in the study sorted sixty photographs from a news magazine eight times, according to different conditions of instruction. Three factors emerged that the investigator describes as showing some narcissistic characteristics but not ones consistent with theory. This, the investigator suggests, is probably because the theory was describing a post-World War II generation, whereas the subject was of a different generation.

Experiments

Slips of the tongue, according to Freud, have hidden meaning and reflect repressed desires that interfere with conscious intentions. A communications specialist (Motley, 1985) reviewed previous findings about slips and related that when someone switches words, the words are usually of the same grammatical category: nouns replace nouns ("go get some bucket in the water") and verbs replace verbs ("he arrives either by driving a bicycle or riding a car"). Even when a person switches a noun and a verb ("the stop bucks here" instead of "the buck stops here") the sentence is grammatically correct. Sometimes the switching is of single sounds (phonemes), as for example when "fresh fish" becomes "fesh frish." These switches are called "spoonerisms."

To further examine the issue the investigator used potential spoonerisms in a study of Freudian

---

2. Stephenson held that Q sorts communicate self-reference. They are subjective in that they are the participant's point of view rather than the experimenter's, but they are subjective *behaviors,* not "mental representations."

slips. Male college students were instructed to read word pairs flashed briefly on a screen. Some subjects were hooked to electrodes and expected to receive a shock, but did not. They often made such errors as "damn shock" for "sham dock." A seductively dressed, attractive young woman presented word pairs to another group of males. The subjects sometimes gave such spoonerisms as "fast passion" for "past fashion" and "bare shoulders" for "share boulders." These results and those of a related experiment support Freud's contentions that anxiety can give rise to errors that might better be unspoken.

In addition to anxieties the experimenter showed that a number of other conflicts can result in interchanges of words and sounds. He found conflicts between (a) the intended utterance and a thought about something else; (b) a related thought which was not intended to be uttered; (c) two different words conflicting for utterance (chilly versus frigid becomes "frilly"); (d) indecision about whether to use a modifier before a noun ("moon rock" becomes "noon mock"); (e) two possible orders for paired words ("said and done" becomes "done and said"); and others.

It seems that while anxieties can produce slips of the tongue as Freud contended, other causes are more prevalent; and these are cognitive indecisions that can be experimentally manipulated.

A psychoanalytic investigator lists four assumptions basic to "psychoanalytic method" that require supporting evidence: (a) an unconscious causes psychological events; (b) free association can reveal unconscious causes; (c) the psychoanalyst's procedures open the free association process for the uncovering of unconscious causes; (d) the unconscious causes arise from the individual's past (Shevrin, 1996).

In a pair of experiments directed toward the first assumption, he found that subliminal stimuli (below threshold) presented in brief exposures turned up in dreams, and that the effects depended on whether the subject is in dreaming or non-dreaming sleep. In a third experiment four psychoanalysts examined the records of cases concerning phobic and pathological grief behaviors

and formulated unconscious causes. They selected words for each patient, some relevant to the unconscious conflict and some neutral. When the words were presented subliminally and supraliminally (above threshold), brain potentials showed that the patients correctly classified words involving unconscious conflict only when they were subliminal; they correctly classified conscious words only when they were supraliminal. The investigator interpreted these results to show that unconscious conflict is independent of the psychoanalytic interpretations, but that they do not directly support the first assumption.

For the second assumption he cited an experiment in which the experimenter's statement about causes created more free associations than did asking a question about causes (Colby, 1961). However, the uncertainty of knowing true causality renders the findings problematical, he notes.

For the third assumption he cited an experiment in which male subjects gave more free associations about people—far more when the experimenter was seated behind the couch than when he or she was not present—suggesting the importance of the analyst's presence to activate object relations patterns of the same sex as the analyst (Colby, 1960). A second experiment showed that the more freely the subject associates, the more likely he or she is to reveal unconscious content (Bordin, 1966).

As for the final assumption, he observed that studies of the relation of individual history to causality provide no clear interpretations, primarily because these studies do not address both necessary and sufficient conditions.

What might we conclude from the investigation of these four assumptions? It appears that the investigator has (a) made some progress in finding experimental procedures that bear on the issues and (b) found some suggestive but not directly applicable evidence.

APPLICATIONS

In addition to psychotherapy, psychoanalysis has applied its theory to such subjects as art, symbols, dreams, history, biography, mythology, literature, and films. For example, Gabbard (1997) avers that when individuals view motion picture films they experience powerful unconscious anxieties that derive from universal experiences in human development. Because they view the anxiety producing conditions distantly in a darkened theater, they can vicariously master the anxieties and leave with a sense of relief and well-being.

The foregoing topics are all theoretical rather than utilitarian applications but the following application is utilitarian and extremely important at that. It makes use of Schafer's action descriptions to suggest a way in which psychiatry can more appropriately provide expert testimony in insanity cases before courts of law (Miller, 1979).

In the United States, interpretations of criminal responsibility center around case law of 1954 known as *Durham*. It states that an accused is not determined responsible for a criminal act if the act was due to "mental disease or defect." This law implies that a "mental disease" is a thing that causes behavior. As such it is subject to the same criticism Schafer has leveled at id, motive, and other psychoanalytic constructs: the person's mental disease, rather than the person, caused the criminal act to occur. In contrast, in Schafer's approach the person's actions *are* the disease. Further, the question of free will versus determinism is a spurious distinction. There are no entities or forces causing the criminal action—no irresistible impulses, no deficiencies of will, no determining powers. Equally, there is no entity or power called will that autonomously made a choice to commit a criminal act. Instead, in action language, " . . . the expert assesses how the accused did what he did at the time of the crime, looks to his explanations and his reasons for this act, and examines these in the light of his past history. The psychiatric expert does not determine what 'forced' the accused to do his criminal act" (Miller, 1979, p. 128).

If a delusion was involved, the accused committed the act delusionally, not *because* of a delusion. For the expert to say that the accused acted delusionally is only to describe the way in which

that person committed the crime. The matter of criminal responsibility remains with the court. Miller finds this approach compatible with the Durham rule in that it does not specify a particular symptom that points to criminal responsibility, and it has the further advantage of indicating:

> that criminal responsibility is a legal convention, not a character trait—a distinction often missing in the courtroom. It is the law that establishes which psychological processes are excusable and which are not. In an action approach, criminal responsibility is understood in terms of how the action was done in relation to some requirement of law . . . The expert's task is to describe the psychological processes of the accused which are relevant to what the law considers in deciding criminal responsibility. The judge's or jury's task is to decide whether the defendant's actions satisfy the legal criteria for an insanity defense. (Miller, 1979, p. 128)

PSYCHOTHERAPY

Psychoanalytic therapy goes hand in hand with psychoanalytic theory. As developed by Freud, therapy is in large part the process of making the unconscious conscious by teaching the patient ("analysand") to "free associate"—say whatever occurs to him or her without self-censorship which the analyst then interprets to the patient in terms of the theory. But attempts at free association meet with "resistance" because of repressed and dangerous thoughts, says the theory. Resistance to free association weakens over time as the analysand comes to trust the analyst. The ego begins to exercise rational control over the impulses, and the libido transfers much of its energy to the analyst, which the analyst applies as counterforce to the resistance. The transference itself must be analyzed until a counter-transference occurs, at which point the analysand becomes independent, thereby completing the therapeutic process. Freud also used dream analysis extensively as an entrée into the unconscious; for dreams, he held, reflect repressed infantile wishes. Consequently, free association of their contents can be invaluable in uncovering repressed memories. Cure is considered to occur when the unconscious becomes conscious.

As indicated in sections above, some newer psychoanalytic procedures can deviate considerably from the orthodox method. Spence's attempt to help clients develop a coherent story as the major goal of therapy is one example.

RELATION TO SOME OTHER APPROACHES

Behavior Analysis

Freud's system was highly mentalistic and at opposite poles from behavior analysis, whose very name stresses an analysis of *behavior* rather than that of a *psyche*. To the behavior analyst, Freud's populating the organism with an array of entities that have causative powers known only through symbolic interpretation in case histories is more like mysticism than science. Kohut's emphasis on "self" would not be much closer to the behavior analysts, but Schafer's action language comes close at times to a radical behaviorism, though it still retains elements of mentalism and consequently seems closer to a methodological behaviorism (see chapter 6).

Dialectical Psychology

Psychoanalysis as a system that posits conflicts as central to its enterprise has formulated a number of polar opposites (also called "dualisms," "binaries," and "two-factor conflicts"). Examples include the life instinct-death instinct, id demands-ego defenses, pleasure principle-reality principle, transference-countertransference, and fixation ("cathexis")-antifixation. Erikson described a dialectical crisis in each of the psychosexual stages whereas Hartmann removed much of Freud's dialectical thinking. Others have carried the modification further, and Schafer has virtually eliminated "dualisms" while retaining the centrality of conflict in psychoanalysis. He regards such polarities as trivial and mechanical, overlooking heterogene-

ity and multidirectionality and serving to maintain such Freudian structures as id and ego. Kohut, on the other hand, conceives of two selfobjects that are polar opposites, one power-seeking and the other idealizing goals. The "tension-arc" (Kohut & Wolf, 1978, p. 414) between these ambitions and ideals activates an intermediate area of talents and skills—a dialectic conflict of thesis and antithesis that produces a synthesis (see chapter 9).

Humanistic Psychology

It is rather ironic that humanistic psychology, which came into existence as a "Third Force" against behaviorism and psychoanalysis, should now find common ground in the theories of some recent theorists of psychoanalysis. Jenkins (1992) attempts to show how Rychlak's logical learning theory (see chapter 4), which provides for considering alternatives and choosing goals (teleology), is consistent with Schafer's approach emphasizing meaning and goal-seeking. Notwithstanding, Schafer's rejection of "self" as an anthropomorphized entity would be anathema to that system. Kohut's theory, giving centrality to self, would find more in common. Sass (1989) describes a number of psychoanalysts moving in the direction of humanistic psychology, especially Kohut; and Kahn (1985) sees the relationship between Kohut and Carl Rogers as providing a bridge between the two systems. The fact that both systems are organocentric facilitates this.

Interbehavioral Psychology

Because interbehaviorism begins its inquiry with events rather than constructs and therefore invokes no mind-body dualism, psychic energies, etc., it has little in common with orthodox psychoanalysis. Schafer's action language approach brings the two closer together, but interbehaviorism goes a step further than Schafer and puts the action not just in the person but in the person-environment relationship. Keeping the action centered on the person as Schafer does, it holds, restricts the number and type of variables that can be considered. Widening the action to the environment adds (a) functional characteristics to the person-object interaction, (b) setting factors, (c) media of contact, and (d) history of the individual as an ongoing interactional development (rather than necessitating endemic characteristics of the infant such as sexuality and aggression). The interbehavioral approach also provides a means of describing the so-called unconscious as action phases of an interaction. No doubt, psychoanalysts would consider the narrower approach of organocentrism superior to contextual interactionism (noncentrism).

Operant Subjectivity

Psychoanalysis puts a premium on subjectivity and has increasingly sought methods of research consistent with the subjective nature of its undertaking. This establishes its interests squarely in accordance with the technique of operant subjectivity, Q methodology. Two studies reported here have employed Q successfully, even though one of these couched the study in terms inconsistent with the scientific philosophy of operant subjectivity. Schafer's insistence that behavior is what observers observe, whereas action is what people observe about themselves, resonates well with operant subjectivity (chapter 11).

In contrast to Edelson's mentalistic interpretation of Q, Goldman (1993), who embraces both psychoanalysis and operant subjectivity, argues against maintaining a mind-body dualism and for moving toward a scientific subjectivism. He notes that others have advocated a shift in this direction but maintains that they have not provided sound methodology or sound theory. He contends that what has been called consciousness or unconsciousness can be handled as operant subjectivity.

> While it is expected that associations will ultimately lead to repressed unconscious material, these narratives, are fundamentally behaviours that were created associatively from other behaviour which may or may not be subject to psychoanalytic interrogations . . . Unconscious-

ness thus is nothing more or less than a construct, a form of life, and behavior that has been classified as such. Its materiality can be probed and symbolized through sound subjective scientific operations. Hence, with Q methodology and its factor analytic quantum based theories of self and subjectivity we can now discard the Cartesian dualisms and mentalisms, and thereby place psychoanalysis within a more contemporary scientific narrative.

Goldman (1997) also notes that Q turns to the behavior of communication through Q sorting that contrasts with such psychoanalytic substantive constructs as intrapsychic conflict, mind, consciousness, unconsciousness, defense mechanisms, and so on. The newer views—such as those of Spence, Schafer, and Kohut—he observes, emphasize subjectivity and empathic knowing, but these approaches are subject to distortion in interpretations of free association whereas Q handles them rigorously. He cites several cases of misunderstandings between client and analyst that illustrate the need for better assessment and describes a Q study of Stephenson's that replaced such distortions with a more accurate view that could be used in planning treatment.

Social Constructionism

A number of theories and practices of psychoanalysis show one degree or another of social constructionism. In Kohut's system the patient is the final judge of what is accurate for him or her; and Schafer, Gill, and Spence insist that there is no one true story line of the patient. Similarly, social constructionism holds that truth is totally relative to each social group and is expressed in the social narrations of the group. Jacques Lacan, a French psychoanalyst, contributed to the narrative movement by introducing linguistics into psychoanalysis and reinterpreting Freud in terms of structural linguistics. Sullivan's ideas about family therapy are similar to social constructionism's use of that therapy. Still, most psychoanalysts are centered on the organism and its putative innate characteristics (organocentric), whereas constructionists are centered on social processes (sociocentric).

CRITIQUE

External vs. Internal Criticisms

Despite the shortcomings or limitations in Freud's formulations that psychoanalysts themselves have found and the various revisions or extensions of his theory they have proposed, few of these reformulators have rejected his work in total. Crews (1996) maintains that the critiques of these partisans are "rarely rigorous or thoroughgoing;" and, despite their recognition of shortcomings, the critics don't agree on how to fix the problems. Nevertheless, psychoanalysis has been evolving ever since the time of Freud's formulation and now exists in forms, as the above sections indicate, that bear only a remote resemblance to his original conceptions. As with all new developments in psychoanalysis, Freud's instinct theory required major change or total abandonment (Eagle & Wolitzky, 1992), and this led to replacement formulations that moved even further away from orthodoxy.

External Criticisms of Freud

Theory. For the most part the external critics (non-psychoanalysts) have failed to recognize the vast changes that have taken place and the radical reformulations of such revisionists as Schafer and Spence. More attention to these would present a very different picture to readers. The external critics have directed most of their criticisms at the original formulation of Freud and occasionally at Jung and a few other "classical" psychoanalysts. The following will serve as important examples of external examinations of Freud's writings.

Salter (1952/1964) made one of the earliest thoroughgoing attacks. In a biting critique he showed the inconsistencies and illogic of the theory and the exaggerated claims of the efficacy of the therapy. He used extensive quotes from Freud to illustrate and document his criticisms. Among his observations is his view of Freud's theoretical procedure of "locating his grotesqueries in a vague place called the 'unconscious.' After all, since no one can possibly know (without an analyst's help) what goes on in the unconscious, who can deny the existence there of the most incredible witches' sabbaths?" (pp. 24–25). Another critic revealed Freud's plagiarism and his self-serving selection of case studies to support his theories (Sulloway, 1991, 1992). Still another pointed out that Freud's entire theory rests on just six published case histories. The subject of one of these—the patient known as the Wolf Man—repudiated Freud's claim by explaining that because he slept in his nanny's bedroom rather than his parents' he could not have interrupted his parents' making love (Dewdey, 1997).

The most acclaimed critique of Freud is Grünbaum's (1984). Surprisingly, his book received considerable attention from the psychoanalysts themselves, who have either criticized it or looked for ways to meet some of Grünbaum's criticisms (for example, Edelson, 1988). The journal *Behavioral and Brain Sciences* published forty peer reviews of the book in its January 1985 issue. Grünbaum points out that because the theory makes claims about the cause of neurosis, it can only receive support by comparing non-neurotic groups with neurotic groups. In other words, it needs to use control groups but has never done so. Instead, it has relied on cures of neuroses that "tally" with the theory's claims of cause and effect. Yet the recovered "memories" that accord with the theory are thoroughly contaminated by suggestion and expectation. The patient learns what the analyst wants to hear and responds accordingly. In addition to these criticisms, Grünbaum refers to studies that show that the rate of spontaneous improvement for neurotic symptoms is as high as it is from psychoanalytic therapy. That is, as a therapy psychoanalysis has no advantage over doing nothing. In a review of Grünbaum's book, Sulloway (1985) points out that a century of research in psychology has shown that human development is not highly sexual and that it is quite malleable and multidetermined. Despite his devastating criticisms, Grünbaum unaccountably allows for the possibility that Freud's theory might eventually be shown to contain some elements of truth.

Another important but little known critique is Macmillan's (1991). He describes the historical evolution of Freud's theory and the fundamental errors of observation and logic that he engaged in. Psychoanalytic theory formation today continues to follow Freud in making the same errors. For example, even the most extreme revisionists accept repression, yet repression has no verification in independent reality. It is only a name of presumed traces of painful memories; thus, it has no explanatory power. After reviewing Macmillan's book Crews (1996) concludes, "a thoroughgoing epistemic critique, based on commonly acknowledged standards of evidence and logic, decertifies every distinctively psychoanalytic proposition" (p. 67). He also observes that the trend toward "recovered memory" (often of those claiming sexual abuse) based on Freud's theory never would have occurred had Macmillan's (1977) earlier critique received attention.

In overview we may note that Freud's claim that this theory was proven by his therapeutic successes overlooks the fact that (a) there was no independent confirmation of his claimed successes; (b) many people with neurotic symptoms improve over time without any therapy; (c) improvement from therapy does not establish that the theory is correct, only that something in the patient-therapist relationship or in their discussions was helpful; (d) if recovery depends on the applications of a valid theory (other therapies are presumably invalid and should not be effective), the rate of success should be higher for analysis than for other therapies, but it is not; and (e) psychoanalysis does not always cure the neurosis (as Freud himself admitted), and those neuroses it claims to cure sometimes recur—hardly a ringing confirmation of the theory and its purported validation in application.

Therapy. Psychoanalysts often report success with their regimes of therapy. However, Wolpe (1981), a founder of behavior therapy, cites "a distinguished psychoanalyst" (Schmideberg, 1970) who reports some appalling failures. Schmideberg blames the profession for making the patient feel that he or she, rather than the system, is the failure. In one case a man with anxieties and inhibitions due only to his inexperience and his being from a poor family spent thirty years in analysis. He had made no improvement and had impoverished himself by paying for thirty years of treatment when he came to Schmideberg. In another case a woman who had no symptoms, but wanted to have a fuller life developed a phobia and went downhill for twelve years under two analysts. Wolpe remarks that he has seen many such cases and finds that analysts tell the patients that their lack of improvement or their deterioration is due to resistance, rather than admitting that the treatment might be inappropriate. Wolpe wonders why a therapist whose specialization is in breaking down resistances, but who cannot succeed in five or ten years would recommend more of the same. All types of psychotherapy have their failures but a continuation of failures for endless years seems restricted to psychoanalysis.

Schafer's Action Psychoanalysis

Schafer continues the Freudian emphasis on infantile sexuality and unconscious influences despite the problems these constructs display. Other criticisms include Leary's (1989) observation that nothing in Schafer's formulation indicates why a retelling around psychoanalytic concepts should be any more therapeutic than a retelling around dialectical or behavioristic concepts. One can make a case for psychoanalysis, she argues, only if the story refers to something beyond itself that falls within the purview of psychoanalysis. Further, she insists, it is the repressed past that is central to psychoanalysis; and to replace it with a construction of the present is to leave little that is psychoanalytic. Berman (1985), however, sees Schafer's approach as (a) providing more flexibility for analysts, as they no longer have to seek "actual" stories; and (b) promoting personality changes in analysands as they drop their defenses and disclaimers, and thereby discover more meaningful versions of their lives.

Barratt (1978) charges that Schafer's action language fails to deal with the vital psychoanalytic concept of alienation that occurs when the ego splits off from the id and the id's repression, thereby undoing the distinction between conscious and unconscious that Schafer subscribes to. In a rejoinder to Barratt, Fourcher (1978) defends Schafer for moving beyond biological metaphors and physical mechanisms into meanings and intersubjective relations. Still others (Ellman & Moskowitz, 1980) find fault with his strictures of using only what is observed in the psychoanalytic situation, this stricture precluding the use of valuable developmental data. Ellman and Moskowitz also complain that his "strict realist position" would eliminate much of what is valuable in psychoanalysis.

CONCLUSIONS

Academic psychology has largely considered psychoanalytic theory unscientific and given it little attention except for an obligatory recounting in textbooks. Critics in psychology, philosophy, and other fields have made a strong case that it has little to offer. They contend, in fact, that it is not a theory which has not yet found empirical support, but is actually a pseudoscience. Given its extensive shortcomings, some critics (Ruse, 1985; Crews, 1996) suggest that what few propositions might, with careful and rigorous research, demonstrate some validity seem hardly worth pursuing. Psychoanalysis itself does not have the organizational structure to engage in programs of research and has no university connections for that purpose. Further, those at universities who are engaged in psychological and psychiatric research usually have little interest in psychoanalysis. Nevertheless, its proponents have shown increasing interest in systematic research, departing from the longstanding view that the procedure of psychoanalysis was itself research and that only that research counted. It is noteworthy that the growing interest in research seems to be accompanied by growing departures from orthodoxy.

Problems abound with psychoanalysis as a form of psychotherapy. It is a slow, ponderous, and expensive procedure. Other psychotherapies can be applied with equal or greater effectiveness in much shorter periods of time. The goal of most psychotherapy today is not toward struggling with hypothetical dark instincts of an individual's past but toward developing new behaviors that enable the individual to cope with his or her world. Nevertheless, the system has legions of partisans among some human service workers, including social workers and art therapists.

Still, psychoanalysis is highly institutionalized as a theory (or variety of theories) and as a therapy. And many non-analysts who are influenced by it do not read the empirical or logical works that point to severe shortcomings, nor do they grasp the theoretical and applied alternatives to it. It seems likely that those within the system, such as Schafer, Gill, Spence, and others who have moved the theory dramatically away from its physicalistic and biological assumptions, will be followed by another generation that will further modify it until it has little identity with Freud. At the same time, others will seek to maintain ties to tradition, thereby assuring its continuation. Such innovations as self-psychology have revitalized some branches of the system, and these will probably continue to develop but will also move both theory and practice further away from orthodoxy.

Because the array of medications now available for maladaptive behaviors usually does not in itself suffice to remedy the problems, and because drugs are entirely inappropriate for many conditions of adjustment, psychotherapy continues to fill a vital need. Various versions of psychoanalysis will probably continue to fill that need along with dozens of other forms of psychotherapy.

REFERENCES

Adler, Alfred. 1917. *A Study of Organic Inferiority and Its Psychical Compensation*. New York: Nervous and Mental Disease Publishing.

————. 1927a. *The Practice and Theory of Individual Psychology.* New York: Harcourt, Brace.

————. 1927b. *Undersanding Human Nature.* New York: Greenberg.

————. 1939. *Social Interest.* New York: Putnam.

Bacal, Howard A. 1995. The essence of Kohut's work and the progress of self psychology. *Psychoanalytic Dialogues* 5: 353–66.

Barratt, Barnaby B. 1978. Critical notes on Schafer's "action language." *Annual of Psychoanalysis* 6: 287–303.

Basch, Michael F. 1995. Kohut's contribution. *Psychoanalytic Dialogues* 5: 367–73.

Berman, Emanuel. 1985. Schafer's contribution: Comments on its continuity and development. *Israel Journal of Psychiatry and Related Sciences* 25: 191–97.

Bordin, E. S. 1966. Personality and free association. *Journal of Consulting Psychology* 30: 30–38.

Colby, K. M. 1960. Experiment on the effects of an observer's presence on the image system during psychoanalytic free association. *Behavioral Science* 5: 216–32.

————. 1961. On the greater amplifying power of causal-correlative over interrogative inputs on free association in an experimental psychoanalytic situation. *Journal of Nervous and Mental Disorders* 133: 233–39.

Crews, Frederick. 1996. The verdict on Freud. *Psychological Science* 7: 63–68.

Dewdney, A. K. 1997. *Yes, We Have No Neutrons: An Eye-Opening Tour Through the Twists and Turns of Bad Science.* New York: Wiley.

Donaldson, Gail. 1996. Between practice and theory: Melanie Klein, Anna Freud and the development of child analysis. *Journal of the History of the Behavioral Sciences* 32: 160–76.

Eagle, Morris N., & David L. Wolitzky. 1992. Psychoanalytic theories of psychotherapy. In *Hisory of Psychotherapy: A Century of Change.* Edited by Donald K. Freedman. Washington, DC: American Psychological Association.

Edelson, Marshall. 1984. *Hypothesis and Evidence in Psychoanalysis.* Chicago: University of Chicago Press.

————. 1988. *Psychoanalysis: A Theory in Crisis.* Chicago: University of Chicago Press.

————. 1989. The nature of psychoanalytic theory: Implications for psychoanalytic research. *Psychoanalytic Inquiry* 9: 169–92.

Ellman, Steven J., & Michael B. Moskowitz. 1980. An examination of some recent criticisms of psychoanalytic "metapsychology." *Psychoanalytic Quarterly* 49: 631–62.

Erikson, Erik. 1963. *Childhood and Society,* 2nd ed. New York: Norton.

————. 1968. *Identity: Youth and Crisis.* New York: Norton.

Eysenck, Hans, & Glen D. Wilson. 1973. *The Experimental Study of Freudian Theories.* London: Methuen.

Fourcher, Louis A. 1977. Adopting a philosophy: The case of Roy Schafer. *A New Language for Psychoanalysis, Existential Psychology and Philosophy* 15: 134–39.

————. 1978. Discussion. *Annual of Psychoanalysis* 6: 303–312.

Freud, Sigmund. 1935. *A General Introduction to Psycho-Analysis,* rev. ed. Translated by Joan Riviere. New York: Simon & Schuster.

————. 1938. *The Basic Writings of Sigmund Freud.* Translated and edited by A. A. Brill. New York: Modern Library.

————. 1969. *An Outline of Psycho-Analysis.* Translated and edited by James Strachey. New York: Norton.

Fromm, Erich. 1941. *Escape from Freedom.* New York: Holt.

————. 1947. *Man for Himself.* New York: Holt.

————. 1955. *The Sane Society.* New York: Holt.

Gabbard, Glen O. 1997. The psychoanalyst at the movies. *International Journal of Psycho-Analysis* 78: 429–34.

Gill, Merton M. 1973. Introduction to George Klein's "Two theories or one?" *Bulletin of the Menninger Clinic* 37: 99–102.

————. 1976. Metapsychology is not psychology. In *Psychology versus Metapsychology: Essays in Memory of George S. Klein.* Edited by M. M. Gill & P. S. Holzman. New York: International Universities Press.

————. 1983. The point of view of psychoanalysis: Energy discharge or person? *Psychoanalysis and Contemporary Thought* 6: 523–51.

————. 1992. Merton Gill speaks his mind. *International Journal of Communicative Psychoanalysis and Psychiatry* 7: 27–33.

Glymour, Clark. 1974. Freud, Kepler, and the clinical evidence. In *Sigmund Freud.* Edited by Richard Wollheim. Garden City, NY: Anchor.

————. 1980. *Theory and Evidence.* Princeton, NJ.: Princeton University Press.

Goldman, Irvin. 1991. Narcissism, social character, and communication: A Q-methodological perspective. *Psychological Record* 41: 343–60.

————. 1993. The psychoanalytic perspective. Paper presented at a panel discussion of "Q methodology in retrospect: Consciousness and subjectivity" at the Ninth Annual Conference of the International Society for the Scientific Study of Subjectivity. Columbia, MO: University of Missouri, October 7–9.

————. 1998. Psychotherapy research. Abstract of a paper presented at the North American Society for Psychotherapy Research, January 31. *Q Methodology Network* [Listserver], 29 September.

Grotstein, James S. 1981. Wilfred R. Bion: The man, the psychoanalyst, the mystic: A perspective on his life and work. *Contemporary Psychoanalysis* 17: 501–536.

Grünbaum, Adolf. 1980. Epistemological liabilities of the clinical appraisal of psychoanalytic theory. *Nous* 14: 307–385.

———. 1984. *The Foundations of Psychoanalysis: A Philosophical Critique.* Berkeley: University of California Press.

Hartmann, Heinz. 1939. *Ego Psychology and the Problem of Adaptation.* New York: International University Press.

———. 1960. *Psychoanalysis and Moral Values.* New York: International University Press.

———. 1964. *Essays on Ego Psychology: Selected Problems in Psychoanalytic Theory.* New York: International University Press.

Holt, Robert R. 1974. The primary process after metapsychology. Paper presented at the Annual Meeting of the American Psychological Association. Cited by Ellman & Moskowitz, 1980.

———. 1989. *Freud Reappraised: A Fresh Look at Psychoanalytic Theory.* New York: Guilford.

Horney, Karen. 1937. *Neurotic Personality of Our Times.* New York: Norton.

———. 1939. *New Ways in Psychoanalysis.* New York: Norton.

———. 1945. *Our Inner Conflicts.* New York: Norton.

———. 1950. *Neurosis and Human Growth.* New York: Norton.

———. 1967. *Feminine Psychology.* New York: Norton.

Jenkins, Adlebert H. 1992. Hermeneutics versus science in psychoanalysis: A rigorous humanistic view. *Psychoanalytic Psychology* 9: 509–527.

Jung, Carl. 1926. *The Psychological Types or the Psychology of Individuation.* Translated by H. Godwin Baynes. New York: Harcourt, Brace.

———. 1927. *The Psychology of the Unconscious.* Translated by Beatrice M. Hinkle. New York: Dodd, Mead.

———. 1928. *Two Essays on Analytic Psychology.* Translated by Beatrice M. Hinkle. New York: Dodd, Mead.

———. 1933. *Modern Man in Search of a Soul.* Translated by W. S. Dell & Cary F. Baynes. New York: Harcourt, Brace, Jovanovich.

———. 1963. *Memories, Dreams, Reflections.* Translated by Richard & Clara Winson and edited by Aniela Jaff. New York: Vintage Books.

Kahn, Edwin. 1985. Heinz Kohut and Carl Rogers: A timely comparison. *American Psychologist* 40: 893–904.

Kavaler-Adler, Susan. 1993. The conflict and process theory of Melanie Klein. *American Journal of Psychoanalysis* 53: 187–204.

Kernberg, Otto. 1992. *Aggression in Personality Disorders and Perversions.* New Haven, CT: Yale University Press.

Klein, George S. 1973. Two theories or one? *Bulletin of the Menninger Clinic* 37: 102–132.

Klein, Melanie. 1935. A contribution to the psychogenesis of manic-depressive states. In *Developments in Psychoanalysis.* Edited by Joan Riviere. London: Hogarth Press.

———. 1964. *Contributions to Psycho-Analysis.* New York: McGraw-Hill.

Kohut, Heinz. 1971. *The Analysis of the Self.* New York: International Universities Press.

———. 1977. *The Restoration of the Self.* New York: International Universities Press.

———. 1979. The two analyses of Mr Z. *International Journal of Psycho-Analysis* 60: 3–27.

———. 1984. *How Does Analysis Cure?* Chicago: University of Chicago Press.

———. 1995. Introspection, empathy, and psychoanalysis: An examination of the relationship between mode of observation and theory. *Journal of Psychotherapy Practice and Research* 4: 163–77.

Kohut, Heinz, & Ernest S. Wolf. 1978. The disorders of the self and their treatment: An outline. *International Journal of Psycho-Analysis* 59: 413–25.

Leary, Kimberlyn R. 1989. Psychoanalytic process and narrative process: A critical consideration of Schafer's "narrational project." *International Review of Psycho-Analysis* 16: 179–90.

Liff, Zanvel A. 1992. Psychoanalysis and dynamic techniques. In *History of Psychotherapy: A Century of Change.* Edited by Donald K. Freedman. Washington, DC: American Psychological Association.

Luborsky, Lester, & Jim Mintz. 1974. What sets off momentary forgetting during a psychoanalysis? *Psychoanalysis and Contemporary Science* 3: 233–68.

Macmillan, Malcolm. 1977. Freud's expectations and the childhood seduction theory. *Australian Journal of Psychology* 29: 223–36.

———. 1991. *Freud Evaluated: The Completed Arc.* Amsterdam: North-Holland.

Mann, David W. 1996. Theories of the self. *Harvard Review of Psychiatry* 44: 175–83.

Meares, Russell. 1996. The psychology self: An update. *Australian and New Zealand Journal of Psychiatry* 30: 312–16.

Mehlman, Elizabeth, & Cheryl Glickauf-Hughes. 1994. Understanding developmental needs of college students in mentoring relationships with professors. *Journal of College Student Psychotherapy* 8: 39–53.

Meissner, W. W. 1979. Methodological critique of the action language in psychoanalysis. *Journal of the American Psychoanalytic Association* 27: 79-105.

Miller, Glenn H. 1979. Criminal responsibility: An action language approach. *Psychiatry* 42: 121–30.

Motley, Michael T. 1985. Slips of the tongue. *Scientifc American* 253, no. 3 (December): 116–27.

Norville, Roxana; Harold Sampson; & Joseph Weiss. 1996. Accurate interpretations and brief psychotherapy outcome. *Psychotherapy Research* 6: 16–29.

Ornstein, Paul H. 1996. Heinz Kohut's legacy. *Partisan Review* 63: 614–27.

Padel, John. 1991. The psychoanalytic theories of Melanie Klein and Donald Winnicott and their interaction in the British Society of Psychoanalysis. *Psychoanalytic Review* 78: 325–45.

Phillips, Adam. 1988. *Winnicott*. Cambridge, MA: Harvard University Press.

Rosbrow, Thomas. 1993. Significance of the unconscious plan for psychoanalytic theory. *Psychoanalytic Psychology* 10: 515–32.

Ruse, Michael. 1985. Philosophy of science and psychoanalysis. *Free Inquiry* 5 (4): 28–30.

Salter, Andrew. 1952/1963. *The Case Against Psychoanalysis*. New York: Citadel Press.

Sampson, Harold. 1992a. A new psychoanalytic theory and its testing in research. In *Interface of Psychoanalysis and Psychology*. Edited by J. W. Barron, M. N. Eagle, & D. Wolitzky. Washington, DC: American Psychological Association.

———. 1992b. The role of "real" experience in psychopathology and treatment. *Psychoanalytic Dialogues* 2: 509–528.

Sandler, Joseph. 1996. Comments on the psychodynamics of interaction. *Psychoanalytic Quarterly* 16: 88–95.

Sass, Louis A. 1989. Humanism, hermeneutics, and humanistic psychoanalysis: Differing conceptions of subjectivity. *Psychoanalysis and Contemporary Thought* 12: 432–504.

Schafer, Roy. 1970. An overview of Heinz Hartmann's contributions to psychoanalysis. *International Journal of Psycho-Analysis* 51: 425–46.

———. 1976. *A New Language for Psychoanalysis*. New Haven, CT: Yale University Press.

———. 1983. *The Analytic Attitude*. New York: Basic Books.

———. 1985. The interpretation of psychic reality, developmental influences and unconscious communication. *Journal of the American Psychoanalytic Association* 33: 537–54.

———. 1995. In the wake of Heinz Hartmann. *International Journal of Psycho-Analysis* 76: 223–35.

Schmideberg, M. 1970. Psychotherapy with failures of psychoanalysis. *British Journal of Psychiatry* 116: 195–200.

Sears, Robert R. 1943. *Survey of Objective Studies of Psychoanalytic Concepts*. New York: Social Science Research Council.

Segal, Hanna. 1988. *Introduction to the Work of Melanie Klein*. London: Karnac Books.

Shevrin, Howard. 1996. Psychoanalytic research: Experimental evidence in support of basic psychoanalytic assumptions. In *Textbook of Psychoanalysis*. Edited by Edward Nersessian & Richard G. Kopff. Washington, DC: American Psychiatric Press.

Silberschatz, G.; H. Sampson; & J. Weiss. 1986. Testing pathogenic beliefs versus seeking transference gratification. In *The Psychoanalytic Process: Theory, Clinical Observations & Empirical Research*. Edited by J. Weiss, H. Sampson, & The Mount Zion Psychotherapy Research Group. New York: Guilford.

Silverman, Doris K. 1996. Arithmetic of a one- and two-person psychology: Merton M. Gill—An essay. *Psychoanalytic Psychology* 13: 267–74.

Spence, Donald. 1982. *Narrative Truth and Historical Truth: Meaning and Interpretation in Psychoanalysis*. New York: Norton.

———. 1994. *The Rhetorical Voice of Psychoanalysis: Displacement of Evidence by Theory*. Cambridge, MA: Harvard University Press.

Spillius, Elizabeth B. 1994. Developments in Kleinian thought: Overview and personal view. *Psychoanalytic Inquiry* 14: 324–64.

Stephenson, William. 1985. Review of "Structures of subjectivity: Explorations in psychoanalytic phenomenology," by George E. Atwood & Robert D. Stolorow. *Operant Subjectivity* 8 (3): 100–108.

Stolorow, Robert D. 1995. An intersubjective view of self psychology. *Psychoanalytic Dialogues* 5: 393–99.

Sullivan, Harry S. 1947. *Conceptions of Modern Psychiatry*. Washington, DC: White Foundation.

———. 1953. *The Interpersonal Theory of Psychiatry*, 3rd ed. New York: Norton.

———. 1962. *Schizophrenia as a Human Process*. New York: Norton.

Sulloway, Frank. 1985. Grünbaum on Freud: Flawed methodologist or serendipitous scientist? *Free Inquiry* 5 (4): 23–27.

———. 1991. Reassessing Freud's case histories: The social construction of psychoanalysis. *Isis* 82: 245–75.

———. 1992. *Freud, Biologist of the Mind: Beyond the Psychoanalytic Legend*, rev. ed. New York: Basic Books.

Viner, Russell. 1996. Melanie Klein and Anna Freud: The discourse of the early dispute. *Journal of the History of the Behavioral Sciences* 32: 4–15.

Wallace, Edwin R. 1988. What is "truth"? Some philosophical contributions to psychiatric issues. *American Journal of Psychiatry* 145: 137–47.

Wallerstein, Robert S. 1996. Outcomes of psychoanalysis and psychotherapy at termination and at follow-up. In *Textbook of Psychoanalysis*. Edited by Edward Nersessian & Richard G. Kopff. Washington, DC: American Psychiatric Press.

Weiss, Joseph. 1986. Part I: Theory and clinical observation. In *The Psychoanalytic Process: Theory, Clinical Observation and Empirical Research*. Edited by Joseph Weiss, Harold Sampson, & the Mount Zion Psychotherapy Research Group. New York: Guilford.

————. 1990. The nature of the patient's problems and how in psychoanalysis the individual works to solve them. *Psychoanalytic Psychology* 7: 105–113.

Winnicott, Donald W. 1951. Transitional objects and transitional phenomena. In *Through Paediatrics to Psychoanalysis*. New York: Basic Books.

Wolpe, Joseph. 1981. Behavior therapy versus psychoanalysis: Therapeutic and social implications. *American Psychologist* 36: 159–64.

Envirocentric Systems

Behavior Analysis: From Operant Conditioning to Behavior Therapy and Rule-Governed Behavior

Chapter Outline

INTRODUCTION

If you select a key and it opens a lock, you are likely to select that key in the future for that lock. If someone tells you how nice you look in your new sweater, you are likely to wear that sweater more frequently in the future. These are examples of the reinforcement principle that is fundamental to behavior analysis. The term "reinforcement" means strengthening or making the behavior more likely to occur again. The term "behavior analysis" stands as a counter to psychoanalysis. Rather than a psyche that undergoes analysis, according to the proponents, it is behavior that does so. And the analysis depends on experimentation rather than case studies. Sometimes the term "experimental analysis of behavior" is used.

FUNDAMENTALS

Most students of psychology have learned about the four basic schedules of reinforcement, usually in the context of rats pressing a bar or pigeons pecking at a disk. These "operations" the animal performs are the basis for the name "operant conditioning." Operant conditioning differs from classical (respondent) conditioning in that the animal must perform an operation to receive a reinforcement, and the operation comes *before* the reinforcement. In classical conditioning, such a Pavlov's dogs which salivate at the sound of a bell because they expected it to be followed by presentation of meat, the animal is passive. It does nothing to "earn" meat reinforcement, and the salivation response occurs *after* the bell rings. (The distinction between operant and classical conditioning is sometimes doubtful [Moore, 1973; Rachlin, 1991a], and recent research in behavior analysis has been exploring the relationships between the two.)

Each of four schedules of reinforcement produces distinctive patterns of behavior (Ferster & Skinner, 1957). The four schedules are called (a) fixed ratio, (b) fixed interval, (c) variable ratio, and (d) variable interval.

On a *fixed ratio* schedule the animal receives a bit of food after each of a fixed number of responses. If it receives the food after each response, this type of fixed ratio is called "continuous reinforcement." If the continuous reinforcement is withdrawn, the animal quickly stops responding—extinguishes. When the ratio is fixed at some value other than one to one—such as one to twenty—the rate of responding between reinforcements is very rapid and extinction is much slower after the reinforcement is withdrawn. Thus, the more strongly reinforced response extinguishes more rapidly than the weakly reinforced response. This is called the Humphrey paradox, after Lloyd G. Humphrey who first demonstrated it experimentally (Rachlin, 1991a).

On a *fixed interval* schedule the animal receives a reinforcement right after the first response, following a designated interval of time. For example if the interval is two minutes, a pigeon receives food after the first peck following the two minute interval. After learning to roughly gauge the time, the pigeon will peck slowly until almost time for the reinforcement and then peck very rapidly. Similarly, many students do not study very much until just before an examination. Then, a day or two—or even the very night—before the exam, they begin intensive efforts, working well into the night to prepare. After the examination they fall back into the pattern of negligence until time for the next exam. College students and pigeons seem much alike in this regard. But what about those few who do perform on a more even and regular schedule? According to the behavior analyst, they have been reinforced to do so—perhaps by praise from parents or by the reinforcement of good results due to following a more rational and effective course of action. Therefore, they are not responding to the fixed interval alone.

If the reinforcement occurs at *variable ratios* or *variable intervals,* it is called "intermittent" reinforcement. In such an arrangement the response rate is fairly even and is the slowest of the four to extinguish after the reinforcement is withdrawn. A pigeon may continue to peck for an hour or more after the last reinforcement, and even then—if it is put back into the situation the next day—it will once again begin pecking at a high rate. Because of the irregular occurrence of the reinforcement, the animal cannot readily detect that reinforcement has been discontinued so extinction is slow to occur. Or, to put it another way, the reinforcement schedule itself is much like extinction conditions; and it is therefore difficult for the animal to distinguish between conditions of extinction and conditions of reinforcement.

The classical example of variable ratio reinforcement is that of gambling. The gambler never knows how many throws of the dice or pulls of the slot machine lever will be necessary in order to obtain a payoff, and that occasional payoff, though usually amounting to less than the gambler spent to play, sustains the gambling. A great deal of human activity is influenced by intermittent reinforcement. A writer may manage to find a publisher for only a small percentage of his or her works, but keeps working because of the occasional payoff. A coin collector searches through thousands of coins and is reinforced to continue searching by occasionally finding a coin that fits into his or her collection. The athlete continues to train because of evidence of improvement and the occasional triumph. A child's temper tantrums are reinforced when the parent finally gives in, and the variable ratio of reinforcement makes the tantrums difficult to extinguish. Similarly, the dog that begs for food at the dining table and finally gets a scrap continues to beg on every occasion.

Over a period of many years behavior analysts have extensively explored various schedules of reinforcement. None of the response patterns that follow can be achieved with punishment. It is only with positive reinforcement that one can build sustained response patterns. And yet much of society's attempts to use the legal system for social control is based on punishment such as fines or imprisonment. The effects of punishment are quite complex, but have little of the consistency in suppressing responses that positive reinforcement has for sustaining them. For example, the recidi-

vism rate for prisoners suggests that prison has little deterrent effect on most crimes. Punishment also has undesirable effects: it is a form of aggression that fosters counter-aggression; it produces fear or dislike of the task connected with the punishment; and it provides no guidelines for what to do as a constructive alternative.

Most professional psychology organizations such as the American Psychological Society and the American Psychological Association require their members to pay annual dues before a designated date in order to avoid paying a late fee. In other words, these organizations emphasize potential punishment if members do not pay by the due date. The Association of Behavior Analysis, on the other hand, couches it differently: if the member pays before a given date the fee is lower. As someone has quipped, behavior analysis is a positively rewarding experience.

Animal studies have demonstrated that the simple S → R model of classical behaviorism cannot account for operant conditioning, because the consequences of the act are an intrinsic part of the behavior and have to be included. The solution to the problem is symbolized by a three-term contingency:

$$S^{Discrim} \underline{\quad\quad} R_{Oper} \underline{\quad\quad} S^{Reinf}$$

or, in more standard form,

$$S^D \underline{\quad\quad} R_O \underline{\quad\quad} S^R$$

where $S^{Discrim}$ = discriminative stimulus; R_{Oper} = operant response; and S^{Reinf} = reinforcing stimulus. (It is also known, more generally, as antecedent stimulus, behavior, and consequence.) A pigeon discriminates that a buzzer is sounding ($S^{Discrim}$), pecks at a disk, and receives a reinforcement such as food (S^{Reinf}). Anything that symbolizes a positive relationship between a reinforcement and a response is a discriminative stimulus. For example, each numbered button in an automatic elevator is a discriminative stimulus for a designated floor (S^{Reinf}). If we push number 4 (R_{Oper}) the elevator will take us to floor number 4, and we are reinforced to press button number

4 the next time (if we want that floor). But if we push number 1 when we want the first floor, and the elevator takes us to the basement, we are less likely to make that response the next time and might try number 2 instead. If number 2 reinforces us, we will most likely repeat that response in the future. We continually encounter discriminative stimuli related to reinforcements: the title of a book on a shelf that indicates it is the one we are searching for, traffic lights that control our stopping or proceeding, the hands on a watch that tell us it is time to leave for a meeting, the spot on a garment that indicates it needs washing, and thousands of others, many of which, as Skinner (1953, p. 75) has noted, are not always obvious to us.

Very little human activity is maintained by such primary reinforcers as food, but secondary reinforcers are very important. A secondary reinforcer is a stimulus that occurs prior to the primary reinforcer and initially has no reinforcing power, but after enough pairings with a primary reinforcer begins to become reinforcing. A powerful secondary reinforcer in our culture is money (actually a "generalized secondary reinforcer" because it reinforces a multitude of behaviors). Coins and currency are almost useless in themselves, but they can be exchanged for food, shelter, and whatever else one finds valuable. Consequently, people work, scheme, steal, plan, and gamble for this secondary reinforcer. Chains of secondary reinforcers sometimes develop. One may engage in work for (a) a promise of (b) a check which can be exchanged for (c) money that is used to buy a product that is sold for profit in the form of (d) another check that is exchanged for (e) money to buy a final product or service.

Behavior analysis is more closely tied to its methodology than any other system except for eco-behavioral psychology (chapter 7) and operant subjectivity (chapter 11). Instead of employing discrete trials or intervals between trials, as most experimental approaches do, behavior analysis provides for free responding at all times. The pigeon can peck at the disk at any moment. The cumulative record shows the responses on a continuous time scale and their relationship to the reinforcements. This methodology is so sensitive to the response rate that a single subject will provide useful and meaningful data and will reveal or demonstrate behavioral principles. No inferential or sampling statistics are necessary, nor is the use of multiple subjects required. Variability is not smoothed out by graphs or canceled out by statistics; nor is it explained away by theory that posits a hypothetical intervening variable—such as a drive or information processing—to absorb it. Rather variability is directly controlled by the experimental procedure and described by it.

EARLY DEVELOPMENT AND SOME ISSUES

Behavior analysis was developed by the man with the best known name in psychology, B. F. Skinner (1904–1990). In a survey of historians of psychology and chairs of departments of psychology (Korn, Davis, & Davis, 1991), he ranked in first place as the most important contemporary psychologist. Although Freud is better known among the general public and more prominent in introductory textbooks (Perlman, 1980), Freud's system is a personality theory and treatment program whose major advocates are in medicine (Freud was a physician) rather than in psychology. Skinner's system, on the other hand, is oriented toward the experimental study of operant behavior and receives most of its support from academic psychology and from such areas of application as training of the retarded, programmed learning, and behavior therapy. Nearly every department of psychology in the universities across the country either gives students experience with operant training of animals or shows them demonstrations of it. And every introductory psychology textbook has a section on operant conditioning. Behavior analysis has become an institution in American psychology.

The principle of reinforcement finds an earlier and more primitive formulation in Edward Thorndike's (1874–1949) Law of Effect. This states that a response is "stamped in" when it is followed by a "satisfying state of affairs." Skinner, in contrast, does not postulate any states, or any "satisfaction," but attempts to rely on a description of relationships: "If the occurrence of an operant is followed by the presentation of a reinforcing stimulus, the strength is increased" (Skinner, 1938, p. 21).

Thorndike's Law of Effect also stated that "an annoying state of affairs" would "stamp out" a response. In his original formulation he held that "satisfying" and "annoying" conditions were equal and opposite: "satisfying" conditions stamped in responses to the same extent that "annoying" ones stamped them out. After further experimental studies he recognized that they were not equal and opposite—that is, the "annoying" conditions did not always "stamp out" responses. Although punishment is usually used with the intention of decreasing the probability of a particular response, Skinner's work and that of many other researchers confirms Thorndike's finding that punishment is *not* very effective in controlling responses. It temporarily suppresses a response but usually does not eliminate it; when the threat of punishment diminishes, the responses return with full vigor (though a *severely* painful stimulus seems to permanently suppress responses in animals).

In addition to punishment, Skinner also recognizes negative reinforcement. This consists of the removal of the stimulus which increases the probability of the recurrence of the response. Thus, both negative and positive reinforcement tend to increase responses. For example, a student might study hard to obtain a good grade (positive reinforcer) or to avoid a bad one (negative reinforcer). A condition that leads to a *decrease* in responding (Thorndike's "stamping out") is a punishment. In all cases, according to the system, *behavior is selected by its consequences.*

John Watson's (1878–1958) behaviorism was also an important forerunner to Skinner's form of behaviorism. It was Watson who influenced psychology (a) to move from the study of mental contents to the study of behavior, (b) to replace the use of introspection with the use of objective methods, and (c) to make the goal of psychology the prediction and control of behavior. Skinner embraced all of these.

One form of behaviorism has traditionally assumed that mental events do not exist and that those behaviors called private or mental (for example, thinking) can be studied once the technology is available. Another form called "methodological behaviorism" held that private mental events exist but can be either ignored or methodologically avoided. Skinner departed from both of these. He insisted that private events and mental events are not the same. Mental events are only fictitious inventions or constructs, but private events have physical status. They are behaviors just as surely as drinking a beer or conversing with a friend is a behavior. Skinner called this approach "radical behaviorism" to differentiate it from methodological behaviorism. (Originally, "radical behaviorism" referred to Watson's rejection of mentalism.) Thus, Skinner accepted private events as behaviors but rejected mentalism as a kind of presumed special power residing in the organism. Unfortunately, the term "radical" has sometimes been taken to mean extremist, but Skinner intended it to refer to a broader, though nonmentalistic, position. Perhaps terming it something like "comprehensive behaviorism" or "naturalistic behaviorism" would have caused fewer problems.

Skinner also departed fundamentally from much of experimental psychology's use of statistics and group comparisons. It had been a standard assumption that the organism will show variability and that this variability must be controlled by use of large groups in which individuals' variabilities cancel each other out; one entire treatment group can then be compared with another entire treatment group. Such group comparisons comprise a between-group design involving statistical control. In contrast, Skinner used within-treatment group designs, often involving a single organism. He assumed that the experimenter imposed the variability and required not a statistical control but an experimental control (such as reinforcement contingencies). His use of single organisms controlled by experimental procedures and his rejection of statistics—including group averages, variances, and the like—left him with little in common with most other psychologists. He was interested only in discovering principles that would provide for highly predictable behavior from a single organism. The pursuit of tiny differences between the means of large groups held no interest for him.

Skinner published his early work in book form; but when his students attempted to publish in the scholarly journals, their work was usually rejected: editors were unfamiliar with the approach and unwilling to approve what they did not understand. The cumulative graphs were also strange to editors.[1] As a result behavior analysts had to establish their own journals.

Skinner was apparently more directly influenced in these revolutionary procedures by T. William Crozier (1892–1953), a physiologist at Harvard University, than by either Thorndike or Watson. Crozier advocated (a) studying a single organism for its variability (stimulus and response relationships as the total cause or description of behavior) rather than studying treatments across conditions that have statistical controls; (b) studying behavior itself, not the nervous system; (c) studying the variability of organisms as a function of changes in the environment and the organism; and (d) establishing empirical relationships rather than developing theory. Skinner accepted all four of these, but went beyond Crozier's principles, which are limited to tropisms of simple organisms such a marine animals.

His work has a parallel with that of Darwin, although Darwin was probably only an indirect influence. Both emphasize selection. For Darwin, it is species that get selected ("contingencies of survival"); for Skinner it is responses ("contingencies of reinforcement"). As organisms emit behaviors, the environment selects some of them through their consequences; that is, reinforced responses are selected for an increased probability of recurring. Thus, both Darwin and Skinner addressed complexity as a function of selection contingencies in nature. Skinner (1989) held that natural

selection accounts for a small amount of human behavior and a large amount of the behavior of nonhuman animals but that most human behavior is selected by reinforcement, especially of a cultural type.

Skinner rejected any unseen determiners of behavior such as drives, mind, or a computer brain. Once the functional relationship in the three-term contingency is described, control is achieved; and the analysis of behavior is complete. Skinner also rejected the notion of an eliciting stimulus for operant behavior. The stimulus does not elicit or set off an operant response. Rather, a response is "emitted" to a stimulus. (It is in respondent or Pavlovian conditioning that the stimulus elicits a response, according to Skinner, and this is emotional behavior.) This means that an operant response merely occurs in coordination with the stimulus. The stimulus does not cause the response. Not even reinforcement causes responses. Rather, reinforcement produces behavior, and the consequences of the behavior are what is learned. It is in the consequences of reinforcement that control is achieved, Skinner maintained, not in an eliciting stimulus or from an inner psychic agent. The orderliness and lawfulness of behavior, he taught, can be discovered by careful analysis of functional relationships. No theory is necessary for generating hypotheses to be tested; for behavior itself, he concluded, will serve as a guide.

VERBAL BEHAVIOR

Skinner considered his work in verbal behavior to be his most important. Verbal behavior, he held, functions in accordance with reinforcing conditions just as do other behaviors. The reinforcer comes from the verbal community of which the speaker is a part. Language is not the product of an inner psychic agent or computer brain, and words are not symbols. Verbal behavior is selected and reinforced by the verbal community (Skinner, 1957).

Skinner identifies two main functions of language; if someone says "hand me the screwdriver," the statement will be reinforced if the speaker

---

1. The line goes up with additions as other graph lines do, but unlike most others it stays steady with zero responses and rises again from that point with any additional responses.

receives the tool. This form of language begins very early as, for example, when a child asks for "doll" and receives it. This is called a "mand" (from *demand*). A more common form occurs when the speaker emits a discriminative stimulus that receives reinforcement. For example, if someone states that a manual for a computer is confusing, a listener could reinforce this by saying, "Yes, I know the problem. Most computer manuals have not been tested on anybody, and the result is confusion." A compliment to someone, a statement about the weather, an inquiry about one's health or children, a philosophical statement or a point of logic—all bring the speaker into *contact* with something in the surroundings and are for that reason called "tacts." A child points to a horse and says "dog" and the parent responds by saying, "No, that's a horse"; when the child then repeats "horse" and hears from the parent, "Yes, that's right, a horse," the parent has reinforced the child's response with the correct tact. Self-description can also involve tacts, as when the gambler laments how unlucky he or she is, or when a person exclaims, "I'm pleased at how much better I look in this new suit."

Verplanck (1992) has extended the tact to verbalizations that we utter to ourselves when observing something. Such a verbalization is the *notate*—we make a verbal note. Two or more notates can become a new unit called a *notant* which shows relationships between notates. For example, if I say to myself, "The wastebasket is overflowing," wastebasket and overflowing are notates that indicate relationships to one another. A series of experiments showed the importance of the notant in replacing "insight" learning. They also demonstrated its role in learning without "awareness" as well as its key role in other situations.

In conversations "intraverbals" come into play. After an initial statement by A, a verbal response by B is intraverbal and reinforces A's initial statement; it is the discriminative stimulus (S^D) for A's next intraverbal statement which reinforces B's previous intraverbal statement. This dual reinforcement continues throughout the dialogue. It might end with the arrival of some other kind of discriminative stimulus, such as the entry of an additional person, a clock that indicates the end of available time, etc. Objects stimulate tacts and words stimulate other words for intraverbals.

Skinner describes a number of other types of verbal behavior, but a brief account of extinction will suffice for this section. Consistent with the research findings from reinforcement and extinction, if one wants to extinguish annoying verbal behavior, one simply withholds reinforcement (for example, by discontinuing nods or replies) until it ceases. That procedure may fail at times, Skinner admits, because the person is reinforced by hearing herself/himself talking. In 1985 the journal *Analysis of Verbal Behavior* was established to publish the work in verbal behavior.

In verbal behavior the speaker's instructions stimulate the listener's behavior, which the listener never emitted and which is therefore not available for reinforcement. Similarly, informational sentences serve the listener for contingencies which the listener has never encountered. Studies of "rule-governed" behavior attempt to address these issues and have become one of the most important research areas in behavior analysis. A rule is a verbal stimulus such as advice, a mandate, a law, or instructions (Skinner, 1969). Rules can be self-initiated as, for example, when one thinks of doing something in a particular way and that thought serves as a rule to initiate and guide the behavior. Rules come from oneself or from the verbal social community and control behavior by specifying what leads to reinforcement. For example, one might say to oneself, "When I measure this board I must allow for the width of the saw kerf in order for the board to be long enough." This designates what behavior must be performed when the measuring is actually performed, as well as the consequences of doing so. If someone else gives the instructions, the principle is the same. Because humans formulate and follow their own rules, rule-governed behavior incorporates thinking; and this takes behavior analysis into more complex behavioral events (Zettle, 1990).

Rule-governed behavior does not require contingencies and may be contrasted with contingency-governed behavior, with its clear reinforcements, that *does* require them. It is shaped by verbal descriptions of contingencies rather than by actual contingencies. Skinner thought that rule-governed behaviors were of more importance for humans than contingency-governed behaviors. This finds support in a study (Lowe & Horne, 1985) in which people formulated rules for reinforcements by which they were able to obtain the reinforcements while avoiding the programmed contingencies; they were also able to convey the rule to others. Although rule-governed behavior was largely neglected for a time, it is now receiving more attention.

Andresen (1992) argues that Skinner's system provides the basis for an analysis of language that takes into account the context of speaking, unlike current linguistic theories which analyze it as structures independent of the context in which speech actually occurs. For most linguists, language is a code for communication in which the speaker encodes a message and the listener decodes it. She points out that discourse analysis, in contrast, treats language as social interaction and has concepts compatible with those of behavior analysis. Discourse analysts, specialists in language acquisition by children, together with behavior analysts "are well positioned" and "well equipped to help shape what promise to be exciting debates in the 1990s" (p. 15), she suggests. They both treat language as a living act that occurs in a social context, not as static structure.

CONCEPTUAL TOPICS

The Question of Control

Skinner illustrates in his novel *Walden Two* what he means by control. The word "control" sounds to some people like an authoritarian condition. Skinner notes that control is being exercised all the time, much of it by means of fear or punishment. But in *Walden Two* people are controlled by their environment, which they themselves administer. This is the arrangement that Skinner advocates in all situations. He also recognizes that con-

trol is a two-way matter. Even in animal operant conditioning, the animal's responses are controlling what the experimenter does. This was depicted in a cartoon in which two rats in a conditioning box were conversing with one another. One said to the other, "I've really got this guy under my control. Every time I press the bar he gives me a bit of food."

Skinner describes his development of behavior analysis as the result of environmental conditions that selected and reinforced his activities, which in turn comprised his formulation, research, writing, and speaking about his system. In a long series of behavioral events, Skinner's increasing success at analyzing the behavior of animals was the reinforcing stimulus that successively shaped his own behavior while at the same time he was reinforcing and shaping the behavior of his animals.

One can also control oneself. The artist who finds it impossible to work during the morning switches to a later hour that is more satisfactory. In a more complex situation, the smoker who wants to quit smoking can get rid of as many discriminative stimulus conditions as possible by, for example, avoiding being around other smokers, not having cigarettes handy, not lingering at the table after meals, and by setting up new reinforcements such as receiving encouragement from others, putting cigarette money in a glass jar to see it accumulate for a desired purchase, and providing frequent self-reinforcers for not smoking (such as allowing oneself to watch a television program, offering self-congratulations, etc.). In other words, we can control ourselves through our selection of discriminative stimuli and reinforcers.

Some might consider control tyrannical and wish to get rid of it all together. But children must be under the control of their parents, pupils under control of the school they attend, and citizens under control of the legal system. All of us are under control of weather conditions and of our culture. The important question, as Skinner sees it, is not whether we should destroy controlling conditions but how we can change them to our benefit. It is not individual people that we need to change so much as the world in which the controls reside.

"Human behavior is controlled not by physical manipulations but by changing the environmental conditions of which it is a function. The control is probabilistic. The organism is not forced to behave in a given way; it is simply made more likely to do so" (Skinner, 1973, p. 259).

But who will make those changes in the world? Who will do the controlling? Who will set the goals? Skinner assumes that in a democratic society these decisions will be beneficent: there will be enough mutual control that a good society rather than a totalitarian one will result. Kvale (n.d.) notes that "While Skinner analyzes the reciprocity in control, he overlooks the asymmetry which usually characterizes control relations. While master and slave mutually control each other, this does not imply that their possibilities of control are equally strong" (p. 11).

Even positive reinforcement can involve deprivation of something that is to be given back by the person in charge. In order to avoid deprivation used as a form of coercion, reinforcers, it may be argued, should be limited to those that occur naturally and should not be imposed (Sidman, 1989). We should not deprive a child of a toy and give it back for a designated behavior. We should look for desirable behaviors to reinforce, but by and large the major form of reinforcement should be social, such as approval for socially desirable behaviors. Others can be something special for special behaviors: we might take a child to a movie for raking the leaves. Here there is no artificial deprivation and coercion is minimized. If the two parties mutually agree upon it, it is behavioral contracting.

Skinner maintains that, if we managed behavior by the scientific principles of behavior analysis, we could end pollution, reduce overpopulation, improve the environment, enhance the health of all age groups, eliminate warfare, foster beauty and art, develop enjoyable and productive vocations for everyone, and bring about general human happiness and well-being. With behavioral management, we would not be automatons or under the dictates of someone else but could have "a world in which people feel freer than they have ever felt before, because they will not be under aversive

control" (Skinner, 1975, p. 47). Inefficient positive reinforcers also need to be replaced with effective ones in order to achieve a good society.

Late in his life he published "Intellectual Self-Management in Old Age" (1983) in which he delineated a number of aids for deteriorating intellectual abilities, especially verbal recall. One aid is simply that of keeping a notebook available to jot down things that one would otherwise forget. He suggests that a "stretched variable ratio" schedule of reinforcement is also useful for some activities: in old age, reinforcements may be less frequent because, for example, there are fewer friends or colleagues in one's field of interest to converse with; but one can still enjoy intellectual exchanges and other such activities if one has adapted to a decreasing frequency of ratios in such situations.

Mind and Brain

Skinner generally rejects any inside-outside distinction, though he inconsistently refers to internal events as lacking consistent reinforcement that external events receive (1963). If we attribute a behavior to a mind, consciousness, or psychic agent or power, we must then explain that power. "The puzzling question of how a physical event causes a mental event, which in turn causes a physical event, remains to be answered or dismissed as unanswerable" (Skinner, 1974a, p. 211). If we go directly to the behavior and the conditions that control it, he argues, we need no further explanation. Where behavior analysis studies the effect of punishment on behavior, mentalistic psychology, in contrast, will resort to postulating anxiety: punishment produces anxiety which produces the behavior. But it then must explain the anxiety, and it never does.

Skinner (1989) finds three meanings of "mind": a place where things happen, an organ that solves problems and carries out other behaviors, and a doer of activities. It is the doer, "the executor of cognitive processing," who cognitivism has emphasized. It perceives the world, organizes sense data into meaningful wholes, and processes information. It is the double of the person. . . ." (p. 17), for it is the person's mind rather than the person, who does these things. Yet, Skinner notes, we could just say that the *person* thinks, comprehends, believes, etc., rather than attributing these behaviors to a separate mind, a double for the person. In actuality "cognitive processes are," Skinner insists, "behavioral processes; they are things people do" (p. 17). People, not minds, are the doers. In tracing the evolution of mentalistic terms, he finds that they originally referred to behavior or to situations in which behaviors occurred.

Mind is often replaced with brain or central nervous system or viewed as its product. Skinner refers to this concept of the CNS (central nervous system) as the "conceptual nervous system" because it has no basis in observation. What we observe in the nervous system are electro-chemical impulses, hormonal and metabolic activities, and other biological events. We do not observe processing, thinking, memories, dreams, colors, or representations of the world. No matter how complete, brain science will never explain how human behavior originates and changes. However, brain science alone, he avers, will explain what happens between stimulation and response and between consequences and change in behavior. "The cooperative action of ethology, brain science, and behavior analysis" will give us a complete account (Skinner, 1989, p. 18).

Skinner refers to the belief that the world is represented internally as the "copy theory." That is, it assumes that there is an external world that is a copy of the internal world. Yet, he points out, if we could somehow coat the brain cells with a developer and obtain an image like a photograph the problem would become even more intractable:

for we should have to start all over and ask how the organism sees a picture in its occipital cortex . . . It adds nothing to an explanation of how an organism reacts to a stimulus to trace the pattern of the stimulus into the body. It is most convenient for both organism and psycho-physiologist, if the external world is never copied—if the world we know is simply the world around us. (1963, p. 954)

Further, "At some point the organism must do more than create duplicates. It must see, hear, smell, and so on, and the seeing, hearing, and smelling must be forms of action rather than of reproduction" (p. 954).

He points out that it is usually visual events that mentalists assume get represented in the conceptual nervous system. Less frequently do they assume that the sounds of a symphony orchestra that we hear come from our inner representation of it rather than from the orchestra, and still less frequently do they assume that tactual events are copied internally.

Because cognitive psychologists assume that mind *is* what the brain *does,* they seek representations, memory stores, feelings, reasoning, etc. in that organ. So far they have not found them "either introspectively or with the instruments and methods of physiology" (Skinner, 1990, p. 1206) and are not likely to; for, he notes, the nervous system cannot be a cause of itself.

The copy theory also extends to memory. The assumption is that events we have encountered or learned are copied into a mental memory store and later retrieved. This is an unfortunate analogy with file drawers, libraries, warehouses, and the like, Skinner holds. In behavior analysis nothing is stored and nothing is engulfed in the organism. Contingencies of reinforcement simply change the organism.

Future stimuli are effective if they resemble the stimuli which have been part of earlier contingencies: an incidental stimulus may "remind" us of a person, place, or event if it has some resemblance to that person, place, or event. Being reminded means being made likely to respond, possibly perceptually. (Skinner, 1974a)

In recalling something, we do not retrieve it from a storage bin but have some probability of making the relevant response.

For the cognitivist, Skinner argues, thinking is the product of an unexplained mind. But for him thinking is behaving. In Rachlin's (1991b) words, "What we think and feel are not causes of individual acts but patterns of acts themselves" (p. 455). And these, the behavior analysts insist (for example, Homme, 1965), are subject to control by reinforcement contingencies as are all other behaviors.

Theory and Metatheory

Skinner directed his objection to theory primarily at the all-encompassing learning theories of the 1940s and 1950s, especially when the proponents drew *deductions* from the theories and attempted to test them. He felt that such theories and their experimental tests only obscured the true controlling conditions; such conditions could be discovered only by experimental exploration of an *inductive* type, such as that which led to his own discovery of operant conditioning principles. Here we can say that Skinner is expressing a metatheory, a theory about theory, but not a theory about actual behaviors. The behaviors are merely described and codified into generalities or principles.

Hypothetical Deduction versus Empirical Induction

The emphasis on an approach that is *empirical* and *inductive* contrasts with those that are *hypothetical* and *deductive,* which occur in such systems as cognitive psychology and methodological behaviorism (see p. 183) of the 1940s and 1950s. These usually start with a theory and then deduce a hypothetical structural condition that causes the behavior: a drive, a computer brain, an instinct, a mind. These structures are intervening variables that come between the environment and the behavior to explain the behavior. To the behavior analyst, these structures or intervening variables in turn need an explanation. Rather than invoking such abstractions, they argue that it is more direct and efficacious to go directly to the behaviors and their functional relationships with the surroundings. Behavior analysis uses empirical (experimental) methods to identify and describe such functional relationships. It rejects as unscientific the deduction of hypothetical structures, and it rejects much of formal theory—theory and hypo-

thetical structure often going hand in hand, it holds, to impede the development of psychology as a science.

Mechanisms versus Contextualism

The behavior analysts have debated numerous issues among themselves. One of these is the role of setting conditions or context (Kantor, 1970). In a presidential address to the Association of Behavior Analysts, Morris (1992) made a case for the need to add context to the three-term contingency. Context allows for specifying factors that influence behavior when the three-term contingency, by itself, cannot; it thereby precludes imposing mentalistic constructs "such as representation, storage, and mediation, to account for variability in stimulus control" (p. 18). Marr (1993) argued, however, in a reply to Morris, that behavior analysis has always been contextualistic as well as mechanistic, and there is no need to abandon mechanism. Shull and Lawrence (1993) agreed with Marr and found that the mechanistic approach of behavior analysis has been the very means of determining contextual stimuli, none of which are revealed in any contextual program.

IMPLICIT POSTULATES

Like most other founders or leaders of systematic positions, Skinner never listed his assumptions, but Delprato and Midgley (1992) worked through his writings and compiled them. The following is based in part on that compilation. Note that postulate 7 seems to contradict the nondualism of metapostulate 3 (metapostulates are assumptions that are broader than postulates). Skinner also objected to an inner-outer distinction, claiming that the skin is not a boundary, while in other places he made a special point of such a distinction. Postulates 4 and 5 are equally inconsistent.

■ *Metapostulates* (supportive assumptions for a particular science)
  1. The primary purpose of psychological science is prediction and control.

2. The subject matter of psychological science is solely behavior.
3. Psychophysical dualism has no validity because only the physical world exists.
4. The environment is the cause of behaviors.

■ *Postulates* (subject matter assumptions)
   1. The environment determines behaviors through selection by means of consequences.
   2. Behavior is determined and lawful.
   3. Behavior is potentially reducible to biology and ultimately to chemistry and physics.
   4. Behavior cannot be reduced to biology.
   5. Private and public events have the same kind of physical dimensions.
   6. External "public" events are consistently reinforced but internal "private" events are not.
   7. The behavioral changes brought about by contingencies of reinforcement are biological.
   8. A methodology of functional analysis relates environmental independent variables to behavioral dependent variables.
   9. Behavior occurs in two major functional classes: respondent and operant.
   10. Operant behavior can be brought under the control of preceding stimuli.
   11. Operant behavior can best be described by three terms (discriminative stimulus, operant response, reinforcing stimulus) and best understood in their functional relationships.

Most of these are apparent from the preceding account but need to be made explicit. Those postulates with apparent inconsistencies point up the importance of such explication. An explicit statement of postulates is also important for comparing fundamental similarities and differences between any two systems, for arguments often occur on matters that never touch the fundamental assumptions underlying two different positions.

Metapostulate 1 may be a statement to which few non-behavior analysts would subscribe. Many psychologists are not interested in prediction or control, but in such varied goals as quantitative,

verbal, or schematic description of events; verification or refutation of hypotheses; personal or subjective meaning of events; and/or statistical comparisons as in surveys. Prediction and control remain legitimate goals for psychology, however, even if not exclusive ones.

APPLICATIONS

Principles. Applied behavior analysis has more complications than does experimental behavior analysis. Behavior analysts can choose a response that is convenient to record and analyze, such as disk pecking or bar pressing, but the conditions governing applied behavior are often social and difficult to control, and the responses are difficult to measure (Krapfl, 1977).

Despite these and other complications, applied behavior analysis has been the most effective means of behavior control to come out of psychology; and it provides solid data about its effectiveness, a claim other approaches have seldom been able to make. As an aid to measuring effectiveness, one must measure base rate responding prior to implementing operant procedures, so that it can be compared with reinforcement responding. The application methods of behavior analysis are also the research methods, and the research methods (contingency or reinforcement management) are also the application methods (Willems, 1977). "The close coordination of the treatment model to the research process surrounds applied behavior analysis with an enviable degree of explicitness, rigor, and precision" (Willems, p. 9).

What is fundamental in operant learning is that it breaks the activity into such small units that one can observe, record, and control. If one wants to assist a severely behaviorally retarded individual to learn to feed him/herself, a discriminative stimulus, a series of selected responses, and the reinforcements can be identified and put into action. Thus, with a series of successive approximations (shaping), the feeding activity begins to resemble normal self-feeding behavior. Applied behavior analysis succeeds in places where all else has failed. The actual implementation requires a trained observer for recording relevant responses and a skillful manager for providing the reinforcement contingencies.

Pigeon-Guided Missiles. One of the most dramatic instances of operant conditioning clearly illustrates Willem's description. This was a military project in which pigeons were trained to peck at a screen showing an image of a target as the missile the pigeon was riding in approached that target (Skinner, 1960). A metal stylus was attached to the bird's beak so that each peck made electrical contact and guided the missile to its target. The pigeons had to peck consistently and rather rapidly in order to keep the missile on course and had to discriminate target from non-target images. They learned to do this with a high degree of reliability. But the pigeons were never actually used in a missile; electronic guidance systems were developed, leaving the pigeons technologically unemployed. It was just as well for them, for the ride would have been one-way.

Psychoanalysis. Many people in various professional services who would never accept that behavior analysis comprises the whole of psychology have nevertheless made good use of its technology. As one example, this writer attended a meeting at which a panel—mostly of philosophers—was giving a very negative appraisal of behaviorism. A member of the audience who identified himself as a psychoanalyst came to the defense of behavior analysis. At first glance, psychoanalysis would seem a very unlikely ally of behaviorism; but, in actuality, it has made increasing use of behavior modification techniques in conjunction with its own therapeutic procedures. The man stated that in his practice there were certain behaviors he could not control or change with traditional psychoanalytic techniques. He found it expedient to employ operant conditioning techniques as a supplement to psychoanalysis in order to achieve a more effective therapy for his patients.

Teaching Machines. This innovation is another important example of the application of behavior analysis to real world problems. In the 1920s, Sidney Pressey developed the first true teaching machine, but it did not present new information.

Instead, the pupil had to study the material prior to using the machine (Ludy, 1988). It was more a *testing* than a *teaching* machine. Skinner incorporated new information in the form of a sentence that requires completion. The information is given in such small steps that the response to it is almost always correct, and the pupil is reinforced by getting it right. The reinforcement comes immediately. Skinner preferred this system to Pressey's multiple choices, which presented a confusing array of wrong answers as well as the single correct one. Skinner called his system "programmed learning." Pupils work at their own pace and learn without the risk of failure or embarrassment. The educator gets regular feedback and can make modifications. This has worked best with simple learning tasks. Other researchers have developed programs involving *branching,* in which pupils explore in whatever directions they choose. The reinforcements are somewhat different in this case.

Programmed learning met great resistance, mostly from charges that were incorrect or from unsupported claims about its negative characteristics. Its use declined after 1962 (Ludy, 1988). Ray (1995) has developed a computerized instructional program teaching operant conditioning that adapts to the rate and level of skill development of the student. It overcomes some or most of the criticisms of previous programs.

Community Conditioning. One of Skinner's most celebrated writings is his novel *Walden Two* (Skinner, 1948), named after Thoreau's *Walden* and its experiment in living. In it Skinner depicts a utopian society based on positive reinforcement, in which punishment is avoided entirely; and everyone lives in pleasurable conditions. Several efforts have been made to develop communities based on the precepts of *Walden Two,* but the closest to Skinner's principles is one founded at Los Horcones in northern Mexico. The participants attempt to live in a community based on cooperation, equality, and sharing and have developed a form of government based on decision by consensus in which nearly all adults participate (Los Horcones, 1989). They consider themselves behavioral scientists in that they regularly collect and publish data on their behaviors and review behavioral principles. According to a newspaper report (Rohter, 1989), Skinner was quite favorably impressed with the results, especially the cooperative and loving nature of the children and the scientific character of the enterprise.

Neighborhood Children. On an informal level, untrained individuals who understand the concept of being positive rather than negative have successfully used the technique. In Watts, a suburb of Los Angeles where many families are on welfare, Stan Myles started a Neighborhood Good Guys Club in 1965. Instead of reprimanding children who were breaking bottles behind his auto repair shop, he gave them soft drinks and told them that they could each earn a dime by cleaning up the broken bottles. He began giving out dimes and other gifts to children for a neat appearance, good grades, obeying their mothers, avoiding fights, and other socially desirable behaviors. In addition to the improved behaviors he engineered, his own shop suffered no vandalism and few items were shoplifted from his premises.

Television Watching and Weight Control. Rachlin (1980) gives a step by step account of helping one individual reduce both the frequency of his television watching and his weight. Both involved the following eleven steps:

(1) establishing baseline and feedback
(2) breaking the chain (changing a series of acts that, in these cases, involved reinforcement for undesired responses— watching television or eating)
(3) stimulus control
(4) increasing alternate rewards
(5) setting goals
(6) selecting signals (establishing a marker for a reinforcement that is otherwise vague: for example, recording calorie reduction even when weight loss does not occur immediately
(7) reducing feedback (beginning to rely on new habits rather than on an artificial situation)
(8) relapsing (preparing for the almost inevitable setback)

(9) resuming feedback (helping to recover from the relapse)
(10) final scheduling
(11) making a commitment—often implicit.

This procedure produced an acceptable rate of television watching and good progress in weight control.

Literacy and Arithmetic. In Seattle, Washington a behavior analysis program at Morningside Academy teaches literacy and arithmetic skills to children and adults. Children advance at the rate of more than two grade levels per year and adults two per month. One auxiliary form of reinforcement allows participants to plot their own response rates and see their progress graphically. From the program, methods are evolving for teaching such important skills as creativity, problem solving, and analytic thinking (Johnson & Layng, 1992).

Behavioral Contracting. Behavior analysts enable clients to select their own means of altering their environments and controlling their lives free of aversive control through "behavioral contracting" (Homme & Csany, 1967; Kirschenbaum & Flanery, 1983). Rather than the practitioner imposing the contingencies of reinforcement on the client, often without informing the client, the client and practitioner discuss and agree on what behaviors will lead to what consequences. For example, a parent and a child can come to an agreement (a contract) that the child's making the bed and picking up his or her clothes every day will result in the granting of a special privilege. Because the contract is a verbal agreement involving rules about what leads to what, it is "rule-governing." This explicit and negotiated approach to the contingencies is more ethical than changing them secretly; it may set a trend toward more rule-governed and less contingency-shaped behavior in therapy (Blackman, 1985).

Performance Appraisal. In business, the application of behavior analysis to performance appraisal has changed this activity from a dreaded event to a productive and pleasant one (Leduc, 1981). By training supervisors to be specific to employees about behaviors that are expected from them (avoiding such vagaries as "good attitudes" and "having spirit") and offering appraisals on a continuing basis (rather than at monthly or quarterly intervals) with plentiful encouragement for properly performed behaviors, the workers and supervisors come to mutually support one another and to meet and exceed goals they have jointly set. A correspondence course for correctional supervisors also uses these principles (Leduc, 1991).

Animal Training. Improved animal training techniques have emerged from behavior analysis. By a technique called "shaping" or "successive approximation," an animal can be quickly taught to perform complex acts. Shaping consists of giving a reinforcement when an animal's response is somewhat in the direction or in the nature of the ultimately desired (target) response. The next reinforcement will require a closer approximation, and so on. For example, if one wants a pigeon to turn in circles, a reinforcement is given when it makes a slight turn. The next reinforcement requires a bit more movement, and the next a bit more. A skillful trainer can get the pigeon to make complete circles after just a few reinforcements. One of Skinner's most famous accomplishments was teaching pigeons to play ping-pong on a specially devised table. Operant animal training has been used for circus acts, in advertising, with monkeys who serve paraplegics, with pigeons which guide missiles to targets (see p. 191), with dogs that detect explosives, and with marine animals that assist in rescuing drowning swimmers and perform spectacular acts for audiences.

This animal work has also revealed that reinforced responses sometimes interfere with operant learning when they are not natural to the way a particular species gets food. For example, when the training of pigs to do complex tasks is pushed too far, they revert to rooting behavior; and under such conditions raccoons will rub or "wash" tokens rather than putting them into a container, though that would result in receipt of food (Breland & Breland, 1961).

More. A list of other areas of application would include psychotherapy (see below), training techniques for retarded individuals, an army training program in which positive reinforcement replaced the conventional brutal treatment at boot camps, creating programs for troubled teenagers, using classroom behavior management or workplace behavior management, studying behavioral effects of drugs (psychopharmacology), curing stuttering and tics, improving attention in classrooms, employing self-help skills with schizophrenics, creating token economies (tokens or points that can be used for privileges awarded when prescribed behaviors occur) in prisons and in boys' detention homes, teaching the management of alcohol and other addictive drugs, and innumerable others. The *Journal of Behavior Analysis* published applied techniques until 1968 when the *Journal of Applied Behavior Analysis* was begun for that specific purpose. Other more specialized applied journals have appeared since that time (such as the *Journal of Organizational Behavior Management,* which deals with applications in business, industry, and other organizations). The thirtieth in a series of volumes entitled *Progress in Behavior Modification* (Hersen, Eisler, & Miller, 1996) appeared in 1996.

BEHAVIOR THERAPY

"Spare the rod, use behavior mod" appeared in *Psychology Today* as a headline slogan. This slogan accurately reflects the avoidance of punishment and its replacement with positive reinforcement that the term "behavior modification" originally advocated. Unfortunately, others used the term to refer to electric shock, psychosurgery, solitary confinement, drugs for aversive conditioning, and other coercive and punitive controls to which Skinner took strong exception (Skinner, 1974b). Nevertheless, Skinner preferred to retain the term while using it in his own way, but other behavior analysts abandoned it. It should be noted that Skinner has not denounced aversive stimulation completely. He concedes that it may be necessary, for example, in the form of drugs or restraint for autistic children who would otherwise hurt themselves and in medicine and dentistry where painful treatment can lead to an improved medical condition (Griffin et al./Skinner, 1988).

Just as many applied behavior analysts reject the term "behavior modification," close followers of Skinner usually also reject "psychotherapy" and "behavior therapy." "Psychotherapy," to them, implies therapy of a *psyche,* and that makes it unacceptable. "Behavior therapy" was first used by those who drew their behavioristic concepts from methodological behaviorism with its theoretical deduction of intervening ("cognitive") variables that account for behaviors (see p. 189); worse, these behavior therapists brought a heavy load of intervening variables into their concepts. As a consequence, many applied behavior analysts reject that term also, even though Skinner has used it. There seems to be no generally accepted term for the type of therapy that applied behavior analysts conduct. Because "behavior therapy" is widely used and seems descriptive of their procedures, it is the term used here.

In the early days of behavior therapy, critics, especially psychoanalysts, charged that using reinforcement to modify behavior was merely attacking the symptom and not the underlying causes. They charged further that the symptoms would reappear in a different form. Both of these charges proved to have little merit; and today reinforcement procedures are often used directly to extinguish symptoms, sometimes in conjunction with other procedures and sometimes as the sole procedure. "The great contribution of behavior therapy has been from the beginning, not only the substantive improvement in clinical practice . . . but even more the insistence on theoretical rigor, experimental proof and clinical check" (Eysenck, 1970, p. 14). In some cases "the treatments developed have been so rigorously specified and standardized, and have so involved readily available personal and environmental variables, that the lay person can easily perform them without the need for professional assistance" (Azrin, 1979, p. 7). That statement requires a caveat, however. The untrained user of these techniques could cause damage. For example, in withdrawing reinforcement in order to bring extinction to self-injury, an "extinction burst" can occur. The uninformed

worker would see the sudden increase in rate of self-injury, sometimes in an altered form, and discontinue the extinction, thereby reinforcing an even more severe pattern of self-injury.

In the *International Handbook of Behavior Modification and Therapy* (Bellack, Hersen, & Kazdin, 1992) are chapters on the treatment of anxiety and fear; depression; schizophrenia; adult medical disorders; alcohol and drug problems; obesity; smoking; crime and delinquency; sexual dysfunctions; sexual deviations; interpersonal dysfunction; obsessive-compulsive disorders; marital distress; habit disorders; retardation; autism; child behavior problems in the home; behavior analysis in classroom teaching; and treatment of childhood medical disorders of asthma, convulsive disorder, and obesity. In other books and in the specialized journals one can find procedures for almost any kind of problem behavior. Most of these require careful adaptation to particular individuals and situations and rigorous monitoring. Among the many behavior problems for which behavior therapy has objective data to demonstrate success rates are depression (McLean & Hakstian, 1979), obsessions, and compulsions (Rachman & Hodgson, 1980).

Applied behavior technology involves such varied procedures as flooding, counter-conditioning, shaping, systematic desensitization, modeling, and others. (Not all behavior analysts would use all of these or even agree that all are consistent with behavior analysis.) The *flooding* procedure floods the client with his or her anxieties until, over a series of sessions, they extinguish. *Counter-conditioning* employs reinforcement of behavior that is inconsistent with the troublesome behavior. *Desensitization* is often coupled with deep relaxation. In the case of a phobia, the client and therapist construct a hierarchy ranging from the most feared thing to one that is minimally feared. During relaxation the client imagines the minimally feared thing and, after suffering any anxiety, relaxes again. By gradually moving up the hierarchy of imagining while using a relaxing procedure, the client eventually imagines without fear the formerly most feared thing. This new response generalizes well to the actual feared object or situation, and the procedure is also used in situ rather than with imagining. *Modeling* is often used with children. The therapist acts as a role model, a discriminative stimulus. The therapist's actions or speech indicate to the child that he or she will receive specific consequences by behaving in the same manner as the therapist and will receive different consequences by behaving in another manner. When the child adopts the therapist's behavior, he or she receives the reinforcement and advances toward the goal of the therapy.

Despite opposition to the negative uses of the term "behavior modification," a number of aversion methods have been developed (not all behavior therapists find these acceptable) and have had significant success, sometimes in combination with other procedures. The conditions to which they have been applied include self-induced vomiting, seizures, enuresis, excessive sneezing, functional or "hysterical" paralysis, writer's cramp, stuttering, and self-injurious behavior such as head-banging and self-biting (Sandler & Steele, 1991). Electric shock is the most common aversive stimulus; others include lemon juice, ammonia, cold water, and, in the case of enuresis, Pavlovian conditioning with a bell.

Operant procedures are now being extended from single individuals to communities and to situations involving the natural environment. The interest in behavior therapy and applied behavior analysis is world-wide. International conferences in a variety of countries discuss techniques for various problem behaviors and the challenges encountered in implementing and evaluating them. Although psychoanalysis had been the most prolific of psychotherapies in publishing its works, applied behavior analysis in a few short years has caught up with or surpassed psychoanalysis in its volume of printed material. All the psychotherapies except behavior therapy show about the same rate of success. It stands above the others in success rate and offers clearer and more objective measures of its success.

RELATION TO SOME OTHER APPROACHES

Cognitive Psychology

Skinner (1990) reserved his most biting criticism for this approach. In his final address a few days before his death, he likened cognitivism to creation science (the religious belief and pressure group movement that seeks to replace the teaching of evolution with a biblical version of divine creation). His comparison was that the cognitivists seek a Self to explain behavior just as the creationists seek God to explain living things. In an earlier work he averred that "no matter how defective a behavioral account may be, we must remember that mentalistic explanations explain nothing" (1974a, p. 224).

The cognitivists hold that the behavior analysts are too mechanistic in confining their search to environmental controls, but the behavior analysts retort that it is not they but the cognitivists who are mechanistic; the behavior analysts deal with mutual actions whereas the cognitivists turn the organism into a hypothetical computing machine. Morris (1992, 1993) presents arguments for a refutation of behavior analysis as mechanistic, but Delprato (1993) claims that the mechanism remains, and Marr (1993) thinks it is mechanistic and should remain so.

Behavior analysis attempts to identify environmental conditions, such as reinforcers, that control such behaviors as thinking, imagining, believing, and other "private" behaviors. Cognitivism assumes that "mental processes" are not behaviors but that they often control behaviors; cognitivists seek these "mental processes" indirectly by experimentation and logically by analogies to computers, holograms, and other technological devices. Behavior analysis assumes that "private" behaviors get reinforced just like all others. Although thinking, as one such behavior, may influence other behaviors and can be a part of causal sequences, it does not initiate behavior (Zettle, 1990). If it initiated behavior it would have to initiate its own actions and omit environmental factors, the behavior analyst argues; a legitimate analysis looks for the controlling stimulus to which the thought occurs which then influences other behaviors. Cognitivism, in contrast, explains thought by attributing power to hypothetical structures, either biological or nonphysical mental ones.

Cognitivism assumes that the environment consists of information that the organism transforms, interprets, refines, filters, expands, contracts, stores, retrieves, and processes. These hypothetical events are not behaviors but are presumed to exist at some other level and to explain overt behaviors. Cognitivists invoke the nervous system but do not derive their constructs from it or from the work of neurophysiology. The constructs are formulated not by physiologists, but by psychologists; and they come not from physiology but from behavior (Marr, 1984a). In other words, to the behavior analyst, the cognitivists have invented fictitious constructs from the events of behavior and assumed that they have some sort of reality which explains the behavior from which they were derived. The behavior analyst, like the cognitivist, accepts the occurrence of thinking, feeling, and imagining, but regards such events as behaviors and holds that these behaviors occur in conjunction with the environment. No hypothetical computer nervous system is needed.

Cognitivism uses a methodology taken over from methodological behaviorism: (a) between-group experimental design involving control groups, and (b) statistical control for variability of large numbers of subjects. Behavior analysis, in contrast, uses single organisms and no control groups. Its controls are entirely by means of the experimental method. Originally, its only statistics were simple counts of response rates to compare with a base rate, but quantification has now become more complex. Its treatment of the organism or subject leaves it free to respond at any time, whereas subjects in cognitive studies are constrained to respond at designated times or under specified conditions. Cognitivism derives from methodological behaviorism with its mediator (brain, instinct, computer, interpreter, mind) be-

tween S and R. Behavior analysis rejects both methodological behaviorism and cognitivism.

Some areas that the reinforcement principle has neglected, cognitive psychology has tried to address. Behavior analysts are well aware of this and are attempting to bridge these gaps. Some psychologists have attempted to combine behavior analysis or its applications with cognitivism. Cognitive-behavior therapy is one example of this hybrid offspring. Most behavior analysts, however, find the mentalistic concepts of cognitivism unscientific (for example, Morris, Higgins, & Bickel, 1982), while others find that some cognitive work can be reconceptualized as behavior and utilized. Still other psychologists attempt to make a hybrid (for example, Bandura, 1989). Those who attempt to combine cognitivism—an organocentric system—with behavior analysis—an envirocentric system—would do well to recognize the fundamental differences in causal assumptions and examine the postulates of each to reveal what will need to change.

Eco-behavioral Psychology

The prospect of bringing eco-behavioral psychology (or ecological psychology) into behavior analysis, especially applied behavior analysis, has received considerable attention (Rogers-Warren & Warren, 1977; Schroeder, 1990), and has been named "ecobehavior analysis." Three major problems have prompted this interest. One of these is that behavior modification often produces unexpected side-effects, sometimes for better and sometimes for worse.

A few examples (Balsam & Bondy, 1983): Behavior modification may result in *responses incompatible with the target behavior.* The child who is offered a reward for taking a nap may become too excited about the reward to sleep. Reinforcement may influence the recipient to cling to, hug, or hold (literally or figuratively) a therapist, teacher, or parent who is providing the reinforcement and interfere with the acquisition of the target behavior. The reinforcing character of therapy may be so strong that the client becomes dependent on it, while the lack of such reinforcement in other situations may produce withdrawal. When a person in rehabilitation leaves that setting, the reinforcements in the way of special recreational equipment or verbal encouragement may no longer be available, and relapse becomes likely. Those in a token economy, similarly, often return to former behaviors upon leaving the program. Perhaps one of the least expected collateral effects is that a child conditioned to attend more to appropriate things and less to inappropriate things then begins to show aggressive and self-injurious behaviors (Herbert et al., 1973).

A second problem is that ignoring *unexplained collateral effects* invites mentalistic explanations for them. By turning to a form of behavior analysis that deals with setting events and does so scientifically, behavior analysis would be in a better position to account for these collateral effects and thereby avoid having mentalists fill the void (Morris and Midgley, 1990).

A third is *generalization*. The gains achieved by reinforcements in the training situation often do not continue in a normal situation or last over time (although some techniques for promoting generalization have been identified [Stokes & Baer, 1977]). Eco-behavioral psychology, which addresses the way in which environment and behavior settings influence behavior, offers some possible help. One example of a way to address the environmental variables come from the Living Environments Group, a team of researchers at the University of Kansas (Risley, 1977) who run an infant daycare project and a toddler daycare project and are also examining the environment of living arrangements for retarded children and for nursing home residents.

Each involves environmental design, the selection of equipment and materials, job specification, training and supervision of paraprofessional staff, general measures of resident participation and staff performance, experimental demonstrations, and program packaging and dissemination. We have found that technical developments in one setting are usu-

ally immediately transferable to the others. (Risley, 1977, p. 151)

In Kansas City, Kansas, the Juniper Gardens Children's Project has been working for nearly thirty years with children living in poverty (Greenwood et al., 1992). In its early strategies, efforts were directed toward language, social, and academic skills. For example, in a second grade class, the children earned points for certain behaviors and traded them for candy and trinkets. This "resulted in dramatic reductions in disruptive classroom behavior compared with the teacher's conventional approach to classroom discipline" (p. 1466). Other activities involved attention and praise as reinforcers and consequences for both individual and group achievements. Measurements of attention to task, assignment completions, conduct, reading, mathematics, and language usage all showed improvements over baselines while disruptive behavior, aggressive behavior, talking-out, and getting out of one's seat all declined. Parents were brought into the program and taught to use rewards for desired behaviors instead of punishment for undesired ones. This increased homework completion and accuracy, and compliance with medical regimens, while reducing rates of complaining, whining, crying, and dawdling. Eventually the program broadened to address a wider range of environmental conditions, and it was found that an improved environment brought improved behaviors beyond the immediate situation. The early work addressed changes in the environment that would bring changes within a year or less. The later work examined the cumulative effect over a period of years and the influences on later life. The project has shown the importance of early intervention, the need for systematically improved conditions over long durations, and other factors.

The work now spanning the themes of consequences, antecedents, functional situation factors, and behavioral development illustrates the trend in behavior analysis toward greater sophistication both in the use of more complex methods for studying interactive and developmental systems and in addressing issues of general concern in psychology . . . . (Greenwood et al., 1992, p. 1472)

Among numerous other applications of ecobehavior analysis are language training for prelanguage children, examination of the settings of residential facilities for the retarded, day treatment programs for developmental disabilities, classroom instruction, and improvement of social and communicative relationships between adults and children (Schroeder, 1990).

Much progress has been made in ecobehavior analysis since 1974 when an ecobehavioral psychologist insisted on the necessity for behavior analysis to include the ecology in its work (Willems, 1974). Behavior analysis responded by giving it serious attention. The fact that the two systems are both envirocentric facilitates their joint efforts.

Interbehavioral Psychology

The two systems hold a great deal of philosophy of science in common. Most fundamentally, they both reject mind-body dualism in all of its many forms and insist on a psychology that focuses on concrete events rather than on hypothetical causative powers. Skinner (1987) has stated that if mind refers to anything it is to "what the *person* does" (p. 784). Kantor (1984), the founder of interbehavioral psychology, states that "scientific psychology embraces all activities and qualities conventionally miscalled mentalistic" (p. 168), but which are actually concrete events. Partly as a consequence of the rejection of dualism, they also reject intervening variables between stimulus and response; physiological reductionism, including brain explanations of behavior (though Skinner seems not entirely consistent on this); and any departure from concrete events. Behavior analysts would probably object to few of interbehavioral formal postulates (chapter 10) but would want to add their own, whereas the interbehaviorists would find a number of the implicit postulates of behavior analysis too restrictive, and numbers 1 and 6 meaningless or misleading.

Interbehaviorism gives a more thoroughgoing emphasis to environment-organism interaction or to the multiplex field character of psychological events, whereas behavior analysis retains an emphasis on the environment as a cause. Earlier it gave almost no attention to setting factors, a part of the interbehavioral field, but it is increasingly doing so, calling them "setting events." Behavior analysis is rooted in its methodology and empirical studies whereas interbehaviorism has only recently begun to develop methodologies and expand its empirical research. From its beginnings in the 1920s, it has given extensive attention to logical and conceptual issues which provide a basis for joining efforts with behavior analysis.

Morris (1982) has attempted to show more specifically how the two might fit together, but no general agreement about such a union exists. As long as one remains envirocentric and the other noncentric, any full rapprochement is unlikely. Skinner and Kantor were colleagues at Indiana University, and many students who studied under both men have utilized the concepts of both (see Fuller, 1973; Lichtenstein, 1973; Morris, 1982). Some interbehaviorists have affiliated with organizations of behavior analysts; and some behavior analysts have been interested in the general philosophy of science that interbehaviorism furnishes, one that might provide behavior analysis with a broader framework. Some researchers have also combined the concept of setting events and the methodology of behavior analysis (see chapter 10).

Along with this goes some friction. Because Skinner (1988a) felt that the interbehaviorists were too critical, he objected to interbehaviorists among behavior analysts. Delprato (1990) countered that the interbehaviorists' criticisms have moved behavior analysis even further toward naturalism, whereas the criticisms of most other parties have been "based on assumptions such as dualism that are tied to the transcendental cultural tradition" (p. 13). For example, the Skinnerian notion of privacy is not fully naturalistic, the interbehaviorists hold, and could become more naturalistic by adopting the position of making no distinction between public and private events: all are human activities, with no meaningful dividing line. Similarly, it could recognize, as interbehaviorism does, the role of biology in psychological events as a necessary, but not sufficient, condition and avoid the inconsistency of advocating both reductionism and nonreductionism. Morris (1993–94) responded to Skinner's objections by noting that both groups "promote a natural science of behavior" and that interbehaviorists' participation in the behavior analyst's organization should be seen as "a compliment, not a complaint" (p. 5).

Phenomenological Psychology

At first glance, phenomenology and its emphasis on meanings or life-as-it-is-lived ("being in the world") might seem the most distant of all orientations from behavior analysis and its response rate measures. To support such differences Giorgi (1975) points out that behavior analysis has a physicalistic orientation: it borrows from the physical sciences to remove all context and all meaning from behavior and to treat it as impersonal, quantitative grist. Further, "So far as I can gather, for radical behaviorism behavior is any measurable movement of a body. For phenomenologists, however, because of intentionality [person-object relationship], behavior simply cannot be adequately described without reference to the situation from the viewpoint of the behaver" (p. 209). Kvale and Grenness (1967) point out that Skinner's physicalism is not totally consistent: he refers to different possible perceptions of the same object but then insists that we function in a world of physics; similarly, he describes meaningful behavior but then reverts to meaninglessness when he separates the subject from the object by asserting that seeing is just a behavior of seeing, for "seeing does not require the presence of things seen" (Skinner, 1963, p. 954). Phenomenology holds, in contrast, that seeing is seeing something, thinking is thinking about something, and so on.

In addition to this major difference Giorgi also finds a number of important similarities: both op-

pose (a) dualism, (b) the hypothetico-deductive method, (c) reductionism of psychology to biology, and (d) introspection of a mind. Both agree on the legitimacy of single subjects for research, use of descriptions for behaviors, and minimization of theory. Kvale and Grenness note that both reject the notion that we live in a double world, one physical and outer and the other a nonphysical inner representation of the outer physical world. (Skinner called this the "copy theory.") They both agree that knowledge or understanding is action. Knowledge comes from acting on the world, behaving toward it: "Man creates and is created—in Skinner's terminology: controls and is controlled. The world is neither given nor created, it is a relation" (p. 140). Kvale and Grenness hold that Skinner has a great deal in common with phenomenology but argue that he needs its concept of intentionality (person-object interdependence) to avoid a number of inconsistencies and logical impasses.

CRITIQUE

Behavior analysis has been a lightning rod attracting vigorous attacks from many sources, but it has also garnered approval for its accomplishments even from some of its staunchest opponents. A few of the criticisms and plaudits follow in no particular order.

Applications

In the applied area, critics have observed that behavior analysis has been quite successful at teaching tricks to animals or eliminating phobias and compulsive-obsessive habits in humans, but they charge that it has been unsuccessful in modifying schizophrenia or manic-depressive psychosis—whereas antipsychotic drugs have been very helpful. Similarly, they charge that programmed learning has been successful only with simple tasks. Behavior analysts reply that their technology is continuing to improve as research proceeds and that their efforts have been more successful than those of most other psychologies.

Kantor's Invited Address

In an invited address to the behavior analysts Kantor (1974) commended them for recognizing that psychological events are solely behavioral concepts: no mentalistic postulates mar the behavioral operations as they do with many others. However, he felt that the preoccupation with animal learning led to simplification of all behavior and a tendency to become so specialized with reinforcement arrangements that all other forms of behavior were neglected. Behavior analysts have responded to this by pointing out that this criticism had some validity in 1974, the date of Kantor's address, but since then humans have often become the subjects of study, and that behavior analysis can now be extended to such behaviors as perception, thinking, and remembering. But Marr (1984b) found merit in the criticism, in that behavior analysis has not adequately adapted its methodology to deal with complex behaviors but should do so rather than leave them to the cognitivists. However, he found little merit in Kantor's criticism of behavior analysis's use of a mechanistic cause and effect; for such mechanism, he maintained, is a necessary part of the important and growing quantitative model of initial conditions and contingencies. Marr agreed with Kantor that behavior analysis has neglected setting factors or context which "in the analysis of verbal behavior and remembering is clearly fundamental" (p. 194) and, similarly, that it has unfortunately ignored the functional meaning of the stimulus as opposed to the stimulus as an object (see chapter 10).

Collected Critical Papers

Skinner's book *Beyond Freedom and Dignity* occasioned a great outpouring of criticisms including a book devoted to the criticisms (Wheeler, 1973). It included eighteen papers and Skinner's replies to them. In 1988 the newly established *Counselling Psychology Quarterly* in Britain published a special issue with articles responding to a paper that the journal had invited from Skinner (1988b). Richelle (1988) argued that Skinner's

and the behavior analysts' position would be much stronger if they would not isolate themselves and ignore or be indifferent to other trends in psychology, some of which might be compatible with their own position. As an example, he noted that ethology has been around for a long time but only recently have behavior analysts discovered and used it. They continue to ignore other developmental studies despite their importance. Foss (1988) listed what he believes to be several shortcomings. One is that complex skills are often organized in a hierarchical arrangement that does not seem analyzable into reinforced responses. This includes social and emotional habits as well as motor skills. Eysenck (1988) believed one shortcoming was in giving no real place to personality, genetics, and individual differences—despite assurances from behavior analysts that these are important—and in denying the relevance of biology. In contrast, Kunkel (1996) argued that behavior analysis has had a great impact on areas of psychology in which it has not received credit. Operant principles, he finds, are used extensively in social psychology, although conventional terminology masks them.

Place (1988b) noted that Skinner maintains that the only way to modify moral behavior is by reinforcement and that this has been offensive to many people because of the deep-seated belief by the culture that we should advance morality by rational argument. And his insistence that we abandon all mentalistic references that are an intrinsic part of ordinary discourse makes it difficult for therapists to communicate with clients; it erects a barrier. Place contended that had Skinner "been a little less dismissive of, and a little more sensitive to, the reasons for resisting his conceptual proposals, behavior analysis might have retained the prestige and influence which it had before the cognitive revolution" (p. 309). He held that agreement with other systems would be especially prominent in Skinner's concept of *rule-governed behavior,* for they would agree that "a substantial part of human behaviour is controlled by what the agent believes about the situation confronting him or her" (p. 309), and belief involves rules. The major disagreement arises in another form of behavior, that of *contingency-* or *reinforcement-shaped behavior:* While the behavior of nonhuman animals and of pre-speech children may be controlled by reinforcement, there is resistance to accepting the principle that the motor and verbal skills of children and adults are so controlled. Yet supporters have pointed out that only behavior analysis can account for most of these latter behaviors.

Hayes and Hayes (1988) contended that the major shortcoming of behavior analysis has been its treatment of verbal behavior, despite its efforts and contributions in this subject. As one example, it has ignored adult pathologies involving high levels of verbalization. As another, in psychotherapy it has conducted most of its work with children and adults in institutions where verbal behavior could be minimized. Though cognitive psychology has been no more theoretically adequate in these situations, cognitivism has transformed verbal behavior into mental processes and gained support for such constructs, apparently because its terminology was consonant with ordinary language usage (Place, 1988b). Hayes and Hayes also pointed out a number of characteristics of language, some of them discovered by behavior analysts themselves, that Skinner's account of language does not address.

Most of the critics in the *Counselling Psychology Quarterly* noted important advantages to Skinner's system. Miles (1988) for example, while partly critical, listed ten positive characteristics and concluded, "All of these are philosophically defensible, and in conjunction they amount to a formidable challenging 'world view'" (p. 303). Cullen (1988) gave unqualified support in his listing of seven principles that apply to counseling. For example, rather than looking for some underlying cause, counselors should be looking at what people *do,* the relation of that doing to the environment, and how that *doing* as a relationship might be beneficially altered. As another of his examples, it is important to seek methods by which clients have the means to alter their environment so as to feel in control of their lives and be free from aversive control. A distinct exception to the other critics was Power (1988) who was totally critical. He argued that behavior analysis has committed "seven sins" and that salvation is through cognitivism. The behavior analyst's reply might be that salvation in the form of self-control and freedom from aversive control is through behavioral contracting, not through cognitivism.

The Effects of Reinforcement

Some of the most important areas of concern lie with the complicated effects of reinforcement itself. Whereas reinforcement must occur within seconds of a rat or pigeon's response in order to control the behavior, in the case of humans the reinforcer can be delayed for hours or even years. This can be an advantage, but conditions are different and the distinction must be recognized. Fagan (1993) reviewed studies that show that the reinforcement principle is a powerful factor in some infant behavior but cannot account for *all* behaviors or for the initial acquisition of some behaviors. He argued for expectancy as a major condition. The behavior analyst might say that if expectancy is a condition, one must, in turn, account for the expectancy.

In McKeachie's (1976) review of the laws of learning as they apply to children in a classroom, he notes the many complexities in the reinforcement principle and that it does not always automatically work. Arousal, intrinsic versus extrinsic reward, feedback (knowledge of results), and motivation are all relevant to effectiveness of reinforcement, and each of these has its own complexities. For example, high achievement children are reinforced by their intellectual achievement itself but low achievement children are reinforced more by praise. Even the *meaning* of reinforcement is important. If a reward is interpreted as the result of continuing a boring task, it will not be as effective as if it is interpreted as the result of making good progress. McKeachie suggests that behavior analysis is "particularly useful in situations that have obvious outcomes with few alternative means to goals" (p. 830). Pfaus et al. (1988) argue that behavior analysts have confined their work to those behaviors that are operant—manipulation of the environment—but have ignored those behaviors that do not fit the definition. Because of what they have ignored, they have never been able to develop comprehensive laws of behavior, only "laws of work." Guttman (1977) makes a related point: "Skinner's analysis of behavior is a special analysis, not a general one; it focuses on certain kinds of relations between action and environment that had not been adequately attended to in previous investigation" (p. 328).

Misconceptions

Numerous authors have pointed out the many misconceptions about Skinner's position. Todd and Morris (1983) have enumerated these in a legion of psychology textbooks. These erroneous conceptions are then passed on to students, some of whom may eventually pass them on on to *their* students. Todd and Morris point out the social and political liabilities these errors bring.

Criticisms of Mainstream Psychology by Behavior Analysts

Behavior analysts offer many criticisms. Among these are psychology's (a) amassing of large amounts of data with little coherence, (b) generating of theories that have scant application, (c) misguided copying of physics, (d) reducing psychology to brain biology, (e) misusing analogies (such as computers), (f) dualizing subject matter into mind (cognition, self, consciousness, etc.) and body. Some behavior analysts consider their discipline a separate science of behaviorology rather than part of psychology.

CONCLUSIONS

Catania (1984) observed that

> Of all contemporary psychologists, B. F. Skinner is perhaps the most honored and the most maligned, the most widely recognized and the most misunderstood. Some still say that he is a

stimulus-response psychologist (he is not); some still say that stimulus-response chains play a central role in his treatment of verbal behavior (they do not); some still say he disavows evolutionary determinants of behavior (he does not). (p. 473)

Skinner's system has shown a strength over a period of sixty years that perhaps no others can match. The very fact that it has drawn so much attention and such extensive criticism is testimony to its power and importance. The system is a philosophy of science as well as a well-honed methodology. As a system of behavior control, it has no peers. The use of rule-governed behavior through language as opposed to contingency-shaped behavior provides additional flexibility and power that has yet to receive adequate attention. To Skinner, "the control exerted by directions, advice, rules, and laws is more conspicuous than that exerted by [environmental] contingencies" (1974a, p. 126). Rule-governed behavior and its role in behavioral contracts are especially important in applied behavior analysis.

Behavior analysis is not just technology. It is basic science, for it starts with basic research and derives its technology from that research. The results have found application in psychopharmacology, psychotherapy, behavior management, education, and other areas. Another point to note about its research is that, unlike most other systems of psychology, its principles are derived from—not imposed on—research; and this research is continuing to address new issues and topics. As it does so, the complexities of behavior become increasingly apparent, with the result that proponents are forced to examine their concepts and seek to modify or further develop them to meet new challenges—including those coming from opponents. An increase in complexity may better address the complexities of the world. The use of ethology, quantification, rule-governed behavior, and setting events are examples of new directions. In addition to these concepts Morris (1982) lists subjects that behavior analysis is now addressing—concept formation, self-control, emotion, social interactions, behavioral medicine, community psychology, social validation, and others. As behavior analysis expands into these areas and develops new concepts to do so, the system may come to resemble its original form less and less. That may be the necessary trade-off for the possibility of becoming broader and more effective.

REFERENCES

Andresen, Julie T. 1992. The behaviorist turn in recent theories of language. *Behavior and Philosophy* 20: 1–18.

Azrin, Nathan H. 1979. The present state and future trends of behavior therapy. In *Trends in Behavior Therapy*. Edited by Per-Olow Sjödén, Sandra Bates, & William S. Dockens. New York: Academic Press.

Balsam, Peter D., & Andrew S. Bondy. 1983. The negative side effects of reward. *Journal of Applied Behavior Analysis* 16: 283–96.

Bellack, Alan S.; Michel Herson; & Alan E. Kazdin, eds. 1992. *International Handbook of Behavior Modification and Therapy*, 2nd ed. New York: Plenum Press.

Blackman, D. E. 1985. Contemporary behaviourism: A brief overview. In *Behaviour Analysis and Contemporary Psychology*. Edited by C. F. Lowe, M. Richelle, D. E. Blackman, & C. M. Bradshaw. London: Erlbaum.

Breland, Keller, & Marian Breland. 1961. The misbehavior of organisms. *American Psychologist* 16, 681–84.

Catania, A. Charles. 1984. The operant behaviorism of B. F. Skinner. *Behavioral and Brain Sciences* 7: 473–75.

Cullen, Chris. 1988. Seven good reasons why counselling psychologists should listen to B. F. Skinner. *Counselling Psychology Quarterly* 1: 273–77.

Delprato, Dennis. 1990. The radical naturalism of interbehaviorism: Who needs it? *ABA Newsletter* 13 (1): 13–14.

———. 1993. Behavior analysis and S. C. Pepper's other mechanism. *Behavior Analyst* 16: 51–53.

Delprato, Dennis, & Brian Midgley. 1992. Some fundamentals of B. F. Skinner's behaviorism. *American Psychologist* 47: 1507–20.

Eysenck, Hans J. 1970. Behavior therapy and its critics. *Journal of Behavior Therapy and Experimental Psychiatry* 1: 5–15.

———. 1988. Skinner, Skinnerism, and the Skinnerian in psychology. *Counselling Psychology Quarterly* 1: 299–301.

Fagan, Jeffrey W. 1993. Reinforcement is not enough: Learned expectancies and infant behavior. *American Psychologist* 48: 1153–55.

Ferster, C. B., & B. F. Skinner. 1957. *Schedules of Reinforcement*. New York: Appleton-Century-Crofts.

Foss, Brian M. 1988. The experimental analysis of behavior and beyond. *Counselling Psychology Quarterly* 1: 311–12.

Fuller, Paul R. 1973. Professors Kantor and Skinner—The "Grand Alliance" of the 40's. *Psychological Record* 23: 318–24.

Giorgi, Amedeo. 1975. Convergence and divergences between phenomenological psychology and behaviorism. *Behaviorism* 3: 200–212.

Greenwood, C. R.; J. J. Carta; B. Hart; D. Kamps; B. Terry; C. Arreaga-Mayer; J. Atwater; D. Walker; T. Risley; & J. C. Delquadri. 1992. Out of the laboratory and into the community: 26 Years of applied behavior analysis at the Juniper Gardens Children's Project. *American Psychologist* 47: 1464–74.

Griffin, James C.; Timothy J. Paisey; Mary T. Stark; & Joseph H. Emerson/B. F. Skinner. 1988. B. F. Skinner's position on aversive treatment. *American Journal on Mental Retardation* 93: 104–105.

Guttman, Norman. 1977. On Skinner and Hull: A reminiscence and projection. *American Psychologist* 32: 321–28.

Hayes, Steven C., & Linda J. Hayes. 1988. Inadequacies not just obstacles. *Counselling Psychology Quarterly* 1: 291–94.

Herbert, E. W.; E. M. Pinkston; M. L. Hayden; T. E. Sajwaj; S. Pinkston; G. Cordua; & C. Jackson. 1973. Adverse effects of differential parental attention. *Journal of Applied Behavior Analysis* 6: 15–30.

Hersen, Michel; Richard M. Eisler; & Peter M. Miller, eds. 1996. *Progress in Behavior Modification*, vol. 30. Pacific Grove, CA: Brooks/Cole.

Homme, Lloyd E. 1965. Control of coverants, the operants of the mind. *Psychological Record* 15: 501–511.

Homme, Lloyd E., & Attila P. Csanyi. 1967. *Con.tingency Contracting: A System for Motivation Management in Education*. Albuquerque, NM: Southwestern Cooperative Educational Laboratory, Inc. (Behavior Systems Department, Westinghouse Learning Corporation).

Horcones, Los. 1989. Personalized government: A governmental system based on behavioral principles. *Behavior Analysis and Social Action* 7: 42–47.

Johnson, Kent R., & T. V. Joe Layng. 1992. Breaking the structuralist barrier: Literacy and numeracy with fluency. *American Psychologist* 47: 1475–90.

Kantor, J. R. 1974. An analysis of the experimental analysis of behavior (TEAB). *Journal of the Experimental Analysis of Behavior* 13: 101–108.

————. 1984. The relation of scientists to events in physics and psychology. *Psychological Record* 34: 165–73.

Kirschenbaum, D. S., & R. C. Flanery. 1983. Behavior contracting. In *Progress in Behavior Modification*, vol. 15. Edited by M. Hersen, R. M. Eisler, & P. M. Miller. New York: Academic Press.

Korn, James H.; Roger Davis; & Stephen F. Davis. 1991. Historians' and chairpersons' judgments of eminence among psychologists. *American Psychologist* 46: 789–92.

Krapfl, Jon E. 1977. Dialectics and operant conditioning. In *Life-Span Developmental Psychology: Dialectical Perspectives on Experimental Research*. Edited by Nancy Datan & Hayne W. Reese. New York: Academic Press.

Kunkel, John H. 1996. What have behaviorists accomplished—and what more can they do? *Psychological Record* 46: 21–37.

Kvale, Steiner. n. d. Some notes on radical behaviorism and dialectical materialism. Manuscript.

Kvale, Steiner, & Carl E. Grenness. 1967. Skinner and Sartre: Towards a radical phenomenology of behavior. *Review of Existential Psychology and Psychiatry* 7: 128–50.

Leduc, Lucien. 1981. *Performance Appraisal: A Practical Guidebook,* Saranac Lake, NY: Tandel Publishers.

————. 1991. *Motivaitng Correctional Staff,* 3 vols. Laurel, MD: American Correctional Association.

Lichtenstein, Parker E. 1973. Discussion: "Contextual Interactionists." *Psychological Record* 23: 325–33.

Lowe, C. F., & P. J. Horne. 1985. On the generality of behavioural principles: Human choice and the matching law. In *Behaviour Analysis and Contemporary Psychology*. Edited by C. F. Lowe, M. Richelle, D. E. Blackman, & C. M. Bradshaw. London: Erlbaum.

Ludy, Benjamin T. 1988. A history of teaching machines. *American Psychologist* 43: 703–712.

MacLean, Peter D., & A. Ralph Hakstian. 1979. Clinical depression: Comparative efficacy of outpatient treatments. *Journal of Consulting and Clinical Psychology* 47: 818–36.

Marr, M. Jackson. 1984a. Conceptual approaches and issues. *Journal of the Experimental Analysis of Behavior* 42: 353–62.

————. 1984b. Some reflections on Kantor's (1970) "An analysis of the experimental analysis of behavior (TEAB)." *Behavior Analyst* 7: 189–96.

————. 1993. Contextualistic mechanism or mechanistic contextualism?: The straw machine as tar baby. *Behavior Analyst* 16: 59–65.

McKeachie, Wilbert J. 1976. Psychology in America's bicentennial year. *American Psychologist* 31: 819–33.

Miles, T. R. 1988. Skinner I and Skinner II. *Counselling Psychology Quarterly* 1: 303–305.

Moore, B. R. 1973. The role of directed Pavlovian reactions in simple instrumental learning in the pigeon. In *Constraints on Learning: Limitations and Predispositions*. Edited by R. A. Hinde & J. Stevenson-Hinde. New York: Academic Press.

Morris, Edward K. 1982. Some relationships between interbehavioral psychology and radical behaviorism. *Behaviorism* 10: 187–216.

————. 1992. The aim, progress, and evolution of behavior analysis. *Behavior Analyst* 15: 3–29.

————. 1993. Behavior analysis and mechanism: One is not the other. *Behavior Analyst* 16: 25–43.

————. 1993–1994. Interbehavioral psychology: Outstanding in the field or out standing in its field? *The Interbehaviorist* 21 (2): 4–8.

Morris, Edward K.; Stephen T. Higgins; & Warrent K. Bickel. 1982. Comments on cognitive science in the experimental analysis of behavior. *Behavior Analyst* 5: 109–125.

Morris, Edward K., & Bryan D. Midgley. 1990. Some historical and conceptual foundations of ecobehavioral analysis. In *Ecobehavioral Analysis and Developmental Disabilities: The Twenty-First Century*. Edited by Stephen R. Schroeder. New York: Springer-Verlag.

Perlman, Daniel. 1980. Who's who in psychology: Endler et al.'s SSCI scores versus a textbook definition. *American Psychologist* 35: 104–106.

Pfaus, J. G.; J. R. Blackburn; T. J. Harpur; M. A. MacDonald; M. J. Mana; & W. J. Jacobs. 1988. Has psychology ever been a science of behavior? A comment on Skinner. *American Psychologist* 43: 821–22.

Place, Ullin. 1988a. Skinner's distinction between rule-governed and contingency-shaped behavior. *Philosophical Psychology* 1: 225–34.

————. 1988b. What went wrong? *Counselling Psychology Quarterly* 1: 307–309.

Power, M. J. 1988. Seven sins of behaviorism. *Counselling Psychology Quarterly* 1: 279–86.

Rachlin, Howard. 1980. *Behaviorism in Everyday Life.* Englewood Cliffs, NJ: Prentice-Hall.

————. 1991a. *Introduction to Modern Behaviorism,* 3rd ed. San Francisco: Freeman.

————. 1991b. A lively ride on a merry-go-round. *Contemporary Psychology* 36: 454–55.

Rachman, Stanley, & Roy J. Hodgson. 1980. *Obsessions and Compulsions.* Englewood Cliffs, NJ: Prentice-Hall.

Ray, Roger, W. 1995. A behavioral systems approach to adaptive computerized instructional design. *Behavioral Research Methods, Instruments, & Computers* 27: 293–96.

Richelle, Marc N. 1988. On Skinner's disenchantment. *Counselling Psychology Quarterly* 1: 317–20.

Risley, Todd, R. 1977. Ecology of applied behavior analysis. In *Ecological Perspectives in Behavior Analysis.* Edited by Ann Rogers-Warren & Steven F. Warren. Baltimore, MD: University Park Press.

Rogers-Warren, Ann, & Steve F. Warren. 1977. *Ecological Perspectives in Behavior Analysis.* Baltimore, MD: University Park Press.

Rohter, Larry. 1989. Isolated desert community lives by Skinner's precepts. *New York Times* (November 7): C1, C8.

Sandler, Jack, & Steele, Holly V. 1991. Aversion methods. In *Helping People Change: A Textbook of Methods,* 4th ed. Edited by Frederick H. Kanfer & Arnold P. Goldstein. New York: Pergamon Press.

Schroeder, Stephen, ed. 1990. *Ecobehavioral Analysis and Developmental Disabilities; The Twenty-First Century.* New York: Springer-Verlag.

Shull, Richard L., & P. Scott Lawrence. 1993. Is contextualism productive? *Behavior Analyst* 16: 241–43.

Sidman, Murray. 1989. *Coercion and Its Fallout.* Boston: Authors Cooperative.

Skinner, B. F. 1938. *The Behavior of Organisms: An Experimental Analysis.* New York: Appleton-Century-Crofts.

———. 1948. *Walden Two.* New York: Macmillan.

———. 1953. *Science and Human Behavior.* New York: Macmillan.

———. 1957. *Verbal Behavior.* New York: Appleton-Century-Crofts.

———. 1960. Pigeons in a pelican. *American Psychologist* 15: 15-37.

———. 1963. Behaviorism at fifty. *Science* 140: 951–58.

———. 1969. *Contingencies of Reinforcement.* New York: Appleton-Century-Crofts.

———. 1973. Answers for my critics. In *Beyond the Punitive Society: Operant Conditioning—Social and Political Aspects.* Edited by Harvey Wheeler. San Francisco: Freeman.

———. 1974a. *About Behaviorism.* New York: Knopf.

———. 1974b. Behavior modification. *Science* 185: 813.

———. 1975. The steep and thorny way to a science of behavior. *American Psychologist* 40: 42–49.

———. 1983. Intellectual self-management in old age. *American Psychologist* 38: 239–44.

———. 1987. Whatever happened to psychology as the science of behavior? *American Psychologist* 42: 780–86.

———. 1988a. The cuckoos. *ABA Newsletter* 11 (3): 7.

———. 1988b. Whatever happened to psychology as the science of behavior? *Counselling Psychology Quarterly* 1: 111–22. [N.B.: Revised version, with new material, of 1987 article.]

———. 1989. The origins of cognitive thought. *American Psychologist* 44: 13–18.

———. 1990. Can psychology be a science of mind? *American Psychologist* 45: 1206–1210.

Stokes, Trevor F., & Donald M. Baer. 1977. Am implicit technology of generalization. *Journal of Applied Behavior Analysis* 10: 349–67.

Todd, James T., & Edward K. Morris. 1983. Misconceptions and miseducation: Presentations of radical behaviorism in psychology textbooks. *Behavior Analyst* 6: 153–60.

Wheeler, Harvey, ed. 1973. *Beyond the Punitive Society: Operant Conditioning: Social and Political Aspects.* San Francisco: Freeman.

Willems, Edwin P. 1974. Behavioral technology and behavioral ecology. *Journal of Applied Behavior Analysis* 7: 151–65.

———. 1977. Behavioral technology and behavioral ecology. In *Ecological Perspectives in Behavior Analysis.* Edited by Ann Rogers-Warren & Steven F. Warren. Baltimore, MD: University Park Press.

Verplanck, William S. 1992. Verbal concept "mediators" as simple operants. *Analysis of Verbal Behavior* 10: 45–68.

Zettle, Robert D. 1990. Rule-governed behavior: A radical behavioral answer to the cognitive challenge. *Psychological Record* 40: 41–49.

CHAPTER 7

Eco-Behavioral Science/ Ecological Psychology: Predictable Patterns in the Interface between Physical Settings and People

Chapter Outline

INTRODUCTION

When we enter a store there are certain patterns we engage in with respect to both the merchandise in the store and the clerks. We go to a grocery store during the hours it is open, obtain a shopping cart, move down the aisles selecting food items and placing them in the cart while avoiding running into other carts, get in line, wait our turn to be checked out, pay the cashier, and carry or cart away the groceries. The pattern is predictable. A description of our behavior in a post office, at a tennis lesson, in a basketball game, or at our workplace would be equally predictable. These are "behavior settings." We follow the expected patterns of the setting; our personalities have little influence. Individuals with very different personalities nevertheless follow similar patterns in a given setting. We even take steps to assure that those patterns continue. For example, if we are attending a meeting at which we wish to use a slide projector but there is no table set up, we will search for and bring in a table. This corrects the deficiencies of the *physical components* that would interfere with or fail to support those patterns. Similarly, we might try to modify nonconforming *behavioral components* by explaining to a newcomer in a coffee shop that one must go to the counter to order. These natural settings, with their orderly and self-regulating character, are the subject matter of *ecological psychology*—now often called *eco-behavioral science* or the *science of behavior settings*—as developed by Roger Barker and his associates.[1]

FUNDAMENTALS OF BEHAVIOR SETTINGS

Standing Patterns

Behavior settings, such as grocery stores, are areas where human activity and physical conditions interact. Here are some additional examples: classrooms, factory shipping rooms, pizza parlors, athletic events, dentists' waiting rooms, card games, courtrooms, and auto repair shops. A behavior setting has several recognizable and orderly characteristics. First of all it has *standing patterns of behavior,* behaviors that recur each time the behavior setting is in operation. In the classroom this includes the students sitting down and facing the front of the room, the instructor facing the students, the instructor taking the lead in discussion or presentation, and the students raising their hands to be recognized by the instructor when they wish to speak.

Synomorphs

The standing behavior patterns are closely tied to the environment, most of it inanimate. In the case of the classroom, there is a chalkboard and chalk, chairs for students, perhaps a table, desk, or lectern in front for the instructor, lighting, heat in cold weather, and walls that shut out distractions. These inanimate components are integral parts of the behavior patterns, and in fact the behavior patterns cannot readily occur without them.

Barker refers to the co-relationship of behavior and physical objects as *synomorphs*—"same structures." A set of synomorphs comprise the structure of the behavior setting. The classroom behavior setting illustrates these structures as examples of behavior patterns interconnected with objects: students sit on chairs and take notes with a pen on a tablet which can rest on the arm of the chair; instructors lecture from notes placed on a lectern and write with chalk on a chalkboard; and this occurs within walls that define the area and limit extraneous sounds and views.

In an iron foundry the melting furnace and the pouring areas are different synomorphs in the same factory but are functionally interdependent and comprise a single behavior setting. However, the shipping room that prepares iron castings for transport acts independently as long as it has a stockpile of castings. What goes on in the manufacture of castings has only limited effect on the shipping activities and vice versa. They are separate behavior settings.

---

1. The term *ecological psychology* is found in the older literature and continues to be used by some writers.

The synomorphs have a degree of interdependence with one another. An institution attempts to schedule events in such a way that no serious time conflicts occur. For example, a department of a university will not schedule classes during a designated period so that faculty can hold department meetings; and a foundry will not schedule maintenance and repair of equipment while production is underway. Any synomorphs that are related in structure but function independently of one another must be parts of separate behavior settings. The criteria of structure and interdependence permit the differentiation of behavior settings from non-behavior settings. Because an iron foundry has functionally independent synomorphs, the whole foundry is not a behavior setting. Neither is a university or even a university department. It is usually easy to assess whether a situation is or is not a behavior setting, but Barker and his associates have developed rating scales for components of the situation to provide a quantitative means of assessment whenever doubt arises.

Because the physical sciences have avoided studying events that include behavior, and the behavioral sciences have avoided studying events involving inanimate objects, the interface between them has been neglected by both. That relationship falls through the cracks, yet it comprises a great deal of human activity. Barker's eco-behavioral science attempts to be a new science that examines some of that activity.

Environment

A behavior setting includes an environment that surrounds the behavior and delimits its geography. For a classroom it is walls. For a factory it is the work area. For a tennis game it is lines around the court. For skiing it is the marked trails along with the lodge and lift-line areas, but it might also include unmarked areas for the more daring skier.

The environment is a well organized arrangement of "nested assemblies" that are like layers of an onion. These layers are circumjacent to each other. Each assembly or unit contains some of the components of the assembly it is circumjacent to,

so that some interdependence occurs. The individual is one such assembly. Each of his or her biological organs is a component of the individual's body, and each in turn is another assembly. For example, the heart is a component of the circumjacent body and a cell is a component of the circumjacent heart. Going the other direction from the individual toward larger units, we find that the behavior setting is an assembly of which the individual is a component, and the behavior setting may be a circumjacent component of an institution such as a factory or a university with numerous behavior settings. Thus, what is a component in one assembly can be an environment in a circumjacent assembly. A unit, then, can be both circumjacent and interjacent.

> There are mutual causal relations up and down the nesting series in which many environmental entities occur; the preperceptual environment is made up of systems within systems. An entity in such a series both constrains and is constrained by the outside unit that surrounds it and by the inside units it surrounds. This means that entities in nesting structures are parts of their own contexts; they influence themselves through the circumjacent entities which they, in part, compose. (Barker, 1963b, p. 23)

Definition of Behavior Settings

A behavior setting consists of five characteristics. It must (a) have standing patterns of behavior; (b) be established in a particular environmental context; (c) occur at a specific place; (d) consist of behavior and environment in synomorphic relationship; (e) involve an environment circumjacent to behavior (Schoggen, 1989, p. 52). Wicker and Kirmeyer (1976) list three more: (f) a hierarchy of positions or roles in the behavior setting, some with more vital function than others (such as a dentist versus the receptionist in a dentist's office); (g) the interchangeability of one participant with another (a replacement dentist or a replacement receptionist would allow the behavior setting to continue without much change); and (h) the control circuits described in the next section.

Control Circuits or Mechanisms

A behavior setting has human components, non-human components, and "control circuits" or "control mechanisms." The term "circuit" refers to the interchange or feedback loops among components (in contrast to a straight line cause-and-effect sequence). The stability of settings with their behavior-environment relationships involves the operation of four types of circuits: goal circuits, program circuits, deviation countering circuits, and vetoing circuits.

Goal Circuits. Every behavior setting exists for some purpose: recreation, production of goods, sale of a commodity, acquisition of knowledge, and so forth. Such a purpose or goal is the behavior setting's *goal circuit*. The goal circuits are procedures for reaching goals satisfying to the participants (Barker calls them "inhabitants,") of the setting. The participants must perceive the goals and the routes to them. When some participants leave, others take their places and receive whatever instruction is necessary for the role. The participants actively attempt to keep the setting operating because its goal provides them with satisfactions. If it fails to be satisfying, they will no longer strive to maintain the setting, and it will go out of existence. People relate to their settings through the pursuit of goal achievement and the satisfaction it brings.

Program Circuits. People also relate to their settings through *program circuits*. Programs are the specifications of behaviors that the participants in the setting carry out, such as rules for a game, production methods in a factory, and procedures for conducting a meeting. One or more participants must know the program and thereby control the sequence of events in it.

Deviation Countering Circuits. These exist when the participants recognize that some person or condition prevents the program of the setting from occurring and acts to remedy the situation. It may involve persuading someone to behave in a

different or more effective manner ("If you don't hurry up, we won't get this job completed by the deadline"). The previous example of explaining to a newcomer to the coffee shop that orders are placed at the counter is also deviation countering. Remedying some fault in the physical environment also falls into this type of control circuit. A speaker with a soft voice may need a microphone; a classroom may need additional chairs; a motor that runs an important piece of machinery on a shop floor needs replacing; a work situation needs a replacement for a person off work because of sickness.

Vetoing Circuits. When deviation-countering circuits are insufficient to bring behaviors into line with the needs of the setting and its goals, *vetoing circuits* come into play. A supervisor discharges an employee who does sloppy or incompetent work; a band leader requests the departure of a player who is high on narcotics; a teacher removes a noisy and disruptive pupil from the classroom. Inanimate components of the setting are also subject to veto: a new lighting device for a theatrical production creates an unsatisfactory effect; loud music at a gathering interferes with conversation; a machine check-out device for library books proves more cumbersome than the old method.

Interplay of Circuits in Achieving Goals. The control circuits change the components in anticipated ways that keep the schedules or programs on course. When one control circuit fails to induce the participant or other component to contribute appropriately to the goal of the behavior setting, participants will activate another. The components and circuits operate as a homeostatic control to keep everything functioning in a predictable and prescribed manner. The foundry worker who is too slow at pouring molten iron into the molds will be pressured to speed up by the worker who is approaching with a huge bucket to resupply the pouring ladles. The person who is going too fast will be limited by the rate at which the molds on the conveyor belt reach him or her. Any improperly filled molds will bring feedback to the pourers and result in correction (deviation countering circuits). The actions of the workers, the physical environment, and the regulating circuits function together to produce a predictable program that meets a goal.

Self Regulation. Barker (1963b) holds that the behavior setting resides not in the behavior or the physical environment but "in the circuitry that interconnects behavior settings, the inhabitants and other behavior setting components" (p. 171). This circuitry enables the setting to be self-regulating.

> *Behavior settings are self-regulating, active systems.* They impose their program of activities on the persons and objects within them. Essential persons and materials are drawn into the settings, and disruptive components are modified or ejected. It's as if behavior settings were living systems intent on remaining alive and healthy, even at the expense of their individual components. (Wicker, 1979b, p. 12)

Additional Factors. Still other mechanisms or circuits can be identified (Stokols & Shumaker, 1981). In order to accommodate more people rather than veto them, overstaffed settings often enlarge themselves. They may also limit admission of newcomers rather than admit people they will then have to veto. Settings vary in how often they are repeated and in their duration. Academic classes and factory work shifts have well defined durations. Both exist for set times and repeat this schedule regularly, but academic classes are discontinued at the end of a semester while work shifts go on indefinitely. A birthday party may have a clear beginning, only a vague ending, and no likely repetition. Some settings remain viable only as long as particular people, such as strong leaders or doers, remain active. Others are quite independent of any particular type of individual, and many are probably in between. The stability of a setting may be threatened by pressing environmental conditions (competing settings, curtailed funding, unavailability of present quarters, hostility of opponents). Unexpected termination can oc-

cur due to fire, hurricanes, or death of a key person such as a store owner. Settings vary in the way they anticipate and prepare for environmental change and crises, and in whether they will stand, fall, or become crippled when such events occur. Sometimes participants change the patterns of the setting to prepare for such events; and sometimes they change them just for variety, efficiency, to upgrade the setting, or for countless other reasons.

EARLY DEVELOPMENT

The Prelude

During a three year period at the College of Education at the University of Illinois, Barker (1979) visited practicing teachers and discovered that he "knew no more about the everyday behaviors and environments of the children of the towns than laymen know" (p. 2150) and that other child psychologists knew no more either. Nor was there any method available for "determining the extent and conditions of frustration, joy, anger, success, conflict, problem solving, fear, and so forth among the town's children" (p. 2150). Later, at the University of Kansas he found a small town nearby where he could begin pioneer efforts toward studying these behaviors in their natural setting. The source of the influences that led him to utilize the natural environment, collect data from an atheoretical view, and deposit the data in archives came from his work in an animal laboratory and a child nursery laboratory. The field work of cultural anthropologists also led him in this direction, and he drew some initial concepts from the social psychologist Kurt Lewin (1951) who held that because the various sciences are incommensurable (a measurement of one is not a measurement of the other; see p. 214), psychological sciences cannot include any other science. His concept that B = f(P,E) (behavior is a function of the person and the environment) was also an influence. Barker began his work with the assumption that its focus would be on individual behavior in naturally occurring environments, but the observed events showed him that it was primarily the context that determined the behavior, not the individual. His formula would be B = f(E).

Stream of Individual Behavior

Barker and his associates began their investigations by studying the ordinary lives of individual children. When they tried to record the children's behaviors and their environments, they "discovered that behavior and environment are inexorably continuous in time, that they are relentlessly ongoing from sunrise to sunrise with no gaps whatsoever" (Barker, 1978, p. 3). While this was not a new revelation it presented problems that the psychology laboratory—with its discrete units such as time periods, trials, tests, and tasks—provided no means of handling. How can one identify the parts of a stream or record it or analyze it? All of this Barker and his associates gradually worked out. They divided the behavior stream into two general categories, behavior episodes and contents.

Behavior Episodes and Contents

The observation and recording of streams of behavior in their natural setting led to the discovery of "behavior episodes." For example, a professor walks to the lectern, spreads out his or her notes, turns to the chalk tray, picks up a piece of chalk, glances at some notes, faces the class, and waits for silence. Episodes are (a) constant in direction, (b) conform to the normal events of a larger unit of behavior, (c) have equal potency throughout their parts, and (d) are of limited size and range. These three characteristics can be illustrated in the example of the professor: (a) the direction of the episode is toward the goal of preparing for the start of class; (b) the episode conforms to the need for the classroom behavior setting to occur and function; (c) none of the components exceed the potency of the whole; (d) the size and range are clearly confined to the start of the class activities. Behavior episodes may occur singly or several may occur simultaneously in any behavior setting. They are molar units of the stream of behavior.

The other category of the stream of behavior, "behavior content," is almost infinitely diverse and comprises whatever the individual is doing.

The number of behavior episodes with even a small number of subjects can be staggering. Barker and associates observed that the 119 children they were observing in a small town engaged in 100,000 episodes every day or 36,000,000 in a year—and even more when the observers broadened the locales in which they were observing. Consequently, a sampling was necessary. The investigators drew three important conclusions from their observations: (a) the episodes change significantly from one situation to another—playground to baseball game to shower room; (b) a child in any given situation displays behavior episodes more like those of other children in that situation than like him or herself in other situations; (c) the whole course of behavior is more closely related to the situation than to parts of the behavior (equal potency). The observation of how behavior episodes relate to the environment was the basis for discovering behavior settings.

Implications

With the assumption that it would be possible to discover important principles of behavior by studying ordinary people (particularly children) in ordinary situations, in 1947 Roger Barker and Herbert Wright set up a field station in Oskaloosa, Kansas.[2] Willems (1990) has noted that

> [they] took this lonely position at a time when the prevailing belief of mainstream psychology held that human behavior could only be studied objectively and scientifically when it was pinned down by the arrangements of an experiment, the probes of a questionnaire, or the guidelines of an interview. I have no idea how many psychologists have been comforted or encouraged or helped by the Barkers' trust, but we

---

2. The station was in the upstairs of an old bank building. For accounts of this station and its involvement with the community, see Barker, 1990; Wicker, 1990; and Willems, 1990.

do know by now that the last 20 years or so have seen an explosion of research in which investigators have looked directly at everyday behavior and, in contrast to the 1950s and 1960s, have not apologized for their work. (p. 473)

Fox (1989) holds that Barker's work has vital implications in the social sciences. ". . . the behavior setting concept may come to play as important a role in the social sciences as the cell concept does in biology" (p. 300). He reviews the far-reaching implications in economics: the economic functioning of organizations, the consumption and replacement of the inanimate objects, investment in durable goods, health and replacement costs of workers as they relate to control circuits, and others.

SOME ISSUES

World of Chaos versus Regularity

It has been a common assumption in psychology that the world is chaotic or has only statistical regularity and that the individual must organize it into some sort of coherency. This assumption goes back at least as far as William James (1890) who tells us in his frequently quoted statement that "the baby, assailed by eyes, ears, nose, skin, and entrails at once, feels it all as one great blooming,[3] buzzing confusion. . . ." which the child must eventually learn to *"fuse into a single undivided object"* (p. 488: italics in original): That is, the individual must put it into order.

Barker observes that the world actually has many organized components. Atoms organize into molecules and these into crystals or into such complex forms as DNA and RNA which organize into complex organisms. We don't need to make order in nature. It is already there in "bounded and internally patterned units that are frequently arranged in precisely ordered arrays and sequences" (Barker, 1963b, p. 22). Because psychologists usually assume that the environment is

chaotic and that the organism must put it in order, they have experimentally manipulated it and imposed order rather than observing the order present in a real-life situation.

Given the fact that each of several persons might describe a situation differently—a library reading room or a courtroom trial or a basketball game—is this not evidence for its lack of regularity, proof that it is not subject to scientific analysis? Barker would hold that these events *are* orderly and even predictable inasmuch as the participants anticipate many of the events and behave according to their expectations. Contrary to the view that prediction is possible only because individuals make generalizations and probability estimates from prior experiences or the idea that regularity arises from each individual's perceptions, Barker argues that the regularity and its predictability are intrinsic to the situation. It is "preperceptual"—existing prior to anyone's perception of it. But because psychologists' traditional methods of research disrupt the normal patterns of behavior, they must resort to the assumption of an internal programming; and in some conceptualizations they have converted this into a computer brain. In this view the program is the major determinant of behavior, and the environment is largely unstructured and passive. The proponents posit the infamous "black box" or computer brain and claim that it turns the inputs into order; it "appears to bring order out of chaos" (Barker, 1969, p. 32).

But to Barker the environment is not passive; it is an active part of the unit of which the individual is a part. Although he started his investigations with person-centered (organocentric) assumptions, he was forced to abandon them when he found that the children in behavior settings showed less variation from one another than they did across settings. They were much like each other in the arithmetic class and much like each other in the ballgames, but the behavior of the same child in the classroom and the ballgame was vastly different. This was difficult to explain with the assumption of an "internal programming people carry around from setting to setting"

---

3. "Blooming" may be a typographical error for "booming."

(1969, p. 34). While acknowledging that individual differences do exist, Barker emphasized that behavior patterns appropriate to a setting occur despite these differences. Environments act as homeostatic systems with control circuits (goal, program, deviation countering, and vetoing) that maintain the characteristic pattern of the setting: classroom, ballgame, workplace, and so on. Hospital patients also showed behavior that was more similar within settings than across settings: the settings accounted for more variance than the patients' individual differences (Willems, 1972).

Barker insists that the individual is a part of the pre-existing order, even though he does not always recognize it as such. We can observe that order when we leave the natural conditions intact. When we do that, the psychologist's mysterious black box as a determinant of behavior becomes entirely superfluous.

It is common in psychology to assume that the environment has no distinct boundaries. For example, a worker at an iron foundry might be in the environment of buckets of glowing molten iron, sand molds moving on conveyor belts, co-workers bustling about performing their jobs, smoke billowing off the poured molds, and machinery clanking and banging as it moves. Further, the worker, together with the factory, is in a neighborhood of workers' houses, in a city beside a river, with mountains visible in the distance, and so forth. In this view the boundaries of what is environment are rather fuzzy and any designation is rather arbitrary. But to eco-behavioral science, the environment is well structured and clearly definable. The regularity and predictability of behavior segments are due in part to the regularity of the environment in its circumjacent layers.

Incommensurability of Units

Eco-behavioral science is not person centered but unit centered. Although the circumjacent assemblies affect one another, they do not account for one another's patterns or functioning characteristics. Each must be studied on its own level. Each is *incommensurate* (not co-measurable) with the other. That is, a measurement of one does not provide a measurement of the other: a behavior setting has principles of its own, which are not reducible to the individuals within it, to the larger society, or to the general physical environment in which it is embedded. This position is a modification of a precept of Kurt Lewin who held that because the various sciences are incommensurate with each other, psychological sciences (subjective sciences to Lewin) could not include any events from any other domain. Barker modified this: it is a unit—in this case, a behavior setting—that is irreducible or incommensurate rather than an entire science.

Eco-behavioral science, as noted above, does not deny the importance of individual characteristics or even deny that they may color a given behavior setting. But in turning to a unit-centered rather than a person-centered approach it brings attention to the importance of regularity and patterning of a great deal of actual human activity in which the behavior setting rather than the individual accounts for most of the event. The setting will even explain much individual behavior.

Transducers and Operators

Eco-behavioral science sees its role as one of "transducer" (from L. *trans,* "across," and *ducere,* "to lead"), not as "operator." As transducer, it records events that it observes in a natural situation and arranges the recordings into categories for storage and analysis. The ongoing psychological events themselves are the operators and the psychologist is a "docile receiver, coder, and transmitter of information" (Schoggen, p. 150). In contrast to this approach, nearly all the vast number of studies of intelligence involve the psychologist as operator, for these studies restrict the subject to standard test items and seldom gather data about the intellectual demands of actual life or their responses to them. Psychologists know about intelligence as responses to test items and its correlation with teacher ratings and job performance but little about intelligent behavior in hunter-gatherer or agrarian societies or in the gangs of a large city.

Similarly, they know how rats behave when crowded in a laboratory experiment but little about humans packed into tenements or prisons. Further, findings from frustration experiments with children (Barker, Dembo, & Lewin, 1941) bear little resemblance to those from life situations (Fawl, 1978). The psychological operator obtains data that are not the same as those obtained by a transducer. Psychologists have discovered quite a lot about how humans behave under experimental conditions but little about behavior in natural conditions. No laboratory will reveal transducer data, the eco-psychologists argue. Such data can be obtained only from real-life. "Psychology has been so busy selecting from, imposing upon, and rearranging the behavior of its subject that it has until very recently neglected to note behavior's clear structure when it is not molested by tests, experiments, questionnaires and interviews" (Barker, 1963b, p. 24).

> Psychology has generally preferred to study elements of the environment under the controlled conditions of the laboratory, in isolation from the complexities of the real-life situations in which they occur—away from ball games, from symposia meetings, from freeways, from music classes. (Schoggen, 1989, p. 4)

Because psychologists usually assume that the environment is chaotic and the organism must order it, they have experimentally manipulated it—imposed order, rather than observing organism-object relationships. They have been operators rather than transducers.

Distribution and Taxonomies of Behaviors

The physical and biological sciences have amassed great amounts of data on the constituents of the earth's surface (and even the moon), of gasses and other elements in stars, of the number of ant species in a tropical forest, of the lengths of flight of migrating birds, etc. But what do they know "about playing, about laughing, about talking, about being valued and devalued, about conflict,

about failure" (Barker, 1963a, p. 145)? What can they say about the frequency with which children play a part in community affairs in various communities or what extracurricular activities they engage in in various sized schools and what effect it has on them for completing their schooling (see pp. 217–220 for some answers)? Just as they know little about the distribution of behaviors, so also do they know little about the taxonomy of behaviors, such as units of behavior and environment, and how these are related. Eco-behavioral science, however, has made some strides in this direction.

Bechtel (1981) studied a community in Alaska in order to determine the types of behavior settings present. In contrast to Barker and Wright's (1955) rather arbitrary designation of government, schools, businesses, churches, and voluntary groups, Bechtel found them to be work, social living, minority groups, and children. But in a similar study of six small towns in Kansas, the settings turned out to be age, number of performers, and duration of setting—suggesting that local variables were the determiners, rather than common variables across locations (Bechtel, 1982a).

Problems and Theories versus Events and Atheory

As Barker (1969) sees it, in psychology's disruption of normal behavior patterns by experiments, questionnaires, and interviews, it has tried to find normality statistically and by "ever more theory-determined, and less setting-determined environmental variables" (p. 32). It is essential, Barker believes, to gather data in a field setting without any guiding theory or any particular problem to be solved and without interfering in any way with the naturally occurring activities. The field psychologist must be as unobtrusive as possible, obtain a reasonably complete record of all that occurs, and place it in an archive. If the field psychologist comes to the situation with a theory or a problem, he or she will gather only that data that is relevant to the theory or problem. But a collection of neutral, archived data will be available to anyone who wishes to use any portion of it from any point of view. Barker cites a number of instances of such usage of his field data. "This experience has taught us that data that are dross for one investigator are gold for another" (Barker, 1969, p. 39).

The analysis of field data requires techniques appropriate to the nature of the data. The data should not be forced into normalized distributions and other hypothesis-testing arrangements, just as subjects should not be forced into counterbalanced groups or control and experimental groups. The events rather than the molds of experimental psychology must determine the method of analysis, Barker insists.

The Theme of Eco-Behavioral Science

Willems (1972) sets forth the differences between eco-behavioral science and more traditional approaches:

The ecologist sees a world characterized by complexity rather than simplicity, a world which obeys laws of balance, reciprocity, and interdependency rather than a world in which independent events occur in isolated fashion. Thus, inevitably, there is a distinctly pluralistic thematic structure or thrust to the way ecologists work . . . The parts of this thematic thrust are (a) documentation of the distribution of the phenomena in nature, (b) taxonomic research, (c) search for basic processes and principles, (d) testing of specific hypotheses, (e) formulation of principles of organization and interdependency within systems, (f) prediction of effects within systems over time, and (g) assessment of predicted effects . . . In the behavioral sciences, there is an acute shortage of specialists for themes a and b and there is little appreciation of their importance. Instead, behavioral scientists rush to themes c and d with various combinations of laboratory and field research. As a result, the behavioral sciences are almost completely unable to fulfill themes e, f, and g, which are dependent on all of the other four.

SEMI-EXPLICIT POSTULATES

Barker has not set forth his postulates in a formal manner but has indicated a number of them more or less directly in various publications. Therefore, they may be regarded as semi-explicit.

■ *Metapostulates* (supportive assumptions for a particular science)
1. Many events of nature, of both the physical environment and of behavior, are ordered and patterned.
2. Many events in nature, including those involving humans, occur in organized circumjacent units that are incommensurate with one another.
3. The environment is not passive but active.
4. Naturally occurring events involving human activity can be understood only if observed in their normal continuity and not interrupted or divided into discrete units.
5. Behavior is a function of the environment.

■ *Postulates* (subject matter assumptions)
1. It is behavior, not a hypothetical mind or other construct, that provides data and that must be used in any description or analysis.
2. Behaviors, together with inanimate objects and conditions, develop patterns that are orderly and self-sustaining and provide a legitimate area of investigation.
3. Causality of behavior lies largely in the behavior setting rather than in individual traits.
4. Behavior and setting are interdependent.
5. Behavior settings are irreducible to any other level of event.

■ *Operating principles*
1. Topics are chosen from areas of investigation rather than from a theory.
2. Data are collected from an atheoretical viewpoint but may then be analyzed theoretically.
3. Observation must be of naturally occurring events and be as unobtrusive as possible.
4. Adequate observation requires locating a research station adjacent to the settings to be

studied. It should be an integral part of the community.[4]

5. It is often expedient to work from the complex to the simple. The complex may comprise an organization that will not be discovered if one starts with parts or attempts to understand the full event by the parts.

6. Long periods of observation may be necessary in order to properly understand interdependencies and cumulative effects.

7. Rate measures, some of them very small and undramatic, should be collected as indicators of ecological relationships.

RESEARCH

"Manning" Theory: Overstaffing and Understaffing

Barker studied behavior settings in a small town in Kansas that he called Midwest (Barker & Wright, 1955) and one in Yorkshire, England that he called Yoredale (Barker & Schoggen, 1973). The residents of Midwest participated in more behavior settings per person and with more frequency than did those of Yoredale. This led Barker to a number of hypotheses about the effects of understaffing and overstaffing (called undermanning and overmanning in earlier terminology) of behavior settings. For understaffing as opposed to overstaffing or optimal staffing, the theory suggests the following (as refined by Barker & Schoggen, 1973):

Task differences:
- more intense efforts or more hours spent to keep the setting operating
- more frequent and more vigorous attempts to deal with threats to the setting
- more frequent and varied efforts to bring deviant behavior into conformity with the needs of the setting

- more appeals to others to help with the tasks of the setting
- each participant serving more frequently in responsible positions
- engagement of each participant in more difficult, more varied, and more essential tasks

Psychological differences:
- each participant having a greater sense of responsibility and perceiving his or her own task as very important
- each participant perceiving both himself or herself and others as job related rather than in terms of personality characteristics
- greater insecurity about the viability of the setting
- increased sense of versatility
- reduced critical attitude toward the performance of others

Additional consequences of understaffing are lower standards of admission to settings, involvement of most individuals in more difficult tasks, a higher frequency of both success and failure, and the greater perceived value of each participant by others in the setting (Wicker & Kirmeyer, 1976). Studies of behavior settings in schools and churches support these theoretical expectations. This applies in the workplace too: in small work units, workers engage in more interaction, feel a stronger obligation to other workers, and participate in more demanding tasks than in large units (O'Donnell, 1980). Crowded settings, on the other hand, reduce the frequency with which newcomers ask questions, apparently because of greater social embarrassment over not knowing relevant information and over appearing to be an outsider (Fuhrer, 1987, 1988).

In their research for *Big School, Small School*, Barker and Gump (1964) studied voluntary behavior settings such as athletic teams, cheerleading squads, bands, and language clubs, and found that such behavior settings don't increase proportionately as school size increases—in fact, enrollment goes up eight times as fast as an increase in extracurricular groups. And there are inherent limits on the number of participants each setting

---

4. Barker (1987) observes that astronomy has its observatories, oceanography its marine stations, geology its observation posts on volcanoes and faults, and biology its research stations; but psychology has had no field stations since the one of twenty-five years duration in Oskaloosa, Kansas, operated by Barker and Wright.

can absorb. The school newspaper or a class play can use only so many individuals. Large school settings averaged three times as many participants as small schools. In contrast with the overstaffing of students in large schools, not only was each setting in the small schools understaffed but the insufficiency of students for the number of settings led to an average participation rate of 3.7 behavior settings for each student. Those who attended large schools participated in only 0.6. The large schools with their overstaffing vetoed 29 percent of the participants whereas the small schools vetoed only 2 percent, the latter more often using deviation countering circuits than vetoing circuits. When a setting is shorthanded, it is important for it to retain as many participants as possible and to try to bring deviants into enough conformity to assist in meeting the goals of the setting.

The small school students reported satisfaction in (a) their accomplishments and in the development of competence, (b) close cooperation with other students, (c) meeting of challenges, and (d) a sense of being valued. Students from large schools reported mostly vicarious satisfaction— association with a large school or with one that won awards or championships. Large schools also had a higher percentage of students who dropped out of school (Schoggen & Schoggen, 1988). Students in small schools held more positions of importance as well as participating more (Barker & Gump, 1964). Because those in smaller schools have more opportunities for participation in voluntary behavior settings, the psychological benefits of a feeling of belonging and of accomplishment probably play a role in keeping marginal students in school. Several studies (Wicker, 1979a) confirm that those in understaffed situations feel more involvement than those in overstaffed situations.

> And this tendency for people to drop out or to be absent as institutions get larger seems to be true for institutions besides the high school. It is true for Rotary Clubs, for mining crews, for textile workers, for airline workers, and so on.

> The old saying, "The bigger the better!" is of dubious worth. (Gump, 1978, p. 255)

In small schools, marginal students, those whose parents had not completed high school and whose intelligence test scores were below average (and likely to be dropouts), felt more social pressure to participate than nonmarginal students. They were outsiders in the large schools, but in the small schools they were valued and their participation solicited (Willems, 1964); the small school was more advantageous for them than for others (Willems, 1967). Seniors from small schools in New York state (Schoggen & Schoggen, 1988) and across the nation (Baird, 1969) participated in a greater variety of behavior settings despite having fewer opportunities than the large schools offered. Those who actively participated, other than in sports, had a higher success rate in college than did those with little participation, independent of socioeconomic status or academic performance (Hanks & Eckland, 1976; Otto, 1975; Spady, 1970). Those from small schools outperformed those from large schools in four out of six areas of curriculum (Baird, 1969). A comparison of a large and a small church found that, like the high schools, the smaller church had fewer participants in each behavior setting than the larger church, its members felt greater social pressure to participate, and the participants held more positions of responsibility and engaged in a greater variety of activities in those behavior settings (Wicker, 1969).

A refinement of the concept of staffing takes into account the minimum number of persons required to move the setting toward its goal (*maintenance minimum*), the maximum number of persons the setting can accommodate (*capacity*), and the total number who wish to participate (*applicants*) (Wicker, McGrath, & Armstrong, 1972). Capacity can involve the size of the physical area, the number of pieces of equipment available, and so forth, as well as the number of behavior roles available. The behavior roles include "performers" and "nonperformers." Nonperformers are consumers, such as the audience at a theater event or spectators at an athletic event. Wicker's analysis of these components means that under-, over-, or adequate staffing depends on the number of applicants to be performers or nonperformers in relation to the maintenance minimum and the extent to which the capacity limits can accommodate performers and nonperformers. Understaffing occurs when the number of applicants is below that required for maintenance minimum, and overstaffing occurs when more apply than the setting can accommodate. This more precise formulation takes account not only of the physical conditions but of performers and nonperformers as well.

Studies of crowding have generally considered it a function of persons per square meter. Wicker's reformulation of staffing emphasizes behavior as a key condition of the effects and allows for a more refined examination. It shows that any solution must go beyond merely expanding space or reducing the number of people.

The behavior settings and the effects of staffing level may also extend to nonhuman animals in ways relevant to survival or reproduction (Schneider, 1990). Such diverse animals as mole rats, wasps, chimpanzees, and wolves establish standing patterns of behavior in conjunction with the inanimate environment. If a mother wolf with pups is killed, another female may begin lactating and taking care of the orphans, thus keeping the behavior patterns alive. Staffing level may have some effects. When a honeybee colony becomes overstaffed, the queen bee is forced out—vetoed—along with workers. When wolf packs become overstaffed with respect to food supply, they invade each others' territories and engage in fights; lower status individuals starve or leave. Small groups sometimes join other groups in order to form a more optimal staffing size for killing prey. The author notes that these similarities with humans are only rough parallels and that many important differences obtain.

In studying three kinds of organizations, Indik (1965) found that participation in group activities was related to greater communication and friendliness among participants in small groups than in large groups. Wicker (1979b) observes that it is not feasible to reduce the size of schools or factories to gain the advantages of smallness, but it may be possible to determine what factors in the small setting could be implemented in the large one. If the cold, impersonal characteristics of a large factory contribute to absenteeism, it might be possible to introduce more friendliness and a sense of caring among employees to lessen absenteeism. But the particular factors would have to be determined for each organization or behavior setting. Wicker's review of research on this matter reveals considerable complexity and few universals.

Wicker (1979b) studied the spontaneous adaptations that occur in settings where more clients appear than the setting can serve. In Yosemite National Park the rangers used more coping strategies as the work load (number of people entering the park) increased; they felt challenged and needed. This feeling gave way, however, to one of overwork and exhaustion as the summer wore on. Wicker (1979a) has summarized additional findings on this topic as well as numerous questions that need investigation. It appears that the effects of staffing level have many complications, including the individual characteristics of participants, a condition that Barker felt was minor.

In an even greater departure from naturalistic observation, Wicker and associates (1976) ran experimental studies to test the effects of staffing levels. Male college students raced toy slot cars under varying staffing requirements. As expected, overstaffing led to less feeling of involvement than did understaffing. Some other predictions from staffing theory were supported and some were not. In an experiment in which subjects undertook the task of building bookshelves out of bricks and boards, individual characteristics as well as the influence of the setting were found to operate (Perkins, 1982). Experimental findings such as these raise the question of whether they will generalize to real life situations.

As an alternative to setting up artificial experiments, Willems (1972a) recommends collecting data from natural experiments—such as increases in population, changes in social programs, institutional changes, changes in transportation systems or routes, modification of buildings, and endless others.

Behavior Setting

Genotype Settings in Schools. When the leaders of one behavior setting or the inanimate objects from it can be placed in another behavior setting, and the behavior setting continues as before, the settings are of the same *genotype*. For example, the players in most games or sporting events can be replaced with others without any major change in the patterns. Similarly with physical objects: if one were to replace the chairs and reception desk in a dentist's office with equally usable items of furniture, the setting would continue unaltered. It would also remain unaltered if one were to replace the dentist with another dentist. These, then, are genotype behavior settings. Barker found 198 genotypes in the small town he called Midwest and 30 in the high school. In "Big School, Small School" Gump (1978) reported that the instructional classes in the two smallest high schools—40 students each—comprised 12.5 genotypes each while the largest—2,105 students—were made up of 28.5 genotypes of instruction. The average size high school had 339 students and 21.5 genotypes. From smallest to largest was a more than 52-fold enrollment increment, but a barely 2-fold genotype increment. From average to largest was a six-fold enrollment increment but only a one-third genotype increment. As Gump noted, "it takes a lot of bigness to add a little variety" (p. 246).

Studies of number of course offerings in New York state high schools— as they related to size of school—showed that the number of courses increased with enrollment up to about four hundred students but showed almost no increase in numbers beyond that. Further, to the extent that course offerings increase, they are mostly additional introductory courses rather than those that build sequentially (Monk, 1987), although some schools do overcome the effects of size (Monk, 1990). The advanced courses that larger schools do offer are taken by relatively few students (Haller et al.,

1990), and these advanced courses are usually mathematics and sciences, not English or social sciences (Monk & Haller, 1993). Although school consolidation has been promoted across the country as providing economy of scale and richer curriculum, the evidence for this is lacking. Data show little gain and many losses with large schools; and, in fact ". . . large, complex and bureaucratic schools are inimical to the social and moral goals sought by reformers" (Haller & Monk, 1988, p. 481). Haller (1992) found that large schools are more disorderly and have more misbehavior than small schools. Monk and Haller (1986) demonstrated that students from small schools performed as well on examinations as those from large schools; and, in agreement with Barker and Gump, their extracurricular participation and social development was superior.

Perhaps these studies will demonstrate how important it is for policy-makers to understand behavior settings. In these studies the focus is on schools, but behavior settings are equally important in prisons, neighborhoods, business and industry, city streets, and so on. They have considerable implications for the conduct of social policy and the well-being of society.

Phenotype Settings. The behaviors that are actually observed are *phenotypes,* behavior episodes that occur regularly in various settings. They do not depend on individuals. They represent function, as genotypes represent structure. They may be found in such social systems as mutual help groups and therapy sessions. In a study of mutual help groups called GROW, which deal with serious problems in living through "caring and sharing," thirteen groups involving 510 meetings were of the same genotype of mutual help but showed differences in four phenotypes: some groups were more personal, some more impersonal; some did more advising, and some engaged in more small talk. One group had poor leadership, was chaotic during meetings, regularly strayed from the task, provided little interpersonal sharing, and engaged in much small talk. Another group had good leadership and kept to the task; members worked with one another outside meetings as well as during meetings (advising). These phenotypic patterns were stable despite considerable turnover of individuals. This variation within the same genotype, a variation in function rather than structure, is overlooked in the original formulation of behavior settings (Luke, Rappaport, & Seidman, 1991).

> One can use the genotype category for those questions dealing with the comparisons across many different types of settings. However, when one is interested in a more fine-grained analysis of the behavioral functioning within a smaller set of more similar settings, the phenotype category will be most useful. (p. 165)

The authors believe that phenotype behaviors in behavior settings have the advantage for eco-behavioral science of (a) emphasizing behavioral variability among settings and (b) providing for application of the theory of behavior settings to small, homogeneous groups. This can also, they suggest, be of value to a wide array of social sciences and to more subjective methodologies.

Behavior Episodes. Barker and Wright (1955) found that four was the maximum number of behavior episodes children engaged in at any one time and rarely more than three simultaneously. This also seemed to be true for teachers (Scott, 1977). In a behavior setting called Large Group Activity, the effective teachers' episodes involved the group more as a whole whereas the less effective teachers' episodes were directed more toward individuals or small groups. Just as Barker and Wright found that children behaved more like each other in the same setting than like themselves in different settings, Scott found this equally true of teachers. Differences were least between effective and ineffective teachers in settings where the behavior was more prescribed and greatest in settings that provided greater individual freedom.

Behavior Mapping. Behavior mapping has been combined with eco-behavioral science to provide a valuable methodology. A behavior map is an analogy with an architectural floor plan. The point of occurrence of a predetermined behavior category is checked off on a diagram of a spatial location. On a data sheet of rows and columns where rows represent space and columns represent precategorized behaviors in a behavior setting, a particular behavior would be represented by the intersection of rows and columns. In one example, a mapping of autistic children in a classroom, the settings consisted of work with teachers, free play, time-out, and group work. The behaviors were out-of-seat echololia, self-stimulation, tantrum, appropriate behavior, work, play, and social. The mapping revealed that high rates of behavior occurred in some settings and low in others. As with normal children, the settings seemed to govern the youngsters' behavior (Charlop et al., 1983).

Scaling. Behavior settings can be measured on several scales. An *autonomy scale* measures where decisions are made about who can participate in the setting. A high of nine is assigned if the decision is made locally and a low of one if it is made by the federal government. Bechtel (1982b) extended the rating to twelve to include decisions made within the setting. A *penetration scale* assigns a high of six to a person whose role is so indispensable to the setting that no substitute is possible: for example, someone who has developed a highly innovative medical procedure, a store or business run by one person, or a professor who teaches a unique university course. When a substitute person is available, the rating is five. Level four consists of those whose role is necessary but is not at the highest leadership level. Barker showed that certain groups, such as women and children, were often limited to this level and excluded from the higher ones. Level one is composed of onlookers who contribute nothing but their presence. The penetration level can be used to measure the number of leadership positions available compared with the population—in other words, where those who aspire to such positions should search for the best opportunities. *Welfare ratings* measure the extent to which behavior settings provide benefits to such groups as minorities while *pressure ratings* indicate the way in which rules of the setting exclude them. These and other ratings can be combined to obtain a general richness index. The higher the number, the more types of behaviors and leadership roles available. This collection of information is a "behavior setting survey." Sometimes it is supplemented by questionnaires to determine attitudes, values, and other subjective behaviors.

Behavior Focal Point. Bechtel (1982b) reviewed seven behavior setting surveys and the information from them that led to implementation of better living conditions. A "behavior focal point" emerged from the studies. It is a behavior setting which is most accessible for the longest time to the largest number of elements in the population: "it is a place where the greatest number of residents can meet face to face" (p. 159–160). Community and housing designs were improved by using information from these studies. The methodology is more encompassing than that from research involving a single hypothesis such as characterizes most of psychology and sociology.

Further Research and Applications. In a residence for women with chronic behavior pathologies, Perkins and Perry (1985) identified ninety-three behavior settings involving either those that the staff organized for the residents or those, such as meals and television viewing, that occurred without staff programming. They examined fifty-five of these to determine what demands the settings placed on the women. Settings involving excursions outside the residence were usually more demanding than those in the residence. A determination of such demands, they suggest, could lead to more suitable structuring for either increased or decreased demands. They also suggested that a study of rewarding as well as coercive features of settings could be helpful.

Despite the ready availability of classrooms for observational study, few researchers have studied the naturally occurring classroom setting. Inspired by the work of Barker and others, Jones (1981) found important characteristics of such conditions

as class size, class structure (method of presentation), and spatial organization (arrangement of seats). For example, in classes of under fifteen students, over 70 percent participated regardless of class structure, but that dropped to as little as 10 percent in a large lecture class. More than fifteen or twenty pupils was not effective for group discussion. Similarly, seating in a circle was awkward and ineffective beyond twenty.

Using the methods of Barker and Wright, Scott (1977) found that effective teachers in preschool programs for disadvantaged children engaged in fewer and longer lasting behavior episodes than did less effective teachers. Their activity was more directed and holistic and was sustained toward a goal. They also more often attained those goals. Their affective behavior also differed: they showed more positive and less negative feelings than less effective teachers, evincing warmth, acceptance, helpfulness, and cheerfulness as opposed to anger, impatience, and rejection.

It is unlikely that anyone will ever again study all the public behavior settings of a complete community such as Barker and associates did with Midwest and Yoredale. Such studies require long-term funding that is now difficult to obtain, and the funding agencies prefer information from urban and suburban areas where most people now live to studies of small towns. As a result, studies have turned toward more specialized or restricted domains.

In what might be the last of the broad domain studies, behavior setting theory provided the means of a comparison of behavior settings in six towns before and after the introduction of a major dam project that flooded a large area (Harloff, Gump, & Campbell, 1981). The greatest change was in the government settings, particularly in the town that is the county seat. Hours of operation of government behavior settings increased by 44 percent while private enterprise settings increased their hours by only 4 percent. Some of the towns showed marked changes during the years of the survey, but in most cases little of it was due to the dam.

Streamlining and Self-Reports

The study of Midwest resulted in 230 data entries for each of more than 800 settings. That amounts to more than 184,000 data entries for that small town. A factor analysis of these data showed that 43 descriptors could be reduced to 9 and still account for 62 percent of the variance (Price & Blashfield, 1975). Others have shortened the survey period and taken other shortcuts. These abbreviated data collection methods should expedite the research on behavior settings.

In a study (a) on the ward, (b) in public areas of the hospital, and (c) in physical therapy of the behavior of individuals with spinal cord injuries, trained observers recorded their behaviors in these three situations. The individuals also provided self-reports of their own behaviors (Norris-Baker, Stephens, and Willems, 1982). The behaviors varied from situation to situation, but the self-reports corresponded well with the observations of the independent observers. The accuracy of these self-reports prompted the authors to suggest that this method could be a cost-efficient means of obtaining large amounts of high quality data "about the patterns of individuals' everyday behavior in various environments, even when the users are mobile" (p. 440).

Intervention

One of Barker's major premises was that the investigator should not interfere in any way with the setting. The investigator should be a transducer, not an operator. Wicker (1979a) argues, however, that intervention is a procedure for learning about how certain changes can improve the well-being of participants, which cannot be discovered in any other way. He found that posts and chains facilitated bus boarding where large numbers of people were involved and that informational signs and silent movies reduced perceived waiting time at a hospital emergency facility. But because of ongoing changes in any situation which can render the experimental results unclear, he urges caution in running intervention experiments. The investigator needs to examine a great many conditions before embarking on the experiment. And then, only those changes that might be relatively permanent if advantageous should be investigated, he cautions.

APPLICATIONS

Most of the pioneering work in eco-behavioral science has been *basic* science rather than *applied* science. Even so, much of it has considerable applicability—for instance, what was learned about the value of small schools and the potential this has for formulating policy about school consolidation. The understanding of control circuits and other factors in settings can be used to restructure the settings in hospitals and other institutions for the betterment of those who work or reside there. Some of the conditions that contribute to the advantages of small settings can be tried in large settings. Increasingly, researchers using this approach have undertaken applied research, sometimes using intrusive measures, to determine what arrangements lead to more pleasant or more efficient operations of bus boarding lines, emergency waiting rooms, and other settings; and behavior setting surveys have been used to improve living conditions. Eco-behavioral science helped paved the way for such disciplines as environmental psychology (chapter 13, p. 376) and community psychology, (chapter 13, p. 370) and contributes to them.

RELATION TO SOME OTHER APPROACHES

Behavior Analysis

After a review of the literature on the influence of behavior settings, Willems (1973a, 1973b) finds himself agreeing with the behavior analysts that the environment selects behaviors. In common with them, he finds that to a large extent the environmental setting controls the behavior occurring in it and that changes in the environment modify behaviors. Winett (1987) notes that he differs with the behavior analysts in that they deal largely with discrete behavior of individuals and engage in experimental research, whereas eco-behavioral science emphasizes the setting level and uses descriptive research. He suggests that the two might be fruitfully combined.

Interbehavioral Psychology

The inclusion of inanimate objects as part of the behavior setting is in agreement with interbehavioral psychology but does not consider the distinction between these objects as objects and the objects as meanings—what the interbehaviorists refers to as stimulus object and stimulus functions, respectively (see Fuhrer below). These and other components of the interbehavioral field might add fruitful dimensions to the eco-behavioral approach. Barker's formula of B = f(E) is highly mechanistic, but some of his followers have considered the interdependence of variables and thereby moved the system in the direction of the interbehavioral emphasis on relationships and away from linear cause and effect.

Operant Subjectivity

The finding that self-report provides accurate accounts of behaviors in varying environments (Norris-Baker, Stephens, Willems, 1982) suggests that the researcher could also use the subjects for more subjective information that is equally objective. Q sorts by the participants in various behavior settings could provide an entirely new range of understanding of these settings. Both the philosophy and methodology of Q sorting seem entirely compatible with eco-behavioral science, although the determination of subjective factors would add a dimension that Barker seemed to prefer to minimize or avoid.

CRITIQUE

Fuhrer (1990) argues for a "gap" between the objective events of the behavior setting and the "per-

son's subjective representation of themselves, their environments, and their behaviors" (p. 520). He sees Lewin's psychology of "life space" (1951) as providing the mentalistic view and avoiding the "empty organism." Fuhrer is arguing for a psychophysical dualism involving a mind or "subjective representation" on the one hand and "behaviors" on the other, an assumption that is inconsistent with eco-behavioral science (see postulates above). But what Fuhrer is expressing dualistically may be expressed without such an assumption: subjective factors—or the objective point of view of the participant rather than that of the observer—have been neglected. The neglect of subjectivity is characteristic of most areas of psychology. As indicted above, Q methodology, which provides an objective measure of subjectivity and assumes no mind-body dualism, could be employed to address this neglect.

Fuhrer emphasizes the distinction between the physical properties of an object and its functional properties and credits Boesch (1980) with this distinction. (This overlooks Dewey's [1896] early recognition of it [see chapter 2], Kantor's thorough development of this distinction in the 1920s [see chapter 10], and Merleau-Ponty's independent recognition of it in the 1960s [see chapter 12].) For example, the functional meaning of a restaurant as a behavior setting differs depending on whether one is with a colleague or a family member. The physical restaurant is the same but its functional characteristics or its meanings change. These variations, he argues, indicate that "behavior settings as *cultural settings* do not simply uniform or homogenize people; they rather set trends from which, in some cases, it allows and in others it even encourages deviation" (p. 533). While Fuhrer's analysis seems useful, these deviations appear to be mostly within the same general overt behavior patterns of the setting—such as those of a restaurant and its physical properties—that Barker indicates. However, the different meanings of the restaurant comprise *covert* and individual behaviors that are important to recognize and to try to understand, perhaps by such Q-sort methodology.

Perkins (1988) maintains that the stable as well as the unstable elements of a behavior setting are important—as, for example, the changes people institute in a behavior setting as an adjustment to changing circumstances: the display area for particular merchandise in a store may be enlarged or reduced as demand changes. In this view, settings are tools that individuals manipulate to meet their needs. They learn to apply deviation countering, vetoes, and fixed boundaries in order to do this.

One criticism of eco-behavioral science is that it neglects individual differences while concentrating on the setting of which they are merely components. It also neglects subjective behaviors. Bechtel (1982b) addresses this by pointing out that individuals can be studied by surveying the types of behavior settings that a child or an elderly person enters during a year, thereby learning much about the life-styles of the individual. Other procedures such as self-reports and Q sorts have considerable potential for providing information about the individual's subjective behavior and its role in the functioning of the setting, but these have been little used. What attitudinal and perceptual behaviors bring individuals to participate in, leave, or modify settings? What roles do interpersonal feelings play, and how do personality conflicts get resolved or become destructive to the setting? What meanings do the settings have for the participants, and what groupings of various meanings and likes and dislikes might be present for the participants (a question that Q method is specifically designed to answer)?

Although eco-behavioral science has been charged with extreme determinism, a behavior setting can influence people's behaviors only as long as it remains satisfying to them. They will participate in the setting patterns and thereby foster its goals only if its goals support their ends. People will abandon the setting when it is no longer satisfying, and it will go out of existence (Wicker, 1979b). This suggests a mutuality rather than a unidirectional determinism. Nevertheless, the system retains a strong element of envirocentrism.

CONCLUSIONS

Eco-behavioral science has broken rank with conventional research methodologies in psychology, and perhaps for that reason has received only fleeting attention. Yet it has revealed important factors about behavior that those conventional procedures could never have uncovered and has done so in natural situations that obviate the question that laboratory studies raise—whether the laboratory results will generalize to the natural world. And rather than using psychiatric patients or conveniently available college students as subjects, it has gone to the real world of ordinary communities with their ordinary activities that occur naturally in all their complexity and diversity. Like any good scientific enterprise, its concepts and methods need continuing refinement and extension; but it has already been one of the most fruitful systems in providing reliable understanding about some important aspects of psychological behavior. It has also been an inspiration in the development of community psychology and environmental psychology (see chapter 13).

REFERENCES

Baird, Leonard L. 1969. Big school, small school: A critical examination of the hypothesis. *Journal of Educational Psychology* 60: 253–60.

Barker, Roger G. 1963a. *Ecological Psychology: Concepts and Methods for Studying the Environment of Human Behavior.* Stanford, CA: Stanford University Press.

———.1963b. On the nature of the environment. *Journal of Social Issues* 19 (4): 17–38.

———.1969. Wanted: An eco-behavioral science. In *Naturalistic Viewpoints in Psychological Research.* Edited by Edwin P. Willems & Harold Rausch. New York: Holt, Rinehart, & Winston.

———.1978. Stream of individual behavior. In *Habitats, Environments, and Human Behavior: Studies in Ecological Psychology and Eco-Behavioral Science from the Midwest Psychological Field Station, 1947–1972, Roger G. Barker and Associates.* San Francisco: Jossey-Bass.

———.1979. Settings of a professional lifetime. *Personality and Social Psychology* 37: 2137–57.

———.1987. Prospecting in environmental psychology: Oskaloosa revisited. In *Handbook of Environmental Psychology,* vol. 2. Edited by Daniel Stokols & Irwin Altman. New York: Wiley.

————.1990. Recollections of the Midwest psychological field station. *Environment and Behavior* 22: 503–513.

Barker, Roger G.; Tamara Dembo; & Kurt Lewin. 1941. Frustration and regression: A study of young children. *University of Iowa Studies in Child Welfare* no. 18: Iowa City.

Barker, Roger G., & Paul V. Gump, eds. 1964. *Big School, Small School: High School Size and Student Behavior.* Stanford, CA: Stanford University Press.

Barker, Roger G., & Phil Schoggen. 1973. *Qualities of Community Life.* San Francisco: Jossey-Bass.

Barker, Roger G., & Herbert F. Wright. 1955. *The Midwest and its Children: The Psychological Ecology of an American Town.* New York: Harper & Row.

Bechtel, Robert B. 1981. Classification of behavior settings. *EDRA Environmental Design Research Association* 12: 101–109.

————.1982a. Classification of behavior settings II. *EDRA Environmental Design Research Association* 13: 112–16.

————.1982b. Contributions of ecological psychology to the evaluation of environments. *International Review of Applied Psychology* 31: 153–67.

Boesch, E. 1980. *Kultur und Handlung.* Bern, Switzerland: Huber.

Charlop, Marjorie H.; Laura Schreibman; Jeanne Mason; & Wade Vesey. 1983. Behavior–setting interactions of autistic children: A behavioral mapping approach to assessing classroom children. *Analysis and Intervention in Developmental Disabilities* 3: 359–73.

Dewey, John. 1896. The reflex arc concept in psychology. *Psychological Review* 31: 357–70.

Fawl, C. L. 1978. Disturbances children experience in their natural habitat. In *Habitats, Environments, and Human Behavior.* Edited by Roger G. Barker & Associates. San Francisco: Jossey-Bass.

Fox, Karl A. 1989. Behavior settings and social systems accounting. In *Behavior Settings: A Revision and Extension of Roger C. Barker's Ecological Psychology.* Edited by Phil Schoggen. Stanford, CA: Stanford University Press.

Fuhrer, Urs. 1987. Effects of social density and preknowledge on question asking in a novel setting. *Journal of Environmental Psychology* 7: 159–68.

————.1988. Learning how to act in behavior settings: The case of newcomers. In *Looking Back to the Future.* Edited by N. L. Park, T. van der Voordt, & H. van Wegen. Delft, Netherlands: Delft University.

————.1990. Bridging the ecological-psychological gap: Behavior settings as interfaces. *Environment and Behavior* 22: 518–37.

Gump, Paul V. 1978. Big schools, small schools. In *Habitats, Environments, and Human Behavior: Studies in Ecological Psychology and Eco-Behavioral Science from the Midwest Psychological Field Station, 1947–1972, Roger G. Barker and Associates.* San Francisco: Jossey-Bass.

Haller, Emil J. 1992. High school size and student indiscipline; Another aspect of the school consolidation issue. *Educational Evaluation and Policy Analysis* 14: 145–56.

Haller, Emil J., & David H. Monk. 1988. New reforms, old reforms, and the consolidation of small rural schools. *Educational Administration Quarterly* 24: 470–483.

Haller, Emil J.; David H. Monk; Alyce Spotted Bear; Julie Griffith; & Pamela Moss. (1990). School size and program comprehensiveness: Evidence from high school and beyond. *Educational Evaluation and Policy Analysis* 12: 109–120.

Hanks, Michael P., & Bruce K. Eckland. 1976. Athletics and social participation in the educational attainment process. *Sociology of Education* 49: 271–94.

Harloff, Hans J.; Paul V. Gump; & David E. Campbell. 1981. The public life of communities: Environmental change as a result of the intrusion of a flood control, conservation, and recreational reservoir. *Environment and Behavior* 13: 685–706.

Indik, B. P. 1965. Organization size and member participation: Some empirical tests of alternative explanations. *Human Relations* 18: 339–50.

James, William. 1890. *The Principles of Psychology,* vol. 1. New York: Holt.

Jones, Elizabeth. 1981. Teacher education in action: Student and instructor in adult learning environments. *Advances in Early Education and Day Care* 2: 91–127.

Lewin, Kurt. 1951. *Field Theory in Social Science: Selected Theoretical Papers.* Edited by Dorwin Cartwright. New York: Harper.

Luke, Douglas A.; Julian Rappaport; Edward Seidman. 1991. Setting phenotypes in a mutual help organization: Expanding behavior setting theory. *American Journal of Community Psychology* 19: 147–67.

Monk, David H. 1987. Secondary school size and curriculum comprehensiveness. *Economics of Education Review* 6: 137–50.

Monk, David, & Emil J. Haller. 1986. *Organizational Alternatives for Small Rural Schools: Final Report to the New York State Legislature.* Ithaca, NY: Department of Education, New York State College of Agriculture and Life Sciences at Cornell University.

————.1993. Predictors of high school academic course offerings: The role of school size. *American Educational Research Journal* 30: 3–21.

Norris-Baker, Carolyn; Mary Ann P. Stephens; Edwin P. Willems. (1982). Behavior varies by environment;

quality of data does not. *Environment and Behavior* 14: 425–42.

O'Donnell, C. 1980. Environmental design and the prevention of psychological problems. In *Psychological Problems: The Social Context.* Edited by P. Feldman & J. Orford. New York: Wiley.

Otto, L. B. 1975. Extracurricular activities in the educational attainment process. *Rural Sociology* 40: 162–76.

Perkins, David V. 1982. Individual differences and task structure in the performance of a behavior setting: An experimental evaluation of Barker's manning theory. *American Journal of Community Psychology* 10: 617–33.

———.1988. Alternative views of behavior settings: A response to Schoggen. *Journal of Community Psychology* 16: 387–91.

Perkins, David V., & Jonathan C. Perry. 1985. Dimensional analysis of behavior setting demands in a community residence for chronically mentally ill women. *Journal of Community Psychology* 13: 350–59.

Price, Richard H., & R. K. Blashfield. 1975. Explorations in the taxonomy of behavior settings: Analysis of dimensions and classifications of settings. *American Journal of Community Psychology* 3: 335–51.

Saegert, S. 1988. The androgynous city: From critique to practice. In *Women, Housing, and Community.* Edited by W. van Vliet. Brookfield, VT: Avebury.

Schneider, Susan M. 1990. Wasps' nests and wolf packs: A note on extending behavior setting theory to non-human groups. *Journal of Environmental Psychology* 10: 371–76.

Schoggen, Phil. 1963. Environmental forces in the everyday lives of children. In *The Stream of Behavior.* Edited by Roger C. Barker. New York: Appleton-Century-Crofts.

———.1989. *Behavior Settings: A Revision and Extension of Roger C. Barker's Ecological Psychology.* Stanford, CA: Stanford University Press.

Schoggen, Phil, & Maxine Schoggen. 1988. Student voluntary participation and high school size. *Journal of Educational Research* 81: 288–93.

Scott, Myrtle. 1977. Some parameters of teacher effectiveness as assessed by an ecological approach. *Journal of Educational Psychology* 69: 217–26.

Spady, William G. 1970. Lament for the letterman: Effects of peer status and extracurricular activities on goals and achievement. *American Journal of Sociology* 75: 680–702.

Stokols, Daniel, & Sally Ann Shumaker. 1981. People in places: A transactional view of settings. In *Cognition, Social Behavior, and the Environment.* Edited by John H. Harvey. Hillside, NJ: Erlbaum.

Wicker, Allan W. 1969. Size of church membership and members' support of church behavior settings. *Journal of Personal and Social Psychology* 13: 278–88.

———.1979a. Ecological psychology: Some recent and prospective developments. *American Psychologist* 34: 755–65.

———.1979b. *An Introduction to Ecological Psychology.* Monterey, CA: Brooks/Cole.

———.1990. The Midwest psychological field station: Some reflections of one participant. *Environment and Behavior* 22: 491–98.

Wicker, Allan W., & Sandra Kirmeyer. 1976. From church to laboratory to national park: A program of research on excess and insufficient populations in behavior settings. In *Experiencing the Environment.* Edited by Seymour Wapner, Saul B. Cohen, & Bernard Kaplan. New York: Plenum.

Wicker, Allen W.; Sandra L. Kirmeyer; Lois Hanson; & Dean Alexander. 1976. Effects of manning levels on subjective experiences, performance, and verbal interaction in groups. *Organizational Behavior and Human Performance* 17: 251–74.

Wicker, Allan W.; Joseph E. McGrath; and George F. Armstrong. 1972. Organization size and behavior setting capacity as determinants of member participation. *Behavioral Science* 17: 510.

Willems, Edwin P. 1964. Forces toward participating in behavior settings. In *Big School, Small School: High School Size and Student Behavior.* Edited by Roger B. Barker & Paul V. Gump. Stanford, CA: Stanford University Press.

———.1967. Sense of obligation to high school activities as related to school size and marginality of student. *Child Development* 38: 1247–60.

———.1972. The interface of the hospital environment and patient behavior. *Archives of Physical Medicine and Rehabilitation* 53: 115–22.

———.1973a. Behavior-environment systems: An ecological approach. *Man-Environment Systems* 3: 79–110.

———.1973b. Behavioral ecology and experimental analysis: Courtship is not enough. In *Life-Span Developmental Psychology: Methodological Issues.* Edited by J. R. Nesselroade & H. W. Reese. New York: Academic Press.

———.1990. Inside Midwest and its field station. The Barker effect. *Environment and Behavior* 22: 468–91.

Winett, Richard A. 1987. Empiricist–positivist theories of environment and behavior: New directions for multi-level frameworks. In *Advances in Environment, Behavior, and Design,* vol. 1. Edited by Ervin H. Zube & Gary T. Moore. New York: Plenum.

Sociocentric Systems

CHAPTER 8

Postmodernism and Social Constructionism: Science and Mythology as Equally Valid, Truth Being Totally Relative

Chapter Outline

INTRODUCTION

The term "postmodernism" may sound strange when we first hear it. After all, isn't this the modern age? Isn't any period up to now the most modern? How can anything be after the modern period when the modern period is still ongoing? Yet "postmodernism" is a term coined to indicate a total revolution in thinking about literary, philosophical, and scientific matters. Postmodernism rejects the heritage of "modern" thinking, which it defines as beginning with the Age of Enlightenment in the eighteenth century. It claims that that modern period is now coming to an end and we are entering the postmodern period. Modernism put humans at the center of importance and holds them to be rational creatures who can use their rational capabilities to acquire knowledge and provide progress for humanity. Postmodernism challenges these contentions of modernism. When the approach is applied to psychology, the term "social constructionism" appears and refers to knowledge constructed by a particular social group with no generality beyond that social group. Some writers in psychology retain the term "postmodernism" or use it interchangeably with "social constructionism."

In brief, postmodernism and social constructionism hold that it is impossible to find objective understanding of the world because all knowledge is socially constructed in words that gain their meanings through social processes, and these meanings vary from group to group and from time to time. Knowledge consists of no more than social agreements in the form of language. Our reality consists of the words with which we describe that reality. We are inextricably embedded in cultural meanings, and these cultural or "local" meanings are all we can ever know. Truth is whatever is coherent, and error is simply disagreement, for each party is right from its own point of view. Postmodernism, according to Kvale (1990), is not so much a systematic theory as it is an interpretation of the present culture.

DEVELOPMENT AND ISSUES

Postmodernism

The term "postmodernism" (sometimes known as po-mo or pomo) first appeared in the 1960s in connection with literary criticism and then spread into architecture, dance, theater, painting, film, music, and finally to the wider culture (R. Brown, 1994). French philosophers such as Jacques Derrida and Michel Foucault were the prime movers of this system. Derrida (1992, 1997) held that language cannot give true expression to anything, including the world. Reality resides only in texts (language), but texts are unstable and self-contradictory. Philosophy, too, consists only of writing. It refers not to mental representations nor to logic nor to evidence but to other writings. Philosophy's search for referents or anchors in the world, Derrida insisted, has been futile—for the only reality is fictional. Reality is whatever is found in a particular pattern of words; this changes for each reader and thereby the reality changes. By means of interpretations from several different readers a story will appear that is a product of these interpreters, not of the author's meaning. Meaning comes from the development of the ever changing present and its context. Because there is no final meaning the only indication of reality is the plausibility of the story or its interest for a particular culture at a particular time. In contradiction, however, Derrida maintained that his own texts had determinate meanings that he could understand.

Derrida also developed what he called "deconstructionism." The term is a combination of *construction* and *destruction* and means that the obsolete is destroyed and replaced with the new. It is a process of undermining a text to demonstrate that its coherence is a result of particular ways of using language and of cultural patterns such as those that have neglected women and nonwhite people while favoring white males. Deconstruction, then, is bringing attention to what has been omitted and made imperceptible. This process causes an undoing or collapse of the text. When applied to scientific writings it can be used to show the historical and social influences that gave rise to a scientific construction and demonstrate that objectivity does not exist. The thrust of this procedure, according to Richter (1992), is more toward destruction than construction.

Foucault (1980) too doubted that language carried any truth. He argued that language determines what we think; and, therefore, thoughts cannot reflect the world. Language receives its form from the power sources in the culture from which it structures our lives. A third French philosopher, Jean-Francois Lyotard, brought the system to the physical sciences by arguing that scientific language is a game in which the richest player has the greatest chance of being right. That is, science becomes a means of domination through its claims. Like Lyotard, Foucault referred to such power influences, especially those of politics and bureaucracy. These powers influence scientific decisions and interpretations and thereby render science less than neutral. Scientific claims attain legitimacy for those who are powerful and serve their personal and social interests, for science is a product of the power sources that feed it. Consistent with the position that sciences are only power tools and have no legitimacy and no claim to truth, postmodernism recognizes that it cannot establish its own legitimacy but is only a pragmatic approach.

Recent literary theory (Eagleton, 1983; Fish, 1980) has also influenced the development of postmodernism and social constructionism. Contrary to a long tradition in which a writing was held to contain information or expressions of an author, the "new criticism" holds that an author has no authority over what he or she intends to convey. Instead, the meaning to the reader is central, and the reader creates what the text means. Each reader reconstructs the text with each reading. Consequently, the text has no single meaning and no enduring meaning.

While deconstruction and literary theory deal primarily with literary texts, postmodernism, as

with Derrida and Foucault, challenges philosophic and scientific claims to objective knowledge. Rorty (1979) follows this line of thinking. He is another philosopher who notes that philosophy (and, we could add, much of psychology) has assumed that mental representations of the world or mental processes make knowledge possible. He calls this viewpoint "mind as a mirror," a mind reflecting the external world. The entirety of Western assumptions about knowledge rests on this metaphor, he holds. As a counter, he argues that we can justify knowing only as a social process involving language, not as a relation between a knowing subject and reality. "We understand knowledge when we understand the social justification of belief, and thus have no need to view it as accuracy of representation" (p. 170). Philosophy's attempt to demonstrate objectivity and rationality as accurate representations of the world, he maintains, is an exercise in self-deception; for the presumed objectivity and rationality consist of nothing more than current discourses or conversations. And these discourses have meanings only within a social context. Mind as mirror also makes possible the separation between philosophy's study of mental events as a source of knowledge and science's study of physical events as a source of knowledge. Philosophy claims to examine the representation and science the object represented. Postmodernism moves away from the conventional search for objectivity or reality outside of any linguistic system and attends to social discourses, the language systems within which we have local agreement about the world.

Because logic and evidence are no longer the basis of knowledge, communication is freed to replace these pillars of Western culture. Communication is democratic, for all can engage in communicating their opinions and beliefs and be informed by others' communications. Knowledge is no longer confined to an elite who use logic and evidence. Postmodernists discard elitists' expertise and authority and become their own experts and authorities. Inasmuch as knowledge belongs to no special group or person, anyone can be a teacher of any subject and teach that subject to anyone else. No one can be a teacher of universal knowledge or truth, for they do not exist. And because there are no final truths, no disagreements are possible: each individual has his or her own truth within a particular social context or "discourse community." Postmoderns, however, engage in a "believing game" in which they surmise a speaker's sincerity before deciding on how much of his or her claims to accept.

Postmodernism challenges not only the assumption that reality can be known apart from the verbal descriptions of it but also the assumption of an individual knower or subjective self apart from a discourse community. The knower merges with the known. Selves, it contends, are social constructions whose experiences are inseparable from social interactions. In fact, people have multitudes of selves, each of which functions in its own way to meet particular social conditions. Because the world and selves are social constructions, human living consists of play. Play replaces the notion of a knowable real world. One can play with one's sense of self. The postmodernist life accepts or even exhilarates in the way things appear in their social context and recognizes what they are not. Some advocates even suggest that postmodernism can provide a solution for society's problems. Yet, contrariwise, postmodernism rejects the notion of human progress. A solution to this inconsistency would consist of a pattern of words that have meanings only as part of local social interactions.

Science, in the postmodernist view, is a set of complex cultural conventions that Western culture has developed in one particular period. Therefore science is not, as we usually assume, an aggregate of knowledge and of methodologies for testing conjectures and theories about nature, but only a discourse or discussion created by one interpretive community as part of a complex of politics, economics, and social context. As with any social group, because the claims to knowledge have their roots in the standards of that group, they have no warrant beyond it. Consequently, science's claim to know the world is only a social convention; its claim to truth is no more valid

than the assertions of soothsayers. As a device for finding presumed truth, scientific methodology is meaningful only within the convention of the scientific social group that gives the methodology its meaning.

According to postmodernism, scientists are the cause of the many ills of society; and education is their handmaiden. Education from primary school to university has taken its form from the Enlightenment and needs replacement. As a counter to the evils of science and education, literature, pseudoscience, and antiscience form the vanguard of postmodern culture, with literature presiding over all.

Postmodernism emphasizes interactions in localized contexts. It sees the subjective individual and objective universal laws as abstractions of human rootedness in the world. What is meaningful and what is truth are matters of decisions and the consequences of those decisions, which people share. Postmodernism replaces universal systems of knowledge with local knowledge and universal meanings with local meanings. Such polar opposites as universal and individual or objective and subjective give way to local context (Kvale, 1990).

Following upon the work of Derrida, Foucault, and Rorty, language plays an important role in postmodernism. Language does not reflect reality, but each language in each local situation provides its own reality. The individual self as speaker gives way to the speaker as a medium. The culture expresses itself through the speaker, who functions as a medium (Kvale, 1990). Therefore language decentralizes the person. Language is not the transmission of information, but a narrative about the culture, a story in which the storyteller and the listener mutually establish their place in the social order. The function of the narrative is to maintain the values and social order of the community of which the participants in the use of language are a part. With the abandonment of the pursuit of universal truth or meaning and an emphasis on communication, the culture finds a new role for the narrator. The narrator is not merely transmitting information to the listener; the two are redefining their positions in the social order.

Much of psychology has attempted to find universal laws; but one system, humanistic psychology (chapter 4), has pursued what Kvale (1990) calls the "cult of individuality" in its emphasis on the self: self-determination, self-actualization, and so forth. Both humanism and behaviorism have removed humans from their context, he argues; this decontextualization occurs both with subjects in experiments and patients in psychotherapy. Kvale finds a double abstraction in modern psychology in that both the person and the person's behavior are decontextualized. He notes that the attempt to quantify all psychological events and the assumption of the uniqueness of the individual gives way in postmodernism to removal of individuals or selves from the center stage they held under behavioristic, humanistic, and cognitive versions of modernism, and situating them as part of language and contextual relationships.

Kvale views modern psychology as misdirected and "out of touch with the social reality of a postmodern age" (p. 50). It is in "intellectual stagnation" as a science and subsists parasitically by attaching itself to neurology, computer science, genetics, linguistics, and the like. Further, "If the psychological constitution of an encapsulated individual self, with an inner psychic apparatus, and the double abstraction of human activity from its context and content, are intellectual dead ends, then psychology as a science of human activity may be beyond repair" (p. 50). But postmodernism has made some inroads. He points to phenomenology (chapter 12), ecology (chapter 7), and role psychology as having an affinity with postmodernism and notes a few other postmodernist developments: social psychology has taken up the issue of power as it involves social meanings, of personal identities as social constructions, and of the use of narratives in the social sciences where a narrative is accepted or rejected on the basis of its coherence—how meaningfully it tells the story. In applied areas, family therapy defines the family social unit as a language system with the therapist serving as a leader of conversation. Pathology now resides in the structure of language rather than in the conscious or unconscious mind.

He holds that research using qualitative analysis can be a central methodology for psychology: it can tap the world of intersubjective meaning. Such qualitative studies represent a linguistic turn in the philosophy of science. A conversation between persons replaces the modernist psychologist's confrontation with nature. Negotiated meaning replaces a search for objective reality.

Social Constructionism

General Assumptions. Although one can find a variety of types of social constructionism, except where otherwise indicated the reference here is to *strict* or *radical* constructionism as exemplified by the work of Kenneth Gergen. The following are some major assumptions set forth by Gergen (1994b), a major architect of strict constructionism:

■ Whatever is, has no requirements for how it is expressed.

■ Relationships among people who are culturally and historically situated determine the forms of expressions by which they understand the world. Neither the world not genetic determinants within individuals produces descriptions or constructions of the world. Such constructions are a result of social interactions. Knowledge is not an individual possession but a byproduct of communal relations.

■ The extent to which any particular account of the world endures over a period of time is a matter of social process, not of any objective validity. An account may continue while the world changes or it may change while the world remains constant. Although scientific methodologies have sustained beliefs that later changed, such methodologies remain relevant to scientific description. Within scientific communities empirical methods relate to truth claims. These communities test theories and accept conclusions from instruments, statistics, and other techniques that are accepted by the community. Their "rituals" can lead to predictions. But the scientific method does not have a "context-free warrant" to claim greater truth than other methods or descriptions.

■ The importance of language arises from its role in patterns of relationships. Language is not a mirror or map of the world, not a referential event or an internal process, but a social interchange. Language is not ideas in people's heads but infinite arrays of signifiers that have no single meaning or signification. Intelligibility comes from repeated patterns of words, and words gain their meaning from contexts of relationships.

■ A social community may evaluate, validate, and invalidate assertions within that community but cannot do so in another. Scientists may evaluate scientists but not cultists and vice-versa. Any evaluation is an evaluation of the culture of which the value is a part. If evaluation by an exterior group can be meaningfully communicated to the group being evaluated, "relational boundaries are softened" (p. 54).

Truth Claims. Constructionists (for example, Gergen, 1985, 1994b) insist that claims about truth are really claims about whether a conclusion is warranted or justified in the sense that others would accept the same group of words about it. (They avoid such terms as verify, demonstrate, show, prove, confirm, corroborate, determine.) They argue that no theory of knowledge can warrant its own truth either with evidence or logic, for to do so would involve circularity: A justifies B and B justifies A. Or, if B is used to justify A, one could use C to justify B; but then we would need D to justify C, and this would go on infinitely. On the other hand, if an empirical approach uses logic or a logical approach uses empirical data to validate its own claims, it thereby subverts its own position. Only "communal convention" is relevant, the constructionists insist. The constructionists also note that all interpretations of observations and empirical data vary from one social group to another and from culture to culture, and even the claims to inherent cognitive knowledge depend on empirical methods. Consequently, there is no way of establishing any *foundation*. All inter-

pretations and all logical arguments depend on the particular social group in which the interpretations are developed and have no coherency or intelligibility beyond it. Because we socially construct things, observation itself is inseparable from these constructions. No scientific foundation of knowledge is possible.

Constructionism makes no denial or affirmation about the world or what is out there or in here. Social constructionism is itself socially constructed and offers its position as a form of intelligibility. Constructionism cannot establish itself as a system with any superiority over other views of knowledge, nor does it seek to replace any of its competitors. It asks only what advantages and disadvantages obtain for each. It does not ask for decisions of truth or error but invites others "to play with the possibilities and the practices coherent with this intelligibility, and to evaluate them against alternatives" (Gergen, 1994b, p. 79). Similarly, it offers no position on moral values but is open to exploration in science and other areas. While it approaches moral and ethical issues as completely relative to a social context, it does not provide a platform from which to observe other positions; for all are interdependent with culture and history, and one cannot judge another. Morality gains its meaning from "cultural intelligibility." It is "a form of communal participation" (p. 103) in a specific community.

Because all facts, all information, all procedures, all intelligibility are social, one cannot test or falsify a theory against a real world. Nevertheless, Gergen's (1994b) position on the human sciences is that with agreements in labeling and consistent patterns of behavior, these sciences can provide useful procedures, information, and programs for the culture of which "theoretical intelligibility" is the most important.

Language. Constructionists hold that all claims to truth are established in the social conventions of language. Because these conventions change from group to group and because language can never be definitive but always has differing meaning across groups and across time, it cannot be used to carry truths about the world. Consequently, it is impossible to test hypotheses, impossible to determine any fundamental truths about the world, for these too are structured in language. In addition to the barriers of differing group meanings, the investigator can always invoke more general assumptions about the context of the hypothesis so that one utterance or another can never establish its validity or its falseness (Stam, 1990).

Although language is not a vehicle for truth or rational thought, it does provide a means of shared understanding; and these understandings depend on social usage. From narrative accounts the participants construct their versions of reality. Scientific writing is one version of reality but has no more claim to accuracy than does fiction. What we call knowledge is what we agree on socially as presented in language. Our knowledge, our realities are comprised of the words that we arrange to describe them. Myths, folklore, science, and the occult are all social conventions that have their foundation in historical and cultural conventions of language. Language, not individual minds or cognitions, provides a way for us to structure the world in accordance with the usages of a particular social group and its context (Gergen, 1994b).

Constructs of Mainstream Psychology. Gergen (1994b) notes that it is difficult to find a referent for such constructs as private experience, awareness, and consciousness; but by asking how the words have been used, what the kinds of discussion of them signify, and what kinds of social discourse comprise them, we can de-objectify these constructs and question whether they represent any reality. In so doing we are using psychological discourse as a means of engaging in social relationships rather than of seeking a reflection of reality. Harré (1986a) maintains that emotions do not exist as things or traits inside people but are socially constructed in substantive form relatively recently. And according to Haley (1963) the notion of getting in touch with our feelings, working through emotions, getting it off our chests, and avoiding holding in emotions is folklore psychology.

Most constructionists have been critical of the construct "mind" and of brain as its surrogate. For Coulter (1989), mind or subjectivity is an interaction. Its attributes such as character and experience are cultural derivatives. He finds that the anthropomorphic characteristics attributed to brain make little sense, such as the claim that one's brain rather than oneself is thirsty. "It is at best a poor joke to propose that it is my brain that requires a glass of water to assuage its thirst" (p. 123). Visual experiences, he contends, are not in the brain or anywhere else, although the brain may facilitate them. The objects of experience such as a sunset have locations but the experiences themselves do not. To claim that we *have* experiences is not necessarily to claim possession and consequently a location. To have money may indicate a location but to have an objection does not. Similarly, to have a visual experience does not indicate location. All that is assumed to be a product of an interior mind or of the brain is a matter of daily interactions.

Gergen (1994b) points out the return of mentalism as cognitivism and outlines the numerous conundrums that ensue with constructs of representations, mental maps, and others. He notes that mental terms are used to define other mental terms. He advocates moving mind out of the head and into the realm of social discourse. Scarr (1985), in contrast, advances a constructionist position that is heavily mentalistic/cognitivistic: "Knowledge of all kinds, including scientific knowledge, is a construction of the human mind. Sensory data are filtered through the knowing apparatus of the human senses and made into perceptions and cognitions. The human mind is also constructed in a social context" (p. 499).

Her last sentence reverts mind back to social constructions, but she seems to give preeminence to mental constructions. Harré (1987) converts mind to conversations that organize around social standards of duties, expectations, and moral relations. That is, conversations construct minds, and therefore minds have no independent existence.

Offenses of Mainstream Psychology. Gergen (1997) lists a number of offenses of which social constructionists hold psychology guilty. These include undermining democracy and community, supporting an ideology of individuality, upholding the system of patriarchy, advancing narcissim, and assisting western colonialism. Because of psychology's attempts at objectivity, he contends, it stifles alternative views and thereby joins with totalitarianism. Its belief in the truth of its method keeps it apart from a dialogue with alternative approaches. Gergen has no objections to conventional psychological research, however, so long as it does not claim any truth beyond the language of the community of researchers. Wexler (1987) accuses psychology of supporting corporate liberal capitalism in which managers and workers have collaborated but proposes that social discourse can help us understand how history produces both culture and human characteristics. Along similar lines, Gergen (1997) believes that the constructionist can add considerable strength to psychological inquiry.

As an example of the shortcomings of decontextualized psychology, Cushman (1991) performs a constructionist critique on Daniel Stern's (1985) book on infant development. Some of the points of Cushman's critique are as follows: Stern's belief that infants begin to distinguish themselves from other things and other persons—the sense of self—is not universal as he claims but an interpretation from the perspective of white, middle-class, late-twentieth-century Western culture. Stern puts *self* inside the organism where it serves as a master for guiding behavior, and he attributes to it other traits as well, which he assumes to be universal. Yet the Chewong of Malaysia locate self in the liver and the Egyptians locate it in the heart. The Tallensi of West Africa believe it belongs to the past and is controlled by an *external* force. Hindus also believe it belongs to the past but is controlled by an *internal* force. Stern ignores these cultural differences that show his model to be characteristic of only a small part of the world and assumes that his conception of the self is innate and universal. If a self is actually innate, it is puzzling why so little of the world corresponds to his model of it. Stern's data is

probably sound, but his interpretation of data is culture bound as is his interpretation of an unconscious, avers Cushman.

> By claiming to have found scientific proof that the human infant automatically emerges as a Western infant, Stern made a profoundly political statement. He implicitly argued that the empty, divided, narcissistic, confused, isolated individual of the modern West who has such difficulty maintaining intimate relationships and cooperating in communal endeavors, is the natural, inevitable shape of human being. (Cushman, 1991, p. 217)

Turning to mainstream psychology, Cushman argues that because human beings are constructed by local groups that psychology ignores, "psychology's program is impossible" (p. 206). And because psychologists stake their claim to truth on the laboratory, a "privileged source" that they assume to be isolated from history and politics, the "decontextualized" psychology that results is "politically dangerous." This, he points out, is illustrated in Stern's attempt to blame the presumed self for isolation and alienation while overlooking the social and political structures that may actually be responsible.

As exemplified in the following passage, proponents of constructionism believe a total demolition of objectivism and its support of evil social forces is imminent:

> There is virtually no hypothesis, body of evidence, ideological stance, literary canon, value commitment or logical edifice that cannot be dismantled, demolished or derided with the implements at hand. Only rank prejudice, force of habit or the anguished retaliation of deflated egos can muster a defence against the intellectual explosives within our grasp. Everywhere now in the academic world the capitalist exploiters, male chauvinist pigs, cultural imperialists, warmongers, WASP bigots, wimp liberals and scientist dogmatists are on the run. Nor are these capacities for deflation and decapitation limited to the academic establishment.

Post-empiricist critique finds ample targets throughout society. Presumptions of empiricism can be located within all domains of high-level decision-making—in government, business, the military, education and so on. . . . The revolution is on, heads are rolling everywhere, there is no limit to the potential destruction. (Gergen, 1994b, p. 59–60)

Other Versions of Constructionism. As an alternative to *strict* constructionism, some have argued that one must consider the constructionist's world to have some objective basis in order to avoid *solipsism*, the assumption that nothing exists besides one's self. Otherwise, research can look only at the social basis of social constructions.

A version called *contextual* constructionism rejects solipsism and allows for a grounding in the world of nature that lies behind the constructions of the social community. It calls for a common-sense view in which knowledge begins in contact with a real world, including the many contextual conditions that influence the constructionist's research. "The very act of obtaining information from an informant influences the form and content of the response. Investigators and analysts in spite of themselves cannot help but import their interests, if not their professional agendas, into their interactions with their informants" (Sarbin & Kitsuse, p. 14).

According to one argument in this direction, in order to more fully understand a construction of the person-in-street, the constructionist must refer to something that can be objectively verified (Best, 1993). Constructionism's social action agenda toward such projects as improving conditions for the underprivileged, the aged, women and minority groups, and toward conserving the world's natural resources also requires a modified approach based on everyday life in the world. This could be along the lines of philosopher and psychologist John Dewey who argued that knowledge consists of the interaction of humans and their world; it does not start with theoretical systems. J. R. Kantor's interbehavioral psychology (chapter 10) takes a very similar position.

An example of contextual constructionism occurs in Andersen's (1994) critique of IQ. He suggests that there are two "metaphors" of intelligence. One states that it is doing problems in the head and the other, a contextual proposal, that it is "the evaluated quality of one's interactions and relationships to one's environment" (p. 126). He observes that "IQ" is often used in place of the more accurate term "IQ test score," resulting in a reification of a construct. Further, when the specific responses of subjects to test questions are transformed into the numerical abstractions of IQ test scores, these scores are creations, not data. Many major intelligence theorists fail to recognize that intelligence is a construction rather than an event in nature. "IQ test scores do exist, but not IQ; IQ is found in that land populated by Easter bunnies, unicorns, tooth fairies, and other mythical creatures" (p. 132). The confusion, Andersen contends, extends to the assertion that IQ is normally distributed, thereby overlooking the fact that the test creators constructed the test to give a bell shaped distribution, one that is not inherent in nature.

Subjectivity, Andersen holds, occurs with the individual; but the social process gives it public objectivity. This he likens to a fire-spotter approach to objectivity in which a number of different spotters at different locations with different subjective perspectives all come to locate the fire in its objective position. Along these lines he indicates that the psychometric approach to intelligence, with its failure to understand the constructed nature of intelligence, is being challenged by a variety of disciplines—each from a different perspective—that may achieve better objectivity about intelligence. The psychometric approach as a mechanistic view of objectivity he contrasts with the contextual constructionist objectivity in which intelligence would be understood as the interaction of examiner and examinee, the context of the testing situation, and the examinee's thinking procedure.

A prominent pioneer in constructionism, Rom Harré (1986b), may also be in the contextual constructionist camp. We come to know about the non-personal world around us, he suggests, by investigating through conversations just as physicists investigate through theories. Our own social system, of course, limits what we can learn but use of conversations provides a practical approach, he argues. An approach to social psychology called "realism" or "transcendental realism" may also be a close kin (Manicus & Secord, 1983). It seeks to discontinue the common practice in social psychology of using unrealistic experiments involving bargaining and prisoners dilemmas and replace them with narratives along the lines of historical research that capture the meaning of things to people in ordinary life. These proponents do not disavow objectivity ("warranted assertibility") or insist on total relativity.

Danziger (1997) distinguishes between a "gentle" or "light" version of constructionism and a "dark" version. Light constructionism not only does not claim that it has the path to truth but counsels tolerance for all paths as long as they do not commandeer authority over the others. Meaning is continually constructed from communities of language. Dark constructionism emphasizes power relationships and that these occur in social structures and in the human body, such as in the biology of gender. Power is established and maintained through conventions of writing and institutionalized social practices. Thus, local social processes, Danziger points out, are unlikely to provide opportunities for social reform; and consequently the postmodernist advocacy of multiple standpoints may not achieve its aims.

Reiss (1993) advocates a "postpositivist" rather than postmodernist position. He agrees with the postmodernists in rejecting final truths and autonomous facts, but he also rejects the postmodernists' total relativism. "Relativism is not acceptable to postpositivists because it eliminates the possibility of gathering fair scientific evidence in accord with the norms of science. Furthermore, if all views are relative then there is no way to justify the effectiveness of one social or personal change over another" (p. 6). He notes that claims to knowledge are published and debated with the intent of arriving at a better understanding of some

event in the world while recognizing that this understanding may change with new perspectives. He emphasizes that the researcher should set forth his or her presuppositions (postulate system) so that others may judge the validity of these as well as the findings that result from them, for facts are such only within a context of assumptions.

Constructionism and Constructivism. Gergen (1994b) differentiates constructivism on the one hand as it appears in the work of Jean Piaget and George Kelly and social constructionism that he himself is advocating on the other. Piaget's child *assimilates* reality but also, through its cognitive system, *accommodates* to the world. Consequently, the individual rather than the social group constructs reality. Kelly's individual privately construes or interprets the world, but an objective world is still there. Thus, both Piaget and Kelley believe in a reality independent of social processes. Greer (1997) similarly points to the constructivists as holding to a more traditional position than the constructionists, one that accepts a reality behind the social constructions of knowledge. Constructionism rejects both "mind" and "world" as having reality apart from a community of discourse, whereas some constructivists assume the reality of these entities.

Both constructivists and constructionists doubt that there is any "foundational" (based on established truths) empirical science that is universal, and each questions whether knowledge is constructed in a mind by observation. Each holds that science's own methodologies shape knowledge rather than discovering it. Constructionists hold that both scientific methodologies and its findings are products of evidence and reasoning that are presented in language and therefore socially "negotiated." Constructivists hold to western individualism with knowledge an inherent process within the individual. For constructionists individuality is a matter of social relationships as are personality, motives, emotions, memory, and thoughts—not components of a mind or self. "Persons are constructed entities; they are theoretical constructions that are social in origin" (Stam, 1990, p. 246). Constructionists assume social causality while some constructivists allow for causality by a free will. The *constructivist* goes even further than the *constructionist* and assumes that language constitutes social reality rather than functioning only as an expression of social agreement (Niemeyer, 1995). Constructivism gives a greater role to biological causality of behavior whereas constructionism gives total causality to social processes (Hardy, 1993).[1]

To continue with Kelly's (1955/1991) "personal construct psychology," it has been the inspiration for an attempt to combine it with social constructionism (Mancuso, 1996). Kelly argues that we interpret the world in terms of our individual cognitive constructs that mediate it for us. It is these mediated interpretations that give it meaning. In Mancuso's version of this theory, the mediators are private meanings. The personal constructs receive inputs from the world and organize them into meanings of things. Each person has a hierarchical system of these constructs and uses different constructs with different inputs that help him or her understand the world. This makes the person's interpretations—rather than those of the social group—central to the system. The theory is closer to notions of cognitive processing than of social constructionism (Wortham, 1996), the latter holding that individual interpreters are part of a larger community of discourse and are "locked in" with the interpretive processes of that community (Burkitt, 1996). Wortham takes issue with the privacy/inner world/mentalism of Mancuso's propositions: "To suppose that we must posit an inner world to explain meaningful experience leads to intractable questions about the accuracy of internal representations, about free-will and determinism, and so on . . . The constructs that give meaning to ourselves and our experiences are so woven into relational context that it does serve us to suppose that they are internalized into individual minds" (p. 81–82).

---

1 Lyddon (1995) outlines a variety of versions of constructivism and classifies them according to Aristotle's four types of causation: material, efficient, formal, and final. Prawat (1996) describes six types, of which the social constructionism of Gergen and the closely related postmodernism of Rorty comprise a single style.

Feminism and Constructionism. Allied with postmodernism constructionism are some of the feminist evaluations of science that show a heavily male bias in methodology and interpretation. Evelyn Keller (1983), trained as a theoretical physicist, points out that women's approach to scientific problems brings a useful perspective that can be quite fruitful, as exemplified by Barbara McClintock's procedure of studying corn genetics by searching for organization and function rather than by treating the gene as an absolute command center. This led to accomplishments for which McClintock received the Nobel Prize for medicine in 1983 but required her to battle male negativism toward some of her concepts and toward her funding for research. Keller maintains that women tend to look for complex interactions while men often seek linear cause and effect. This leads men to overstate the controlling role of DNA while failing to take account of its interactions with other molecules. Making a similar observation is Bonnie Spanier (1995), a microbiologist and specialist in women's studies. In spite of the evidence for the interactional role of a variety of complex molecules, her survey of textbooks and journal articles showed a continuing pattern of attributing to the gene a controlling function at the top of a hierarchy of molecules in the cell.

Most feminist scientists want to bring more women into the sciences and to add a qualitative dimension to science while retaining the quantitative (Nemecek, 1997). In addition, they want science to take account of the social values and gender biases that influence scientists. It is noteworthy that the recognition of biases that influence experiments on the part of both the investigator and the subject led to the use of double blind controls in experiments. Many older studies are of questionable value because of the many years that such controls were lacking. But many feminists want to go beyond methodological controls. Their call is for a move away from science as a male preserve to science as a human endeavor, one that uses diverse viewpoints and relinquishes the male intellectual dominance—a dominance based on power politics rather than science even when that is unintended and unrecognized. A broadened approach, they hold, will improve science, not degrade it. "Nature itself is an ally that can be relied upon to provide the impetus for real change: nature's responses recurrently invite re-examination of the terms in which our understanding of science is constructed" (Keller, 1995, p. 175–76).

Criticisms similar to those about genetics could be made about mainline psychology: the use of quantitative methods to the exclusion of qualitative ones and the assumption of linear cause and effect in the assumption of a brain-directed body or environment-caused responses.

Inroads. During the past twenty years constructionism has become of major importance in women's studies and in sociology, particularly in the study of social problems, and in some of anthropology. It has made less headway in psychology (Sarbin & Kitsuse, 1994) except in social psychology and educational psychology where it has found a prominent home. (Cognitivism has also become influential in social psychology, while most traditional social psychology has moved to business schools.) Gergen (1985) would like to move constructionism into all of psychology, for he considers psychology—and other sciences as well—to be "a form of social process" (p. 266).

SEMI-EXPLICIT POSTULATES

The following postulates are those that Gergen seems to exhibit. Most are fairly explicit in his writings but a few are more inferential:

- *Protopostulates* (general guiding assumptions about science or, in this case, general inquiry)
  1. No universal truths about the world can be established.
  2. The only events in nature that can be known are social events.
  3. Individuals do not possess knowledge. Knowledge is simply a type of relationship that occurs in a community.
  4. Knowledge comes neither from a mind in which the world is represented and geneti-

cally organized nor from observations of the world.
  5. Relationships among people, who are culturally and historically situated, determine the forms of expression by which we understand the world.
  6. Science, logic, mythology, religion, mysticism, opinion, and fiction all have equal claims to truth as social conventions.
  7. Social constructionism can make no greater claim to truth than any other approach. Like the others, it seeks intelligibility from repeated patterns.
  8. A social community can evaluate or validate its own claims for its own community but, because of cultural differences, cannot evaluate those of another community.
  9. Science can provide "theoretical intelligibility" as its most important contribution to a culture of which science is a part.
  10. Use of logic and evidence have no warrant beyond the social groups in which they are historically and culturally situated, yet logical coherency may be used as a part of the formulation of social constructionism and in the questioning of other stances. Reference to evidence may be used hand-in-hand with this rationality.
- *Metapostulates* (supportive assumptions for a particular science)
  1. Having abandoned truth claims, social constructionism invites others to entertain the possibilities that make up intelligibility and to consider alternatives.
  2. Holding to a total relativism, social constructionism takes no position on any issue—whether scientific, moral, political, etc. Such issues are to be judged only within the context of a particular culture.[2]

---

2. Gergen (1985) claims that because (a) constructionism follows normative rules of the community, (b) rules can be critiqued historically and culturally, and (c) constructionism evaluates the morality of scientific action from the perspective of the general society, the approach is not entirely relativistic.

3. Individual characteristics may be reduced to discourse of the social group.

4. We structure the world linguistically rather than cognitively. A truth claim is a juxtaposition of words containing a proposition.

5. Social discourse is the only form of knowledge, and it does not extend beyond the social group in which the discourse occurs.

■ *Postulates* (subject matter assumptions)

1. Psychology studies social discourse as the only basis of knowledge.

2. Social discourse carries truth or knowledge only on the local level at which the discourse is created.

3. Causality does not arise from internal determiners such as minds, brains, will power, or other individual constructs but only from the social community.

RESEARCH

Constructionist research uses any procedures that provide intelligibility within a single social community. Interviewing and narrative-writing are commonly used. A more sophisticated procedure used by some constructions is Q methodology (chapter 11), which provides a rigorous and powerful quantitative device for discovering the various combinations of subjectivity in which people cluster together on their social constructions. Topics include lesbianism and feminism (Kitzinger, 1986, 1987; Kitzinger & Stainton Rogers, 1985), feminism and pornography (Gallivan, 1994), child abuse (Stainton Rogers & Stainton Rogers, 1989), social and behavioral texts (Curt, 1994; McKeown, 1990), and psychopathy (Stowell-Smith, 1997). Some constructionists advocate the narrative as the most useful means of reporting constructionist research and concepts (Sarbin & Kitsuse, 1994). In still another procedure five investigators wrote their own memories and reflections on emotional events, discussed them as a group, looked for patterns across memories, and analyzed ways in which meanings were constructed in their social contexts (Kippax et al., 1988; Crawford et al., 1990).

Gergen (1994b, 1997) lists such topics as hostility, cognition, attitudes, love, smells, sincerity, sexuality, intention, personality structure, emotions, child development, and physical pain, as well as anxiety, schizophrenia, depression, anorexia and bulimia, multiple personality, and other psychiatric classifications as receiving research attention as social constructions. That is, these are constructions from the community and have no further generality. Constructionists are also interested in the viewpoints of others in order to provide alternatives to conventional views and policies as, for example, emotions that are specific to cultures. They are interested in the changing historical concepts of children, cross-cultural comparisons of children, and variations in mother love. They have examined passion, jealousy, and sense of smell and taste as social processes. They have studied changing conceptions of psychology of the person, of subjects in research, and of the character of experimental psychology. They have also provided accounts of the constructed nature of the body, sex differences, medical disease, pregnancy, childhood, intelligence, wife abuse, and life course. They have presented gender roles, criminal offenses, and aggression as results of interactions rather than of inner impulses and have given attention to gender bias, plight of minorities, racism, and other social problems.

Many of these are empirical studies; but according to proponents they provide no truth or warrant for the validity of the propositions. They only provide a construction of social life in new ways and dramatize accounts of reality, setting them in a new perspective and providing alternative approaches to action. "Each form of theoretical intelligibility—cognitive, behaviorist, phenomenological, psychoanalytic, and the like—provides the culture with discursive vehicles for carrying out social life" (Gergen, 1994b, p. 142). All have a role to play and all can be part of the constructionist social landscape, the constructionists allow, but none should be dominant. One will not find in constructionist research any of the traditional research efforts of psychology—those that look for generalities such as whether massed or spaced practice is a more efficient way to learn, what response patterns result from different reinforcement schedules, or what conditions maintain or change perceptual constancies (although constructionists might be interested in cultural differences in these behaviors). One will not even find anything in social psychology, the home base of constructionism, along the lines of Sherif's classical demonstration using the natural setting of a boys' camp to show that warfare can be incited between groups, and then these enemy groups can unite against a common threat and even become allies and friends.

In examining postmodernist research in education, Constas (1998) argues that its narrative methodology should not be used exclusively over systematic study but should take its place as one of many methodologies. He denies that "ordered thinking and rational inquiry stifle the human spirit and oppress the political rights of the people we study" (p. 28). He finds that much postmodern research avoids coming to conclusions or offering recommendations; it is so vague as to be of little use to educators. Similarly, postmodern research reports heavily freighted with academic literary tradition—as most of them are—will only widen the gap between educational practitioners and researchers. If, however, they are presented in a form such as that employed by novelists and social critics, they could greatly assist communication. An important role that narrative research can play, he believes, is in joining with narrative presentation of findings so that the researcher can meaningfully communicate those findings to teachers, educational administrators, and the public.

PSYCHOTHERAPY

Principles

Conventional psychotherapy is often preoccupied with individual perceptions and understandings. Constructionist therapy replaces interest in the individual with a focus on the social process of language. It asks whether a particular self-description can be recast into a new form or whether alternative descriptions handle the facts equally well (Gergen, 1994b). The therapy sets in progress a new set of constructions that provide alternatives to the old ones (Fruggeri, 1992). Being sick or having problems becomes a cultural construction rather than an independent reality. Dysfunctional families, anxiety, depression, and suffering are social perspectives. Diagnosis is unnecessary and a cure is a reconstrual of social perspectives. The view that a change is needed and that the therapist will bring it about is replaced. Instead, the therapist is a participant-observer who collaborates with the client to produce a context in which new and more satisfying realities can develop (Hardy, 1993). Therapy is a process of developing meanings specific to a particular therapist-client relationship in which therapist and client co-evolve meanings through their dialogue.

Efran and Clarfield (1992) view therapy as an educational enterprise in which teacher and student negotiate an agreement that will operate within the limits of the community and that establishes goals and procedures. Therapist and client are not subject and object but joint participants; and thinking, feeling, and imagining are not inner mental events but are constituted by the participation. The medium of the participation is language. The therapist, they hold, must accept responsibility for the consequences of his or her own opinions and values and should encourage the client to do likewise. In this scenario the therapist helps the client view symptoms or problems as a part of social patterns of living rather than inner forces or a disease. The "warfare of life" is not between thoughts and feelings but between conflicting demands of different social contexts (Efran & Fauber, 1995).

Who Is in Charge?

In constructionist therapy the therapist loses his or her position of authority and knowledge and takes on different ways of interacting and describing that foster alternative constructions while the client looks at choices and their outcomes and at the various possibilities these have for developing new meanings. The therapist takes the role of "a conversational artist—an architect of the dialogical process" as "a participant-observer and a participant facilitator" (Anderson & Goolishian, 1992). While abandoning the view of the therapist as a change agent, constructionism also abandons the doctrine that clients resist change (Fruggeri, 1992). Some constructionist therapists have become as non-directive as the Rogerians (chapter 4) according to Efran and Clarfield (1992), who suggest that this is an unnecessary extreme.

Who Knows?

Clients are encouraged to explore a variety of narratives but not to commit to one as true. Narratives are a way of producing meaning as well as helping the client and therapist understand meaning as part of a context that has no finality or truth. Through the narrative experience they will recognize that one narrative is no better or more important than another (Gergen, 1994b). According to Anderson and Goolishian (1992), narration gains its transformational strength by the way in which it expresses life meanings in a new context. The therapist indicates to the client that the therapist does not have any presuppositions, answers, or expectations—does *not-know*—but does have great curiosity and wants to hear more. Therapists cannot avoid acting to help overcome problems for the clients who ask for a change, but they can change the social expectations of the therapist as an expert (Fruggeri, 1992). Neither can therapists avoid their knowledge and biases or the referral information they receive, but they can preclude closing off new meanings by taking a don't-know point of view. As Anderson and Goolishian (1992) describe the therapy, in the not-knowing process the therapist avoids leading questions or interrogation and attempts to encourage the client to bring the therapist to new understandings. The not-knowing questions lead to a locally constructed vocabulary and understanding between the two as the story is repeatedly retold and developed. This provides a coherent account of feelings, history, and perceptions. Such an approach,

Anderson and Goolishian hold, fosters a sense of liberation in a therapy deemed successful.

One example of this form of therapy is that of a forty-one-year-old man who was certain he had a contagious disease and was a menace to other people. When he persisted in this belief after medical examinations ruled out the possibility of any contagious disease, he was referred to psychiatric services but gained no benefit from them. A psychiatrist finally referred him to Goolishian who did not challenge the man's story but expressed an interest in it. That seemed to relax him. By asking such questions as "How long *have you had* this disease?" the therapist encouraged him to retell the story in such a way as to reveal new meanings. This not-knowing approach seemed to have beneficial results. When the man returned to his psychiatrist, the doctor reported that his life was better and that he was dealing with vocational and marriage problems rather than with the question of infection. The not-knowing fostered a new beginning in the therapeutic process.

Some Procedures

The therapeutic procedures constructionism has used include: discussion of solutions instead of problems (de Shazer, 1993), assistance to clients for writing letters and other works in which they reconstruct their lives (White & Epstein, 1990), negotiations between therapist and client through varied conversational means (O'Hanlon & Wilk, 1987), focus on clients' positive characterizations of themselves (Friedman & Fanger, 1991; Durrant & Kowalski, 1993), and work with disabled adolescents through narrations of their condition using puppets (Coelho de Amorim & Cavalcante, 1992).

Family Therapy

This therapy, of which there are numerous varieties, has become prominent in constructionist clinical practice. It sees behavior as a part of the family system involving circular causality among members of the family rather than as a linear causality of past events acting on the individual. The feminist movement, social constructionism, and cultural relativism have all been important in reshaping family therapy (Hardy, 1993). Feminism has brought attention to the fact that we live in a patriarchal society in which men give directives and women follow them; cultural relativism has insisted that all aspects of life are influenced by culture and that therapy cannot ignore culture. What is functional or dysfunctional varies with different cultures, as Afro-American traditions rooted in Africa value the unity of the group over the rights of individuals.

The family itself is a type of unit in which the therapist as well as the client is a member. Because of this experience in common with the client, the therapist participates in constructing individual family problems, some of which may be those the client faces. As with individual constructionist therapy, the therapist is no longer an authority or expert but a co-interpreter.

Sauber et al. (1993) offer the following operational characteristics of family therapy:

■ The entire family is the unit and any number of members could participate in the therapy in any combination.

■ The combination can vary from time to time.

■ The family identifies the patient, who represents the maladjustments of the entire family.

■ A diagnosis is made for the entire family and the treatment goal is for the entire family.

■ Rather than maintaining confidentiality of an individual, all materials are shared with the family members.

■ The therapist focuses on relationships and meanings within the family and emphasizes ways in which healthy interactions can be achieved.

■ Some family therapists go beyond the family to the community, and this brings the approach into the realm of community psychology (chapter 13, p. 370).

Hoffman (1991) identifies five "sacred cows" and "a super sacred cow" in mainstream psychology and indicates their implications for family therapy:

(a) the belief in *objective social research* is based on myth; and, similarly, objective diagnostic processes for insurance reimbursement that require the diagnosis of a biological illness are of doubtful validity.

(b) *The self* as an inner cognition or emotion is problematic. In family therapy the individual becomes part of an ecology.

(c) *Developmental psychology* has assumed universal stages of development such as those of Piaget or of psychoanalysis, but forms of development are highly variable. Traditional psychotherapy has similarly assumed a predetermined path of change, but change is equally variable.

(d) The supposition that *emotions* have a universal form and exist inside people gives rise to the belief that they must be released or expressed, or that they are things to get in touch with. Psychologists and social workers believe they must help people "work through" their emotions when disaster strikes. Family therapists have long attacked these various repression theories.

(e) The notion of *levels,* such as the belief that a symptom means an underlying disorder, can be replaced with what is communicated in various contexts.

Finally, the super sacred cow is *colonialism* in which the researcher or the therapist takes a position of authority, and the subject or the client is submissive. That is, the therapist is the colonial administrator over the client. Family therapy has moved away from this, and in one version uses a "reflecting team" that discusses the family in front of the family members and then invites their commentaries. Hoffman describes the relationship between client and therapist as a partnership. She does not hesitate to tell her own stories along with ones she encourages the client to tell, and she expresses her feelings rather than maintaining a position of privacy and being above it all.

Little information is available in psychology about how beliefs arise or how they change (Fruggeri, 1992). In constructionist family therapy, the client does not determine change by selecting what is useful any more than the therapist determines it. A systematic analysis of sessions of family therapy showed that the therapist's questions challenging the coherence of beliefs brings the participants to develop a new coherence, and the greatest change in narrations occurs when the therapist connects multiple and diverse accounts. This suggests that merely providing multiple viewpoints is insufficient. The therapist must show how they all connect (Fruggeri & Matteini, 1991, as cited in Fruggeri, 1992).

Constructivist Therapy. Neimeyer (1995) describes one form of constructivist therapy called "narrative reconstruction" in which the first step is to "externalize" a problem such as depression, making it exterior to the individual. Then the therapist guides the client in developing narratives that relate the conditions of living that produced the problem. With the distancing, the client can better develop an alternative story which allows him or her to take control of the problem. The therapist helps validate the story by awarding diplomas of mastery, or writing letters that either describe the client's success or look to future narrational developments. This procedure seems to use reinforcement techniques in accord with behavior analysis/behavior therapy. Similarly, in treating "intractably aggressive" patients by shifting emphasis from something wrong with the person to "structures of interactive patterns among the people involved with the problem" (Caldwell, 1994), the procedure amounts to behavior therapy. The social reinforcers for the aggressive behavior are withdrawn and that behavior gradually declines. These versions of social constructionist/constructivist therapy are joined with behavior therapy.

Challenging constructionist/constructivist rejection of a knowable reality, Speed (1991) contends that while emphasizing how clients construct their ideas, constructivists therapists ignore

what goes on in clients' lives. Where, he asks, do clients' ideas come from? Why do clients construct one idea rather than another? He considers constructivism valuable in helping therapists see that their idea of truth is not the only possibility, but he believes that opposing any objective truths is going to an extreme and has "taken family therapists up a blind alley" (p. 407). He advocates "co-constructivism," which recognizes a structured reality of which different aspects become important according to individual or group situations. The therapist, together with the family, constructs an account of the events.

Some constructivist therapists employ cognitive concepts and techniques, and some prefer a version of self-psychology which constructionists and other constructivists would reject. Kelly's personal construct theory (pp. 240, 241) also provides a constructivist approach. The "therapist as research consultant" (Kelly's words) helps clients to formulate their personal constructs to more effectively deal with important questions and to increase their alternative views of life's possibilities (Efran & Fauber, 1995).

Hermeneutical Therapy. Hermeneutics, as an interpretation of language, has much in common with constructionism but retains an orientation toward an objective world. Woolfolk (1992) prefers it to constructionism and argues that we can evaluate truth by using a variety of methods in a variety of contexts. Only by justifying objective truth can we defend the traditions and practices of our culture, he contends. As an approach to psychotherapy, hermeneutics involves technology, values-clarification, self-discovery, and self-interpretation.

Postmodern Therapy and Academic Psychology

Polkinghorne (1992) holds that psychotherapy, when conducted by skilled practitioners, is effectively a postmodern practice, an alternative to academic psychology. Such psychologies as behavior analysis, Rogerian self-psychology, and psychoanalysis can be reinterpreted as metaphors for discovery and as cognitive schemas by which clients organize their experiences. Therapists, he documents, seldom find any useful information in psychological research and have to develop their own body of knowledge. They do this not by drawing on a body of presumed truths that academic psychology has established but by observing surrounding conditions and using their own patterns of thought to construct a body of knowledge that is utilitarian for the therapy. One can best deal with academic psychology, he argues, as a subdivision of the psychology of practice. Because postmodernism is already dominant in practice, he claims, academic psychology then becomes a subdivision of postmodernism.

APPLICATION

Constructivism (more than its close relative constructionism) has turned some of its efforts to education (for example, Jones & Maloy, 1996; Marlowe & Page, 1998; Palinscar, 1998; Richardson, 1997). It does not emphasize knowledge but instead "facility with discourse, norms, and practices associated with particular communities of practice" (Palinscar, 1998, p. 365). Efforts to improve education should include an emphasis on informal knowledge, accepting a multiplicity of correct answers for many kinds of problems, and "promoting the social construction of some types of knowledge" (Berliner & Biddle, 1995, p. 327). The following are measures the proponents advocate:

(a) fostering social construction of meanings rather than objective knowledge

(b) learning across, rather than within, academic disciplines

(c) encouraging social justice and democratic discussions rather than corporate domination of democracy

(d) understanding meanings mutually arrived at rather than obtaining knowledge from adults

(e) constructing meanings while reading, computing, and discussing rather than obtaining knowledge from the previous generations

(f) discussing what is important in the future for individuals and society rather than learning a standardized body of knowledge on which to be tested (Jones & Malloy, 1996, pp. xvi, 362).

Constructivists try to convey a liking for science more than proficiency in science and a liking for mathematics more than proficiency in it. What is needed in a democracy, the constructivists contend, is not so much technical or professional knowledge and proficiency as healthy mutual respect for genders, classes, and races. In fact, they state, experts make too much of the importance of empirical knowledge. It is common sense, experience, and thoughtful appraisal that keep the world running. A comparison reveals how similar these principles are to humanistic education (chapter 4, pp. 124–126 and 134–136).

RELATION TO SOME OTHER APPROACHES

Cognitive Psychology

Most constructionists reject an agency in the head that causes behavior and look to the social community as the source of action and meaning. Memories, emotions, beliefs, perceptions, and so on are to be found in social structures, not in constructed representations and schemas attributed to the brain or mind. On the other hand, cognitivists would reject the constructionist propositions that cognitive empirical studies consist of no more than social discourse and have no generalizability beyond local groups. Another important difference is that constructionists reject "mind as a mirror" of the world whereas most cognitivists advocate it in the form of some version of mental representation, either consisting of, or produced by, neural action.

Postmodernist/constructionists have in common with cognitivists the belief that a barrier stands between knowers and the world of nature.

For some constructivists and some postmodernists language comprises reality and the rest of nature is unknowable. For the constructionists, social constructions as reflected in language are all that is knowable. Cognitivists claim that the internal representations of the world are knowable but not the external real world. These differences squarely reflect the organocentric versus the sociocentric postulates of the respective systems.

Interbehavioral Psychology

A comparison with interbehaviorism is rather complex. Constructionism denies any distinction between subject and object as it denies mind as a mirror of the world. It accepts the event of social construction in which language is shared understanding, but it denies any independent truth to other events. Interbehaviorism, in contrast, puts no limits on what events may be a part of nature. But it agrees with constructionism that mind and mirrors are constructs, not events, and would insist that they not be confused with events. Language, to interbehaviorism, is bistimulational interactions in which a person tells someone about something. Unlike constructionism, interbehaviorism does not treat language as a grand schema that constitutes or structures all knowing, but it does agree that language is not the transference of a mental content from one mind to another and that it functions as shared meanings. (Interbehaviorism maintains, apparently in agreement with constructionism, that social psychology itself is a study of shared meanings [Kantor, 1929, 1982].) When constructionism states that language is a sign or a signifier, interbehaviorism would agree— if it means written language. But interbehaviorism argues that spoken language is concrete bistimulational interactions, not signs or symbols. Everyday understandings (Semin & Gergen, 1990) are the beginning points of knowledge for both systems, but interbehaviorists seek to build upon this to achieve scientific knowledge while the constructionists believe this to be the end as well as the beginning of knowledge.

The constructionist's refusal to accept individual action that is not totally "situated" in a social context may be due in part to the assumption that individual action requires a construct of mind or brain power to cause the action. While invoking no such constructs, interbehaviorism proposes that individual action can be understood as interactions between the individual and objects that occur in a setting (social or non-social) in which there is a history of past interactions, all of these factors jointly comprising the cause of the action, whether thinking, believing, practicing and improving skills, remembering, acting habitually, conversing, or developing social constructions. Mind, will, brain power, and other constructed causal agents become irrelevant when only events rather than constructs are part of the interactional field. In contrast to interbehaviorism's recognition of all events, the strict constructionist insists that we cannot know events apart from the social process and recognizes only the event of the social process itself. Contextual constructionism (p. 239), on the other hand, is more noncentric than sociocentric and has more in common with the interbehavioral position.

Operant Subjectivity

For Stephenson, communication is between persons rather than groups, and subjectivity and objectivity are only differences of standpoint—my standpoint or yours. For Gergen, communication is social, and objectivity exists only in the social process. Subjectivity smacks of individuality, and its quantitative character makes it even more suspect. Even so, a number of social constructionists have found Stephenson's Q method well suited to their interests and have conducted studies with it that determine the subjectivity involved in social constructions, the way in which individuals do or do not share viewpoints in various combinations. Narrations interest constructionists, but it is all too easy for the person collecting the narration or conducting the interview to control it. In Q methodology people tell their own stories by the ways in which they sort statements.

Phenomenological Psychology

Giorgi (1992) suggests that postmodernism and constructionism have attested the importance of subjectivity but have left it so enfeebled that it has little remaining consequence. Subjectivity, for some constructionists, refers to individuality, and individuality must be subsumed under social processes. While phenomenology emphasizes meanings of things to people, these meanings are usually individual rather than social. Constructionism recognizes only social meanings. There is no individual point of view. Constructionism would also reject Husserl's concept of intuiting meanings—such as apprehending the three corners that characterize a triangle—that cross boundaries of cultures, opinions, biases, or theories and would insist that meanings are restricted to "local" groups.

Psychoanalysis

A few psychoanalysts have modified their system by borrowing from social constructionism. For example, Merton Gill replaces Freud's biological and physicalistic concepts with social constructionism and hermeneutics, interpretations (see chapter 12) in which the participants in the therapeutic process, analyst and analysand (patient), construct meanings together. No single interpretation is the correct one, but the best is the one that seems most coherent at that time (although it might change at another time). Roy Schafer, similarly, looks for no true interpretation but turns to narration as a procedure for constructing events in the present and, in so doing, discards the traditional role of psychoanalysis, that of reconstructing the past. Telling the story is the only reality. Donald Spence takes the analytic session to be narrations about fables in which fact and fantasy, such as posited memories of childhood incest, cannot be separated. Because truth can never be known, in his version the analyst must construct stories coherent enough for the patient to believe and benefit from. These psychoanalysts have moved considerably from the traditional organo-

centric position of psychoanalysis toward a sociocentric position.

CRITIQUE

Because postmodernism and social constructionism have been so critical of the entire scientific enterprise of both physical and social sciences, they have provoked considerable response. The responses have been quite varied and are not easily grouped. The following is only a loose grouping, ending with a few efforts proposed by proponents to modify the position in an effort to meet some of the challenges.

Use of Logic to Discredit Logic

The constructionists and postmodernists use logic to attack other positions and argue for the advantages of their own position involving social, linguistic, historical, and other matters that are superior to logic and evidence. Thus, they—the strict constructionists, at least—implicitly employ the very procedures they disparage. Nowhere do they engage in irrationality such as inconsistencies or contradictions—in fact, they point them out in other systems. Nor do they even employ a "local" social group as the basis of their position, for that would warrant the appropriateness of postmodernism/constructionism for only that social community. Although these proponents disclaim any special warrant for their own position, they make a concerted effort to show the shortcomings of other positions and the strength of their own. Even though they state that constructionism is only an alternative to the others and has no special claim to truth, they attempt to show that no other system can be justified.

Consider the following: "it may be argued that there is no theory of knowledge—whether empiricist, realist, rationalist, phenomenological, or otherwise—that can coherently furnish warrants for its own truth or validity" (Gergen, 1994b, p. 77). What is the basis for this claim to truth? Do negative claims such as this one stand alone while positive claims are only social constructions? And, since the author seems to be addressing a wider audience than his brand of social constructionism, does not "may be argued" imply a rational statement that has some "warrant for its own truth" beyond his local group?

Redhead (1995), a philosopher of physics, wonders why it is that, since the constructionists consider everything to be relative to a viewpoint, they bother to argue. Their own arguments are mere opinions or viewpoints. Yet they imply the truth of relativism. "The relativists regard their position as the height of postmodernist sophistication, but in fact the whole position totters toward incoherent absurdity" (p. 14).

Use of Empiricism to Discredit Empiricism

Constructionism's broad conclusions—(a) statements about knowledge are always dependent on context and (b) because context is always shifting there is no knowledge or truth—are claims based on empirical observations. "Thus social constructionism is revealed as unwittingly but firmly embedded in the empiricist tradition" (Terwee, 1995, p. 193). Yet while using this procedure, constructionism denies any broad validity to empiricism.

Which Events Count?

Does not the claim by constructionists that people in social groups create their own understanding of the world confuse social interaction with what is interacted with? The event of knowing is not just something emitted from a social group; it is comprised of interactions with people and other things. If the constructionist deems the people and objects interacted with to be unknowable, would not their constructions be equally unknowable? It seems strange that constructionists accept the social process of construction as a knowable event of nature but allow for no other event as knowable.

Reference Point

Mascolo and Dalto (1995) contend that in order for observation to be intelligible, it must be an-

chored in a framework of actual experiences. Similarly, Nettler (1986) points out that some empirical foundation is required as a reference point from which to advance, and without it the result is "a new variety of occult speech" that does not permit challenges to objectivity its proponents claim. She avers that the truths the system contains get "stretch[ed] beyond good sense" (p. 480). Gergen (1986) replies that he has no interest in "good sense," which consists of no more than "socially sanctioned conventions" (p. 481). Yet he also recognizes that all intelligibility is based on a cultural framework ("forestructure") and that once he has deconstructed this framework and converted it to language, he has nothing on which to base his arguments: if a real world is not relevant, then his own arguments cannot be based on a real world (Gergen, 1994a). Related to this is a major criticism of postmodernism and strict constructionism: it provides only propositions about propositions; it cannot get beyond words (Caputo, 1983; Prawat, 1996).

The Question of Relativism

Relativism versus Social Agenda. The constructionists' interest in social issues such as eliminating racial and gender discrimination and bringing democratic dialogues into the sciences suggests an implicit acceptance of some universal values. The system draws on cross-cultural studies and history to demonstrate its points; and these, despite the disclaimers, suggest some acceptance of evidence beyond the local discourse community for supporting a position. Further, the proponents do not make clear just what constitutes a "local" community. Is American culture local, or would local refer to some subdomain, such as American psychologists? Is local a sub-subdomain such as cognitive psychologists? Or an even finer division, such as connectionists among cognitivists or a subdomain of those? Or does local community refer to Norwegian vs. Bantu culture? Apparently all of Western culture is "local" when postmodernists attack the Enlightenment tradition, sometimes referred to by radical feminists as "dead, white, male Anglo-Europeans." One proponent (Danziger, 1997) recognizes a divergence of opinion among postmodernists between (a) the "discourse of emancipation" (promoting social justice) and (b) the position of knowledge as totally relative to social constructions. He suggests that the system may be "potentially self-destructive" (p. 409).

No doubt what is local changes from situation to situation, but what criteria do proponents use (and if they use any, would not such criteria comprise a universal?) to determine whether it is appropriate within the constructionist system for one social group to challenge another. Gergen (1994b) states that such challenges cannot meaningfully occur. Why then can a postmodernist or constructionist group challenge a science group? Is it because they are both part of Western culture, even if not of the same subculture? If postmodernism can challenge science, why can't science challenge occult claims?

A prevailing point of view in American culture has denied equal opportunities to women and minorities. Postmodernists/constructionists have inveighed against this as an injustice. They wish to empower the disenfranchised, democratize choice and values, support environmental protection, etc. How do they select these social goals if they have no warrant beyond the social groups of which they are a part and if it is the social relationships of these groups that determine the values the constructionists are ready to change? A strict constructionist such as Gergen would say that these goals, indeed, have no warrant beyond the social group, either as desirable or undesirable; but other constructionists do give them special status—as does Gergen himself when he advocates "democratization."

Taking a position on social issues can be a two-edged sword for a postmodernist/constructionist. Cutting in one direction is the proclamation that social constructions about race and gender inferiority have led to discrimination. Cutting in the other is the interpretation that discrimination is a social construction and therefore has no objective reality. The double edge slices equally well on all social issues.

Relativism versus Commonalities Among Cultures. By demanding total relativism, suggest Martin and Thompson (1997), constructionism denies basic human experiences and the possibility of communicating across cultural boundaries. In its extreme form, the authors note, such relativism would make psychology impossible and reduce human experience to nothing but local occurrences with only fleeting meanings. Further, any such totally relativistic position constitutes in itself a universal that constructionism claims to oppose.

The strict constructionists have turned all knowing into language conventions that depend on culture and history while disregarding how much knowledge all humans have in common that overrides all cultural differences. Few would question that history and culture influence our ways of construing many aspects of the world, such as whether a particular food tastes good or bad or whether an object has magical powers or adheres to laws of nature. But no matter what culture or subculture we belong to, nearly everyone recognizes that jumping from a high place will result in a rapid fall and probable injury, that infants require a long period of care before they can even minimally take care of their own needs, that health is better than sickness (witness healers from shamans to physicians), that food and water are required to maintain life, and so on. Even though these matters are handled differently in different cultures, the basic principles are accepted by all; they are *not* culture specific, and they provide a ground for common understanding.

In a survey of 220 cultures Murdock (1945) found a large array of distinctly cultural "elements" common to all. At one end of the alphabet they ranged from age-grading, athletic sports, and bodily adornment to, at the other end, visiting, weaning, and weather control. However, considerable variety exists within each of these categories specific to the "responses of the behaving individuals and of the stimulus situations in which the responses are evoked" (p. 125). What they have in common is "a uniform system of classification, not a single fund of identical elements" (p. 125). The most selfsame is the family, its form fundamentally the same everywhere without exception. What Murdock's survey indicates is that what is culturally alike or different is not a matter of Norwegian versus Bantu or scientist versus nonscientist, but that specificity rules. If we accept empirical findings at all—and constructionists do make empirical cross-cultural comparisons—the findings indicate that we cannot speak in blanket terms about what is local or nonlocal but must specify what categories are alike, what elements within the categories are different, and which of these is relevant to understandings we have in common—or not in common. Also deserving of attention is what means might be used to bridge the gap when communication is hampered by social differences. Lewis Wolpert (1993) takes up some of the issues considered in this chapter to provide such a bridge between scientists and nonscientists.

Just how much postmodernism itself is relevant to other cultures is open to question. A Q-sort (see chapter 11) study of environmental groups in India did not support the postmodernists' claims about transitions[3] from modern to postmodern society (Peritore, 1993). In the Indian culture the emerging environmental groups and their relationships are quite different from those of the West. It is rather ironical that postmodernism has pointed to cultural differences as a major argument against foundationalism and for localism, and now cultural differences suggest that postmodernism may have no relevance beyond a local group, in this case Western culture.

Relativism versus Realism. Greenwood (1992a, 1992b), a philosopher, contends that the following two major arguments of the constructionists do not hold: (a) no means exists to compare independent reality with descriptions, and (b) the language in which theoretical descriptions occur has no objectivity. He notes that discourse between himself and the constructionists is deemed objective and concludes that there is no reason for the language of scientific theory to be any less objective. The agreement of meaningful descriptions, he holds, occurs because we all make the same kinds of discriminations about a wide range of things around us. Also because of this agreement we can develop metaphor and theory about events that we cannot directly perceive. In addition to such agreement we must add shared social conventions. Common descriptions together with social conventions provide the opportunity to develop meaningful descriptions that can be tested. Cromer (1997), a physicist, argues that science is indeed objective and that the basis of that objectivity is repeatability together with theoretical knowledge of what is relevant to be repeated. Redhead (1995) takes a similar position. Referring to subatomic particles he notes that we may never know with certainty about their existence, but experimental evidence provides degrees of support, and the reliability of experimental reports can be assessed through testing and calibration. He finds that he must "reject the apparently liberal, openminded and egalitarian but ultimately destructive doctrines of the relativists and the social constructivists" (p. 16).

The constructionists, Greenwood insists, have provided no evidence that "descriptions *cannot* be adjudicated" (1992b, p. 189), and consequently there is no reason to resort to alternatives such as those derived from literary theory. Further, the claim that multiple theories could fit any data set, and therefore there is no way to eliminate the false ones, is untrue. Often, not even a single theory will account for an observation, he notes. Perhaps a good example of this is in cosmology (the study of the origin and evolution of the universe) in which the continuing flood of data from ever-improving telescopes makes finding a theory to fit the data a challenge that has not yet been met. In psychology the theories that have been proposed to account for such personality characteristics as liberal and conservative have also been unsuccessful. But where multiple theories in psychology can account for the observations, this is due,

---

3. Transitions would include new meanings of information, a service component that depends on knowledge, and government that assumes increasing roles in regulating a market economy and in protecting consumers (R. Brown, 1994).

Greenwood suggests, to "the artificiality of many experimental and other empirical studies" (1992b, p. 189). The problem could be avoided, he avers, by adopting a realist position of "the social relational dimensions of *mind and action*"(1992b, p. 189).

Most scientists, including those in the psychological sciences, would probably agree with Greenwood about scientific realism, but some would disagree with the psychophysical dualism of *"mind and action."*

Reductionism and the Double World

S. Brown (1995) notes that constructionism is reductionistic in that it reduces individual activity to an operation of the social group—that individuality is a function of a more fundamental unit. This reductionism prevents constructionism from accounting for individual creativity or for intellectual ideas that individuals formulate prior to submitting them to any discourse community and that community's social construction. Similarly, Fletcher (1992) suggests that the "extreme brand" of constructionism assumes an "oversocialized" conception of human activity that provides no room for individual characteristics or creativity. Judging from Gergen's statement about writing, one might conclude that he would reply that all seemingly individualistic actions are embedded in a history of prior social interactions and are an inextricable part of them: "Let us consider the possibility that writings are never the works of single individuals. They are products of historical conventions or participatory systems in which individuals are mere conduits of communal forms" (Gergen, 1986, p. 482). Still, by attempting to explain one form of behavior (individual) at another level that constructionism assumes to be more fundamental (social), this approach remains reductionistic. It denies that the functioning level, individual behavior in this case, has any relative independence or any operational principles of its own.

S. Brown also points out that not only does constructionism have to accept that it too is a social construction (as Gergen does) but must also acknowledge that within that system even its account of social constructions would be reduced to a social construction. It appears that constructionism may be caught in an infinite regress in which one goes infinitely backward in search of a beginning point of constructions.

In addition to reductionism, does constructionism assume a dual world, one that is socially constructed and another that the construction is based on, the latter unknowable in actuality? If so, this suggests roots in the work of Immanuel Kant, the nineteenth century German philosopher who argued that because the real world is only a representation in the mind, it is unknowable. Kant, in effect, declared that we live in two worlds, a real one that we can't know and a mental one that we do know, which represents the real world. And that takes us back to mind-as-mirror that Rorty and other postmodernists/constructionists have claimed to reject. If constructionism does not accept that constructions are based on actual events, then it accepts only abstractions—the constructions themselves—as having existence, a kind of solipsism.

Postmodernism versus Physical and Biological Sciences

Two scientists, Gross and Levitt (1994), have written an extensive rejoinder to postmodernism's attack on science. The authors note that postmodernists assume that Western civilization is on the verge of collapse and cannot creatively meet the future. The postmodernists, they point out, credit themselves with great moral authority in making pronouncements but show only superficial understanding of science. These proponents claim that science is prejudiced and a social artifact and that their own system offers new wisdom that can evaluate scientific questions. Yet the proponents are not even technically competent to do so, for few postmodernists are scientists or have studied science intensively enough to have any detailed knowledge or facility with it. Gross and Levitt see postmodernism as a threat to science in that it endangers the capacity of the broader culture to utilize scientific achievements and to intelligently evaluate the findings of science.

Postmodern skepticism about science does not extend to the pronouncements the proponents make about the merits of postmodernism itself. Postmodernists "deny any special privilege to science as compared with intuition or myth, but claim just such privilege for postmodern criticism" (Smith, p. 393). Another inconsistency, Gross and Levitt note, is that these proponents attack both the foundations of science and the conclusions of science by the very procedures of logic and evidence that science uses. They appeal to rather standard measures of truth that can form a logical coherency. Further, postmodernism abandons all universal theories and embraces indeterminate meanings, instability, and total relativism, which its proponents claim will free us from the oppression and ecological disaster that science is imposing. Is this not itself a universal theory, Gross and Levitt ask?

Rather than scientific language being a game that only the rich and powerful can play, as the philosopher Lyotard claims, Gross and Levitt argue that scientific language is open to all. With its objective description of findings about the world, all can communicate about those findings and share in them. The poorest people want the benefits of science. To deny those benefits would be inhuman. "To put the matter brutally, science *works*" (p. 49). A philosopher, Paul Kurtz (1994), expresses the matter similarly: "The scientific approach to understanding nature and human life has been vindicated by its success" (p. 257).

Gross and Levitt remind us that one legacy of the Enlightenment was to build a unified body of knowledge about the world, but postmodernism holds itself opposed to this, insisting that the pursuit of knowledge is hopeless, a delusion and even oppressive to some social groups. It insists that no universal knowledge is possible, for all knowledge is situated in local conditions as a product of social class and formed by the prejudices and historical existence of that social class. Instead of knowledge, we have only stories or narratives that

help us make sense of the world; but, as Gross and Levitt observe, such postmodernist understanding is expressed in terms of the prejudices and self-interests of the narrator.

> In scorning the Enlightenment, the postmodern left is clearly cutting away the roots, emotional as well as intellectual, that formed and sustained its most deeply held egalitarian ideals . . . The doctrine, at its most virulent, is hardly distinguishable from the moral blankness . . . upon which fascism was erected in the first half of this century. (Gross & Levitt, p. 73)

Englebretsen (1995), a philosopher, views the effects of postmodernism in a manner similar to that of the scientists Gross and Levitt. He believes it has a pernicious effect on science and education. These subjects are "compromised, contorted, denigrated, denied" (p. 53) by postmodernism's blaming them for all social evils and its determination to replace them with local beliefs and to eliminate distinctions between teacher and student. He finds that while postmodernism emphasizes tolerance for all ideas, whether rational or irrational, it is intolerant of people. This intolerance arises from its insistence on local truths that divide people according to their locality, and that locality may be based on race, age, nationality, or gender. "When my truth and your truth are different depending on the differences between us, then the differences between us cannot be ignored—they matter too much" (p. 53).

Gross and Levitt observe what they consider the pernicious effects of postmodernism on the social sciences—that anthropology has given over to the postmodernists and dropped its scientific principles for antiscientific relativism, and that some of sociology and some of social psychology have replaced rigorous research with storytelling.

Postmodernists draw from Thomas Kuhn's claim in his celebrated book on "paradigms" (conceptual frameworks) in science that new paradigms successfully replace old ones only when the advocates of the old ones leave the scene and a new generation takes over. The paradigms, Kuhn indicates, are incommensurate with one another.

Postmodernists also draw from the Willard Quine's contention that any number of scientific theories could fit a given set of data. (Kuhn is a historian and Quine a philosopher.) These authors appear to demonstrate that science has no absolute truths and that knowledge is totally relative to social and historical circumstances. But Kuhn has distorted the actual progress of science by using selective examples from its early history to claim a series of revolutions that have little continuity (Cromer, 1997). Wolpert (1993), a research biologist, gives numerous examples to illustrate that in many instances both Kuhn and Quine are wrong. Further, he denies that science seeks absolute truth. What it seeks are theories that provide a better understanding of the events observed. "While the initial stage of acceptance of one or other of competing theories may have a strong social aspect that involves fashion, power groupings and so on, the main criterion will eventually be how well the theory explains the phenomena" (p. 103). A half century earlier, Kantor (1942) was reacting to similar questions: "While constructions are different from the original data and are influenced by the instruments and hypotheses of the investigator, they are neither arbitrary nor simply impositions upon the events through the influence of traditions" (p. 177).

Wolpert points out that the relativists' claim that science and beliefs are both socially constructed and equivalent as truth fails to take account of the closed nature of belief—acceptance with little scrutiny—whereas scientific claims are open to challenge and change. In fact a great strength of science is that it provides procedures for gathering information, testing claims, and drawing inferences that are open to others. As indicated above, scrutiny by women has shown the need for modifications to gender-biased science. Andersen (1994) suggests that the objectivity of science is a social process in which many people participate in questioning, challenging, agreeing, revising, replicating. With a variety of different people with different perspectives studying a question about nature, some tentative finding emerges that may be less than perfect and may

need changing or modifying later but that provides some understanding, some objectivity, for the moment.

One such understanding has resulted in the acceptance of vaccines for prevention of disease in Japan, China, Egypt, and tribal Africa as well as in Europe and North America. Such achievements are clearly more than local even if a few groups reject them. Many cultures and subcultures can come to recognize and accept the scientific and technological advantage of vaccines and telephones—that, to repeat Gross and Levitt's words, "science *works*." Do the postmodernists/constructionists really want to insist that the lengthened life span in many countries that has resulted from a scientific understanding of sanitation, disease, and nutrition is merely a social construction? If so, whose construction?

The universality of science itself is underscored by the growing participation in scientific and technological research around the world. International scientific conferences and international collaboration are commonplace. Scientific journals and books often contain contributions from many different cultures and nations, not all of them from the West. Many countries comprising greatly diverse cultures but without facilities for training students in the sciences are sending their students to those countries that can provide the training. The interest in pursuing science is based on a widespread recognition that science does work and on a desire to gain its benefits. Of course, science and technology can be used for evil purposes or can have damaging results, but so can just about anything else. That is where the importance of broad democratization as a control system together with dissemination of scientific knowledge becomes important.

The constructionist proponents Semin and Gergen (1990) admit "the constructionists have failed as yet to render compelling accounts of the origins of discursive practices, the relationships between language and behaviour, and the significant gains by the natural sciences" (p. 16). R. Brown (1994) concedes that the social sciences, too, have made contributions to society. They have championed "academic freedom, professional judgment, civil liberties and due process of law" and been an important force in "the victory of civility over violence, reason and evidence over passion and prejudice, clear communication over cloudy commitment" (p. 26). Even so, he concludes, "foundationalism has become philosophically untenable" (p. 26).

Influence on Education

Constructivism, Cromer (1997) finds, has permeated public school standards. It results in a form of science education, supported by grants from the National Science Foundation, that is based on a discovery process which is ineffective, highly misleading, and often erroneous. Cromer charges,

> In the United States, pre-high school science education, such as it is, is controlled by professional science educators, trained in schools of education which have been notorious for a hundred years for their low academic standards. Rare is the science educator who knows even the science expected of an eighth grader. It's this group which has enthusiastically endorsed constructivism because it allows them to speak only about process (whatever that is) rather than content (of which they are ignorant). And it's this group that writes the frameworks, standards, and textbooks for elementary and middle schools. (p. 11)

Constructivism, he further charges, has vilified objective knowledge and provided the rationale for educators to reject academic science and to perpetuate ignorance. Teachers (a) functioning only as facilitators and (b) facilitating pupils to construct their own frameworks as a replacement for universal frameworks of knowledge have undermined education. He reviews science education in Greece and finds that after nine years—and with no emphasis on self-esteem—Greek pupils have a far better grasp of science than American pupils after twelve years. Extensive research on self-esteem shows no relation to either performance or personal goals (Bandura, 1997).

Cromer also challenges the constructionist's assertion that literature is the master science. While recognizing the critical importance of language in education, he suggests that most of culture is transmitted without language. Manual skills are difficult to describe in language and are mostly learned by imitation, and pictures can often instruct or illustrate better than any words. Art, music, athletics, and crafts may use words to encourage or to correct, but demonstration is more often fundamental. Derrida and Foucault and the constructivists have it backwards, he contends, when they argue that scientific knowledge is impossible because (a) only language provides thinking, and language cannot properly represent reality; and (b) empirical approaches cannot validate themselves. This, he suggests, is a reversion to a medieval version of Aristotle in which logic and discussion would lead to truth. Newton, he notes, showed the immense power of reasoning (Platonic rationalism) combined with observation (Aristotelian empiricism). Empirical observation and reason as equal partners opened the whole world to inquiry.

Much of what Cromer attributes to constructivism began in teacher training colleges in the 1930s, well before constructivism made its appearance (see chapter 4, p. 125). Nevertheless, constructivism is compatible with the educational policy that Cromer refers to and that dominates public schools in the United States. Further, constructivists are introducing additional or modified points of view to that policy. For example, while traditional policy has given a back seat to academic achievement (while denying this neglect), constructivism soft-pedals it even more and offers group consensus as a replacement. In at least some cases, constructivism has rejected evaluation of its results so that the opportunity to experiment would not be discouraged (Sykes, 1995). The National Commission on Excellence in Education sounded the alarm with its publication of *A Nation at Risk* (U.S. National Commission, 1983). It documented low expectations and poor performance in the schools. Since that time, further comparative evaluations of American students with those of other industrialized countries show a dismal performance of the former. Whatever the contributions of constructivism and humanistic psychology (see chapter 4, pp. 124–126 and 134–136, especially table 4.1) may be to social constructions and self-enhancement respectively, together with long-standing educational policy in teacher training colleges with which they are largely compatible, they have been severely injurious to academic achievement. Overwhelming evidence shows no possibility that these approaches can ever reverse that effect (Stebbins et al., 1977; Watkins, 1988; Adams & Engelmann, 1996).

Another negative result among many is that those in higher education, except for highly selective institutions, have to contend with numerous poorly prepared and poorly motivated students and provide remedial courses for their deficiencies. The laments of undergraduate instructors are legion, and the grade inflation in colleges and universities from the pressure to accept lower performance is pervasive.

Modifications of Constructionism

In order to avoid some of the extreme conclusions of strict constructionism, such modifications as contextual constructionism have arisen (p. 239). This provides an alternative to the constructionist position in which a knowing relationship consists of an interaction in a context of a knower and a knowable world. Upon this knowing interaction we can strive to develop additional knowledge about nature, including social relationships and the role of language so important to the constructionist. In actuality, as Woolgar and Pawluch (1985) point out, constructionists engaged in research necessarily use an interpretive framework that anchors itself in this common-sense world. It allows them to observe and analyze the social constructions that they report.

Along similar lines, Foster (1987) shows by historical example that, contrary to some constructionist claims, scientific knowledge *does* accumulate and *can be* objective. The fact that knowledge of an object is never complete or may be erroneous

on initial contact does not support absolute unknowability. With successive contacts with the object, knowledge increases; and it is contact with the object, not a philosophical position, that shapes our understanding. Only by denying that we have contacts with objects can the constructionist maintain a position of relativism against objectivity. Relativism, he notes, has been linked politically with anarchism and fascism; he quotes Mussolini (ruler of Italy 1922–1943 and an ally of Hitler) on the advantages of relativism (see also quotation above from Gross & Levitt). Similarly, a statement by Hitler makes the same arguments as the postmodernists about objectivity, science, truth, morals, power, and relativism (Rauschning, 1940). R. Brown (1994), however, claims that relativism has produced fewer atrocities than absoluteness and asks which is worse: evil justified as cultural relativism or evil justified by insistence on absolute truth? He insists that tyranny depends on absoluteness whereas democracy depends on relativism for exercising judgment.

Another proposed modification—among many—would recognize social influences while retaining a construct of self as a causative agent (Mascolo & Dalto, 1995). This proposal would utilize probabilistic epigenesis (see chapter 13, p. 380) in which the organism is one of the interacting components in a hierarchical development system of organism-environment interaction; and, by analogy, the self is a level within that system. Note that this proposal has a construct (self) interacting with objects or events (organism and environment). (See chapter 11, pp. 322–323 for an alternative, non-dualistic approach to self.)

CONCLUSIONS

Postmodernism is based in art and literary criticism but has made a contribution to science by showing the subjectivity, the value-laden characteristics, and the cultural and gender biases of much of science and the need to take these into account. However, the extremism of postmodernists in scorning and denigrating the sciences has earned them the opprobrium of scientists and others, and some of the influences of social constructivism in education may be more detrimental than helpful. It has become prominent in women's studies, sociology of social problems, social psychology, and educational psychology. But few in the physical and biological sciences or in most of the other areas of psychology have accepted it as the queen of the sciences or the master science. Increasingly, postmodernism is regarded as just another art style and not having anything worthwhile to say about the structure of knowledge or science.

Danziger (1997) sees constructionism as playing primarily a critical role, one of challenging the assumptions of mainstream psychology. It is his hope that in this role it may help reduce dogmatism. And because it has served primarily as a critic, it is dependent for its existence on the very system it seeks to change. Therefore, it may be called "parasitic" or perhaps "symbiotic," he notes. This dependence leads it to take a much more traditional position than might be expected from its propositions, Danziger concludes.

That conclusion seems to square with some of the points suggested above (Critique), that postmodernism/constructionism seems to make use of at least four principles that appear contrary to its agenda: (a) use of rationality beyond any local group, (b) crossing of social group boundaries to make comparisons, (c) use of empirical evidence, (d) a social reform orientation that ignores relativism, (e) implicit recognition of the actuality of non-social events.

It seems clear that social constructionism is playing an important role in pointing up a number of important conditions and shortcomings in psychology of which the following may be mentioned: the subjectivity in the planning and interpretation of research; the values inherent in research; the limitations of "objective" methodologies in experimental psychology; the authoritarian role of the therapist assumed by some psychotherapies; the inextricable role of context and history in any scientific enterprise; and the social and historical origins of some of the common constructs in psychology such as mentalism, representationism, and biological reductionism.

Few in psychology or other sciences, however, are ready to give up observations and relegate all knowledge and all procedures to mere language conventions as strict constructionism requires. Contextual constructionism with its continuing ties to the commonplace world and that world's contextual relationships might enjoy a somewhat better reception. "The liberation of psychological theories from narrowly-defined (but not necessarily from all) observation statements may yet be [constructionism's] strongest legacy" (Stam, 1990, p. 251).

REFERENCES

Adams, Gary L., & Siegfried Engelmann. 1996. *Research on Direct Instruction: 25 Years Beyond Distar.* Seattle, WA: Educational Achievement Systems.

Anderson, Harlene, & Harold Goolishian. 1992. The client is the expert: A not-knowing approach to therapy. In *Therapy as Social Construction.* Edited by Sheila M. McNamee & Kenneth J. Gergen. London: Sage Publications, pp. 25–29.

Andersen, Milton L. 1994. The many and varied social constructions of intelligence. In *Constructing the Social.* Edited by Theodore R. Sarbin & John I. Kitsuse. London & Thousand Oaks, CA: Sage.

Bandura, Albert. 1997. *Self Efficacy: The Exercise of Control.* San Francisco: Freeman Press.

Berliner, David, & Bruce J. Biddle. 1995. *The Manufactured Crisis: Myths, Fraud, and the Attack on America's Public Schools.* Reading, MA: Addison-Wesley.

Best, Joel. 1993. But seriously folks: The limitations of the strict constructionist interpretations of social problems. In *Reconsidering Social Constructionism: Debates in Social Problems Theory.* Edited By J. A. Holstein & G. Miller. Hawthorne, NY: Aldine, DeGruyter.

Brown, Richard H. 1994. Reconstructing social theory after the postmodern critique. In *After Postmodernism: Reconstructing Ideology Critique.* Edited by Herbert W. Simons & Michael Billig. London: Sage Publications.

Brown, Steven R. 1995. Q methodology, postmodernism, and social constructionism. Q Methodology Network [Listserver], May 29.

Burkitt, Ian. 1996. Social and personal constructs: A division left unresolved. *Theory and Psychology* 6: 71–77.

Caldwell, Michael J. 1994. Applying social constructionism in the treatment of patients who are intractably aggressive. *Hospital and Community Psychiatry* 45: 597–600.

Caputo, J. D. 1983. The thought of being and the conversation of mankind: The case of Heidegger and Rorty. *Review of Metaphysics* 36: 661–85.

Coelho De Amorim, Annibal, & Fatima G. Cavalcante. 1992. Narrations of the self: Video production in a marginalized subculture. In *Therapy as Social Construction*. Edited by S. MacNamee & K. Gergen. London: Sage Publications.

Constas, Mark A. 1998. The changing nature of educational research and a critique of postmodernism. *Educational Researcher* 27 (2): 26–33.

Coulter, Jeff. 1989. *Mind in Action*. Atlantic Highlands, NJ: Humanities Press.

Crawford, June; Susan Kippax; Jenny Onyx; Una Gault; and Pam Benton. 1990. Women theorising their experiences of anger: A study using memory-work. *Australian Psychologist* 25: 333–50.

Cromer, Alan. 1997. *Connected Knowledge: Science, Philosophy, and Education*. New York: Oxford University Press.

Curt, Beryl C. 1994. *Textuality and Tectonics: Troubling Social and Psychological Science*. Philadelphia: Open University Press.

Cushman, Philip. 1991. Ideology obscured: Political uses of the self in Daniel Stern's infant. *American Psychologist* 46: 206–219.

Danziger, Kurt. 1997. The varieties of social construction. *Theory and Psychology* 7: 399–416.

Derrida, Jacques. 1992. *Margins of Philosophy*. Translated by Alan Bass. Chicago: University of Chicago Press.

———. 1997. Deconstruction in a Nutshell: A Conversation with Jacques Derrida. New York: Fordham University Press.

de Shazer, S. 1991. *Putting Differences to Work*. New York: Norton.

Durrant, M., & K. Kowalski. 1993. Enhancing views of competence. In *The New Language of Change: Constructive Collaboration in Psychotherapy*. Edited by S. Friedman. New York: Guilford Press.

Eagleton, Terry. 1983. *Literary Theory: An Introduction*. Minneapolis: University of Minnesota Press.

Efran, Jay S., & Leslie E. Clarfield. 1992. Constructionist therapy: Sense and nonsense. In *Therapy as Social Construction*. Edited by Sheila McNamee & Kenneth J. Gergen. London and Newbury Park: Sage Publications.

Efran, Jay S., & Robert L. Fauber. 1995. Radical constructivism: Questions and answers. In *Constructivism in Psychotherapy*. Edited by Robert A. Neimeyer & Michael J. Mahoney. Washington, DC: American Psychological Association.

Englebretsen, George. 1995. Postmodernism and new age unreason. *Skeptical Inquirer* 19, no. 3 (May/June): 52–53.

Fish, Stanley E. 1980. *Is There a Text in This Class?* Cambridge, MA: Harvard University Press.

Fletcher, Garth J. 1992. The social construction of our bodies. Review of *Physical Being: A Theory for a Corporeal Psychology* by Rom Harr. Oxford, England: Basil Blackwell, 1991. *Contemporary Psychology* 37: 1186.

Foster, James. 1987. An appeal for objectivism in psychological metatheory. In *The Analysis of Psychological Theory: Metapsychological Perspectives*. Edited by H. Stam, T. B. Rogers, & K. J. Gergen. Washington, DC: Hemisphere Publishing.

Foucault, Michel. 1980. *Power/Knowledge*. New York: Pantheon.

Friedman, Steven, & Margot T. Fanger. 1991. *Expanding Therapeutic Possibilities: Putting Grief Psychotherapy to Work*. New York: Livingston.

Fruggeri, Laura. 1992. Therapeutic change as the social construction of change. In *Therapy as Social Construction*. Edited by Sheila McNamee & Kenneth J. Gergen. London and Newbury Park: Sage Publications.

Fruggeri, Laura, & Matteini, M. 1991 La struttura della narrazione terapeutica. In *Soggetto, Emozioni, Sistema*. Edited by V. Ugazio. Milan: Vita e Pensiero.

Gallivan, J. 1994. Subjectivity and the psychology of gender: Q as a feminist methodology. In *Women, Girls, and Achievement*. Edited by J. Gallivan, S. D. Crozier, & V. M. Lalande. Toronto: Captus University Publications.

Gergen, Kenneth J. 1985. The social constructionist movement in modern psychology. *American Psychologist* 40: 266–75.

———. 1986. Elaborating the constructionist thesis. *American Psychologist* 41: 481–82.

———. 1994a. The limits of pure critique. In *After Postmodernism: Reconstructing Ideology Critique*. Edited by Herbert W. Simons & Michael Billig. London: Sage.

———. 1994b. *Relations and Relationships: Soundings in Social Construction*. Cambridge, MA: Harvard University Press.

———. 1997. The place of the psyche in a constructed world. *Theory and Psychology* 7: 723–46.

Giorgi, Amedeo. 1992. Whither humanistic psychology? *Humanistic Psychologist* 20: 422–38.

Greenwood, John D. 1992a. Realism, empiricism and social constructionism: Psychological theory and the social dimensions of mind and action. *Theory and Psychology* 2: 131–51.

———. 1992b. Realism, relativism and rhetoric: A response to comments on "Realism, empiricism and social constructionism." *Theory and Psychology* 2: 183–92.

Greer, Scott. 1997. Nietzsche and social construction: Directions for a postmodern historiography. *Theory and Psychology* 7: 83–100.

Gross, Paul R., & Norman Levitt. 1994. *Higher Superstition: The Academic Left and Its Quarrels with Science.* Baltimore, MD: Johns Hopkins University Press.

Haley, Jay. 1963. *Strategies of Psychotherapy.* New York: Grune & Stratton.

Hardy, Kenneth V. 1993. Live supervision in the postmodern era of family therapy: Issues, reflections, and questions. *Contemporary Family Therapy* 15: 9–20.

Harr, Rom. 1986a. *The Social Construction of Emotions.* Oxford, England: Basil Blackwell.

———. 1986b. *Varieties of Realism: A Rationale for the Natural Sciences.* Oxford, England: Basil Blackwell.

———. 1987. Grammar, psychology and moral rights. In *Meaning and the Growth of Understanding: Wittgenstein's Significance for Developmental Psychology.* Edited by M. Chapman & R. A. Dixon. Berlin: Springer-Verlag.

Hoffman, Lynn. 1991. A reflexive stance for family therapy. *Journal of Strategic and Systemic Therapies* 10 (3 & 4): 4–17.

Jones, Byrd L., & Robert W. Maloy. 1996. *Schools for an Information Age: Reconstructing Foundations for Learning and Teaching.* Westport, CN: Praeger.

Kantor, J. R. 1929. *An Outline of Social Psychology.* Chicago: Follett.

———. 1942. Preface to interbehavioral psychology. *Psychological Record* 5: 173–93.

———. 1982. *Cultural Psychology.* Chicago: Principia Press.

Keller, Evelyn F. 1983. *A Feeling for the Organism: The Life and Work of Barbara McClintock.* San Francisco: Freeman.

———. 1995. *Reflections on Gender and Science.* New Haven, CT: Yale University Press.

Kelly, George. 1955/1991. *The Psychology of Personal Constructs.* London, New York: Routledge.

Kippax, Susan; June Crawford; Pam Benton; Una Gault; & Jenny Noesjirwan. 1988. Constructing emotions: Weaving meaning from memories. *British Journal of Social Psychology* 27: 19–33.

Kitzinger, Celia. 1986. Introducing and developing Q as a feminist methodology: A study of accounts of lesbianism. In *Feminist Social Psychology.* Edited by S. Wilkinson. Philadelphia: Open University Press.

———. 1987. *The Social Construction of Lesbianism.* London: Sage.

Kitzinger, Celia, & R. Stainton Rogers. 1985. A Q-methodological study of lesbian identities. *European Journal of Social Psychology* 15: 167–87.

Kurtz, Paul. 1994. The growth of antiscience. *Skeptical Inquirer* 18: 255–65.

Kvale, Steiner. 1990. Post modern psychology: A contradictio in adjecto? *Humanistic Psychology* 18: 35–54.

Lyddon, William J. 1995. Forms and facets of constructivist psychology. In *Constructivism in Psychotherapy.* Edited by Robert A. Neimeyer & Michael J. Mahoney. Washington, DC: American Psychological Association.

Mancuso, James C. 1996. Constructionism, personal construct psychology and narrative psychology. *Theory and Psychology* 6: 47–70.

Manicus, Peter T., & Paul F. Secord. 1983. Implications for psychology of the new philosophy of science. *American Psychologist* 38: 399–413.

Marlowe, Bruce A., & Marilyn L. Page. 1998. *Creating and Sustaining the Constructivist Classroom.* Thousand Oaks, CA: Corvin Press.

Martin, Jack, & Janice Thompson. 1997. Between scientism and relativism: Phenomenology, hermeneutics and the new realism in psychology. *Theory and Psychology* 7: 629–52.

Mascolo, Michael F., & Carol A. Dalto. 1995. Self and modernity on trial: A reply to Gergen's *Saturated Self. Journal of Constructivist Psychology* 8: 175–91.

McKeown, Bruce F. 1970. Q methodology, communication, and the behavioral text. *Electronic Journal of Communication* 1. Troy, NY: computer file, access via electronic mail "send mckeown v1n190" Comserve@rpitsvm.

Murdock, George P. 1945. The common denominator of cultures. In *The Science of Man in the World Crisis.* Edited by Ralph Linton. New York: Columbia University Press.

Neimeyer, Robert A. 1995. Constructivist psychotherapies: Features, foundations, and future directions. In *Constructivism in Psychotherapy.* Edited by Robert A. Neimeyer & Michael J. Mahoney. Washington, DC: American Psychological Association.

Nemecek, Sasha. 1997. The furor over feminist science. *Scientific American* 277 (January): 99–100.

Nettler, Gwynne. 1986. Construing the world. *American Psychologist* 41: 480.

O'Hanlon, Bill, & James Wilk. 1987. *Shifting Contexts.* New York: Guilford Press.

Palinscar, A. Sullivan. 1998. Social constructivist perspectives on teaching and learning. *Annual Review of Psychology* 49: 345–75.

Peterson, Patrick. 1993. Environmental attitudes of Indian elites: Challenging Western postmodernist models. *Asian Survey* 33: 804–818.

Polkinghorne, Donald E. 1992. Postmodern epistemology of practice. In *Psychology and Postmodernism.* Edited by Steiner Kvale. London: Sage.

Prawat, Richard S. 1996. Constructivisms, modern and postmodern. *Educational Psychologist* 313: 215–25.

Rauschning, Hermann. 1940. *The Voice of Destruction* (cited in Cromer, 1997). New York: Putnam.

Redhead, Michael. 1995. *From Physics to Metaphysics*. Cambridge: Cambridge University Press.

Reiss, Ira L. 1993. The future of sex research and the meaning of science. *Journal of Sex Research* 30: 3–11.

Richardson, Virginia, ed. 1997. *Constructivist Teacher Education: Building New Understandings*. Washington, DC: Falmer Press.

Richter, Paul. 1992. An introduction to deconstructionist psychology. In *Psychology and Postmodernism*. Edited by Steiner Kvale. London & Newbury Park, CA: Sage.

Rorty, Richard. 1979. *Philosophy and the Mirror of Nature*. Princeton, NJ: Princeton University Press.

Sarbin, Theodore R., & John I. Kitsuse. 1994. A prologue to constructing the social. In *Constructing the Social*. Edited by Theodore R. Sarbin & John I. Kitsuse. London and Thousand Oaks, CA: Sage.

Sauber, S. R.; L. L'Abate; G. R. Weeks; & W. L. Buchanan. 1993. *The Dictionary of Family Psychology and Family Therapy*, 2nd ed. Newbury Park, CA: Sage Publications.

Scarr, Sandra. 1985. Constructing psychology: Making facts and fables for our times. *American Psychologist* 40: 499–512.

Semin, Gün R., & Kenneth J. Gergen, eds. 1990. *Everyday Understanding: Social and Scientific Implications*. London: Sage Publications.

Smith, M. Brewster. 1995. About postmodernism: Reply to Gergen and others. *American Psychologist* 50: 393.

Spanier, Bonnie. 1995. *Im/Partial Science: Gender Ideology in Molecular Biology*. Bloomington, IN: Indiana University Press.

Speed, Bebe. 1991. Reality exists, O.K.? An argument against constructivism and constructionism. *Family Therapy* 13: 395–409.

Stainton Rogers, Wendy, & Rex Stainton Rogers. 1989. Taking the child abuse debate apart. In *Child Abuse and Neglect*. Edited by W. Stainton Rogers, D. Hevey, & E. Ash. London: Batsford.

Stam, Henderikus J. 1990. Rebuilding the ship at sea: The historical and theoretical problems of constructionist epistemologies in psychology. *Canadian Journal of Psychology* 31: 239–53.

Stebbins, S. L.; R. G. St. Pierre; E. C. Proper; R. B. Anderson; & T. R. Cerva. 1977. *Education as Experimentation: A Planned Variation Model*, vol. IV A–D. *An Evaluation of Follow Through*. Cambridge, MA: ABT Associates.

Stern, Daniel. 1985. *The Interpersonal World of the Infant: A View from Psychoanalysis and Developmental Psychology*. New York: Basic Books.

Stowell-Smith, Mark. 1997. Identity dilemmas and psychological discourse: The case of psychopaths in a secure psychiatric hospital. *Operant Subjectivity* 20: 143–58.

Sykes, Charles J. 1995. *Dumbing Down Our Kids: Why America's Children Feel Good about Themselves but Can't Read, Write, or Add*. New York: St. Martin's Press.

Terwee, Sybe J. S. 1995. Deconstructing social constructionism. In *Trends and Issues in Theoretical Psychology*. Edited by Ian Lubek, René van Hezewijk, Gail Pheterson, & Thomas W. Tolman. New York: Springer.

U.S. National Commission on Excellence in Education. 1983. *A Nation at Risk: The Imperative for Educational Reform*. Washington, DC: The Commission-Superintendent of Documents.

Watkins, Cathy L. 1988. Project Follow-Through: A story of the identification and neglect of effective instruction. *Youth Policy* 10 (7): 7–11.

Wexler, Philip. 1987. After social psychology. In *The Analysis of Psychological Theory: Metapsychological Perspectives*. Edited by H. J. Stam, T. B. Rogers, & K. J. Gergen. Washington, DC: Hemisphere Publishing.

White, Michael, & David Epstein. 1990. *Narrative Means to Therapeutic Ends*. New York: Norton.

Wolpert, Lewis. 1993. *The Unnatural Nature of Science*. Cambridge, MA: Harvard University Press.

Woolfolk, Robert. 1992. Hermeneutics, social constructionism and other items of intellectual fashion: Intimations for clinical science. *Behavior Therapy* 23: 213–23.

Woolgar, S., & D. Pawluch. 1985. Ontological gerrymandering: The anatomy of social problems explanations. *Social Problems* 32: 214–27.

Wortham, Stanton. 1996. Are constructs personal? *Theory and Psychology* 6: 79–84.

Noncentric or Interactional Context Systems

CHAPTER 9

Dialectic Psychology: Conflict and Contradiction as a Basis of Change

Chapter Outline

INTRODUCTION

Probably everyone has been in an argument. One party presents his or her side of the issue and the other presents counter arguments. This is one form of dialectic. Even a discussion in which there is a simple interchange of ideas or information is a dialectic process. A monologue by one person is not dialectic. There must be a dialogue or interchange.

The word "dialectic" derives from Greek *dia-*, meaning between, and *legein*, meaning to argue, reason, talk—talking between two persons. More generally, it is the logical examination of ideas, often by means of questions and answers, for the purpose of arriving at some determination of their validity. A famous example is that of the dialogues of Plato in which Socrates raises questions with various figures in the city of Athens about such topics as virtue and the good, then continues probing each of the answers he receives until he reaches some better understanding.

Dialectics can also mean defining a concept or principle and testing it by showing all its consequences, both negative and positive. It is a way of probing for new alternatives, finding still other meanings. A reviewer of these many meanings concluded that "If there is any core meaning of dialectic, it would seem to be the idea of bipolarity, opposition, or contradiction. To be a true dialectic, one end of the bipolarity must directly imply the other" (Rychlak, 1976, p. 14). Perhaps three characteristics would be accepted by most dialecticians:

1. All reality consists of a whole with interrelated parts.
2. Reality consists of opposing forces rather than static states, and any resolution of these opposite forces creates new opposites.
3. Reality is constantly changing (Koerner and Linehan, 1992).

To some dialecticians "opposites" can refer simply to non-being: when we recognize any existing thing we automatically recognize its opposite or its negation, its non-being (Georgouldi, 1983).

Dialectic can also mean the analysis of a concept or thesis that reveals an antithesis, the opposite of the thesis. Continued analysis produces one or more syntheses of the thesis and antithesis. Each dialectical event, when it is developed, produces its own negation—its non-being as an opposite. The antithesis does not have to come from elsewhere (Buss, 1976). Many dialecticians hold that the synthesis will, in turn, produce a new thesis and this another antithesis (Fig. 9.1): in thesis-antithesis to synthesis, the dialectic process is infinite. No final resolution is possible, for every thesis (or synthesis) implies its opposite.

In psychology, the dialectic process presupposes that human interaction between the individual and the world is a developmental process that never ends. Every dialectical exchange brings changes in both the person and the world that lead to ever new interchanges. And this occurs in a context involving meanings that are part of the ever-changing dialectic. The person and the world are not independent of each other, and neither is one of them *in* the other. Rather, they

> are intertwined in an individual-world field that comprises their unity. Within this gestalt, various aspects (e.g., individual, world) may be distinguished, but they are always parts of the field and refer to it for their identity. The individual requires the worldly context for the content of his thoughts and actions, for the ranges of possibilities (of thinking and acting) among which he can choose. Without this common ground people's ideas and behaviors would be random and chaotic, having nothing to delimit them and nothing to refer to. (Ratner, 1971, p. 83)

Where Ratner refers to the person and the world in "an individual-world field" with a unity, Kvale

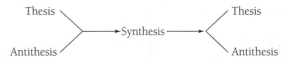

Figure 9.1. One Conception of the Dialectic Process.

(1977) similarly tells us that "dialectics focuses on development and interaction that exist as aspects of a totality . . ." (pp. 165–66) and "emphasizes the interdependence of man and world" (p. 166). Dialectical psychology, then, focuses on the meaningful relationship between the person and the world rather than on one pole of the dialectic. That is, dialectics puts no premium on either the individual or the world but on the interaction between them—the field of relationships involving the person and surroundings. And because each component of the "individual-world field" is influenced by other components and derives some of its quality from them, the field of relationships is not reducible to any of its components. For example, learning, remembering, and believing cannot be accounted for by the brain or by culture or by the environment, although each one plays a role in the total field. For those dialectical psychologists who hold this view, causation is not internal (a brain or mind) or external (the world); rather, causality resides in the field, the dialectical interchange with its history and context. Others, however, implicitly reject this when they assume an internal cause.

Kvale (1977) expressly excludes the inner-outer dichotomy: "A dialectical approach to psychology rejects the subject-object dichotomy and the dualism of an inner consciousness and an outer behavior. . . ." (p. 166). Further, "meaning is located neither inside nor outside, but exists in man's continual dialogue with the world" (p. 172). And "behavior is no mere indicator of an inner state, man is his behavior to the world" (Kvale & Grenness, 1967, p. 132).

Dialectics has a role in the theory about motivation and control of behavior that has affected more people than any other on earth. The Bolshevik revolution, which espoused a radically modified version of the dialectics of Karl Marx, led to the formation of the Soviet Union. That political state affected nearly everyone on earth either directly or indirectly, and the lives (and deaths) of hundreds of millions were directly caught up in it. The dialectical views of Mao Zedong (Mao Tse-Tung in earlier spelling conventions) and his

revolution directly affected the lives of more than one fifth of the people on earth (Ho, 1988). Yet these psychological concepts have received little attention in the West.

EARLY DEVELOPMENT AND SOME ISSUES

Chinese Dialectics

The oldest known usage of dialectic occurred in China, where it was practiced 3000 years ago in the Chou dynasty. It held that opposing forces exist throughout nature. Centuries later the Chinese used the term yin to indicate the passive but creative force and yang for the active or bold principle. The active yang brought rain to its opposite, the passive earth, so that life multiplied. Thus yin became dark, negative, and female; yang became light, positive, and male. Together they provide a balance in nature involving not so much a clash— as do opposites in European dialectics—as a harmony. The Chinese identify themselves more with yin than yang: their passive character, like running water on a rock, eventually wears down opposition (Kuo, 1976).

A Chinese story about a fir tree, yin, in a snowstorm, yang, illustrates these concepts. As the storm progresses, snow piles up on the limbs of the tree, and the limbs begin to droop lower and lower. Eventually the snow is so heavy and the limbs so low that the snow slides off and the limbs spring back up. Passive yin prevails over active yang (until the next snowstorm when the dialectic interchange begins again).

The ancient Chinese identification with dialectic processes made it easy in the present century for the Chinese led, by Mao (1893–1976) to adopt Marxian (actually Leninist) dialectics in opposition to another ancient Chinese concept, Confucianism, which began nearly 2500 years ago. Confucius held that people should show proper deference to those above them and respect for those below. By virtue and honesty in social relationships, one became worthy of one's station in life and honored one's ancestors. Proper respect for people's titles and their relative permanence was necessary for stability and a well-functioning society. Hence, Confucianism is non-dialectic, but it has lived side by side with dialectic thinking since the time of its advent. Unfortunately, Confucianism was used as an excuse for maintaining the position and wealth of landlords and keeping the peasantry in abject poverty—even starvation. Marxist-Leninist dialectics then became the political theory on the basis of which Mao conducted his campaign against the Nationalists and Confucianism. But after the death of Mao, Confucianism—which lay dormant during the Mao's purges of the Great Leap Forward beginning in 1958 and the Cultural Revolution of 1966–1976—began to return, along with its ancestor worship. In psychology Confucianism has provided a basis for teaching moral development.

Dialectical Idealism

The use of dialectics in Europe began around the fifth century BCE in Greece (about 500 years later than in China), but its modern beginnings lie in the work of philosopher Immanual Kant (1724–1804), who treated it as form of transcendental (beyond the physical world) logic in which contradictions appeared in thought when thought was not related to experience. G.W.F. Hegel (1770–1831), another philosopher, took up dialectics as a method of logic that, contrary to Kant, started with direct experience of the world. Despite this more concrete and naturalistic beginning, he formulated a cosmic mysticism in which thought is identical with the life of the universe and is present throughout it. Such thought reaches its highest form in rational beings. The entire process of the universe is rational thought or spirit in which humans as spirit are identical with their own thought. This is called "dialectical idealism."

Dialectical Materialism

Friedrick Engels (1820–1895) and Karl Marx (1818–1883) converted "dialectical idealism" to "dialectical materialism," a term coined by Joseph Dietzgen (1828–1888; see Buick, 1975). Engels and Marx held that everything is material, not spiritual, and all things exist in the world independent of human perception. Further, all things are in conflict; and from this conflict comes growth, change, and development—"a struggle of opposites." In the case of humans, their economic needs produce social classes, which lead to class conflict and the need for social reform. Marx (1932) believed that because capitalist society contains inherent contradictions, these contradictions must lead to a workers' revolution against oppression and to the overthrow of the class system. The workers will then own the means of production and distribute the fruits among themselves. After the triumph of the working class, the struggle will end. Such a conclusion, some dialecticians hold, does not represent a true dialectic, for the dialectic process is eternal: any working class victory will have within it inherent contradictions that will begin the process anew.

The dialectics of Lenin and Trotsky, who applied Marx to their own revolution in Russia, continued the old dichotomy of mind and matter. Thinking is due to the mechanical movement of mental atoms. Dietzgen called this a "mechanical materialism." To Dietzgen and Marx, the world is naturalistic and dialectical. Mind and matter are abstractions that do not even have referents to actual events, and, therefore, one cannot cause the other. The natural world that is important to humans, they held, is a meaningful world; meanings are not made up of atoms or mechanical cause and effect but consist of people, houses, books, trees, clothing, and social relationships. The world of chemical reactions and the world of social relationships co-exist, but each is on a different level of organization. Their materialism, then, unlike the mysticism of Hegel, dealt with real breathing people standing on a solid earth and was dialectical in that it emphasized bipolar interactions. Marx and Engels (1972) argued that people are not only products of their upbringing and circumstances but that they can also change their circumstances. That is, people both determine and are determined by their society; they are both products and producers of society; they are in dialectical relationship with nature; and nature includes people, society, and the inanimate world. To Marx and Dietzgen, everything is interconnected and only the study of each thing in its context will provide understanding.

Russian Undialectics

Unlike Dietzgen and Marx who held that thoughts were part of the world of natural events, Lenin claimed the contrary and was quite undialectic in his views, but he continued to use the term "dialectical materialism" in connection with his revolution. He also changed the concepts of Marx when he set up state capitalism in the Soviet Union, a system in which the government rather than the workers owned the means of production. This totalitarian government was also nondialectic, unlike a democratic government (which Marx favored) in which various parties change and are changed by one another.

DIALECTICAL PSYCHOLOGY IN CHINA

Mao's views as described by Ho (1988) are as follows: He held that the major factor distinguishing humans from other things in the universe is their ability to convert subjective behavior into overt behavior, what he called "voluntary activist capability." This allows them to conceive of social possibilities and then to test their validity against social practice. The transformation back and forth between overt and covert behaviors, conception and application, is a never-ending dialectic. Mao considered the human factor to be more decisive in a war than economic or military power; for economic change to be successful, *people* must change. For this reason the masses must have an ideological education, and leaders must appeal to their class consciousness. They will be most motivated by ideological factors, not by material incentives, he maintained. And because the limits of human potential change as the group changes, human potential as part of a group is unlimited.

Chinese psychology takes much of its orientation from Marx and Lenin.[1] From the latter comes the view that psychology is primarily a function of the brain, and psychological events are approximate representations of reality (Yue, 1994a). Some, however, would not consider brain activity the same as psychological activity but would nevertheless continue to attribute to the brain considerable power in determining events.

Indigenous Chinese thinking seems not to assume mind-body dualism (Smith, 1985; see Fig. 2.2). As with many pre-dualistic cultures, the seat of some or many psychological functions lies in the heart (Smith, 1985, 1990): the Chinese word for psychology is "xinli xue," "study of the rule of the heart" (Petzold, 1987). The Chinese make no conscious-unconscious distinction and have no "sophisticated philosophical and psychological systems to explain the 'soul'" (Petzold, 1987, p. 215).[2] But many Chinese psychologists have studied in the West or been influenced by the West (Yue, 1994b; Petzold, 1994), and the influence of Buddhism has probably also left its mark (Kuo, 1976). Consequently, it is not surprising to find mind-body dualism in the form of brain determiners—as it occurs in the West—and also in the more direct form of an internal world and an external world, of inner causes and exterior causes, of mind as a function of body, and a dualism of body and brain (Gao, 1979, cited by Yue, 1994a; Kuo, 1971; Pan, 1987).

For example, Chu (1962, cited in Kuo, 1971) holds that a human psyche emerges from the brain and reflects reality. The contradictions that reality contains then occur in the psyche. He indicates that because objective reality changes constantly, it presents each person with continuing problems

---

1. However, Wang (1993) reviews various domains of study in current Chinese psychology and makes no reference to dialectics.

2. Petzold assumes this is due to the Chinese lack of distinction between knowing and acting. He overlooks the possibility that a nondualistic culture would regard knowing as a form of acting and that such forms of dualism as conscious-unconscious would have little meaning in that framework. This tendency to impose Western thinking on all peoples is pervasive in the West.

to resolve. This produces a conflict between the person and the objective world, and as a result the person must change the world, himself/herself, or both in order to achieve balance. But any balance is only temporary, he believes, because new demands and new contradictions will arise between subjectivity and objectivity, these contradictions being the basis of personality.

DIALECTICAL PSYCHOLOGY IN THE UNITED STATES

Dialectical psychology seems moderately strong in Europe, especially in Scandinavia, most notably perhaps in Denmark (Dreier & Kvale, 1984). It has been widely used in conjunction with phenomenological and existential psychologies (see chapter 12), somewhat as an adjunct. It came to the United States largely as a transplant, mostly through the energetic and persevering efforts of Klaus Riegel (1925–1977). Riegel, a developmental psychologist of German origin and a professor of psychology at the University of Michigan, was its most prominent proponent until the time of his early death. His writings continue to be of central importance.

Riegel (1976, 1979) argued that we should reject the notion of stable traits and abilities, for stability is only transitory. We should also reject intelligence and need for achievement, for these are abstractions whose investigations outside a cultural-social context lead to the assumption that they are fixed entities; the reification of intelligence, he maintains, interferes with understanding humans as continually changing in a continually changing world. Similarly, in assuming a need for tranquility for individuals or for groups, we have overlooked the advantages of conflict, change, and excitement. And instead of asking how we solve problems and find answers we should ask how we create problems and raise questions. We should not, for example, settle for Piaget's stages of development, which give no attention to how the child progresses from one stage to the other; and we should note that while

Piaget gives attention to the role of objects, he gives none to that of social interactions. Petzold (1987) cites a Chinese study that changed some of Piaget's experimental arrangements and found that the developmental stages, rather than being fixed, were influenced by educational and situational conditions.

For Riegel, much traditional psychology has attempted to study the organism without its cultural matrix and often without its developmental character. It is change over time in a historical-social context that is basic to all psychological events, Riegel insists, and it is dialectics that addresses this. In fact development in its very nature, he holds, is dialectical, proceeding along four dimensions at the same time: inner-biological, individual-psychological, cultural-sociological, and outer-physical. These four apparently exhaust all the possibilities.

When conflict occurs in any one of these or between any two, development progresses.

■ *Inner biological conflict* could include a broken leg or a bad cold.
■ *Individual-psychological conflict* could be an altercation between parent and child or failure to achieve a goal.
■ *Cultural-sociological conflict* could include a child's rejection by peers or a woman's inability to advance in her career because of sexist male attitudes.
■ *Outer-physical conflict* could be due to soil erosion that renders a farmer's fields no longer productive or warfare that destroys a way of life.

Stability or plateaus occur when the individual completes a phase of development, but at that point new questions or problems arise and further change occurs.

Riegel distinguishes between long-term and short-term dialectics. The four dimensions above are long-term dialectics and are along the lines of life-span development. Short-term dialectics involves short episodes of social interactions in which a dialogue between two persons is typical. Mother and child dialectics involve ongoing short interactions between them that, over time, become long-term dialectics. He also distinguishes between inner and outer dialectics. The inner form includes memory, thinking, imagining; the outer form is commonly some type of social intercourse, especially where speaking is involved, but it can involve any sort of interaction with the surrounding world.

Riegel's dialectical psychology with its development through the four dimensions gives equal emphasis to all stages of development. This is unlike traditional developmental psychology which treats mostly child and adolescent development and ignores adulthood on the assumptions that (a) the earlier periods complete most of the process, and (b) adulthood is a period of largely stable unchanging behaviors. But Riegel's use of the four interrelated and interacting dimensions makes development a continuing event throughout each individual's life. Marriage, divorce, advent of children, children leaving the home, retirement, financial windfalls or setbacks, change of careers, death of a spouse, etc. are all a part of ever changing adulthood that the dialectical dimensions attempt to address.

Riegel feels that we must use dialectics to move psychology away from the mechanism that gripped it for most of its history in which all meaning was removed from human tasks, and subjects were grouped into statistical categories in which all individuality was lost (see ch. 11 for a proposed corrective). This, he notes, began with Ebbinghaus who invented the nonsense syllable to study memory specifically so it would be devoid of meaning and therefore a mechanistic task. Kvale (1975) points out that Ebbinghaus's nonsense syllables provided a substitute for sensations that introspectionists such as Titchener were looking for. Titchener tried to train his subjects to avoid any context or meanings and report only isolated sensations. The associationists, Kvale observes, also found nonsense syllables useful; for they represented outer forms of the inner sensations or mental units that could be held together by associations. These associations provided a kind of mental glue that would string to-

gether memories and reactions. A third group, the behaviorists, he finds, transformed the syllables into stimulus and response, the external form of the introspectionist's mind. Both behaviorism and associationism are mechanistic systems that dialectics can improve or replace.

In its use of nonsense syllables, words on memory drums, and the like, psychology was attempting to imitate the prestigious advances of physics and chemistry and has continued this pursuit, one that Riegel believes overlooks much of what is uniquely human in human activity. He would agree with Koch (1959) that "man's stipulation that psychology be adequate to science outweighed his commitment that it be adequate to man" (p. 783). As a result psychology has looked for external mechanical causes of behavior or has turned to ghostly internal causes from mind or brain. In his "Manifesto for Dialectical Psychology" (1976) Riegel presents the problem:

> A specter is haunting western psychology: the specter of scientific dialectics. The scaffold of the academic world is shaking; the time for its transformation is near. By segregating the subject from the object, we escaped into abstract formalism; by preferring static traits and equilibria, we substituted for the human being a mechanistic monster or a mentalistic mirage; by disregarding our commitment to the human being and to human culture, we increased our self-constriction instead of our self-awareness; by focusing on static universality, we forgot that the human being is a changing being in a changing world. (p. 696)

He then presents a five-point summary of the conditions involved and gives a ringing cry for revolution: "Dialectical psychologists unite! You have nothing to lose but the respect of vulgar mechanists and pretentious mentalists; you will win a world, a changing world created by ever changing human beings" (p. 697).

Riegel wrote an introductory text to psychology with the enticing title of *Psychology, Mon Amour: A Countertext* (1978). In it he attempted to address basic issues in psychology which the popular glitzy textbooks overlook, issues that carry distinct assumptions and biases about psychology which the authors never disclose and of which they are perhaps never even aware. His book also ". . inverts the traditional way of studying psychology. It is problem-oriented, and thus puts theory before research, thinking before reading, and understanding before memorizing." Yet it is not a replacement for standard textbooks, he insists, but only a supplement to them. (For a history and evaluation of Riegel's work see Ijzendoorn, Goossens, & Veer, 1984.)

According to Georgoudi (1982), in application to social psychology, dialectics rejects the convention of treating individuals as passive creatures shaped by their social situations. It rejects the proposition that the group is independent and responds to pressures from members of the group and from social demands. It offers as a replacement the proposition that the individual and the social situation are interdependent and mutually influence one another. The social event is not in the individual or the group but in the relationship. It is a process in which changes are ongoing over time; and thus social psychology is historical and developmental. As transformations occur historically, the activity points in a direction—that is, it has purpose. Creativity, purposiveness, and intentionality consist of "the juxtaposition of relationships of human activities one to another" (Georgoudi, 1982, p. 87). And what about individuality? Where does it come in, if at all? Individuality comes not from standing in isolation against the social context of which that individual is a part but from the relationship in which the person's uniqueness transforms the social group and is transformed by it. Individuality "is a way of speaking about particular aspects of a larger configuration" and "can only develop within the presence of social relations" (p. 85).

SEMI-EXPLICIT POSTULATES

Riegel did not make his basic assumptions explicit—nor has any other dialectical psychologist—

but what he wrote provides the basis for making a reasonable inference about them. Metapostulate 4 (Riegel, 1978) is inconsistent with the rest of the postulate system:

■ *Metapostulates* (general guiding assumptions about science)
1. All that exists in the world is in a state of constant and necessary change.
2. Contradiction, opposition, and conflict comprise these changes. Contradiction is inherent in everything. It is the source of change. *Corollary:* Science is itself in constant conflict and by this means creates constantly changing understanding.
3. Human dialectics is not organism- or environment-centered but stresses interactive, reciprocal relationships between humans and the world.
4. Dialectics can be inner and outer, and their interface is psychic activity.

■ *Postulates* (subject matter assumptions)
1. Humans continually act upon and change the world and in turn are changed by it.
2. Behavior occurs in a continuous manner rather than in discrete units, but changes may involve dialectical leaps.
3. Behavior occurs in a context and develops historically.
4. Equilibrium and stability are only temporary conditions that result from resolution of contradictions and lead in turn to further contradictions.
5. Because of continual change, the assumption of such internal entities or fixed features as intelligence, traits, and competencies are invalidated.

Like Riegel, Buss (1978, 1979) has called for revolution in psychology. Instead of seeing the object acting upon the subject or the subject acting upon the object, the dialectical position he notes, insists on recognizing a reciprocal or interactive relationship between subject and object "such that each may serve as both subject and object." With this orientation psychology "can complete the revolution to end revolutions" (1978, p. 62).

RESEARCH

Dialectics has no specific research methodology but may use almost any technique including experimentation, phenomenological methods (see chapter 12), surveys, and qualitative and quantitative analyses (Kvale, 1977). But it does turn to the commonplace and to the meaningfulness of situations, and it puts these in a social context. These may be short-term interactions or long-term developmental events. It seeks no constancies or ideal sequences of development. What it does look for is ever-changing characteristics in natural situations. The following are a few examples of dialectic research and its findings.

Riegel (1972, 1973) studied long-term retention by asking undergraduate college students to write down in six minutes as many names of people they had known as they could think of. Most of those the students listed they had met either early in their lives (primacy effect) or relatively recently (recency effect). They listed few in the middle. Males listed their parents more often than females and thought of the father or mother first equally often. Females always thought of their mothers first. When Riegel conducted the experiment on middle-aged people there was no primacy effect and only a slight recency effect. On elderly subjects neither effect showed up. One can see in these experiments changing patterns with time from young to elderly subjects. Riegel interpreted the results to indicate changing importance of time periods to various age groups.

Rather than regarding memory as a sort of stored copy of something, Kvale (1974b) studied memory of a word in a sentence in its temporal context as something meaningful; its meaning is interconnected with the words that have already preceded it and with the words that will follow it in the future, which have not yet been uttered. Kvale offers these two sentences:

- "In order to illuminate this better, I shall find another lamp for you."
- "In order to illuminate this better, I shall give yet another example."

The listener does not know that "illuminate" refers to a "lamp" or to "example" until the sentence is nearly completed. Only retroactively does "illuminate" take on a specific meaning. The meaning depends on context; and context in this case is temporal, relying on words that come before and those that follow. Kvale (1974a) also presented ambiguous figures for two seconds each and defined them retroactively. When one rather bulbous figure was defined retroactively as a pear, subjects drew a pear. When it was defined retroactively as a bottle, they drew a bottle. Meaning, he concluded, is never independent of context. Nor are memories things that get stored in some fixed way. A change of meaning that depends on the retroactive context indicates this lack of fixity of memories and raises questions about the storage notion: the word or form that is remembered is not distinctly established until after it has passed out of existence—hardly a candidate for storage when its occurrence is already in the past.

In order to study the dialectics of mature thought, Basseches (1980) developed a dialectical schemata framework of twenty-four typical moves that the thinker engages in: for example, (a) thesis-antithesis-syntheses movement in thought, (b) assumption of contextual relativism, (c) and recognition of reciprocal relationships. Using freshmen, seniors, and faculty from a liberal arts college, he tape recorded twenty-seven interviews about education then coded and analyzed them statistically. He found that the more academically advanced the individuals, the more dialectical schemata they used: faculty the most, seniors intermediate, and freshmen the fewest.

Dialectics assumes that relationship maintenance as a dialectical enterprise is an ongoing process among romantically paired couples: the couple must continually adapt to contradictions in order for the relationship to continue (Montgomery, 1993). For example, each member of the pair must sacrifice some autonomy, which contradicts the need to avoid dependence. This is autonomy-connection dialectic. A dialectic also occurs in predictability-novelty and in openness-closedness (what to say and what not to say). A questionnaire study of these three dialectic processes—involving couples ranging from casual dates to married couples—identified some strategies the couples used to maintain satisfaction with the relationship. The most prominent findings were that time spent together was used to limit autonomy, and predictability was more satisfying than excessive novelty. But "excesses in autonomy, predictability and closedness are common dialectical problems experienced by couples" (Baxter & Simon, 1993, p. 239).

PSYCHOTHERAPY

Principles

The dialectical approach to psychotherapy has in some cases used general dialectical principles without applying any specific techniques, and in others it has developed techniques unique to dialectics. The following are principles of the general type: change is not a future goal in dialectic therapy but an ongoing process that is happening now and at every moment. Because every change will, at some point, be transformed into its opposite, such changes are bipolar and not always positive (Kaminstein, 1987). The goal is to have all changes, even if they are disappointing or painful or regressive, contribute to an ever higher level of attainment. The dialectical therapist would not single out the client's problem so much as he or she would emphasize the social context of the problem and attempt to understand it within that context. Short and Boon (1990) hold that the counselor is a mediator between the values of the society and the needs of the individual, and the complex dialogue that this necessitates must take in the whole social context as well as counselor and client. They insist that social roles of counselor and client be abandoned in order to facilitate openness to change on the part of both, for the dialectic process does not allow for the counselor to remain static while attempting to change the client; rather, both must change together.

The Linehan Procedures

In working with borderline personality disorder behaviors (hypersensitivity to affective situations and inability to adequately control affect), Koerner and Linehan's (1992) strategy is for the therapist to communicate to the client that truth cannot be grasped at one instant, is not totally absolute or relative, and must be constructed over time. Each truth the therapist and client come to understand together will contain its paradoxical opposite; they must examine these opposites together while searching for truths that they have overlooked. The truth will become increasingly whole as the dialectic continues. These procedures therefore differ from those of cognitive therapy, which seeks rationality; for in the dialectic, nonrational thought is as valid as rational thought. The two also differ in that cognitive therapy attempts to change painful affect whereas dialectic therapy encourages the client to accept painful affective situations.

The following dialectical devices are used in the therapeutic session (Linehan, 1993).

Paradox: (a) The therapist accepts the client as neither good nor bad but as understandable while insisting that he/she must nevertheless change. (b) What the client wants or holds to be true may be in opposition to what is realistic. For example, the therapist will be on vacation for two weeks and not available to the client during that time. The client wants the therapist to cancel the vacation. The therapist admits it would be better for the client if the therapist canceled the plans and met with the client but continues to hold to the plan. (c) The therapist helps the client but insists that the client help him/herself.

Storytelling: As a means of clarifying problems, the therapist may tell stories involving conflicting duties and desires. They are often very interesting and easy to remember, and they present lessons the client can consider without feeling threatened or being controlled. For example, the therapist and client are adrift on a raft in the ocean; the client is in pain from an injury and the therapist has a few pain tablets. Should the therapist immediately give the client as many as the client needs or ration them for longer-term use? Might the client believe the therapist has more but is a drug addict and wants them for him/herself? Stories are often useful when they involve the harmful effects of the client on someone else or behavior of the client that interferes with good interpersonal relationships. Stories can come from children's or adult literature, Eastern philosophies, religions, biographies, folklore, and so on.

Playing Devil's Advocate. The therapist presents an extreme position, a thesis. The client counters with an antithesis. The ensuing dialogue results in synthesis. The maladaptive position of the therapist forces the client into an adaptive one.

Turning Liability into an Asset. Often what the client takes to be a liability has within it the basis of an asset than needs only to be recognized and developed.

The Omer Procedures

Omer (1991) reviews a number of procedures and the unique dialectic techniques involved. The following is a summary of some of the strategies, cases, and explanations in three of the five general categories that he provides. Some therapists did not label the procedures as dialectical even though they were so in principle.

Dual Therapists. In one arrangement the client has two therapists so that he or she is challenged in opposite ways. The two therapists involve the client in thesis and antithesis. This dilemma, it is indicated, mobilizes the forces of change and neutralizes resistance. One of the two, the "bad" therapist, is critical and obnoxious. The other, the "good" therapist, is warm and supportive, and gradually comes to defend the client against the "bad" one.

A case study illustrates this treatment strategy: The "bad" therapist tells a five-year-old who has become mute that she is childish and incapable of acting like others of her age. The "good" therapist tells the "bad" that such a judgment, based on a single meeting, is unjust. The "bad" therapist holds up a pack of candy and tells the girl that if she doesn't speak a single word to her kindergarten teacher during the coming week, he will give the candy to her and her brother (who is present with the rest of the family). If she *does* speak, they have to bring him candy. As the girl and her family are leaving, the "good" therapist whispers to her that the "bad" therapist is wrong to call her stubborn and childish and will come to regret it. The treatment is effective in overcoming the muteness, and at the next session the "bad" therapist apologizes to the girl and tells her he had learned his lesson.

The "good" therapist developed a warm alliance that facilitated the girl's confidence, while the "bad" therapist encouraged antagonism to himself and roused her desire to defeat him by talking. This bipolar encounter built up conflicting motives, the girl's desire to speak and be like other children on the one hand and the opposing need to remain mute because of anxiety and negativism on the other. The latter force blocked the motive to speak, resulting in "tense immobility." The dialectical strategy took the two forces apart by channeling the negativism to the "bad" therapist and the desire to speak to the "good" one. Thus the "bad" therapist's act served the "good" therapist's efforts.

Alternating Antitheses. Opposing forces can also be pulled apart by alternating them. Consider a family with one authoritarian and one permissive parent and an anorexic daughter. The therapist's strategy is to have one parent try to induce the girl to eat while the other avoids interfering; then they alternate. Each goes considerably beyond the point when the other would ordinarily have intervened. If both fail, the therapist declares the girl the winner but a destructive tyrant. This counters the parent's efforts, which are blocking each other and improves the chances that each will succeed.

A client who shows contrary behavior is asked to role-play each pattern in turn, then to admit to both behaviors. This produces a new synthesis out of thesis and antithesis. The contrary forces of the authoritarian and the permissive parents, and the opposed behaviors in the role-playing cancel each other by alternation. The client comes to recognize both sides as right and is ready to cooperate.

A fifteen-year-old boy has dropped out of school for more than a year and spent his time playing computer games. The parents' continual entreaties to get him to return to school have failed as have seven therapy sessions. In the conflict between parents and child, the latter is stronger, but the parents cannot let up because that would mean to them that they have failed. The dialectical strategy involves instructing the parents to take turns pleading and remonstrating to the boy in his room for two hours every morning. After a week of this, the parents are unable to continue. The therapist tells them they have done their best, that they can now restore their own lives, and that they should tell the boy he has won—they will no longer ask him to return to school. The parents feel relief that they are not blamed, and a month later the boy decides on his own to return to school. A year later he is still continuing his education.

Contrary Twist. In this strategy the therapist inflates the dysfunctional behavior in order to more firmly counter it later. This was used with a boy at school who remained isolated and believed that all adults were intent on persecuting him. In response to a deliberate set-up that induced him to run away, he did run away and returned after ten days, disheveled, hungry, and exhausted. The adult in charge brought him to the dining room, but the boy was too upset to eat. The adult then took him to the kitchen where he was able to eat as much as he wanted. Then the adult suggested that it was too late for him to go to the dormitory, so he fixed him a bed in the hall. Before leaving, he patted the boy on the head and spoke kindly to him. After that the boy's relationship with the school and the adults changed considerably and rehabilitation proceeded.

Omer concludes that dialectical strategies differ from nondialetical ones in that the latter have either a single maneuver or a series of stages with no change in direction, whereas the former is always bidirectional. Further, dialectic strategy clearly displays elements of the strategy: the forces of opposition—resistance and cooperation—are easy to see. Dialectical tactics have a distinct advantage: they can be employed not only in a game plan that is dialectic from the outset but also in a unidirectional course of action for "driving apart the forces of resistance and cooperation" (p. 570).

RELATION TO SOME OTHER SYSTEMS

Behavior Analysis

Both dialectics and behavior analysis hold that society's problems derive not from individual people but from their social environments. Dialectics attempts to delineate these social conditions, often along Marxian lines, whereas behavior analysis does little to analyze them. Dialectics deals with meanings as part of social contexts, while behavior analysis treats the organism as an object in a physicalistic universe. Krapfl (1977) finds that one group of dialectical psychologists, whom he calls cognitive dialecticians, are distinctly mentalistic and are to that extent inconsistent with behavior analysis. They put "too much emphasis on the thing and not enough on the process" (p. 309); that is, they seek explanations in terms of powers or things rather than in concrete activities. They assume a consciousness that reflects the world, the notion of an inner world that copies an outer world.

The following are some of dialectical psychology's similarities with behavior analysis, as observed by Krapfl (1977). The experimenter in behavior analysis controls the experimental subject and in turn is controlled by that subject. Each influences what the other does. There are no "well-defined beginnings and ends" (p. 304), and thus a dialectical exchange occurs. Similarly, interaction and contradiction occur between behavior and the environment. The environment controls behavior by acting on it to alter the probability of recurrence, and behavior changes the environment. In this interactive or bipolar event, environment and behavior contradict each other as each controls and is controlled by the other. Krapfl finds additional similarities in that both systems oppose reduction of behavior to physiology, both oppose static states such as traits and Piagetian stages, and both hold to an active organism in interaction with an active environment, with neither organism or environment having any distinct independent status.

Cognitive Psychology

Dialectical psychology insists on dealing with meaningful behavior and meaningful information. Some dialecticians observe that the information processing of cognitive psychology is meaningless. In the technical sense of communication theory, information is only channel capacity. Bits of data have no meaning to a machine and are not information in that sense, and cognitivists have followed this pattern of meaninglessness. Yet cognitive behavior itself is mostly meaningful behavior. Human cognition, the dialectician argues, can only be treated meaningfully as a dialectic process; and must therefore be studied dialectically, not as machine analogies (Westcott, 1987). Reese (1977), however, argues for the value of merging the concepts of information processing with those of dialectical psychology.

Humanistic Psychology

Some humanistic psychologists employ dialectical concepts, but one major difference lies in the fact that dialectical psychology puts all human events into a social context whereas humanistic psychology, as an organocentric system, has a self-centered orientation as indicated in its emphasis on such terms as self-actualization and self-realization. It has even been called narcissistic. Its repudiation of statistical and experimental data also distinguishes it from a dialectic orientation. Its mind-body dualism differs from the noncentric dialectical psychologists but would be acceptable to those who are organocentric.

Interbehavioral Psychology

According to Hillner (1984),

> The conceptual correspondence between Kantor's system and Riegel's dialectics is so pervasive that the former even includes the notion of implicit interactions, such as thinking, reasoning, and imagining, that involve invisible substitute stimuli: The concept of an implicit interaction is analogous to that of an internal dialogue. (pp. 294–95)

Although this statement is a little misleading, the two systems do have a number of important points in common, and Ratner's (1971) description of an individual-world field (see p. 266) points in that direction. The similarities include focusing on (a) the bidirectionality or interaction of behavior; (b) the contextual or field nature of behavior; (c) the historical and developmental character of human events; and (d) the avoidance of mentalism, mechanism, and organocentrism. Nevertheless, if one examines the formal statement of postulates of interbehaviorism (chapter 10), one finds some important differences as well. For example, interbehaviorism does not assume that everything in the world is necessarily in a state of conflict or contradiction. And it more thoroughly replaces such constructs as mind, consciousness, traits, and other agents, powers, or fixed entities with concrete events; dialectics, on the other hand, retains a lingering mentalism (see Riegel's postulates, p. 272, and the "Critique" p. 278) and sometimes a physiological reductionism to which it attributes causality.

Operant Subjectivity

As noncentric systems, both Stephenson's and Riegel's oppose mechanism and mentalism, and both emphasize the importance of meanings of things to people. They also wish to preserve individuality in bodies of data. Dialecticians seem not to have used Q methodology but many find it useful for their purposes.

Phenomenological and Existential Psychology

For phenomenology, especially Merleau-Ponty, the subject matter of psychology is consciousness of something ("intentionality"); for existentialism, especially in Sartre's formulation, it is the dialectical relation between a person and that person's world (Dreier & Kvale, 1984). For dialectics, as for existentialism, psychology consists of the conflicts each individual must deal with whose resolution leads to development but also to more conflict. The fact that in some versions both are noncentric systems contributes to the correspondence.

Psychoanalysis

Classical psychoanalysis posits conflicts and their resolution within the individual. In Mao's dialectical psychology, in contrast, the internal conflicts merely reflect external events and can be resolved by class struggle. Mao emphasized character as defined by what a person does in society and each person's struggle as related to another person's struggle; psychoanalysis, on the other hand, gives paramount importance to a person's internal struggles. To Mao, the struggle is a quite conscious one, nothing like the psychoanalyst's focus on unconscious events (Ho, 1988).

Freud's constructs of polar conflicts between life and death instincts, id versus ego demands, pleasure principle versus reality principle, and fixation versus anti-fixation were distinctly dialectical. One goal of therapy was to resolve the conflict between the life and death instincts. Many of his followers rejected the life and death instincts, and Hartmann, in his thorough revision of psychoanalytic theory, removed all of the dialectical conflicts. Consequently, while the classical form of psychoanalysis has much dialectical character to it, some of its revisions moved away from that character.

CRITIQUE

Observation supports the dialectic contention that everything in the world is constantly undergoing change. That such change invariably involves contradictions is not quite so clear from observation, but some dialecticians turn conflict into a causative and explanatory power. The assumed ubiquity of bipolarity or contradiction is more of a construct than an observed event and is so loose or broad that it is always possible to find ways of making the observed events fit the construct: one can always find some way of construing two events as being in conflict or an event's opposite as its non-being. In another context Johnson (1996) refers to "a compulsion to divide the world into dualities: positive and negative, matter and antimatter, good and evil, summer and winter, north and south" (p. 199). This would seem to apply to the dialecticians. It may be argued that many of these opposites have graduations. Seasons graduate into each other as night does into day. Few people are totally moral or totally immoral; in fact, because most of our activities do not require moral choices, most people are amoral most of the time. On the other hand, some events in physics such as negative versus positive charge, matter versus anti-matter, and waves versus particles do seem to occur in opposites. Most human events do not.

One finds among the Chinese dialecticians and those strongly oriented toward Marxism frequent efforts to relate psychological events to social class struggles or at least to a social context. Some of this may be justified, but at times the effort seems rather strained. Under Mao and Marx dialectical psychology gave little place to individuality, but for Georgoudi it is a part of the social process (1983).

Some dialecticians denounce mentalism but inadvertently subscribe to it nevertheless. Mentalism is implicit in Riegel's work though he gives limited place to it; it is more blatant in the work of others. For example, according to Kaminstein (1987), ". . . what happens in people's minds influences their everyday life, and what happens in the outside world influences their emotional life as well. It is a truly interactive relationship. Dialectically speaking, there is no separation between inner and outer, but a continuum" (p. 97).

On the one hand Kaminstein fully embraces mentalism and on the other denies it. Referring to it as a "continuum" only adds to the confusion. Similarly, Georgoudi (1983) argues that no human activity including cognitive behavior is independent of environment; and to assume that it is independent "is to adopt a traditional form of dualism which the dialectic orientation calls into question" (p. 83). But as a basis for this statement he himself implies such a dualism: "Dialectics can neither be placed exclusively in the realm of ideas [mind] . . . nor exclusively in the realm of the material . . . but only within human action. It is neither a mental nor a situational phenomenon" (p. 82). For Shames (1984) "a dialectical conception of the social organization of psychological individuality requires a clear formulation of the relation of the psyche to the physical body" (p. 61). Kvale (1977), on the other hand, seems to consistently avoid mentalism.

CONCLUSIONS

An important strength of dialectics lies in its emphasis on bidirectionality, not on bipolar conflict so much as on interaction or mutuality. It is this bidirectional character that phenomenology and existentialism have utilized and which is characteristic of noncentric systems. Such an emphasis recognizes the "individual-world field" character of the organism and environment as they change each other and the need to examine the interaction rather than attempting to isolate causality in the organism though some dialectics—especially that of the Chinese—attributes psychological events to the brain. Dialectics draws attention to (a) change that is continuous, (b) the historical-social context of which change is a part, and (c) change as development across the lifespan. It has provided other psychologies with these valuable perspectives. Dialectics has also challenged other psychologies by rejecting stable traits and IQs, stages of development that provide no understanding of how progression occurs, stored memories, and research that deals with meaningless and decontextualized tasks. Such challenges may induce those who accept them to reexamine old assumptions or to recognize what assumptions they are making.

Although the bidirectional character of dialectical psychology has been useful to a number of other systems, few systems show much interest in bipolarity. In fact some psychoanalysts recommend removing such dichotomies from their own theory and replacing them with continuities. It seems likely that bidirectionality will continue to be of more interest than bipolarity to a number of systems of psychology, but the latter is so much a fundamental part of dialectical psychology that it will probably retain its prominence in that system.

REFERENCES

Basseches, Michael. 1980. Dialectical schemata: A framework for the empirical study of the development of dialectical thinking. *Human Development* 23: 400–421.

Baxter, Leslie A., & Eric P. Simon. 1993. Relationship maintenance strategies and dialectical contradictions in personal relationships. *Journal of Social and Personal Relationship* 10: 225–42.

Buick, Adam. 1975. Joseph Dietzgen. *Radical Philosophy* 10: 3–7.

Buss, Allan R. 1976. Development of dialectics and development of humanistic psychology. *Human Development* 19: 75–88.

———. 1978. The structure of psychological revolutions. *Journal of the History of the Behavioral Sciences* 14: 57–64.

———. 1979. *A Dialectical Psychology*. New York: Irvington Publishers.

Chu, Chih-Hsien. 1962. Critique on modern bourgeois social psychology. *Acta Psychologica Sinica* 2: 106–113.

Dreier, Ole, & Steiner Kvale. 1984. Reviews of Scandinavian psychology I. Dialectical and hermeneutical psychology. *Scandinavian Journal of Psychology* 25: 5–29.

Gao, Juefu. 1979. The historical teaching of psychology. *Acta Psychologica Sinica* 2: 148–53.

Georgoudi, Marianthi. 1983. Modern dialectics in social psychology: A reappraisal. *European Journal of Social Psychology* 13: 77–93.

Hillner, Kenneth P. 1984. *History and Systems of Modern Psychology: A Conceptual Approach*. New York: Gardner Press.

Ho, David Y. F. 1988. The conception of human nature in Mao Tse-Tung thought. In *Asian Contributions to Psychology*. Edited by Anand C. Paranjpe, David Y. F. Hoe, & Robert W. Rieber. New York: Praeger.

Ijzendoorn, M. H. van; F. A. Goossens, & R. van der Veer. 1984. Klaus F. Riegel and the dialectical psychology: In search for the changing individual in a changing society. *Storia e Critica della Psicologia* 5: 5–28.

Johnson, George. 1996. *Fire in the Mind*. New York: Knopf.

Kaminstein, Dana S. 1987. Toward a dialectical metatheory for psychotherapy. *Journal of Contemporary Psychology* 17: 87–101.

Koch, Sigmund. 1959. Epilogue. In *Psychology: The Study of a Science*, vol. 3 in *Formulations of the Person and the Social Context*. Edited by Sigmund Koch. New York: McGraw-Hill.

Koerner, Kelly, & Marsha M. Linehan. 1992. Integrative therapy for borderline personality disorder: Dialectical behavior therapy. In *Handbook of Psychotherapy Integration*. Edited by John C. Norcross & Marvin R. Goldfried. New York: Basic Books.

Krapfl, Jon E. 1977. Dialectics and operant conditioning. In *Life-Span Developmental Psychology: Dialectical Perspectives on Experimental Research*. Edited by N. Datan & H. W. Reese. New York: Academic Press.

Kuo, You-yuh. 1971. Psychology in communist China. *Psychological Record* 21: 95–105.

———. 1976. Chinese dialectical thought and character. In *Contributions to Human Development*. Edited by J. F. Rychlak. Basel, Switzerland: Karger.

Kvale, Steiner. 1974a. Permanence and change in memory, I: Reproduction and recognition of visual figures. *Scandinavian Journal of Psychology* 15: 32–42.

———. 1974b. Permanence and change in memory, II: Reproduction and recognition in sentences. *Scandinavian Journal of Psychology* 15: 139–45.

———. 1975. Memory and dialectics: Some reflections on Ebbinghaus and Mao Tse-Tung. *Human Development* 18: 205–222.

———. 1977. Dialectics and research on remembering. In *Life-Span Developmental Psychology: Dialectical Perspectives on Experimental Research*. Edited by N. Datan & H. W. Reese. New York: Academic Press.

Kvale, Steiner, & Carl E. Grenness. 1967. Skinner and Sartre: Towards a radical phenomenology of behavior? *Existential Psychology and Psychiatry* 7: 128–50.

Linehan, Marsha M. 1993. *Cognitive-Behavioral Treatment of Borderline Personality Disorders*. New York: Guilford.

Marx, Karl. 1932. *Capital: The Communist Manifesto and Other Writings by Karl Marx*. New York: Modern Library.

Marx, Karl, & Friedrich Engels. 1972. *Feuerbach: Opposition of the Materialistic and Idealistic Outlook*. Moscow: Progress Publishers.

Montgomery, Barbara M. 1993. Relationship maintenance versus relationship change: A dialectical dilemma. *Journal of Social and Personal Relationships* 10: 205–223.

Omer, Haim. 1991. Dialectical interventions and the structure of strategy. *Psychotherapy* 28: 563–71.

Pan, Shu. 1987. On the so-called relationship between mind and body. *New Explorations in Psychology* 3: 1–16.

Petzoldt, Matthias. 1987. The social history of Chinese psychology. In *Psychology in Twentieth-Century Thought and Society*. Edited by Mitchell G. Ash & William R. Woodward. Cambridge: Cambridge University Press.

———. 1994. Chinese psychology under political pressure: A comment on Guoan Yue. *Theory and Psychology* 4: 277–79.

Ratner, Carl. 1971. Principles of dialectical psychology. *Telos* 9: 83–109.

Reese, Hayne W. 1977. Discriminative learning and transfer: Dialectical perspectives. In *Life-Span Developmental Psychology: Dialectical Perspectives on Experimental Research*. Edited by N. Datan & H. W. Reese. New York: Academic Press.

Riegel, Klaus. 1972. Time and change in the development of the individual and society. In *Advances in Child Development and Behavior*, vol. 7. Edited by H. Reese. New York: Academic Press.

———. 1973. The recall of historical events. *Behavioral Science* 18: 354–63.

———. 1976. The dialectics of human development. *American Psychologist* 31: 689–700.

———. 1978. *Psychology, Mon Amour: A Countertext*. New York: Houghton Mifflin.

———. 1979. *Foundations of Dialectical Psychology*. Ann Arbor: University of Michigan.

Rychlak, Joseph F. 1976. The multiple meanings of "dialectic." In *Contributions to Human Development*. Edited by J. F. Rychlak. Basel, Switzerland: Karger.

Shames, Carl. 1984. Dialectics and the theory of individuality. *Psychology and Social Theory* 4: 51–65.

Short, Robert H., & Brian J. Boon. 1990. Counseling as a dialectical process. *International Journal for the Advancement of Counseling* 13: 129–43.

Smith, Noel W. 1985. Belief systems—A psychological analysis. *Mankind Quarterly* 25: 195–225.

————. 1990. Psychological concepts under changing social conditions in ancient Egypt. *Mankind Quarterly* 30: 317–27.

Wang, Zhong-Ming. 1993. Psychology in China: A review dedicated to Li Chen. *Annual Review of Psychology* 44: 87–116.

Westcott, Malcolm R. 1987. Minds, machines, models, and metaphors: A commentary. *Journal of Mind and Behavior* 8: 281–90.

Yue, Guoan. 1994a. Theoretical psychology in China today. *Theory and Psychology* 4: 261–75.

————. 1994b. More on Chinese theoretical psychology: A rejoinder to Matthias Petzold. *Theory and Psychology* 4: 281–83.

CHAPTER 10

Interbehavioral Psychology:

The Event Field as Observable Interactions Replacing Assumptions of Mind and Brain

Chapter Outline

INTRODUCTION

It should not be hard to find agreement that humans—and non-human animals as well—respond to objects and events around them. We might also agree that to respond to objects visually we must have light and to respond auditorily we must have sound. Perhaps most people will also concur that how we respond to something depends on the situation in which it occurs. For example, a smile in a joyous circumstance would be perceived as happy, but the same smile in a tragic setting would seem evil or sadistic. It might be less obvious, but once it is pointed out we would probably agree that we respond to objects not so much on the basis of their physics or chemistry but on the basis of what they mean to us. A book is not just paper and ink but something that functions to provide us with reading material. It might also function as a paperweight, a doorstop, or material for starting a fire. Just as any given object may have more than one function, so too, any response to an object may have more than one function. We may read the book to gain information or for entertainment, but it is the same response—reading. Finally, we are all aware of the fact of our historical development: as we encounter new things and situations these encounters influence our subsequent actions.

To interbehavioral psychology these are the ingredients of psychological behavior or *interbehaviors*. They comprise the *interbehavioral field*. Notice that all of them are observable and can be identified by anyone. Interbehavioral psychology insists that we must start any investigation with observables—unlike those systems of psychology that start with constructs of brain powers, information processing, memory storage, drives, minds, and other unobservables. We must also interpret our investigative findings in terms of these same observables.

Interbehaviorism was founded in the 1920s by J. R. Kantor. He worked largely alone but taught his system to his undergraduate and graduate students and continued writing until his death in 1984 at the age of ninety-five. His system was largely neglected until the last part of the twentieth century, at which time it began to attract increasing attention (Morris & Midgley, 2000).[1]

FUNDAMENTALS AND ISSUES

The Interbehavioral Field

Stimulus Functions. With a little more elaboration, the components of a psychological event sketched above will provide the fundamental program of interbehavioral psychology. Interbehaviorism calls the object that we respond to a "stimulus object," and the meaning or function that it has in any given situation is the "stimulus function." The functional characteristics of the book described above is one illustration. Our own behavior patterns can also be stimulus functions. We see ourselves as successful, unhappy, independent, unworthy, etc., yet we are a single organism just as the various functions of the book are of a single book. (Note how this differs from referring to an unhappy self, an alcoholic self, etc. and treating these selves as entities or causal agents—that is, as *mind*.) The interbehavioral claim that our interactions with objects are actually with the stimulus functions of those objects eliminates the need to assume some unknown mental process that interprets the physical stimulus and gives it meaning.

The system delineates several types of stimulus functions, but the "substitute stimulus function is especially important." If you look at your watch and decide it is time to go to your classroom, it is not the classroom that is stimulating you but the watch that substitutes for it. All "reminders" are stimulus substitutes. The mousetrap that is sprung but holds no mouse becomes the substitute stimulus for inventing a better trap. That is, it is the stimulus object for developing a better device—a device that is not present.

---

1. Listserver subscription to announcements and discussion about the system is available by sending to listproc@list.emich.edu the following message: subscribe IB-L <your name>. One interbehavioral web address is http://web.utk.edu/~wverplan/kantor/kantor.html.

Interbehaviorism holds that all inventions, formulae, metaphors, poetry, fiction and nonfiction writing, remembering, inferences, financial transactions, myth, religion, theories, and scientific development consist largely of substitute rather than direct stimulus functions. A conversation, too, utilizes substitute stimulation in that the thing or situation the speaker refers to (and the listener hears about) is often not present.

Response Functions. The "response" to the stimulus consists of body activity, but the functional character of that response is called the "response function." We may go from A to B by walking or by riding a bicycle. They are different responses, but all have the same response function of getting us from A to B. Moreover, we can walk from A to B to get from one point to the other, or we can walk from A to B for the exercise. In that case the response is the same but the function is different. As a further example, consider the following dialogue:

"Do you have any popcorn left?"
"Yes."
"Did you eat all of the popcorn?"
"Yes."

The "yes" is the same response but a different response function in the two instances.

A response and its response function occur in response to something—a stimulus object and its stimulus function. When we are stimulated by an object, we are responding. Neither can occur independently. Therefore, they are interdependent. This immediately replaces the notion of dependent-independent variables, the assumption that the response is *dependent* upon the stimulus and the stimulus stands *independent* or the organism.[2] To show this *interaction* or mutual relationship between stimulus and response, interbehaviorism uses a double headed arrow (Fig. 10.1). Because of this interdependence, whether we say that a book

stimulates us to read it or that we respond to it as something to read depends entirely on which side of the interaction we wish to emphasize.

Setting Factors. The smile that had different meanings in different settings illustrates the *setting factor.* The plant that we regard as pleasant beside the stream but a nuisance in our garden is another example. Setting factors can be part of the organism or external to the organism. (a) Examples of organismic setting factors: When we have a cold we respond to things differently than when we feel well. If we go to a grocery store before a meal, we buy more than if we go after a meal. A person who is ordinarily mild-mannered might be ready for a fight when drunk. (b) Examples of setting factors external to the organism: Usually we interact differently with instructors in the classroom than in their offices or in bars. A dog that barks at people from its home area, its territory, will not usually do so when walking down a street that is not its territory. The varieties of non-organismic settings are almost infinite.

Media of Contact. According to the interbehaviorist, every object we see, hear, smell, taste, etc., occurs by means of a medium. Sound waves are necessary for hearing and light for seeing.[3] Interbehavioral psychology insists that we not confuse media with stimulus functions. If we do confuse them, we might conclude that we see only light waves, not a flower; we hear only sound waves, not a siren.[4] Those psychologies that assume that a medium is the stimulus have to invent some mechanism to convert the vibrations back to an appearance of the object. That mechanism is a hypothetical brain or mind power which then produces an appearance of the object "out there." The

---

2. The "dependent" variable is actually an uncontrolled variable, and the "independent" variable is controlled. The interbehaviorist views the inappropriate terminology as symptomatic of misunderstandings of psychological events.

3. Some media consist of pressure, and taste is a chemical medium involving solubility in saliva. Pain requires a tissue-insulting medium.

4. The medium, the stimulus object, and the stimulus function can all coincide if, for example, we listen to a tone or notice the color of a light.

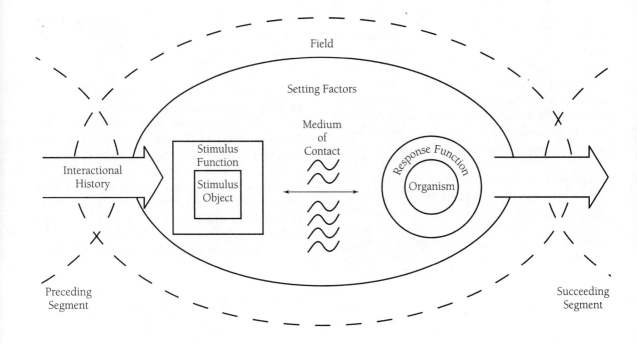

Figure 10.1. The Field of Interacting Events Comprising a Psychological Field. Each stimulus object may have any number of stimulus functions and each response any number of response functions. A slice in time of continuous interactions is the behavior segment. The overlapping segments indicate the continuity of the events and the interactional history. Reprinted by permission of the Psychological Record.

interbehaviorist holds that we don't see or hear waves and then "mentally" interpret them. Rather, we see or hear objects—not waves of energy—that have meanings in accordance with our past histories and present settings. "To lose sight of the genuine distinction between media and stimuli spells disaster for the whole psychological system" (Kantor, 1924, p. 55).

Interactional History and Personality. Finally, our history of interactions is of utmost importance, the interbehaviorist insists. From the time of our birth until our death we continue to develop our *interactional history* and this influences everything we do. It is, of course, interdependent with stimulus functions and response functions:

we develop these functions from our history with objects and conditions, and even the effect of settings is influenced by our history with them. Functionality is even more important in psychology than in biology, for "organisms do not simply react to objects on the basis of their physiochemical properties but also on the basis of their functions developed in previous interbehavior" (Kantor, 1978/1984, p. 145).

Up to this point the descriptions have been of what the system identifies as component events of the field. But our responses, the system insists, are not isolated. Every action influences every other action, and these successions of mutual influences develop into organized ways of performing that form a unity. That unity is *personality,* the stable and enduring organization of responses of each individual.

Field or Behavior Segment. The interrelated components that comprise the interbehavioral field are shown in figure 10.1 as a behavior segment. Each such behavior segment is specific and unique. Interbehaviorists call this the specificity principle. In regard to specificity, Pronko (1988) notes that "If you want to know the planets of the sun in any thorough fashion, you will have to focus on them individually, for each is unique" (p. 208). One cannot give a single explanation of why some students spend their time in bars rather than maximizing their academic opportunities or why some abused children grow up to abuse their own children and some become good parents. Each instance, the interbehaviorists insist, involves a unique complex of field factors, although similarities may permit grouping and generalization. Generalizations are made up of descriptions and interpretations; and these, too, are "born of specificities" (Kantor, 1978/1984, p. 153). The consequences of specificity include (a) pointing us to observable events of the field, (b) replacing vagaries and abstractions with concrete events, and (c) directing us to interdependent relationships (Pronko, 1988). Stephenson (1953) observes that specificity is "the principle by which the scientist keeps his feet firmly planted on reality. Without it he loses himself playing a scientific game according to rules" (p. 341) rather than according to observation.

At first glance, the complex interdependence of field factors may seem to be too much to deal with; but, the interbehaviorists claim, interdependence is more realistic than simple causation by single events, and we might as well get on with dealing realistically with this complexity. Further, it is possible to study some components in relative isolation, but they must always be put back into the field and their interdependence noted: "any factor dissected out for research purposes must always be handled with direct reference to the entire unit from which it was taken" (Kantor, 1959, p. 19). This is much like the biologist's procedure.

The biologist may extract a component of the organism—structural or functional—for study but then must examine it in its relationship with other components. As the review of research below (p. 298) will show, some investigators have successfully studied concurrent multiple factors.

The failure to consider the various field factors is what leads to the invention of unscientific constructs, argue the interbehaviorists. For example, Gewirtz (1967) proposed a drive to account for his experimental results with children; but upon learning about setting factors he was able to turn from unseen drives to observable setting events. Similarly, the interbehaviorist notes, brain processing, mind, consciousness, and other hypothetical powers are invoked from the culture or from analogies with other sciences (information processing, for example) when concrete specifics of the field are overlooked.

For illustration, consider a specific behavior segment in the life of a hypothetical individual. Professor Ossify, a specialist in the Lower Paleolithic (Old Stone Age) culture, picks up an object from the ground and uses a soft brush to gently remove the soil. She had found an important fragment of the skull of an ancient human-like creature, perhaps *Australopithecus afarensis*. As a stimulus object the piece consists of weathered and mineralized bone. But it has the stimulus function to her of a skull component of an early hominid who once walked the earth. Her response is to use a brush to remove the soil, which has the response function of allowing her to better examine it. Alternative responses would be to wipe it off with a cloth or to blow it off; these would have the same response function of allowing more careful inspection. The setting consists of an exploratory search for such fossils in a desert landscape strewn with small rocks and barren soil in East Africa. It occurs in a medium of sufficient light for visual interaction and identification. Her interactional history consists of extensive training with such materials and thus the ability to recognize the fossil amid stones on the ground or other bone fragments that look similar. This behavior segment is specific to that individual in that situation. No other behavior segment has ever been precisely like it, and it will never occur again—such specificity and uniqueness being true of all events in nature.

Note than interbehaviorists specify the functional details of the action rather than resorting to a general explanatory abstraction. Whereas most psychologies assume that thinking, decision making, and emotions are internal events, the interbehaviorist approach makes this assumption meaningless. In this case and in all others interbehaviorists propose no internal causes such as mind, information processor, or drives. Nor do they propose an external cause of environmental conditions, for they assume no internal-external dichotomy. Nor is there any place in the integrated field for such abstractions to fit (consider fig. 10.1 in this light), and none of them are necessary or even useful in the system. The interbehaviorists hold that when the specific functional relationships of field factors have been described, that completes the scientific account—just as it does with any other event in nature. This description of the components of a natural event in strictly observational terms and closely connected inference, always tied to events, is the way in which a scientific psychology must proceed, the proponents insist.

Kantor (1959) has summarized the interbehavioral field in the following descriptive formula:

$$PE = C(k, sf, r, rf, hi, st, md)$$

PE is the psychological event, C the entire field, k the specific event, sf the stimulus function, r the response, rf the response function, hi the history of interactions, st the setting, and md the medium. Note that no hypothetical constructs are included, and in fact they would be superfluous to this system.

In sum, to put the system in its simplest form, it begins with a biological organism and a world. Their interactions constitute psychological events. The history of those interactions changes further interactions.

Phases of the Interaction. A stimulus and response interaction is quite complex, but it is possible to analyze out of it the fundamental action components that comprise the interaction. Kantor called these *reaction systems*. They are *phases of the interaction, action phases, or action patterns* (the last two terms are used in this chapter). The simplest response is a reflex action such as jerking away from a hot object. The object has only a single stimulus function (an intrinsic property of the object—hotness), and the response to it is composed of only a single action phase. Similarly, the startle response to a sonic boom consists of a single action phase. The action phases of a coin collector searching through a pile of coins are quite different (Fig. 10.2). She attends to each one, perceives its identity, decides that it is or is not needed for her collection, moves it aside, and repeats the process with the next one. If she perceives one as quite rare she might feel excited, look at with a magnifier, and then complete the action pattern by putting it in a special holder.

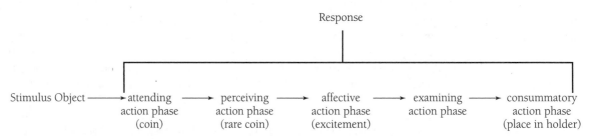

Figure 10.2. Action Phases of a Response. The attending, perceiving, and consummatory are minimal components of the response. Others such as affective phases may or may not be involved in any given interaction.

The system holds that except for reflex actions, all responses consist of a minimum of three phases: (a) attending to or actualizing the stimulus, (b) perceiving, and (c) a final or consummatory action.[5] It is mostly the consummatory action that we notice, but the first two must precede it. The totality of individual action phases is the *personality* or the *behavior properties* or *attributes* of the individual and in various combinations of interactions comprise his or her information, abilities, skills, habits, and other attributes. Personality is a product of interactional history.

Attending and Perceiving. The action phases *attending* and *perceiving* bear a little further scrutiny. Until we have attended to one stimulus out of any number of other possible ones, we cannot react to it. But once a potential stimulus object has become an actual stimulus object, we discriminate or perceive its functional meaning to us, and then we can complete a response to it. If the telephone rings (a) I attend to it (and discontinue attending to whatever else I was interacting with at the moment), (b) I perceive that it is in fact the telephone and that someone is trying to speak to me, and (c) I finalize the interaction by picking up the phone and saying "hello." Likewise, when the caller (a) actualizes as a stimulus my "hello," (b) perceives—perhaps—that it is my voice, and (c) finalizes that interaction by stating who is calling, I now have a new stimulus to actualize, etc.

Attending brings an organism and a particular object into interaction. How one actualizes any given stimulus is influenced by a host of variables. On the stimulus object side it may be the condition of size (newspaper headlines, for example), motion, color, repetition (the advertising jingle), and others. On the response or organism side are immediate interests (the need to find a rest room), personality (likes, dislikes, habits, knowledge, etc.), and personal conditions (worry, depression, excitement, absorption in task, health, etc.). The stimulus and organism conditions can be combined. For example, computer buffs encountering new computers on display are stimulated by the powerful new models and at the same time are receptive to these stimulus objects because of their own personality organization involving their knowledge and interest in computers. They actualize stimulus objects involving computers that others might not.

Although all actions are actually indivisible and unitary, each phase of the action pattern occurs as "a behavior configuration, a way in which the organism distributes itself in relation to the space in which both it and its interaction objects are located" (Kantor & Smith, 1975, p. 54).

We can now consider in more detail the example of Professor Ossify (above) who found a human fossil fragment. Based on her interests of the moment and her behavior characteristics, at that point she attended to that particular stimulus object rather than to other inanimate objects in the landscape. Subtle color differences from the surrounding stones and the object's configuration might have been salient object conditions for her. Upon attending, she perceived that it was probably a section of a fossil skull, perhaps hominid, and completed the interaction by bending over and picking it up. Additional action patterns might have also occurred—as wondering whether it might prove to be an animal rather than a hominid fragment, hoping that it would not crumble into smaller pieces, wondering if other pieces might be close by, and being excited over its potentialities. That behavior segment would be followed by others in which she would attend to various components of the fossil as stimulus objects/functions and respond with her tentative identification of *Australopicthecus afarensis*.

An account of Professor Ossify along conventional lines of psychology would say that she has an internal filter which selects what she attends to. Light waves reflecting off the fossil, not the fossil itself, serve as stimuli that cause the neurons to conduct "messages" to her brain where they become "sensations." Another unseen process combines these sensations into an internal perception that her brain then interprets as meaning hominid

---

5. Sometimes the perceiving and consummatory acts are combined as when one appreciates the beauty of a symphony, the lively colors of a bird, or the magnificent antlers of a deer.

fossil. Therefore, the fossil that Professor Ossify perceives is a creation of her mind or brain. It is said to be a *representation* or *image* inside her head and has no certain objective existence. To the interbehaviorist, in contrast, Professor Ossify has interacted with the fossil by means of light as a medium. The light is not the stimulus object, and no filters, sensations, representations, or conversion processes are assumed. The object's meaning does not come from a "mental process" but is comprised of her present interactions, which in turn are interdependent with her past interactional history. The entire event is a field of *observable* interactions that can be specifically identified (the specificity principle), not an *unobservable* biological conversion in the head.

The action phase of *perceiving,* the system notes, provides a degree of independence from the object. In the case of a reflex response to a hot object, the response is to jerk away. The response is totally dependent on the intrinsic character of the object. But in the case of most objects, according to interbehaviorism, perceiving occurs as a phase of the interaction in which any number of possible consummatory actions can follow as the final phase of that interaction. In the case of a mountain hiker who encounters a gargantuan boulder, the final or consummatory phase of the interaction might be to contemplate its magnificence, tell a story about how it was once a giant bear, judge its weight, note its composition and its likely origin, attempt to climb over it, or in the setting of a strong wind use it as a shield. As this example suggests, perceiving may be followed by either *covert* (or *implicit*) consummatory actions (contemplation, judging) or *overt* consummatory actions (climbing, telling a story, using it as a windbreak). Often we perceive more than one meaning: the boulder can be magnificent but an impediment to one's hike up a mountain. We may also perceive more than one action that can follow, such as climbing over the boulder, working our way around it, or tuning back.

Voluntary Interactions. After the hiker perceives more than one possible way to get past the boul-

der, the selection that he or she makes is voluntary behavior. According to interbehaviorism, two or more such perceptions, or the perception of having the choice to act or to refrain from acting, are fundamental to choosing. Language often plays an important role in such selections; but the individual's personality attributes such as knowledge, preferences, skills, judgment, etc. weigh even more heavily, the interbehaviorist maintains. Settings are also relevant. A student might choose to mark up a library book in private but not in the presence of a librarian. Choice is also "guided or influenced by consequences" (Kantor, 1926, p. 313); but because consequences are often not clear until the action is completed, the person must react to the consequences covertly by means of substitute stimulation.

The free will versus determinism conflict does not arise in the interbehavioral framework. The interbehaviorist insists that *choosing* as well as any other psychological interaction does not arise from such an abstraction as free will or determinism but is comprised of a field of events. The field also comprises causality. They do not differ. In this system, to account for a choosing event we must describe the perceiving of choices, the setting in which the choosing takes place, and the interactional history and resulting personality attributes. Weighing or pondering the choices might also be phases of the interaction. For example, a student might need to choose whether to enroll in an advanced course that will be valuable to his or her career or to take an easier but less valuable course. The student considers his or her capabilities and past experiences with such courses, study habits, time available for studying the contemplated course in addition to other courses, what the academic advisor might recommend, possible career consequences, and similar matters (note the extensive number of substitute stimuli in these covert acts). The consummatory action of choosing and thereby completing the interaction is the outcome of these correlated events. Once we have described these specific events, we have, from an interbehavioral perspective, accounted for the choosing event. To add an abstraction such as willpower or determinism would be contrary to the specificity principle.

Awareness, or Witting and Unwitting Interactions. We all experience the frustration of putting down a key, eyeglasses, a paper, a tool, or some other item and being unable to recall where we put it. Putting it down without observing the location is an example of unwitting behavior. On the other hand, we often know exactly what we have done in the past or are doing at the present. This is witting behavior. We can also refer to these behaviors as awareness and unawareness.

In witting behavior, the interbehaviorist holds, a series of action patterns precede the consummatory act "which refer to some past contacts of the individual with the stimulating objects, or else to some phase of the object that is not then serving the stimulational function" (Kantor, 1924, p. 46). In putting one's keys down, one may note the convenience of the location as a temporary resting place or say to oneself, "I'm leaving the keys on the lamp table for now." Or in entirely different stimulus conditions that comprise witting behaviors the mountain hiker may notice characteristics of the stimulus object: the muddiness of a section of the trail up the mountain and the rocks sticking up through the mud. Note here the interdependence of the object and its functional meaning: mud means something to avoid stepping in and rocks mean stepping platforms to avoid the mud. Other choices, such as going around or jumping over might be available: such recognition of choices, too, is witting behavior; for one has to consider alternatives and their consequences. Speaking, writing, and various covert acts such as pondering, appreciating, judging, and recognizing are also witting interactions.

In unwitting behaviors the various phases of the interaction present in witting behavior—such as thinking and other cognitive acts, language, preparation for choosing, or reference to some characteristics of the object—are absent. If, in putting my keys down, I do so without any of these action phases, I am left detached from the object although interacting with it.

Unwitting behavior, the interbehaviorist claims, is distinct from not observing what is in our field of vision. For example, even avid card players seldom know what the queen of hearts is holding in her right hand even though they have looked at the card innumerable times. This is not unwitting behavior but failure to attend to that particular detail. Similarly, as we walk along or drive a car, thousands of objects enter our field of vision. We simply do not actualize most of them as stimulus objects. Likewise, out of the myriad of sounds in a large city, we notice—attend to—only a relative few.

Habit, the system holds, also plays a role in awareness. Habit consists of interactions in which the final phase of that interaction, through repetitive occurrence in conjunction with the stimulus object, becomes tightly connected to it. The attending and perceiving phases are extremely weak and so tightly integrated with the consummatory act that they may be inseparable from it. This is part of personality attributes and makes it possible to drive a car while conversing or knit a sweater while watching television. Driving is an enormously complex activity that habit, in part, makes possible. Knitting is a simpler one that habit makes efficient. With habit we can interact without awareness while engaging in other activities that require awareness. Some of the belief in a subconscious may derive from these occurrences, suggests Kantor (1924, p. 444); but one need not invoke any special power or entity, such as a subconscious, to account for such events. A descriptive account derived from observation is sufficient, he insists.

Sometimes individuals develop habitual interactions to the point of dissociation: "we may organize these complex habits without in the least knowing at the time that such an acquisitional process is going on," but this provides no basis for "some mysterious 'subconscious'" (p. 445). Such constructs, he holds, are not derived from ongoing events but from non-scientific sources.

Habits can interfere with the need for contrary responses. If we move our residence to a new location, it is all too easy to make the habitual response of turning left when we now need to turn right. A new behavior pattern requires careful attending with cognitive action phases and use of substitute stimuli to begin building up a new habit to replace the old one. As the new integration develops, the cognitive action patterns can cease.

We can respond either deliberately to an object or mechanically and in a detached way to the same object. This has inspired jokes about absent-minded people and has provoked assumptions about an unconscious or a subconscious. To the interbehaviorists, *people* are not divided into parts controlled by separate things such as a conscious, an unconscious, or a subconscious. However, it is possible, interbehaviorists claim, to abstract out components of *interactions* between persons and objects to see how they comprise the functional relations that may be described; and they have tried to do this.

Some Implications of the System

Nonreductionism. The field comprising a psychological system means, interbehaviorists contend, that the event cannot be reduced to biology or to culture. We are not in lockstep with culture although it is one participating condition, sometimes as stimulus function, sometimes as setting, and often as part of our personal history. The brain, too, is a participating condition but does not contain or produce psychological events. It is not the boss of the organism or of the field of interactions. In short, it is not a psychological organ but a biological organ. As a biological organ it serves a vital function of coordinating the organism, but it does not think or interpret or decode "messages" from the nerves. The nerves transmit electro-chemical *impulses,* not "messages." The brain participates in all our activities and is necessary for them. But this does not make it the determiner or cause or even the locus of psychological events.

The entire field, the interbehaviorists contend, is the locus. Just as Copernicus moved the earth

from the center of the universe around which the sun and stars turned, Kantor has moved the psychological event not only out of the brain but also out of the organism. The organism's behavior is an interrelationship with its surroundings, and to understand relationships we must study all components and their mutual influences, not just a single one that we presume to be the determiner of all the others.

On the biological level, neurons, hormones, immune system, cardiovascular system and many others interact so that no one of them is a master or a director of the others. Each influences and is influenced by the others. On another level, the interbehaviorists argue, the organism with its biological components interacts with its environment, and this level of organization is different from that of any of the components. This level of organization has principles of its own that must be understood at that level, not at a lower level such as that of the brain. This level of organism-object interaction, not the level of biology, is that of psychology, and it is there that we must seek psychology's principles.

> "Can't you give me brains?" asked the Scarecrow.
> "You don't need them. You are learning something every day. A baby has brains but it doesn't know much. Experience is the only thing that brings knowledge, and the longer you are on earth the more experience you are sure to get." (Frank Baum, *The Wizard of Oz*)

We often hear of a "biological basis" of psychology, but interbehaviorism holds that no science is a basis for any other. While the events of one may participate in the events of another—chemistry in psychology, psychology in sociology—each has its own level of organization whose principles are different from those of any of its constituents. Culture, biology, chemistry, physics, and sociology find their full roles in the interbehavioral field but are never determiners of the entire field.

What seem to be discrepancies between biological conditions and non-responses to them have puzzled investigators: (a) Where the optic nerve leaves each eye we have a *blind spot* covering about six degrees of arc where no photoreceptors exist, yet we never notice a hole in our vision. (b) Our eyes make rapid jerky movements about five times per second called *saccadic eye movements,* but we perceive our world smoothly. (c) Our *visual field* takes in about 180 degrees, but we usually observe only a small part of it. To illustrate the last point, notice the visual objects outside the pages of this book while still looking at the pages. You did not previously see them even though they were in your visual field. How do the traditionalist and the interbehaviorist, respectively, account for these conditions?

The traditionalist invokes a hypothetical brain process to "fill in" the hole in the blind spot of each eye and another one to smooth out our visual perceptions despite the saccadic movements. The interbehaviorists invoke no such brain constructs but suggest that we can account for these events quite simply by what we don't have: we lack the biological equipment to perceive the blind spot or the rapid visual fixes (Smith, 1997). As for our field of vision, the traditionalists propose that the brain turns on and off what we see. The interbehaviorist observes that retinal stimulation is biological but holds that seeing is a psychological field. We perceive only what we attend to regardless of its presence in the visual field, and attending depends on the factors described earlier.

Biology and Beyond in the Psychological Field. Biology participates not only structurally and functionally in all psychological interactions but ontogenetically as well. As the child develops more biological equipment—its ontogenetic development[6]—it is able to interact in more complex ways with its surroundings and advance its interbehavioral capabilities—such as knowledge, reasoning, judging, etc. When biological equipment

is well developed and further biological change is in the direction of decline (beginning about age twenty),[7] psychological development may continue in relative independence of biology and in some activities reach new heights into old age: creative writing, inventions, artistic production, financial skills, and so forth. J. R. Kantor, the founder of interbehavioral psychology, continued his analytic writing until the night before his death at the age of ninety-five. In his old age, Frank Lloyd Wright, the eminent American architect, said that solutions he had struggled so hard to create in his younger years he could now just shake out of his sleeve. Delprato (1980) reviews research that supports this lack of parallel between biological and psychological development and notes a number of developmentalists whose concepts are moving in a direction similar to that of interbehaviorism. Herrick (1983) uses Kantor's procedure of historico-critical analysis to show the origins of the belief that psychological decline parallels aging and to show how the social consequences of ageism have resulted from that belief. The interbehaviorist recognizes all psychological events as biological but insists at the same time that they are much more than biology.

Mind-Body Dualism. In this system, not only is there no reductionism to biology or other sciences, there is also no mind-body dualism. No mind in a body. No body without a mind. No declarations that body and mind are one. The mind-body issue is totally irrelevant to the interbehavioral field. Mind is a construct, not an event. For if we ask what is mind apart from the events and relationships in the interactional field, we find no separate concrete referent. Finding no separate referent, the interbehaviorist concludes that these

---

6. "Ontogenetic" can refer to either biological or psychological development.

7. After age twenty the decline is indicated by such measures as a slowing down in reaction time, declining numbers of T-cell lymphocytes that are important in the immune system, and others. It may come as a shock to college students to learn that as they leave their teens they are "over the hill," but they can take consolation in the fact that psychological development continues well into old age.

are constructs that consist only of verbal utterances. We have not observed mind but have imposed it on what we do observe. In contrast, the interbehavioral field, proponents claim, is a construct derived from observation of actual events. By including all the identified events and their relationships it leaves no room and has no need for additional hypothetical determiners.

Causality. There are two major views about causation in psychology: the organism's actions are caused by something inside, or they are caused by something outside. If inside, the cause is said to be a mind or brain; if outside, it is the environment. When any of the various psychologies assert that the organism or the organism's brain is the cause of action, the interbehaviorist asks what in turn causes the brain to act. Can it cause its own actions? And if the brain interprets or sees images on the retina, what sees what the brain sees? Or if the brain shuttles information around inside itself from one hypothetical processing unit to another, what directs it? Can it direct itself? One finds only an occasional attempt to answer such questions and only an occasional recognition by those who assume brain causation of behavior that these questions logically arise from the assumption; the implication of these hypothetical brain powers is that the organism or the brain is self-caused or engages in self-action.

If, on the other hand, the cause is said to have an outside origin, the assumption is of a passive organism shaped by its environment in a rather mechanistic fashion. This shows up in the notion of independent and dependent variables and in forms of behaviorism that propose a stimulus eliciting or evoking a response.

Sometimes causes are conceived as pushers and pullers. An inside force of mind, will, drive, or instinct is a pusher; and an outside force such as an incentive or a stimulus that elicits a response is a puller. Emotion has been proposed as an internal cause infusing energy into the organism, thereby being the motive power that causes it to act. Sometimes motives are said to be both pushers and pullers. Most motivational concepts have been so

cloudy or fraught with problems that they have gradually lost much of their former prominence in psychology.

When the stimulus conditions are the same but responses vary, in this system it is not necessary to assume a drive (Gewirtz, 1967) or a "person" or "self" (Hamachek, 1987) between stimulus and response. Rather, setting factors and evolution of stimulus functions are specific, identifiable field conditions that can be examined for their effects.

As for the internal cause in which the organism causes its own behavior, the interbehaviorists point out that we know of nothing in the universe that is self-caused. Self-causation is another unscientific construct, and we don't need it. Nor do we need to assume that the environment causes a passive organism to act. We can, they argue, forego both organocentrism (centered on the organism: pushers) and envirocentrism (centered on the environment: pullers). We can replace them by turning to a field of interactions. An active organism interacts with an active world, and we can study the development of those interactions in various settings to understand human activity. Just as the system has no need for mind-body dualism or for reduction of psychology to some other science, it also has no need to assume inside-outside distinctions, pushers or pullers, or self-causation or elicitors. They are not observed events but constructs that have been imposed on the events.

In short, in the interbehavioral approach the organism does not cause its own behavior; and neither does the environment cause behavior. Rather, causation is comprised of a field of interacting person and surroundings. This position renders meaningless the question of internal willpower versus external determinism. There is no assumed power called will or determinism to contend with. These are merely versions of mind-body dualism, the system argues.

Examples of How the System Operates. It may be helpful to see how this system would deal with a classical problem, that of perceptual *constancies*. Why do we see a person as a constant size whether that person is one meter from us or one hundred? The size of the points of light on the retina that correspond to the object varies greatly with distances from one meter to one hundred. The fact that we see the person as a constant size is called *size constancy*. Another form of constancy is that of shape: as a rectangular door swings on its hinges and we view it from edge-on to a full frontal view, the angle corresponding to the points of light that strike the retina changes. We do not say, however, that the door changes shape. We perceive it as rectangular from all angles. This is called shape constancy. The traditionalist would say that our mind or brain receives the various retinal images and continuously reinterprets them for us, or that the brain is a computer that encodes the retinal size of the person, or that the retinal angle of the door gives us a decoded read-out. (But what reads the read-out?) The read-out tells us that this is a normal size person or a rectangular door.

The interbehavioral approach is radically different. Rather than imposing such constructs as a computer brain, it begins with the observed components of the field. Because of our history with tables and doors and similar objects and with viewing them from various angles, we recognize the features that mean rectangularity. Given those stimulus functions of the stimulus object in connection with our history with them and a normal setting (unusual settings can be constructed to produce other perceptions), interbehaviorism argues that we perceive the object in terms of what it means to us: the door means rectangular object regardless of viewing angle, and the person means normal size regardless of distance.

The term *psychosomatics* implies that psyche (mind) acts on the soma (body). It is said to be implicated in asthma, high blood pressure, and other disorders. Rather than assuming a construct (mind) acting on an object (body), the interbehaviorists observe that the total pattern of interactional components in any situation includes biological components, some of which may be injurious to the body. Similarly, in a stress situation, such as a student's presentation before a class, the student may have dry mouth, sweaty palms, elevated blood pressure, and pounding heart. These are a part of the total pattern of the interaction, not a mind acting on a body.

Current conventional psychology views *thinking* as a processing of information by the brain. Interbehavioral psychology, in its steadfast fashion, turns to an examination of observable events. Thinking, it holds, consists of overt or covert manipulations that pave the way for something to follow. Planning, evaluating, and choosing are examples of thinking. These interactions consist of applying information gained from one situation to another similar situation. If the thinking occurs as a single behavior segment, as when one perceives on a road map the combination of roads that offer the shortest route to one's destination, the interaction consists of a series of action phases that precede and anticipate a finalizing phase—recognizing that best combination of roads. If the thinking is more complex, it consists of a series of behavior segments, the preliminary ones anticipating the final one of the series. For example, someone who thinks about how to overcome a slump in sales at a store actualizes a number of substitute stimuli, each of which has a number of phases of interaction. These behavior segments may themselves serve as stimuli for the next behavior segment until a final behavior segment involving a plan of action is reached.

Mainstream psychology holds that *memories* are encoded by neurons and then decoded and retrieved when needed. Interbehaviorism rejects analogies and constructed mechanisms such as coding, storage, and retrieval. It argues that recollection (which it distinguishes from memory) is not a thing that can be stored but an interaction. Recollecting or recalling is a reestablishment of an earlier field of interactions with a substitute stimulus for the thing remembered. Whether or not biological changes have occurred that might comprise one necessary condition in the recall, recall is a re-enactment of an earlier event. Nothing is stored.

How do we manage *contingencies*, situations we have not encountered before? Clark and Toribio (1994) argue that meeting contingencies or engaging in abstract organizing *requires* that we "invoke the idea of an internal representation" (p. 420). Interbehaviorism, in contrast, treats contingencies as adaptations to relatively new and unfamiliar situations. Such adaptations utilize (a) re-ordering and readjustment of existing action patterns and (b) new action patterns based on reflexes, earlier established action patterns, and cultural and individual behaviors.

Some contingencies we plan for. The student whose instructor may give unannounced quizzes tries to prepare for the most likely questions. In both planned and unplanned contingencies, the more action patterns we have built up that are related to the contingency, the more adequately we deal with it. The interbehaviorist always rejects imposed constructs such as internal representations and turns to functional relationships that we can observe. When we cannot identify what actual events are involved or make closely connected inferences from observations, it is better to admit ignorance, proponents insist, than to invent "dryads" (chapter 2, p. 53).

How can we respond to the *absent* and the *nonexistent,* to something that is not present? Does this not require a mind? Clark and Toribio (1994) believe that it does. We must have, they claim, "some inner resource which enables appropriate behavioral co-ordination" (p. 419) when there are no constant inputs from the environment to guide us. But we have already seen that interbehaviorism takes note of stimulation that substitutes for the thing that is absent (p. 284, above). Language is the most common example, but almost any object or event can become a substitute for the original. Interbehaviorism maintains that when we observe these substitutions and how they function, we have no need to invent mental constructs.

Forms of Behaviorism. Interbehaviorism can be distinguished from two other forms of behaviorism (Kantor, 1976). One of these is derived from physiological reflexes. In this scenario a stimulus elicits or evokes an action of the organism and is the primary causative agent of the psychological event; the organism is largely passive. This form of behaviorism may be represented as S $\longrightarrow$ R.

Another form, that of behavior analysis (see chapter 6), has the action originating from the organism; the stimulus is only an occasion for the organism to act and is essentially passive: the organism *emits* a response to the stimulus. This may be represented as S $\longleftarrow$ R. In contrast to these two forms of behaviorism, interbehaviorism, as noted above, regards the stimulus object with its functions and the responding organism with its functions as actively interacting: an active organism in an active world—hence interbehaviorism. This approach may be represented as S $\longleftrightarrow$ R or, better, $S_{func} \longleftrightarrow R_{func}$.

Neither S $\longrightarrow$ R nor S $\longleftarrow$ R behaviorism recognizes the stimulus functions that inhere in a stimulus object. Yet this recognition is critical. Without it one must assume either (a), as cognitive psychology has done, a mind or brain power that interprets the stimulus object into something meaningful, or (b), as a form of behaviorism has done, leave the stimulus as a meaningless object that mechanically elicits a response or to which a response is emitted.

EXPLICIT POSTULATE SYSTEM

Unlike all other systems, interbehavioral psychology is the only one that makes explicit exactly what it assumes. Kantor (Kantor, 1959; Kantor & Smith, 1975) does this by setting forth a hierarchical list of postulates that make it clear precisely what the system assumes at all levels of generality. The following postulates and the commentaries on them are from Kantor & Smith (1975, pp. 412–17) (italics added to quotations). Many of the postulates will already be apparent to the reader from the preceding description of the system. (A more complete postulate system that addresses investigation, data, and construction of laws can be found in Kantor, 1959).

■ *Protopostulates* (general guiding assumptions about science)
   A sample of two out of the ten protopostulates will suggest their character.
   1. *"No science is concerned with existences or processes which transcend the boundaries of*

scientific enterprises. No scientific problem is concerned with a 'Reality' beyond confrontable events and their investigation."

This postulate tells us that science deals only with concrete events of nature and may not assume anything beyond those "confrontable events."

2. *"Scientific construction—the formulation of (a) hypotheses and (b) theories and laws— must be derived from interbehavior with events and not imposed upon the events or scientific enterprise from nonscientific sources."*

This postulate is basic to the entire interbehavioral field construction. All of the components—stimulus object and stimulus function, response and response function, contact media, setting factors, and interactional history—are those the interbehaviorist claims can be observed or reasonably inferred from observation.

■ *Metapostulates* (supportive assumptions for a particular science)

1. *"Psychology is a relatively independent Science, though in constant interdisciplinary contact with other relevant sciences."*

Psychology has its own subject matter. It is not based on biology, chemistry, or any other science, nor can it borrow constructs from other sciences. This precludes the use of "information processing" from computer science or adopting from physiology the imposed construct that the brain creates colors. It may, however, use data from other sciences as participating conditions in the interactional field.

2. *"An adequate psychological system should take account of events, operations, and theory construction."*

Behaviorism has confined itself largely to learning and conditioning; and cognitive psychology has only begun to give attention to feelings, individual differences, or abnormal behavior. Interbehavioral psychology insists on giving attention to all psychological interactions including choosing, knowing, orienting, volitional acts, desiring, anticipating, implicit interbehaviors, contingential,

and others that receive little attention from other systems.

3. *"Psychological systems are irreducible."*

Because no science is basic to another, the traditional hierarchies of science are unsatisfactory. Each science has its own level of organization of events in nature, and such organization has principles or laws of its own that are not reducible to any other. To use one science to explain another, such as biology to explain psychology, misconstrues both sciences.

4. *"Psychology must be freed from all traditional philosophies."*

Philosophies that do not adhere to observing and describing events are not appropriate to scientific work.

5. *"All scientific systems are subject to change."*

With change in observational procedures and with improved understanding of events, systems must change to conform to those events.

■ *Postulates* (subject matter assumptions)

1. *"Psychology Studies Interbehavioral Fields."*

It is not minds, or information processing, or other constructs that psychology studies, but the concrete events of organisms interacting with objects, events, or other organisms. These interbehavioral fields range from manipulating objects as in planting a garden to subtle reasoning and imagining.

2. *"Psychological Fields Are Multiplex."*

In addition to organisms and objects psychological fields include media of contact, interactional history, and setting conditions.

3. *"Psychological Interbehavior Involves the Performance of Entire Organisms, Not Special Organs or Tissues."*

This postulate follows from the preceding postulate. The multiplex field precludes confining the activity to the brain or the entire organism as the sole cause of the event. The locus of the psychological event is in the field rather than in the organism.

4. *"Psychological Events Occur without Any Internal or External Determiners."*

Naturalistic descriptions of observable field events replace all constructed internal events such as consciousness, mental states, drives, instincts, brain powers, and information processing and such an external cause as environment.

5. *"Psychological Events Are Ontogenic."*
Psychological events are historical or developmental.

6. *"Psychological Constructions Are Continuous with Crude-Data Events."*
This postulate is continuous with the first protopostulate and specifies that interbehavioral constructs are drawn from "confrontations with ongoing events" and not from convention. All descriptions, hypotheses, and theories must be "derived directly from the observations of actual interbehaviors" (p. 417).

7. *"Psychological Events Are Interrelated with Societal Events as Well as with Events Studied by Physicists, Chemists, and Biologists."*
This is continuous with the first metapostulate listed above. Psychology is relatively independent of other sciences but interdependent with them.

8. *"Psychological Events Are Evolved from Bioecological Interbehaviors."*
All psychological interactions develop from bioecological interactions just as organisms have developed from prior forms of organisms. Biology participates in every action organisms engage in.

Why does Kantor consider it so important to lay out his postulates? Because he emphasizes the crucial role that such fundamental assumptions play in the formulation of various psychologies and stresses that these assumptions usually go unrecognized. Whether psychological events are said to occur by means of an information-processing brain (cognitive psychology), by reinforcing contingencies (behavior analysis), by dialectical processes (dialectical psychology), by unconscious motives (orthodox psychoanalysis), by behavior settings (eco-behavioral science), by self-fulfillment (humanistic psychology), or by fields of interactions depends on our postulates—whether implicit or explicit. This in turn affects

the design of research studies and how their results are interpreted as well as in such applications as business and psychotherapy. By setting an example of making the postulates explicit and thorough, he showed what kind of psychology could emerge from what he held to be sound scientific principles—drawn directly from the world of nature—that these assumptions incorporate. Similarly, he could show how unsatisfactory are psychologies that arise from implicit assumptions derived from nonscientific sources.

RESEARCH

Because organisms interbehave with objects as part of a field and investigators interbehave with the field of interbehavior they are investigating, all research, Kantor (1963–69) claims, is interbehavioral. But the interpretation of the research is interbehavioral only if the investigator begins with observations and draws constructs directly from them. What often happens, instead, is that investigators start with such constructs as information processing, consciousness, mind, or brain powers and interpret the results in terms of the constructs with which they began. Ray and Delprato (1989) hold that research also fails to meet interbehavioral criteria or those of the physical sciences when it employs a mechanistic view of unidirectional chains of cause and effect.[8] The physical sciences replaced mechanistic constructs with interacting field events, but much of psychology continues to employ mechanistic constructs by assuming the stimulus to be "independent" of the response and by measuring a single response, which is regarded as "dependent" on the stimulus. Ray and Delprato (1989) note that investigators usually ignore the interdependencies among classes even when they do measure more than one response class. The first of the following six sections is a sample of interbehavioral research that gives special attention to interdependencies.

---

8. This is an assumption of straight-line cause and effect: A causes B causes C. For example, a stimulus leads to information processing which leads to behavior (S ⟶ Info Proc ⟶ R).

Multiple Measures of Interdependencies

A number of studies have demonstrated that only the examination of multiple variables can adequately account for experimental behaviors and that using a field approach to relate these multiple variables is more fruitful than resorting to single variables and linear mechanical approaches (Delprato & Rusiniak, 1991; Keehn & Nobrega, 1978; Ray & Brown, 1975; Ray & Delprato, 1989; Ray, Upson, & Henderson, 1977; Upson & Ray, 1984; Wong, 1977). The importance of multiple variables to account for behavior were found in such varied animals as rats, orcas (killer whales), and humans.

Proponents of interbehaviorism point to instructional situations as displaying the interbehavioral field with particular clarity. By employing the field concept for classroom research, it is possible to evaluate settings, people, and responses, and the way in which many classroom events "have the propensity to affect many others in a multidirectional fashion" (Hawkins, Sharpe, & Ray, 1994, p. 245). Sharpe and Hawkins (1992a, 1992c) investigated the multiple variables of the field in physical education instruction by videotaping instructional lessons of master teachers and using raters to analyze the complex variables and enter them into a computer. This permitted the investigators to determine categories of responses, organismic and environmental setting elements, and stimulus objects. From this, they (Sharpe & Hawkins, 1993; Hawkins, Sharpe, & Ray, 1994; Sharpe, Hawkins, & Ray, 1995) developed two computer programs, the Behavior Evaluation Strategy and Taxonomy (BEST) and coordinated with it the Temporal Analysis System (TAS). With these tools teachers can quickly learn improved teaching techniques (BEST) and evaluate the results (TAS). BEST gives the teacher immediate feedback and opportunity for modification of teaching procedures.

In an effort to find a better technique for describing the operating characteristics of an interbehavioral field, Ray (1992) used a computer to simulate the interbehavioral field of a monkey in a cage engaging in the simple actions of sitting, standing, walking, climbing, turning, and eating. This semi-realistic portrayal allowed the investigator to determine what is overlooked in a complex field of interactions. Even though Ray had twenty years of experience in researching behavior systems and movements, he "did not fully anticipate the need for *field-specific* [emphasis added] matrix construction or for reinforcing the field probabilities directly. Nor did [he] think the implications of stimulus setting factors versus stimulating events would be so different" (p. 112).

Ray then developed two additional computer programs, Cyberat and MediaMatrix (Ray, 1995a; 1995b). Cyberat provides model descriptions of fields of events by using descriptive arrays and commands that enable a student to operant condition a rat that appears in video clips. MediaMatrix follows a similar course in that it instructs the student with a program that systematically adapts to the student.

Setting Factors

The types of populations on which setting factor studies have been conducted include small children, rats, students, and elementary pupils. Behavior analysts, among others, have examined setting factors with a number of types of populations and settings, and those are included in the review.

Small Children. Brown, Fox, and Brady (1987) showed that three- and four-year-olds engaged in more social interaction in a small free-play area than in a larger one. They suggest that the use of this setting arrangement offers opportunities for improving social development. In investigating some intellectual activities that Piaget has delineated, three Italian investigators (Caracciolo, Moderato, & Perini, 1988) found that such field factors as interactional history and settings were more important in performance than the children's intellectual level.

Rats and Students. Ray and his associates (Ray, Upson, & Henderson, 1977; Ray & Delprato,

1989) showed that rats slow their activities as environmental conditions slow down and that college students slow their rate of choosing different setting conditions as conditions slow (Upson, Carlson, & Ray, 1981). The students participated in three conditions. In the first the experimenter specified each setting that the subjects had to participate in; these were college events such as listening to music, dancing, and sitting in chapel. In the second the students chose their own campus setting. In the third they spent four days on a Bahamian Island with few of the sources of entertainment to which they were accustomed but with free selection of activities. The last was the slowest environment and resulted in the slowest rate of transition from one setting to another.

Elementary Pupils. The great range of setting conditions in the elementary classroom—such as whether seats are in rows, circles, or clusters—can influence the educational outcome; the judicious use of physical, social, and programmatic settings can promote learning and reduce behavior problems (Rosenfield, Lambert, & Black, 1985). The way in which setting conditions interact also have an effect (Greenwood et al., 1990; Nordquist & Twardasz, 1990), and a better understanding of these interactions could be used to "influence the rate of students' academic growth" (Greenwood et al., 1990, p. 59).

Behavior Analysis and Setting Events. Applied behavior analysis has discovered that setting factors, which they have renamed "setting events" (Bijou, 1976; Bijou & Baer, 1961), are important and sometimes even crucial to the success of reinforcement and contingency management. The following is a sample of these studies.

Setting events may play a crucial role in reinforcements. Bloom (1974) demonstrated that setting events consisting of eye contacts with infants were necessary in order for reinforcement of responses to be effective. She described the setting as a "catalyst" for reinforcement and learning. A series of studies have employed setting events in mother-child conflict. Wahler (1980) successfully taught mothers operant procedures for the management of

their children's anti-social behaviors, such as hitting, verbal abuse, fighting, destroying property, refusal to comply with requests, and stealing. But the mothers' original unsuccessful and counterproductive behavior, such as screaming at the children, returned when the mothers had aversive contacts with social agency workers. Further studies (Dumas & Wahler, 1985; Whaler & Graves, 1983) showed that additional setting events of mothers, such as poverty and lack of friends, were correlated with conflict with their children. The investigators recommended improving setting events as a prerequisite to training. Because parents are influenced by a host of field conditions, Brown, Bryson-Brackmann, and Fox (1986) suggest that applied behavior analysis, in order to be more effective, needs to deal with these conditions.

Interactional History

All interactions between persons and things around them are interdependent with their history. Some studies, however, have focused specifically on the effects of the history. Two studies with children will illustrate the role of interactional history. Krantz and Risley (1977) found that kindergarten children were generally inattentive to their teacher during story-telling if they had previously engaged in boisterous play. Replacing the boisterous period with a rest period prior to the storytelling improved the attention level as much as did a contingency management procedure. Quilitch & Risley (1973) found that the replacement of "isolate" toys with "social" toys raised cooperative and social behavior from 16 percent to 78 percent. An interactional history with these toys, even if it was short, influenced behavior.

Overt and Covert Interactions

Interbehaviorism does not recognize a mind-body dualism but observes that many interactions are very subtle and not easy to detect except by one who is engaging in the interactions. These *covert* or *implicit* interactions differ in degree of observability from those more *overt* or *explicit* but are the same in principle, they claim. Three studies have tested these claims and found supporting evidence for them. Ackerman (1972) demonstrated that the covert desire to smoke or to consume soft drinks could be extinguished by the same operant procedures as overt responses. Smith and Delprato (1976) also studied covert desires to smoke and found that these desires followed the same reinforcement principles as overt responses. Delprato (1977) examined the claims that, due to psychic powers, a hand-held pendulum would move toward an object the subject was thinking about. He showed that these movements could be explained interbehaviorally and therefore naturalistically: recourse to nonphysical mental or psychic powers was totally unnecessary.

Stimulus Functions in Problem Solving

A concept of fixity of function, or "functional fixedness" (Duncker, 1945), describes a situation in problem solving in which a given usage of a stimulus object interferes with recognition of a different usage of it, one that is required for solving the problem. This readily translates to "stimulus function" and "stimulus evolution" (stimulus functions that develop with time and situations) of interbehaviorism. Swartz (1955) performed an experiment with playing cards in which the subjects would not be able to find the solution if the stimulus function of the cards remained fixed but could do so if the red cards evolved into one stimulus function and the black cards into another— but with different functions for each. He found that it was difficult for subjects to evolve new stimulus functions when the stimulus objects shared a common property.

A series of studies of a ring and peg problem by Scheerer (1963), although conducted totally independently of interbehaviorism, well illustrates the interrelationship of such field factors as stimulus function/response function, interactional history, and setting. The task consisted of putting rings on a peg from a point six feet away, where the subject had to stand when placing the rings. Two sticks were also available to the subject, each stick two feet in length. In the first condition of the experiment a string was hanging on the wall. All subjects solved the problem by taking down the string, tying the sticks together, and using them to place the rings on the peg. This was a base measurement or control condition. In the first experimental series the string held up one of three useless objects: a blank piece of cardboard, an outdated calendar, or a cloudy mirror. Nearly all of the subjects solved the problem. Here the string was perceived as lacking any useful function but as available for use with the problem. In the second experimental series the string held up a current calendar, a no-smoking sign, or a clear mirror. Over half failed to solve the problem with the calendar and the sign and nearly 70 percent with the mirror. Subjects had been instructed to think aloud, and all immediately mentioned the need for a string. The string was in full view, as in the other test; but the subjects perceived it as having the function of holding up a utilitarian object, not as something to be used in the task. During the entire twenty-minute test period they recognized the need for a string but did not change their perceptions.

In a variation on these tests, the subject was performing a written task when a secretary entered the room, apologized for interrupting, explained that mirrors were being placed in all the experimental rooms for a forthcoming experiment, and asked if the subject would hang up the one she was carrying. After doing so, the subject returned to the task and fifteen minutes later confronted the peg and ring problem with the mirror on the wall that he or she had placed there. Despite this direct experience with handling the string, about half the subjects failed to solve the problem. The interactional history with the string in this setting was consistent with its use as a utilitarian object unrelated to the problem. In a second experiment subjects were given a task called "manual dexterity" in which they tied the string with tweezers and then hung up the cardboard, outdated calendar, or clear mirror. Fifteen minutes later when they confronted the peg and rings all but one of thirty-six subjects solved the problem. This particular setting and the interactional history, in which the string was a manipulable object and part of an experiment, made it easy for the subjects to perceive the stimulus function/response function of the string that they needed.

Linguistic Interactions

The interbehaviorist treats language as "bistimulational interaction" involving the speaker interacting simultaneously with two stimulus objects: (a) the thing the speaker is referring to and (b) the listener (Kantor, 1928, 1977). Language is telling someone about something. Living, ongoing speech behavior, unlike fixed written language, includes such components as gesture, intonation, context or setting, and what the speaker assumes about the listener's understanding of the subject. On the part of the listener, linguistic interactions include context of prior verbal statements as well as general surroundings that might be relevant. It also includes what the listener knows about the speaker's mode of reference, gestures, and intonation, as well as a mutual sharing of sounds that have a particular reference. Thus, the emphasis is on specific identifiable events that are in constant flux as the speech adjustments continue, rather than on such constructs as brain processing or abstracted grammatical structures.

The earliest interbehavioral language studies were tests of bistimulation, and they found supporting evidence for that concept (Briones, 1937; Bucklew, 1943; Herman, 1951a, 1951b; Ratner & Rice, 1963). Another early test focused on a widespread assumption that language consists of sound symbols that pass from the mind of the speaker to the mind of the listener, producing the same or similar mental images or ideas in the mind of the listener as are in the mind of the speaker. The test found evidence for the bistimulational event rather than for these traditional constructs (Pronko, 1945). Turning to assumptions about biological determinants of speech, Wolf (1958a) conducted experiments on those with aphasia, brain damage that results in some loss of language usage or comprehension. He found that aphasics performed better if familiar objects—items of a table setting—were in their normal context rather than in some irregular arrangement. This indicated that aphasic linguistic behavior includes both setting factors and biology as participants in the interbehavioral field. In a second study (1958b) he examined the reaction to stimulus objects comprising a table setting and showed that errors were not random but relative to the arrangement of the items, and therefore not fixed by tissue impairment.

In more recent research, using a manual they had developed for identifying and analyzing linguistic interbehaviors, Bijou and his associates (Bijou, Chao, & Ghezzi, 1988; Bijou et al., 1986; Bijou, 1989; Ghezzi & Bijou, 1994) generated a procedure for helping mildly retarded children improve their language skills. The investigators videotaped two children talking to each other, one normally developed and the other mildly retarded and socially withdrawn. They used raters to analyze the language behavior—including gestures—of the speaker and listener, and the roles of the referent and the setting. The ratings were used as one of the selection criteria to determine which children might profit from training and for determining the linguistic shortcomings of those children. For training, the investigators used videotapes to show the target children their desirable and undesirable linguistic interactions and to teach them to identify those characteristics independently and to practice helpful alternatives. A second procedure trained the children to initiate and sustain conversations through role playing. In a third method, seven- and eight-year-old normally developing children were taught to assist a target child in conversation. All three procedures produced marked improvement in the target child's initiating and sustaining conversations as measured by specifications of the manual. Still other improvements occurred without instruction. Thus, the interbehavioral method developed for analysis also provided measurements for improvements with training.

The Bijou manual has also proved useful for research into the linguistic interactions of schizophrenics and college students. Ratings of schizophrenics and normals (non-schizophrenics) based on the manual's program disclosed that schizophrenics referred extensively to themselves but normals did so very little (Williamson & Lyons, 1988; Williamson et al., 1987; Williamson et al., 1986). When the manual and raters were applied to listeners and speakers among college students (Chiasson & Hayes, 1993), it showed that fresh-

men did not initiate as many interactions with seniors and graduate students or spend as much
time talking with them as they did with other
freshmen. Their peers comprised a setting factor
that facilitated more language interactions than
did a setting factor of advanced students.

APPLICATIONS

A number of applications appeared in the section
on research, above, as outcomes of interbehavioral
research. Setting factors assumed an important role
in such widely varied applications as managing antisocial behavior of children, facilitating social behavior of preschool children, improving attentional
behavior of kindergartners, promoting achievement of Piagetian intellectual tasks, and assisting in
achieving educational goals. Research attention to
additional components of the field has influenced
the development of computerized instructional
programs: BEST, MediaMatrix, and Cyberat. Analysis and training of language interbehaviors of
slightly retarded children was used to promote socialization. Some additional applications follow:

Business Management, Space Program

Fuller (1987) combined behavior analysis and
interbehaviorism for application to business management, the space program, and various educational and clinical problems. In business, rather
than giving directions, he facilitated a cooperative
arrangement among relevant jobs and stressed
positive interpersonal relationships with an attention to settings. "Those professionals who have
previous contacts with psychologists find this experience different, due to the comprehensive, positive, achievement-oriented approach and the
process of interaction between people working together" (p. 28). In the space program a benefit
"has been the merging of the psychological
systems approach with the engineering systems
approach . . . high speed digital computers,
systems-engineering developments, and manual
and optimal control theory combined with interbehaviorism to give us a powerful tool for research
and application" (p. 29).

Education

Sharpe and Hawkins (1992b) cite research to
show that expert instructors use instructional
techniques within the appropriate context whereas novice teachers seem to be "rule-governed"—
that is, they use what may be good rules but use
them out of context. This fact leads the authors to
recommend dispensing with "an isolated-element
approach to teacher preparation" and adopting a
field model that will "enable teachers to more adequately conceptualize their enterprise in its interdependent, interconnective framework and thus
operate more effectively within their particular
context" (p. 82). They maintain that use of theory
for applications must meet the requirements of
good science, science that accurately reflects the
interrelationships of the appropriate variables, and
must foster an understanding of how science and
technology are related. Their research program
(see p. 299) in teaching physical education instruction is so directed. This "field systems evaluation" involves use of portable computers to
record instruction as it occurs and give the instructor immediate feedback on such complexities
as "system coherence, velocity, rate of responding,
rapid response timing, and context specific instructional pattern recognition" (Sharpe, 1996).

Baxter (1994), drawing on the work of the interbehaviorists and of Engelmann and Carnine
(1982), demonstrates in the teaching of young
children the specifics of principles similar to those
set forth above by Sharpe and Hawkins. He notes
that when a learning problem occurs, such as reversal of numbers by a kindergarten child, the typical response is to focus on the child by (a) attributing the cause to delayed development or (b)
producing a clinical diagnosis of a perceptual
handicap. In this scenario one can wait for further
development or attack the perceptual problem. In
the case of waiting, if the child is still reversing at
age eight, no remedy is offered. In contrast to both
the waiting and the perceptual diagnostic approach, the interbehaviorally oriented teacher recognizes that the mistakes children make in learning are primarily due to confusion in context
(such as similar numerals introduced at the same

time), and this results in learner misgeneralization (such as confusing a 4 with a 9). Consequently, according to an interbehavioral view, the teacher's role is to observe the type of misgeneralization the child is making and then replace the teacher-learner context with one that eliminates the confusion. Such a teacher is aware that writing digits from 1–9 falls into three different groups, each of which involves drawing lines in different directions. For example, a 4 starts with a line down and then to the right, a 7 with a line to the right and then down, and a 9 with a loop and then a line down to the right. When the teacher clusters the groups according to sameness and teaches them some time apart—while demonstrating sameness both within and between groups—children no longer reverse them. Reversal, Baxter holds, is due to a failure to observe and teach specifics ("communication"), and not to a child's failure to develop or to the effects of a perceptual handicap.

Similarly, the child who spells words correctly in a list but incorrectly in a sentence is not suffering from "visual imagery long-term memory deficit" or some other clinical construct, Baxter contends. Rather, the learning situation is not being properly addressed. Instead of blaming some shortcoming of the pupil, the teacher needs to emphasize spelling in context as well as in lists, give practice in the two, and show that they are identical. A third example is of a child who demonstrates proficiency on the day of learning but fails to repeat it at a later time. Rather than blaming the learner, the teacher should use distributed review with interrupted practice to correspond to the need for recall at unpredictable times. In these three examples, the interbehavioral specificity principle emerges clearly. Baxter's observations receive strong support from a billion-dollar study funded by federal grants that demonstrated that children's achievements were a result of instructional method rather than of any shortcomings in the children (Stebbin et al., 1977; Watkins, 1988) and by follow up studies (Adams & Engelmann, 1996). Baxter maintains that

the primary focus in effective teaching, as in any interbehavioral event, is not just on the learner,

but is a study of a multitude of interacting variables. In the case of the natural event of teaching, the primary variables are the instructional communications, in accompaniment with other interacting variables that define the event, such as those of the teacher-learner interaction, setting, and event history . . . If we are to be successful in creating effective change in education we must make it known to teachers that there is a psychology that is an alternative to those psychologies that use a mythological language that immobilizes the teacher and prevents him/her from becoming effective. (pp. 29–30)

Baxter's reference to a "mythological language" is similar to the criticisms by other investigators of the impediment to understanding imposed by abstract constructs, which can be removed by specifying concrete events (Farrington, 1972; Knapp & Delprato, 1980. See "Clinical Psychology," below).

Cornwell and Hobbs (1986) began an attempt to apply the principles of behavior analysis to teacher education in Scotland; but as they become more involved in the specifics of it, they moved increasingly toward an interbehavioral approach. This came about in the development of a system called EXRIB—Example, Rule Indicator, Behavior—for analyzing teaching. The Rule Indicator provides a stimulus function that directs pupil behavior toward stimulus objects in other categories. The system also includes categories of "contextual stimuli" and "contextual responses" in its trifold division of observations into (a) pupil behaviors, (b) conditions, and (c) teacher evaluations of pupil behavior. As opposed to the vagaries of "mental work" (Hobbs & Kleinberg, 1978; Hobbs, Kleinberg, & Crozier, 1980), EXRIB involves specific objectives, observations, and conditions—instances of the specificity principle.

Psychotherapeutic Applications

Combined with applied behavior analysis, Wahler and Hann (1987) have used interbehavioral concepts for children and their families who engage in oppositional or antisocial behavior (see p. 300). The concept of interdependence between setting and stimulus-response is "the hallmark of interbehavioral clinical psychology" (p. 75).

Ruben and Ruben (1987) have subjected assertiveness training to interbehavioral treatment. They reject the notion that changes can be made inside the person and emphasize the learning of new skills. They suggest two means of doing this. (a) Because behavior does not reside within the person, replace teaching the person as an isolated entity with interaction of person and events; this involves employing "functional descriptions" that consist of specific gestures—for example, use of fingers and avoiding of wrinkling forehead in specific settings, such as "when people are looking at you" or "in showing surprise." (b) Because skills do not readily transfer by some "intrapsychic dynamics" from the training situation to the one where they will be applied, teach "through a series of successive situations (fields)" (p. 108) that begin to approximate realistic settings rather than just the training setting.

Behavioral medicine with interbehavioral characteristics began with a demonstration of the role of enduring setting events (pain medication, food, nurse call-button) and changing setting events (laboratory procedures, physician visits) in pain and distress of cancer patients (Redd & Rusch, 1985). Another approach to interbehavioral medicine applies interbehavioral principles to research and relates it to some interbehavioral postulates (McGlynn, Cook, & Greenbaum, 1987). After reviewing innovative clinical methods in behavioral medicine when the specialty was still quite young, Delprato and McGlynn (1986) argued that unrecognized interbehavioral thinking was at the heart of many modern applications of psychological principles in medicine; and they foresaw advantages of explicitly adopting interbehavioral postulates in the discipline. Ruben (1992), in turning to interbehaviorism for treatment of alcohol and drug abuse, adapts from Delprato and McGlynn (1986) six postulates for an interbehavioral clinical psychology while recognizing that as "guide-

lines" they are only "introductory" to dealing with the problem.

The approach to obesity has been dominated by the assumption of a "set point," a presumed biologically determined weight that the individual is seldom able to obtain. Stevenson and Hemingway (1987), like Ruben, adapt the postulates of Delprato and McGlynn (1986) for a behavioral/interbehavioral medicine that greatly broadens the approach:

> The field-factor approach helps the scientist-practitioner confront the multitude of biological and psychological factors one encounters in obesity and risk-factor management. The systemic view of obesity leads us to take data on body composition, blood pressure, lipids, and other measures of organismic functioning, rather than focusing on weight alone. We examine patterns and composition of intake rather than a single measure such as Kcal/day. Instead of citing insufficient willpower we examine cultural, familial, and personal interaction patterns. (pp. 120–121)

They have developed a systematic program that incorporates these principles, and their data show encouraging results.

Legal deviance (or "crime and delinquency") has been traditionally treated from a mentalistic framework (Morris et al., 1987). This sometimes focuses on genetic traits and sometimes on biological or hypothetical mental mediators—such as purported criminal thought patterns—between person and surroundings. Another approach uses "situationism," in which the individual's environment is blamed. This, however, fails to account for those persons from the same environment who do not turn to legal deviance. The interbehaviorist, Morris et al. note, recognizes that similar environments can have quite different meanings (stimulus functions) for different individuals, depending on the individuals' interactional histories; further, an investigation of interactional histories may disclose why certain functional meanings develop and how they might be altered. A treatment program, they hold, must identify the contributions of each field factor before effective intervention is possible—another example of the interbehavioral specificity principle.

Daurelle et al. (1987) have combined the interbehavioral field with the three-term contingency of behavior analysis to train parents to deal with developmentally delayed children. A review of studies shows the shortcomings of procedures that have not taken into account the broader field factors of which families are a part. Scafasci (1987) emphasizes the role of the psychologist as part of the interbehavioral field in working with these populations.

In sum, interbehavioral psychology does not provide a specific procedure for clinical psychology but does emphasize the necessity to take account of the larger context of which the individual is one part and to be specific about behaviors and conditions. The section below further addresses these matters.

CLINICAL PSYCHOLOGY

Because interbehavioral psychology is a scientific system oriented toward the understanding of psychological events rather than toward applications, it has no defined psychotherapy. Nevertheless, it has been possible to derive some important guidelines from it for clinical practice. The use of setting factors with children as reviewed in "Setting Factors," above, is one such example. Perhaps two general guidelines for clinical work can be identified from its fundamental principles: (1) Any therapeutic process that expects to be effective and enduring should take account of more elements of the field than just the organism. Most therapies, whether psychoanalysis, behavior therapy, gestalt therapy, reality therapy, humanistic therapy, existential therapy, or others attempt to change the individual while ignoring the context within which the individual operates. A major exception is community psychology (see chapter 13) that attempts to work with the individual in the workplace, the school, the family, and other places that are parts of the individual's life. This approach is more consistent with interbehaviorism than are the tradi-

tional therapies.[9] (2) Any clinical evaluation or description must be specific to observations: the client's demographic information, history, behavior observations, and statement of the problem. The inferential constructs that the clinician draws, such as diagnoses and prognoses and the basis for the treatment plan, must be consistent with these observations. The clinician should avoid starting with constructs such as ego strength, intrapsychic drives, psychosexual stages, mental states, and internalization and imposing these on the client.

Requirements for a Clinical Psychology

Kantor (1987) observes that competence in clinical practice requires a scientific orientation. The clinician should not "confound diagnoses and treatment with notions of internal mental states or imaginary brains" (p. 7) or with presumed heredity for which there is no evidence (p. 7). Psychiatrists, he notes, seldom reject mind-body dualism or have a command of psychological, ecological, and sociological conditions; but psychiatrists are important in treating physiological deficits that may preclude normal interactions. An interbehavioral psychology, he holds, is in the best position to deal with the complex field factors that comprise maladaptive behaviors and to clarify the proper roles of medical practice and clinical psychology. Cromwell and Snyder (1993) have incorporated these principles into their approach to schizophrenia.

Pronko (1987) argues that everyone operates from some sort of theoretical orientation, even those who use haphazard or eclectic methods. Therefore, it is not a question of theory or no theory but of bad theory versus good theory. Much bad theory, he contends, is self-actional. That is, it

---

9. One of the pioneers in community psychology was Jerry Carter, Kantor's first doctoral student. Though rarely cited, he carried interbehavioral principles into that field and in 1970 received from the Division of Community Service of the American Psychological Association a Distinguished Service Award for "a lifetime of significant contributions to community mental health and community psychology." From the Division of Psychologists in Public Service he received the Hildreth Memorial Award.

is organism-centered and assumes that the organism causes its own behaviors. This takes such forms as attributing causation to the brain, a mind, or destructive thinking. He cautions against (a) using haphazard methods and hoping to stumble onto something that will work, and (b) using bad theory that imposes self-actional constructs. He recommends examining the interactional history, setting factors, and other relevant field events.

Among the principles that Delprato (1995b) suggests for an interbehavioral approach to clinical psychology are the following:

(a) Causality of the client's problem arises not from some hypothetical outside force such as an environment or in some hypothetical inside force such as a mind or cognitive processing. It is comprised of the field of relationships, and it is those relationships that need attention.

(b) Because maladaptive behaviors are multifaceted and require modifying field factors, clinical services should apply an interdisciplinary approach and include social, biological, educational, vocational, and other relevant conditions. At the same time a field system with its nonreductionistic postulate precludes the assignment of final authority to those, such as medical personnel, who work within a biological orientation.

(c) The emphasis should be on the construction of behaviors that build on potentials rather than on the elimination of behaviors.

(d) The first approach to complaints or problems should be to explore the conditions—usually social—that contribute to the complaint and attempt to modify them rather than trying to modify the person.

(e) The clinician should de-emphasize intervention and resolve the problem as quickly as possible by making use of whatever resources, such as friends or school, are available in the community: "to solve problems in highly artificial ways (e.g., physical restraint, contrived reinforcers [conditions not found in the normal environment]) is to make transition to everyday life . . . difficult. Two guidelines to address are: make the initial phase of services as minimally artificial as possible and fade out artificiality as quickly as possible" (1995b, p. 627).

The following is a selection from Delprato's (1995a) list of his positive and negative biases for clinical psychology:

Table 10.1

Biases about Clinical Psychology

Biased for	Biased against
Observation	Intuition
Events	Speculation
Observation of events	Reliance on cultural tradition and authority
Interpretation and explanations based on events	Reliance on what one learned in graduate school
Data	Casual observations
Empirically validated clinical procedures	Evaluation of services only by asking clients how they feel
Claims of expertise supported by data	Alleged expertise based on credentials or on personal experience
Clinical psychology as it can be	Clinical psychology as it has been

Source: Dennis Delprato, "Admitting Bias," *Behavior Therapist* 18 (1995): 108.

The subjectivity or feeling states that are measured objectively by Stephenson's (1987) Q methodology use assumptions that draw explicitly from interbehaviorism and are eminently suitable for an interbehavioral clinical psychology, proponents claim. It provides a means of assessing feelings—the all-important client's point of view rather than that of the clinician—before treatment and at any point during treatment. "By way of Q technique and its methodology we can fathom what a patient is substituting for action, what [the patient] is deceptive about, what thoughts are hidden, and indeed whether [the patient] has any thoughts at all. Q-sorting is backward looking (though it can also look forward, especially about intentions), and there are thousands of selves to preview . . ." (Stephenson, 1987, p. 104). Cromwell and Snyder (1993) state that while interbehaviorism expunges mind-body dualism, it accepts subjectivity as "constructions of events" as long as such variables "enter into reliable relationships with other variables derived from the event field" (p. 9).

Interbehaviorism would hold that the constructs of some of the traditional therapies as well as those of many individuals do not optimize the therapeutic situation. Farrington (1972) studied prison inmates' use of constructs such as mind, ego, need, and unconscious in group therapy sessions. The inmates modeled the constructs on the speech of therapists and on texts that they had read and regarded them as the terms of professional language. When asked to define the constructs, they did so with additional constructs. Some used them because they believed that the constructs helped with communication in therapy; others used them in an effort to appear sophisticated before parole boards. She suggests that replacing "constructs which reify and which have no referent in crude data" (p. 393) with the identification of concrete conditions that might lead to improved behaviors would be advantageous.

Knapp and Delprato (1980) found among respondents to a questionnaire a strong belief in the construct "willpower" and the belief in the necessity of the strength of willpower to overcome such "self-indulgences" as overeating and smoking and such "non-self-indulgences" as shyness and fear of flying. The authors observed that few behavior therapists would hold that clients can overcome their behavior problems by application of "willpower" and that some evidence indicates that belief in willpower interferes with the therapeutic process. They call for research that would show the way toward overcoming this belief and observe that scientific psychology has had little influence in countering this cultural construct. That many of the respondents had studied one or more psychology courses and that these experiences were unrelated to the belief in willpower raises questions, they note, about what the students are learning in psychology courses that they carry beyond the classroom.

Kantor's System of Abnormal Psychology

After thoroughly reviewing the meaning of "abnormality" Kantor (1926; see also Kantor & Smith, 1975, Chp. 23) identifies three categories: (I) unusual interbehavior, (II) unadaptive interbehavior, (III) defective or pathological interbehavior. The third is divided into (a) undeveloped, (b) defectively developed, (c) disintegrated, (d) dissociated, (e) degenerated, (f) disorganized, and (g) traumatic or truncated. The bases for these abnormalities lie in defects of the action system, in personality patterns, or in the individual interactional history involving the entire interbehavioral field. Biological impairments can play a role. Any number of particular conditions could be classified in any of the three, depending on the degree of severity.

Lundin (1987), who summarizes this system, finds a number of advantages. (a) It does not follow a medical model with its invoking of "mental diseases" that supposedly parallel "physical diseases." (b) It recognizes a continuum from the mildest form of disorders, the unusual, through the intermediate, the unadaptive, to the most severe, the pathological. (c) The description of each behavior characteristic is able to handle several different classes of personality disorder. (d) Rather than using categories of symptoms as is standard, the system uses observable descriptions of behaviors that result from different interactional histories. It might be added that this system, like the larger interbehavioral system of which it is a part, avoids centering on the organism and turns to the field of interactions. Lundin suggests that the system might be helpful in various treatment approaches.

An Interbehavioral Description of a Case Study

An example of a pioneering interbehavioral description and treatment of a clinical case (Carter, 1937) is that of a thirteen-year-old girl with symptoms of a partially paralyzed left leg, extreme jitteriness, and loss of appetite. She began to avoid social interactions and developed the paralysis when it was time for recess at school, an apparent means of avoiding the social activities of the recess. The diagnosis in interbehavioral terms was *reactional dissociation*. These symptoms developed in conjunction with her parents' involvement in a triangular infidelity and the continuing stormy aftermath, including a threatened divorce. Even the thought of the events was extremely disturbing to her. The therapy consisted of encouraging her to describe the events repeatedly in a nonthreatening situation to the therapist or to a confidant or to herself. Her distress became less with each telling, and after four months she could relate the events without disturbance though doing so remained unpleasant. The symptoms disappeared and she began behaving normally.

Up to the time of the domestic turbulence her personality attributes had been developing well, but during the two years of upheaval "the various objects, persons and situations did not constitute a homogeneous unity" (p. 224) with the result that the personality attributes she developed during that time were not well integrated. When she was faced with the recess period and the social interaction she did not wish to engage in, a component of an action pattern—use of her left leg—did not function. She was engaging in *reactional dissociation*. Rather than merely restoring the malfunc-

tioning interaction phase, the treatment strategy was to replace the inadequate behavior attributes with a more satisfactory adjustment. By re-experiencing under supportive conditions the events that lead to the abnormal attributes she was able to develop new behavior attributes that were more satisfactory.

In the interbehavioral system no case would be referred to as "mental disease" or "nervous breakdown" or "emotional problem" or other such terms that impose cultural constructs and avoid specifics. Instead, the reference would be to interbehaviors that are unusual, unadaptable, or pathological. The case above is *pathological, dissociative type* in Kantor's system or *reactional dissociation*. In the psychiatric system it would be called a "conversion reaction," meaning that a nonphysical, mental event had converted to a physical (biological) event. According to interbehaviorists, dissociative individuals develop what appear to be normal behavior attributes, but they have the capability of disconnecting from the rest of the organized personality at a later time. During this development, objects and persons are not homogeneous; and the behavior characteristics are not integrated into a whole. Consequently, under stress, the behavior attributes separate into whatever will function under the circumstances. The action phases of interactions are left in abeyance and do not respond to the usual stimulus functions of objects involved in ordinary activities. These non-functioning action phases can include paralysis or insensitivity of parts of the body, blindness, deafness, and loss of memory. Those with a group of different dissociative action phases are multiple personalities (now called "dissociative identity disorder" in *DSM-IV* [Maxmen & Ward, 1995]) or dissociated personalities. (See chapter 11 for a description of a multiple personality case.)

RELATION TO SOME OTHER APPROACHES

Behavior Analysis

This system shares much in common with interbehaviorism in its philosophy of science.

Interbehaviorists are one of the Special Interest Groups of the Association of Behavior Analysis, and they present papers at the annual meetings of the behavior analysts. The review of research, above, shows that behavior analysts have drawn from interbehavioral concepts for research and that interbehaviorists have used behavior analysts' methodology. A similar mutual borrowing has occurred in clinical psychology. Nevertheless, differences remain, although they are becoming somewhat fewer as behavior analysis broadens its scope to take account of contexts and ecological relationships and extends the topics it will address. Still, behavior analysis remains largely envirocentric in its orientation toward reinforcement contingencies whereas interbehaviorism is committed to a field system.

Cognitive Psychology

While interbehaviorism welcomes the attention to what it considers cognitive interbehaviors, it parts company with cognitivism's separation of cognition from behavior. This separation it regards as another form of mind-body dualism. It holds that cognitivism has formed a mental mechanics by converting mind to brain and brain to a computing machine. It notes that cognitivists seldom even acknowledge that "information processing" is a construct, not an event; yet their literature is replete with references to the brain's information processing as if this were an observed event. The world, interbehaviorism maintains, is not a matter of representations but a source of stimulus objects with which the individual interacts. Even images are not representations but interactions with substitute stimuli. Cognitivism, interbehaviorism insists, is guilty of (a) reductionism, (b) assumptions of linear cause and effect and self-causation, (c) confusion of constructs with events, (d) confusion of necessary with sufficient conditions, and (e) mind-body dualism. Yet much of its research could be of value if it were described in terms of actually-observed events that their experiments actually show, instead of in terms of imposed constructs. Perhaps cognitivists would find fault with interbe-

haviorism for its lack of reductionism, failure to assume self-causation and linear cause and effect, obsession with a distinction between events and constructs, failure to recognize the duality of mind and body, and lack of creativity in not imposing constructs from the outset of investigations.

Some movements within cognitivism, especially those influenced by Gibson (chapter 13, p. 374), are in the direction of interbehaviorism, but the mainstream is dedicated to organocentrism. The two systems are unlikely to have much in common in the foreseeable future.

Dialectical Psychology

The two systems agree on the bidirectionality of organism and object, that such bidirectionality occurs in a context and that it develops historically. Riegel, the major promoter of dialectical psychology, rejects mechanism and mentalism—though mentalism nevertheless appears in the writing of a number of dialecticians and even in Riegel's own writings (see chapter 4, pp. 270–273). A great deal of reductionism to hypothetical brain powers is found in Russian and Russian-influenced dialectical psychology, such as that of the Chinese. The assumption of ubiquitous conflict is also unique to dialectical thinking. In sum, the two share some important general concepts about interactional development in a context but differ where dialectical psychology invokes such traditional constructs as mentalism and reductionism.

Operant Subjectivity

Stephenson (1982) found in interbehaviorism a basis for Q's concepts. Both he and Kantor rejected consciousness because of its mind-body dualism and recognized subjectivity as self-reference. Q's objective method of measuring subjectivity, though it has been little used by interbehaviorists, provides a potentially important methodology for interbehavioral research as well as for clinical work in such covert interbehaviors as feeling, knowing, orienting, imagining, and others (Smith & Smith, 1996). Brown (1995) has indicated how

Q could be used to study each of the components of the field as they involve feelings about things.

Phenomenological Psychology

The psychology of Merleau-Ponty and Sartre has a number of important points in common with interbehaviorism. Merleau-Ponty distinguishes the stimulus function from the stimulus object, the response function from the response, and the medium from the stimulus object; he notes the interdependence of the response with the setting. Both systems reject inner-outer distinctions and linear causality. Both recognize the role of biology as a participant rather than a cause, producer, or container (of, e.g., memories) of behavior; and both agree on the importance of meanings as lived. (Meanings, interbehaviorism holds, are involved in all behavior segments except reflexes.) However, Merleau-Ponty is not entirely consistent about rejecting mentalism and uses "consciousness" in ways that are sometimes unclear or questionable to interbehaviorism. According to Bucklew's (1955) analysis, in Merleau-Ponty's attempt to avoid psychophysical dualism (mentalism), he has substituted subjective philosophy for psychology. An additional difference is that he has never combined into an integrated field system the components of psychological activity he has identified. Finally, inerbehaviorism would accept a broader range of research methodologies than the single one promoted by phenomenology.

Social Constructionism

Those social constructionists who reject such constructs as mind, information processing, and knowledge as internal representation would agree with interbehaviorism on those points and on their cultural and historical basis. Kantor has documented the historical and social conditions that give rise to these artifacts (1963–1969). Both systems recognize the cultural influence on what the scientist does and concur that it is impossible to be totally culturally free in our propositions and other constructs. But interbehaviorism parts company with the more radical social constructionists who believe that these constructions are all we can ever know, that any one social construction cannot be established over any other, and that observation is not a basis of knowledge (Gergen, 1985, 1994). Kantor (1959) proposes interbehaviorism "as a means of studying psychological events with the *least possible interference by cultural traditions* [emphasis added]. Banished are all constructs, such as mind, body, ego, sensation, which lack correspondence with events" (p. 19). He also rejects pursuits of absoluteness or relativity of knowledge—major concerns of constructionism—as pseudoproblems and irrelevant to scientific enterprises (Kantor, 1959). Kantor gives recognition to *all* events, whereas the social constructionists acknowledge only *social* events.

CRITIQUE

One major criticism of interbehavioral psychology is that it has not demonstrated its mettle with empirical research. That criticism is now being met by the research reviewed earlier in this chapter. Considerable potential for interbehavioral research lies in use of Q methodology (chapter 11) that could help to examine and further illuminate its detailed analyses (Kantor, 1924, 1926) of intricate and complex human activities (Lichtenstein, 1984, 1988). (For a more detailed account of interbehavioral research see Morris & Midgley, 2000.) In a larger sense, it could be argued that the system has always used empirical research in that the entire system is based on close observation of human activity in natural conditions, observation that controlled laboratory experiments could never provide. Interbehaviorism could also turn around the argument about lack of empirical research as a major failing and point out that experimental psychology has its own major failing—not examining its implicit postulates about linear cause and effect with the result that it has produced the mechanistic psychologies of behaviorism and cognitivism.

Thus, interbehaviorism's failure to engage in formal research has a good start on being remedied while its postulate system and logic of science are highly developed and extensive. Experimental psychology's research is extensive but its attention to postulates and logic of science is inadequate.

A study of how others evaluated Kantor showed that most criticisms were rather minor (for example, too negativistic about other approaches, not enough of a role given to internal determiners, too objective). It is especially noteworthy that not a single one found fault with the field conception (Smith, 1981; Smith & Ray, 1981). A survey of behavior analysts showed that their criticism of interbehaviorism was mostly about lack of empirical research (Morris, Higgins, & Bickel, 1983).

Among the strengths claimed for the system are those of (a) insisting on separating events from constructs and basing scientific work on observation of events from which constructs are developed, (b) making its postulate system explicit at all levels of generality and keeping research operations harmonious with the postulates, (c) emphasizing interdisciplinary studies, (d) providing a clear alternative to mechanism and mentalism and emphasizing the interdependence of multiple factors in all psychological events. The age-old dilemmas of mind-body dualism and the mechanism of a brain processor or an environmental (stimulus) input and an organismic (response) output are replaced with an interbehavioral field.

As early as 1935, Bentley found that Kantor was able to use his system to cover the entire field of psychology.

> He attains lucidity as well as completeness and shows a technique well adapted to expansion of observation, discrimination, and terminological precision. He can discuss in great detail intricate psychological problems that run far beyond the possibilities of the behaviorist technique. He is free from dependence upon terms that eventually prove to be nothing more than mechanistic changelings for the implications of the old mind-language. . . . '[T]he environment,' so necessary to the physiological psychologist as a general dominating principle,

does not enter into Kantor's work at all. That which enters is always the *specific case* [emphasis added] of organism *and* object in functional activity. (1935, pp. 94–95)

Bentley, however, does criticize Kantor for not giving as much attention to human-human interactions as he does to human-object interactions. One may wonder whether Bentley would consider Kantor's book *Psychological Linguistics* (1977) or *Cultural Psychology* (1982) to have addressed the problem.

If the system gains more attention it will probably also provoke more criticisms. That seems to be inevitable with all systems. But if it provides a viable alternative to received doctrine it will have served its purpose.

CONCLUSIONS

The proponents argue that one of the strengths of Kantor's system is that it rejects traditional constructs that have descended from theology and culture, and replaces them with those derived from observation. It is a naturalistic system through and through. It makes no use of biological reductionism, no analogies from other sciences even in such sophisticated technological forms as computer processing, no hypothetical neuronal interpreters or mediators of the world, no drives to make the organism go, no incentives to pull it around, no dualizing of the organism into mind and body, no reduction of complex interactions to linear cause and effect or to single causes, and no self-causation. Yet it attempts to handle the most subtle of human activities, such as imagining, believing, and desiring. It deals with psychological events at their own level of organization rather than relegating them to other sciences at some other level. It is a system that largely relies on observation (experimental, naturalistic, etc.) of observable events and draws descriptive constructs (verbal, quantitative, diagrammatic, etc.) of their functional relationships from them. Its emphasis on naturalistic description does not preclude prediction, however. To the extent that one can identify and describe the functional relationship of salient factors in the field, to that extent one can make a probabilistic prediction. And that is characteristic of the sciences in general. Even its emphasis on a field is paralleled by similar directions in physics (relativity and quantum field theory) and biology (ecology) in which interrelationships of events rather than linear chains of cause and effect have been fruitful directions of theory and research. Its emphasis on specificity, including the specification of its own postulates at all levels of generality, could serve as a valuable model for other systems.

Perhaps its major obstacle is that it has attempted to cut through the thoroughgoing confusion of constructs with events that has plagued psychology throughout its history, and to that extent it meets the resistance or incomprehension of those whose professional abilities, habits, and preferences—personality attributes—are built around those constructs. But, as Delprato (1995b) sees it, "When all remnants of nonscientific (i.e., non-naturalistic) thinking have vanished from how we approach human behavior, interbehaviorism will no longer be necessary, because what it offers (for example, a field/system perspective) will have been incorporated into psychology itself" (p. 618).

REFERENCES

Ackerman, Paul D. 1972. Extinction of covert impulse responses through elimination of consummatory events. *Psychological Record* 22: 477–86.

Adams, Gary L., & Siegfried Engelmann. 1996. *Research on Direct Instruction: 25 Years Beyond Distar.* Seattle, WA: Educational Achievement Systems.

Baxter, Charles. 1994. An interbehavioral approach to teaching and problem solving in education. *The Interbehaviorist* 22 (1): 26–30.

Bentley, Arthur. 1935. *Behavior, Knowledge, Fact.* Bloomington, IN: Principia.

Bijou, Sidney W. 1976. The basic stage of early childhood. In *Child Development,* vol. 3. Englewood Cliffs, NJ: Prentice-Hall.

———. 1989. Psychological linguistics: Implications for a theory of initial development and a method for research. In *Advances in Child Behavior and Development,* vol. 21. Academic Press.

Bijou, Sidney W., & Donald M. Baer. 1961. A systematic and empirical theory. In *Child Development,* vol. 1. Englewood Cliffs, NJ: Prentice-Hall.

Bijou, Sidney W.; C. C. Chao; & P. M. Ghezzi. 1988. Manual of instructions for identifying and analyzing referential interactions II. *Psychological Record* 38: 401–414.

Bijou, S. W.; J. Umbreit; P. M. Ghezzi; & C. C. Chao. 1986. Manual of instructions for identifying and analyzing referential interactions. *Psychological Record* 36: 491–518.

Bloom, Kathleen. 1974. Eye contact as a setting event for infant learning. *Journal of Experimental Child Psychology* 17: 250–63.

Briones, Ignacio T. 1937. An experimental comparison of two forms of linguistic learning. *Psychological Record* 1: 205–214.

Brown, Steven R. 1995. Q methodology as the foundation for a science of subjectivity. Paper read at the Eleventh International Conference of the International Society for the Scientific Study of Subjectivity. College of Medicine, University of Illinois, Chicago, October 12–14.

Brown, William H.; William Bryson-Brockmann; & James Fox. 1986. The usefulness of J. R. Kantor's setting event concept for research on children's social behavior. *Child and Family Therapy* 8: 15–25.

Brown, William H.; J. J. Fox; and M. P. Brady. 1987. The effects of spatial density on the socially directed behavior of 3 and 4 year old children during freeplay: An investigation of a setting factor. *Education and Treatment of Children* 10: 247–58.

Bucklew, John. 1943. An exploratory study in the psychology of speech perception. *Journal of Experimental Psychology* 32: 473–94.

———. 1955. The subjective tradition in phenomenological psychology. *Philosophy of Science* 22: 289–99.

Caracciolo, Ettore; Paolo Moderato; & Silvia Perini. 1988. Analysis of some concrete-operational tasks from an interbehavioral standpoint. *Journal of Experimental Child Psychology* 46: 391–405.

Carter, Jerry W. 1937. A case of reactional dissociation (hysterical paralysis). *American Journal of Orthopsychiatry* 7: 219–24.

Chiasson, Carmenne A., & Linda J. Hayes. 1993. The effects of subtle differences between listeners and speakers on the referential speech of college students. *Psychological Record* 43: 13–24.

Clark, Andy, & Josefa Toribio. 1994. Doing without representation? *Synthese* 101: 401–431.

Cornwell, David, & Sandy Hobbs. 1986. What interbehavioral psychology has to offer education now. Paper presented at the annual conference of the Experimental Analysis of Behavior Group, University of St. Andrews, St. Andrews, Scotland, April 2–4.

Cromwell, Rue L., & C. R. Snyder. 1993. *Schizophrenia: Origins, Processes, Treatment, and Outcome.* New York: Oxford University.

Daurelle, Lynne A.; James J. Fox; William E. Maclearn; & Ann P. Kaiser. 1987. An interbehavioral perspective on parent training for families of developmentally delayed children. In *New Ideas in Therapy: Introduction to an Interdisciplinary Approach.* Edited by Douglas H. Ruben & Dennis J. Delprato. Westport, CT: Greenwood.

Delprato, Dennis J. 1977. Observing overt behavior ("mind-reading") with Chevreul's pendulum. *Psychological Record* 27: 473–78.

———. 1980. The reactional biography concept: Early contribution to a perspective for the psychology of aging. *Human Development* 23: 314–22.

———. 1995a. Admitting bias. *Behavior Therapist* 18 (5): 108.

———. 1995b. Interbehavioral psychology: Critical, systematic, and integrative approach to clinical services. In *Theories of Behavior Therapy: Exploring Behavior Change.* Edited by W. O'Donohue & L. Krasner. Washington DC: American Psychological Association.

Delprato, Dennis J., & F. Dudley McGlynn. 1986. Innovations in behavioral medicine. In *Progress in Behavior Modification,* vol. 20. Edited by M. Hersen, R. M. Eisler, & P. M. Miller. New York: Academic Press.

Delprato, Dennis J., & Kenneth W. Rusiniak. 1991. Response patterns in shock avoidance and illness aversion. In *Fear, Avoidance, and Phobias.* Edited by M. R. Denny. Hillsdale, NJ: Lawrence Erlbaum Associates.

Dewey, John, & Arthur F. Bentley. 1949. *Knowing and the Known.* Boston: Beacon.

Dumas, Jean E., & Robert G. Wahler. 1985. Indiscriminate mothering as a contextual factor in aggressive-oppositional child behavior: "Damned if you do and damned if you don't." *Journal of Abnormal Child Psychology* 13: 1–17.

Duncker, Karl. 1945. On problem-solving. *Psychological Monographs* 58 (no. 5, whole no. 270).

Engelmann, Siegfried, & Douglas Carnine. 1982. *Theory of Instruction: Principles and Applications.* New York: Irvington.

Farrington, Jacqueline. 1972. Utilization of psychological constructs by group therapy participants. *Psychological Record* 22: 387–94.

Fuller, Paul R. 1987. From the classroom to the field and back. In *New Ideas in Therapy: Introduction to an Interdisciplinary Approach.* Edited by Douglas H. Ruben & Dennis J. Delprato. Westport, CT: Greenwood.

Gergen, Kenneth J. 1985. The social constructionist movement in psychology. *American Psychologist* 40: 266–75.

———. 1994. *Relations and Relationships: Soundings in Social Construction.* Cambridge, MA: Harvard University Press.

Gewirtz, Jacob L. 1967. Deprivation and satiation of social stimuli as determinants of their reinforcing efficacy. In *Minnesota Symposia on Child Psychology,* vol. 1. Edited. By John P. Hill. Minneapolis: University of Minnesota.

Ghezzi, Patrick M., & Sidney W. Bijou. 1994. Social skills training for withdrawn mildly retarded children. In *Psicologia Inerconductual: Contribuciones en Honor J. R. Kantor.* Edited by L. J. Hayes, E. Ribes, & F. Lopez-Valedez. Guadalajara, Mexico: Universidad de Guadalajara.

Greenwood, Charles; Judith J. Carta; Debra Kamps; & Carmen Arreaga-Mayer. 1990. Ecobehavioral analysis of classroom instruction. In *Ecobehavioral Analysis and Developmental Disabilities: The Twenty-First Century.* Edited by Stephen R. Schroeder. New York: Springer-Verlag.

Hamachek, Don E. 1987. Humanistic psychology: Theory, postulates, and implications for educational processes. In *Historical Foundations of Educational Psychology.* Edited by John A. Glover & Royce R. Ronning. New York: Plenum.

Hawkins, Andrew; Tom Sharpe; & Roger Ray. 1994. Toward instructional process measurability: An interbehavioral field systems perspective. In *Behavior Analysis in Education: Focus on Measurably Superior Instruction.* Edited by R. Gardner, D. M. Sainato, J. O. Cooper, T. E. Heron, W. L. Heward, J. W. Eshelman, & T. A. Grossi. Pacific Grove, CA: Brooks/Cole.

Herman, David T. 1951a. Linguistic behaviors: I. Some differentiations in hearer responses to verbal stimulation. *Journal of General Psychology* 44: 199–213.

———. 1951b. Linguistic behaviors: II. The development of hearer interaction with holophrastic language stimuli. *Journal of General Psychology* 44: 273–91.

Herrick, James W. 1983. Interbehavioral perspectives on aging. *International Journal of Aging and Human Development* 16 (2): 95–123.

Hobbs, Sandy, & Sue Kleinberg. 1978. Teaching: A behaviour influence approach. In *Understanding Classroom Life.* Edited by Ray McAleese & David Hamilton. Windsor, Berkshire, England: NFER.

Hobbs, Sandy, Sue Kleinberg, & Sheena Crozier. 1980. Doing mental? *Scottish Educational Review* 12: 32–39.

Kantor, J. R. 1924. *Principles of Psychology,* vol. 1. New York: Knopf.

———. 1926. *Principles of Psychology,* vol 2. New York: Knopf.

———. 1928. Can psychology contribute to the study of linguistics? *Monist* 38: 630–48.

———. 1929. *An Outline of Social Psychology*. Chicago: Follett.

———. 1959. *Interbehavioral Psychology: A Sample of Scientific Science Construction*. Bloomington, IN: Principia.

———. 1963–1969. *The Scientific Evolution of Psychology*, 2 vols. Chicago: Principia.

———. 1970. An analysis of the experimental analysis of behavior (TEAB). *Journal of the Experimental Analysis of Behavior* 13, 101–108.

———. 1976. Behaviorism, behavior analysis, and the career of psychology. *Psychological Record* 26: 305–312.

———. 1977. *Psychological Linguistics*. Chicago: Principia.

———. 1978/1984. The principle of specificity in psychology and science in general. In *Selected Writings in Philosophy, Psychology and Other Sciences, 1929–1983*. Chicago: Principia. (Originally published in *Mexicana de Análisis de la Conducta* 4: 117–32.)

———. 1982. *Cultural Psychology*. Chicago: Principia.

———. 1987. What qualifies interbehavioral psychology as an approach to treatment? In *New Ideas in Therapy: Introduction to an Interdisciplinary Approach*. Edited by Douglas H. Ruben & Dennis J. Delprato. Westport, CT: Greenwood.

Kantor, J. R., & N. W. Smith. 1975. *The Science of Psychology: An Interbehavioral Survey*. Chicago: Principia.

Keehn, J. D., & Jose Nobrega. 1978. Stereotyped behavior during acquisition and extinction in rats. *Psychological Record* 28, 245–51.

Knapp, John R., & Dennis J. Delprato. 1980. Willpower, behavior therapy, and the public. *Psychological Record* 30: 477–82.

Krantz, P. J., & T. R. Risley. 1977. Behavioral ecology in the classroom. In *Classroom Management: The Successful Use of Behavior Modification*, 2nd ed. Edited by K. D. O'Leary & G. O'Leary. New York: Pergamon.

Lichtenstein, Parker E. 1984. Interbehaviorism in psychology and in the philosophy of science. *Psychological Record* 34: 455–75.

———. 1988. Interbehavioral psychology and Q methodology. *Operant Subjectivity* 11: 53–61.

Lundin, Robert W. 1987. The interbehavioral approach to psychopathology. In *New Ideas in Therapy: Introduction to an Interdisciplinary Approach*. Edited by Douglas H. Ruben & Dennis J. Delprato. Westport, CT: Greenwood.

Maxmen, Jerrold S., & Nicholas G. Ward. 1995. *Essential Psychopathology and Its Treatment*, 2nd ed., revised for DSM-IV. New York: Norton.

McGlynn, F. Dudley, Edwin W. Cook III, & Paul E. Greenbaum. 1987. In *New Ideas in Therapy: Intro-duction to an Interdisciplinary Approach*. Edited by Douglas H. Ruben & Dennis J. Delprato. Westport, CT: Greenwood.

Morris, Edward K.; Stephen T. Higgins; & Warren K. Bickel. 1983. Contributions of J. R. Kantor to contemporary behaviorism. In *Reassessment in Psychology: The Interbehavioral Alternative*. Washington, D. C.: University Press of America.

Morris, Edward K.; Lisa M. Johnson; Lynda K. Powell; & James T. Todd. 1987. Interbehavioral perspectives on legal deviance: Some considerations of context. In *New Ideas in Therapy: Introduction to an Interdisciplinary Approach*. Edited by Douglas H. Ruben & Dennis J. Delprato. New York: Greenwood.

Morris, Edward, & Bryan D. Midgley, eds. 2000. *Modern Perspectives on J. R. Kantor and Interbehaviorism*. Westport, CT: Greenwood.

Nordquist, Vey M., & Sandra Twardasz. 1990. Preventing behavior problems in early childhood special education classrooms through environmental organization. *Education and Treatment of Children* 13: 274–87.

Pronko, N. H. 1945. An exploratory investigation of language means of oscillographic and reaction time techniques. *Journal of Experimental Psychology* 35: 433–58.

———. 1987. Theory versus practice? In *New Ideas in Therapy: Introduction to an Interdisciplinary Approach*. Edited by Douglas H. Ruben & Dennis J. Delprato. Greenwood.

———. 1988. *From AI to Zeitgeist: A Philosophical Guide for the Skeptical Psychologist*. Westport, CT: Greenwood.

Quilitch, H. Robert, & Todd R. Risley. 1973. The effects of play material on social play. *Journal of Applied Behavior Analysis* 6: 573–78.

Ratner, Stanley C., & F. Edward Rice. 1963. The effect of the listener on the speaking interaction. *Psychological Record* 13: 265–68.

Ratner, S. C.; J. J. Gawronski; & F. E. Rice. 1964. The variable of concurrent actions in language of children: Effect of delayed feedback. *Psychological Record* 14: 47–56.

Ray, Roger. 1992. Interbehavioral methodology: Lessons from simulation. *Journal of Teaching in Physical Education* 12: 105–114.

———. 1995a. A behavioral systems approach to adaptive computerized instructional deisgn. *Behavior Research Methods, Instruments, & Computers* 27: 293–96.

———. 1995b. Media Matrix: An authoring system for adaptive hypermedia teaching-learning resource libraries. *Journal of Computing in Higher Education* 7: 44–68.

Ray, Roger, & Douglas A. Brown. 1975. A systems approach to behavior. *Psychological Record* 25: 455–78.

Ray, Roger, D., & Dennis J. Delprato. 1989. Behavioral systems analysis: Methodological strategies and tactics. *Behavioral Sciences* 34: 81–127.

Ray, Roger, D.; James D. Upson; and B. J. Henderson. 1977. A systems approach to behavior III: Organismic pace and complexity in time-space fields. *Psychological Record* 27: 649–82.

Redd, William H., & Frank R. Rusch. 1985. Behavioral analysis in behavioral medicine. *Behavior Modification* 9: 131–54.

Rosenfield, Peter; Nadine M. Lambert; & Allen Black. 1985. Desk arrangement effects on pupil classroom behavior. *Journal of Educational Psychology* 77: 101–108.

Ruben, Douglas H. 1992. Interbehavioral analysis of adult children of alcoholics: Etiological predictors. *Alcoholism Treatment Quarterly* 9: 1–21.

Ruben, Douglas, & Marilyn J. Ruben. 1987. Assumptions about teaching assertiveness: Training the person or behavior? In *New Ideas in Therapy: Introduction to an Interdisciplinary Approach.* Edited by Douglas H. Ruben & Dennis J. Delprato. Westport, CT: Greenwood.

Scafasci, Mary Ann. 1987. Community-based psychological services for developmentally retarded persons. In *New Ideas in Therapy: Introduction to an Interdisciplinary Approach.* Edited by Douglas H. Ruben & Dennis J. Delprato. Greenwood.

Scheerer, Martin. 1963. Problem-solving. *Scientific American* 208, no. 4 (April): 118–28.

Sharpe, Tom. 1996. Using technology to study daily teaching practices. *Teacher Education and Practice* 12: 47–61.

Sharpe, Tom, & Andrew Hawkins. 1992a. Field systems analysis: Prioritizing patterns in time and context among observable variables. *Quest* 44: 15–34.

———. 1992b. The implications of field systems for teacher education. *Journal of Teaching in Physical Education* 12: 76–84.

———. 1992c. Strategies and tactics for field systems analysis. *Journal of Teaching in Physical Education* 12: 9–23.

———. 1993. Behavioral field systems evaluation in movement education classrooms: Practice and implications. *Studies in Educational Evaluation* 19: 327–46.

Sharpe, Tom; Andrew H. Hawkins; & Roger D. Ray. 1995. Interbehavioral field systems assessment: Examining its utility in preservice teacher education. *Journal of Behavioral Education* 5: 259–80.

Smith, George S., & Dennis J. Delprato. 1976. Stimulus control of covert behaviors (urges). *Psychological Record* 26: 461–466.

Smith, Noel W. 1981. Annotated citations to and bibliography of the interbehavioral psychology of J. R. Kantor. *JSAS Catalog of Selected Documents in Psychology* 11 (no. 1): 13. (Ms. 2198)

———. 1997. Consciousness: Construct or event? In *Investigations in Behavioral Epistemology.* Edited by Linda J. Hayes & Patrick M. Ghezzi. Reno, NV: Context Press.

Smith, Noel W., & Candace E. Ray. 1981. A citation study of the interbehavioral field psychology of J. R. Kantor. *Revista Mexicana de Análisis de la Conducta* 7: 117–34.

Smith, Noel W., & Lance L. Smith. 1996. Field theory in science: Its role as a necessary and sufficient condition in psychology. *Psychological Record* 46: 3–19.

Stebbin, S. L.; R. G. St. Pierre; E. C. Proper; R. B. Anderson; & T. R. Cerva. 1977. *Education as Experimentation: A Planned Variation Model,* vol. IV, A-D of *An Evaluation of Project Follow Through.* Cambridge, MA: ABT Associates.

Stephenson, William. 1953. *The Study of Behavior: Q-Technique and Its Methodology.* Chicago: University of Chicago Press.

———. 1982. Q-methodology, interbehavioral psychology, and quantum theory. *Psychological Record* 32, 235–48.

———. 1987. Q methodology: Interbehavioral and quantum theoretical connections in clinical psychology. In *New Ideas in Therapy: Introduction to an Interdisciplinary Approach.* Edited by Douglas H. Ruben & Dennis J. Delprato. Westport, CT: Greenwood.

Stevenson, Dallas W., & Michael J. Hemingway. 1987. Multidisciplinary approach to obesity and risk-factor management. In *New Ideas in Therapy: Introduction to an Interdisciplinary Approach.* Edited by Douglas H. Ruben & Dennis J. Delprato. Westport, CT: Greenwood.

Swartz, Paul. 1955. Stimulus evolution in problem solving behavior: An interbehavioral analysis. *Psychological Reports* 1: 425–32.

Upson, J. D.; M. L. Carlson; & R. D. Ray. 1981. Setting changes and the quality of human life. In *Applied Systems and Cybernetics.* Edited by G. E. Lasker. New York: Pergamon.

Upson, J. D., & R. D. Ray. 1984. An interbehavioral systems model for empirical investigation in psychology. *Psychological Record* 34: 497–524.

Wahler, Robert G. 1980. The insular mother: Her problems in parent-child treatment. *Journal of Applied Behavior Analysis* 13: 207–219.

Wahler, Robert G., & Marilyn G. Graves. 1983. Setting events in social networks: Ally or enemy in child behavior therapy? *Behavior Therapy* 14: 19–36.

Wahler, Robert G., & Della M. Hann. 1984. The communication patterns of troubled mothers: In search of a keystone in the generalization of parenting skills. *Educaiton and Treatment of Children* 7: 335–50.

————. 1987. An interbehavioral approach to clinical child psychology: Toward an understanding of troubled families. In *New Ideas in Therapy: Introduction to an Interdisciplinary Approach.* Edited by Douglas H. Ruben & Dennis J. Delprato. Westport, CT: Greenwood.

Wahler, Robert G., & E. E. Stambaugh. 1976. *Ecological Assessment of Child Problem Behavior: A Clinical Package for Home, School, and Institutional Settings.* New York: New York: Pergamon.

Williamson, P. N., & C. A. Lyons. 1988. Interactional components of psychotic language. Paper presented at the Association for Behavior Analysis, Philadelphia, PA.

Williamson, P. N.; C. A. Lyons; B. B. Abney; & A. Gonzales. 1987. Listener effects on linguistic interactions of psychotic adults. Paper presented at the Association for Behavior Analysis, Nashville, TN:

Williamson, P. N.; C. A. Lyons; B. B. Abney; A. Gonzales; & M. Galligos. 1986. Analysis of linguistic interactions of psychotic adults. Paper presented at the Association for Behavior Analysis, Milwaukee, WI.

Wolf, Irvin S. 1958a. Stimulus variables in aphasia: I. Setting conditions. *Journal of the Scientific Laboratories, Denison University* 44: 203–217.

————. 1958b. Stimulus variables in aphasia: II. Stimulus objects. *Journal of the Scientific Laboratories, Denison University* 44: 218–28.

Wong, Paul T. P. 1977. A behavioral field approach to instrumental learning in the rat: I. Partial reinforcement effects and sex differences. *Animal Learning and Behavior* 5: 5–13.

CHAPTER 11

Operant Subjectivity:
Objectivity of Subjectivity

Chapter Outline

INTRODUCTION

We would probably all agree that everyone has preferences, opinions, and feelings. But are these behaviors? Aren't such things mental rather than behavioral? Well, let's change the nouns to verbs and refer to preferring, opining, and feeling. Now would these qualify as behaviors? Are they acts we perform? If so, aren't they behaviors? The system developed by William Stephenson (and some other systems as well) insists that they are. But can we measure these as behaviors or study them scientifically? Again, Stephenson would maintain that we can and that his method provides a scientific and rigorous method of doing so. He makes another claim that might seem even more radical: that we can have a science of studying single individuals. We are accustomed to rating scales, IQ tests, personality tests, and questionnaires that use standardized test items and sample from large populations. But one subject?

Actually, single-subject psychology is not new. Much of the earliest experimental psychology, such as that of Wundt and Külpe, developed individual profiles of each subject's responses. Ebbinghaus, Pavlov, Piaget, and Skinner used single subjects, and their findings are some of the most enduring in the history of psychology. Had they used group averages it is unlikely that they would have made these findings at all, for the averages would have masked them. "In sharp contrast to this focus on the single organism, the central datum in much psychological research is the group mean. This measure is a quantitative abstraction utilized both for its summaritive properties and its compatibility with parametric statistical analyses, not because it represents any essential dimension of behavior" (Morgan, 1998, p. 450).

The present procedure of averaging subjects to look for population trends began in the 1890s and has continued to the present day. The statistics used in these studies in which large numbers of individual responses are combined for group characteristics or where large populations are tested to determine some hypothetical trait such as "mental ability" is called R after the Pearson product-moment correlation that is designated by *r*. A few

systems of psychology, such as behavior analysis (chapter 6) and sometimes eco-behavioral sciences (chapter 7), do perform single subject studies and seldom use R; but they do not examine the subject's frame of reference. Humanistic psychology (chapter 4) attempts to do so but lacks a method of doing it rigorously, while psychoanalysis (chapter 5) imposes its own frame of reference. Clinical and counseling psychology and other human services often use the single case study. Most of academic psychology and other human sciences use R methodology almost exclusively. Investigators who employ R require large populations, score the responses objectively, and look for population differences. Both undergraduate and graduate students learn R methodology and are seldom exposed to any alternative—or even informed that an alternative exists.

The one system that (a) provides the alternative to R, (b) consistently maintains the subjectivity of subjects, and (c) has a rigorous and objective method of doing so is called *operant subjectivity* or *Q methodology*[1] to distinguish it from R methodology. This system, like behavior analysis and eco-behavioral science, has an interdependent philosophy and research methods. "Operant" means that when individuals are given sample of statements to be sorted according to some preference or judgment or feeling about them, they *operate* with them in such a way as to indicate their viewpoint; and this is independent of any constructed effects (such as those of rating scales) on the part of the investigator. Those statements they agree with or like in some way and those they dislike are operant for each individual. Thus, "operant" applies to *events* on both the stimulus side and the response side of the interaction. It involves both Q items and people. "Operant subjectivity," then, is subjective behavior as it manifests itself through Q methodology.

More specifically, Q method consists of a group of statements (or pictures or other items) about a topic, and subjects (in the fullest sense of that

---

1. Smith and Smith (1996) referred to this system as "quantum subjectivity" because of its parallels with quantum mechanics in physics (Stephenson, 1982, 1988–1989, 1989).

word) are instructed to sort them into subjective categories such as "like best" (+5) to "like least" (−5). They could do this to describe Psychology 101 or a past love affair. The resulting sort is called a Q sort. Those who sort items in similar ways will correlate with each other. This differs from correlations between tests or measurements, for it is correlations of people. From the individual correlations, clusters of correlations are extracted, and these are called factors. The factors show the ways in which people share viewpoints in various combinations— the response patterns that are present. Those who have sorted in a similar fashion will cluster together in a factor. They are similar to each other on that factor and different from those who cluster on another factor. Each factor represents a common viewpoint of those who cluster on that factor.

Q is taught as an alternative to R in a few universities but not in psychology departments. Psychology has sometimes employed Q sorting but has usually treated it as R, ignoring subjectivity; and psychology departments sometimes teach it in this form. Psychology journals have also shunned Q. For more than fifty years the Journal *Psychometrika* has excluded articles on Q (Stephenson, 1990). Mainstream journals in psychology have typically never been receptive to revolutionaries: The editors of these journals prefer what they are familiar with. For example, Skinner's students could find few publication outlets until they established their own journals (Krantz, 1971). Skinner himself published his early work in book form and avoided the problem. Similarly, few of Barker's eco-psychology works were published in establishment journals; and Sommer (1977) reported difficulty in publishing studies based on observations in the field rather than on experiments in a laboratory.

FUNDAMENTALS AND ISSUES

Development of the System

Stephenson developed both the concepts of the Q system and its techniques. He was an Englishman who completed his doctorate in nuclear physics but whose broad interests took him into experimental psychology and psychological measurement. In 1935 he announced his inversion of the use of intercorrelations so that individuals were measuring themselves rather than being measured by a researcher. How people felt about things would become the center of measurement in place of such abstractions as ego strength, extraversion, intelligence, capacities, and other traits. In contrast with R methodology Stephenson correlated people rather than tests items. He continued to develop and expand the system and called it Q methodology. *Methodology* refers to the philosophy of science behind the system and *method* to the particular procedure. Since the time of his death in 1989, his former student Steven Brown has been the leader of this system, explaining its philosophy and technicalities, teaching it to others, demonstrating its wide applicability and efficacy, and assisting others to apply it in various domains.

Stephenson considered his system behavioristic, but this behaviorism embraced subjectivity and seemed incongruous to behaviorists of the 1940s and 1950s who had rejected all subjectivism as mentalistic and contrary to objective human science. They associated "subjective" with the discredited introspection of the mind and, as a result, largely ignored such subtle human activities as thinking and imagining. Stephenson refused to accept any actual separation between objective and subjective and was not alone in his conception of behavior as embracing all human activity, including the subjective. As early as the 1920s Arthur Bentley with his "transactionalism" and J. R. Kantor with his "organismic psychology" (later called "interbehavioral field psychology") argued that the psychological event is not localized inside in a mind or outside in a body but is a relationship between the person and the object, and that this relationship can be studied scientifically: there is no inside or outside, no mind-body, but rather concrete transactions (Bentley) or interactions (Kantor) between persons and their surroundings. Stephenson drew some of his inspiration from these men for his insistence that beliefs, feelings, opinions, and the like were concrete behaviors that could be communicated and systematically analyzed by Q methodology. The prevalent view, however, was that a scientific study of the individual (i.e., Stephenson's goal) was impossible . . . Science must search for general laws and universal principles; it could not be founded upon the study of intra-individual behavior or subjectivity. Thus, studies based on single cases, which Q methodology promoted, were considered unscientific, despite the sophistication of Q methodology's quantitative and multivariate techniques. (Febbraro, 1995, p. 145–46)

Stephenson's approach to measurement, philosophy of science, statistics, and psychological principles was a revolution that psychology was not ready for. Operant subjectivity has now outlived most of its critics but without being widely adopted. Nevertheless, a scattering of interests has coalesced, due especially to the indefatigable leadership of Brown. As this has occurred, vehicles to serve its advancement have developed: The International Society for the Scientific Study of Subjectivity brings people together annually from a wide array of disciplines and from a variety of countries to discuss applications and issues. The journal *Operant Subjectivity* provides an outlet for research publications and other relevant materials. The Q Methodology Network, a computer e-mail Listserver is an information source and a discussion forum for technical issues. In a video program Brown demonstrates how to perform and analyze a Q sort.[2] Computer programs can now perform the necessary calculations (Atkinson, 1992; Stricklin, 1990).[3]

---

2. The video tapes are available in two versions and three formats from the Stephenson Research Center, 120 Neff Hall, School of Journalism, University of Missouri, Columbia, MO 65211.

3. Inquiries about the program for personal computers (including Macintosh and OS2) can be e-mailed to p4lbsmk@unibw-muenchen.de or mstrick@unlinfo.unl.edu. The program for IBM mainframe computers can be obtained by e-mailing to listserv@listserv.kent.edu the message GET Q-METHOD PACKAGE. For Vax mainframe computers send to the same address the message GETVAXQPACKAGE. Both of these will bring GET commands for the series of files. Forward these to listserv@listserv.kent.edu for the program files. Such statistical programs as SPSS, SAS, and BMPD will also analyze Q sorts but are designed for R methodology and are not as satisfactory as those designed for Q.

Scientific Orientation

Operant subjectivity rejects not only mind-body dualism but also

- Self as an entity
- The traditional distinction between objectivity and subjectivity
- Behavior as a function of neural determiners.

Its rejection of dualism carries with it the rejection of the assumption that there exist both an external behavior subject to observation and measurement and a separate internal or mental state that cannot be observed or measured but only inferred from behaviors. Stephenson replaces consciousness with subjectivity: witness the title of one of his papers, "Consciousness Out—Subjectivity in" (1968). And he replaces the Cartesian assumption of *privacy* (no one can know another's mind) with the concrete events of *communicability,* communication of subjectivity through Q. "Q methodology provides the basis for a science of subjectivity, and it does so by the simple expediency of replacing the metaphysics of consciousness with the empiricism of communicability" (Brown, 1986, p. 74).

Stephenson uses "self" as a reference to the individual's own subjective viewpoint. Q sorting determines subjectivity operantly by "self-reference." But Stephenson rejects what he calls the "categorical self," a hypothetical agent that initiates action or sits inside the head and takes in pictures of the world. "Self" in that sense is another word for mind. When an unseen agent is used to explain observable behavior, that agent in turn requires explanation and then it too requires explanation, and so on infinitely. For example, if anxiety accounts for behavior what accounts for the anxiety and what accounts for the account? For Stephenson (like Skinner [chapter 6] and Kantor [chapter 10]), we must deal with the behavior directly, observe what specific conditions relate to it, and avoid imposing unobservables. He turns to concrete behavior, particularly behavior from the viewpoint of the subject as he rejects categorical self, mind, and consciousness.

The word "subjective" has been used by some to refer to a mind or inner experience and the opposite of "objective," but Stephenson (1953) uses it strictly as a point of view and as totally objective in the sense that it is concrete behavior that can be measured and studied "with full scientific sanction, satisfying every rule and procedure of scientific method" (p. 25). It is "what one can converse about, to others, or to oneself. It has form which can be reached purely operantly, that is, not by prior definitions of consciousness, self, or the like, but by way of Q sorts and factor-analysis" (1968, p. 501). The only difference between objectivity and subjectivity, he insists, is point of view. What is subjective from my point of view is objective from yours. Subjectivity has self-reference; objectivity does not. People refer to their subjective feelings; a tree does not. Q's *object* of study is the *subject*. Hence, no distinction about inner and outer or mind versus body or privacy versus public behavior has any meaning beyond different standpoints of observation. And rather than assume that behavior is the manifestation of some hypothetical neural determiners, it is specific behavior itself that is of interest and that can be measured by Q technique. "Behavior is neither mind nor body nor physiology: it is simply behavior, whether subjective to a person or objective to others" (Stephenson, 1953, p. 23). Imagining and riding a bicycle are equally behaviors to Stephenson, and so he identifies himself as a behaviorist but is critical of behaviorism for its rejection of subjectivity—despite the fact that subjectivity is as objective as the behavior of the rat that behaviorism used so extensively for experimental purposes. He insists that "all experience is behavior" (p. 86) even though "it has not been usual to think of it in this way" (p. 87). Behavior can be made operant and measured with Q just as blood pressure that cannot be observed unaided is made operant and measured with an air pressure cuff and a listening device (Dennis, 1986).

The system rejects all absolutes and all universals such as Spearman's g (general intelligence), hypothetical-deductive methods, or other ultimate powers. It rejects the common procedure of proposing a theory, deducting hypotheses, and then testing this with group averages. Each experiment is unique and requires treatment specific to it. After Kantor, Stephenson (1953) notes "that all scientific behavior is *concrete inferential interbehavior,* that is, relatively specific to each experimental situation . . . no single set of procedures can fit all the inferential interbehavioral settings of science . . . the precise form of analysis undertaken is determined by the experimental situation" (p. 40).

Rather than making predictions, Q seeks to make discoveries. Stephenson was never one to build grand theories but was "more interested in *understanding* than in explanation, and in determining *how* things worked as opposed to *why* in some ultimate sense they did so" (Brown, 1995c). Stephenson (1953, p. 40), after C. S. Lewis, remarks that it is easy to examine a garden's soil and its bacteria and yet miss its beauty; similarly a theory may influence the investigator to assume that verbalizations are manifestations of unconscious forces or of thought processes and overlook what the person is saying.

The Q Method

A set of statements developed around a topic is called a "*concourse* (from Latin *concursus,* meaning 'a running together,' as when ideas run together in thought), and it is from this concourse that a sample of statements is subsequently drawn for administration in a Q sort" (Brown, 1993b, p. 94). A concourse is often obtained by interviewing the subject(s) but could be from writings or any other verbal source. But it may be other than verbal, such as drawings, musical excerpts, flavors, odors, tactile materials, or any other item that is relevant to the project. Brown (1993a) expresses the character and potential of concourses:

> Concourse is the very stuff of life, from the playful banter of lovers or chums to the heady discussions of philosophers and scientists to the private thoughts found in dreams and diaries. From concourse, new meanings rise, bright ideas are hatched, and discoveries are

made: it is the wellspring of creativity and identity formation in individuals, groups, organizations, and nations, and it is Q methodology's task to reveal the inherent structure of a concourse—the vectors of thought that sustain it and which, in turn, are sustained by it. (Brown, p. 95)

We could obtain a concourse of behavior therapy clients by asking them what the therapy is like, their expectations, their complaints, and so on. In an industrial situation we could ask workers their feelings about their supervisors, company policies and practices, advancement, job security, fellow workers, management, and future prospects. The responses are not statements of fact but opinions, statements of self-reference. Studies using surveys and questionnaires often use categories that the investigator imposes on the responses. Q, on the other hand determines "categories that are *operant,* i.e., that represent functional as opposed to merely logical distinctions" (Brown, 1993a, p. 97). That is, they are functional to the subject rather than logical to the investigator.

Once the concourse is completed, the next step is to take from it a sample of items that subjects will sort into categories. At this point, Q investigators may temporarily resort to imposing some categories. An inspection of the concourse may show that behavior therapy clients seem to be either enthusiastic or uncertain about the therapy and some have participated in other forms of therapy while others have not. As shown in table 11.1, this provides a 2 × 2 matrix of four cells: uncertainty versus enthusiasm on one dimension, experience with other therapies versus behavior therapy alone on the other. We might then take ten statements from each of the four cells in order to get a good distribution of statements. These statements so categorized and so sampled could have quite different meanings to the subjects. Consequently, they have no systematic meanings beyond their utility as a device for sampling.

Each of the statements (forty in the hypothetical example) is written on a card and randomly

Table 11.1		
Categories from a Concourse		
	Experience with behavior therapy alone	Experience with other therapies
Enthusiastic	10	10
Uncertain	10	10

assigned a number.[4] The cards are shuffled and the subject is asked to sort the cards into piles from "strongly agree" to "strongly disagree" or from "most like" to "most dislike" or whatever terms are chosen. The subject sorts according to some "condition of instruction." It might be "sort according to the way you felt when you began therapy." If it is a single-subject experiment, the subject will do additional sorts such as "according to the way you feel about therapy now" and "according to the way you expect to feel when you finish therapy." Or the single subject can do the sort "according to the way you feel about therapy now" at the beginning of therapy and at intervals as it continues. If several subjects are used, they can all do one and the same sort, or they can all do multiple sorts, as in the example of the single subject.

The sorting is usually laid out on a table surface with the distribution from +5 to −5 or, if using a smaller number of statements, +4 to −4 or even +3 to −3. The investigator usually suggests that the subject start with three piles, the most positive, the most negative, and those that are neutral. Once this is completed the subject can further divide them into the remaining categories, putting the largest number at 0, the fewest at the extremes, and an intermediate number in between 0 and the extremes so that a symmetrical curve is produced approximating a normal curve's bell shape. (The

---

4. Due to the fact once a number is selected it is not replaced—making the selection of each remaining number increasingly probable—the numbers are not strictly random, but only quasi-random. As long as they are not in any systematic order, however, it doesn't matter.

number required for each category is specified so as to give this configuration.) If the subject departs somewhat—or even markedly—from this shape it is of no consequence for the outcome of the computations (Brown, 1971). Q has the special merit that it permits subjects to place items that they are unfamiliar with or uncertain about in the neutral categories. This helps assure that the results will reflect "an individual's views in a manner consistent with his/her own experience" (Stephen, 1985, p. 205).

Using the numbering on the cards as the designation of placement of statements in the distribution, a correlation matrix is computed from which factors are determined. (The investigator can simply put the numbers on the cards into a computer program according to the way the subject sorted them, and it will do all the calculations.) One group might correlate highly with another but have a low correlation with a second group. Two distinct groups of subjectivity would then be revealed by the factor scores. The factors, however, are merely numerical values and do not tell us what characterizes each of the two groups. To obtain that information, we must return to the original Q statements contained in the correlations. In addition to examining the statements that underlie the factors, the investigator will often interview the subjects about why they put particular statements at the extreme high and low ends which, due to squaring, contribute the most to factor values. (Often, immediately after the subject completes the sort, the investigator will ask the reasons.) Sometimes the statements from such interviews are used in a new concourse for another Q study that will further refine the investigator's understanding of the subject's reactions to the topic.

Questionnaires and Rating Scales versus Q Methodology

Rating scales (such as those of Likert type) and tests come in for considerable criticism from Q proponents; and, because they are so uncritically accepted in psychology and other behavioral and social sciences, it is worth considering some of this criticism in detail so that the alternative offered by Q will be clearer.

Brown (1980) advances the following arguments. Rating scales are not free of subjectivity as the formulators and users of them usually assume. They have meanings of their own that involve the biases of the investigator which is then imposed on the subject. The investigator defines what a response will mean prior to its occurrence, thereby imposing that meaning and interpreting the subject's responses accordingly. This "is more akin to creativity than to measurement"; further, "for an investigator to regard his own understanding as in some sense objective or correct is therefore pretentious in the extreme" (p. 3). Similarly, Delprato (1997) notes that humans construct and select their variables and that "mainstreamers have a lot to learn about the subjectivity of their operations and interpretations. Inferential statistics was once the hope of pristine objectivity. Only the most naive, I would think still hold to this."

Trait theory endows rating scales and other test items with meaning and interprets responses to them according to population norms on those items. To expect an item to have fixed meaning (a) gives the item too much responsibility, (b) gives the response to it too little, (c) ignores the interactions between the item and the person, and (d) ignores the changes that occur with changing situations. Although, Brown observes, social science has honed "the science of asking important questions" it has not given equal attention to how to listen to the responses but has "transform[ed] them, through a kind of behavior alchemy, into something else" (p. 3).

The concreteness of the response is bypassed in favor of the "objective" meaning of the scale. The individual's independent point of view, in effect, is considered to be dependent on the prior meaning of the scale. As a consequence, the statistical analysis of scale scores rarely eventuates in any real advance in knowledge since the investigator, when called upon to explain or interpret his results, is forced to return to his original scale constructions (liberalism, anomy, etc.) which have been superimposed on the actual behavior under scrutiny. (Brown, 1980, p. 4)

In scaling procedures, investigators often start with theoretical constructs (anything constructed rather than observed—inference, conclusion, comparison, description, hypothetical condition such as a trait or IQ, etc.) from which hypotheses are deduced. They create a scale to measure the construct, and the scale often defines the construct itself. The score on the scale defines how much of the trait the subject has: intelligence, anxiety, self-efficacy, ego-strength, dominance, and so forth. Brown (1980) observes that behavioral and social scientists have typically assumed that thoughts, feelings, preferences, and the like are traits or internal states that can be measured only indirectly by such devices as tests and scales. Q reverses the scaling approach. Rather than defining and imposing constructs such as intelligence or anxiety and then interpreting the results in terms of these same constructs, it observes an event, such as an expression of feeling or opinion, and then uses Q method to develop a construct from it. The Q statement has no meaning apart from that given to it by the subject.

Q may be used to test a theory but is mostly used for discovering what was previously unknown. Because Q does not seek predetermined traits or assume any norms but aims toward determining individual characteristics, the question of internal reliability or consistency is not relevant. It does not need support from such auxiliary constructions as validity and reliability, as R does. However, a test-retest procedure can be used to determine stability of response. The reliability studies that have been run show high correlations—greater than .90 for short intervals (Fairweather, 1981) and .81 for an eleven-month period (Kerlinger, 1973). Because no right or wrong exists for subjective operants, there is no need for the absolutistic concept of validity; for the subject's own opinion has no criterion of validity. But scales, in contrast, usually assume a continuum in

a single straight line from one extreme to the other (introversion to extroversion, for example) in which a participant receives a mean score. The continuum suggests that such a dimension exists in nature, but this is only an arbitrary construction and the data from such a continuum arise from the arbitrary construction.

With scales "it is almost true to say that no one knows what he is measuring," Stephenson maintains (1953, p. 5). One could throw away all of them and still measure thinking activities, beliefs, attitudes, desires, social interactions, personality characteristics "and all else objective to others and subjective to himself; and we can do all this scientifically" (p. 5). Psychometrics with its large number of cases, standardized tests, scales, and group averages has inundated us with categories of all sorts, such as personality and intelligence, that are only illusions of particular behaviors. Sometimes a standardized Q set such as the California Q-SET (see p. 327, below) can serve a useful purpose but must be justified in each application. Never can it be a general rule, for each situation is specific. As both Stephenson and Kantor have observed, no single logic covers all cases. Even generalizations are derived from specific conditions.

Stephenson (1980b) contends that Q provides (a) "facts in the inductive frame of subjective science" and (b) "understandings which could not be grasped before by application of questionnaire to thousands of persons" (p. x). He argues (1980a) that the "abortive" research results given in the Report to the Surgeon General in 1972 on the effects of television violence on children could have been reversed with a Q study. Each of the thirty researchers could have conducted a Q sort on one child each, asking the children to sort still photographs taken from the violent scenes on videotapes. Stephenson suggests several conditions of instruction such as "Which frightened you most?" and "Which do you feel your mother would object to?" These thirty children would have produced valuable information that the researchers' ten thousand subjects failed to provide. The failed research, he remarks, did not allow the children to speak for themselves, only to respond in accor-

dance with the "preconceptions of the investigators" (p. 19).

R versus Q

Comparisons. Intimately related to the question
of *scales* versus Q is that of *R* versus Q. The users
of R methodology make objective measurements
of some construct formulated about people, such
as a trait, and assume that the differences are only
quantitative. Subjectivity and difference between
one person and another becomes an "error term"
that must be reduced—partialed out—as much as
possible. Because it is uncorrelated with anything
else, R thinking goes, it is scientifically useless.
Brown (1972) quotes a statistician who referred
to this "error term" as "psychometric slop." To the
Q methodologist, however, the "error" is "merely
a person's own point of view—what the individual himself was willing to say, to himself or to
others—made objective (i.e., public) through
formal representation in a Q sort" (Brown, 1972,
p. 62). The so-called error or psychometric slop
becomes central in Q methodology.

In experimental procedures, similarly, uniqueness becomes the error term within each treatment
group. In contrast, Q emphasizes uniqueness. It
makes no predictions and looks for no tests of hypotheses. It emphasizes the discovery of unexpected characteristics—R's error term—and gives
these discoveries center stage. In R research designs, subjectivity, as Brown (1980) notes, is accidental and randomly distributed; whereas in Q
methodology objectivity is randomly distributed
and accidental, the relative subjective importance
of one statement to another being the aim of measurement. Q correlates persons whereas R correlates tests (variables). This puts Q in the position of
being able to measure between-person relationships (Stephen, 1985) rather than treating them as
an "error." R assumes that the constructed trait
stands alone, autonomous and fixed, and that the
process of measurement is independent of that absolute trait. In R methodology such an assumption
is necessary for correlating traits. Q, in contrast, assumes that measurement is interdependent with
meanings and that the meanings that subjects give
to Q items are created in the very act of sorting. And
so, in Q, persons rather than test items are the variables. In Q, subjects are measuring themselves as
they sort. In R, someone else is measuring them. In
Q, individuals are separated and sorted into similar
factors. In R, everybody is averaged, and individual
characteristics are lost. In addition, each subject is
usually measured only once or a few times, so the
means reflect few observations whereas single-
subject designs require numerous measurements
and thereby gain a high reliability (Morgan, 1998).
In Q the size of the concourse determines the number of measurements of an individual.

The most frequent use of Q sorting has been to
convert it into R methodology by averaging,
thereby obscuring all subjective structures that
would have emerged in the factors. Summing
scores "can conceal factorial differences and often
produces a mish-mash average of all the factors,
hence is representative of none" (Gargan &
Brown, 1993). Brown cites an early recognition of
this problem:

> If masses of items, which have evidently been
> variously influenced by quite independent
> causes, are taken together in a series the aver-
> age so computed has little scientific value, since
> it does not express the activity of a unified com-
> plex of natural or social causes and is, as a rule,
> poorly adapted to purposes of comparison.
> (Zizek, 1913, p. 65)

The traditions centering around R and Q go
back to the nineteenth century. In the German tradition of experimental psychology of Wundt and
Fechner, any variability—whether within individual measurements or between individuals—was
an error that deviated from some "true" value.
This is the R tradition. In Britain, in contrast, the
work of Galton and Pearson held variability between individuals to be of central importance
rather than an error, and Darwin's use of variability as the basis from which natural selection
worked became the core of British psychology.
This study of variability between individuals made

use of correlations, norms, and other statistical techniques pioneered by Pearson and others. At the outset this approach rejected true values and hidden causes; but Spearman, turning more toward the German tradition, brought in such hidden causes as "general intelligence" and "specific intelligence" to account for variability and employed normal distributions to deal with it. Continuing along that path, experimental psychology fashioned itself after physics, and variability was treated like the observational errors of astronomy. Presuming subjectivity as error, mainstream psychology has attacked it by treating it as a random variable or by averaging over individuals (Gigerenzer, 1987a, 1987b). Longitudinal studies have shown that R measurements of personality as traits that are universal, normally distributed, and fixed in early childhood turn out to have little consistency across childhood and adolescence (Kohlberg, 1969; Kohlberg, LaCrosse, & Hicks, 1970). Q has the advantage, Kohlberg (1972) holds, of emphasizing the lives of people rather than traits. In Q studies, subjects are truly subjects, not objects as they are in R.

In personality measurement "The Big Five" or five-factor model (Block, 1995; McCrae & Costa, 1997)—consisting of surgency or extraversion, agreeableness, conscientiousness, emotional stability, and openness to experience—are instances of recent trait constructions derived from R factor analysis. Stephenson (1953) earlier noted that R methodology has tried to assemble all human attributes and then reduce them to "atomic-like order" (p. 344), and The Big Five are recent examples. In contrast, Q deals with concrete human behavior as found in specific instances. It does not seek generalities or potentialities. The Big Five—along with I.Q., aptitude, and other traits and potentialities that emerge from R analysis—are not self-referential whereas behavior as actual events is always self-referential. Consequently, according to Q proponents, the traits constructed by R proponents mask or replace the actual events of nature with artificialities.

Q does not need large numbers of subjects as does R, for it can reveal a characteristic independently of the distribution of that characteristic relative to other characteristics—just as the occurrence of blue eyes in a population of varicolored eyes does not depend on the proportion of blue in the population (Stephenson, 1953). And because it proposes no absolutes or universals but turns always to specifics, large populations are irrelevant. By correlating persons instead of items, it is possible to do factor studies with a large number of test items and a small number of persons whereas the standard procedure of correlating tests requires large populations to which only a small number of tests can be given. With Q, the test items rather than people comprise the sample and each condition of instruction is a variable.

R methodology is entirely appropriate in brewing and agriculture where it originated for testing samples of different vats of brew and of potatoes raised under different conditions of manure. It is also useful in the human sciences where questions of fact or information are involved—where self-reference does not occur. It is less than satisfactory, Q proponents argue, when it is used to test hypotheses about constructs concerning human behavior: R gives false validity to the constructs and masks genuine, specific, human behavior. Similarly, Layzer (1974) has pointed out that IQ scores are purely instrumental—that is, products of the instruments or IQ tests that produce them—and offer no scientifically objective measurement. Therefore, using them to provide heritability estimates is invalid. This obvious fact is widely ignored in the pursuit of the degree of contribution to IQ by genes or environment. Stephenson (1974), citing Layzer, goes on to note that this holds true in all attempts to use norms for psychological measurement. In order to advance our science, we must, he holds, turn from these operational definitions (defined by responses to tests) and make use of operants (events).

Psychophysics is another area of psychology where R methodology has blinded investigators to the crucial role of subjectivity. Weber and Fechner pioneered the work in this field, the latter developing a formula (derived from Weber's work) that claimed to mathematically relate nonphysical mental sensation to the physical intensity of the stimulus. For example, how much must physical brightness increase before the nonphysical mind has the "sensation" of a difference? Fechner and others failed to recognize the impossibility of relating the physical and nonphysical, mind and body, but unknowingly circumvented the problem by actually dealing with the magnitude of the stimulus and the magnitude or sensitivity of the response. "Sensitivity," however, "is not an absolute condition but exists under specific conditions including instructions, attentiveness, nature of the task and many others" including particular measurement procedures (Smith, 1993, p. 270). It is subjective from the subject's perspective. When S. S. Stevens became the major research figure in psychophysics, he assumed that such responses ("sensations") as those to pitch, loudness, and electrical stimulation should be objective and therefore independent of the measurement procedures; and various experimental procedures would be directly related to one another. When they were not, he abandoned one of two procedures and kept the other so that with only one it would be objective and accurate (Gigerenzer, 1987b). Had Stevens oriented himself to an examination of specific events under specific conditions, Q proponents would say, it might have been clear to him that responses are not independent of the measurement procedures but are interdependent with them. They would also hold that if Stevens had been equipped with Q method, perhaps forming a Q set from the stimulations, he might have discovered some operants, some genuine effects. "In Q, only the person can measure his or her own subjectivity, and this is what renders meaning and measure inseparable . . ." (Brown, 1993c).

Q and R each have their appropriate applications. Q proponents maintain that Q is much better suited for communication of subjective responses where such traditional devices as psychological tests, questionnaires, and rating scales have been employed. R is best suited for gathering and analyzing information—that is, for events where self-reference is impossible.

The California Procedure. A major modification of Stephenson's Q methodology was developed by Block (Block, 1961; Block & Haan, 1971) at the University of California at Berkeley. Block and his followers considered this a refinement and improvement on Stephenson (for example, Jones et al., 1993). Others hold that it has some limited utility but is by and large a corruption of Q methodology. They have called it the "California Q syndrome" to indicate its pernicious effects, the label "syndrome" indicating a group of symptoms characteristic of a disease. Far more studies have been conducted with the Block approach than with Stephenson's, and Q is much more widely known in the Block version. That version uses a Q set of 100 statements of assessment, written in clinical terminology and sorted by professionals. Block has developed sets for a variety of clinical conditions whose sufferers are described as paranoids, hysterics, narcissists, etc. The assessments and the sorting are always done by professionals, never by patients. This "external" viewpoint is a legitimate one, Q methodologists hold, but not to the exclusion of the "inner" viewpoint, that of the subject of the inquiry. Such an exclusion implies that the client's viewpoint is untrustworthy or worthless.

The proponents of the California Q-Set (CQS) typically average together separate sortings so that the resulting single perspective obscures differences among the sorters (Brown, 1994b). For example, in one application therapists' viewpoints about three separate sessions with one client become a single viewpoint (Miller, Prior, & Springer, 1987), and this general procedure has been followed by several other investigators. In the Georgia Family Q-sort, modeled after the CQS (Wampler et al., 1989), observers sort descriptions of families, and the investigators draw conclusions about the families, but the families never do any sorts. The practitioners of the California procedure (a) seldom permit the subject of the investigation to do the sorting and (b) consistently engage in averaging, thereby losing the differences between their own sorters' views of the subjects (Brown, 1994b).

In one CQS study the authors correlated self with ideal at ages 14, 18, and 23 as a measure of self-esteem (Block & Robins, 1993). Subjects did their own sorting on a Self-Descriptive Q-Set. This was the "subjective part." Then clinical psychologists sorted the California Adult Q-Set as a measure of the same subjects' personalities; and these were, in turn, correlated later with other performances. As Brown (1995d) sees it,

> The first thing to note is that one can come away from a reading of Block and Robins without the faintest idea about the ways in which any of these individuals think of themselves, nor with any sense of the nature of the ideals to which their various selves are to a greater or lesser extent correlated: This information should be at the very heart of a science of subjectivity, but it is locked up tight as a drum with the self-ideal correlation coefficient. . . .

Further, although the investigators start with measures of subjectivity by means of a Q sort,

> they have not displayed or examined this information; rather they have correlated this subjectivity with some other subjectivity (the same person's ideal Q sorts), and then have retained the resulting correlations as indicative of self-esteem, as if esteem were like electric current— a quantitative variable of which some people have more than others. The use of Q sorts notwithstanding, the above strategy [reference to statistical usage and Brown's technical analysis of it] is a textbook example of R methodology, and many other characteristic features of R pervade it. The language is of variables, for example, as well as of individual differences, personality characteristics, and predictability. In addition, data reports are mainly of group means (e.g., average self-ideal correlations for females vs. males) and inter-individual correlations (e.g., of self-esteem with various personality characteristics across subjects), and all hypothesis testing is from within the hypothetico-deductive framework. In conceptualization, strategy, execution, and interpreta-

tion, therefore, this study has far more in common with R than with Q methodology, and its conclusions, however interesting in and of themselves, seem remote from what would be considered useful to a science of subjectivity." (Brown, 1995d)

Communicability

Communication versus Information. Self-reference is communication of one's subjectivity by means of Q method. Information, which never has self-reference, must be distinguished from communication, which always has self-reference. Or one could substitute "subjectivity" and "objectivity" for self-reference and non-self-reference, respectively. Stephenson (1980a) points to the statement "the sun is shining" as one that is factual in nature and informational. But any number of additional statements cannot exhaust what "the sun is shining" may mean subjectively. However, Q may provide a systematic and rigorous understanding of some of the subjective meanings. Q is preeminently a system of communicating what is otherwise often not apparent.

McKeown (1998) likens the communication of self-reference through Q to hermeneutics (see chapter 12) in which a text provides a means of interpretation. Q is not just what people are saying but an attempt to understand what they mean. The factors are interpretations of what they are saying which the subjects themselves would be unable to tell us. That is the discovery character of Q.

Consciring versus Consciousness. Stephenson (1980a, after Lewis, 1960) points out that "consciousness" was originally "consciring" (from Latin *conscire*), meaning sharing knowledge. This acquired the connotation of a shared secret or a conspiracy. Then in the seventeenth century René Descartes made "consciousness" a synonym for consciring, a private knowledge that characterizes the nonphysical mind side of his mind-body dualism. And so consciousness became the secrecy of the mind or its mystery, and in this form was imported into English from French.

The fact that this term did not come into English until the middle of the seventeenth century indicates that it is not a reference to something intrinsic in us for which we should have had a term going back over the millennia, but a recent invention. Stephenson (1980a) suggests using the predecessor term of consciousness, consciring, in its original meaning as the sharing of knowledge that characterizes Q.

> *"Thus, all, and we mean all, subjectivity is rooted* in conscire, *in the common knowledge, the sharable knowledge known to everyone in a culture. The sharing is what should have been called consciousness, and it meant merely being communicable in common."* (p. 15; italics Stephenson's, 1980a)

Brown (1991) asks if "consciousness" is really necessary or is only a non-entity that concrete communicability can replace. Q does not ask people to emit a stream of consciousness or to introspect on some mysterious mind. Subjectivity is only what one can say to oneself or to others.

Consciring as Self-Reference versus Information Exchange. Q methodology, its proponents point out, has amply demonstrated that it is able to capture the unstructured, unbounded, continuously changing, interdependent, and unique events of communication as self-reference and to do it rigorously and scientifically. These proponents further contend that the specificity of behavior—which both Stephenson and Kantor (chapter 10) emphasize as intrinsic to the natural world of which behavior is a part and which must be scrupulously followed if scientific progress is to ensue—is well observed in Q.

Today we give great attention to cybernetics, recording, feedback loops, decision making, and so on. This, Q methodologists point out, is communication as information exchange. It completely ignores communication as consciring which is really at the core of the meaningful everyday communication of human beings. The communication of feelings, preferences, judgments, and other personal or subjective responses are bypassed and ignored as specialists race in pursuit of the machine and its technology. These developments in the discipline of communication have a parallel development in psychology where, it may be argued, cognitive psychology—with its computer analogy and the construct of "information processing" by the brain—has imposed these mechanistic structures on the actual events of behavior and has mechanized objectivity while totally ignoring subjectivity.

In short, subjectivity is communication that occurs in self-reference statements, and "these can be sampled and operated upon by the subject to represent his or her existence" (Stephenson, 1974, p. 14).

The Single Case and the Question of Generalization

One must distinguish between a single case and a single test. A single case—that is, an individual—is often the focus of clinical psychology and of remedial or special education. In testing a new drug, a single test (the drug) is the focus, and measurement of its effects on a large population is appropriate. In selecting the make-up of the population for drug testing, it is important to take account of gender, age, and sometimes other characteristics, such as whether subjects are smokers or nonsmokers. Here non-self-reference rules, and various experimental designs and R statistics are indispensable. The same may be true about a taboo word versus a non-taboo word flashed on a screen. But we could also ask a single subject to Q-sort taboo words and non-taboo words according to several different instructions and might make some discoveries that could be further elucidated by interviews and/or additional Q sorts. This would provide quite a different understanding, one that is closer to everyday life than responses to the words flashed on a screen.

Often this question arises about Q methodology: How can one generalize from a single case? This is not a logical question, any more than asking it about a single clinical case study. For a particular purpose, a single case is important in itself. "What is at issue, always, is how far sound scientific procedures are involved, whether for one case or many, one experiment or several. . ." (Stephenson, 1974, p. 3). Specificity, as both Q methodologists and interbehaviorists have argued in other contexts, is a necessary condition for any scientific enterprise. Similarly, Brown (1933/1994) suggests, "It is therefore not in the averaging of responses taken *en masse* that the laws of behavior are to be found, but in generalization induced from examination of single cases in all their specificity" (p. 46).

Stephenson (1974) notes that the classical learning studies of Ebbinghaus were performed with a single subject. So were those of inverted vision (wearing an optical device that inverts the visual world), and single cases are commonplace in clinical psychology and psychiatry. Chasson (1979) describes an array of single cases—or what he calls "intensive design"—that include Q methodology. The Gestalt experiments were also done with single subjects, as were those of Piaget and those of behavior analysts and applied behavior analysts. Similarly, Barker and Wright (1951) recorded in great detail one day in the life of a young boy. The point of these studies is not to generalize "from N = 1 to N = population" (p. 7); rather, they are important for theoretical reasons. For example, what does inverting the visual world tell us about how we adapt the coordination of our visual and motor responses and what seeing "right-side-up" means (Smith, 1993)? What does a severe hydrocephalic whose skull contains only 5 percent brain but who is behaving normally and is an intellectually high-achieving individual (Lewin, 1980) tell us about the assumptions we make about the role of the brain in behavior? Stephenson (1974) cites the case of an eight-year-old boy who could understand language even though he lacked the motor capabilities to produce speech, thereby discrediting the belief that children must hear themselves babble in order to learn to understand speech. Population sampling is unnecessary in these cases; and science would

gain more by sampling *problems* rather than persons, Stephenson maintains, though we rarely do this. Survey studies almost never include a representative population of stimulus conditions or problems, only a population of persons; yet problems have wide variability. Further, he notes, when we sample populations of people we are rarely clear about who should be included: the incarcerated? the elderly? infants? psychotics? the homeless? particular ethnic or vocational groups?

Most misapplications of Q methodology, Q proponents say, fail to sample problems and, instead, sample persons. Researchers set out with operational definitions—derived from responses to a testing device—of such constructs as self and ideal-self and try to find these in populations of people rather than to discover what is subjective to the Q sorter, the operants, the actual events.

> The aim [of science] is not to gather facts but to reach understandings. If operants are available the scientist can have no truck with operational definitions of his constructs or concepts: in our case, therefore, no Q-samples are standardized to measure anyone's concept of self, ideal-self, or whatever—though for practical purposes no doubt some use can be found for such categories. (Stephenson, 1974, p. 24)

Brown (1996b) observes that Q factors themselves comprise generalizations. If two factors, A and B, emerge from a Q sort of several individuals, the individuals represented by A have, in general, that type of viewpoint and those represented by B another. "Factors represent qualitatively different modes of thought that retain their distinctive features no matter how many persons of each kind are included in a study"; consequently, "large number of cases are not required to reach generalizations of this kind" (Brown, 1995b). This is why dependent and independent variables are inappropriate to Q. To return to Stephenson's (1953) analogy with eye color, just as one individual's blue eyes are not dependent on anyone else's eye color or on the distribution of that color in any population, the subjectivity revealed by Q is not dependent on its proportion in any population. Subjectivity, like eye color, simply *is*. Such specific events can be demonstrated reliably and scientifically. "That existence *is* the single case in operation should, of course be the primary concern" of science (Stephenson, 1974, p. 14). Q sorting of both multiple and single cases is important for providing communication about those cases and for addressing theoretical questions. Even when several subjects sort the same Q set, each is a concrete, specific case; how each one contributes to particular factors is a part of the analysis.

In addition to the single case's value for discovery, it also lends itself to testing. Brown (1993/1994) used a single case to test a voting theory and another to test a philosophy of the political self. Both the voting theory and the self theory started with presupposed categories rather than with observed events. The Q studies provided observations of subjectivity that differed from the categories that the theories presupposed. The natural or observational categories of the Q sorts represented subjective behaviors at variance with the theorists' logical categories.

Generalization can be statistical, can be an inference about a population from a sample, or can be a higher order abstraction—as when Galileo generalized from balls rolling down a plane to all falling bodies (Brown, 1997). Scientific advancement is typically of the Galilean type, not a matter of determining how many or how much of this or that occurs. The latter may be of interest, but secondarily to the scientific principle. Going from the single case to the more abstract is more fundamental to science than going from the few to the many. Brown (1997) points to (a) the fame that Kepler gained in the history of science for showing that the planet Mars followed an elliptical path around the sun and (b) that Borelli, who demonstrated that ellipticity applies to the planets more generally, is barely recognized. R methodology focuses primarily on quantitative generalization and is parallel with Borelli's work. Q focuses on principles and is parallel with Kepler's work.

How many persons should be used in a Q sort? It often takes only a few, perhaps five or six, to define a factor, and additional persons will add noth-

ing. Five sorts with a test-retest reliability of .80 will result in a factor reliability of over .98 (Brown, 1993b). If factors A and B are well-defined by a few sorters and their meaning is clear from the items they contain, the major goal of the procedure has been achieved. Further understandings may be achieved by interviews with the sorters about why they placed certain key items in the categories they did. But factor C, which was unknown, might be represented by fewer people than A and B. It might require forty or fifty subjects to capture C. (Q cannot indicate what percentage of a population holds a particular view shown in Q analysis, only that the view exists.) Because Q methodology is a process of discovery rather than of theory, deduction, prediction, and hypothesis testing, a sparsely held view is never known until the sorting and analysis are completed.

But if one suspects that some segments of a population might have certain views different from those of another, then those segments should be included. For example, if we want to know students' viewpoints about a psychology department's undergraduate program, we would include psychology majors but we might also want to include students who take courses as electives or to fulfill requirements in other departments. This sample of persons is called a P-set. The P-set is not used for generalization to a larger population but to provide opportunity for all viewpoints about the department's program to show up—not as quantitative differences but as differences in the ways of thinking about the program. With a single case, the uncertainty about what will emerge is even greater than with multiple sorters; and, of course, no P-set is possible.

The Q methodologist argues that after the factor structure reveals the points of subjectivity involved, one can proceed to count heads on a more informed basis—if doing so is still important. In the above example, we might find three quite different viewpoints about the psychology program and a fourth opinion that two of the three groups have in common. The survey results, however good the sampling, would probably have missed all these relationships. With this structure established, one could then conduct a much more informed survey of how many comprise each group.

IMPLICIT POSTULATES

In various writings Stephenson provides considerable information about what he regards as proper science and investigative procedures. In one source he (Stephenson, 1967) sets forth a list of "principles," "postulates," and "pragmatics," most of which are tied to the topic of the book but a few of which have more general application. The following may be inferred from his statements.

- *Protopostulates* (general guiding assumptions about science)
  1. Science is concerned solely with concrete events. Science does not deal with such non-physical constructs as minds, mindless bodies, consciousness, or selves.[5]
  2. Each event in nature is specific and unique, and such specificities come before generalities and comprise them.
- *Metapostulates* (supportive assumptions for a particular science)
  1. Psychological events consist of levels of organization that differ from those of physiology or physics.
  2. No internal or external determiners or mind-body distinctions are relevant to a science of psychology.
  3. Whatever is not subject to observation is not a part of a science of psychology. It must be possible to manifest such things in some reliable operation, such as measuring blood-pressure with a pressure cuff and gauge or ascertaining subjectivity with Q methodology.
  4. Each scientific investigation consists of concrete inferential interactions specific to each situation, and each requires a different analysis tailored to that experimental situation.
  5. Operants or events, not constructs, are the beginning points of investigation.
  6. Communication (and hence, data) occurs between persons, not groups, but can occur within oneself.
  7. Subjectivity or meaning arises from persons, not groups.
- *Postulates* (subject matter assumptions)
  1. Psychological events consist of a field of interactions of organisms and objects that develop historically in settings. (Stephenson adopts Kantor's formula [see chapter 10, p. 288]: PE = C(k, sf, rf, hi, st, md).)
  2. Psychological events are both subjective and objective. They are subjective from one's own point of view (self-reference) and objective from some other person's point of view (other's-reference).
  3. Much of psychological behavior that has been called mind, consciousness, and/or self is subjective or self-referential behavior (the remainder being objective behavior). Hence, it is best understood through procedures that allow the subject to measure him- or herself and by quantification methods that preserve these meanings and determine how they are shared by individuals.
  4. Averaging techniques that replace the meanings of things to subjects with experimenter-determined meanings are suitable only when information or facts are important—and not necessarily even in those instances.[6]

RESEARCH

Q has found its most frequent use in communication, political science, nursing science, and developmental psychology, but it is equally applicable to economics, social psychology, industrial rela-

---

5. As this chapter has tried to show, Stephenson rejected "self" as a substantive thing or an agent, but did use the word to refer to "my reference point as demonstrated in my Q sort" as opposed to "your reference point as expressed in your Q sort."

6. The author is grateful to Steven Brown for his critique of two drafts of these postulates.

tions, business, law, literature, women's studies, and all other disciplines involving human behavior. And that includes the human side of chemistry, physics, geology, and so forth. The number of published Q studies exceeds twenty-five hundred although many of these are attenuated by R methods. Following are a few studies, *not* corrupted by R, that are relevant to psychology and will suggest Q's claimed potential.

How might preschool children communicate their subjectivity? Because written statements could not be used, Taylor, Delprato, and Knapp (1994) used a Q set of pictures of children engaged in various activities. The children sorted into seven categories of subjectivity following a distribution guide that allowed them to see the distribution required, but the administrator put the items in place after the children made their choices. They sorted according to eight conditions of instruction, such as "most like you/not like you" and "what teacher thinks is most like you/what teacher thinks is not like you." Each child showed organized experience as evidenced by the 3–4 significant factors for each, but each child was unique as indicated by different sorts under different conditions of instruction. Because a limited number of factors emerged, the children probably shared common variance. Additional information would be required to better understand the findings, but they indicate that Q Method can be applied even to three- and four-year-olds and can reveal differences between and within children.

Chusid and Cochran (1989) used Q to show how family themes related to vocational choices. They asked six men and four women who had changed careers to sort forty-six adjectives to describe each of several family members and vocational figures. The results of the Q sorting showed patterns of relationships between family experiences and career changes which were then examined by interviewing the subjects. An analysis of the interviews provided case portraits of each subject, and the subjects reviewed these portraits for accuracy. The final product showed family themes ("drama") shifting from the old career to the new career or a different family theme arising in the

new. Consistent with most Q studies, the subjects were unaware of these relationships or aware in only limited ways as "when they described coworkers in virtually the same way as they did family members" (p. 39).

Gallivan (1993) studied characteristics that make for a sense of humor by having forty-one participants sort seventy-nine statements selected from a concourse made up of "people's descriptions of someone with an excellent sense of humor." She found four factors or groups. The first enjoyed humor that disparages someone. Members of the second group considered themselves very poor at producing or enjoying humor. A third group disliked disparaging humor. The fourth group was more complex: these individuals tended to reject disparagement and to feel positive about their own use of humor—as did the first and third groups—but were unique in feeling the importance of their own use of humor in coping with everyday life.

Dennis and Goldberg (1996c) used fifty-four women as subjects. They averaged 10 percent over their ideal body weight and were participating in a nine-month weight-loss program involving both nutritional and behavioral components. Two groups emerged, one called "assureds" and the other "disbelievers." The assureds had higher self-efficacy beliefs and lower depression than the disbelievers. The assureds lost an average of six kilograms and the disbelievers seven, a statistically significant difference. In post-treatment the disbelievers who became assureds lost twice as much as those who began and remained disbelievers: ten kilograms vs. five kilograms. The assureds indicated higher self-esteem and better mood and eating patterns. Q's establishment of different behavioral characteristics, those of self-efficacy, which relate to success suggest that a program to help improve self-efficacy should go hand-in-hand with the nutritional program. Brown (1996a) comments on the work that

> Dennis and Goldberg's study is among the first to be able to demonstrate significant weight loss between categories of persons. All prior

studies, of course, have relied upon objective categories—such as age, number of previous diets, trait anxiety, intro- and extroversion, eating pattern, degree of obesity, etc.—for predicting either obesity or weight loss, but none has proven consistently successful, which leads the authors to suggest "the potential use of a Q methodology as a new direction for matching clients to obesity treatments."

It appears that subjectivity was much more closely related to successful weight loss than trait measures.

APPLICATIONS

Q has applications ranging from discerning similarities and differences between persons or between conditions for a single person on the one hand and on the other large-sample research of public opinion (Stephen, 1985). Brown (1993b) has surveyed some of the many areas in which Q methodology has been used, such as patient control in hospitals, training of nursing-home staff, analyzing decision-making settings, studying the effects of pornography, devising political campaign strategy, teaching environmental values, integrating refugees, studying ethics and corruption, analyzing public reaction to scandal, distinguishing among authoritarian personalities, communicating, critiquing family videos, and others applicable to particular countries. It has found favor in some quarters of feminist studies because of "the focus on 'persons' (the realm of the interpersonal or relational) rather than on 'tests'" (Febbraro, 1995, p. 147).

Stephen (1985) points out a "vexing problem" in qualitative research: that of resolving discrepancies in what independent researchers discover about the same matter. The common referents in Q items provide a means of finding a resolution. After developing a concourse and Q set around the characteristics that focus on the discrepancies, each independent investigator can do a sort that can be factor-analyzed to show similarities and differences in the approaches to these common referents.

CLINICAL PSYCHOLOGY

Because Q is the specialist of the single case, it is eminently suitable for use in clinical psychology. A concourse made up of (a) the client's history, (b) an interview with the client, or (c) information from other relevant sources can be the basis for a Q set. The sorts can be done quickly in the therapy session; or with suitable instructions, the client can take the cards home and sort them according to the conditions of instruction decided by the therapist and client. The client could even decide to do additional sorts by adding his or her own conditions of instruction. An office clerk can enter the numbers into a computer program which will quickly yield the factors. The clinician with a little training can complete the analysis—perhaps consulting with the client in the process. The analysis of a Q sort and a follow-up discussion with the client about the results can be used as an aid in diagnosis or in treatment planning. The results of Q sorts at the outset of psychotherapy and at various points in its course can become part of the therapeutic process, assisting both the therapist and the client. A good example (Goldstein, 1989) is in connection with the case of a thirty-three-year-old male who had suffered abuse as a child and stuttered when trying to speak in the presence of co-workers. He sorted twenty-four adjectives under nineteen conditions of instruction to refer to each person—girlfriend, boss, ideal mother, ideal father, brother, therapist, and others—who was important to him. Three factors surfaced that represented interpersonal relations. These the therapist and client discussed in order to develop goals and treatment procedures.

Q sorting become popular in clinical and counseling research about mid-century (for example, Rogers & Diamond, 1954); but usually someone other than the client did the sorting, thereby completely eliminating the viewpoint of the most important person in the setting. For example, in a study of two clients in psychoanalytic therapy (Jones, Cumming, & Pulos, 1993), the sorters were "clinical judges," not the client. They used a standardized Q sort, not one drawn from a concourse relevant to the two individuals. And, of course, the statistical analysis was R, not Q.

A Q study of a Freudian, an Adlerian, a Jungian, a Sullivanian (see chapter 5 for an account of these four psychoanalysts), a nondirectivist (chapter 4, pp. 126–127), and a personal construct theorist (chapter 8, pp. 240–241) showed that each interpreted an attempted suicide case from his own theoretical perspective (Kelly, 1963). Stephenson (1974) points to a clinical case in which the therapist's Q sorts showed a view of the client radically different from that of the client's own Q sorts. Even the goals of what the client wanted for herself were different from what it meant to the therapist. The *objective* view point of the therapist was totally incongruent with the *subjective* viewpoint of the client (Parloff, Stephenson, & Perlin, 1963). Similarly, in Q studies of Myra, one of the Genain quadruplets—all of whom were schizophrenic—the therapist and Myra had entirely different goals for therapy. Further, the therapist's Q sorts showed that his views about how Myra perceived him were at variance with her actual perceptions (Stephenson, 1980). This kind of discovery in a clinical situation should be of major importance in adjusting the therapist-client relationship and the treatment process.

In one application of Q (Stephenson, 1985), the method was used as a way of moving away from the analyst's interpretation of free associations of the client or even of the analyst's attempts at empathy (Atwood & Stolorow, 1984)—as opposed to interpretation. Q would produce a concrete measurement of the client's actual feelings as provided by that client's sorts. Both analyst and client (P-set = 2) performed a Q sort of ninety-six items involving the analytic situation to test the claim of transference. Three factors emerged. One of these supported the claim by showing a strong transference from the patient to the analyst. Another factor suggested a possible transference from the analyst to the client.

In another instance, Q was used to examine some of the separate identities in a case diagnosed as dissociative identity disorder (DSM-IV), formerly called multiple personality (Brown & Smith,

unpublished). This was a thirty-four-year-old female. The most frequently occurring or *presenting* identity, Lonnie, provided the names and descriptions of ninety-six identities in the system. These names became both the concourse and the Q set. The six most active members of the system sorted names of the ninety-six according to the following six conditions of instruction: most to least (a) similar to me, (b) comfortable to be with, (c) influence with the system, (d) understanding, (e) cooperative, (f) informed about the system.

Although some of the identities had names that were witty metaphors of their functions in the psychological system of this individual, in order to protect the subject's confidentiality they have been changed. The six identities presented themselves to participate in the Q sort.

- In day to day events, Lonnie was most frequently present and took responsibility for the actions of the entire system. Some of the identities were hostile toward her and had injured her.
- Arthur was a young male who kept order and did much of the planning. He was friendly and diplomatic with all members of the system.
- Wendy, a saucy eighteen-year-old who looked for a good time, was cooperative and friendly with Lonnie but had been hostile in the past and had injured her.
- At the opposite pole, April and Sally were hostile to Lonnie. April was the guardian of the family honor and induced guilt by accusing Lonnie of failing to uphold that honor.
- Sally planned to seduce men in order to humiliate them as revenge for the damage she believed they caused the system.
- Playing a rather different role, eight-year-old Robin was friendly and merry. She presented when the system was overwhelmed or in danger of self-injury.

The thirty-six sorts yielded three factors. The Q sorts for "influence" and "understanding" dominate the first factor. That is, all six sorters agree about which other personalities have the most influence and understand most about the system.

More complex is Lonnie's Q sort for "similarity" and "comfort." "Similarity" is significantly associated with the first factor but not with the second or third, whereas "comfort" is significantly associated with the second factor. Apparently, those to whom Lonnie sees herself as similar are different from those with whom she feels comfortable.

Factor two consisted mostly of Arthur's "similarity" sort and Wendy's "similarity" and "comfort" sorts. This reflects the good working relationship between Wendy and Arthur.

The third factor represented considerable polarity. Both April's and Sally's "similar" Q sorts for Pursuit (a terrifying identity who has inflicted injury) and Gloss (a female who insists that all is well but fronts for those who inflict injury) define the factor positively. They also agree on their dissimilarity with Smoke (a child of four who carries all the shame of the system and will not show her face) and Jove (a gleeful, magical character who provides safety to the children of the system). Eight-year-old Robin's "similar" Q sort is highly negative on this same factor; she is most similar to Jove and Smoke and most different from Pursuit and Gloss. Perhaps Robin's friendliness and warmth counter the unfriendliness of April and Sally—hence, the bipolarity.

Immediately after sorting, each identity was asked why he or she placed the particular items (names) in the two highest and two lowest categories. These statements would be used for a concourse in the second phase of the study. Here is an example of Lonnie's statements about those she placed at −5 on "most/least comfortable with": "I am scared of some of them. I feel bad about putting Smoke in the −5 column. Smoke is ashamed and connected with abuse but I'm not comfortable with what she's about. I don't dislike Smoke; I just don't feel comfortable with her. April is about guilt. Sally is about sex. Fear, Shame, Guilt. The four people [Pursuit was the fourth] in this pile may be the most in need of working in therapy. This is a real eye-opener for me." Robin gave the following statements for her four +5 placements on "most/least cooperative": "I always try to help everyone I can. Celeste [a guardian] is

probably why everyone inside is still alive. Kenny keeps order and balance. Arthur helps everybody."

The subject used the findings from this first phase of the study in discussions with her therapist. Happily for her, after the first phase was completed she began the long and difficult but successful struggle to integrate the identities and to move toward healthy behavior. Consequently, some of the identities were no longer presenting so the second phase was no longer feasible (Brown & Smith, p. 325).

RELATION TO SOME OTHER APPROACHES

Cognitive Psychology

This approach, which is organocentric and emphasizes cognitive acts such as imagining and thinking, would seem to put a premium on subjectivity. But, in fact, it almost totally ignores subjectivity except where objective variables give rise to it. This seemingly anomalous situation arises because cognitive psychology uses R methodology which it derives—along with its mechanistic and mentalistic orientation—from methodological behaviorism. Its major departure is to shift from the mechanism of classical conditioning to the mechanism of computers as an analogy for human cognition.

Because Q methodology as a noncentric system abjures psychisms, hypothetical-deductive methods, biological reductionism, and construct-imposed approaches and because these are endemic to cognitivism, the two are in many ways poles apart. Cognitivism could make good use of Q for its studies of perception, imagining, and other topics but is unlikely to do so without converting it to R methodology, thereby losing Q's unique advantages.

Humanistic Psychology

This system emphasizes *the* self and the study of what is meaningful in human life. It generally rejects psychological research because of its neglect of the individual's point of view. Despite some overlap of interest with Q methodology, humanistic psychology's philosophy makes the categorical self or mind, rather than simply self-reference, its centerpiece; so it does not comport with the scientific philosophy of Q. Nevertheless, the two do share an interest in meaningful human behavior ("experience," in humanism's terms), and Q methodology could greatly improve humanistic psychology's qualitative research by supplementing or replacing its limited and cumbersome methods with the rigorous and efficient method of Q. The strengths of both qualitative and quantitative approaches are combined in Q (Brown, 1996). The research that humanistic psychology rejects is the R type, with which Q methodology also has quarrels. Carl Rogers (Rogers & Diamond, 1954), a major figure in humanistic psychology, used Q method in his study of the effects of psychotherapy, but he combined it with problematic R analysis. A fuller use of Q would be more consistent with humanism's own principles.

Humanistic psychology could also make valuable use of Q in psychotherapy. Its insistence on the client's full participation as an equal with the therapist in the treatment process can be satisfied by Q. The client would participate in the planning, performance, and analysis of Q sorting and in its application to the treatment process.

Interbehavioral Psychology

Stephenson (1982, 1987) rests his Q methodology on Kantor's (1959) interbehavioral field construct. His emphasis on *operants,* which interbehaviorism calls *events,* is considered by both to be the fundamental data on which a science of behavior must depend. In other words, rather than imposing such constructs as motivation, intelligence, self, consciousness, aptitudes, traits, and the like, investigation must deal with what individuals are doing—whether writing letters or sorting Q statements. Both systems insist that specificities come before generalities and that specificities are more fundamental to science than generalities. They agree that laws are not universals but are specific to situations. They regard experience and subjec-

tivity as concrete behaviors rather than as existing apart from behaviors, and they reject the notion that minds contain private contents known only to the presumed minds that contain them. For Kantor, so-called privacy is nothing more than uniqueness of occurrence, which is characteristic of every event in nature. Privacy can be nothing more than the particular vantage point from which occurrences can be observed. In a psychological field several components of natural events are available for observation by various means and vantage points. By turning to communicability through Q sorting, Stephenson also rejects the privacy assumption. Accordingly, they both underscore the objectivity of subjectivity and its availability for study. They reject such constructs as mind-body dualism, consciousness as a thing or process, and the reduction of psychology to neurology. Both reject all absolutes and recognize the changing nature of human interactions from one situation to another. Despite their rather different aims, the two systems are remarkably consistent in their philosophy of science—and this is precisely what should occur if they are both focused on operants/events from which constructs are derived.

Phenomenological Psychology

Brown (1972) compares Sartre's statement about the distinction between facts and essences with that of R and Q respectively. The traits that R seeks to measure can never reveal subjectivity. Although Merleau-Ponty, the pioneer of phenomenological psychology and, an associate of Sartre, holds to a broad kind of behaviorism that gave preeminence to an interdependent person and world and in that respect comes close to the philosophy of Q, he remains somewhat entangled in the construct of consciousness and never entirely frees himself from mentalism. Consequently, in those ways his phenomenological psychology remains disjunctive from operant subjectivity. Nevertheless, Q methodology would serve phenomenology's research purposes quite well by providing the rigor and clarity that "the phenomenological method" lacks. By orienting their Q study of preliterate children toward phenomenology, Taylor, Delprato, and Knapp (1994) provide an example of this usage.

Postmodernism and Social Constructionism

Brown (1995a) points out that because behavioral science at one point in its history treated subjectivity and mentalism as the same and rejected both, postmodernists concluded that the rejection of subjectivity was a derision of humanity, and, therefore, they totally rejected science. This was unfortunate because subjective science, Q methodology, would have supported postmodernism in its criticism of the exclusion of subjectivity from science while still retaining a scientific approach to human behavior.

Social constructionism has made use of Q in diverse areas: for example, studies in connection with lesbianism (Kitzinger, 1996), psychoanalysis (Edelson, 1989), feminism and pornography (Gallivan, 1994), and child abuse (Stainton Rogers & Stainton Rogers 1989).

CRITIQUE

Some confusion could be avoided if Q methodology consistently used behavioral rather than mentalistic terminology but references to "internal" and "external" or "inner" and "outer" viewpoints and to "states of mind" are used by Q methodologists. For example, Q is said to deal with "states of mind" rather than with "objective states" or with "internal" rather than "external" perspectives. Even though Q methodologists define these to mean only the subject's framework, our culture is so steeped in mind-body dualism that these terms suggest such dualism and can only contribute to misunderstanding. For example, Duijker (1979) attempts to understand Q methodology as a thoroughgoing mind-body dualism and to further explicate it in those terms. It appears that some of these usages contributed to his misinterpretation or at least reinforced his assumptions. Stephenson did eventually recognize that "my"

view and "your" view were better referents than "inner" and "outer." Despite the frequent usage in the psychological literature of "subjectivity" as "mental," the term probably cannot be avoided, and the Q literature has made diligent efforts to clarify its usage as *behavior.*

In terms of economics, because Q studies require fewer subjects than R studies, they are often less costly; but this advantage is offset somewhat by the fact that Q sorting requires careful explanation of the procedure to each subject and often follow-up interviewing. Usually only one subject at a time sorts, but it is possible to conduct sorts on a group basis. In addition to the foregoing advantages (and limitations), Dennis (1986) lists a variety of additional advantages including highly reliable data, no missing data, no "undecided" responses, and—because of self-reference—no environmental bias.

CONCLUSIONS

Q is not just another way of obtaining ratings or just another way to measure opinions and preferences, nor is it an assessment or personality device. It is not in the usual R tradition of quantitative research, nor does it follow the footsteps of qualitative research which usually searches for patterns or special features in interviews. In contrast to the latter, it provides subjects with specific items to react to—items to sort into categories according to their subjective meaning to each subject. And this categorical sort provides the basis for a rigorous mathematical analysis. In its best usage, Q offers "unique insights into the richness of human subjectivity" (Dennis, 1996, p. 7).

Q might seem more a technology than a philosophy of science, simply one faction in a Q versus R quarrel. But "the concern is with far more than the simple operations called 'Q-technique.' Rather, it is with a comprehensive approach to the study of behavior, where man is at issue as a total thinking and behaving being" (Stephenson, 1953, p. 7).

Despite the great advances in objective science and technology, those developments have brought liabilities as well as benefits. A major role for subjectivity as a balancing force is sorely needed, Brown (1994a, after Stephenson, 1978) contends:

> We remain largely ignorant of the subjectivity paralleling these events—ethics, fears, hatreds, ethnic loyalties—so that our own thinking and motivation as well as our understanding of them remain virtually as they were in Newton's time, replete with modern versions of witch-hunts, social and religious intolerance, and intergroup violence. One cannot help wondering if things might have been otherwise had more resources been devoted to understanding the human condition—to finding the human causes of war, for example, rather than material ways to wage it—but this would have required a different outlook toward subjectivity and a willingness to place it on an equal scientific footing with objectivity. Science's shame is that it has not done this, and shows few signs that it plans to. (Brown, 1994a)

REFERENCES

Atkinson, J. 1992. Q Method. Kent, OH: Computer Center, Kent State University (computer program).

Atwood, George E., & Robert D. Stolorow. 1984. *Structures of Subjectivity: Explorations in Psychoanalytic Phenomenology.* Hillsdale, NJ: Analytic Press.

Barker, Roger G., & Herbert F. Wright. 1951. *One Boy's Day: A Specimen Record of Behavior.* New York: Archon Books.

Block, Jack. 1961. *The Q-Sort Method in Personality Assessment and Psychiatric Research.* Springfield, IL: Thomas.

———. 1995. A contrarian view of the five-factor approach to personality description. *Psychological Bulletin* 117: 187–215.

Block, Jack, & Norma Haan. 1971. *Lives through Time.* Berkeley, CA: Bancroft.

Block, J., & R. W. Robins. 1993. A longitudinal study of consistency and change in self-esteem from early adolescence to early adulthood. *Child Development* 64: 909–23.

Brown, Steven R. 1971. The forced-free distinction in Q technique. *Journal of Educational Measurement* 8: 283–87.

———. 1972. A fundamental incommensurability between objectivity and subjectivity. In *Science, Psychology, and Communication: Essays Honoring*

William Stephenson. Edited by S. R. Brown & D. J. Brenner. New York: Teachers College Press.

———. 1980. *Political Subjectivity: Applications of Q Methodology in Political Science.* New Haven & London: Yale University Press.

———. 1986. Q technique and method: Principles and procedures. In *New Tools for Social Scientists: Advances and Applications in Research Methods.* Edited by William D. Berry & Michael S. Lewis-Beck. Newbury Park, CA: Sage.

———. 1991. The two containers. Q Methodology Network [Listserver], 24 October.

———. 1993a. Methodology query. Q Methodology Network [Listserver], 20 November.

———. 1993b. A primer on Q methodology. *Operant Subjectivity* 16: 91–138.

———. 1993c. Q and amplification. Q Methodology Network [Listserver], 14 November.

———. 1993/1994. The structure and form of subjectivity in political theory and behavior. *Operant Subjectivity* 17: 30–47.

———. 1994. Belated reply to Peter Schmolck's introduction. Q Methodology Network [Listserver], 18 February.

———. 1994b. The "California way" in Q methodology. Q Methodology Network [Listserver], 23 November.

———. 1995a. SB "behavior." Q Methodology Network [Listserver], 29 October.

———. 1995b. SB1: Open questions. Q Methodology Network [Listserver], 30 October.

———. 1995c. SB2 Overview of chapter 2 of *The Study of Behavior.* Q Methodology Network [Listserver], 5 November.

———. 1995d. The "California way" in Q methodology. Q Methodology Network [Listserver], 23 January.

———. 1996a. Q bibliography: Dennis & Goldberg, weight loss strategies. Q Methodology Network [Listserver], 31 March.

———. 1996b. Frequently asked questions about Q methodology. Q Methodology Network [Listserver], 6 July.

———. 1996c. Q methodology and qualitative research. *Qualitative Health Research* 6: 561–67.

———. 1997. Re: The problem of generalization. Q Methodology Network [Listserver], 12 March.

Brown, Steven R., & Noel W. Smith (unpublished). A Q-sort by six identities of a dissociative identity disorder.

Chasson, J. B. 1979. *Research Design in Clinical Psychology and Psychiatry,* 2nd ed. New York: Irvington.

Chusid, Hanna, & Larry Cochran. 1989. Meaning of career change from the perspective of family roles and dramas. *Journal of Counseling Psychology* 36: 34–41.

Cronbach, L. J., & G. C. Gleser. 1954. [Review of] *The Study of Behavior,* by W. Stephenson. *Psychometrika* 19: 327–30.

Delprato, Dennis. 1997. Theoretical rotation. Q Methodology Network [Listserver], January 22.

Dennis, Karen E. 1986. Q methodology: Relevance and application to nursing research. *Advances in Nursing Science* 8: 6–17.

Dennis, Karen, & Andrew P. Goldberg. 1996. Weight control self-efficacy types and transitions affect weight-loss outcomes in obese women. *Addictive Behaviors* 21: 103–116.

Duijker, Hubert C. J. 1979. Mind and meaning. *Operant Subjectivity* 3: 15-31.

Edelson, Marshall. 1989. The nature of psychoanalytic theory: Implications for psychoanalytic research. *Psychoanalytic Inquiry* 9: 169–92.

Fairweather, John. 1981. Reliability and validity of Q-method results: Some empirical evidence. *Operant Subjectivity* 5: 2–16.

Febbraro, Angela. 1995. On the epistemology, metatheory, and ideology of Q methodology: A critical analysis. In *Trends and Issues in Theoretical Psychology.* Edited by I. Lubek, R. van Hezewijk, G. Pheterson, & C. W. Tolman. New York: Springer.

Gallivan, Joanne. 1993. Humor appreciation: A Q-methodological study. Paper read at the Canadian Psychological Association Annual Meeting, May 29.

———. 1994. Subjectivity and the psychology of gender: Q as a feminist methodology. In *Women, Girls, and Achievement.* Edited by J. Gallivan, S. D. Crozier, & V. M. Lalande. Toronto: Captus University Publications.

Gargan, John G., & Steven R. Brown. 1993. "What is to be done?" Anticipating the future and mobilizing prudence. *Policy Sciences* 26: 347–59.

Gigerenzer, Gerd. 1987a. The probabilistic revolution in psychology—An overview. In *The Probabilistic Revolution,* vol. 2, *Ideas in the Sciences.* Edited. By L. Krüger, G. Gigerenzer, & M. S. Morgan. Cambridge, MA: MIT Press.

———. 1987b. Probabilistic thinking and the fight against subjectivity. In *The Probabilistic Revolution,* vol. 2, *Ideas in the Sciences.* Edited by L. Krüger, G. Gigerenzer, & M. S. Morgan. Cambridge, MA: MIT Press.

Goldstein, David M. 1989. Q methodology and control systems theory. *Operant Subjectivity* 13: 8–14.

Jones, Enrico E.; Janice D. Cumming; & Steven M. Pulos. 1993. Tracing clinical themes across phases of treatment by a Q-Set. In *Psychodynamic Treatment Research: A Handbook for Clinical Treatment.* Edited by N. E. Miller, L. Luborsky, J. B. Barber, & J. P. Docherty. New York: Basic Books.

Kantor, J. R. 1959. *Interbehavioral Psychology: An Example of Scientific System Construction.* Bloomington, IN: Principia Press.

Kelly, George A. 1963. Nonparametric factor analysis of personality theories. *Journal of Individual Psychology* 19: 115–17.

Kerlinger, Fred. 1972. Q-methodology in behavioral research. In *Science, Psychology, and Communication.* Edited by S. Brown & D. Brenner. New York: Teachers College Press.

Kitzinger, Celia. 1987. *The Social Construction of Lesbianism.* London: Sage.

Kohlberg, Lawrence. 1969. Stage and sequence: The cognitive-developmental approach to socialization. In *Handbook of Socialization Theory and Research.* Edited by D. Goslin. New York: Rand McNally.

———. 1972. Chicago, 1948–1956. ["Introduction: William Stephenson," by O. L. Zangwill, L. Kohlberg, & D. J. Brenner]. In *Science, Psychology, and Communication: Essays Honoring William Stephenson.* Edited by S. R. Brown and J. Brenner. New York: Teachers College Press, pp. xi–xviii.

Kohlberg, L.; J. LaCrosse; & D. Hicks. 1970. The predictability of adult mental health from childhood behaviors. In *Handbook of Child Psychopathology.* Edited by B. Wolman. New York: McGraw-Hill.

Krantz, David L. 1971. Schools and systems: The mutual isolation of operant and non-operant psychology as a case study. *Journal of the History of the Behavioral Sciences* 8: 86–102.

Layzer, D. 1974. Heritability analyses of IQ scores: Science or numerology? *Science* 183: 1259–66.

Lewin, R. 1980. Is your brain really necessary? *Science* 210: 1232–34.

Lewis, C. S. 1960. *Stuides in Words.* Cambridge: Cambridge University Press.

McCrae, Robert R., & Paul T. Costa. 1997. Personality trait structure as a human universal. *American Psychologist* 52: 509–516.

McKeown, Bruce. 1998. Circles: Q-methodology as a hermeneutical science. *Operant Subjectivity* 21: 112–38.

Miller, M. J.; D. Prior; & T. Springer. 1987. Q-sorting Gloria. *Counselor Education and Supervision* 27: 61-68.

Morgan, David L. 1998. Selectionist thought and methodological orthodoxy in psychological science. *Psychological Record* 48: 439–56.

Parloff, Morris B.; William Stephenson; & Seymour Perlin. 1963. Myra's perception of self and others. In *The Genain Quadruplets.* Edited by David Rosenthal. New York: Basic Books, pp. 493–501.

Rogers, Carl R., & Rosalind F. Diamond. 1954. *Psychotherapy and Personality Change: Co-ordinated Research Studies in the Client-Centered Approach.* Chicago: University of Chicago.

Smith, Noel W. 1993. Sensing is perceiving: An alternative to the doctrine of the double world. In *Greek and Interbehavioral Psychology: Selected and Revised Papers,* rev. ed. Edited by N. W. Smith. Lanham, MD: University Press of America.

Smith, Noel W., & Smith, Lance L. 1996. Field theory in science: Its role as a necessary and sufficient condition in psychology. *Psychological Record* 46: 3–19.

Sommer, Robert. 1977. Toward a psychology of natural behavior. *APA Monitor* (January).

Stainton Rogers, W., & R. Stainton Rogers. 1989. Taking the child abuse debate apart. In *Child Abuse and Neglect.* Edited by W. Stainton Rogers, D. Hevey, & A. Ash. London: Batsford.

Stephen, Timothy D. 1985. Q-methodology in communication science: An introduction. *Communication Quarterly* 33: 193–208.

Stephenson, William. 1935. *Technique of factor analysis. Nature* 136: 297.

———. 1953. *The Study of Behavior: Q-Technique and Its Methodology.* Chicago: University of Chicago Press.

———. 1954. Comments on Cronbach and Gleser's review. *Psychometrika* 19: 331-33.

———. 1968. Consciousness out—subjectivity in. *Psychological Record* 18: 499–501.

———. 1974. Methodology of single case studies. *Journal of Operational Psychiatry* 5 (2): 3–16.

———. 1977. Factors as operant subjectivity. *Operant Subjectivity* 1: 3–16.

———. 1978. The shame of science. *Ethics in Science and Medicine* 5: 25–38.

———. 1980a. Consciring: A general theory for subjective communicability. *Communication Yearbook 4.* Edited by Dan Nimmo. New Brunswick, NJ: Transaction.

———. 1980b. Foreword. In *Political Subjectivity: Applications of Q Methodology in Political Science,* by Steven R. Brown. New Haven and London: Yale University Press.

———. 1982. Q-methodology, interbehavioral psychology, and quantum theory. *Psychological Record* 332: 235–48.

———. 1985. Review of *Structures and Subjectivity: Explorations in Psychoanalytic Phenomenology,* by George E. Atwood & Robert D. Stolorow. Hillsdale, NJ: Analytic Press. Originally published 1984 in *Operant Subjectivity* 8 (3): 100–108.

———. 1987. Q methodology: Interbehavioral and quantum theoretical connections in clinical psychology. In *New Ideas in Therapy.* Edited by D. H. Ruben & D. J. Delprato, Westport, CT: Greenwood Press.

———. 1988–89. The quantumization of psychological events. *Operant Subjectivity* 12: 1–23.

———. 1989. Quantum theory of subjectivity. *Integrative Psychiatry* 6: 180–95.

———. 1990. Fifty years of exclusionary psychometrics: I–II. *Operant Subjectivity* 14: 105–120, 141–62.

Stricklin, M. 1990. p.c.q.: Factor analysis programs for Q-technique (version 2.0). Computer program. Lincoln, NE 68502.

Taylor, Priscilla; Dennis J. Delprato; and John R. Knapp. 1994. Q-methodology in the study of child phenomenology. *Psychological Record* 44: 171–83.

Wampler, K. S.; C. F. Halverson; J. J. Moore; & L. H. Walters. 1989. The Georgia Family Q-Sort: An observational measure of family functioning. *Family Process:* 223–38.

Zizek, F. 1913. *Statistical Averages: A Methodological Study.* Translated by W. M. Persons. New York: Holt.

CHAPTER 12

Phenomenological Psychology:
Meaning, Consciousness, and Relating to the World

Chapter Outline

INTRODUCTION

The word *phenomenon* (singular; plural is *phenomena*) refers to an appearance. Many psychologists believe that phenomenological psychology claims to study a mind or subjective experience—appearances—and is a form of introspection. This, however, is a misconception. According to Kruger (1983), phenomenological psychology may be defined as "The study of the nature of our *presence to the world*" (p. 19)." When we think, we think *about something;* when we are angry, we are angry *about something;* when we remember, we remember *something.* Such relationships involve meanings, and phenomenological psychology investigates these meanings of things to us and of us to them, rather than using the impersonal mode of the physical sciences that much of psychology has adopted. The world to humans, phenomenologists insist, is not a collection of bare or impersonal objects, nor is the body's role that of a computing machine that processes information or neurally interprets the world. The world has meaningful structure and our bodies live as part of that meaning. "Man *is* his lived bodiliness, his attunement to the world, his life history and lived time. . . The world always appears to us as a meaningful structure; it is not mere brute materiality, it always has a face" (Kruger, 1983, p. 19).

EARLY DEVELOPMENT AND SOME ISSUES

In the nineteenth century psychology began breaking away from theology and philosophy by imitating the physical sciences, especially physics and chemistry. These two sciences served as prestigious models, and the mechanistic philosophy of British empiricism added to the orientation. The early investigators held that their task was to determine how the organism used its physiological equipment to differentiate color, sound, brightness, size, and even feelings about the physical objects around it. Ebbinghaus, in the nineteenth century, began his pioneering studies in memory by inventing nonsense syllables to represent memorized items. (He assumed that the syllables represented the atoms that comprised a mind, as propounded by the British empiricists; the syllables were an outer form of inner mental atoms.) He wanted to know how people learned what was devoid of meaning and for this he employed nonsense. Similarly, the behaviorists and more recently the cognitivists regarded the world as a series of stimuli to the organism, stimuli with the physical properties of contours, loudness, number, size, and so forth. The current major form of behaviorism, behavior analysis, holds that reinforcements *shape* the organism's behavior. Cognitivists hold that the organism is a computing machine that *processes* information. For both behaviorists and cognitivists, research in psychology is largely confined to the laboratory where researchers set up experiments from their own point of view, strive to keep all conditions as mechanistic as possible, and direct the "subjects" to their tasks in such a way as to minimize any possibility that they might be subjective. They take measurements of subjects' responses to stimulus objects when those responses are assumed to be *dependent* on the stimulus and the stimulus *independent* of the subject. Cognitivists amalgamate all data so that individuality is replaced with a population characteristic.

What is missing in all this? According to the phenomenologists, it is *meaning*. To them, we perceive not stimuli but the *meanings* of objects and conditions. The task of psychology should be to study the meanings of things to people. A desk is not just a rectangular configuration made of atoms and molecules. It means a surface on which we can write or place certain objects. Meanings may also involve feelings, values, and judgments. And these meanings will change in different contexts. It is these meanings, phenomenologists insist, that should be central to any investigation of human activity, and meanings always involve a relationship between the person and the world. We cannot study the person or the person's world in isolation—only as a relationship.

The modes of expression available in our language do not readily allow us to express this mutuality. We regularly refer to the automobile we see or the child we hear, but it is difficult to express the way in which the automobile or the child acts on us. (Aristotle noted the same problem.) In order to indicate that action, Kruger (1981) refers to "that which shows itself" and Zaner (1985) to "the *awareness-of-something,* and *that-of-which* there is the awareness" (p. 620) as a corelationship.

Consciousness and mind are redefined by phenomenology. Consciousness is said to point beyond itself to an object—either an actual object or one thought about. Therefore consciousness is not something in the person nor do objects occur in consciousness. As Sartre (1956) puts it: "a table is not in consciousness—not even in the capacity of a representation. A table is *in* space, beside the window, etc." And according to Lyotard (1991):

> We arrive at a new locus of the "psychological" which is no longer interiority, but intentionality— that is, the relation between the subject and the situation, it being understood that this relation does not unite two separable poles, but on the contrary that the ego, like the situation, is definable only in and by this relationship. (p. 80)

Mind-body or inner-outer dualism—along with consciousness as a receptacle for objects of the world or as a representation of an outer world— are all rejected and replaced with relationships. Consciousness is the process of being present to something else. Similarly rejected is the explanation of psychological events in terms of physiology. For example, Giorgi (1976) notes of the trace theory of memory, "memory always involves the awareness of the past as past from the present" (p. 305). If memory were the activation of a trace, the memory should appear in the present as its trace does, yet it appears to be in the past. He notes further that researchers have searched for the trace in the neuron and the synapse, in RNA and in DNA. "Thus in the history of the search, one moves nonchalantly from anatomical, to functional, to chemical conceptions without blinking" (p. 306). Arcaya (1989) gives an extended argument against the notion of memory traces and stored memory and indicates that phenomenology replaces the assumption of memory storage with memory as part of a temporal context that involves a way of relating to the world. The notion that the brain is an interpreter of an outside world

also comes in for criticism: Kruger (1981) insists that he is not sitting in his brain looking out at the world and interpreting it. Rather, he is present in the world, a part of it, interacting with people and other components of it.

A key concept, one used by Lyotard in the quotation above, is "intentionality," the word referring to relatedness. The concept of intentionality comes from the scholastics of the Middle Ages, especially Thomas Aquinas, and is derived from Latin *intendere,* meaning "to stretch forth." In this view a mind is directed to or intends its object, which is not necessarily a real thing but is what the mental act is about. In the nineteenth century Franz Brentano (1838–1907), a docent and priest at the University of Vienna,[1] employed the concept in his psychology: the mental content is physical but the act of judging, representing, or valuing it comes from the nonphysical soul. *Intentionality* refers to the psychical, and *extensionality* (having extension or dimensions in space) refers to the physical. Edmund Husserl (1859–1938), a professor of philosophy and mathematician by training, used intentionality in his development of phenomenological philosophy.[2]

For Husserl, phenomenology was the attempt to describe the essence of consciousness of things rather than the features of the physical world. This means that even purely imaginary things such as mermaids and ghosts, as well as objects such as trees and the sublime sounds of symphony orchestras, could be included. Essence is what makes things what they are. It is what gives existence and stability to things and determines their

---

1. He later resigned both his position at the university and his priesthood rather than accept the doctrine of papal infallibility promulgated in 1870.

2. For the psychologists Merleau-Ponty and Sartre (see below), it included not just cognitive acts but the relationships between one's body and an object prior to any verbalization or other recognition, for the body has a rapport with a situation and an understanding of its possibilities, even prior to explicitly recognizing it or reflecting on it. For example, one jumps out of the path of a moving car seen only in peripheral vision; one has a reply to a verbal statement prior to reflecting upon it. Intentionality also came to mean a direct dialectic, a bidirectionality between person and world. See Eckartsberg (1989) for the evolution of "intentionality."

characteristics. To determine the essence of the experience of things one must suspend or "bracket" (as brackets are used in algebra) all biases and other habitual modes of thinking and engage in an intense concentration on the object. By this means one obtains an intuition of the essence (hence "phenomenology"). This is the first step—separating the experience from all assumptions of causality and existence. The second step is to analyze the essence by examining the components and how they are related. A third, "eidetic reduction," is to apprehend the essence by surveying or imagining particular instances of something more general: one imagines form, color, extension of the object or any similar object and thereby apprehends seeing not just that object, a dog for example, but any visual object. Thus, the intrinsic structures of the experience are revealed, and this structure is the essence of experience. Finally, one describes the essence. The vagueness of this procedure led to varied interpretations among Husserl's followers.

Experience, Husserl argues, is not *caused* by an external object or stimulus that is independent of the experience. Instead, what one experiences is a meaning quality that comprises an interdependence of the thing and the person. A slice of lemon on one's plate means sourness and flavoring; this meaning is a quality of the person's experience with the lemon and the presence of the lemon in that particular context. Similarly, anger is not something in itself but is a way of relating to something. Anger is always anger *about* something, not isolated physiology of glands or action of the nervous system.

But phenomenology is not just subjective experiences or the particular point of view of each individual. It is, according to Husserl and his followers, a way of obtaining absolute knowledge through intuiting the essence of conscious events. One may intuit that a square has four right angles of ninety degrees each, and this can be ascertained as a universal, eternal truth by anyone in any culture at any time period. Consciousness along with mathematics and other essences, he claims, is not in time and space as is the natural world.

Phenomenologists argue that psychology commits an error when it treats mind or consciousness as connected with the body and as a part of the natural world that obeys natural law. Psychology cannot experiment on the essence of consciousness, but philosophy can do this and at the same time provide a foundation for empirical psychology that will enable psychology to become scientific. This is where bracketing comes in. One suspends the *attitude* of a natural world (not belief in the *existence* of a natural world) to achieve pure consciousness. By stripping away all of our presuppositions about something's existence or nonexistence we take on a new attitude or new focus in which essences can be apprehended. This Husserl calls "transcendental reduction" in which one no longer studies the object of consciousness but focuses on essences which provide meaning to those objects and events. One can, for example, reflect on a visual object such as a book and—by imagining various characteristics of it such as its weight, its appearance from various angles, its print with readable characters, and its shape—can intuit its essence and that of similar objects. This procedure apprehends the process by which the characteristics of objects come to have a unity and wholeness to us despite their diverse features, features by which we know the object and which persist on subsequent contacts with it. These characteristic meanings differ from the natural ones that the chemist or physicist would describe.

As an example, consider figure 12.1. The investigator could, following a physicalistic model, ask participants to measure the length of each arrow shaft and report the results. This would destroy the illusion that would occur in a phenomenological procedure. In another example, Purkinje, a Czech physiologist, observed a color shift in his

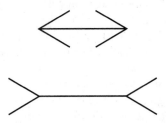

Figure 12.1 The Müller-Lyer Illusion. To the phenomenologist what is important is not knowing that the shafts are of equal length but recognizing how they appear to us.

flower garden at dusk. Reds turned to grays while blues became lighter and retained their color after other colors had faded. By holding a neutral attitude—bracketing or accepting what he saw instead of interpreting what he "knew" to be reds and blues—he discovered the true essence under those lighting conditions. This color shift could not be learned from readings of instruments because it is strictly organismic. Today it is known as the Purkinje effect and has applications in studying what colors show up most or least in varying intensities of light. Phenomenologists cite this finding as an example of the fruits of the phenomenological method and as indispensable to psychology (although Purkinje did not knowingly use such a method).

Attitudes about natural events arise from a particular time and context or a particular theory. For example, Newtonian physics considered gravity to be a force acting at a distance between bodies in space; general relativity physics considers gravity equivalent to acceleration in a space distorted by bodies of mass. In contrast to these theories, the knowledge of essences—such as the apparent difference of arrow-shaft lengths in the Müller-Lyer illusion—is, according to Husslerians, free of all theories, opinions, assumptions, biases, cultural beliefs, and so forth. It is absolute, nonrelative, and eternal. A stone age woman or a Wall Street broker would intuit the same essence. Some phenomenological psychologists reject the claims of absoluteness (for example, Snyder, 1988); some even reject Husserl altogether (for example, Henley, 1988). Still others maintain that phenomenological philosophy with its trancendental reduction (often referred to as "phenomenological reduction" or merely "reduction") is a necessary foundation for scientific psychology (for example, Davidson, 1988; Jennings, 1986).

Toward the end of his life Husserl began developing a phenomenological psychology in which he accepted experimental methods as aids to the phenomenological method. But he always rejected the collection of correlated facts as making for an empirical psychology. For him it was the discovery of the meanings of things as people orient toward the world that remained paramount, life as it is lived.

Husserl's student, Martin Heidegger (1889–1976), pointed out that there is no consciousness apart from the world and no method for finding absolute certainty. Heidegger discarded transcendental reductions and argued that humans are bound to the world—they interact with their world in social environments. Consequently, the most fundamental things we know are from the community—communal knowing—and from day to day practical living. Knowing is not individual. Philosophy derives from this communal knowing and is not itself a beginning point of knowledge as philosophers have supposed. However, he retained the phenomenological principle by maintaining that philosophy is not based on empirical information but on insight that is self-evident from the structure of experience.

THE FRENCH CONNECTION

Merleau-Ponty

It was in France that a more direct effort to apply phenomenology to psychology was developed. The principal figure in this event was Maurice Merleau-Ponty (1908–1961) who held an appointment in psychology and child pedagogy at the Sorbonne in Paris and later received an appointment in philosophy at the Collège de France. (Jean Piaget later filled his position at the Sorbonne and replaced his phenomenological psychology of children with structuralistic/cognitive child psychology.) It was his work in phenomenology that came to the attention of American psychologists. His book, *The Structure of Behavior* (1963), as the title suggests, has important points in common with behaviorism. However, this is not the mechanistic behaviorism of Watson but behaviorism as broadly conceived. In Kvale and Grenness's interpretation (1967), behavior is "man's meaningful relatedness to the world" and in such a relationship "neither can be defined independent of the other" (p. 137).

Merleau-Ponty's major goal was to study the relationship between consciousness and nature, and he found consciousness to be a form of behavior. He rejected the assumption of consciousness as pure subjectivity. To him behavior is part of a structured context and replaces the mind-body distinction. Structure refers to the dialectic process or relationship as part of a context. These relationships involve a more or less stable form. For example, joy will differ in its character from one situation and one time to another. It is never the same twice, but it has a meaningful commonality, form, or structure that runs through all instances.

In his analysis, a presumed transcendental mind and mechanistic reactions to stimuli give way to an interaction or dialectical interchange between the person and that person's world. That is, rather than assuming a ghostly guiding agent inside the organism or responses caused by conditioning, he looks for concrete interchanges between the person and the person's world. The organization of the human body with its particular sensory organs, mobility, and capabilities for thinking, perceiving, and the like select for the behaviors that occur in this circular dialectic. These behaviors in turn provide further selection to the body's participation and to the qualities of the behaviors. This dialectic process comprises meanings.[3]

Rather than a stimulus that elicits a response. Merleau-Ponty finds that one cannot identify a stimulus apart from a response, as for example in a painful stimulus. Further, the stimulus is actually both "the physical event as it is in itself, on the one hand, and the situation as it is 'for the organism,' on the other, with only the latter being decisive in the reactions" (p. 129). In other words, it is not the physical properties of the stimulus that are important in behavior but what the object or event means to the person. Fine wine may mean a delightful tasting experience to a wine connoisseur but an evil liquid to a Muslim. Its physical properties such as water, alcohol, and esters have no direct relevance to the dialectic process.

Just as stimulus separates into two distinct characteristics, so too does response. The "sum of the movements actually executed" have an "objective relation with the physical world" whereas these same movements as "behavior so-called" have an "internal articulation as a kinetic melody gifted with a meaning" (p. 130). That is, movements as mere movements are physicalistic and devoid of meaning but movements as behavior (in interdependence with the stimulus as meaning, presumably) are a part of the meaningful world, the world as experienced. Both stimulus and response "are linked internally by their common participation in a structure" (p. 130) involving a circular process rather than cause and effect. A stimulus does not cause a response, but the two interact with each other and give rise to ever changing meanings.

Merleau-Ponty's *Phenomenology of Perception* is aimed more at providing a basis for his philosophy than at establishing a model for psychology. Nevertheless, it provides much that is relevant to psychology; and, like *Structure of Behavior,* it draws heavily on research available at that time from psychology, psychopathology, and clinical medicine (especially on brain injuries), often with a point by point reference to that research.

He discards Husserl's bracketing, for experience of the world is primary, and perception provides this primary experience even though it is limited in this capacity. Because we necessarily operate from a body that has its own position in space, we always view things from that limited perspective. Therefore, we are always limited in what we can know. Nevertheless, it is perception, he holds, that provides "a window" to meanings. It is a way of understanding the dialectic between consciousness and the world. Fundamental to perceiving is attending. In an objectivist's world, he notes, there

---

3. Husserl referred to our meaning-making activity as the "intentional arrow of consciousness." This comes from two sources: the *inner horizon* of our consciousness with its domain of meanings and the *outer horizon* of objects and the meaning context in which they are embedded. Although Merleau-Ponty adopted the concept of a dialectic to indicate this relationship, Kwant (1966) holds that near the end of his life he replaced dialectic, a kind of duality, with reversibility, and interchangeability or intercommunicability from one mode of responding to another—touch to sight, perception to speech, and even reversibility between different persons. Further, "reversibility manifests itself in the relationship between man and world: man is part of the world, but he is a part which possesses the whole . . . There is an interpenetration of man and world" (pp. 90–91).

would be no way for us to attend to one object or situation rather than another. But the experience of attention establishes figure on what was previously ground. Now we see the bird in the tree as figure where we previously saw only the tree, the ground. Attending provides the unity of new meanings but does not constitute new meanings or provide for their origin. New meanings occur in perception as happens in examining a cube (treated primarily in *Structure of Behavior*). In a phenomenological reduction, one finds that a cube never presents itself as having six sides with equal angles at each corner. Instead, "it presents itself in a series of profiles, each of which announces the cube in its entirety but without revealing it" (Brannon, 1967, p. 29). What it shows is affected by its context, such as lighting, the viewing angle, and the viewer's distance from it. Never does it present itself as a six-sided figure. That would be possible only in a completely disembodied consciousness. By redefining and recognizing the object and the consciousness of it in terms of the experience in which both occur, one can function phenomenologically.

Rather than regarding perception as a product of the body's physiology, Merleau-Ponty regards the body as providing the condition for perception of objects and the meanings that come from the perception. An object is a structure for consciousness, and consciousness is always of some object. Consciousness of something and the structure for consciousness that the object provides would each cease to be without the other.[4] This is a dialectical relationship. Each implies the other, its opposite. The body is completely constituted only with consciousness. The object then is a counterpoint to the body and to existence in which the body provides stabilized structure. Meaning is as much a part of the body as it is of the object: in Merleau-Ponty's expression, "j'en suis" (I am of it). Giorgi (1975) makes the same point when he says, "Sleekness belongs to the airplane as much as it

does to my perceiving it" (p. 207). It is not that one is objective and the other subjective. Both are objective in their own ways.

In Merleau-Ponty's analysis of the senses, each sense—taste, vision, hearing, smell—involves a different behavior structure which cannot be interchanged but can nevertheless interpenetrate one another. We look at a drum and see its loudness. We read a maxim and see its lesson. We see strength in a steel beam and weight in a boulder; we hear fire in a "hot" trumpet; we listen to a lively rhythm and feel energized. Perceptual synthesis comes through the body, not through thought, not through interpretation. Although we see our world through two separate eyes, the single view of that world we experience is not created by transformation by neurons or because we think about the merger of two images or reinterpret two images as one but because of body organization as it relates to the perceived world. Intersensory events (hearing fire in the sound of a trumpet) involve a perceptual synthesis similar to that of intrasensory events (seeing a single object with two eyes). Sensing involves the whole body but particularly the sense modality involved. No interpreter—neuronal or intellectual—is needed. Instead, there is a unity involving visual intentionality with the object seen. Merleau-Ponty refers to "the roots of the mind in its body and in its world" (1964b, p. 3) in opposition to perception as a result of mechanical actions of stimuli on the sense organs and to consciousness or mind as an interpretive agent sitting in the body. Perhaps a statement about color expresses as well as any the thoroughgoing interdependence of the body and its world that Merleau-Ponty emphasizes: "colors . . . are themselves different modalities of our co-existence with the world" (1964b, p. 5).

An important question in understanding perception is that of *constancies*. In the case of size constancy, for example, why do we see an adult at a distance not as small but as the same size as when the person is close? For Merleau-Ponty it is not because a disembodied mind or brain is reinterpreting the size as the distance changes. Rather, it is because the perception as lived, as

---

4. Kwant (1963) notes that he refers to consciousness as "'a presence of man to himself'" (p. 228) but that he provides no analysis of it.

experienced, is one of same-size adult at different distances against the appropriate ground. He (1964a) treats a number of other constancies in a similar manner.

The role of illumination in perception is not, he insists, one of the brain converting light waves into color or into an object. We don't see illumination; we see *according to* it; it is a medium for those things we do see. Illumination mediates color and provides a condition of seeing.

Because he holds that the person and the person's world comprise one another, he finds that psychological events do not involve cause-effect relationships. The world does not cause the person to behave. This means that phenomenological psychology does not use the experimental study of cause and effect; and for the same reason rejects independent and dependent variables, control groups, and testing of hypotheses. Hypotheses imply that some hidden condition is causing the observed event, and so this cause-effect assumption, too, is replaced with descriptions of the lived world.

Merleau-Ponty approaches thinking as expressing experience we have previously lived (*Structure of Behavior*). However, it not only involves previous meanings but also gives new meanings to things. Thinking, he concludes, is not located in us but is intentional with the thing thought about and therefore has no location except as a relationship— but the relationship excludes itself. That is, it does not reflect back on itself. Like perception and other psychological behaviors, thinking is not a product of neurons, though it depends on the body. It too is a dialectical process.

His analysis of these psychological events indicates that he attempts to avoid both mind-body dualism and physiological reductionism in favor of an organism-environment relationship. "Truth does not 'inhabit' only the 'inner man,' or more accurately, there is no inner man, man is in the world, and only in the world does he know himself" (Merleau-Ponty, 1962, p. xi).

Sartre

Some of Merleau-Ponty's work was done in association with the playwright, novelist, and existentialist philosopher Jean-Paul Sartre who was also at the Sorbonne. Existentialism focuses not on essences of things, as in Husserl's phenomenology, but on *existence* as experienced by each individual, especially nonrational experience. It abjures the lawful, predictable, cause-and-effect world of physics in favor of the personal, the human. Physical items *possess* existence but humans *are* existence. Our existence is what we are, our combined acts. For Husserl, essence comes before existence; but for Sartre, existence comes first and all else flows from it. That is, all human characteristics result from human existence. Humans are what they are because of their existence. It is existence that is concrete while all else is abstraction. Human existence is always in the process of change. A person is continually becoming, continually changing and developing.

Heidegger was a major influence on Sartre and others. Although he disclaimed the appellation of existentialist, he nevertheless exemplified some of the philosophy's features. He succeeded Husserl at the University of Freiburg and renamed intentionality "being-in-the-world" or, in the original German, *Dasein*, "being (*sein*) there (*da*)." The study of philosophy, Heidegger held, is not the study of consciousness but the study of being. People are present to the world. He emphasized "being" as a verb as opposed to "being" as a noun. Because people are alienated from being as the action of living (being-in-the-world) and closely bound to being as objects, the task of psychology is to examine the mode of being-in-the-world of each individual. If people remain alienated from their own being-in-the world, they are fragmented and may become psychotic. Because they find themselves in an incomprehensible world and facing inevitable death, they feel anguish and dread. They try to overcome this dread by cloaking it in conformity and conventional thought and speech, in which case they are not being authentic. To be authentic and free, humans must be true to themselves by accepting the subjective meaning of death and its nonbeing. Anxiety is rooted in the fear of the nonbeing that comes with death and in the unwillingness to confront it. Once we accept our finitude we can begin to comprehend our true existence as opposed to the nonexistence of death. Heidegger also examined the relation of human existence to care and mood, arguing that we do not have moods; we do not *feel* joy or sadness. Rather, we *are* joy or sadness.

What is the meaning of human existence, Sartre asked? His conclusion was that neither human existence nor the world's existence has any meaning whatsoever. There is no reason why either should exist at all. There is no possibility for a god to exist; in fact, a god would be a contradiction. Humans create God, and the essence of God is human existence. Yet humans and their consciousness exist, he declares, and this is totally inexplicable.

According to Sartre, what is most characteristic of humans is their ability to make choices. They are free. In fact, for him humans do not *possess* freedom; they *are* freedom. They are doomed to continually make choices and reap the consequences. Because God does not exist, humans are alone and must look not to a god for divine guidance but to themselves for decisions and the consequences of those decisions. This is an enormous burden which they may wish to escape. Exercising their freedom can lead to anxiety and despair, which they must learn to live with. By making decisions, however, they obtain personal growth and self-definition. One form of existential psychotherapy deals with the despair that existentialists believe comes from recognition of one's freedom in various contexts.

Among Sartre's books are *Psychology of Imagination* (1948) and *The Emotions* (1953). To him, images are acts, not things, and consist of consciousness of things. There are no images in consciousness, but images are a *type* of consciousness. As for emotions, they provide a means of transforming the harshness of reality into an unreal world. One may react to a painful situation, for example, by denying it or by other unrealistic reactions. One may react to a knotted shoe lace by angrily jerking or tearing at it rather than dealing with it rationally. An orderly relationship can give way to an irrational one. Phenomenological reduction, he holds, allows one to understand why one reacts in emotional ways rather than in a more reflective manner. Here again is the seed of a therapeutic procedure. Sartre's existentialist task was to interpret the individual's history of life-choices as they are embedded in contexts. Existentialism turns to "emotions and [the] burning questions of the meaning of life, suffering, and death . . . [and] unique individual problems of everyday existence . . . [It] centers its attention on man as he exists in the world and on his relation to the world and to his fellow men" (Misiak & Sexton, 1973, p. 81). While phenomenology restricts itself to what it calls "consciousness" (perception, memory, thinking, etc.), existentialism puts these in a context of life-as-it-is-lived.

Sartre, Merleau-Ponty, and Heidigger regarded human reality as being-in-the-world. However, Sartre posited two kinds of reality—(a) the nonhuman that is inanimate and deterministic, which he called *en soi* (being-in-itself), and (b) pure consciousness of human reality, which he called *pour soi* (being-for-itself). Thus, he held to a form of psychophysical dualism.

PHENOMENOLOGICAL PSYCHOLOGY IN THE UNITED STATES

In the United States the center for this brand of psychology is primarily at Duquesne University in Pittsburgh, Pennsylvania, where Adrian van Kaam from the Netherlands established a psychology department expressly to teach phenomenological psychology. The department launched the *Journal of Phenomenological Psychology* in 1971 and in the same year began publishing the *Duquesne Studies in Phenomenological Psychology*. Much of the content of these volumes deals with methodological and measurement issues in phenomenological and clinical psychology. In 1983 the fourth volume celebrated the twenty-fifth anniversary of the department. It reported that the graduates were teaching in twenty-five institutions of higher learning in the United States—an impressive record, especially when one considers that most graduates have become clinicians. The University of Dallas in Irving, Texas, also offers phenomenological psychology.

One of this psychology's American proponents is Amedeo Giorgi, who describes its content as contextualized and situated experiential-behavioral relationships of man with himself, the world, and others. Thus the basic unit of psychological analysis is the situation and one must always begin with the concrete behavior and experience of the person in a given situation, but these must not be understood merely physically. The future horizons (i.e., the intentions, expectations, etc.) and the history (memories, habits, and past interpretations) of both behavior and experience *belong* to the concrete situation that forms the basic unit. Similarly, the network of lateral relations with significant others that influence specific behavior also belongs to the situation. Concreteness if defined by what spontaneously belongs to a situation according to the subject rather than what is merely perceptually present to the researcher. (Giorgi, 1976, p. 330)

The phrase "behavior and experience" is used regularly in this system and seems to imply a mind-body dualism. However, the two nouns are not used additively as the word "and" might suggest. They are perspectives of either the observer or the actor. Behavior is what I do from your point of view; experience is what I do from my point of view. The "and" signifies a dialectical relation between the observer and the actor involving changing perspectives between them. Experience and behavior involve "one reality, human action, seen in two different ways" (Romanyshyn, 1978, p. 34). This is further suggested in Giorgi's reference to "contextualized and situated experiential-behavioral relationships of man with himself, the world, and others" in the quotation above. From the perspective of the observer, the action may be either visible or invisible and the same is true of the actor.

The study of child development has also been used to question the interior-exterior or mind-body distinction. Sims (1993) relates that children do not distinguish inside from outside (mind vs. body), and their drawings illustrate the meanings the world has to a child, those things that they choose to represent and the way they represent it:

for example, fingers coming from the head, a house with two ends visible, a cat with two legs extending straight out from each side of its body. The world is

> shot through with vectors of meaning, rather than built up out of the elements of conceptual thought . . . Merleau-Ponty's notion of the "lived body" implies that we experience our bodies not as anatomical, scientific, outside shells to our psyches, but as powers that interact with the environment . . . The child living her body does not experience it as an object, but as entwined with a situation in a meaningful way. There is no subjective inside nor an objective outside to the lived body, but a flow of gestures between self and other. (p. 36)

Sometimes phenomenological psychology is combined with existentialism for a system with the unwieldy name of existential-phenomenological psychology. The "existential" part refers to strictly human characteristics of existing such as freedom, hope, love, happiness, despair, worry, pride, and determination. The phenomenological part refers to the descriptive method of determining the structure, essence, or form of the meaningful world. The world and the person have no existence apart from one another. They coexist and coconstitute each other, just as the famous reversible face and vase coconstitute one another. Without one the other has no meaning (Valle & King, 1978).

IMPLICIT POSTULATES

As the founder and major figure in phenomenological psychology, Merleau-Ponty is the logical choice for a list of postulates for that system. Some of his postulates are fairly clear from his writings but others are difficult to infer. The following list is quite tentative.

Protopostulates (general guiding assumptions about science)

1. Nature is not comprised of everything in total interdependence so that distinctions do not ex-

ist, nor as a composite of isolated processes. It consists of structures that involve continuous relationships that are properties of wholes.
2. Science seeks laws about these structures.
3. Structure and law are dialectical or reciprocal counterpoints, not separate beings.

Metapostulates (supportive assumptions for a particular science)

1. Psychological events are not reducible to biology, chemistry, or physics; but these do provide conditions for behavior.
2. The world has meanings as well as physical characteristics. The meanings are of primary concern to psychology.
3. No internal or external determiners are relevant to a science of psychology.

Postulates (subject matter assumptions)

1. Behavior is not mechanical responses to stimuli, nor is it caused by an internal mind.
2. Behavior is an interaction, a dialectical exchange, a relationship.
3. Meaning behaviors consist of relationships between person and object, but the person is more important than the relationship.
4. Objectivity and subjectivity differ only as frames of reference.

The inconsistency of postulate 3 with the other postulates is due to the construct of intentionality in which directionality is primarily from the person to the object, rather than a true dialectical exchange.

RESEARCH

Perhaps the most celebrated research using a phenomenological viewpoint in an experimental setting was conducted by Albert Michotte (1881–1965) at the University of Louvain in Belgium. Michotte studied perceived causality. In one experiment he projected two spots of light on a screen. Depending on how they came together, joined, and parted, subjects saw one or the other

spot as causing the actions of the other. He discovered several principles including *launching* and *entrainment*. The impression of launching occurs if object A moves against B and comes to rest while B moves off in the same direction as A was previously moving. Subjects see A as shoving B. Entrainment occurs if A continues its movement along with B's; one object seems to have captured the other and carried it along with itself. But the effects vary under different patterns of stimulus conditions that Michotte explored very carefully. He was able to show the character of perceived causal meanings. Others have been able to replicate and thereby validate Michotte's findings.

What was important was not what the subjects knew about causality in terms of laws of physics involving mass, velocity, and momentum. The objects of observation in these experiments were merely surfaces of light. What is important is how things are experienced. Causality, Michotte indicates, exists phenomenologically apart from knowledge of physics and sometimes even in contradiction to physics. He concludes that perception is not an interpretation (we see, then we mentally interpret what we see) but a way of directly experiencing (Michotte, 1963, 1991). In another series of experiments he examined apparent permanence. He showed under what conditions an object that goes out of sight—for example, moves behind a screen—is still perceived as existing (having permanence), and under what conditions it evaporates or goes out of existence. Still other work shows the way in which people perceive a two-dimensional picture as three-dimensional. Because the stimulus pattern accounts for this perception, no cognitive interpreter need be assumed. This work closely accords with the later work of Gibson's ecological perception (Gibson, 1979; see chapter 13, p. 374). Michotte's work shows the way toward a rigorous methodology of studying meaning, which involves both phenomenology and experimental procedures and which could not be accomplished without either one.

In the case of decision making, the phenomenological method yields different results than the method of cognitive psychology. The cognitivist uses the experimental method to find the rule or strategy that a person uses in making a choice. One such finding is that a person assigns attributes to each possible choice, sums them up, and selects the one with the highest sum. The phenomenologist regards this as ignoring context as well as historical and cultural connections in the abstract strategies that result from the experimenter's imposed structures. At the same time, the results fail to adequately reflect the person's experiences of making choices. This is not surprising inasmuch as the cognitivist sets up the experimental situation to seek only strategies, and is unlikely to find alternatives or additional operations. In a phenomenological study the investigator attempts to describe the *process* of choosing by asking the subjects to think out loud while he records their reports (Karlsson, 1987, 1988, 1992). An analysis of the reports shows that the use of strategies is only one of several operations or phases. These are, first, seeking and clarifying information; then evaluating and comparing alternatives; then rejecting and choosing alternatives; and, finally, strengthening the choice.

Most cognitive psychologists consider thinking, perceiving, and remembering as the processing of information, a concept borrowed from computer science. They also hold that the thinking involved in chess playing can be simulated with computers and have given heavy emphasis to such computer programs. To test the similarity of computers that play chess with humans who play chess, Aanstoos (1983, 1987) asked skilled chess players to think out loud as they played. He found that human approaches were quite different from those of computers. Computers try out millions of possible combinations of moves and outcomes in order to make an advantageous selection. Even those computers specially programmed to search more selectively check out several thousand possibilities. In contrast, human chess players adopt a perspective or plan and consider a few possible alternative moves within it. Computers rely on predetermined guidelines whereas humans use these only as questions to be answered negatively or positively and sometimes to be reconsidered later.

Finally, the computer uses symbols for manipulation and mathematical calculations, whereas human chess players use symbols to refer to the total relationships among the chess pieces.

Phenomenological research has taken up a variety of topics. The two preceding studies used a method of thinking out loud and were designed to test assumptions of cognition. Sometimes the thinking out loud method and the analysis of audio or video tapes is referred to as an existential-phenomenological method. The analysis of texts and other works such as those of literature, art, ceremonies, films, plays, autobiography, and television is called hermeneutical-phenomenological psychology. It takes its name from the hermeneutics (from Greek *Hermes,* the messenger god, and *hermeneutes,* an interpreter) in which scholars attempt to work out critical explanations or analyses in biblical texts. (See Eckartsberg [1986] for an account of these methodologies and examples of the research.) Hermeneutics has also been extended to discourse and to psychotherapy (see p. 357).

The following will suggest a few of the many additional topics that phenomenological psychology has addressed. Rahilly (1993) used the bracketing and analysis method to study experiences of authenticity. In this case, the researcher used an existential-phenomenological method to study an existential concept. Kvale (1983) interviewed and recorded Danish children about their school grades and analyzed them for six phases of meanings. He compared this with the qualitative procedure used by marketing researchers in which interviews of consumers are used to determine hidden meanings such as the value of a car beyond mere transportation—prestige, sex appeal, machismo—and these themes were then used effectively in advertising.

In a study of shame, Ablamowicz (1992) tape recorded separate interviews with each of eight graduate students. He then listened to the tapes for developing a phenomenological description followed by a reductive analysis and then a phenomenological interpretation. By examining the phenomenology of shame rather than shame as a principle or substance, he found that it is not primarily an experience to be avoided but a part of one's life world, a universal natural experience, the recognition of which can facilitate interpersonal communication. Daniluk (1993) studied women's experience of sexuality by tape recording their discussions of it. Two female graduate students, one of whom was a participant, analyzed the contents. The two then met with the researcher, also a participant, to synthesize and integrate the themes the two reviewers had extracted. Finally, the original participants responded to these themes, further refining them. Among the several findings was the fact that the women felt that medicine and religion, each with its male-dominated orientation, had been "severely disenabling" to them.

Seamon (1982, 1987) has reviewed phenomenological research and methodological contributions to environmental psychology. Q methodology provides still another type of procedure. Because the verbal limitations of young children make it impossible for them to adequately express their experiences, Q methodology involving the sorting of pictures into piles of "most like me" to "least like me" and factor analyzing the results provides an objective measure of children's subjectivity (Taylor, Delprato, & Knapp, 1994). Finally, a survey of forty-eight papers on schizophrenia published in the *British Journal of Psychiatry,* showed that twenty-four were of a phenomenological nature (Mortimer, 1992). The employment of a phenomenological research orientation with its somewhat varied methodologies seems to be gaining an ever-growing following.

PSYCHOTHERAPY

Because the phenomenological approach uses immediate experience as a "given" and as a starting point, it comes before explanation. To recognize the essential nature of anything, including problems of adjustment or behavior pathology, we must observe the behavior before we try to explain it or discover a cause (just as we must see colors, smell objects, and experience illusions before we try to explain them). In the clinical domain we must first determine what the drug addict or

the depressive is experiencing and then seek an explanation.

A commentary by a schizophrenic (Tomecek, 1990) illustrates this theme. This individual criticized an article in *American Psychologist* (the flagship of the American Psychological Association) in which the writer called for the elimination of schizophrenia. Tomecek does not want his schizophrenia eliminated.

> I like it. I need it in order to survive, and it does not necessarily come into conflict with the rest of society, for I have found positive ways of dealing with it, and of enriching it through my art and my writing . . . To me, normalization and conformity are not acceptable because they would necessarily reduce my creative abilities, my potential to find the joy in life that I now experience according to my personal modes of learning, communicating, and living. (p. 550)

He rejects the medical model which considers the schizophrenic primarily in terms of biology and which subjected him to medication and shock treatment that nearly drove him to suicide. He also rejects the notion of rehabilitation. He wants only the help that will enable him to meet his needs and minimize his stress. This viewpoint can be understood only by seeking it from the person involved, not from those who would impose their own viewpoints. And such a client-centered view as opposed to a therapist-centered view is necessary for the development of an appropriate explanation (if explanation is needed at all) and treatment plan.

The same point is made by Lora and Reba Schappell, conjoined ("Siamese") twins who are attached at the head and who face in different directions. Despite the awkwardness of the situation, they have no desire to be separated (Angier, 1997). Such a refusal is difficult to understand for surgeons and sometimes parents who want to bring "normality" to the individuals' lives. Should such congenital abnormalities as ambiguous genitals and deafness be repaired on children too young to make a decision? Some later resent the repairs or refuse repairs at a later age. Should the genital mutilation of circumcision be performed on males before they can give consent? Considerable protest—even from the United Nations—has arisen over the forced genital mutilation of girls that occurs in some parts of the world. The phenomenological perspective of the person involved bears hearing.

Phenomenological psychology has remained largely an academic discipline and has given only minor attention to psychotherapy. Existentialism, however, has been extensively involved in therapy. Although no clear guidelines and no standard techniques have emerged for conducting this therapy, it has developed some fairly uniform concepts that use such terms as "existential neurosis," "becoming," "authenticity," and "encounter." "Existential neurosis" is the living of an inauthentic existence because of a failure to find meaning in life. "Becoming" means developing into someone better than one was before. "Authenticity" means being aware of existence, both the way things were and the way they are; a more extended meaning includes making one's own decisions, exercising one's own freedom to live a meaningful life in the face of the dread and anxiety that freedom brings.[5] "Encounter" refers to the relation between therapist and client, in which "something totally new is revealed, new horizons open, one's [view of life] is revised, and sometimes the whole personality is restructured" (Ellenberger, 1958, p. 119).

According to May (1958), an important pitfall is guilt. He holds that it arises from failure to fulfill responsibilities. Because recognition of one's freedom to choose brings dread, the client must learn to accept dread, guilt, and anguish as being-in-the-world—that is, life as it is lived, the meaning that life holds. The client must exercise the now recognized freedom of choice and must not let others make decisions for him/her. To do so is to live a life of inauthenticity. Recognition of death as nonbeing or nonexistence also creates anxiety.

In addition to freedom, guilt, and recognition of death, there are two additional conditions of existence: isolation and meaninglessness (Yalom, 1980). Isolation involves the aloneness that one feels in an indifferent world. A sense of meaninglessness arises from the lack of absolutes in the world: transcendental gods, truths, givens. These conditions of existence occur not separately but interdependently, and therapy must deal with them in whatever form or relationships they arise for each individual.

Where psychoanalysis emphasizes removing resistance and repression, existential analysis emphasizes removing the blocks to freedom and potentials (May, 1958). It does not cure any crisis, solve any problem, or seek any remedy, nor does it regard the client as pathological. Its goal is "to make manifest or real [the client's] own existential potential for authenticity" (Anderson, 1978, p. 333). Once one can accept one's anxiety and dread and make decisions (become authentic), one can find meaning.

Victor Frankl (1963) developed what he called *logotherapy* (Greek *logos* = spirit or meaning). It is also known as the "Third Viennese School of Psychotherapy" (the first two are Freud's and Adler's approaches). As a survivor of Nazi death camps, Frankl learned that the final freedom that every human has is the ability to choose an attitude. He observed that among those the Nazis did not execute, the ones who clung to a desire to live survived disease and starvation. Those who lost all meaning in life deteriorated and died.

Frankl believes that suffering is a necessary part of life and gives meaning to it. His approach to therapy is to search for the meaning of life, the meaning of one's own existence in which one will obtain a rational understanding of emotional pain, of suffering. That understanding will give meaning to the suffering. A tool to facilitate this search is tragic optimism with which one converts suffering into experience that has meaning. This helps one develop a positive and healthy outlook on those experiences. Because no universal meaning exists, each individual must find his or her

---

5. Rahilly (1993) reviews a variety of meanings of "authenticity" that various writers have given, most of them closer to the usages of humanistic psychology than to those of existentialism.

own. And there will be many of these as life continues.

Frankl encourages his clients to set goals for their lives. Setting and working toward goals mobilizes creativity and energy. Striving for goals and seeking meaning require a spiritual (*logos*) quality, he believes—spiritual in the sense of will and self-dependence. It is spiritual health that enables survival and recovery in the face of adversity.

Another widely known form of existential psychotherapy is the *existential analysis* of Ludwig Binswanger, a Swiss psychiatrist. Binswanger was originally a psychoanalyst but came under the influence of Heidegger and incorporated his concepts. This therapy examines the client's "existential modes," the relationships the client establishes with the world and with other humans. The therapist encourages the client to become authentic, to behave in a manner that is true to himself and thereby become free.

A variation on existential psychotherapy is hermeneutical psychotherapy. Because Ricoeur (1970, 1974) has argued that Husserl's procedure does not provide pure essences of things, psychotherapy cannot use this procedure and expect to apprehend the real. Therefore, it is necessary to deemphasize the real, turn to what the client has narrated, and try to understand it. Meanings, assumptions, and preconceptions may be hidden but acted upon. These need to be discovered in their context and articulated. It is often necessary even to construct a new meaning. This new meaning, when it is coherent and plausible, helps the patient relate his or her beliefs, dreams, feelings, and perceptions to other events. Although "meanings are created rather than recovered" (Bouchard & Guérette, 1991, p. 392), objective truth and phenomenological truth do play roles in that they provide the context for meanings that can be developed in a client's narration. Consciousness is the speech of the narrative. Through a dialog between client and therapist, the goal of hermeneutical therapy is "to galvanize the client's life energies toward healing" (p. 387).

In 1979 existentialists founded Burch House in Littleton, New Hampshire as a residential center for disturbed adults that would employ existential principles such as self-responsibility and future-directedness (Symmes, 1989). Clients and staff share the daily living chores. Because clients are involved in scheduling and doing normal activities, they maintain their skills and initiative in these matters and avoid the dependency and lethargy of institutionalization. Psychotherapy is non-authoritarian and therefore offers no solutions or interpretations but encourages clients to recognize the source of their pain and to use their own abilities to find better resolutions. Burch House claims a 60–70 percent success rate defined as "the ability to live constructively in the larger community" (Symmes, 1989, p. 16). The figure includes those called "improved" who require continuing support.

The highlights of a case study will suggest the Burch House approach. A thirty-year-old man who had completed graduate studies after the death of his mother could find only a traveling job, and the job eventually became intolerable. His distress brought him to Burch House. After several weeks of therapy he came to recognize an unresolved grief over his mother and hostility toward relatives on whom he was dependent. Upon entering Burch House, he suffered withdrawal distress and nightmares, but after ten weeks he began to improve and to engage in maintenance work on the house. He worked out his conflicts with his relatives, found a suitable job, and became self-supporting.

RELATION TO OTHER APPROACHES

Behavior Analysis

Giorgi (1975) lists a number of points of convergence between phenomenology and one major form of behaviorism—radical behaviorism or behavior analysis. Both oppose psychophysical dualism, including the notion of inner representations of an outer world and other conscious states ("the illusion of the double world" Kvale and Grenness [1967] call it; Skinner calls it the "copy theory"—the outer world is copied onto the brain which then interprets it); both oppose the hypothetico-deductive method so widespread in psychology; both oppose interpreting behavior in terms of physiology or introspection; both record behavior descriptively and minimize theory. Kvale and Grenness (1967) point out that both Skinner and Merleau-Ponty hold that behavior is the fundamental principle in psychology and that "behavior is no mere indicator of an inner state, man is his behavior to the world" (p. 132).

Among the differences between these two systems, phenomenological psychology attempts to discover meanings people live, not means of prediction and control (as behavior analysis does). Its emphasis on these meanings contrasts sharply with behavior analysis's operant conditioning and shaping strategies. The latter shows no interest in meanings, only in conditions of reinforcement that lead to one or another behavior. Meaning itself would be a product of reinforcement. As an envirocentric system, behavior analysis draws from the natural sciences while phenomenology, as a largely noncentric system, draws from life as it is lived; the latter wants to broaden science to include these strictly human events. Although both utilize description, behavior analysis applies it to any body movement in conjunction with reinforcing stimuli. Phenomenology, in contrast, applies it to "the situation from the viewpoint of the behaver" (Giorgi, 1975, p. 209), which is intentionality.

Cognitive Psychology

Cognitivists assume internal structures involving long and short term storage depots, feedback loops, attenuators, and so forth that organize knowledge and determine how it will be developed and utilized. They use experimental procedures and collection of quantitative data and pay little attention to contexts. This differs radically from the procedures of phenomenology which seek meanings as part of specific contexts. As with behaviorism, cognitivism's "subject" is allowed to be only nonsubjective whereas phenomenology seeks subjectivity. The differences

between an organocentric system and a noncentric system make a striking comparison in these two instances.

Dialectic Psychology

Although the dialectic process serves as a description for much of the interdependence and interaction of events for phenomenological psychology, the latter does not explicitly assume (as do the dialecticians) that everything in the universe is in conflict. Dialecticians assume a thoroughgoing bidirectional relationship between the person and that person's world; phenomenologists give priority to the person's role in the relationship and fall short of a true dialectic.

Both agree on the importance of context and of the individual's historical development. Both oppose the notion of a fixed or stored memory, and some of the dialecticians agree with the repudiation of the brain as a seat of psychological activity; but others, especially the Russian and Chinese dialeticians are highly reductionistic.

Humanistic Psychology

Humanistic psychology is sometimes used interchangeably with phenomenological-existential psychology. It is true the former has borrowed such concepts as intentionality, becoming, and authenticity from the latter, but important differences remain. Much of the writing of humanistic psychology is mentalistic and assumes self-causation. Whereas phenomenologists have attenuated (though not eliminated) the physical-nonphysical, interior-exterior constructs of Cartesian dualism, humanistic psychology has not. Phenomenologists emphasize human-object relationships (intentionality)—even if not in a fully bidirectional or mutual manner (Bucklew, 1955; Ratner, 1971); humanistic psychologists use the term "intentionality" mentalistically and emphasize the autonomous self.

Phenomenologists also show little interest in teleology or purposiveness that is fundamental to humanistic psychology. Humanistic psychology sometimes refers to choices as totally free. To phenomenology, choices are always part of a situation and can operate only within that situation. Further, the making of a choice changes the situation, and that new situation changes further choices. Turning to a comparison with the existential side of the existential-phenomenological pairing, humanistic psychology tends to see human activity in an optimistic and positive way with everyone having valuable potential; existentialism is quite gloomy, emphasizing anxiety and dreadful freedom. Humanistic psychology advocates the self-actualization or self-fulfillment of each individual and the goal of reaching peak experiences; existentialists emphasize becoming, authenticity, and meanings.

A symposium held at Rice University in 1963 entitled "Behaviorism and Phenomenology: Contrasting Bases for Modern Psychology" (Wann, 1964) actually contrasted humanistic and behavioristic psychologies. One commentator noted, "this symposium may well rank in future years as the most misunderstood and misguided symposium in the history of psychology" (Egan, 1970, p. 567). This comment was in the context of a later paper (Hitt, 1969) that excerpted mentalistic ("phenomenological") and behavioristic statements from the presentations at the symposium in an effort to show that each provided certain truths and that together they could provide a more complete psychology. Perhaps two of the most striking errors were (a) the assumption that phenomenology deals with *interior* human activity and (b) the failure to realize that phenomenology is itself a form of behavior, not a contrast with it. The misunderstanding and the "caricature of phenomenology" (Egan, p. 567) illustrate both the common misunderstanding of phenomenology and the confusion with tenets that are closer to those of humanistic psychology.

Interbehavioral Psychology

If we compare Merleau-Ponty's phenomenological psychology with J. R. Kantor's interbehavioral psychology, we find many similarities and a few differences. Both distinguish between the functional or meaning character of a stimulus and its physical characteristics; both similarly distinguish the response from the response function; both consider the stimulus and response to be interdependent; both indicate the interdependence of setting and response; both reject an external environmental stimulation or an internal physiological cause of responses and emphasize interaction or dialectical interchange between the person and surroundings; both reject an internal-external distinction; both consider light to be a medium of contact rather than a stimulus to be converted into an object; and both reject causality as a linear chain of events. Further, Merleau-Ponty's concept of the "lived body" as potentials that interact with the surroundings seems consistent with interbehaviorism's stress on biology as a participating factor (a necessary but not a sufficient condition) in all psychological events.

They differ in that Merleau-Ponty retains in some sense the idea of the mental, or consciousness. Through the concept of intentionality, which puts more emphasis on the person than on the relationship, he seems to contradict his attempt to move toward a thoroughgoing dialectic of person-world interchange. This is also reflected in the use of intentionality as a response to objects that are not present—as in imagining—as if they were created by a mind. Interbehaviorism, on the other hand, points out substitute stimulus objects that are a part of the organism-object interaction. Interbehaviorism holds that to the extent that the "mental" refers to anything beyond historically invented abstract constructs, it can refer only to concrete events that comprise the field of interactions. Thus, enjoying, believing, perceiving, and so forth are interactions and are not reducible to physiology or to something special to the organism. As the phenomenologists insist, when we enjoy we enjoy *something*; when we believe, we believe *something*; when we perceive, we perceive *something*. Interbehaviorism emphasizes these relationships (while recognizing that some acts involve the organism and its own response-produced stimulation more than others) as field events to the exclusion of any additional mentalistic constructs. Phenomenology, on the other hand, retains some mentalism and organocentrism, of which the unidirectionality and the implied creation of imagined objects it assigns to intentionality are examples.

Interbehaviorism accepts the importance of meanings as lived (the interbehavioral field comprises meaning) and agrees that research with that emphasis is indispensable; at the same time it finds merit in the more traditional research as well. Perhaps this is not entirely inconsistent with Merleau-Ponty if one considers his position that factual information can serve as a basis for phenomenological information. Interbehaviorism rejects causality and hypothesis testing only if these are linear but accepts them if they refer to field interactions. Apparently, phenomenological psychology cannot accept them under any conditions.

Operant Subjectivity

The search for subjective meanings to which phenomenological psychology is dedicated is closely related to Q methodology (see chapter 11). Both share a determination to avoid imposing the researcher's objective structure on the person, to find what things mean to the person, and to do this objectively. Q methodology provides a rigorous way to do exactly this in almost any situation and with almost any subject matter, even with very young children (for example, Taylor, Delprato, & Knapp, 1994).

A phenomenologist's characterization of psychology is quite apropos to Q methodology:

> an intersubjective communicative science, systematically studying the structure of human existence by explicating lived (historical) experience . . . While the word "intersubjective" indicates that psychology is to be a shared, validated enterprise, the word "communicative" indicates that the psychology as a science, must be built up by what people can communicate about their experiactions.[6] (Kruger, 1983, p. 19)

Communication of subjectivity is exactly what Q methodology is all about. William Stephenson (1988), the founder and developer of Q, recognized its relationship with phenomenology and advocated its use for that orientation. He noted that (a) communicability would replace consciousness; (b) events of experience would provide for the concourse (population of statements from which Q items are selected); and (c) Q-sorts would allow for grasping essences—but those of the subject rather than those of the investigator. When factor analysis reduces the self-references to clusters of factors, new understandings of subjective meanings emerge.

Postmodernism and Social Constructionism

Heidigger's contention that knowing does not begin with individuals but is a communal matter is fundamental to social constructionism, and that system acknowledges his contribution to its development. It has much less in common, however, with the phenomenological psychology of Merleau-Ponty despite Heidigger's influence on phenomenology.

CRITIQUE

The mode of expression and terminology in phenomenology is notorious for its difficulty of comprehension. One finds any number of writers trying to explain what Husserl, Merleau-Ponty, and others mean. Even the terminology is confusing. For example, the difference, if any, even between two fundamental terms—consciousness and intentionality—is not clear. Karlsson (1992) apparently considers them synonymous: he refers

---

6. "Experiaction" is one of phenomenology's neologisms; it indicates that experience is an action or behavior, not a separate event. It also signifies that there is no dualism of experience *and* behavior, that is, mind and body. There is only a single unified behavior but with the emphasis on subjectivity or meaningful behavior that the world "experiaction" suggests.

to "consciousness as intentionality." Valle and King (1978) leave the matter unclear: "when speaking of consciousness one is either implicitly or explicitly referring to its *intended object* as well" (p. 13). If consciousness does not exist apart from its object, and the object together with consciousness comprise intentionality, how do they differ? And if they do not differ, why not drop one of the terms and avoid the confusion?

Giorgi (1976) seems to use the term "consciousness" and "intentionality" inconsistently with his other accounts of the phenomenological event. Although he tells us that the sleekness of an airplane is not in the plane or in the person but in the relationship between them (1975), he defines consciousness as "a stream of activity that keeps bursting forth toward the world and needs, so to speak, objects in the world to help stop its centrifugal movement" (1976, p. 311). He also says of intentionality that it is "intrinsically directed toward the world" (p. 311). He seems to be telling us that it is unidirectional in that it comes from the person and goes to the object. This contradicts the account of sleekness as one of bidirectionality and interdependence comprising a dialectic process. And his reference to consciousness as a "medium of access" implies an intervening variable that would be in league with cognitivism and its claim to mind as a mediating agent. Yet phenomenology strives to distinguish itself from consciousness as a mediator or internal agent. It appears that the mentalistic meaning of the term consciousness intrudes itself and produces the inconsistency.

In a similar connection, Ratner (1971) points out that both Merleau-Ponty and Sartre tend to give priority to acts being determined by the individual and do not give full accord to the reciprocal action of the world. That is, their use of the term "consciousness" includes considerable attention to how it is organized but not the nature of the world it refers to. Phenomenologists and existentialists exhibit

a fundamental unwillingness to take serious account of the world, to recognize its full impact on our acts, and to acknowledge that it can be dealt with in a manner than can enrich human existence. There is a deep seated mistrust of the world and of our ability to know and affect it, and this leads to ignoring it as something beyond us. (p. 97)

Bucklew (1955) finds the same shortcoming. In light of phenomenology's effort to stress the interdependence of object and subject, this seems to be a major inconsistency and may be a legacy of Husserl's notion of intentionality, a largely unidirectional concept: consciousness reaches forth to the world. Due to this formulation of intentionality, the dialectic or bidirectionality that the phenomenologists lay claim to is never fully realized. In the case of Merleau-Ponty, the influence of William James on him may have been a factor in his failure to break completely with this organocentrism. Existential psychotherapy and hermeneutical psychotherapy follow the same organocentrism. They attempt solely to change the individual. Existential therapy seeks to help the individual to become and to be more authentic. Hermeneutic therapy seeks to construct new meanings. Neither tries to help the individual change such circumstances as a demoralizing job, conflict with a family member, or inadequate preparation for university study.

Phenomenologists explain that they want to conceive of the mental differently from René Descartes with his sixteenth-century dualism. Despite the fact that the Husslerians stress the need to avoid presuppositions, the very fact that they assume the legitimacy of the "mental," even as something to be reinterpreted, is itself a presupposition, one that is fraught with problems. Similarly, they employ "consciousness," "psyche," "nonphysical events," and other mentalistic references. If, instead of starting with these constructs, they started with observations of meaningful actions and the context of which they are a part, perhaps they would construct a psychology more consistent with their stated objectives. Perhaps they would produce a psychology that is clearer, more concrete, and less subject to confusion with un-wanted constructs. Apropos of this possibility, in a discussion after an address that Merleau-Ponty made on perception, Beaufret charged that Merleau-Ponty did not go far enough in modifying Husserl: he should have abandoned mentalistic terms and concepts completely (Merleau-Ponty, 1964a, p. 41–42). We may note that had Merleau-Ponty done so, his work might not have generated this distorted interpretation: "Merleau-Ponty argued that people's minds and bodies are always interrelated. At any given moment, people's lives are both mental and physical. To be human is to be simultaneously mind and body" (Becker, 1992, p. 16).

A criticism from the social constructionists (chapter 8) is that the phenomenologists fuse subject and object, the experiencer and the experienced world, and claim that one can understand the individual only by entering his or her world and then clarifying and reflecting on that understanding (Semin & Gergen, 1990). How, they ask, can science deal with a fused subject and object? And what is the scientist's role if experience is the only world, as they claim? If science is a reflection on experience, someone outside of the scientist's experiences must comprehend the reflections. This seems hardly feasible, they note. The experiencing person is another form of mind, they argue, and phenomenology's use of it reestablishes psychophysical dualism.

On the positive side, phenomenological psychology's emphasis on studying meanings in life is one that the larger body of psychology can hardly afford to continue ignoring. Nor are phenomenology and the traditional natural world approach necessarily mutually exclusive methods. We would not want to abandon what we have learned about perception as it applies to improving the safety of pilots approaching a landing strip. We also need, however, to explore perceptions as meanings, while recognizing that when meaning to the pilot is not consonant with the character of the physical world the result is tragic. We would not want to abandon operant conditioning where it has vastly improved educational achievement of

underprivileged children or self-care by the retarded, but we might also make advances in helping underprivileged children or the retarded if we tried to better understand things from their point of view (note the statements above by the schizophrenic and the conjoined twins). Environmental psychologists have found that playground design, as one of many examples, is vastly different when children and adolescents are asked what they want than when the designer merely observes children at playgrounds and records statistics or—worse yet—merely assumes he or she knows what they want. As for laboratory studies, ecological psychology (chapter 7) shows us the value of getting out of the laboratory and into the world of various behavior settings. These and a variety of other methodologies such as Q (chapter 11) will no doubt be necessary for obtaining a major advancement in understanding the complexities and richness of "the structure of behavior" and human "experiaction" to which phenomenological psychology has made important contributions.

CONCLUSIONS

Perhaps only behavior analysis has been more misunderstood than phenomenological psychology. Much of this seems due to some American psychologist's use of "humanistic" and "phenomenological" interchangeably and to considering these systems to be at least continuous with each other. That leads to the assumption that "phenomenological" means "mental." One finds psychologists from a number of different persuasions using "phenomenological" in just that way, and the confusion shows no signs of clearing. In actuality, phenomenological psychology played an important role in making large strides toward an alternative to the old mentalism.

While criticizing psychology's century-long engagement in laboratory experiments that eliminate meaning, phenomenological psychology provides compelling research demonstrations of the importance of meaning that the rest of psychology will ignore to its own detriment. Perhaps this is its major contribution and will continue to be its most important source of strength. Its counterpart in the clinical area, existential psychology, has developed some distinctive forms of therapy that appear to be useful, at least to selected clients. How effective they may be compared with other forms of therapy remains to be demonstrated.

REFERENCES

Aanstoos, Chrisopher M. 1983. A phenomenological study of thinking as it is exemplified during chess playing. In *Duquesne Studies in Phenomenological Psychology*, vol. 4. Edited by A. Giorgi, A. Barton, & C. Maes. Pittsburgh: Duquesne University.

———. 1987. A critique of the computational model of thought: The contribution of Merleau-Ponty. *Journal of Phenomenological Psychology* 18: 187–200.

Ablamowicz, Halina. 1992. Shame as an interpersonal dimension of communication among doctoral students: An empirical phenomenological study. *Journal of Phenomenological Psychology* 23: 30–49.

Anderson, Tom G. 1978. Existential counseling: An introduction to existential-phenomenological thought in psychology. In *Existential-Phenomenological Alternatives for Psychology*. Edited by Ronald S. Valle & Mark King. New York: Oxford University.

Angier, Natalie. 1997. Joined for life, and living life to the full. *New York Times*, December 23: B11, B15.

Arcaya, José. 1989. Memory and temporality: A phenomenological alternative. *Philosophical Psychology* 2: 101–110.

Becker, Carol S. 1992. *Living and Relating: An Introduction to Phenomenology*. Newbury Park, CA: Sage.

Bouchard, Marc-André, & Louis Guérette. 1991. Psychotherapy as a hermeneutical experience. *Psychotherapy* 28: 385–94.

Brannon, John F. 1967. *The Philosophy of Merleau-Ponty*. New York: Harcourt, Brace & World.

Bucklew, John. 1955. The subjective tradition in phenomenological psychology. *Philosophy of Science* 2: 289–99.

Daniluk, Judith. 1993. The meaning and experience of female sexuality. *Psychology of Women Quarterly* 17: 53–69.

Davidson, Larry. 1988. Husserl's refutation of psychologism and the possibility of a phenomenological psychology. *Journal of Phenomenological Psychology* 19: 1–17.

Eckartsberg, Rolf von. 1986. Life-World Experience: *Existential-Phenomenological Research Approaches in Psychology*. Washington, D.C.: Center for Advanced Research in Phenomenology and University Press of America.

———. 1989. The unfolding meaning of intentionality and horizon in phenomenology. *Humanistic Psychology* 17: 146–60.

Egan, Leroy J. 1970. Comment on Hitt's analysis. *American Psychologist* 25: 567.

Ellenberger, Henri F. 1958. A clinical introduction to psychiatric phenomenology and existential analysis. In *Existence: A New Dimension in Psychiatry and Psychology*. Edited by R. May, E. Angel, & H. F. Ellenberger. New York: Simon & Schuster.

Frankl, Viktor. 1963. *Man's Search for Meaning: An Introduction to Logotherapy*. New York: Pocket Books.

Gibson, James J. 1979. *The Ecological Approach to Visual Perception*. Boston: Houghton Mifflin.

Giorgi, Amedeo. 1975. Convergences and divergences between phenomenological psychology and behaviorism. *Behaviorism* 3: 200–212.

———. 1976. Phenomenology and the foundations of psychology. In *Nebraska Symposium on Motivation–1975*, vol. 23. Lincoln: University of Nebraska Press.

Henley, Tracy B. 1988. Beyond Husserl. *American Psychologist* 43: 402–403.

Hitt, William D. 1969. Two models of man. *American Psychologist* 24: 651–58.

Jennings, Jerry L. 1986. Husserl revisited: The forgotten distinction between psychology and phenomenology. *American Psychologist* 41: 1231–40.

Karlsson, Gunnar. 1987. *A Phenomenological Psychological Method: Theoretical Foundation and Empirical Application in the Field of Decision Making and Choice*. Stockholm: Akademitryck.

———. 1988. A phenomenological psychological study of decision and choice. *Acta Psychologica* 68: 7–25.

———. 1992. The grounding of psychological research in a phenomenological epistemology. *Theory and Psychology* 2: 403–429.

Kruger, Dreyer. 1981. *An Introduction to Phenomenological Psychology*. Pittsburgh: Duquesne University Press.

———. 1983. Psychotherapy research and existential-phenomenological psychology—An exploration. In *Duquesne Studies in Phenomenological Psychology*, vol. 4. Edited by A. Giorgi, A. Barton, & C. Maes. Pittsburgh: Duquesne University Press.

Kvale, Steiner. 1983. The qualitative research interview. *Journal of Phenomenological Psychology* 14: 171–96.

Kvale, Steiner, & Carl E. Grenness. 1967. Skinner and Sartre: Towards a radical phenomenology of behavior. *Review of Existential Psychology and Psychiatry* 7: 128–50.

Kwant, Remy C. 1963. *The Phenomenological Philosophy of Merleau-Ponty*. Pittsburgh: Duquesne University Press.

———. 1966. *From Phenomenology to Metaphysics: An Inquiry into the Last Period of Merleau-Ponty's*

Philosophical Life. Pittsburgh: Duquesne University Press.

Lyotard, Jean-Francois. 1991. *Phenomenology*. Translated by Brian Beakley. Albany: State University of New York Press.

May, Rollo. 1958. Contributions of existential psychotherapy. In *Existence: A New Dimension in Psychiatry and Psychology*. Edited by R. May, E. Angel, & H. F. Ellenberger. New York: Simon & Schuster.

Merleau-Ponty, Maurice. 1962. *Phenomenology of Perception*. Translated by Colin Smith. London: Routledge & Kegan Paul.

———. 1963. *The Structure of Behavior*. Boston: Beacon Press.

———. 1964a. The primacy of perception and its philosophical consequences. Translated by James M. Edie. In *The Primacy of Perception and Other Essays on Phenomenological Psychology, the Philosophy of Art, History and Politics*. Edited by James M. Edie. Evanston, IL: Northwestern University Press.

———. 1964b. An unpublished text by Maurice Merleau-Ponty: A prospectus of his work. Translated by Arleen B. Dallery. In *The Primacy of Perception and Other Essays on Phenomenological Psychology, the Philosophy of Art, History and Politics*. Edited by James M. Edie. Evanston, IL: Northwestern University Press.

Michotte, Albert. 1963. *The Perception of Causality*. Translated by T. R. & E. Miles. London: Methuen.

———. 1991. *Michotte's Experimental Phenomenology of Perception*. Edited by George Thinés, Alan Costall, & George Butterworth. Hillsdale, NJ: Erlbaum.

Misiak, Henryk, & Virginia S. Sexton. 1973. *Phenomenological, Existential, and Humanistic Psychologies: A Historical Survey*. New York: Grune & Stratton.

Mortimer, Ann M. 1992. Phenomenology: Its place in schizophrenic research. *British Journal of Psychiatry* 161: 293–97.

Rahilly, Deborah A. 1993. A phenomenological analysis of authentic experience. *Journal of Humanistic Psychology* 33: 49–71.

Ratner, Carl. 1971. Principles of dialectic psychology. *Telos* 9: 83–109.

Ricoeur, Paul. 1970. *Freud and Philosophy: An Essay on Interpretation*. Translated by Denis Savage. New Haven, CT: Yale University Press.

———. 1974. *The Conflict of Interpretation: Essays in Hermeneutics*. Edited by Don Ihde. Evanston, IL: Northwestern University Press.

Romanyshyn, Robert D. 1978. Psychology and the attitude of science. In *Existential-Phenomenological Alternatives for Psychology*. Edited by Ronald S. Valle & Mark King. New York: Oxford University Press.

Sartre, Jean-Paul. 1948. *The Psychology of Imagination*. New York: Philosophical Library.

———. 1953. *The Emotions: Outline of a Theory*. New York: Philosophical Library.

———. 1956. *Being and Nothingness*. London: Methuen.

Seamon, David. 1982. The phenomenological contribution to environmental psychology. *Journal of Environmental Psychology* 2: 119–40.

———. 1987. Phenomenological and environment-behavior research. In *Advances in Environment, Behavior, and Design*, vol. 1. Edited by Elwin H. Zube & Gary T. Moore. New York: Plenum.

Semin, Gün R., & Kenneth J. Gergen, eds. 1990. *Everyday Understanding: Social and Scientific Implications*. London: Sage Publications.

Sims, Eva-Maria. 1993. The infant's experience of the world: Stern, Merleau-Ponty and the phenomenology of the preverbal self. *Humanistic Psychology* 21: 26–40.

Snyder, Douglas M. 1988. Comment on Jennings. *American Psychologist* 43: 403–404.

Stephenson, William. 1988. William James, Niels Bohr, and complementarity: V.—Phenomenology of subjectivity. *Psychological Record* 38: 203-219.

Symmes, Catherine B. 1989. An existential demonstration. *Psychosocial Rehabilitation* 13 (2): 9–17.

Taylor, Priscilla; Dennis J. Delprato; & John R. Knapp. 1994. Q-methodology in the study of child phenomenology. *Psychological Record* 44: 171–83.

Tomacek, Odile. 1990. A personal commentary on "Schizophrenia as a brain disease." *American Psychologist* 45: 550–51.

Valle, Ronald S., & Mark King. 1978. An introduction to existential-phenomenological thought in psychology. In *Existential-Phenomenological Alternatives for Psychology*. Edited by Ronald S. Valle & Mark King. New York: Oxford University Press.

Wann, T. W., ed. 1964. *Behaviorism and Phenomenology: Contrasting Bases for Modern Psychology*. Chicago: University of Chicago Press.

Yalom, Irvin D. 1980. *Existential Psychotherapy*. New York: Basic Books.

Zaner, Richard M. 1985. The logos of psyche: Phenomenological variations on a theme. In *A Century of Psychology as Science*. Edited by Sigmund Koch & David E. Leary. New York: McGraw-Hill.

Additional Systems in Brief

From Community to Probabilities: Six Systems

COMMUNITY PSYCHOLOGY

Community psychology along with environmental psychology was influenced in its inception by calls in the 1960s for social reform and by the advent of social activism. It had its beginnings in the treatment of behavior pathologies, and it was critical of clinical psychology's deference to illness rather than health, to treatment rather than prevention, and to the individual rather than to the person-situation (Heller & Monahan, 1977). During President Kennedy's tenure, legislation establishing community mental health facilities also promoted its growth. One pioneering study involved a program that set out to reduce the extent to which psychiatric patients labeled themselves negatively. It taught competency in matters of patients' daily living and offered group support (Fairweather et al., 1969). After only limited success, the researchers revised the program to include a community lodge system so that feelings of deviance that began in the psychiatric ward could be reversed over a period of time before the individuals left the lodge for a more independent life.

Community psychology has expanded from applications in behavior pathology to use in nursing homes, schools, prisons, and other institutions, and beyond into broader communities. It takes as its subject matter the person-in-social-context. Like Roger Barker (chapter 7), it borrows some of its inspiration from Kurt Lewin, especially from his concept of behavior as a function of person and environment. It also draws on Barker's demonstration of the way in which the behavior setting determines behavior patterns. A behavior setting can be a discotheque, a shopping mall, an office, a post office, a factory work station—any situation in which patterns of behavior are predictable. In a behavior setting the community is an ecosystem with standing patterns of behavior in an environment that surrounds it. The community has implicit rules for conducting events, and people within the setting know and follow the rules for the behavior patterns. They see to it that others also follow the rules or face expulsion. By this means the community is self-regulating and stable

(see chapter 7 for more on behavior settings). These standing patterns of behavior and physical conditions together with such factors as exchange of resources, interaction of one behavior setting with another, and social climate are dealt with by community psychologists in conjunction with the individual who is a part of the community setting.

Most of psychology emphasizes the person or even a part of the person—such as neurons—and tries to understand behavior from this organocentric stance. Where remediation is necessary, it tries to change the *person*. This is true of nearly all psychotherapy. Individual intervention neglects the conditions at a level different from that of the individual and may appear to blame the victim (Ryan, 1971). Changing the individual while leaving intact the situation that caused the problem is likely to lead to only temporary gains, if any, and may reinforce the person's belief that he or she is at fault and has failed once again. Dissatisfaction with this traditional emphasis on treatment and on the person as a passive recipient ("patient") is countered by community psychology's dual goals of prevention and empowerment. "Empowerment" means enabling individuals who are underprivileged or of marginal status—whether from physical or behavior disabilities or from social or demographic conditions—to take charge of their own lives (Fawcett, 1990; Rappaport, 1990) and to want to contribute to their communities. It tries to understand the community of which people are a part and to promote improved well-being by changing the person-situation interaction. The community psychologist attempts to work with social networks and in such varied settings as the home, the neighborhood, and the medical clinic or hospital.

Using Barker's five major types of behavior settings—governmental, workplaces, schools, voluntary groups, and religious groups—Shinn (1987) reviewed the research in each and suggested how community psychology can work for "both understanding and intervention at levels beyond the individual" (p. 568)—that is, at the behavior setting level. Orford (1992) points out that communities involve social settings at a variety of levels, including socioeconomic, gender, age, and disability, and must address all of them. In examining the role of ecological psychology (ecobehavioral science) in community psychology, O'Conner and Lubin (1984) consider the levels somewhat differently—those of individual, family, community, and socio-cultural conditions.

A few brief quotations suggest the contextual, multidimensional, and interrelational approach of the system:

- "Multilevel, multistructured, multidetermined social context" will best provide understanding in community psychology (Kingry-Westergaard & Kelly, 1990, p. 27).
- "Multidimensional analysis of systems, rather than identifying a single cause" is necessary in order to meet the interests of community psychology" (Tolan et al., 1990a, p. 7).
- "Relationships are reciprocal: Persons affect settings, and settings affect persons, persons influence other settings, and one setting affects another setting" (Kingry-Westergaard and Kelly, 1990, p. 28).
- Research in community psychology should be "in the context of the people of concern" (Rappaport, 1990, p. 55).

Community psychology ties in with environmental psychology as well as with ecobehavioral science. Both environmental and ecological psychology have been important in planning social interventions in the community (Rappaport, 1977). In many instances the research, the aims, and the methods that environmental and community psychology use are indistinguishable from one another (Holahan & Wandersman, 1987) as in the example cited below. ("Environmental Psychology") in which the community and school participated in the design of a schoolyard. In general, community psychology focuses on behavior problems in conjunction with the individual's institutions (Levine & Perkins, 1997) whereas environmental psychology looks for ways to design the environment to improve social well-being. However, the distinction is often a matter of degree rather than of kind.

Unfortunately, according to some proponents (Lounsbury et al, 1985; Heller, 1990), most of the research reported as applying to community psychology has not lived up to its aims but has conventionally focused on the person. Some of the problem is that no adequate research methodology for studying interdependent individuals comprising a community has yet been developed nor are good methodologies available for studying community change except at an overly simple level (Heller, 1990). However, the situation may be improving (Orford, 1992) as indicated by the papers in recent volumes on research in community psychology, some of which are cited here (Tolan et al., 1990b).

DIRECT REALISM

Because the arguments for direct realism in psychology have been advanced primarily by Australians, it might also be called Australian realism. The prime mover for this position in psychology is J. R. Maze (1983, 1991) who attacks cognitive psychology's assumption that we know the world only by mental representations inside us which stand for the real objects in the world. Because it assumes that we construct our world rather than know it directly, this cognitivist view is also called "constructivism" (not to be confused with social constructivism which assumes social rather than mental constructions). It goes back to the eighteenth-century German philosopher Immanuel Kant and has become so dominant a psychology in the United States and some other countries that it is sometimes called the "establishment" position. It is perhaps best known by its reference to psychological events as "information processing."

Constructivism, in its computational or information-processing form, dominates cognitive science . . . According to this thesis, the business of psychology is to explain how the brain constructs, or 'builds up', knowledge of the external world by manipulating, organizing and interpreting the imperfect data available. That the brain works with symbols or representations of the world, rather than real objects, is usually taken as self-evident; and it is taken as self-evidence because the existence of error demonstrates that there is often a discrepancy between what we seem to perceive and what is really the case. (Rantzen, 1993, p. 147)

Michell (1991) believes cognitive constructivism gained its dominant position because of (a) its association with the prestige of the computer and the well-funded research support that has resulted from this association; (b) a bias in our culture that views cognition as an internal event; and (c) the reliance of psychologists on experiments rather than logic. It is logic, not experiments, that can challenge the assumptions.

Maze (1991) argues that since the representational view maintains that the object of knowing is always a mental representation and never an object in the world with independent existence, this leaves no real world object to be represented. It leaves no way to distinguish between truth and error. Denying this problem, the representationist proposes that if the representation is like the thing it represents, it constitutes a true belief, and if not, a false belief. Further, according to representationism, the fact that errors occur proves that we are not responding directly to the world but only to internal images. This, notes Maze, "presupposes that we can on occasion step outside the representationist framework and examine the external objects directly, so as to make the comparison with their images, and that would mean that representationism was unnecessary as a general theory of knowledge" (p. 169). Apropos of this view, Tolman (1991), who is not identified with direct realism, comments: "Any organism requires an objective assessment of its environment for survival. An organism that responded only to a world created 'in its head' would not survive for long—indeed it would never have evolved in the first place" (p. 159).

Knowing, unlike cognitive psychology's "representations," is treated by the direct realist as a relationship with objects of the world through our biological organization. The nervous system is necessary for cognitive acts but is not itself a cognitive act. It *enables* cognitive relationships to occur. One of Maze's arguments against representationism is that nothing can have relationships intrinsic or internal to itself inasmuch as the object of cognition is external to the nervous system. To say that consciousness is intrinsic to thoughts or that mental images are intrinsic to awareness ignores the existing relationships. "To be conscious of, to be known, are relations, and a relation can hold only between two or more terms" (Maze, 1991, p. 182). Further, cognitive representations cannot represent anything, for they involve circularity: they require for operation the very knowledge they claim to explain. One can only know what an internal representation means if one already knows the relation between the representation and the object it represents. Or to put it another way, *if one knows only the representation, one cannot specify anything it refers to*. This, for the direct realist, is a fatal blow to the representational construct—whether it is taken to be neural codings or mental states—for the meanings cannot be intrinsic. By rejecting internal relations—those intrinsic to itself—one also rejects "self-directed activating energies with which the theory of motivation is cluttered" (p. 182). This statement puts direct realism in accord with Dewey and Bentley (1949) in their objection to self-action, and with the noncentric systems.

Direct realism claims that cognition can to some extent be directly observed. According to Maze (1983), when we perceive an organism's behavior, we perceive some of its cognitions. For example, in describing someone's actions, such as opening a door, one assumes that that person's movements are guided by his or her perceptions. Cognition is observable in the organism's behavior, in the way it relates to an object. However, Maze always refers to cognition and behavior separately, indicating a remaining dualistic assumption in common with cognitive psychology, despite their other differences.

Maze argues for determinism as the basis of action in psychology and for instinctual drives (derived from psychoanalysis) that shape behavior through cognition. He explains the instinctual drives this way: Each of us has many knowers, and these are components of the central nervous system. The knowers are instinctual drives that enter into cognitive relations via the perceptual system (Maze, 1983). When these drives are aroused or excited by exciting conditions, motor pathways in the brain are aroused and innately produce an action. Knowing involves a drive system and brain structures that enable cognition to occur. This formulation gives the system a somewhat organocentric twist.

Carrying Maze's arguments for direct realism further, Michell (1988) contends that a representation cannot be intrinsic or internal; a representation has no way to contain meaning, for that is logically impossible, and no empirical evidence can apply, for "there can be no empirical support for a logically incoherent theory" (p. 230). Because a cognitive representation requires an intrinsic reference that it does not have, and a computer's internal representation has no meaning, he rejects the analogy that makes the human brain an information processor like a computer. A computer's meaning lies in extrinsic reference, that of the programmer or the user. The computer does not process information but determines which internal-state structures partially cause which outputs. He dismisses entities that refer to *inner* things but wishes to retain mental terms that refer to relations such as perception, imagination, and memory.

Representation theory usually takes the form of information processing, but direct realism rejects all assumptions about the transmission of information. Neither physiology of neurons nor experimental cognition can reveal anything about representations, notes Michell (1988). Studies of neurophysiology can reveal only neurophysiology. Experimental research of cognition can reveal only behavior.

In experimental investigations of cognition, as in all psychological experiments, all that is observed is behaviour occurring under controlled conditions. All references to "information," "coding," "representations," "storage," "computation," and cognate concepts is interpretation guided by theory. Hence, a further implication of direct realism is that all such research requires reinterpretation. (p. 246)

Direct realism emphasizes "identif[ying] events that constitute the necessary and sufficient conditions for cognition in various circumstances" (p. 246). It can, claim the realists, directly observe cognition in behavior and therefore treat it as a dependent or independent variable. This occurs "where bodily movements are sensitive to the full propositional content of environmental situations" (Michell, 1988, p. 247).

Rantzen (1993) takes up the issue of cognitive error as central to the clash between direct realism and representationism. Because the latter holds that the brain constructs knowledge out of imperfect bits of information received from the senses, it concludes that we know the world only in this indirect and constructed form, with all of its errors. Given the fact of perceptual errors, how then can direct realism be credible? How can it account for errors? For hallucinations and delusions? According to Rantzen, "we cognize not symbols or representations but real situations existing independently of our knowing them" (p. 148). Error is not erroneous cognition but the absence of cognition. He proposes that errors occur when (a) the individual does not have the opportunity for cognition, (b) the individual does not have the cognitive capability that the situation requires, or (c) the situation blocks some fact that the individual needs. "Direct realism finds no place for mediating entities; instead it takes the organism's interactions with the environment to be the true theatre of cognition" (p. 168). He also argues that direct realism has major advantages for research.

Michell (1988) notes the similarity of direct realism with Gibson's ecological perception which also holds to a direct relationship between the knower and the known and rejects any assumption of mediation through cognitive representations (see p. 374). This is also true of Merleau-

Ponty's phenomenological psychology (chapter 12), Kantor's interbehavioral psychology (chapter 10), Stephenson's operant subjectivity (chapter 11), Riegel's dialectical psychology (chapter 9), Skinner's behavior analysis (chapter 6), and Kuo's probabilistic epigenetic psychology (p. 380). The advocacy of determinism agrees with Skinner but does not seem to be assumed in the others, and in interbehaviorism it is explicitly rejected along with will as an unscientific construct imposed on events. The emphasis on relations between organism and object rather than on an internal mediator is also characteristic. Maze's proposal of instinctual drives finds echoes in psychoanalysis, from which it derives, and in humanistic psychology (Maslow's "instinctoids" and Rogers' innate "true self") but is at odds with most versions of cognitive psychology and also with the noncentric systems (with which it is otherwise closely allied).

ECOLOGICAL PERCEPTION/ECOLOGICAL REALISM/ECOLOGICAL PSYCHOLOGY

Inasmuch as James Gibson's (1979) ecological perception embraces only one topic, it is not a broad system, but more of a theory about that topic. Nevertheless, it has implications well beyond perception and, as already noted, has influenced a number of theorists. It is sometimes appropriately called "ecological realism." The implications extend into the very question of what constitutes a psychological event—an internal biological interpreter or complex interactions between organism and surroundings. Increasingly, the system is being called *ecological psychology,* a term that is still in use for Roger Barker's quite different system (chapter 7), although Barker used the term *eco-behavioral science.*

Gibson's account of perception evolved from the traditional mentalistic account to an ecological one over a period of years (Smith, 1993). Only the latter will be described here.

Gibson relates the large number of characteristics of physics, chemistry, and geometry that psychologists and others have inappropriately applied

to perception and notes that sensations from the sense organs were considered raw data to be converted into meaningful perceptions. His argument goes as follows: Because we can use the *effects* of light on the environment but *not light itself,* the traditional assumption of sensations of light converted to mental perceptions is without foundation. We perceive not stimuli but conditions of the environment; we do not perceive sensations, hear cochlear hair cells, or taste our taste buds. Neither do neurons transmit or analyze messages or information. A neural impulse does not specify whether it comes from eye, ear, nose, or other receptor. There are no signals or messages and no sender or receiver that requires an infinity of interpreters. Information is present and available. We do not create it or convert it.

Further, retinal images are a myth. Any such image would present a tilted world when we tilt our heads. We perceive the world directly, not through "*retinal* pictures, *neural* pictures, or *mental* pictures" (p. 147). No message, no sender, no information processor, no storage depositories in which memory connects the present with sensations from the past. No series of sensations to produce perceptions; no pictures of the past or present or neural engrams to make up memory. Perceiving does not divide past and present but is ongoing. It does not require memory, mind, cognition, or processing by the brain. "*Direct perception* is the activity of getting information from the ambient array. I call this a process of *information pickup* that involves the exploratory activity of looking around, getting around, and looking at things" (p. 147).

Disputing the claims of the empiricists (associationists), he argues that our perceptions are not a matrix of separate spots held together by the mental glue of learned associations. And similarly challenging the nativists (Gestaltists and others), he denies that such a matrix is conjoined by a mysterious innate process. Rather, he holds, we perceive a hierarchy rather than a matrix. The visual array is filled—not merely "speckled"—and smaller components fill the larger ones in the hierarchy.

What we have called "cues" to depth, he argues, have been confused with natural perspective. Natural observation involves movement whereas perspective—both in nature and in pictures—is static. As movement occurs, some features of the visual array change and some do not. We see a table top as rectangular from all angles even though the angles and proportions change. But "the unchanging relations among the four angles and the invariant proportions over the set . . . are equally important" (p. 74). Reciprocal variance and invariance provide the information for our perspective.

It has been generally assumed that the retina receives a two dimensional image, and the lost third dimension must be restored in the brain by means of "cues." In contrast, Gibson argues that we see three-dimensional space by "the relations of surfaces to ground and to one another" (p. 148).

Perception, he tells us, does not occur in a mind or in a brain but *in the living observer*. It is an ecological event of person and object in relationship to one another. "Perceiving is an achievement of the individual, not an appearance in the theater of his consciousness. It is a keeping-in-touch with the world, an experiencing of things rather than a having of experiences" (p. 230). It consists of information pickup involving surfaces of objects and the person in visual interaction. Rather than being simply an interpreted retinal image, it consists of the way the object is laid out, its invariants, changes, textures, edges, affordances (possibilities or potentialities), occlusions, and other visual conditions as well as continual surveying of eye, head, and body movement. The muscles of the body adjust to these factors and coordinate with the sense organs. The brain is not a "seat of vision" (p. 309) but "only the central organ of a complete visual system" (p. 1).

Because of attempts to relate the static and artificial conditions of pictures to the natural world, he holds, some erroneous assumptions about perception have developed. And this error has been repeated in experiments with perception. Experiments reoriented toward the actual ecological condition lead him to reject traditional assumptions and to adopt a direct approach.

Gibson's concept of "information pickup" should not be confused with "information processing." He rejects the latter unequivocally:

Note that modern theories of so-called "information processing" *accept* the doctrine of afferent neural inputs inasmuch as what their adherents call incoming *information* is a pattern or sequence of inputs. In my opinion, they cheat by simply *calling* inputs information. They try to substitute Claude Shannon for Johannes Müller! They attempt to slip around the old perplexities. They neglect the history of sense perception; they do not seem to know sense physiology. Signal detection indeed! (1985, p. 227).

Gibson's objections to conventional doctrine about perception (and the characteristics of perception that he provides as a replacement) are not entirely original with him, as he attests. Similar points were advanced earlier by Woodbridge (1909, 1913a, 1913), Kantor (1920, 1924; Kantor & Smith, 1975), and Merleau-Ponty (1962). As early as the fourth century BCE, Aristotle described perception as the joint actualization of two potentials: the potential of the organism to sense and the potential of the object to be sensed (see chapter 2, p. 16). He described the role of the medium of contact and distinguished it from the sensible object (stimulus). That several investigators would arrive at similar views quite independently of each other and at variance with convention suggests that they have been observing, describing, and analyzing the same events. Their account of these events would seem to deserve as much attention as does the conventional view. Gibson's work has brought increased attention to this alternative.

Neisser (1982, 1985) notes the lesson of Gibson's ecological realism for naturalistic studies and for the role of the environment, rather than artificial laboratory tests, in such areas as memory and concept formation as well as perception. He argues for the value of extending it to those areas. Eleanor Gibson (wife of James Gibson), an eminent developmental psychologist, has extended her husband's concepts along with her own to the developmental process (E. Gibson, 1969, 1982, 1997; E. Gibson & Walker, 1984). An edited work, influenced by the ideas of James and Eleanor Gibson combines ecological realism, dynamic systems, and epigenetic systems (see Dent-Read & Zukow-Goldring, 1997). These editors describe ecological realism as dealing with the way in which organism and environment adapt to each other, a way in which all knowing develops in that relationship. They describe dynamic systems as the way in which organism and environment interact to form a system that becomes self-organizing. This approach examines various levels of these interactions that lead to species-typical activities such as walking. Much of the focus of dynamic systems is on motor activity. Probabilistic epigeneticism (see p. 380) studies organisms in their natural environments (sometimes called "internal and external environment") to determine the way in which they influence one another and bring about changes in the entire system, not merely in specific parts. By bringing these three together, the editors hoped to show similarities and differences among them as well as the contribution each makes to understanding human development as organism-environment relationships rather than as mechanistic, psychoanalytic, or cognitive processes.

As might be expected, Gibson's work has drawn criticism from conventionalists. But it has also elicited criticisms from those who essentially agree with him. For example, Costall (1986) finds Gibson inconsistent about the mutuality of organism and environment, often giving preeminence to the organism. Like all important intellectual contributions, Gibson's ecological perception is not to be held sacrosanct but to be further refined and advanced.

ENVIRONMENTAL PSYCHOLOGY

Environmental psychology (also called "environment and behavior") began developing in the 1960s, but the name came into use in the 1970s when researchers called attention to the effect on human behavior of the environment constructed by humans. According to Holahan (1982, p. 21) "the historical roots of environmental psychology can be traced to the research carried out by Barker and Wright at the Midwest Psychological Field Station in the 1950s" (see chapter 6), but a number of factors coalesced to produce it (Moore, 1987; Sommer, 1987) including such diverse influences as Lewin's emphasis on behavior as a function of person and environment and the movement toward social reform in the 1960s. Psychology departments of the 1960s began offering courses in environmental psychology and degree programs followed. Across the United States and Canada, there are now over twenty offering Ph.Ds and more offering the master's degrees. They are spread over departments of psychology, geography, architecture, sociology, and natural resources.

Environmental psychology deals with such topics as perception of the environment; privacy; crowding; fear of crime; noise, temperature, and pollution; personal space and territoriality; design of buildings, furniture, and playgrounds; development and environment; perception and environment; stress and environment; preservation of the environment; natural and technological disasters; and city planning. It seeks to find ways in which people can react to the environment, control it, or design it better so as to improve human well-being.

No fully satisfactory definition of environmental psychology exists, but the following two definitions capture much of what it is about:

1. "Environmental psychology is the study of the interrelationship between behavior and the built and natural environments" (Fisher, Bell, & Baum, 1984, p. 6).
2. "Environmental psychology is the discipline concerned with the interactions and relationships between people and their environments" (McAndrew, 1993, p. 2, after Proshansky, 1990).

Most forms of psychology include the environment. This necessarily follows from taking account of the stimulus. The stimulus is environmental, even when it involves the individual's body. Consequently, the dividing line between environmental psychology and other forms of psychology is not clear-cut and may be compared with eco-behavioral science (chapter 7) in which the differences between it and other psychologies are even less clear. The differentiation, however, is in the emphasis, the conventional approach centering on the organism while eco-behavioral science focuses on well-defined behavior settings and environmental psychology focuses on the broader relationship of environment and person. Sometimes studies of behavior settings (such as Bechtel's [1982b] cited above) that are used to evaluate environments merge with environmental psychology. Two other examples of such mergers—in this case, architecture—are found in the work of Gump & Good (1976) who used small synomorphs (chapter 7) called "segments" to evaluate two types of school architecture on a number of educational measures, and the work of Osborn (1988) who studied personality traits in the behavior settings of interior designs. Regardless of the distinctions between environmental and eco-behavioral science the fact that ". . . schools, hospitals, and other community settings are continually being constructed with only minimal attention to the interacting of their sociophysical milieu with desired setting behavior attests to the needs for further emphasis on ecological psychology" (Winett, 1987, p. 38).

Operant conditioning also emphasizes the effects of the environment on behavior (see chapter 6). Its role in environmental psychology includes studies showing how operant conditioning can reduce littering, improve water and energy conservation, increase use of public transportation, and increase the selection of self-help material on dietary improvement and implementation of dietary changes (Winett, 1987).

A few examples from research hint at the breadth of environmental psychology.

Investigators have shown that adults have little understanding of *the play needs of children,* and they design play spaces based on false assumptions (Bishop & Peterson, 1971). Play serves a variety of needs such as socialization with peers, energy release, exploration of the world, conversation, and acting out situations with imagination and creativity. Fixed equipment can meet these needs only in limited ways. Typical playground equipment such as swings, slides, and climbing devices receives only a small percentage of children's play time. A study using recordings of behavior settings, interviews with children, and behavior mapping in three types of playgrounds found that the most popular components of each playground were those that provided greatest freedom of play, especially for older children who used a clubhouse more than any other component. Sand and water were also popular in the two playgrounds that offered them (Hayward, Rothenberg, & Beasley, 1974). Playgrounds with such items as clubhouses, sand, and water promote pretend play; and it is these, Susa and Benedict (1994) indicate, that facilitate creative behavior. One attempt to meet the need for improved design of children's play areas involved an international student competition for design of two community schoolyards in Harlem, New York. In conjunction with the school and the community, the best ideas were put together for implementation (Hart et al., 1992).

Safety for children is a critical environmental concern. To improve safety conditions, we must seek input from parents as well as from children (Garling, 1985), for parents overestimate their children's ability to manage hazards and have different estimates of the degree of hazard presented by a given piece of equipment (Valsiner & Mackie, 1985). The U.S. Consumer Product Safety Commission (1975) found that children's playgrounds and stairs are among the greatest hazards, and the surface under play equipment is a major culprit. In 1981 the Commission (U.S. Consumer Product Safety Commission, 1981) developed and issued national standards for playground safety.

Attention to environmental supports for women's projects is important. These include neighborhood service centers (Wekerle, 1988) and urban housing structured to facilitate women's work, childbearing, and child-rearing (Saegert, 1988).

Control of youth gangs works best where the community has both formal and informal social networks. Crimes against people and property go up with social disorganization (Sampson & Groves, 1989). Fear of crime is reduced when people feel a part of the community (Hunter & Baumer, 1982). Perceived social control goes up and fear of crime goes down as the percentage of single family houses increases (Gates & Rohe, 1987). Recent research has included community problem solving, environmental pollution, national and international violence, effects of technological change on people and groups, promotion of community health, and design of environment for an aging society (Stokols, 1995). A review of research activity from 1984–1994 found an increasing number of studies in natural settings, an expansion of types and number of publications, and an increasing diversity of research settings (Sundstrom et al., 1996).

Craik (1996) sees as central to the field the theoretical and research issues of person-environmental interactions within life-span development as they occur on a daily basis in ordinary life. To Bechtel (1996), on the other hand, applied contributions are central, especially in evaluating architecture's suitability for its occupants. Issues on theory, methodology, basic science, and applied science abound in environmental psychology. The issues expand more rapidly than the resolutions, but this is typical of a vigorous science. What is regrettable is that it receives little attention either in psychology in general or in society despite its potential to contribute so much to both. However, the field has now broadened to an international scope, which is contributing to its vitality (Stokols, 1995). Stokols (1996) suggests that in the future environmental psychology may be more effectively advanced in interdisciplinary programs than in traditional psychology departments.

EVOLUTIONARY PSYCHOLOGY

This system draws one of its two major premises from the events of evolution and the other from the constructs of cognitive psychology. From evolutionary biology comes the principle of natural selection. Over many generations, a characteristic that fosters survival and reproduction becomes established in a population. The antelope that runs fastest and escapes predators will survive to pass on its fleetness. From cognitive psychology comes the construct of mental mechanisms that process information in such a way as to lead to desires, urges, preferences, and the like that, in turn, are presumed to produce certain behaviors. The system proposes that these had survival value in ancestral environments and became established in the brains of the population that survived because of them. (A further assumption is that the brain produces behavior.) For evolutionary psychology, then, it is not *behaviors* that are selected but *mental mechanisms* or *instincts*. These mechanisms are specific to a particular species and produce correlated behavior in that species. Observed regularities in behavior lead the evolutionary psychologist to a search for evolved psychological mechanisms that underlie the behavior.

For example, the observation that males are more often sexually promiscuous than females might lead to a search for an adaptive mechanism that leads males to seek multiple partners and for a counter-mechanism that causes females to seek a single partner. So, in the ancestral environment, multiple partners gave males a better chance of reproductive success, and their preferences for multiplicity would be selected as a brain mechanism. That same ancestral environment might offer females a better chance in a monogamous relationship that provided a stable family situation for raising children to reproductive age, thus continuing her line of descent. Such a mental mechanism could be selected and passed on.

Some mechanisms are fairly easy to see in accordance with this scheme, especially in male-female relationships. Others require considerable ingenuity to ferret out. Consider a hypothetical evolutionary function: Women prefer men who are kind, understanding, and dependable. The brain structures that prefer these characteristics are adaptations geared to successful child-rearing which, in turn, leads to the continuation of women's progeny. Or observe that young men tend to be risk-takers, which gets them more potential mates and thus more opportunities for reproduction when there is competition for mates. A male's preference for young, attractive females would more likely lead to reproductive success than a preference for old or unhealthy ones. However, a critic can counter that a female body most likely to manage pregnancy and childbirth (e.g., wide-hipped) is not the current male ideal.

Perhaps male jealousy of a mate functions to keep other males away and maximizes the likelihood of paternity for the jealous male, but jealousy has complications. To study the complexity of jealous behavior, Buss (1995) asked men and women whether they would be more upset by the thought of their mates having sex with someone else or by the idea of their mates developing a close emotional relationship with someone else. All but a few women found the emotional attachment more upsetting, whereas most men found the sexual relationship worse—but only at a ratio of 60 percent–40 percent. Subjects' physiological reactions during the imaging were consistent with the answers. For many men, the alternative they chose depended on whether they had ever experienced a committed sexual relationship. The emotional attachment took first place for the majority that *had* experienced a committed sexual relationship and the sexual infidelity for those who *had not* experienced one. Thus, according to the researcher, context and individual differences as well as evolutionary mechanisms play important roles.

Moving away from male-female relationships, Dunbar (1996) argues that gossip replaces the grooming that primates engage in. These animals remove debris, matted hair, and flakes of dead skin from each other's coats. The standard interpretation of this activity is that it fosters group cohesion. In humans, according to Dunbar, language is its substitute. The origin of language, particularly of gossip, serves no purpose of planning food gathering or hunting. It functions solely as a social cement. And a large brain is needed to keep track of the complex social relationships that develop. Dunbar finds a correlation between the size of the neocortex and the size of groupings of animals. In humans the maximum group size is about 150. Within a group of this size each person can know all the others and know how they relate to each other. One hundred fifty is the size of clans in hunter-gatherer groups and the number of workers in a business that can function without a bureaucracy. Dunbar's theory about the origin of language is quite different from that of Pinker (1994), though both operate within an evolutionary framework. Pinker argues for a language instinct. Among the many behaviors receiving attention from an evolutionary psychology perspective are cooperative behavior (Ridley, 1997), perception (Shepard, 1992), and sex differences in social behavior (Archer, 1996). A list of thirty recent studies on adaptation and selection ranges from evolved landscape preferences to mother-fetus conflict (Buss et al., 1998).

Tooby and Cosmedes (1992) and Cosmedes and Tooby (1997) set evolutionary psychology apart from the mainstream by rejecting what they call a Standard Social Science Model. This model proposes general mechanisms such as reasoning, learning, and memory which have no innate content and must derive all content from the world. In contrast, they hold that a large number of standard circuits specializing in certain specific tasks develop in all minds/brains. These "domain-specific" mechanisms descend from biological evolution and "generate behavior" appropriate to the environment. Because they evolved during millions of years of hunter-gatherer life, these mechanisms often do not fit present needs very well; but because of their great number, humans have many to draw from and gain great flexibility (Buss, 1995). According to the proponents of this system, in today's world of complex technology, business, and commerce, the way in which genes function selfishly is often hidden beneath layers of behavior patterns. The evolutionary psychologist recognizes that these behaviors are often unrelated to reproduction—watching movies, getting addicted to tobacco, following through on careers, writing poems, etc.—and must be separated from behaviors that are related. One proponent seems to regard evolutionary biology as only a stepping-stone to a different level of organization involving complex interactions: "human beings evolved by one set of laws, those of natural selection and genetics; and how they interact with one another according to another set of laws, those of cognition and social psychology, human ecology, and history" (Pinker, 1997, p. 208).

PROBABILISTIC EPIGENETIC PSYCHOLOGY

"Epigenesis" refers to the development of new properties or activities not present in an earlier stage of an individual's history. The adjective "epigenetic" is applied to approaches as diverse as psychoanalysis and cognitive psychology. Usually these usages mean only that later development is influenced by earlier development. "Probabilistic epigenesis" (Gottlieb, 1970; Lerner, 1976) goes much further and refers to a non-linear (i.e., not consisting of a chain of A causing B and B causing C) mutual influence of biology and environment both within the organism and between the organism and its surroundings. The organism contributes to its surroundings and is changed by them. There is a thoroughgoing interdependence and an ongoing mutual interchange between organism and environment. This is also called "environment-organism interaction".[1] The term "probabilistic" (Gottlieb, 1970s) refers to the fact that in naturalistic interactions, as opposed to contrived ones in a laboratory, a "sequence or outcome of individual behavioral development is probable (with respect to norms) rather than certain" (p. 123). The interaction of components does not always occur at precisely the same time and, as a result, characteristics do not emerge at the same time, for the same duration of time, or even in the same sequence for all individuals of the same species (Lerner, 1978). Therefore, the emergence of any given characteristic at any point

or duration of time or in any sequence can have only some probability of occurring. Not all children begin to talk or walk or complete toilet training at the same time or in the same sequence. Not all college students develop at the same time or in the same sequence such mature behaviors as moderating alcohol consumption, driving carefully, or studying regularly and diligently.

This approach to development differs from (a) a conditioning approach such as that of behaviorism, and (b) a predeterministic approach such as that of orthodox psychoanalysis or of Piaget's stages (Lerner, Hess, & Nitz, 1991). Some behaviorists assume that environment and continual, quantitative additions of S–R units determine behavior. Predeterminists assume that biology unfolds in an unvarying sequence to some predetermined end state, and environment can change only the rate of that sequence. This latter approach may be called "predetermined epigenesis" (Gottlieb, 1983). Probability epigenesis, on the other hand, holds that behavior patterns are produced not by biology or by environment but by a relationship between the two. The meaning or significance of a particular behavior lies neither in the person nor the environment but in that relationship and in a particular context. Consequently, to understand behavior pathology or criminality we must look at interactions, and to modify them we must deal with the interactions—for they are comprised of such interactions (for a closely related view, see chapter 10).

Although one may cite a number of progenitors of probability epigenesis, Zing-Yang Kuo was perhaps the most far-reaching pioneer in both experimental and theoretical contributions. Kuo (1967) defined "epigenesis" as a "continuous developmental process from fertilization through birth to death" with emphasis on

> diversification and modification of behavior patterns . . . as a result of the continuous dynamic exchange of energy between organism and its environment. . . . At every point of energy exchange, a new relationship between the organism and the environment is established;

---

[1]. Such terms as "transactional," "contextual," and "individual-socioecological" (Gottlieb, 1991) and "developmental contextualism" (Lerner, 1989) are also used.

the organism is no longer the same organism and the environment no longer the same environment as they were at the previous moment. (p. 11)

Lerner (1978) cites the dialectical psychology of Riegel (see chapter 9) as advancing this view, and one could also add the interbehavioral psychology of Kantor (see chapter 10).

Kuo was a native Chinese who undertook his graduate studies with Tolman at the University of California at Berkeley. He rejected Tolman's purposive behaviorism in favor of Watson's radical behaviorism but found that it too had shortcomings. He conducted experiments, now classics (for example, see Kuo, 1930), that challenged the instinct doctrine and, because he eschewed traditional constructs, was considered quite radical. While still a graduate student, he conducted and published his first challenge to the instinct doctrine (Kuo, 1921) and received numerous reactions from eminent psychologists of the period. His freedom from Western culturalization may have played a role in some of what he rejected and some of what he advocated, although Gottlieb (1976) attributes his rebelliousness to his upbringing.[2] His interest in prenatal and neonatal behavior led him to devise the first improvement on Aristotle's method of breaking an egg open at different stages to study the embryo's development. Kuo put a window in the egg so he could continually observe the embryo's behavior as it developed. Upon returning to China, he set up animal research compounds and conducted research on birds, cats, and dogs. The political upheavals in China put an end to most of his work, but he managed to summarize the experiments in a book (1967).

For Kuo, behavior is bi-directional. Every behavior pattern results from the "dynamic relationship" or "interlocking reactions" between organism and surroundings, not from passive stimulation. Body structures and their functions set

limits on behavior but do not determine it: a dog can bite an adversary but not throw a stone at it; the potential to bite is enabled but not determined by biology. The range of behavior ("behavior potentials") that an organism can enter into depends on its history in its environmental context as well as on structures and functions. Physiological and behavioral characteristics interact as the organism develops. The limits set by anatomical and physiological components of the organism in turn affect further biological and behavioral development. Biological characteristics provide conditions for certain behaviors to occur and, as behavior develops, that very behavior affects the development of the physiological and anatomical components of the organism. As the organism develops, its repertoire of responses becomes more restricted—a decrease in behavior potential—and more specific as a result of its developmental history. And as the organism becomes more biologically capable it extends its interactions in more complex ways. An organism's interactions with stimuli continually build and adapt as both organism and conditions change. Every neonate among social animals has great behavioral potential—of which very little is realized during a lifetime—and is limited only by its body structures.

Kuo puts considerable emphasis on the "behavior gradient" in which, in any given response, the entire organism is involved but with some components participating more intensely (higher on a gradient) than others and with interactions and feedbacks. This includes chemical events as well as gross anatomy. These variations and their feedbacks form complex, interdependent, orderly patterns of behavioral gradients that constantly change and vary in intensity and extensity. Psychology's job is to uncover these changing patterns and their laws. The patterns are not just physiological counterparts of behavior but are intrinsic components of the total pattern. Variation of the different parts of the gradient patterns depends upon (a) the stimulating object, (b) the total environmental context, (c) the status of anatomical structures and their functional capacities, (d) the physiological (biochemical and biophysical)

---

2. For a short biography of Kuo and a list of his publications, see Gottlieb (1976).

conditions of the organism, and (e) the organism's developmental history.

In short, according to this system, we cannot understand behavior unless we examine development in its context. Nor can we understand it without the gradations of intensity and extensity of interactions in their correlated multilevel and multivariate forms. We cannot separate physiology from behavior or the innate from the learned. We can only examine the behavior gradients in their interdependent complexity as development proceeds. Accordingly, Kuo (1967) dismisses physiological psychology, a physiological basis of behavior, mind and body, innate and learned, and other dichotomies. He distinguishes between "explicit gradients" and "implicit gradients" only as a matter of the extent of their visibility (observability). "What has been commonly known as behavior (overt or gross movement visible to the naked eye—the molar level) is merely an integral part of the total response of the animal to the environment, involving every part of the whole organism." Even so, within "this total response— *behavior*—of the organism, there are differentiations of intensity and extensity among the different parts of the body," the behavior gradients (Kuo, 1970, p. 189). In other words, "behavior" covers a broad spectrum of coordinated events. Kuo would have found the distinction between behavior and cognition or behavior and experience to be without foundation.

Kuo rejects attributing such behaviors as learning, memory, and emotion to functions of the brain. The brain, he insists, is only the body's coordinating center for the system of behavior gradients. He "welcomes all laboratory information on the function of the nervous system . . . [but] has no desire to make the central nervous system the strategic sanctuary of his scientific ignorance" (1967, p. 193). That is to say, attributing behavior to the brain is a matter of ignorance about how behavior actually occurs.

Kuo emphasizes the variability and complexity of all behavior. He conducted a series of experiments with dogs, cats, and birds in natural environments to demonstrate that what have been

considered biologically fixed behaviors are quite modifiable depending on the interaction of these components in various environmental settings. The results support his rejection of both innate and acquired characteristics as well as behavior genetics. In his view, these constructs simply do not deal adequately with the complex of factors nor do they make useful dichotomies. Similarly, he insists that the work of Pavlov, Watson, and Skinner is over simplified; and he rejects the work of the European ethologists because they assume instincts and fail to recognize the role of the animal's history of interactions.[3] It is little wonder that during his time many considered him to be radical.

Although Kuo focused on animal studies, he suggested that his work pointed the way toward modifying human as well as animal behavior without changing the genetics of the species. This could be accomplished by controlling the environmental context at an early stage of development. In reviewing studies of sensing and learning in the newborn, Lipsitt (1977) similarly concluded that it should be possible to increase the range of human capabilities, just as increasing knowledge has made it possible to continually improve the performance of athletes. He also holds that this has clinical implications: Behavioral and environmental psychologists can rigorously study the influence of environmental conditions on normative behavior and on individual differences and can transfer this to the control of aberrant or pathological behavior.

Behavior potential or plasticity is not, however, infinite. Despite the best techniques in teaching rapid reading, for example, there is a maximum speed for any given individual. Still, if we offer long-term training beginning in childhood (such as some musicians receive), we don't know what the limits might be. And plasticity may have negative as well as positive consequences. Changes

---

3. Apparently, Kuo did not know about the work of Hinde (1966), who dismissed the instinct doctrine by bringing together comparative psychology and ethology, thus adding development to ethology and rendering it epigenetic, anti-instinctive, and holistic.

at one level could affect another. For example, genetic engineering of a biological trait might reduce or improve a behavior potential. Without knowing these outcomes in advance, only "scientifically conservative steps are warranted" (Lerner & Hood, 1986, p. 146).

In probability epigenesis the organism itself actively contributes to its own development (Lerner, 1989), and numerous experiments on various species support this. For example, a series of studies on human infants shows how crawling, usually between six and nine months, contributes to further development (Bertenthal, Campos, & Kermoian, 1994). Fear of heights arises so suddenly during the third quarter of the first year of life that it is commonly assumed to be related to biological maturation, having evolved as survival value for the individual and thus the species. It may be true that biological maturation makes such fear possible, but experiments show the interplay of other conditions. In the well-known visual cliff test, infants are slowly lowered over a cliff. Those with experience in crawling show an increase in heart rates; those of the same age who are not yet crawling maintain a constant heart rate. As a further test, precrawling infants are given experience in a walker and then tested. They show increased heart rates whereas control subjects of the same age show none. In a third test, infants' willingness to cross the visual cliff is tested at eleven or forty-one days of crawling experience. Duration of crawling experience, not age, relates to willingness to cross the cliff. The experimenters conclude that "crawling experience contributes significantly to the development of fear of heights" (p. 142). Additional experiments showed that crawling also contributes to the ability to find a hidden object, possibly because of greater variety of experiences that occur during or as a part of the locomotion. This experience includes improved orientation. According to the experimenters, contrary to the traditional view that such accomplishments are only end products of development, infants' own activities provide some of their most important early experiences. And contrary to linear models of development (straight-line sequence), development is "respon-

sive to multiple factors that interrelate and subsume organism-environment coactions. From this perspective, behavioral development is multidetermined, relational, and emergent" (p. 145).

Mainstream developmental psychology has been largely influenced by population genetics, which focuses on sources of variance (Gottlieb, 1995). This assumes that genes set the upper and lower limits of behavioral development; consequently, knowing the results of one condition of rearing will allow one to predict the upper and lower limits of another condition of rearing. The relationship is linear. Yet empirical studies flatly contradict this. In contrast, probabilistic epigenesis emphasizes development as the emergence of a different level of organization, one that is nonlinear and unpredictable. This has been well demonstrated, as Gottlieb (1995) notes. Interactions can occur on horizontal levels—such as between genes, cells, organisms or contexts—or on vertical levels—as between gene and cell or organism and culture. Genes are not independent causes, he argues, but part of the developmental process and influenced by other levels of the system. Causes do not arise from any single level but from relationships among levels; and analysis of variance, which ignores the individual in its averaging procedures, "is not the same as the analysis of causes" (p. 139).

Nevertheless, the developmental psychology textbooks that Gottlieb surveyed generally hold to the traditional view of behavior genetics and analysis of variance. The misappropriation of a biological concept is perpetuated in these textbooks when it is not even accepted in the form of linear causation in biology.

After working with Kuo's window-in-the-egg and other data-collecting procedures, Gottlieb (1997) concluded that "instinctive" behavior, such as bird calls, is regulated by prenatal interactions—mutual influences—that include the levels of genes, neurons, behavior, and environment. Causality is co-action of these structure-function relationships, not a linear event consisting of genes causing behavior or even behavior causing structures. "Innate" refers not to genetic determination but to performance specific to the species, independent of direct learning but dependent on experience in a broad sense. In fact, behavior may drive evolutionary change. A population of animals (including humans) that begins to live in a new place must adapt and change its behaviors. Within the population, such a change leads to the marshalling of resources favoring greater strength or dexterity or visual acuity, and that changes anatomy and physiology. This change, in turn, may eventually lead to changes in the genetic composition of the population. The entire developmental system changes. Some latent genes become active. Because only a tiny portion of genes in the entire bank of genes (the genome) is expressed, the potential for others to act is huge. One example of such activation is the growth of a tooth in a bird when its epithelial cells are subjected to altered conditions of development. Even when genes mutate they cannot by themselves change traits, for they are only part of the developmental system. Gottlieb calls his approach to psychobiology "top-down" (behavior to genes) in contrast to the "bottom-up" (genes to behavior) approach that seeks explanation of behavior and its changes in the genes. He argues that the interactions, the mutual influences, through all levels—genes, neurons, behavior, and environment—must be taken into account.

Oyama (1985), who argues similarly for discarding the dichotomy between genes and environment, suggests that the traditional dichotomy may be retained because it apparently "gives more clarity, more coherency, more consistency" (p. 9). Perhaps some resistance arises from the comparative ease of attributing outcomes to genes *or* environment *or* instinct as against dealing with the complexities of interacting events. Keller (1983, 1995) and Spanier (1995) contend that the problem lies in male dominance of science and the patriarchal perspective of males which assigns a hierarchical command center and overlooks interaction. Whatever the reason for dichotomies and assumptions of linear cause and effect, probabilistic epigenetic psychology finds interactions taking place.

REFERENCES

Archer, John. 1996. Sex differences in social behavior. *American Psychologist* 51: 909–917.

Bechtel, Robert B. 1982b. Contributions of ecological psychology to the evaluation of environments. *International Review of Applied Psychology* 31: 153–67.

———. 1996. The paradigm of environmental psychology. *American Psychologist* 51: 1187–88.

Bertenthal, Bennett I.; Joseph J. Campos; & Rosanne Kermoian. 1994. An epigenetic perspective on the development of self-produced locomotion and its consequences. *Current Directions in Psychological Science* 3: 140–45.

Bishop, R. L., & G. L. Peterson. 1971. A synthesis of environmental design recommendations from the visual preferences of children. Northwestern University Department of Civil Engineering. Cited by Hayward, Rothenberg, & Beasley (1974) in "Children's play and urban playground environments: A comparison of traditional, contemporary, and adventure playground types." *Environment and Behavior* 6: 131–68.

Buss, David M. 1995. Evolutionary psychology: A new paradigm for psychological science. *Psychological Inquiry* 6: 1–30.

Buss, David; Martie G. Haselton; Todd K. Shakelford; April L. Bleske; & Jerome C. Wakefield. 1998. Adaptations, exaptations, and spandrels. *Scientific American* 53: 533–48.

Cosmedes, Leda, & John Tooby. 1997. Evolutionary psychology: A primer. Available at www.psych.ucsb.edu/research/cep/primer.htm.

Craik, Kenneth H. 1996. Environmental psychology: A core field within psychological science. *American Psychologist* 51: 1186–87.

Dent-Read, Cathy, & Patricia Zukov-Goldring, eds. 1997. *Evolving Explanations of Development: Ecological Approaches to Organism-Environment Systems*. Washington, DC: American Psychological Association.

Dewey, John, & Arthur F. Bentley. 1949. *Knowing and the Known*. Boston: Beacon.

Dunbar, Robin. 1996. *Grooming, Gossip and the Evolution of Language*. Cambridge, MA: Harvard University Press.

Fairweather, G. W.; D. H. Sanders; D. F. Cressler; H. Maynard; & D. S. Black. 1969. *Community Life for the Mentally Ill*. Chicago: Aldine.

Fawcett, Stephen B. 1990. Some emerging standards for community research and action: Aid from a behavioral perspective. In *Researching Community Psychology: Issues of Theory and Methods*. Edited by P. Tolan, C. Keys, F. Chertok, & L. Jason. Washington, DC: American Psychological Assoc.

Fisher, Jeffrey D.; Paul A. Bell; & Andrew Baum. 1984. *Environmental Psychology*. Philadelphia: Holt, Rinehart & Winston.

Garling, Tommy. 1985. Children's environments, accidents, and accident prevention: An introduction. In *Children Within Environment: Toward a Psychology of Accident Prevention*. Edited by Tommy Garling & Jaan Valinser. New York: Plenum.

Gates, Lauren, & William Rohe. 1987. Fear and reactions to crime: A revised model. *Urban Affairs Quarterly* 22: 425–53.

Gibson, Eleanor J. 1969. *Principles of Perceptual Learning and Development*. New York: Appleton-Century-Crofts.

———. 1982. The concept of affordances in development: The renascence of functionalism. In *The Concept of Development: The Minnesota Symposia on Child Development*, vol. 3. Edited by W. Andrew Collins. New York: Wiley.

———. 1997. An ecological psychologist's prolegomena for perceptual development: A functional approach. In *Evolving Explanations of Development: Ecological Approaches to Organism-Environment Systems*. Edited by Cathy Dent-Read & Patricia Zukov-Goldring. Washington, DC: American Psychological Association.

Gibson, Eleanor J., & A. S. Walker. 1984. Development of knowledge of visual-tactual affordances of substance. *Child Development* 55: 453–60.

Gibson, James. 1979. *The Ecological Approach to Visual Perception*. New York: Houghton Mifflin.

———. 1985. Conclusions from a century of research on sense perception. In *A Century of Psychology as a Science*. Edited by Sigmund Koch & David E. Leary. New York: McGraw-Hill.

Gottlieb, Gilbert. 1970. Conceptions of prenatal behavior. In *Development and Evolution of Behavior: Essays in Memory of T. C. Schneirla*. Edited by L. R. Aronson, E. Tobach, & T. C. Rosenblatt. San Francisco: Freeman.

———. 1983. The psychobiological approach to development issues. In *Handbook of Child Psychology: Infancy and Developmental Psychobiology*, 4th ed. Edited by M. M. Haith & J. J. Compos. New York: Wiley.

———. 1991. Epigenetic systems of human development. *Developmental Psychology* 27: 33–34.

———. 1995. Some conceptual deficiencies in "developmental" behavior genetics. *Human Development* 38: 131–41.

———. 1997. *Synthesizing Nature-Nurture: Prenatal Roots of Instinctive Behavior*. Mahwah, NJ: Erlbaum.

Gump, Paul V., & Lawrence R. Good. 1976. Environments operating in open space and traditionally designed schools. *Journal of Architectural Research* 5: 20–26.

Hart, Roger; Cindi Katz; Selim Iltus; & Maria Rosario Mora. 1992. International student design competition of two community elementary schoolyards. *Children's Environments* 9: 65–92.

Hayward, D. Goeffrey; Marilyn Rothenberg; & Robert R. Beasley. 1974. Children's play and urban playground environments: A comparison of traditional, contemporary, and adventure playground types. *Environment and Behavior* 6: 131–68.

Heller, Kenneth. 1990. Social and community intervention. *Annual Review of Psychology* 41: 141–68.

Heller, Kenneth, & John Monahan. 1977. *Psychology and Community Change*. Homewood, IL: Dorsey.

Hinde, Robert A. 1966. *Animal Behaviour: A Synthesis of Ethology and Comparative Psychology*. New York: McGraw-Hill.

Holahan, Charles J. 1982. *Environmental Psychology*. New York: Random House.

Holahan, Charles J., & Abraham Wandersman. 1987. The community psychology perspective in environmental psychology. In *Handbook of Environmental Psychology*, vol. 2. New York: Wiley.

Hunter, Albert, & Terry Baumer. 1982. Street traffic, social integration, and fear of crime. *Sociological Inquiry* 52: 122–31.

Kantor, J. R. 1920. Suggestions toward a scientific interpretation of perception. *Psychological Review* 27: 191–216.

———. 1924. *Principles of Psychology*, vol. 1. New York: Knopf.

Kantor, J. R., & Noel W. Smith. 1975. *The Science of Psychology: An Interbehavioral Survey*. Chicago: Principia.

Keller, Evelyn F. 1983. *A Feeling for the Organism: The Life and Work of Barbara McClintock*. San Francisco: Freeman.

———. 1985. *Reflections on Gender and Science*. New Haven: Yale University Press.

Kingry-Westergaard, Cynthia, & James G. Kelly. 1990. A contextualist epistemology for ecological research. In *Researching Community Psychology: Issues of Theory and Methods: Issues of Theory and Methods*. Edited by P. Tolan, C. Keys, F. Chertok, & L. Jason. Washington, DC: American Psychological Association.

Kuo, Zing-Yang. 1967. *The Dynamics of Behavior Development: An Epigenetic View*. New York: Random House.

———. 1970. The need for coordinated efforts in developmental studies. In *Development and Evolution of Behavior: Essays in Memory of T. C. Schneirla*. Edited by L. A. Aronson, E. Tobach, D. S. Lehrman, & J. S. Rosenblatt. San Francisco: Freeman.

Lerner, Richard M. 1976. *Concepts and Theories of Human Development*. Reading, MA: Addison-Wesley.

————. 1978. Nature, nurture, and dynamic interactionism. *Human Development* 21: 1–20.

————. 1986. Plasticity in development: Concepts and issues for intervention. *Journal of Applied Development* 7: 139-52.

————. 1989. Developmental contextualism and the life-span view of person-context interaction. In *Interaction in Human Development*. Edited by Marc H. Bornstein & Jerome Bruner. Hillsdale, NJ: Erlbaum Associates.

Lerner, Richard M.; Laura E. Hess; & Katherine Nintz. 1990. A developmental perspective on psychopathology. In *Handbook of Child and Adult Psychopathology: A Longitudinal Perspective*. Edited by Michel Hersen & Cynthia G. Last. New York: Pergamon Press.

Levine, Murray, & David V. Perkins. 1997. *Principles of Community Psychology: Perspectives and Applications*, 2nd ed. New York: Oxford University Press.

Lipsitt, Lewis P. 1977. The study of sensory and learning process of the newborn. In *Clinical Perinatology* 4: 163–86.

Lounsbury, J.; M. Cook; D. Leader; & E. Mears. 1985. A critical analysis of community psychology research. In *Community Research: Methods, Paradigms and Applications*. Edited by Edwin C. Susskind & Donald C. Klein. New York: Praeger.

Maze, J. R. 1983. *The Meaning of Behavior*. London: George Allen & Unwin.

————. 1991. Representation, realism and the redundancy of "Mentalese." *Theory and Psychology* 1: 163–85.

McAndrew, Francis T. 1993. *Environmental Psychology*. Pacific Grove, CA: Brooks/Cole.

Merleau-Ponty, Maurice. 1962. *Phenomenology of Perception*. Translated by Colin Smith. London: Routledge & Kegan Paul.

Michell, Joel. 1988. Maze's direct realism and the character of cognition. *Australian Journal of Psychology* 40: 227–49.

Moore, Gary T. 1987. Environment and behavior research in North America: History, Developments, and Unresolved Issues. In *Handbook of Environmental Psychology*, vol. 2. Edited by Daniel Stokols & Irwin Altman. New York: Wiley.

Neisser, Ulrich, ed. 1982. Memory Observed. San Francisco: Freeman.

————. 1985. Toward an ecologically oriented cognitive science. In *New Directions in Cognitive Science*. Edited by Theodore M. Schlechter & Michael P. Toglia. Norwood, NJ: Ablex Publishing.

O'Conner, William A., & Bernard Lubin. 1984. *Ecological Approaches to Clinical and Community Psychology*. New York: Wiley.

Orford, Jim. 1992. *Community Psychology: Theory and Practice*. New York: Wiley

Osborn, Don R. 1988. Personality traits expressed: Interior design as behavior-setting plan. *Personality and Social Psychology Bulletin* 14: 368–73.

Oyama, Susan. 1985. *The Ontogeny of Information: Developmental Systems and Evolution*. Cambridge, England: Cambridge University Press.

Pinker, Steven. 1997. *How the Mind Works*. New York: Norton.

Proshansky, H. M. 1990. The pursuit of understanding: An intellectual history. In *Environment and Behavior Studies: Emergence of Intellectual Traditions*. Edited by Irwin Altman & Kathleen Christensen. New York: Plenum.

Rantzen, Andy J. 1993. Constructivism, direct realism and the nature of error. *Theory and Psychology* 3: 147–71.

Rappaport, Julian. 1977. *Community Psychology: Values, Research and Action*. New York: Holt, Rinehart & Winston.

————. 1990. Research methods in the empowerment social engender. In *Researching Community Psychology: Issues of Theory and Methods*. Edited by P. Tolan, C. Keys, F. Chertok, & L. Jason. Washington, DC: American Psychological Association.

Ridley, Matt. 1997. *The Origins of Virtue: Human Instincts and the Evolution of Cooperation*. New York: Viking.

Ryan, William. 1971. *Blaming the Victim*. New York: Random House.

Saegert, S. 1988. The androgynous city: From critique to practice. In *Women, Housing and Community*. Edited by Willem van Vliet. Brookfield, VT: Avebury.

Sampson, R., & W. Groves. 1989. Community structure and crime: Testing social-disorganization theory. *American Journal of Sociology* 94: 774–802.

Shepard, Roger N. 1992. The perceptual organization of colors: An adaptation to regularities of the terrestrial world. In *The Adapted Mind: Evolutionary Psychology and the Generation of Culture*. Edited by J. Barkow, L. Cosmedes, & J. Tooby. New York: Oxford University Press.

Shinn, Marybeth. 1987. Expanding community psychology's domain. *American Journal of Community Psychology* 15: 555–74.

Smith, Noel W. 1993. Sensing is perceiving: An alternative to the doctrine of the double world. In *Greek and Interbehavioral Psychology: Selected and Revised Papers*. Edited by N. W. Smith. Lanham, MD: University Press of America.

Sommer, Robert. 1987. Dreams, reality, and the future of environmental psychology. In *Handbook of Environmental Psychology*, vol 2. Edited by Daniel Stokols & Irwin Altman. New York: Wiley.

Spanier, Bonnie. 1995. *Im/Partial Science: Gender Ideology in Molecular Biology*. Bloomington: Indiana University Press.

Sundstrom, E.; P. A. Bell; P. L. Busby; & C. Asmus. 1996. Environmental psychology, 1989–1994. *Annual Review of Psychology* 47: 485–512.

Stokols, Daniel. 1995. The paradox of environmental psychology. *American Psychologist* 50: 821–37.

———. 1996. Bridging the theoretical and applied facets of environmental psychology. *American Psychologist* 51: 1188–89.

Susa, Anthony M., & James O. Benedict. 1994. The effects of playground design on pretend play and divergent thinking. *Environment and Behavior* 26: 560–79.

Tolan, Patrick; Fern Chertok; Christopher Keys; & Leonard Jason. 1990a. Conversing about theories, methods, and community research. In *Researching Community Psychology: Issues of Theory and Methods*. Edited by P. Tolan, C. Keys, F. Chertok, & L. Jason. Washington, DC: American Psychological Association.

———. eds. 1990b. *Researching Community Psychology: Issues of Theory and Methods*. Washington, DC: American Psychological Association.

Tolman, Charles W. 1991. Theoretical indeterminacy, pluralism and the conceptual concrete. *Theory and Psychology* 1: 147–62.

Tooby, John, & Leda Cosmedes. 1992. The psychological foundations of culture. In *The Adapted Mind: Evolutionary Psychology and the Generation of Culture*. Edited by J. Barkow, L. Cosmedes, & J. Tooby. New York: Oxford University Press.

U. S. Consumer Product Safety Commission. 1975. *Hazard Analysis of Injuries Relating to Playground Equipment*. Washington, DC: U.S. Consumer Product Safety Commission.

———. 1981. *A Handbook for Public Playground Safety*, 2 vols. Washington, DC: U.S. Government Printing Office.

Valsiner, J., & C. Mackie. 1985. Toddlers at home: Canalization of climbing skills through culturally organized physical environments. In *Children Within Environment: Toward a Psychology of Accident Prevention*. Edited by T. Garling & J. Valinser. New York: Plenum.

Wekerle, Gerda R. 1988. From refuge to service center: Neighborhoods that support women. In *Women, Housing and Community*. Edited by Willem van Vliet. Brookfield, VT: Avebury.

Winett, Richard A. 1987. Empiricist-positivist theories of environment and behavior: New directions for multi-level frameworks. In *Advances in Environment, Behavior, and Design*, vol. 1. Edited by Ervin H. Zube & Gary T. Moore. New York: Plenum.

Woodbridge, F. J. E. 1909. Consciousness, the sense organs, and the nervous system. *Journal of Philosophy, Psychology, and Scientific Method* 7: 449–55.

———. 1913a. The deception of the senses. *Journal of Philosophy, Psychology, and Scientific Method* 10: 5–15.

———. 1913b. The belief in sensations. *Journal of Philosophy, Psychology, and Scientific Method* 10: 599–608.

PART

VII

Retrospective

CHAPTER 14

Looking Back and Sorting Out

CAUSALITY AND THE SYSTEMS

One form of categorizing used to compare systems involves determining where to place causality. This presents four categories: (a) organocentric—causality centered in the organism; (b) envirocentric—causality centered in the surrounding environment; (c) sociocentric—causality centered in the social group; and (d) noncentric (or "contextual interactionist")—causality not centered in any single source but comprised of relationships or a field of events. Most systems fall more or less into one of these categories but a few are a little ambiguous, vary from one proponent to another, or have not established a clear position about causality—either implicitly or explicitly.

The most ambiguous are these: (a) Environmental psychology is rather nonspecific about causality; it is primarily concerned about the effects of the environment on people but defines itself in terms of mutual relationships. If it is interactional, as it appears to be, it belongs in the noncentric category along with community psychology (with which it has much in common). If it is closer to Barker's assumption that behavior is a function of the environment, it is envirocentric. (b) Dialectical psychology is sometimes reductionistic to biology and in those cases it is organocentric. (c) Phenomenological psychology retains some mental causality from its theological heritage and to that extent is organocentric. (e) Direct realism is organocentric to the extent that it draws on psychoanalytic instincts but is otherwise distinctly noncentric. In addition, social constructionism is a specialized form of envirocentrism in that the social community, which determines all that we can know about anything, is part of the environment; the system might equally well be placed in the envirocentric category. Notwithstanding, table 14.1 shows the sixteen systems treated in this volume in the four categories.

What is striking about the table is that so many systems are noncentric, or at least predominantly so. What this may suggest is that an appreciable number of psychologists have been dissatisfied with traditional organocentric systems and that their observations about psychological events have brought them independently to a similar alternative. However, the total influence of the group in the United States is very small, and most of the systems are known by relatively few psychologists and therefore not available to them to consider as alternative approaches. Gibson's ecological perception is the best known and has had a small but noticeable influence. In Europe, existential-phenomenological psychology may be the most influential of these.

Table 14.1			
Systems of Psychology Categorized by Causality			
Organocentric	Envirocentric	Sociocentric	Noncentric
Cognitive psychology	Behavior analysis	Social constructionism	Community psych.
Evolutionary psychology	Eco-behavioral science		Dialectical psych.
Humanistic psychology			Direct realism
Psychoanalysis			Ecological perception/ realism/psychology
			Environmental psych.
			Interbehavioral psych.
			Operant subjectivity
			Phenomenological psych.
			Prob. Epigenetic psych.

CHARACTERISTICS OF EACH CAUSALITY CATEGORY

Organocentrism

Theory. Organocentrism has its roots in the eighteenth-century rational philosophy of continental Europe—especially Germany, France, and Scotland. In a simple form it goes back to animistic beliefs of hunter-gatherers in which the heart or some other organ was the locus of psychological events. The Hellenic Greeks replaced animism with a fuller naturalism, and Aristotle formulated a noncentric psychology. But organocentric psychology returned with Patristic theology and has continued to the present in references to the psyche, soul, mind, brain, consciousness, and self, and in constructs of processing. Drawing from the rationalists' influence in Continental Europe, it posits innate knowledge or innate mechanisms to handle external stimulation, and the stimulus then represents the world in one form or another. Thus, it assumes a double world, a physical one outside and a mental one inside. The inside one is often converted to biology, especially the brain, which then produces behavior and is itself self-caused. Frequently analogies are used to facilitate this conversion and explain its operation, the most common today being the computer and computer programs. Because the inside-outside dichotomy is a form of mind-body dualism, questions arise. Is the mind the same as the brain? Or is the mind an emergent phenomenon, an epiphenomenon, of the brain? Usually some form of the latter is assumed (chapter 2, pp. 56–59).

The organocentric systems invariably begin their inquiry with constructs such as neural networks and computer programs (cognitivism), self-actualization (humanistic psychology), and instincts (evolutionary psychology and psychoanalysis), and interpret the results of investigations in terms of these same constructs. All these systems except cognitivism give a fairly prominent role to the environment. Cognitivism, in contrast, treats the environment as little more than inputs to be arranged and acted on by the innate mechanisms of the brain. Some cognitivists, however, attempt to give a larger role to the environment, but the future of that effort is uncertain.

- *Cognitivism* or *cognitive psychology* remains the dominant player in this group and, for that matter, in the entirety of American psychology. It gives organocentrism the lion's share of psychology today. Except for a few decades of behavioristic dominance—and methodological behaviorism had a strong organocentric ingredient even then—organocentrism has been the prevailing view in psychology, and cognitivism continues that tradition. Rather than the drives and instincts of the recent past, however, it posits mechanisms analogous to computer programs and refers to psychological events as "processing."
- *Evolutionary psychology* appeals to some cognitivists and might even be considered one subdomain of cognitivism or cognitive science, like artificial intelligence or psycholinguistics. But it gives more attention to the environment than cognitivism usually does. On a time dimension, evolutionary psychology and humanistic psychology stand at opposite poles on causality. The former looks to the past for mental adaptations that influence behavior, whereas the latter looks to the future for purposes and goals (teleology) that influence behavior.
- *Humanistic psychology* attributes causality to the self, and the self is self-caused ("self-actualization"). Because it has little room for social factors and focuses on enhancement of the self, it is egocentric as well as organocentric.
- Some proponents of *psychoanalysis* have transformed that system so radically that, in some instances, instinctive drives are gone and only remnants of Freud's original theory remain.

Perhaps Woodworth's S–O–R (chapter 2, p. 44) or S → O → R can symbolize the construct approach common to the organocentric systems, as well as their essential linearity. S is the stimulating environment that provides inputs into O, the organism's brain. R is the response output or behavior, only a manifestation or sign of something hidden or private. O may also be called experience, self, information processing, cognition, mind, id, intellect, connectionist networks, motivation, and any number of other constructs to be interposed between two observable events. These systems, especially cognitivism and evolutionary psychology, are hypothetico-deductive in that they emphasize deductions from theoretical constructs, which they test experimentally as hypotheses. This practice, along with the use of R methodology to compare group averages (chapter 11), follows in the mode of methodological behaviorism.

Proponents of these systems seem less aware of alternatives than proponents of any of the others. It is in these systems (and in social constructionism) that we most often find statements, either direct or implied, that no other possibilities exist. Perhaps this is because they are deeply rooted in traditional modes of thought, whereas the others have departed to some degree from that tradition and to that extent are more familiar with alternatives.

Research. To test deductions from the variety of theories that have come out of it, cognitivism has spawned a huge volume of research. It has taken over the "R" methodology of behaviorism—which behaviorism borrowed from agriculture and brewing—for finding group differences. Evolutionary psychology has also been very productive in research, especially considering its relatively recent arrival on the scene. Psychoanalysis has taken a serious attitude toward research in recent years, has sought appropriate methodologies, and has completed some well designed studies. Still, it is handicapped by few university connections for research support. Humanistic psychology generally scorns experimental and quantitative research, but a few proponents have turned to it. Most of their research has been qualitative in nature. The system has also been resistant to studies of the efficacy of its psychotherapy. Humanistic psychologists contend that objective data cannot adequately reflect its subjective effects Even so, researchers conducted some of the earliest studies on the effectiveness of psychotherapy—client-centered therapy—with this system.

Applications. Psychoanalysis has always been a procedure for psychotherapy as well as a theory of personality, and it continues along those same lines. The system is now tackling more difficult clinical cases and developing new theories. Cognitive psychology's primary application is in psychotherapy; humanistic psychology's in education, industry, and psychotherapy. In education, the humanistic approach coincides rather closely with the "experience curriculum" begun in American education in the 1930s. Although the extent of humanistic psychology's actual influence on education is unclear, some critics blame its avoidance of direct instruction for the decline of pupil performance.

Envirocentrism

Theory. These systems continue seventeenth-century British empiricism's emphasis on the environment as molder and director of the individual and positivism's insistence on confining science to observable events. Again, in continuity with British empiricism, these systems put greater emphasis on inductive evidence than on deduction. (Deduction is more characteristic of organocentrism which often tests its deductions from theoretical constructs.)[1] They begin their inquiry with observations (the inductive emphasis) which they systematize into constructs. Eco-behavioral science's tenet that behavior is a function of the environment (metapostulate 5) seems to come closest of any current system to classical behaviorism's S → R. Although behavior analysis accepts the same tenet (metapostulate 4), to handle its data effectively, it moves beyond S → R to the three-term contingency of S^D—R_O—S^R indicating stimulus antecedent, behavior, and consequence. Perhaps if eco-behavioral science formally worked

---

1. The hypothetico-deductive method deduces hypotheses from theoretical constructs, such as a connectionist network, and then runs experimental tests of the hypotheses. The empirico-inductive method gathers data (induction) from experiments or systematic observations (empirico-) and from these looks for patterns of regularity.

out the stimulus and response relationships of the behavior setting, those relationships, too, would be rather complex.

Behavior analysis works primarily with single organisms to find consistent behavior patterns—whether of humans or of other animals—rather than looking for average trends in large populations. Its findings of responses to schedules of reinforcement are among the most stable and consistent principles in all of psychology for prediction and control but are nevertheless far from absolute. Eco-behavioral science turns to natural settings ignored by others—such as the school band, the church supper, and the corner drugstore—and finds patterned behaviors and the mechanisms that control them. These too are highly predictable but under control of the behavior setting itself rather than that of the investigator. Mind-body issues, analogies, and biological reductionism never enter into these systems. Barker emphasizes the need for investigations to be setting-determined (event-based) rather than theory-determined (construct-based). Skinner, too, keeps his events and constructs distinct and always begins with observation of events. Although he frames it differently, he is sharply critical of the widespread practice in psychology of starting with constructs. It might be asked of both systems, however, if they have taken an adequate sample of events (see p. 399, below).

Research. Behavior analysis produces great volumes of findings both for basic science and for applications, all oriented toward procedures that result in high levels of predictability for a single subject. Over the years behavior analysts have broadened the scope of research from animal conditioning to complex human activities and continued the flow of findings. Because eco-behavioral science, in contrast, has only a small following, its volume of research is small. What it has accomplished, however, is disproportionate and adds a whole new dimension to our understanding of human behavior that occurs in ordinary settings in conjunction with physical components of the setting. Its findings about small schools versus large

schools is important to the well-being of public education even though those findings have been generally ignored. Barker avoided intervening in the behavior setting he was studying, but some of his successors introduce interventions in natural settings as an expeditious way of obtaining information, much in the manner of European ethologists.

Applications. Probably behavior analysis is second in eminence only to cognitivism. This eminence is due in part to rigorous research that obtained remarkable and repeatable findings, and in part to its unmatched success in treating a great variety of applied problems in psychology. In psychotherapy its success rate is better than that of other techniques, many of which combine behavior therapy with their own methods.

Although eco-behavioral science is not used very much in application, its findings about staffing, control circuits, school size, and effects of changing the characteristics of physical components of behavior settings offer considerable potential for social benefits. The applied systems of community and environmental psychology have been inspired by this research.

Sociocentrism

Theory. Sociocentrism, of which postmodernism/social constructionism is the only system, is largely a late twentieth-century development. Among its precursors are (a) Plotinus, the third-century mystic who merged the knower with the known; (b) nineteenth-century experiments with social utopias (with writings going back to 1516); (c) Marxism, which holds that people determine their society and are in turn determined by it; (d) the German philosopher Martin Heidigger, who taught that human knowing comes fundamentally from social relationships and the meeting of practical needs, rather than from the individual or from philosophy, and (e) American philosopher Thomas Dewey, who rejected the proposition that knowledge begins with theories of knowledge and insisted that knowledge consists of interactions between humans and their surroundings, acting and being acted upon—a mutuality.

Social constructionism holds that all knowledge is relative to the social group that constructs it, and the knower is inseparable from the community of discourse that provides the constructions. Perhaps the system's approach can be represented as Group → R. Most proponents reject objective knowledge, but a few allow room for knowledge that holds across social groups though they maintain that such knowledge is never entirely free of social influences. Proponents have attacked psychologies influenced by rationalism, positivism, and empiricism. They reject causation by mind, brain, and environment. They reject what they regard as mainstream psychology's errors, including the cult of the individual, adherence to quantitative methods to the exclusion of qualitative ones, and assumption of linear cause and effect. Because they also regard their own system as a construction, they are much clearer about the nature of constructs in various systems than are the proponents of organocentric systems. They attempt to avoid dualism by invoking social reductionism, just as cognitivism and evolutionary psychology attempt to avoid it by resorting to biological reductionism.

Research. Social constructionists have researched a variety of topics. They use any number of research methods, primarily interviews and the writing of narratives. Q method (chapter 11) is increasingly popular. Cross-cultural comparisons and women's issues are frequent topics, but a plethora of others regarded as social constructions, including psychopathology, also receive attention.

Applications. One area of application is education, where social constructionism attempts to teach social discourse, social meanings, and a liking for subjects in place of learning subject matter. Knowledge, they contend, is relative to any given social group and has no truth beyond that group. Some of these objectives are similar to humanistic psychology's approach to education. A second area

of application is their own brand of psychotherapy, of which family therapy is an important form.

Noncentrism

Theory. Noncentrism has antecedents in Columbia University's natural philosophy and in pragmatism. It even parallels some of the principles of Aristotle. Dialectical psychology, however, has roots in ancient China and pre-Socratic Greece; and phenomenological psychology's "intentionality" comes from the philosophy of Thomas Aquinas in the thirteenth century. The others are twentieth-century developments that have stepped outside tradition to one degree or another and have little influence on traditional philosophy. Each of the nine systems in this category seems to have developed independently of the others. What they have in common is a focus on relationships or interdependencies as comprising psychological action rather than on linear causality, either from the environment or from the organism. To varying degrees they have also begun their inquiry with observed events rather than with constructs. Because they are dealing with interdependent relationships as ongoing events, they do not need and do not invoke mind-body dualism or any form of reductionism. Interbehaviorism has been especially critical of confusing constructs with events. The proponents of these systems know the alternatives to mainstream organocentrism, for they are among those alternatives.

We may represent noncentrism in its simplest form as S ←→ R. The double headed arrow indicates that the relationship between the stimulating world and the responding organism is not inputs and outputs and not linear cause and effect but mutuality or interaction, and it is this interaction that comprises all psychological events, however overt or subtle. Also contributing to the interaction are such participating conditions as the context in which the interaction takes place, the biological organization of the particular organism along with any impairments, and the history of interactions. No hypothetical causal agent such as mind, cognition, instinct, brain or the like is required.

A brief comment on each of the nine systems in the order (alphabetical) that they appear in table 1.1:

■ *Community psychology* is an applied system that attempts to improve the person-situation relationship rather than to change the person to adapt to the situation. Hence, its focus is not primarily on the environment or the person but on the joint action.

■ Intrinsic to *dialectical psychology* is give and take, reciprocal change. In the interchange or interaction both the person and the world change in a context of meanings that also change. Because this system emphasizes developmental changes, it is not surprising that it usually finds supporters in developmental psychology.

■ *Direct realism* has not yet developed a research program or applications. Its effort has been toward providing a logical replacement for the representationism of cognitive psychology. In so doing, it has developed a largely noncentric position. Most proponents seem less inclined than Maze, the progenitor of the system, to invoke psychoanalytic drives.

■ *Ecological perception/realism/psychology* rejects the construct of sensation that has long influenced philosophy and psychology and with it the hypothetical internal brain interpreters. It turns to the direct interaction of sensing person and sensible world in a manner similar to both Aristotle's and interbehaviorism's accounts of perceiving. The system has been extended to memory, concept formation, and developmental processes, and has been combined with dynamic systems and probabilistic epigenesis. Despite its original specialization in perception, in the United States it is the most influential of the seven systems.

■ *Environmental psychology* focuses on the object side of the organism-object interaction. It has researched a plethora of topics, from pollution and violence to playgrounds and public housing, and continues to expand. As humans rapidly change earth's environmental conditions, environmental psychology's work of finding better approaches to environmental situations gains an increasingly critical potential for improving or mitigating the consequences.

■ *Interbehaviorism* is the most thoroughly worked out and systematic of the noncentric systems. It views observed stimulus functions and response functions, interactional history, setting, and media of contact as a multiplex field of interactions that comprises the psychological event. It has worked out in considerable detail a great range of psychological events as fields, some of which have received little attention elsewhere, and provided an entire volume on the postulate system at all levels of generality. With this plenitude of observed field components, it needs no hypothetical constructs nor does it leave any room for intervening variables. The field is the antithesis of linear causality.

■ *Operant subjectivity* adopts the interbehavioral system and brings to psychology (and numerous other disciplines) a rigorous methodology for measuring subjectivity objectively. Through item sorting it allows subjects to measure themselves on the relative subjective importance of one item over another and groups together those persons who show similar subjective dimensions. This contrasts with conventional "R" methodology, which discards individual characteristics, and can measure subjectivity only from the point of view of the investigator (rating scales, for example), not that of the subject.

■ *Phenomenological psychology* emphasizes meanings—life as it is lived. It takes account of all the field conditions of interbehaviorism but does not systematize them into a field. It refers instead to a dialectical relation between person and the world and the integral nature of the person with meanings in the world. Some proponents maintain the historical directionality meaning of intentionality rather than holding to a mutuality. The emphasis on meanings is congruent with interbehaviorism's identification of stimulus functions and response functions.

- Although *probabilistic epigenesis* deals primarily with non-human animals and interbehaviorism primarily with humans, the two are the most similar systems among the nine in their stress on the interdependence of biology, environment, and individual history.

Research. With two exceptions noncentric systems are eclectic in their use of research methodologies. The two are (a) phenomenological psychology, which uses solely qualitative methods such as analyses of audio- and videotapes; and (b) operant subjectivity, which has its own Q-sort methodology. Q sort has proven valuable to both centric and noncentric systems by providing subject-centered measurements that are completely untapped by the averaging techniques used in R statistics. Dialectical psychology insists that whatever method is used must deal with meaningful relationships that are natural and in context. Community psychology has yet to find fully appropriate methodologies, but most of the nine systems include bodies of research that usually have implications beyond the particular system from which the research came.

Applications. Whether in industry and organization, education, individual adjustment problems, or other applied situations, the noncentric systems point to the need to deal with person-environment relationships rather than with just one or the other.

Summary

This section has been an overview of the four major proposals for causal conditions that we find in psychology: the organism, the environment, the social group, or interdependent relationships. Causality for each is represented symbolically in table 14.2.

- **Organocentric:** For these systems the middle term—whether called mind, brain, information processing, or other construct—not the S of the environment, is the major causative power. This is the only category that gives preeminence to a construct as a causal condition.
- **Envirocentric:** Causality in envirocentric systems—as with the three-term contingency—can be more than simply behavior as a function of the environment.
- **Sociocentric:** Social constructionism is not so much concerned with causality as with knowing. Therefore, the arrow emanating from "Group" should be regarded as more of an indication of source of knowing than of causality. Possibly, it should be double-headed.
- **Noncentric:** Causality is linear for organocentrism and envirocentrism. For noncentrism, causality has no special meaning. The interdependent events occur, and a description of their functional relationships is the sole task of a scientific psychology. This occurrence can be designated causality or the term can be discarded.

From these we have four choices of what causes behavior (or is knowable): the organism, the environment, the social group, or relationships. And within each of three of these, additional choices are available. Even the sociocentric category offers some choices, such as strict or radical constructionism, contextual constructionism, constructivism, and other variations.

Table 14.2			
Symbolic Representation of Causality			
Organocentric	Envirocentric	Sociocentric	Noncentric
$S \rightarrow O \rightarrow R$	$S \rightarrow R$ $S^D \rightarrow R_O \rightarrow S^R$	$Group \rightarrow R$	$S \leftrightarrow R$

CRITERIA FOR SCIENTIFIC CONSTRUCTS

The criteria for scientific constructs are repeated below from chapter 2, pp. 52–53. They are consistent with progress in science, but not everyone would agree with all of them. The social constructionists, for example, argue that all observation—observation being emphasized in these criteria—is affected by social or cultural influences, and for that reason knowledge has no generality beyond the social community that constructed it. Humanistic psychologists totally reject objective events for psychology and insist that psychology should be solely subjective—that is, mental. It should be construct-based rather than event-based, contrary to these criteria, and some might wish to add other criteria. Still, most psychologists (with the possible exception of the social constructionists and humanistic psychologists) would probably agree with at least some items in the list. The first seems most fundamental. We have to recognize what is part of nature and what we are only constructing before we can build a science that reflects nature rather than our presupposed constructs. Here again, however, social constructionists say that such a distinction holds only for the group that constructs it. At least by being explicit about criteria, we have clearer alternatives. The reader may come to a better understanding of these alternatives by considering the usefulness of each criterion against science in general and against each of the systems in particular.

- Distinguish carefully between constructs of all types and the original events.
- Begin all investigations with observations from which constructs may be derived; avoid starting with constructs and interpreting results in terms of those constructs.
- Keep interpretive constructs consistent with the events observed; do not base them on other constructs.
- Avoid all constructs derived from traditional cultural and philosophical sources.
- When means for obtaining critical information is lacking, keep constructs extremely tentative and never base them on unobservables.

- Avoid adopting unobservable constructs or analogies for what is unknown and regard admission of ignorance as a scientific virtue.
- Note that only constructs derived directly from observed events have the potential for validity.
- Take an adequate sample of events so that the interrelationships of events may be observed.
- Anchor all constructs such as intelligence, motivation, and attitudes in observed referents and avoid giving them independent existence as things or causes.
- Avoid turning participating conditions, or those that may be necessary for the event, into determining conditions.
- Recognize the different levels of organization of things and events, and keep explanatory constructs consistent with the corresponding level.
- Use only those constructs that are observable at least in principle.
- Derive postulates from observation.
- Distinguish between the knower and the thing known and avoid merging them.
- Use only those constructs that are corrigible.

METHODOLOGY

Psychology's mainstream methodologies of laboratory experiments and R-type statistical analyses have been borrowed largely from biology and physics. Koch (1959) notes that "Sciences won their independence and ultimately institutional status, by achieving enough knowledge to become sciences. But at the time of *its inception, psychology was unique in the extent to which its institutionalization preceded its content and its methods preceded its problems*" (p. 783, author's italics). Some reviews of research using mainstream methods paint a rather dismal picture (Furedy, 1990). For example, despite volumes of research on memory, little progress is apparent (Tulving, 1979). Textbook citation of what is important in that area shows almost no agreement. Physiological psychology (Melzak, 1989), too, shows little advancement, and experiments in social psychology are so far removed from ordinary behavior as to be nearly meaningless (MacIntyre, 1985). Further, eleven eminent psychologists agree on almost nothing about serious problems in psychology (Wade, 1982).

A number of systems have called for either abandoning the traditional methodologies or for supplementing them with such methods as observations in natural settings, interviews, Q-sorting, and others. For example, Barker (chapter 7) insisted on systematic observations with no intervention of any kind. He objected to the mainstream construct in psychology that the world is chaotic and must be put into order experimentally. He demonstrated that one could observe the order that is already there without interfering with it. Stephenson (chapter 11) has called for putting the subject back into research and allowing self-reference so that the subject rather than the experimenter defines the meaning. Social constructionism, humanistic psychology, and psychoanalysis have relied primarily on qualitative studies and Q methodology. Behavior analysis and operant subjectivity seek regularity in single subjects rather than in large group averages.

Operant subjectivity, phenomenological psychology, and others object to mainstream psychology's use of the hypothetico-deductive procedure which starts with a theoretical construct such as drives or memory stores (sometimes operationally defined), deduces hypotheses, and then experimentally tests each hypothesis against the construct. They argue that this procedure uses constructs to support constructs. Behavior analysis, eco-behavioral science, and operant subjectivity use only the empirico-inductive method: they start with observations and then gather data either experimentally (behavior analysis and operant subjectivity) or by systematic field observations (eco-behavioral science) and draw constructs, such as observed regularities, from their investigations rather than from an initial construct. The empirico-inductive procedure is event-based; the hypothetico-deductive procedure is construct-based. Just as some systems are founded on constructs, so too are some methodologies; and just as some systems are founded on events, so too are

some methodologies. Scaling methods, for example, start with such constructs as intelligence or personality and then revert back to the scale to interpret the results. Oddly, both kinds of methodologys have been used across the categories of systems.

It is clear that a single methodology, such as R, can never be adequate for all of psychology although it will remain useful for instances of fact and information. Others such as Q and procedures for analyzing audio- and videotapes are opening new dimensions, though gaining little recognition beyond a few dedicated users. The use of computer analysis of multiple components of videotaped events (chapter 10) opens still further avenues. In making informed choices, knowing about these methodologies is as important as knowing about the various systems that are available.

CONCLUSIONS

Is psychology about how the mind or the brain generates behavior? Is it about mental processes? Is it about how reinforcement contingencies determine behavior? Is it about self-actualization? Or intentionalities? Or dialectical conflicts? Or individual-environment interactions? Perhaps it is time to examine constructs and postulates of the systems both in and out of the mainstream and make comparative evaluations of their scientific suitability. Rather than arguing about cognitivism versus social constructionism, for example, it might be more fruitful to decide what postulates can be justified logically and observationally at each level of generality and how constructs will be handled.

Although few of those in the mainstream know the full range of current alternatives, if this volume has even approximated its goals, readers will be in a better position than most mainstream specialists to make informed judgments.

REFERENCES

Furedy, John J. 1990. A realist perspective. *Canadian Psychology* 31: 254–61.

Koch, Sigmund. 1959. Epilogue. In *Psychology: A Study of a Science,* vol. 3. Edited by Sigmund Koch. New York: McGraw-Hill.

MacIntyre, Alasdair. 1985. How psychology makes itself true—or false. In *A Century of Psychology as Science.* Edited by Sigmund Koch & David E. Leary. New York: McGraw-Hill.

Tulving, Endel. 1979. Memory research: What kind of progress? In *Perspectives on Memory Research.* Edited by Lars-Goren Nilsson. Hilldale, NJ: Prentice-Hall.

Wade, N. 1982. The editorial notebook: Smart apes, or dumb? *New York Times,* April 30.

Collected
Postulate
Systems

Postulates of Each System

These postulate systems are taken from the chapter on each system and presented here for direct comparison. *Protopostulates* are general guiding assumptions about science, *metapostulates* are supportive assumptions for a particular science, and postulates are assumptions about the subject matter.

ORGANOCENTRIC SYSTEMS

Implicit Postulates of Cognitive Psychology (H. Simon: chapter 3)

Protopostulates

1. Science involves both observation of events and the employment of cultural constructs such as mind and body.
2. Knowledge comes from interpreting observation of events in terms of these constructs.

Metapostulates

1. Psychology is based in biology.
   Corollary: Psychology is not an autonomous science but is dependent on biology.
2. Biology includes the dual role of biological functions and psychological functions.

3. Psychological events are produced by specialized biological tissue and do not involve the entire organism.

Postulates

1. Humans are part body and part mind, and mind is different from behavior.
2. The construct of existential mind includes storage and transformational properties.
3. Experience is produced by the person's mind.
   Corollary: Mind is self-causative.
4. Mind construction acts to transform information.
   Corollary: Humans live in a double world—an outside world that is physical and an inside world that experiences the outside world as it is transformed and reconstructed by the mind.
5. Causation is linear: inputs are processed in a sequence of coding, storage, and reconstruction.
6. Human cognition is sufficiently similar to computer programs that it can be effectively studied as analogous to them.
7. The only role the environment plays in cognition is to provide sensory inputs from which the brain creates its own world.
8. Psychology gives preeminence to constructs; events are merely indicators of these constructs.

Semi-Explicit Postulates of Humanistic Psychology (A. Maslow: chapter 4)

Metapostulates

1. Psychological events are "biologically based."
   Corollary 1: Psychology is dependent on biology.
   Corollary 2: Psychological events are caused by biology or biology's mind.
2. Psychological events are partly unique and partly universal—the universal component being the biological influence.
3. Psychological events are not mechanisms but meanings.
4. Psychological events are both natural and mystical.

Postulates

1. Humans are part body and part mind or self, and self is different from behavior and from body.
   Corollary: Psychology gives preeminence to constructs.
2. The self has biologically determined values that are socially neutral or good rather than destructive or evil.
3. The biological determinants are weak and easily changed by the environment.
4. Biology presents a hierarchy of needs from tissue needs to social and personal needs.
5. Humans are self-causative.

Semi-Explicit Postulates of Psychoanalysis (R. Schafer: chapter 5)

Protopostulates

1. Reality consists not only of events of physics, chemistry, and biology but also of the meanings of things to people ("psychic reality").
2. Only through use of language rules do we come to systematically understand anything. Such rules provide coherency, establish facts, and determine criteria of consistency.

Metapostulates

1. Psychological events have meanings and cannot be accurately described by the terminology of physics or biology. These meanings are those of the person whose actions comprise them and in that sense are subjective.
2. Individuals consciously control their own choices and determine their own destinies.
3. Description is explanation. A description of reasons as actions replaces physicalistic ("dynamic") constructs.
4. Actions of people are paramount, and explanations by entities must be abjured along with the distinction between internality and externality (or mind and body).

Postulates

1. Psychological events consist of actions and must be referred to in action language.
2. Actions of humans involve choosing, setting goals, striving for goals, and finding meanings.
3. Actions need not necessarily be visible. Thinking, knowing, feeling, fearing, ideating, and fantasizing are as fully action events as are audible verbalizations.
4. Erotic and aggressive actions and conflicts are endemic to childhood and are influential in later behavior.
5. Many actions are unconscious, preconscious, or conscious.
6. Actions are products of both person and circumstance.
7. Language as narration comprises experiences, and present reality is constructed from such narration. No one narration is more true than another, but each is a different way of representing reality.

ENVIROCENTRIC SYSTEMS

Implicit Postulates of Behavior Analysis (B. F. Skinner: chapter 6)

Metapostulates

1. The primary purpose of psychological science is prediction and control.
2. The subject matter of psychological science is solely behavior.

3. Psychophysical dualism has no validity, because only the physical world exists.
4. The environment is the cause of behaviors.

Postulates

1. The environment determines behaviors through selection by means of consequences.
2. Behavior is determined and lawful.
3. Behavior is potentially reducible to biology and ultimately to chemistry and physics.
4. Behavior cannot be reduced to biology.
5. Private and public events have the same kind of physical dimensions.
6. External (public) events are consistently reinforced, but internal (private) events are not.
7. The behavioral changes brought about by contingencies of reinforcement are biological.
8. A methodology of functional analysis relates environmental independent variables to behavioral dependent variables.
9. Behavior occurs in two major functional classes: respondent and operant.
10. Operant behavior can be brought under the control of preceding stimuli.
11. Operant behavior can best be described by three terms (discriminative stimulus, operant response, reinforcing stimulus) and best understood as their functional relationships.

Semi-Explicit Postulates of Eco-Behavioral Science (R. Barker: chapter 7)

Metapostulates

1. Many events of nature, both of the physical environment and of behavior, are ordered and patterned.
2. Many events in nature, including those involving humans, occur in organized circumjacent units that are incommensurate with one another.
3. The environment is not passive but active.
4. Naturally occurring events involving human activity can be understood only if observed in their normal continuity and not interrupted or divided into discrete units.
5. Behavior is a function of the environment.

Postulates

1. It is behavior, not a hypothetical mind or other construct, that provides data and that must be used in any description or analysis.
2. Behaviors, together with inanimate objects and conditions, develop patterns that are orderly and self-sustaining and provide a legitimate area of investigation.
3. Causality of behavior lies largely in the behavior setting rather than in individual traits.
4. Behavior and setting are interdependent.
5. Behavior settings are irreducible to any other level of event.

Operating principles

1. Topics are chosen from areas of investigation rather than from a theory.
2. Data are collected from an atheoretical viewpoint but may then be analyzed theoretically.
3. Observation must be of naturally occurring events and must be as unobtrusive as possible.
4. Adequate observation requires locating a research station adjacent to the settings to be studied. It should be an integral part of the community.
5. It is often expedient to work from the complex to the simple. The complex may comprise an organization that will not be discovered if one starts with parts or attempts to understand the full event by the parts.
6. Long periods of observation may be necessary in order to properly understand interdependencies and cumulative effects.
7. Rate measures, some of them very small and undramatic, should be collected as indicators of ecological relationships.

SOCIOCENTRIC SYSTEMS

Semi-Explicit Postulates of Social Constructionism (K. Gergen: chapter 8)

Protopostulates

1. No universal truths about the world can be established.

2. The only events in nature that can be known to exist are social events.
3. Individuals do not possess knowledge. Knowledge is simply a type of relationship that occurs in a community.
4. Knowledge comes neither from a mind in which the world is represented and genetically organized nor from observations of the world.
5. Relationships among people, who are culturally and historically situated, determine the forms of expression by which we understand the world.
6. Science, logic, mythology, religion, mysticism, opinion, and fiction all have equal claims to truth as social conventions.
7. Social constructionism can make no greater claim to truth than any other approach. Like the others, it seeks intelligibility from repeated patterns.
8. A social community can evaluate or validate its own claims for its own community but, because of cultural differences, cannot evaluate those of another community.
9. Science can provide "theoretical intelligibility" as its most important contribution to a culture of which science is a part.
10. Use of logic and evidence have no warrant beyond the social groups in which they are historically and culturally situated, yet logical coherency may be used as a part of the formulation of social constructionism and in the questioning of other stances; reference to evidence may be used hand-in-hand with this rationality.

Metapostulates

1. Having abandoned truth claims, social constructionism invites others to entertain the possibilities that make up intelligibility and to consider alternatives.
2. Holding to a total relativism, social constructionism takes no position on any issue—whether scientific, moral, political, etc. Such issues are to be judged only within the context of a particular culture.

3. Individual characteristics may be reduced to discourse of the social group.
4. We structure the world linguistically rather than cognitively. A truth claim is a juxtaposition of words containing a proposition.
5. Social discourse is the only form of knowledge, and it does not extend beyond the social group in which the discourse occurs.

Postulates

1. Psychology studies social discourse as the only basis of knowledge.
2. Social discourse contains truth or knowledge only on the local level at which the discourse is created.
3. Causality does not arise from internal determiners such as minds, brains, will power, or other individual constructs but only from the social community.

NONCENTRIC SYSTEMS

Semi-Explicit Postulates of Dialectical Psychology (K. Riegel: chapter 9)

Metapostulates

1. All that exists in the world is in a state of constant and necessary change.
2. Contradiction, opposition, and conflict comprise these changes. Contradiction is inherent in everything. It is the source of change.
   Corollary: Science is itself in constant conflict and by this means creates constantly changing understanding.
3. Human dialectics is not organism- or environment-centered but stresses interactive, reciprocal relationships between humans and the world.
4. Dialectics can be both inner and outer, and their interface is psychic activity.

Postulates

1. Humans continually act upon and change the world and in turn are changed by it.

2. Behavior occurs in a continuous manner rather than in discrete units, but changes may involve dialectical leaps.
3. Behavior occurs in a context and develops historically.
4. Equilibrium and stability are only temporary conditions that result from resolution of contradictions and lead in turn to further contradictions.
5. Because of continual change, the assumption of such internal entities or fixed features as intelligence, traits, and competencies are invalidated.

Explicit Postulates of Interbehavioral Psychology (J. R. Kantor: chapter 10)

Protopostulates

1. "No science is concerned with existences or processes which transcend the boundaries of scientific enterprises. No scientific problem is concerned with a 'Reality' beyond confrontable events and their investigation."
2. "Scientific construction—the formulation of (a) hypotheses and (b) theories and laws— must be derived from interbehavior with events and not imposed upon the events or scientific enterprise from nonscientific sources."

Metapostulates

1. "Psychology is a relatively independent Science, though in constant interdisciplinary contact with other relevant sciences."
2. "An adequate psychological system should take account of [all relevant] events, operations, and theory construction."
3. "Psychological systems are irreducible."
4. "Psychology must be freed from all traditional philosophies."
5. "All scientific systems are subject to change."

Postulates

1. "Psychology Studies Interbehavioral Fields."
2. "Psychological Fields Are Multiplex."

3. "Psychological Interbehavior Involves the Performance of Entire Organisms, Not Special Organs or Tissues."
4. "Psychological Events Occur without Any Internal or External Determiners."
5. "Psychological Events are Ontogenic."
6. "Psychological Constructions Are Continuous with Crude-Data Events."
7. "Psychological Events Are Interrelated with Societal Events as Well as with Events Studied by Physicists, Chemists, and Biologists."
8. "Psychological Events Are Evolved from Bioecological Interbehaviors."

Implicit Postulates of Operant Subjectivity (W. Stephenson: chapter 11)

Protopostulates

1. Science is concerned solely with concrete events. Science does not deal with such nonphysical constructs as minds, mindless bodies, consciousness, or selves.
2. Each event in nature is specific and unique, and such specificities come before generalities and comprise them.

Metapostulates

1. Psychological events consist of levels of organization that differ from those of physiology or physics.
2. No internal or external determiners or mind-body distinctions are relevant to a science of psychology.
3. Whatever is not subject to observation is not a part of a science of psychology. It must be possible to manifest such things in some reliable operation, such as measuring blood pressure with a pressure cuff and gauge or ascertaining subjectivity with Q methodology.
4. Each scientific investigation consists of concrete inferential interactions specific to each situation, and requires a different analysis tailored to that experimental situation.
5. Operants or events, not constructs, are the beginning point of investigation.

6. Communication (and hence, data) occurs between persons, not groups, but can also occur within oneself.
7. Subjectivity or meaning arises from persons, not groups.

Postulates

1. Psychological events consist of a field of interactions of organisms and objects that develop historically in settings. (Stephenson adopts Kantor's formula [see chapter 10, p. 288] of PE = C[k, sf, rf, hi, st, md].)
2. Psychological events are both subjective and objective. They are subjective from one's own point of view (self-reference) and objective from some other person's point of view (other's-reference).
3. Much of psychological behavior that has been called mind, consciousness, and/or self is subjective or self-referential behavior (the remainder being objective behavior). Hence, it is best understood through procedures that allow the subject to measure him- or herself and by quantification methods that preserve these meanings and determine how they are shared by individuals.
4. Averaging techniques that replace the meanings of things to subjects with experimenter-determined meanings are suitable only when information or facts are important—and not necessarily even in those instances.

Implicit Postulates of Phenomenological Psychology (M. Merleau-Ponty: chapter 12)

Postulates

1. Nature is not comprised of everything in total interdependence so that distinctions do not exist, nor is it a composite of isolated processes. It consists of structures that involve continuous relationships that are properties of wholes.
2. Science seeks laws about these structures.
3. Structure and law are dialectical or reciprocal counterpoints, not separate beings.

Metapostulates

1. Psychological events are not reducible to biology, chemistry, or physics; but these do provide conditions for behavior.
2. The world has meanings as well as physical characteristics. The meanings are of primary concern to psychology.
3. No internal or external determiners are relevant to a science of psychology.

Postulates

1. Behavior is not mechanical responses to stimuli, nor is it caused by an internal mind.
2. Behavior is an interaction, a dialectical exchange, a relationship.
3. Meaning behaviors consist of relationships between person and object, but the person is more important than the relationship.
4. Objective and subjective differ only as frames of reference.

Author Index

Page numbers in italics indicate reference sources.

Subject Index